FALL OF CIVILIZATIONS

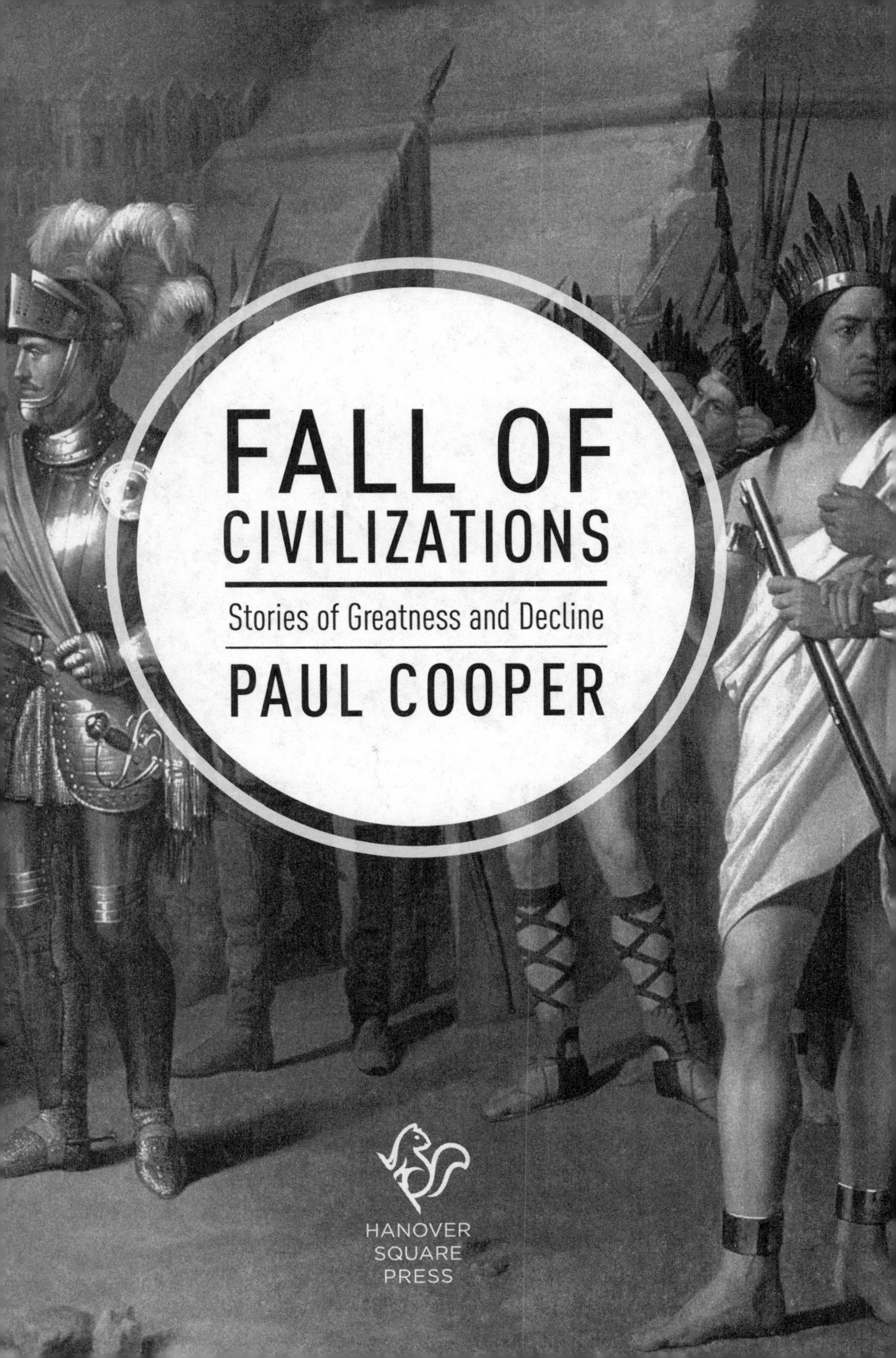

FALL OF CIVILIZATIONS

Stories of Greatness and Decline

PAUL COOPER

HANOVER
SQUARE
PRESS

HANOVER
SQUARE
PRESS™

ISBN-13: 978-1-335-01341-5

Fall of Civilizations

First published in 2024 by Duckworth. This edition published in 2024.

Hanover Square Press
22 Adelaide St. West, 41st Floor
Toronto, Ontario M5H 4E3, Canada
HanoverSqPress.com

Printed in U.S.A.

To Annie, my first listener

Also by Paul Cooper

River of Ink

All Our Broken Idols

FALL OF CIVILIZATIONS

CONTENTS

TIMELINE OF CIVILIZATIONS

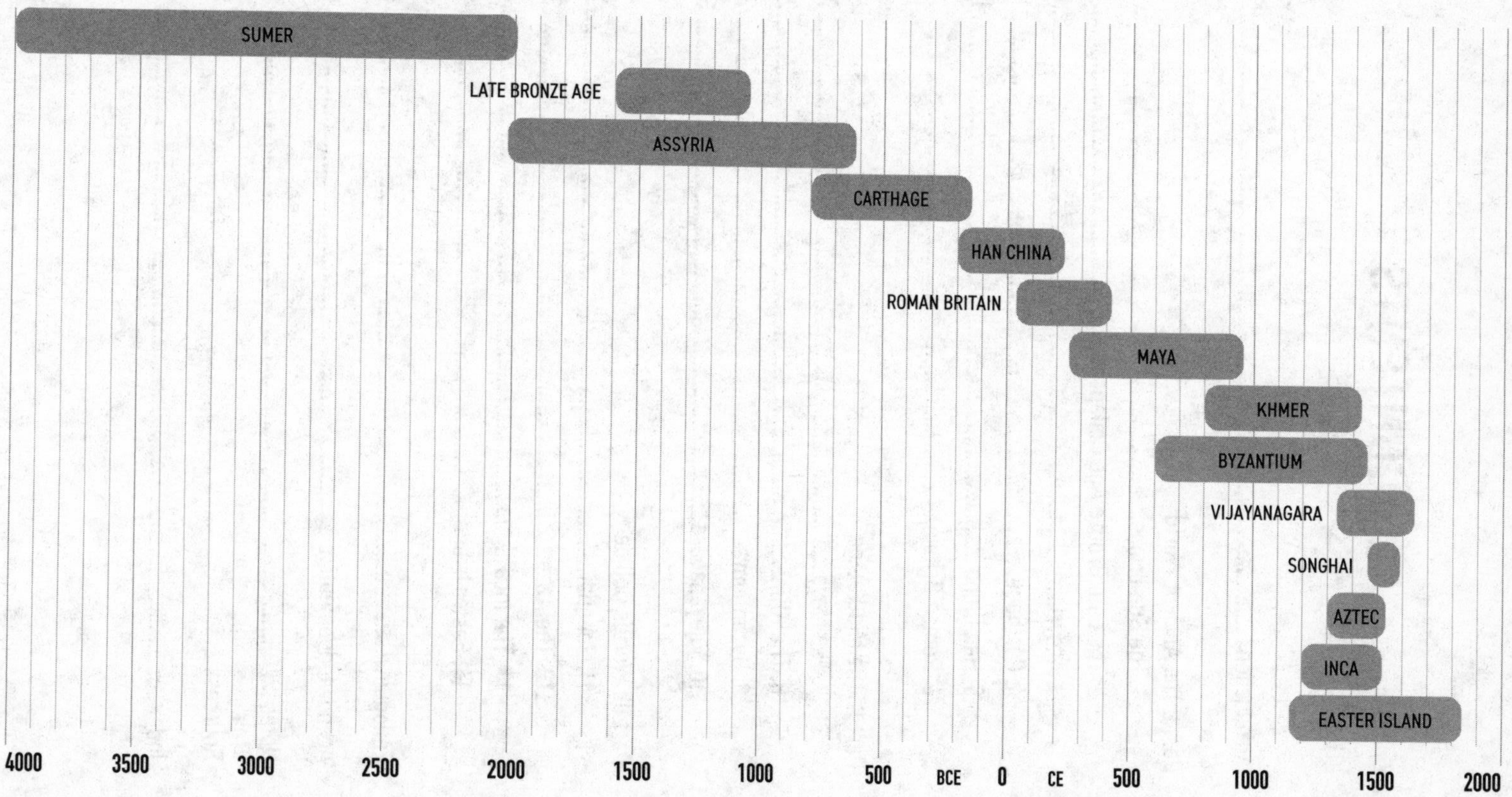

INTRODUCTION

This is how one pictures the angel of history... Where we perceive a chain of events, he sees one single catastrophe which keeps piling wreckage upon wreckage and hurls it in front of his feet. The angel would like to stay, awaken the dead, and make whole what has been smashed. But a storm is blowing from Paradise... The storm irresistibly propels him into the future to which his back is turned, while the pile of debris before him grows skyward. This storm is what we call progress.

Walter Benjamin, *Theses on the Philosophy of History*, 1940

In 2016, I visited the remains of one of the most opulen palaces built by Saddam Hussein, the deposed dictator of Iraq. It's a domineering sight, rising from the top of an artificial hill outside the city of Hillah, on a branch of the Euphrates River—all angular facades and empty windows, almost too bright to look at in the baking Iraqi sun. In the thirteen years since the toppling of Saddam's government, its once-neat gardens have overgrown and now burst with scrub and weeds collecting scraps of windblown rubbish. Once you step inside the cavernous space, emptied of all furniture, you can still see the traces of finery, the mantles and doorways in mock-baroque style—but now the plaster is cracked, the walls are scrawled with graffiti, and local children play football in the echoing space. Glass beads from the chandelier in the main hall are scattered on the floor coated with a thin layer of dust. It's said that after building this palace at enormous expense, Saddam only visited once—but every night, his cook would prepare him dinner just the same, in case he ever showed up.

As I walk out through the empty windows and on to the panoramic balcony of the main bedroom, the plains of the Euphrates Valley stretch out before me, and another ruin fills my view: a lunar landscape the colour of lion's fur, the sprawling mass of broken walls and ancient architecture that shows where, 2,500 years before, the city of Babylon once stood. Saddam had hoped that building his palace here would encourage comparisons with the ancient rulers of Mesopotamia. Perhaps he imagined that he would step out onto this balcony and feel inspired by the deeds of those ancient kings: Sargon, Esarhaddon, and Nebuchadnezzar. During his twenty-four years in power, Saddam embarked on many ill-conceived restoration projects of these ruins. When he learned that ancient kings used to stamp their names on the bricks they used, he was inspired to do the same—now many of the ancient walls have been rebuilt using bricks bearing the inscription: 'From Nebuchadnezzar to Saddam Hussein.' Today, the remains of his palace stand over the ruins of Babylon like a bad joke—the palimpsest of human history forever being written and rewritten, scrubbed out and started again.

The world is full of such ruins. Sometimes it seems as if there are more of them than anything else. From Rome's Colosseum to the rusting factories of Northern England and the crumbling suburbs of Detroit; from the pyramids of Giza to the ghost villages wiped off the map in the devastation of the First and Second World Wars; from the vine-wreathed temples of the Maya to the cracked star forts of European colonizers; from the emptied shopfronts of our high streets to the shell-pocked buildings of Bakhmut, Mosul, Aleppo and Gaza. Each of these ruins means something different, but they have one thing in common: these are all places where one day the future was cancelled.

As countless people have found throughout history—many of them included in these pages—a ruin is a place where the mind can't stay quiet. As we walk among the fallen walls and crumbling stones of an ancient temple, a palace or fortress, we can't help but imagine the world as it once was—and as it might have continued to be. Our minds fill in the gaps in the stones to make them whole. We sketch in the upper floors of towers and keeps that have long since rotted or burned away, and we hear the thud of footsteps across those vanished floorboards. We picture the lives that passed through the corridors and halls and left the stone steps worn in the middle like used bars of soap; human lives as a geological force, flowing like water through the broken cloisters.

A ruin is a paradox. Each one shows us the fearsome power of time, while simultaneously standing in defiance of it. Being such powerful imaginary spaces, ruins have always spurred human creativity. From the dawn of history, people have written about the poignant and difficult feelings they provoke: that peculiar mix of awe and melancholy. One Babylonian world map from the sixth century BCE, inscribed on a clay tablet, shows how ancient people conceived of the earth: divided into quadrants, it includes lands of serpents, dragons and scorpion-men, the far northern regions 'where the sun is never seen', and a great body of water they called 'the Bitter River'. The map also describes 'ruined cities…watched over by…the ruined gods'. These ruins were thought to be places of magic, the haunts of ghosts and evil spirits. Ruins haunt us still. This haunting finds a new expression in countless video games, books, films and television series that depict post-apocalyptic wastelands, where the familiar modern world around us is turned into a bleak and hostile place, and the comforts of modern society are stripped away. The ruins of the past and countless imagined futures remind us that history is not a linear progression from worse to better, from ignorance to knowledge, from war to peace. It has always been characterized by periods of flourishing, periods of fallowness, and periods of wanton destruction.

When I first began telling these stories in the form of an audio podcast at the start of 2019, I expected to reach an audience of perhaps a few thousand like-minded listeners—but at the time of writing, as the series enters its fourth year, it has been listened to more than 100 million times by listeners all around the world. This book is in part dedicated to all the people who have supported the project through the years and buoyed it up with their kindness, their knowledge and their passion. For those who have been following the series since the start, I hope that when they hold this book in their hands, they will know the part they had in making it.

Our word 'dilapidated' comes from the Latin for stone: *lapis*. *Dilapidare* means 'to scatter stones about'. And as Ecclesiastes tells us, there is 'a time to cast away stones, and a time to gather stones together'. This book is an attempt to gather a number of different stones. It does not pretend to be an exhaustive account of every significant civilization in history, and there are notable omissions that I hope will rebalance the attention that certain periods in history receive. However, I aim to tell as complete a story of the history of human collapse as could be achieved without significant repetition. The chapters of this book are designed to stand alone as self-contained narratives, allowing a reader to dip in and out wherever they please—but I have placed them in a loosely chronological order, so that those who wish can see the interconnected ebb and flow of history down the ages. The book is divided into three parts. The first is the 'The Ancient World', in which we see the formation of the earliest city-based societies in Mesopotamia and the Eastern Mediterranean, giving way to the rising classical powers of Carthage and ultimately Rome, and on the other side of the world, the Han Dynasty of China, before these too break apart. The second is 'The Middle Age', in which societies and empires around the globe like the Maya, the Khmer, Vijayanagara and Byzantium struggle to hold themselves together against the centrifugal forces of dissolution, as the world changes from under them and new technologies shake up long-established power structures. The final section, 'Worlds Collide', will look at the great mass extinction event of human societies that took place during the colonial period, and the peoples that were ground into dust to make way for modernity. Finally, in the epilogue, I will look ahead at what the future may hold for our own modern world.

The book defines a 'civilization' as any large and organized society. My interest is not in the simple disintegration of empires, and I have left out examples such as the British, Ottoman, Spanish and Soviet empires, where administrations simply transitioned from one government to many. I have restricted my stories to those in which a significant abandonment of population centres took place—where the social fabric disintegrated, cities were left empty and buildings fell into disuse and disrepair. I have not attempted to systematize collapse or come up with a grand unifying theory for why it occurs. I tell these stories not to file them away into a neat system where they cannot hurt us, but because they *do* hurt us. These stories of loss and failure are all of our stories, and they are as much a part of us as any exalted monument or grand epic. However, it cannot escape the reader's attention that the stories share common themes. Many of these societies collapsed because the climate or environment changed around them in ways that they could not foresee or control. Many kept their populations in states of staggering inequality, which destroyed their social fabric and reduced their abilities to react to crises. Some collapsed because the interconnected systems of trade and exchange they were a part of disintegrated. Others sowed the seeds of their own destruction with excessively cruel or bellicose treatment of their neighbours. In virtually all, the productive forces that once nurtured their growth eventually turned into liabilities—but they found themselves unable or unwilling to change course.

As a result, this book should also be read as a call to action. While no one knows what the future will hold, the coming century will present perhaps the greatest series of challenges that humanity has ever faced, and the actions required to correct our current course are significant. Every ruin in this book should thus be understood as a warning and a challenge: take nothing for granted, resist those who have mortgaged our future for their greed, and fight with every inch of your being to build a better world.

PART 1

The Ancient World

And on the pedestal, these words appear:
My name is Ozymandias, King of Kings;
Look on my Works, ye Mighty, and despair!
Nothing beside remains. Round the decay
Of that colossal Wreck, boundless and bare
The lone and level sands stretch far away.

Percy Bysshe Shelley, *'Ozymandias'*

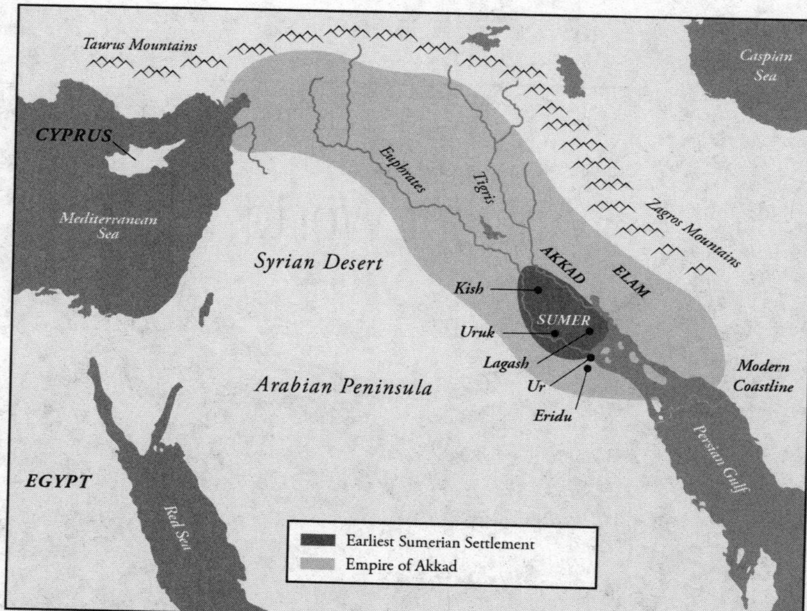

Taurus Mountains
Caspian Sea
CYPRUS
Euphrates
Tigris
Mediterranean Sea
Zagros Mountains
Syrian Desert
AKKAD
ELAM
Kish
SUMER
Uruk
Lagash
Ur
Eridu
Modern Coastline
Arabian Peninsula
Persian Gulf
EGYPT
Red Sea
Earliest Sumerian Settlement
Empire of Akkad

1

The Sumerians

c. 4000 BCE–2004 BCE

In 1625, an Italian nobleman named Pietro Della Valle went on a tour of the Middle East. Della Valle was an eager traveller, and spent much of his life in Persia, North Africa and India. He married an Assyrian Christian princess in Damascus, and the two journeyed together across Mesopotamia, trekking on horses and camels across the deserts of what is now Iraq, accompanied by local guides. At the time, travel in this region was perilous. The Ottoman and Persian empires were at war, fighting over who would rule in Baghdad, and meanwhile, local bandits took advantage of the chaos to prey on travellers. As if that wasn't enough, lions roamed in the hills. Alert to these dangers, the guides were constantly on edge, and on 18 June, they spotted a distant group of Bedouins watching them from a dune. Unsure of their intentions, Della Valle's group beat a hasty retreat. They fled across the desert, searching for somewhere defensible to hide. That's when they spied a looming mass on the horizon, a strange form rising out of the desert. As they drew near, they saw that they were approaching a series of enormous and very ancient ruins. 'For more security we removed a mile further,' Della Valle later wrote, 'and took up our station under a little hill near some ruins of buildings, which we saw from far away.'[1]

Illustration of the Great Ziggurat of Ur, as it appeared in 1857.

Della Valle's group camped in those ruins for several nights while the guides negotiated with the local chieftain for safe passage. During the day, under the intense heat of the Iraqi sun, Della Valle passed the time by walking among those crumbling monuments, as he later wrote in his memoirs:

> Our removal hence being still deferr'd... I went in the forenoon to take a more diligent view of the ruins of the above-said ancient building. What it had been I could not understand; but I found it to have been built with very good Bricks, most of which were stampt in the midst with certain unknown letters which appear'd very ancient. I observ'd that they had been cemented together in the Fabrick, not with lime, but with bitumen or pitch.

Della Valle was fascinated by the broken fragments of clay brick, and impressed by the unfamiliar symbols that littered the ground of this ruined place. He explored further, and copied down some of the marks that he saw:

> I found on the ground some pieces of black Marble, hard and fine, ingraven with the same Letters as the Bricks; which seem'd to me to be a kind of Seal... Amongst other letters which I discover'd in that short time, two I found in many places, one of which was like a jacent Pyramid...and the other resembled a Star of eight points.[2]

Although they couldn't have suspected it then, Della Valle and his wife had stumbled across the ruins of a city that had once been called Ur. It had been at the heart of one of mankind's first true civilizations—the society of Sumer. It was here, in this now inhospitable waste, that much of the world we know today had its beginning.

Cuneiform tablet impressed with Sumerian writing, ca. 2040 BCE.

Eventually, negotiations with the local leader fell apart, and Della Valle's group left in the dead of night. In his bags, he carried away with him a few of the clay tablets that he had found at the site, which he took home as curiosities. They would be the first examples ever seen in Europe of a language that had not been spoken for millennia. Della Valle must have turned these fragments over in his hands, peered at their strange symbols, and wondered: Who had built such enormous mounds of brick out there in the middle of the desert? What did the marks on those broken pieces of clay mean? And if a great city had once stood there, what in all the world could have happened to it?

★★★

Mesopotamia is a name that in classical Greek means 'between the rivers'—and since ancient times it has been given to the lands that lie between the rushing Tigris and the winding Euphrates rivers, and which today we call Iraq. Since the earliest recorded history, Mesopotamia was also home to two distinct major cultures: the peoples of Sumer and Akkad.

We know a reasonable amount about the Akkadian people in the north. They spoke a language in the Semitic group—the family of Aramaic, Hebrew and Arabic—and which was indigenous to the region, sharing grammar and words with other languages originating nearby. But the Sumerian people of southern Iraq are more mysterious. In fact, the question of where they came from remains such a mystery that archaeologists have referred to it as 'the Sumerian Problem'.

Sumerians spoke what we call a language isolate—that is, it has no relation to any of the languages around it, and was effectively in a linguistic family all of its own. Sumerian was so alien to the region that early scholars who discovered its first texts didn't believe it could be a real language at all, and assumed it was a kind of code. This alone has led some to question whether the Sumerians arrived in southern Iraq from somewhere else.

The Sumerian culture centred on the coast of Iraq's far south, and so it has been suggested that they may have arrived by boat, possibly from Oman or Qatar. Early Sumerian legends refer to an ancestral homeland known as Dilmun, an Edenic paradise where 'the raven uttered no cries…the lion killed not, the wolf snatched not the lamb, unknown was the kid-killing dog, unknown was the grain devouring boar'.[3] Further support for this theory may come from the writings of the Roman historian Flavius Josephus, who recounts a legend from the now vanished writings of a Hellenic-era Babylonian priest named Berossus. It tells the story of a figure called Oannes, half-man, half-fish, who walked out of the sea and taught the people of Mesopotamia the secrets of culture.

> He had the whole body of a fish, but above his fish's head he had another head which was that of a man, and human feet emerged from beneath his fish's tail; he had a human voice... He taught them the use of letters, sciences and arts of all kinds, the rules for the founding of cities, and the construction of temples, the principles of law and of surveying; he showed them how to sow and reap.[4]

Having revealed these secrets, Oannes leaped back into the sea and swam away. It's possible that in this myth, ancient storytellers have preserved a memory of the arrival of the Sumerians, landing *en masse* by boat and bringing with them their strange language and advanced urban culture. Some have even argued that the Sumerians may have come from as far afield as the Indus Valley in modern Pakistan—and genetic analysis has shown that certainly some population exchange took place between the Persian Gulf and the Indus Valley during the civilization's long history. Meanwhile, others have proposed a more outlandish theory, which once again finds its roots in mythology. The Sumerians believed that in the time of their distant ancestors a great flood had washed over the world. This same story would later pass into the legends of the Babylonian Empire, and from there to the Hebrew poet-historians who wrote the first books of the Bible. The story of the great flood is perhaps the oldest continuously told story, and it's in this legend that we might find a clue to Sumerian origins.

The story of the flood is so striking that many historians—and no shortage of pseudo-historians—have tried to come up with a historical event that may have inspired it. But it may genuinely find its roots in real human experience. When the last ice age, or glacial maximum, began to end around 18,000 years ago, global temperatures started to rise, and would ultimately increase between 4 and 7 degrees. Up to that point, immense ice sheets had reached from the North Pole as far south as modern-day Berlin. But as temperatures rose, these ice caps melted, and their water poured back into the oceans. Combined with the expansion of oceanic water on a warming planet, this caused global sea levels to creep up by an average of 2.5 centimetres a year, until they had risen 120 metres, or enough to submerge a forty-storey building. The sea engulfed vast regions of the coast. The land bridge that had once connected Russia and Alaska was inundated, separating Asia and the Americas, as were the low-lying regions of what is now the North Sea, turning Great Britain into an island. In Mesopotamia, the effects were just as dramatic.

During the ice age, the Tigris and Euphrates had flowed on for a further 900 kilometres down a flat fertile valley of marshlands and forests, emerging into the Indian Ocean beyond where the Strait of Hormuz is today. It would have been the perfect place for human settlements, and it's likely that people made their homes here. But this landscape's days were numbered. As the glaciers melted, the Strait of Hormuz opened around 14,000 years ago. After that, the coastline moved inland across the flat riverine landscape at an average rate of more than 60 metres a year, or more than a metre every week—although the flooding likely happened in fits and starts as it moved over the landforms. For any humans living in this region at the time, this event must have been utterly terrifying. These people could have watched the sea advance by kilometres in their lifetime, and the next centuries would see them driven north by the encroaching waves, which swallowed whole forests and villages. They would have been unable to settle anywhere for very long, and been forced to adapt as they went. This gradual flight would have continued until the planet's temperature stabilized, and the coast reached its highest point around 5000 BCE. This happens to be right around the time that Sumerian culture as we know it burst onto the historical stage. At the same time, Semitic farmers speaking an ancestor language of Akkadian were moving down the rivers from the northern mountains. They would have met this beleaguered and unfamiliar population fleeing from the south, carrying everything they owned with them, and telling tales of a flood that had drowned the whole world.

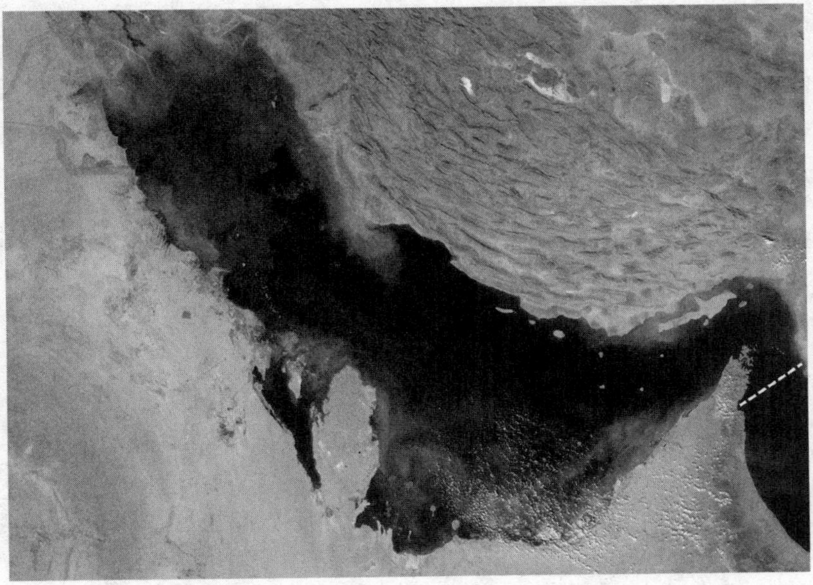

The Persian Gulf today (NASA). The white dotted line shows the approximate position of the former coastline.

However the Sumerians arrived, their relationship with the more northerly Akkadian peoples formed one of the earliest and most successful examples of cultural symbiosis in the ancient world. The Sumerians referred to themselves as *ùĝ saĝ gíg ga*—or 'the black-headed people', and the Akkadians called them *tsalmat-qaqqadi*, which meant the same thing in their own language. This suggests that something about their appearance may have set them apart from other peoples in the region. Some early anthropologists even resorted to studying the skulls they found in Mesopotamia and comparing them to depictions in Sumerian carvings—a discredited practice—but even in the age of DNA analysis, we don't have a clear idea of who the Sumerians were. Human remains in this region are usually badly preserved, and even if it were possible to get good readings on DNA, it would be difficult to link any one genetic group to the ancient Sumerians with any certainty. Bilingualism was clearly widespread for much of their history, and vocabulary and cultural practices flowed back and forth between groups, further blurring distinctions.

But one thing we know: over the following centuries, the Semitic Akkadians and the Sumerians lived side by side in such a way that their cultures ran in parallel, just like their two great rivers. They shared their successes and advances, and they shared the cities that by 4000 BCE were quickly growing to become the largest yet seen. But they would also share their failures, and for the next 2,000 years, their fates were inextricably entwined.

★★★

From carvings and other artefacts that depict Sumerians, we can see how they wore their hair: curly on top and cut short on the sides. Common men wore sheepskin kilts, while the rich wore coloured fabrics spun from wool, decorated with tassels and beads. Among the wealthy, both men and women wore jewellery: anklets, bracelets, necklaces and ear ornaments made of copper and sometimes gold.

The Sumerians believed that the world was a roughly circular landmass, surrounded on all sides by a huge body of water. They believed that another ocean also lay above their heads, held in place by the solid structure of the sky, which occasionally let some of this water through as rain. Sumerians called their homeland *ki-en-gi(-r)*, which means 'the land of the noble lords'. To describe the settled societies of the Sumerians and Akkadians, they used the word *kalam*, meaning 'civilized', while *kur*, which was used to describe the mountainous zones bordering the plains, came to have an additional meaning: rebellious, barbarous and wild. And that's how the outside world must have looked to them. To their south and west, the desert of Arabia yawned: a rolling sea of sand dunes where no crops could grow, home to nomadic warrior clans. To the north, the rocky Taurus mountains hemmed them in, full of hardy mountain people, while the Zagros mountains of Iran formed the edge of their world to the east.

The Sumerians made use of the pottery wheel, the wagon wheel, the plough and the sailboat. Their buildings used complex arches and domes—and in fact their builders mastered all the architectural techniques that would go on to be used before the age of steel and concrete. They worked out how to cast metals such as copper and later bronze. They were avid mathematicians and accountants, and developed complex systems of measurement, as well as methods for dividing and multiplying, even writing down the first ever multiplication tables on clay tablets. In fact, we still use Sumerian mathematics every day. Their number system worked on a base of sixty, rather than our decimal system, and they divided time into the units we use to this day—sixty seconds in a minute, sixty minutes in an hour—as well as the 360 degrees in angle measurement. It's thought they would count to twelve using the three bones in each of their four fingers, tapping each one with their thumb, while keeping count of the twelves on their other hand's fingers. Once five fingers were held up, they had reached sixty.

Thanks to this spark of ingenuity, Sumerian society grew at a steady pace despite the challenges of their landscape. They had little stone or wood, so instead they learned to build with the river mud, mixing it with straw, gravel and broken pottery, and baking the resulting bricks in the sun or in kilns. With clay, they made everything from pots and plates to sickles and writing tablets. Just as they are in the Iraqi marshes today, buildings were also constructed out of reeds, bound together in huge quantities into strong beams up to a metre thick. They dug networks of irrigation canals that extended the agricultural zone around the rivers and facilitated the transportation of goods by boat. They built dams to regulate the flow of the rivers and control the spring floods, and used a grand array of words for all the different water control mechanisms they used. Gradually, the landscape of southern Iraq transformed from dusty salt flats and marshy swamps to a green patchwork of farmland, where wheat, millet and sesame could be grown. The Sumerians planted orchards of nutritious dates, and in the shade beneath these tough palms they planted more delicate pomegranates, grapes, figs, chickpeas, lentils, leeks, garlic, cucumbers and watercress. Archaeological evidence shows that the Mesopotamians of antiquity enjoyed a richer diet than their neighbours, and we have even uncovered Sumerian recipes on clay tablets. The recipe for a dish they called '*Tuh'u*' gives a sense of the variety they enjoyed.

> *Tuh'u*. Leg meat is used. You prepare the water. You add fat. You sear. You fold in salt, beer, onion, arugula, cilantro, Persian shallot, cumin, and red beet, and [you crush] leek and garlic. You sprinkle coriander on top.[5]

Many historians have argued that it was the digging of these canals and watercourses that led to the developing social organization of the Sumerian Period. Extensive systems of water management required careful planning, engineering expertise and mathematical calculations—not something that could be achieved without significant planning. Work teams needed to be organized and paid in food and beer, foremen and overseers appointed, complex water systems mapped out. All of this led to a kind of early bureaucracy that in turn gave rise to the first true states. It's no coincidence that for these early Sumerians, the god of water, Enki, sat at the top of their pantheon. One Sumerian myth credits him with bringing order to the southern marshes.

> The plow and the yoke he directed,
> The great prince Enki…,
> Opened the holy furrows,
> Made grain grow in the perennial field
> The lord, the jewel and ornament of the plain,
> Fitted out on its strength, Enlil's farmer,
> Enkimdu, the god of the canals and ditches,
> Enki placed in their charge.[6]

According to Sumerian texts, the first city in the region was Eridu. One document known as the Sumerian King List describes it as the place where Enki first decided that a king should rule: 'When kingship from heaven was lowered, the kingship was in Eridu. In Eridu, Alulim became king; he ruled for 28,800 years. Alalngar ruled for 36,000 years.'[7] Archaeology shows that the city of Eridu was founded around 5400 BCE, and was populated by Sumerian speakers. Soon it was just one of a constellation of small Sumerian cities that dotted southern Iraq. At that time, populations of woolly mammoths, survivors of the end of the ice age, still roamed in remote parts of the Arctic.

The cities of Sumer were not the first large human settlements. Excavations at the sites of Çatalhöyük (7500 BCE) and the even older Göbekli Tepe (9500 BCE) have shown that humans had already lived in so-called 'proto-cities' for millennia. These were often anarchic, self-organized communities that looked something like a Brazilian favela, and their constructions showed no evidence of central government or urban planning. In Sumer, we see the rise of the first true city states. These were relatively small, the most populous probably having no more than about 10,000 inhabitants, and were centred around their temples and ruled by priest-kings, known as ensi. Records show that an ensi was often assisted by a semi-democratic council of elders, which included both men and women. Their borders were defined by the courses of canals and by specially carved boundary stones. During this time, art and architecture began to take on the style that we would consider distinctively Sumerian, and technology also took leaps forward. What's more, this early era seems to have been one of relative peace. There is little evidence for organized warfare or the keeping of professional soldiers in these early cities, and most towns went without walls. But this would not last for long. One ancient Sumerian myth, called *The Gifts of Inanna*, seems to capture some of the spirit of this period of transition. It describes technology and the refinements of settled society being handed down by Enki to his daughter, the goddess Inanna, who later passes them down to the people of Sumer.

> Holy Inanna received the craft of the carpenter, the craft of the coppersmith, the craft of the scribe, the craft of the smith, the craft of the leatherworker, the craft of the builder, the craft of the reed-worker… Holy Inanna received wisdom, attentiveness, holy purification rites, the shepherd's hut, piling

> up glowing charcoals, the sheepfold. Respect. Awe. Reverent silence.[8]

Enki teaches Inanna about family, the proper laws of inheritance and the art of good judgement. But he also goes on to give her other gifts which show that the darker side of civilization was already making itself known: 'Holy Inanna received deceit, and the rebel lands… Holy Inanna received heroism, power, wickedness. The plundering of cities, and the making of lamentations.'[9]

From their peaceful beginnings, the Sumerians were already learning what Walter Benjamin would one day write: 'There is no document of civilization that is not at the same time a document of barbarism.'[10] Nevertheless, their cities grew, drawing in more people—creating their own gravity, putting pressure on various systems. Out of that pressure, some time around 3200 BCE, came an extraordinary invention, like the birth of a star that would flood the era with light: the written word.

★★★

One Sumerian epic poem called *Enmerkar and the Lord of Aratta* gives the first known story about the invention of writing, by a king who has to send so many messages that his messenger can't remember them all.

> His speech was substantial, and its contents extensive… Because the messenger, whose mouth was tired, was not able to repeat it, the lord of Kulaba patted some clay and wrote the message as if on a tablet. Formerly, the writing of messages on clay was not established. Now, under that sun and on that day, it was indeed so.[11]

The Sumerians had two things in virtually limitless abundance: the clay beneath their feet, and the reeds that grew on the marshes and riverbanks—and these combined to create the written word. They made marks on palm-sized tablets of wet clay with the ends of cut reeds, and the distinctive shape of these impressions gives this form of writing its name, from the Latin for 'wedge-shaped': cuneiform. The oldest cuneiform clay tablets come from the Sumerian city of Uruk, and date to the late fourth millennium BCE. They are ergonomically shaped to the human hand, and as a result are roughly the dimensions of a modern smartphone. Cuneiform was at first made up of some 1,500 pictograms that each represented a whole word—but scribes had to work fast, copying hundreds of documents throughout their day. Over time, the original pictographs naturally became simpler and more abstract. Around this time, someone had the bright idea that each symbol could also stand for a certain sound, instead of a whole idea, and after 3000 BCE, this meant the number of symbols was reduced from some 1,500 to about 600. These were the beginnings of the first alphabets. The human brain would never be the same again—and in large part thanks to this new ability to record and pass on knowledge, the technology of Sumer made even greater leaps forward.

This phase of Mesopotamian history is known as the Uruk Period, which lasted until the end of the fourth millennium BCE. One of the key markers of the shift into this period is a dramatic change in the region's pottery—but it did not become more sophisticated and ornate as technology improved. In fact, the pottery of the preceding Ubaid Period was exceptionally beautiful, made on a device known as a slow wheel and painted with distinctive geometrical designs in brown or black glaze. These were luxury items for the wealthy few. The Uruk Period, by contrast, saw a significant increase in the amount of pottery produced—but the quality fell dramatically. Thanks to the new 'fast wheel', clay jars and pots could be made in great numbers by workmen in intensive workshops, and they could now be afforded by everyone. This was the first era of mass production.

In their clay documents, the buzzing economy of the Sumerian cities comes to life in a slew of numbers. We know that in Girsu, for instance, 15,000 women were employed in the textile industry. One factory produced 1,100 tonnes of flour a year, but also bread, beer and linseed oil, as well as grindstones, woven reeds and clay pots. This factory employed 134 specialists, and 858 skilled workers, of which 669 were women, 86 were men, and 103 were teenagers of both genders. Since there was no currency at this time, workers were paid directly in food and other goods. The minimum ration of an unskilled factory worker consisted of 20 litres of barley a month, along with 2 litres of oil and 2 kilograms of wool per year, while their supervisor might earn twice this ration. Poorer workers sometimes had to supplement their income by borrowing commodities—like silver, grain or wool—from lenders, always at crushing interest rates.

Tablet of the *Epic of Gilgamesh* (obverse).

Of all the Sumerian settlements, the one that would rise to the greatest heights was the one that gave the period its name: Uruk. By the end of the fourth millennium BCE—when the earliest of the Egyptian pyramids was still at least 400 years in the future, and the large stones at Stonehenge would not be laid for another 800 years—the city of Uruk and its surrounding metropolitan area had swelled to some 90,000 inhabitants and covered 2.5 square kilometres. It was the largest settlement the world had yet seen.

Humanity's earliest surviving work of literature, the *Epic of Gilgamesh*, begins in Uruk. The real King Gilgamesh probably ruled over the city in the early third millennium BCE, and made enough of an impression that he went down in legend as a mythical hero, two-thirds god and one-third man. Over the centuries that followed, his stories were likely passed by word of mouth, before being set down on clay by later Babylonian and Assyrian scribes. Although it contains far more myth than historical fact, the *Epic of*

Gilgamesh does tell us about how Sumerian society was changing. For one thing, it's evident that warfare had begun to increase. As the tale opens, one feature of the city is repeatedly mentioned as a source of pride: a ring of enormous, fortified walls.

> Ascend and walk about on the wall of Uruk,
> Inspect the corner-stone, and examine its brick-work,
> Are its walls not made of burned brick, and its foundation overlaid with pitch?[12]

We can surmise that city walls were by now necessary for a powerful metropolis like 'strong-walled Uruk'.

> Three years the enemy besieged the city of Uruk;
> the city's gates were barred, the bolts were shot.
> And even Ishtar, the goddess, could not make head against the enemy.[13]

At the centre of the city rose a temple to the goddess Ishtar, and also the famous White Temple, a four-storey sanctuary dedicated to the sky god Anu, which could be seen from some distance across the plain of Sumer. It was covered in white gypsum plaster that would have reflected the sunlight during the day and moonlight after dark. The *Epic of Gilgamesh* gives us a sense of the bustling religious life of these temples.

> Three shar of oil the men carried, carrying it in vessels.
> One shar of oil I kept out and used it for sacrifices,
> while the other two shar the boatman stowed away.
> For the temple of the gods I slaughtered oxen;
> I killed lambs day by day.
> Jugs of cider, of oil, and of sweet wine,
> like river water
> I poured out as libations.[14]

If you walked the streets of Uruk during this time, you would see markets full of produce—beans and lentils, pomegranates and dates, jars of date syrup and oil—and smelled the smoke from kilns and bread ovens, and all the pungent aromas of an ancient city. In the richer parts of town, houses were built from baked bricks, but elsewhere, the clay-built houses were crowded into a chaotic labyrinth of alleys and warrens likely covered by reed matting to keep out the midday heat, as people still do today in parts of Iraq. You would see farmers carrying large sheaves of reeds and wheat on their backs and drovers bringing their long-haired sheep and oxen in from the fields, while women worked as weavers, ground flour, towed boats along canals, gathered clay and sand, and wove baskets out of rushes. You would have seen circles of men in shaded courtyards, sharing a large jar of beer flavoured with herbs and honey, all sipping through long straws made of hollow reeds.

With trade routes reaching as far as India, the influence of the metropolitan Uruk civilization spread like ripples on a pond—and its success soon spawned local copycats. As the third millennium drew to a close, another Sumerian city state was rising that would soon take Uruk's place as the pre-eminent regional power. The name of that city was Ur.

★★★

Ur was a coastal city, situated right at the point where the Euphrates River met the sea, and this made it a booming trade hub. As we've already seen, if you needed clay or reeds, southern Iraq was the place to be—but virtually every other resource the Sumerians required, they had to import. Fortunately, they always had something to trade. They were alone among almost the whole of the ancient Near East in producing a large surplus and variety of food, and so they quickly became the breadbasket of the region. In return for these staples, valuable goods flowed back. Copper came down from the mountains of north-western Iran, Armenia, and later by ship from the island of Cyprus, while tin to make bronze travelled through the long mountain passes from Afghanistan. Silver came down the Euphrates on barges from Turkey's Taurus mountains, while gold came overland from Egypt and by ship from India. Ordinary timber for building work could be chopped in the Zagros mountains of Iran, to the east, but for finer constructions, for palaces and ornate city gates, only the prized timber of the cedar tree would do. This was brought overland and then down the Euphrates from the mountains of Lebanon. One episode in the *Epic of Gilgamesh* relates the king's quest to slay a monster in these hills, steal this beautiful wood from the forest it guards, tie the lumber into a raft and float it back downriver to Sumer.

From their tiny coast on the Persian Gulf, the Sumerians sent their ships out to ports in modern Bahrain and Oman, and from there along the coast to trade with another of the world's most ancient and mysterious cultures: the people we know today as the Indus Valley Civilization. This was the likely source of all kinds of spices, and gemstones like carnelian and brilliant blue lapis lazuli, which the Sumerians adored and used to make jewellery and amulets, inlays in gaming boards, musical instruments and sculptures of delicate beauty. Grave goods uncovered in Ur show not only incredible wealth concentrated in the hands of its elite, but also magnificent craftsmanship, suggesting a sophisticated community of artists.

One such artefact found in a royal tomb in Ur gives an unparalleled insight into the lives of the ancient Sumerians. It is a small ornate decorative piece of furniture, inlaid with an intricate mosaic of shell, red limestone and lapis lazuli that depicts detailed scenes from everyday life 4,600 years ago. Today, it is called the standard of Ur. On one side, it shows images of the Sumerians at war: the four-wheeled chariots pulled by donkeys, the soldiers wearing leather capes and helmets, the men carrying spears and axes. On the other, it portrays the Sumerians at peace: a row of farmers and herders at work, shaved-headed scribes sitting at their desks, a musician playing a lyre for the King.

★★★

By the mid-third millennium BCE, urbanism in the Sumerian world was reaching its peak, and the economic might of Ur reigned supreme. But within only a handful of centuries, the influence of Ur began to wane. A new militarized age dawned, city walls were thrown up around the region, and the power of trade and diplomacy seems no longer to have been sufficient. One city which came into its own in this new era of violence was Lagash. This was a slaving city on the river Tigris that had grown rich by raiding villages in the hills, kidnapping people and trafficking them across the region. Some time around 2500 BCE, the ruler of Lagash, a man named Eannatum, fell out with the neighbouring city of Umma, seemingly over a stretch of farmland along the river. The two cities went to war, and one carved stone monument captures something of the spirit of this age. It is known as the Stele of the Vultures. The upper part of the stele shows King Eannatum of Lagash leading his soldiers into battle, armed with spears and javelins. The inscription reads:

> A man of the wind
> ...
> Eannatum, in Umma
> like a destructive storm of rain
> he left behind a deluge.
> ...
> Umma he defeated,
> and twenty ruin mounds for it
> he heaped up there.[15]

The carving is explicit and violent. As the soldiers of Umma try to flee the bloody battlefield, the soldiers of Lagash cut them down and trample them beneath their feet. Overhead, vultures wheel, with the severed heads of the soldiers of Umma in their beaks. They feast on the tongues and eyes. There's a particular kind of nasty, pitiless relish in this portrait of the massacre that seems to embody a change in the spirit of Sumerian warfare.

Detail from the Stele of the Vultures, showing carrion birds carrying off the heads of killed soldiers.

Perhaps aided by the merciless ethos depicted in the carving, the slaving city of Lagash went on to conquer much of Southern Mesopotamia and establish what some historians have called the first true empire in the world. But this Empire of Lagash would last for only about a hundred years. In these times, administrating even one city could be a challenge, and Lagash was soon critically overstretched. King Eannatum passed his throne on to his brother, and then down a succession of kings until a man named Uru-ka-gina sat on the throne. It was at this point that the subjugated city of Umma seized its chance, led by a ruler named Lugal-zage-si.

It's not clear exactly what made Lugal-zage-si so successful, but he seems to have fostered an ardent desire for revenge against the Empire of Lagash. He quickly toppled the kings of Kish and Larsa, who were still loyal to the empire, and then marched on Ur and Uruk. These fell in turn, and Lugal-zage-si moved his capital to the mighty walled fortress of Uruk. Finally, he marched on Lagash itself. The king of Lagash, Uru-ka-gina, didn't hold out for long. Lugal-zage-si burst through its walls, sacked the city and burned it to the ground. Even by the standards of the time, this was a shocking act, and one recovered clay tablet, apparently written by a scribe or priest living in Lagash, recounts with rage and sorrow the sacking of the city:

> The men of Umma, by the despoiling of Lagash, have committed a sin against the god Ningirsu! The power that is come unto them, from them should be taken away! Of sin on the part of Urukagina, king of Girsu, there is none. But as for

> Lugal-zaggisi, patesi of Umma, may his goddess Nidaba bear this sin upon her head![16]

After sacking Lagash, Lugal-zage-si's momentum was unstoppable. He worked his way north, up the course of the two rivers. Soon, he had conquered all the regions that Lagash had once claimed. One inscription written by him even claims to have conquered all the lands between what he calls the upper and lower seas, meaning all the way from the Persian Gulf to the Mediterranean coast:

> When the god Enlil, the king of the lands had bestowed upon Lugal-zaggisi the kingdom of the land…he had conquered them from the rising of the sun unto the setting of the same, at that time he made straight his path from the Lower Sea over the Euphrates and the Tigris unto the Upper Sea. From the rising of the sun unto the setting of the same has Enlil granted him dominion.[17]

This is probably an exaggeration, and in fact archaeology shows that the Sumerians were never able to maintain distant colonies for very long. More likely Lugal-zage-si pulled off a successful raiding party on the Mediterranean coast, burning and looting and bringing treasure back to Uruk. Still, this was the first time that a Sumerian prince had ever made such a bold claim, and it would leave a lasting impression. From then on, the idea of a king who could conquer all the lands between the seas would possess the imaginations of all the rulers who came after.

Despite his successes, King Lugal-zage-si, like the rulers of Lagash before him, soon found himself overstretched. His empire simply grew too big for the administrative capacity of the time, and before long, civil wars and rebellions broke out between the various Sumerian city states. In this time of chaos, the other great people of Mesopotamia began to fancy their chances at ruling—the people who up until this moment had been something of a junior partner in the civilization of southern Iraq: the Akkadians. One man would soon lead them in an outright civil war against the ruling Sumerians. He would go down in history with a name that in Akkadian means 'the one true king'. That name was Sargon, and he ushered in the twilight of the Sumerian Age.

★★★

Like many episodes from the mythologized history of Mesopotamia, the origin story of Sargon of Akkad is one that might be familiar to anyone brought up on Bible stories. He was a speaker of the Akkadian language, born around the middle of the twenty-fourth century BCE to a poor mother who abandoned him in a reed basket on the river, as one later Babylonian text records.

> My lowly mother conceived me, in secret she brought me forth. She set me in a basket of rushes, with bitumen she closed my door; She cast me into the river, which rose not over me. The river bore me up.[18]

According to the legend, the baby Sargon is found by a labourer digging a canal nearby, in the royal palace of the Sumerian city of Kish. He raises the child as his own, and brings him up as a gardener: 'Akki, the irrigator…lifted me out, Akki, the irrigator, as his own son…reared me, Akki, the irrigator, as his gardener appointed me.'[19]

But, like the biblical Moses, this foundling child was not to stay in his lowly position. Sargon clearly had no shortage of charisma, and this young Akkadian man was soon taken on as a cupbearer in the palace, bringing wine to the Sumerian lords and royalty of the kingdom. In a remarkable reversal, he somehow rose to overthrow the old king, and rule Kish in his place, as the Sargon myth recounts: 'Four years I ruled the kingdom. The black-headed peoples I ruled, I governed; Mighty mountains with axes of bronze did I destroy. I climbed the upper mountains; I burst through the lower mountains.'[20]

But Sargon didn't stop there. Kish was still subservient to King

Lugal-zage-si, the man who had united Sumer into one kingdom. Sargon dreamed of using his newfound power to throw off Sumerian rule, and form a new Akkadian power. To do this, he would have to strike at the heart of Lugal-zage-si's empire—the capital city of Uruk itself. He found his moment when King Lugal-zage-si was away on campaign, probably fighting to extend his power in the Mediterranean. With the Sumerian forces away at war, Uruk would be lightly defended. But it was still a daunting task. The tall city walls of Uruk, immortalized in the *Epic of Gilgamesh*, must have loomed ahead of Sargon and his men as they readied their attack. Nevertheless, Sargon's plan was a success. His men poured over the walls and the defenders fled. Sargon captured the city, and before reinforcements could arrive, he broke down several sections of those famous walls. It was both a deeply symbolic act and a strike against the might of Lugal-zage-si's Sumerian Empire.

King Lugal-zage-si swung around from his distant war-making and marched back home, gathering all his subject kings to him as he went. Inscriptions record that as many as fifty kings may have marched under his banner. Their task was easy enough: to crush the forces of one small city state. But Sargon seems to have been one of those generals—like Hannibal or Napoleon long after him—who seemed able to turn battles in their favour no matter the odds. We don't know the details of how he did it, but in a pitched battle with the amassed forces of the empire, it was Sargon's modest army that emerged victorious.

Sargon captured King Lugal-zage-si, and marched him through the gates of the holy city of Nippur wearing a wooden yoke on his neck like an ox. This would have been humiliating of course, but Sargon clearly had a merciful streak that stands out as rare in the ancient world. He spared Lugal-zage-si's life, and even allowed him to take up the role of governor of Uruk, so long as he swore allegiance. Sargon founded a new city to act as his empire's capital, and named it Akkad. An inscription on a statue from Nippur claims that he went on to conquer much of the empire formerly controlled by Sumerian Kish, and even up to the forests of Lebanon, and the grey Taurus mountains of Turkey.

> Sargon, the king of Kish, triumphed in thirty-four battles, up to the edge of the sea, and destroyed their walls... Sargon, the king, prostrated himself before [the god] Dagan... and he (Dagan) gave him the upper land...up to the cedar forest, and up to the silver mountain.[21]

At each city he conquered, Sargon made a point of destroying the walls, reducing the likelihood of rebellion. He even ceremonially demonstrated his mastery over the whole land by washing his weapons in the waters of both the Persian Gulf and the Mediterranean. Once the dust of war had settled, he turned to policy. He made efforts to strengthen the centralized administration and thus the stability of the empire, and even reformed the calendar. By the standard of the times, he was a relatively progressive ruler. But Sargon was also Akkadian, and he was what we today might call a nationalist.

Until now, Sumerian had been the language of royal inscriptions on palaces and temples, but during Sargon's reign, Akkadian was used in official inscriptions for the first time. The cuneiform writing system, initially designed to encode Sumerian, was re-engineered to write Akkadian. Sargon also gave himself the new title 'King of Akkad', appointed fellow Akkadians to key government positions, and garrisoned Sumerian cities with Akkadian troops. The two peoples of Mesopotamia, who had lived and grown together for millennia, now saw a wedge driven between them. Sargon ruled for fifty-five years, but towards the end of his reign, simmering resentment in the southern Sumerian-speaking cities finally boiled over. 'Afterward in his old age all the lands revolted against him,' one later Babylonian text recalls. 'And they besieged him in Agade [Akkad]; and Sargon went forth to battle and accomplished their defeat; Their overthrow he brought about, and their wide spreading host he destroyed.'[22]

But his military talent could only hold the empire together for so long. After Sargon's death around 2279 BCE, his sons Rimush and Manishtushu spent years bitterly trying to subdue the southern Sumerian cities of Ur, Umma, Lagash and Adab with less success. It would be Sargon's grandson, Naram-Sin, who restored peace to the empire, crushing the Sumerian rebellion in its southern heartlands. Afterwards, he sought to reconcile the two intertwined peoples of Mesopotamia, breaking from his father's title, 'King of Akkad', and ruling under the more diplomatic title, 'King of Sumer and Akkad'.

But the truth is, the Sumerian people were no longer the primary cultural force in the region. Akkadian was gradually replacing Sumerian not only as the official language of kingship but increasingly as the *lingua franca* of commerce. As a language isolate in a linguistic family of its own, Sumerian was difficult for others in the region to learn, while many of the empire's surrounding trading partners spoke Semitic languages that were close cousins of Akkadian. For merchants and traders in nearby provinces, learning Akkadian might have been like an English-speaker learning German or French, while learning Sumerian would have been like attempting Korean or Hungarian. The peoples of Mesopotamia had been largely bilingual for centuries, but gradually, all Sumerians learned to speak Akkadian, and fewer and fewer Akkadians spoke Sumerian. The Sumerian language faded away, and with it, some of the unique cultural signifiers that set them apart from their neighbours began also to fade from the historical record. However, the days of the Akkadian Empire were also numbered—and the Sumerians would get one more chance to leave their mark on history.

***

When the peacemaker Naram-Sin died, his son Shar-Kali-Sharri—Sargon's great-grandson—took over. Four years into his reign, a celestial sign appeared in the skies overhead. Around 2215 BCE, nearly 200 million kilometres out into space, a giant ball of ice and dust 40 kilometres across flew past Earth. This was the comet Hale-Bopp. It would spend the next 4,200 years or so hurtling through our solar system on its deep elliptical orbit until it returned to our night skies again as a blazing streak of light in 1997.

At that time, it was the brightest comet with the longest tail ever to be observed. It remained visible with the naked eye for eighteen months.

In 1997, the sight of the comet in San Diego, California propelled thirty-nine members of an apocalyptic cult, Heaven's Gate, to take their own lives by drinking a lethal mixture of vodka and phenobarbital. They believed that their souls would be carried away on a spaceship that was hidden behind the iridescent tail of the comet. In ancient Sumer 4,000 years earlier, we can only imagine what effect the sight of this comet might have had. Some might have looked up and seen the blessings of the gods, smiling on the lands of Sumer. Others might have stared at that lonely cosmic traveller and seen a sign of doom. Ultimately, it was these latter who proved correct.

During the reign of Shar-Kali-Sharri, the global climate underwent a sudden and mysterious shift. This change is known only by the cryptic name, the '4.2-kiloyear event'. It has been tentatively connected to changes that took place in the sea ice of the North Atlantic, causing ripples throughout the world's delicately interlinked climate systems. Whatever the cause, its effects were dramatic. In various places around the globe, the event coincided with periods of reduced rainfall. Studies of sedimented dust layers in Iraq and elsewhere in the Middle East have shown that annual rainfall dropped dramatically and the climate became much more arid. The annual river floods, on which agriculture depended, routinely failed, and famine set in. This period of drought and famine lasted for well over a century, and some believe for the next 300 years. It was mentioned in Egyptian texts of the time and has been linked to a number of other collapsed societies, notably Egypt's Old Kingdom, the Indus Valley Civilization in India, and the Liangzhu culture in China.

In Mesopotamia, still ruled over by the Akkadian Empire, it's clear that resources became suddenly scarce. The days of a booming food surplus were over, and some towns and cities in the drier zones of the north were abandoned. After the death of Shar-Kali-Sharri around 2193 BCE, a period of chaos and bitter civil war descended on the lands of Akkad. The Sumerian King List records this period in an almost sarcastic tone: 'Then who was king? Who was *not* king? Irgigi was king, Nanum was king, Imi was king, Elulu was king; those four kings ruled three years.'[23]

This turmoil did not go unnoticed. In the mountains overlooking the plains of Mesopotamia, a nomadic tribal people known as the Guti were watching. Who the Guti were, what language they spoke, and which gods they worshipped, we have no idea—but ancient texts like the Esagila Chronicle reserve particular contempt for these nomads: 'The Gutians were unhappy people unaware how to revere the gods, ignorant of the right cultic practices.'[24] The Guti had raided and plundered along the borders of the Akkadian Empire for years, burning villages and stealing cattle. In a letter dating from the reign of Shar-Kali-Sharri, an Akkadian lord who owned land on the borders of Guti territory tells his labourers to ignore the Guti attacks and get back to work, although it's clear he himself is maintaining a safe distance:

> Cultivate the field and watch over the cattle! Do not tell me, 'The Guti enemies are around, I could not cultivate the field.' Post sentries at one-mile intervals, and if the Guti try to attack you, take all the cattle into the village. Now I swear on the life of King Shar-Kali-Sharri that if the Guti men drive off the cattle, and you cannot pay for them yourself, I won't pay you any silver when I come to town.[25]

In Akkad's moment of drought-stricken weakness, the Guti made their move. They rode down from the hills, this time not to raid, but to invade and take the lands of Sumer for themselves. One remarkable literary text written a few centuries later is called *The Curse of Akkad*, and it relates how the god Enlil, angered by the King of Akkad, summons the Guti as a punishment. The hill people are imagined as monstrous creatures, with a language that sounded to the Sumerians like the barking of dogs.

Gutium, the land that brooks no control,
Whose understanding is human, (but) whose form (and) stuttering words are that of a dog.
Enlil brought them down from the mountain.
In vast numbers, like locusts, they covered the earth.
Their 'arm' stretched out...like an animal-trap,
Nothing escaped their arm,
No one eluded their arm
...
All the lands raised a bitter cry on their city walls.[26]

It seems the Guti practised hit-and-run tactics, raiding supply lines and leaving scorched earth behind them. They swept down on the capital city, Akkad, and so thoroughly destroyed it that the ruins have never been found. Their attacks devastated the economy, and the already weakened, drought-ridden and war-torn society folded under the onslaught.

The Guti attempted to set up their own dynasty and rule over Sumer and Akkad—but as invaders of Mesopotamia have found in our own time, it's much easier to conquer a society than to rule it. Cuneiform sources suggest that the Guti administration showed little concern for maintaining agriculture, written records, or public safety. They were not literate and must have struggled to administer an empire that had relied for centuries on the written word. For reasons known only to them and perhaps relating to their nomadic lifestyle, they didn't believe in keeping animals in pens, and apparently released all of the farm animals to roam about the countryside freely. Their policies soon brought further famine and a massive increase in the price of grain. Infrastructure began to crumble, as *The Curse of Akkad* relates:

> On its canal bank tow-paths, the grass grew long. On its highways laid for wagons, the grass of mourning grew. Moreover, on its tow-paths built up with canal sediment, wild rams and alert snakes of the mountains allowed no one to

pass. On its plains, where fine grass grew, now the reeds of lamentation grew.[27]

The Guti occupied southern Iraq for more than 150 years, and it was by all accounts a time of suffering, a miniature dark age in which written records became scarce and unsophisticated. But as resentment to their rule grew, some among the newly marginalized Sumerian population saw the opportunity that this teetering occupation presented. One such Sumerian was Utu-hengal, who may have been the governor of Uruk. Around 2114 BCE, he seized his chance, at the moment when a new Guti king named Tirigan had just ascended to the throne. Amassing his rebel force, Utu-hengal stopped off at the temple of Ishkur, the Sumerian god of storms, to make an offering. He may have sacrificed a lamb or goat and sung an ancient prayer before the altar, before marching to meet the Guti generals on the plain. He and his Sumerian forces were victorious. The King List describes how he routed Tirigan's armies, and the Sumerians finally rejected the dominion of both the Akkadians and the Guti.

Utu-hengal ushered in an era known today variously as the Third Dynasty of Ur, or the Neo-Sumerian Empire. Some historians have even called it 'The Sumerian Renaissance'. It was to be the final flourishing of Sumerian culture.

★★★

Despite bringing the kingship back to Sumer, the rebel king Utu-hengal didn't rule for long. He died in unusual circumstances after only seven years, supposedly killed when a river dam that he was inspecting burst and swept him away. One of Utu-hengal's more ambitious governors, a man named Ur-Nammu, came to the throne soon after, and some historians have certainly raised questions about whether he had a hand in that dam bursting—if, indeed, any dam burst at all.

Regardless of how he rose to power, Ur-Nammu proved to be an effective ruler and an outstanding administrator. He standardized the bronze weights that merchants used in the market and established a conventional unit for measuring out silver, the *mina*, equivalent to sixty shekels, thus laying the foundations for the first currencies. He also leaves us the earliest surviving example of a legal code, known as 'the Code of Ur-Nammu', three centuries older than the more famous Code of Hammurabi. It ensured a two-shekel reward for anyone returning a runaway slave to their master, and set the compensations in silver for various kinds of injury. If a man were to put out the eye of another man, the code dictates he should pay the injured party half a *mina* of silver—and if he cut off his foot, ten shekels. This code of laws influenced those that came after, and its echoes can be found in the Hebrew Bible.

Ur-Nammu was also a prodigious builder. He constructed buildings at the cities of Nippur, Larsa, Kish, Adab and Umma. He rebuilt the kingdom's roads and irrigation ditches after the long decades of neglect under Guti rule. More than anything, Ur-Nammu loved to build ziggurats. A ziggurat was a kind of stepped tower that acted as a focal point of Sumerian worship, built in layers like a wedding cake. Soon, every Sumerian city had a ziggurat at its centre. The greatest of these was the ziggurat that Ur-Nammu built in his home city of Ur.

The Ziggurat of Ur was enormous, soaring to a height of 30 metres, or about ten storeys, and towering over all the other low-lying buildings in the city. It was built from baked-clay bricks, held together with bitumen. It's thought that it would have taken at least 1,500 workers more than five years just to build its base. Farmers up to 20 kilometres away would have been able to see this enormous shape rising on the horizon. To them, it would have testified to the power of Ur, and the god who lived there. But despite this late flourishing, the age of the Sumerians was definitively passing. Part of the reason for this lay in the soil beneath their feet.

All river water contains small amounts of salts and other minerals, and the waters of the Tigris and Euphrates, flowing over the limestone rocks of the Taurus mountains, contain more than most. The Sumerians had grown to such heights partly due to their mastery of irrigation systems, but when ancient farmers diverted water into their fields to feed their crops, the hot sun would evaporate the water, and these traces of salts were left behind. In places with a reasonable amount of rainfall, these salts are washed away—but in the arid conditions of Iraq, the salt builds up over time and makes it difficult for plants to grow.

The meticulous records of the Sumerian scribes, maintained year on year, paint a bleak picture. From around 2350 BCE, they show the gradual reduction of crop yields across the region, and one telltale detail reveals that the salt content of the soil might have been to blame. While yields of hardy, salt-tolerant barley remained near-constant, the Sumerians' main crop of wheat kept reducing over the centuries. Texts recovered from the city of Girsu show that around 3500 BCE, wheat and barley were being produced in equal amounts, but after a thousand years of irrigation, wheat accounted for only one-sixth of the crop. Only a few centuries later, in the twenty-first century BCE, wheat was less than two per cent of the annual harvest. This points to a sharp increase in the salt content of the soil, and a desperate attempt by the Sumerians to adapt to the new conditions.

The Sumerians didn't stumble blindly into their salinity crisis. As well as switching their staple crop to barley, they also developed new methods for draining the soil—but soil salinity is still a challenge for farmers in Iraq today, despite all our technology and scientific knowledge. While the ancient people worked hard to mitigate their agricultural decline, the overall trend was slow but unstoppable. The soil was failing year by year, and with the population of Sumerian cities growing, and the 100-year drought dragging on, the demands on this farmland were only increasing. Eventually, a thick layer of salt encrusted the topsoil, and little grew at all. Today when you walk around the deserts of Iraq, the soil in some areas has a crumbly crust that cracks underfoot, peeling like old paint on a wall. This is the salt that more than 4,000 years ago choked the life from the civilization of Sumer. However, the final death blow for Sumerian culture would come not from the soil, but at the tip of a spear.

★★★

As the Sumerians struggled to eke ever-decreasing yields from their salinized earth, hostile outside forces once more sensed weakness. After their failed attempt at empire-building, the Guti had retreated to their nomadic mountain lifestyle, but they still posed a threat to Sumerian lands, raiding border towns and stealing cattle. In a desperate blow to the empire, King Ur-Nammu died in battle, apparently while trying to chase off these raiders. An epic poem entitled *The Death of Ur-Nammu* describes the ensuing death spiral of the Sumerian Empire: 'Silence descended. As he, who was the vigour of the Land, had fallen, the Land became demolished like a mountain; like a cypress forest it was stripped, its appearance changed.'[28]

Four further Sumerian kings followed Ur-Nammu. Some, like King Shulgi, who came to the throne in 2094 BCE, enjoyed successes on the battlefield, and developed and reformed the economy as much as they could—but their reigns were characterized by drought, reduced crop yields and ongoing threats from the mountain regions. As drought tightened its grip and food got scarcer across the whole region, more and more nomadic people were driven to raiding and plundering to feed themselves. The Guti were far from the only people who now threatened the border of Sumer and Akkad.

One tribe known as the Martu posed a particular threat. They were a Semitic sheep-herding people from the mountains of Syria and Lebanon, and around this time, drought and famine were pushing them south, into the lands of the Sumerians. Like the Guti, the Sumerians considered them wild and barbarous, and tended to describe them in contemptuous but also fearful terms:

> Their hands are destructive and their features are those of monkeys; he is one who eats what Nanna forbids and does not show reverence. They never stop roaming about...they are an abomination to the gods' dwellings. Their ideas are confused; they cause only disturbance. He is clothed in sack-

> leather...lives in a tent, exposed to wind and rain, and cannot properly recite prayers.[29]

Despite the weakened Sumerian state, the later kings of the Neo-Sumerian Empire were determined to stop the Martu incursions. One king named Shu-Sin, whose reign began in 2037 BCE, even ordered the construction of a wall that stretched almost 300 kilometres between the Tigris and Euphrates rivers. It came to be called the Martu wall, and sometimes 'The Wall Facing the High Lands'. What exact form this took is unknown, since its remains have never been found, but it was likely an earthwork rampart dotted with forts, and perhaps fronted with a moat fed by canals. It was more than twice the length of Hadrian's Wall, and essentially turned the farmland between the Tigris and Euphrates into a moated fortress, with the rivers on either side, the sea to the south, and the wall to the north. But ultimately the wall would prove useless. It would only have been effective when constantly manned by garrisons—something that the Sumerian state was increasingly struggling to do. The building of this wall was not an act of strength, but the last resort of an empire falling in on itself.

★★★

The last Sumerian king was Shu-Sin's son Ibbi-Sin, who took the throne in 2028 BCE. In the first year of his reign, the eastern city of Eshunna broke free from the empire, and in the third year, Susa, a city in the region of Elam, successfully rebelled. The fracturing empire could no longer maintain its defences along the 300 kilometres of the great Martu wall that his father had built. In the fifth year of his reign, it failed. The Martu poured over the defences and overran the rich farmlands behind it.

The effect on the Sumerian economy was devastating. Food shortages ran rampant. In years seven and eight of Ibbi-Sin's kingship, the price of grain increased to sixty times the usual cost. Facing threats on multiple sides, the king attempted a frantic series of last-ditch measures. He sent a general named Ishbi-Erra to supervise the transport of a large grain shipment from the nearby city of Isin at many times market value. But when he got to his destination, Ishbi-Erra betrayed the king: he decided to keep the silver and the grain, and declared himself the king of Isin. With no grain and now another city gone, the frantic Ibbi-Sin ordered fortifications built at Ur and Nippur, but these efforts too were in vain. The Sumerian Empire fell apart, and only the city of Ur remained, surrounded by hostile forces.

Soon the Elamites, former subjects based in the mountains of modern Iran, marched down from the hills and laid siege to Ur. Ibbi-Sin made one last attempt to beat them back. He even tried to enlist the help of his worst enemies, the wild Martu tribesmen, and even, humiliatingly, the new King of Isin, the backstabbing Ishbi-Erra. But it was useless. The Elamites burst through the walls of Ur and set the city on fire. They plundered its sacred precinct and temples. The surrounding fields were burned, and the waterways became contaminated with the dead.

The armies of Elam stormed the royal palace and took Ibbi-Sin away in chains. This last king of Sumer, a civilization that had endured for millennia, died in chains, imprisoned by his enemies in a foreign land. And, as one lament had it, 'like a swallow that has flown from its house, he should never return to his city'.[30] The Sumerians who witnessed the destruction of their cities recorded their sorrow in the way that humans always have: they wrote poetry. For each of their great ruined cities, they wrote a lament. Five of these epic poems survive. *The Lament for Ur* relates with tangible anguish the horror of that time:

> In the city the wife was abandoned, the child was abandoned, possessions were scattered about. The black-headed people were carried off from their strongholds. Ningal like a bird in fright departed from her city. All the treasures accumulated in the Land were defiled. In all the storehouses abounding in the land fires were kindled… They broke up the good house with pickaxes. They reduced the city to ruin mounds. Its queen cried, 'Alas, my city', cried, 'Alas, my house'… Your song has been turned into weeping before you.[31]

The fall of Ur marked the end of the unified Sumerian state. Over the following years, a great population movement took place, from the south of Mesopotamia to the north. The Martu, those wild hill people so detested by the Sumerians, themselves settled in the cities they had conquered along the river valley, and their descendants laid the foundations for the superpowers that arose from the ashes of Sumer—the civilizations of Babylon and Assyria. The Sumerian language had been dying for centuries, but now the last of its speakers were scattered to the winds, and it would never again be spoken on the streets. It did, however, remain in ceremonial use for at least another 2,000 years, preserved in the temples and scriptures of later empires, just as Latin survived in the churches of medieval Europe after the fall of Rome. For these peoples, Sumerian became the language of myth and magic, the language of the gods. The Kings of Ur passed into legend, with some later revered as deities, and all the kings of the new Mesopotamia, for the next 2,000 years, would rule under a title that gave them a kind of ancient legitimacy reaching back to the first age, to the dawn of mankind's journey into civilization: 'King of Ur, King of Sumer and Akkad'.

Some time around the year 1700 BCE, when the Kings of Ur were already a distant memory, on the other side of the world, on the edge of the Arctic Ocean, on a small rocky outcrop known as Wrangel Island, the last woolly mammoth ever to live on earth lay down and died. Sumerian society in its imperial form rose, lived out its golden age and died, outlived by the woolly mammoth.

***

Today, if you stand in the ruins of Ur, the sea that once lapped its shores is nowhere to be seen. Archaeologists who began visiting the site in the nineteenth century were astonished to see millions of seashells scattered in the sand of this lonely stretch of desert. By then, continual deposits of alluvial silt, along with global changes in sea level, had combined over the millennia to push the Gulf coast back to its present position, about 150 kilometres to the south. The Euphrates River, which once brought the rich bounties of trade down to the city of Ur from the north, is also nowhere to be seen, its course having changed over the centuries. In fact, stretching away from the barren mounds of earth where Ur once stood, there's nothing but the lone and level sands of the Iraqi desert, boundless and bare for miles around.

The Great Ziggurat of Ur, as it appeared in 1932.

Water had always been Ur's lifeblood, and the loss of the river and the sea spelled its death. People abandoned their homes. They stopped working its fields and maintaining its irrigation canals. The land dried up, and the topsoil blew away. The priests extinguished the fires that burned in the top chamber of Ur's ziggurat and ceased leaving their offerings to the moon god Sin. The markets closed and the mud-brick buildings began to crumble. The wooden beams of the roofs rotted and fell in. The desert winds rolled the sand through its streets and buried them. Before long, the city was only a mound of ruins where the occasional desert traveller passed by, and where the explorer Pietro Della Valle would one day take shelter from a band of threatening Bedouin.

Following the collapse of Ur, Uruk went into a similar steep decline. Today, the walls of Uruk, boasted of in the *Epic of Gilgamesh*, are still visible as heaps of ancient brickwork emerging 15 metres tall from the flat lunar landscape, washed by a tide of broken pottery and bones. The English archaeologist William Loftus was the first European to rediscover the ruins of Uruk. 'I know of nothing more exciting or impressive,' he wrote, 'than the first sight of one of these Chaldaean piles, looming in solitary grandeur from the surrounding plains and marshes… Of all the desolate sites I ever beheld, that of Warka [Uruk] incomparably surpasses all.'[32]

Buried in the ruins of these, the world's first cities, lay the clay tablets on which were written the records and recipes of the Sumerian people, their music and prayers, their loves and grief, their triumphs and their beautiful, sorrowful lamentations. Somewhere buried in those sands would lie the fragments of the *Epic of Gilgamesh*, which contains what may as well be the final epitaph of Sumer:

> As long as houses are built, as long as tablets are sealed,
> as long as brothers are at enmity,
> as long as there exist strife and hatred in the land,
> as long as the river carries the waters to the sea,
> no man can tell when his own time might come.
> The great gods assemble,
> and the goddess of fate, she who with them determines fate,
> will do so,
> For they alone determine death and life.
> But the days of death are unknown to mankind.[33]

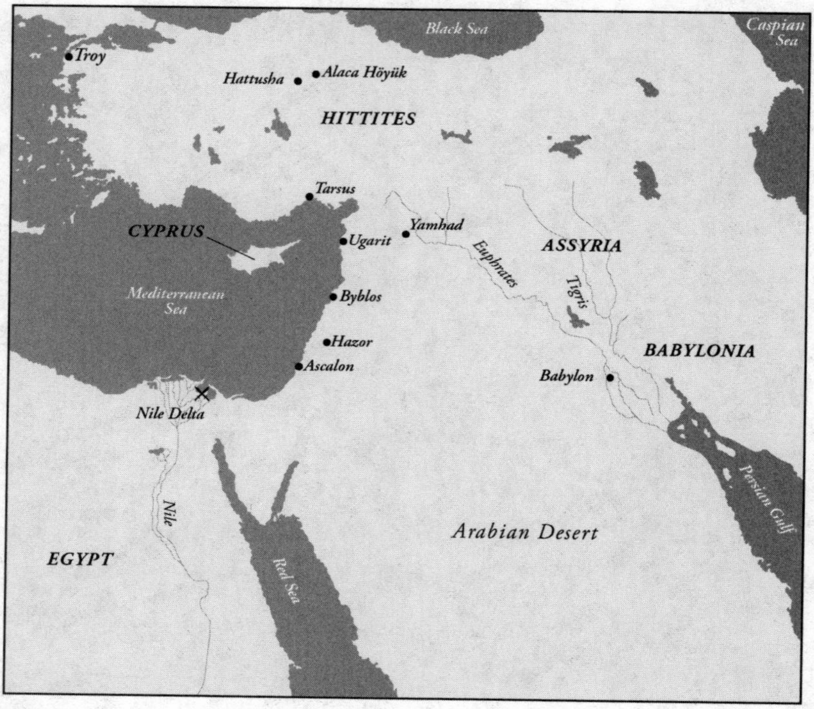

Black Sea
Caspian Sea
Troy
Hattusha
Alaca Höyük
HITTITES
Tarsus
CYPRUS
Ugarit
Yamhad
Euphrates
ASSYRIA
Tigris
Mediterranean Sea
Byblos
Hazor
Ascalon
BABYLONIA
Babylon
Nile Delta
Nile
Persian Gulf
Arabian Desert
EGYPT
Red Sea

2

The Late Bronze Age Collapse

c. 1600 BCE—*c.* 1150 BCE

From the ashes of Sumer, a host of successors arose in the millennium that followed, and by 1200 BCE, the eastern shores of the Mediterranean Sea were ruled by a diverse scattering of kingdoms, minor empires and city states. Languages and cultures mingled as trade routes criss-crossed land and sea. Markets bustled in the thriving cities of Ugarit, Hattusha, Mycenae and Babylon, and the Mediterranean experienced a golden age of literacy and culture. But within just a few decades, every one of these cities lay in ruins. Their stones were scattered, their libraries burned, their people left unburied in the streets. The world as it once was came to an end, and only ash and desolation were left behind. This was one of the worst disasters of ancient history, an event that historians have come to call the 'Late Bronze Age Collapse'—and exactly what happened is still one of history's most fiercely debated mysteries.

***

The ruins of the city of Hattusha are a melancholy sight: crumbling walls of grey limestone stand out against the tawny yellow grassland and rocky outcrops of the surrounding hills. Even now, one look will tell you that Hattusha was once a mighty fortress, built in the rocky Çorum province of the Black Sea Region of Turkey, within a great bend of the Kızılırmak River. Its double wall was defended by more than a hundred towers, its thick gateways decorated with carved sculptures of lions. For centuries, this was the prosperous capital of the Hittite Empire. But if you were to dig down into the ruins of Hattusha, you would find a thin black layer right above the floor level of its buildings. This layer is made up of ash, charred wood and rubble scorched in a fierce fire, and it dates to around 1200 BCE. Archaeology paints a picture of total destruction: walls and roofs collapsed, bricks shattered and melted. After that event, the archaeological record ends. Except for occasional signs of a few scattered scavengers eking out an existence among the rubble, the ruins of Hattusha remained empty for centuries—a haunted place, where it seems most feared to go.

We find the same evidence 20 kilometres north of Hattusha, at the site of the ancient city of Alaca Höyük, where the Hittites buried their kings in opulent tombs. Like Hattusha, it is completely covered by ash and rubble at the same level. And 100 kilometres to the east of that, another fortified Hittite town known as Maşat Höyük, with a strong citadel and spacious palace, was also burned around the same time. In nearby Karaoğlan, you can find arrowheads littering the earth like fallen leaves, and the bones of men, women and children left lying in the streets, right where they fell over 3,000 years ago. In fact, almost anywhere you go in the Eastern Mediterranean, across an area spanning over 1,000 kilometres, you will find this layer of destruction. Archaeological evidence is quite explicit: at some point between 1200 and 1100 BCE, civilization in this region simply came to an end. The historian Robert Drews puts it succinctly:

> Within a period of forty or fifty years at the end of the thirteenth and beginning of the twelfth century [BCE] almost every significant city in the eastern Mediterranean world was destroyed, many of them never to be occupied again… It is safe to say that for a long time after the year 1200 [BCE] there were no cities in the [Eastern Mediterranean] area.[1]

It took some of these areas nearly a thousand years to recover. Powerful and well-established empires like those of the Hittites, Ugarit, the Minoans and the Mycenaean Greeks collapsed so completely that they disappeared from the historical record altogether, and their descendants were left to live among the ruins.

***

One of the ways in which the memory of the Late Bronze Age Collapse may have survived is through the epic poetry that was composed about this time. The most famous of these relates the destruction of a walled city in the Eastern Mediterranean called Troy.

The "Grave of Agamemnon" at Mycenae.

The epic poems known as the *Iliad* and *Odyssey* are attributed to the author Homer, who may or may not have existed. Recent scholarship now generally holds that these epics were passed down as oral poetry for centuries through the period known as the Greek Dark Ages, which followed the chaos of the Bronze Age Collapse. These poems survived by word of mouth, with each poet-singer using astonishing skills of memory to recite them, lengthening and embellishing them along the way, until they were finally written down by an anonymous scribe around the eighth century BCE. The poetry of the *Iliad* especially relates the story of a ten-year war that took place in the Eastern Mediterranean, and which occupied much of the warrior classes of Greece. This war was supposedly led by Agamemnon, a king of the Greek city state of Mycenae.

In the second millennium BCE, Mycenae was one of the major centres of Greek civilization, and from around 1400–1200 BCE was the predominant power of the Peloponnese. Lying about 90 kilometres south-west of Athens, it was a military stronghold that held sway from its mountainous perch overlooking the plains of Argos, and had a population of over 30,000 people at its height. Like Hattusha, its citadel gates were decorated with carved stone lions, and its people made armour out of ivory taken from the tusks of wild boars. Over a millennium later, in the second century CE, the Greek travel writer Pausanias wrote breathlessly about his visit to its ruins, the large stones of which were so impressive that he believed them to have been built by giants:

> The wall, which is the only part of the ruins still remaining, is a work of the Cyclopes made of unwrought stones, each stone being so big that a pair of mules could not move the smallest from its place to the slightest degree. Long ago small stones were so inserted that each of them binds the large blocks firmly together…[2]

For a long time it was thought that the Trojan War was an invention of a poet's imagination, and that the city of Troy itself was a myth—but that all changed with the discovery of the ruins of Troy at the end of the nineteenth century, at a place called Hisarlık at the mouth of the Dardanelles in what is today Turkey. This location would have placed Troy on the periphery of the Hittite Empire, and as a major rival to Mycenaean power.

Many scholars now believe that the Trojan War as related by Homer does reflect real events, or at least a composite of several events, filtered through the lens of mythology and oral storytelling. The historian Eric Cline points out that a Hittite artefact known as the Milawata letter describes a conflict that seemingly occurred between the Hittites and the Mycenaeans over a city that they called Wilusa—which may have been the Greek Ilion, or Troy. This conflict may not have been particularly large, but in the time between the real event and the writing of the epics, the entire region underwent the catastrophe of the collapse. Over that period, these epics may have preserved at least in hazy form an authentic memory of those days—not just a clash between two powerful Bronze Age empires, but the feeling of apocalypse that must have washed over the region, the trauma of a period of warfare and destruction that seemed to dwarf all others.

The site of Troy has now been extensively excavated, and we have learned that throughout the Bronze Age, Troy was indeed a grand city much as Homer describes. It was topped with an impressively fortified citadel, and contained artefacts that suggest trade links to the Hittites, Assyrians and Babylonians. This layer of the city's archaeology is known as Troy VI, and it lasted from about 1750 BCE until about 1300 BCE. According to the Greek epics, its walls were built by the gods Poseidon and Apollo, and in reality they were certainly impressive: 9 metres high, with towers soaring up to 18 metres. Around the citadel replete with royal palaces, a long curtain wall enclosed a larger urban area. But unfortunately for historians, the ruins of Troy are strangely silent—that is, there has been almost no writing uncovered in any excavations of the city, and it's unclear even what language the people of Troy spoke.

The grand royal city of Troy VI was destroyed around the year 1300 BCE, possibly by an earthquake—there is widespread damage to the foundations of the buildings, and some sign of fire damage to the city's stones—but others argue that it could have been sacked, and that this is the event that Homer's *Iliad* remembers. After this disaster, people rebuilt many of the monumental palaces, and reinhabited the city in a somewhat diminished form—but then around 1190 BCE, the city was burned again, right as that wave of destruction passed over the whole region. Here, significant traces of fire can be found on its stones, while human remains were found in houses and in the streets. Near its north-western ramparts, a human skeleton with skull injuries and a broken jawbone was unearthed, and bronze arrowheads litter the ground in the citadel. In fact, it seems Troy was burned twice towards the end of the thirteenth century BCE. It's not clear who the perpetrators of this massacre were—but we can imagine that the poetry of the *Iliad* captures something of the violence of warfare in that time.

> Then rose too mingled shouts and groans of men
> Slaying and slain; the earth ran red with blood.
> As when, descending from the mountain's brow,
> Two wintry torrents, from their copious source
> Pour downwards to the narrow pass, where meet
> Their mingled waters in some deep ravine,
> The weight of flood, on the far mountain's side
> The shepherd hears the roar; so loud arose
> The shouts and yells of the commingling hosts.[3]

The Hittitologist Trevor Bryce speculates that it was this final abandonment of Troy's population centre that inspired Greek poet-singers to assemble the material of the *Iliad*:

> All this contributed to the making of the epic: a long tradition of conflicts between western Anatolian peoples and the Mycenaean Greeks…the final abandonment of the citadel of this state… They now saw before them Troy's ultimate fate—its destruction and abandonment.[4]

The Greek city state of Mycenae would itself face a similar fate. By 1200 BCE, its power was waning—but then, within a short time, all the palace complexes of southern Greece, including Mycenae, were burned to the ground. But before we go into the causes of the Bronze Age Collapse, we need to understand what was lost—this vibrant and varied region that had prospered for so many centuries, and fell so completely and so suddenly.

***

We often make the mistake of thinking about the ancient world as a series of insular and isolated states, and it is true that their worlds were smaller than ours. The 'known world' for someone living in the Eastern Mediterranean around 1200 BCE would have extended from Greece to perhaps the Zagros mountains of western Iran. It was populated by the Mycenaean people of Greece in the west and the New Kingdom of Egypt in the south, which was just emerging from a period of civil war. It took in the islands of Cyprus and Crete, as well as coastal cities along the Levantine coast like the Phoenician city of Byblos—then an Egyptian colony—and the wealthy port city state of Ugarit. To the east in the verdant marshes of southern Iraq, the city of Babylon was at that time ruled by a dynasty known as the Kassites, and to the north of them was the bellicose Empire of Assyria, which governed the plains of northern Iraq and Syria.

These kingdoms, empires and city states could be suspicious and rivalrous and often went to war—but this wasn't the whole story. The societies of the Bronze Age were in many ways as entangled and interdependent as the nation states of our globalized world today. Firstly, trade across the Mediterranean Sea was essential to the economies of these civilizations. One shipwreck found off the coast of Uluburun in south-western Turkey offers a glimpse into the rich exchange of materials that occurred during this time. Built of Lebanese cedarwood, the ship has been dated to about 1300 BCE, and was likely sailing to a Mycenaean port when it sunk. Among its cargo, archaeologists found 10 tonnes of copper smelted into more than 350 ingots, 1 tonne of tin, logs of ebony, elephant and hippo tusks along with more than a dozen hippopotamus teeth, a jar filled with glass beads, more with olives and terebinth resin, almonds, pistachios, figs, grapes and coriander, whole pomegranates and a golden scarab beetle inscribed with the name of the Egyptian queen Nefertiti, arrowheads, daggers, turtle shells and ostrich eggs, quartz crystals and gold, pottery and oil lamps from Cyprus, along with blocks of raw coloured glass in cobalt blue and lavender—altogether goods from at least seven different lands.

It's easy to see how this rich trade would have drawn all these disparate civilizations together. People, too, passed between them. We know that Minoan artists from Crete, for instance, came to decorate the walls of Egyptian palaces in the Pharaonic naval base of Peru-nefer. Kings requested the services of 'physicians, artisans, weavers, musicians, and singers'[5] from other kingdoms. And intermarriage was also fairly common, especially among the elites. To give just one example, we know from court records that Ammurapi, the last king of Ugarit, married and subsequently went through a bitter and lengthy divorce with a Hittite woman.

While much of the trade in the region was in luxury goods, other materials that flowed down these trade routes were utterly essential to the survival of these large, complex nations—and of all these, the most critical Bronze Age resource was of course the one that gives the era its name. Bronze is a reddish-gold alloy of copper and tin, on a roughly 10:1 ratio. It was the sharpest and hardest metal yet available, and since its discovery some time in the fourth millennium BCE, had become critical to the manufacture of just about every weapon, tool and household object. Like aluminium or steel today, it had become completely indispensable to the societies it supported. Without a steady supply of high quality bronze, armies would have no weapons; chariot wheels would go rimless; craftsmen would have no tools. The historian Carol Bell describes this early period of globalized supply.

> The availability of enough tin to produce what I like to call weapons grade bronze must have exercised the minds of the great king in Hattusa and the Pharaoh in Thebes in the same way that supplying gasoline to the American SUV driver at reasonable cost preoccupies an American President today.[6]

For the manufacture of all this bronze, copper was relatively easy to find—but tin was a rare metal. At the time, the primary source was a series of mines in the Badakhshan region of Afghanistan. From there, it had to be brought overland on caravans of donkeys, following the ancient route that would one day be known as the Silk Road. It was a long and perilous route that crossed mountains and rivers, until it reached the cities of Mesopotamia. From there, the cargo of tin spread out across the region, and over the sea to Greece. Studies of isotope and chemical composition have even shown that tin mined in south-western England—in the present-day counties of Devon and Cornwall—was making its way into the furnaces of the Near East around this time. The entire military might of the region's superpowers—Egypt, Assyria, the Hittites, Ugarit, Babylon and Mycenae—all depended on these precarious supplies, which must have felt at the time as fragile as a cobweb.

Tied together by these interrelations of trade and supply, these nations were not entirely distinct and separate entities, so much as a complex and entangled mesh of societies, each as dependent on each other as the next. While peace largely held in the region and trade could continue, they achieved a kind of stability. But for a number of reasons, peace wasn't to last.

★★★

When casting around for the causes of the Late Bronze Age Collapse, historians have long alighted on one particular set of culprits. These they refer to as the 'Sea Peoples', a moniker coined in the nineteenth century. This name seems to evoke something terrifying and foreign, like monsters rising up from the depths to wreak devastation on the land. Who exactly the Sea Peoples were, where they came from or what language they spoke are all uncertain. Many historians have offered their guesses, ranging from Sardinia and Sicily to Libya or the Aegean, or closer by in the Eastern Mediterranean. But wherever they originated, one thing is certain: around the time of the great collapse, these invaders began landing on the shores of the Eastern Mediterranean in large numbers and with fearsome force. An account of this armada is given on the walls of the mortuary temple of Pharaoh Ramesses III at Medinet Habu, near the Valley of the Kings.

> The... [Northerners] in their isles were disturbed, taken away in the [fray]—at one time. Not one stood before their hands, from Kheta, Kode, Carchemish, Arvad, Alasa, they [all] were wasted... They desolated his people and his land was like that which is not... These lands were united, and they laid their hands upon the land as far as the Circle of the Earth. Their hearts were confident, full of their plans.[7]

At least some of the societies that caved in at the end of the Bronze Age fell because of this single cause. One example is the city state of Ugarit, a booming trade city whose ruins lie at the site of Ras Shamra on the coast of northern Syria.

Ugarit had ruled over a small coastal kingdom of merchants and sailors for at least six centuries. It stood at the very end of the trade routes that snaked across the Asian landmass, and dispersed goods from its port all over the Mediterranean. Ships full of all the items found nestled in the hold of the Uluburun shipwreck would have passed through Ugarit, and each one of them would have been taxed. With this wealth its citizens built a resplendent city by the sea. Like most successful trading towns, Ugarit was multicultural and diverse, using at least seven languages in its records. It was a city in love with the written word and it kept expansive libraries in its palaces and temples. It even fostered some of the earliest known private libraries, one of which we know belonged to a diplomat named Rapanu. To Ugarit, we owe the oldest surviving complete piece of written music in the world, a hymn dedicated to the moon goddess Nikkal, which can still be played today.

But this prosperity was soon to come to an end. In Ugarit, archaeologists have found a clay tablet containing a letter from King Ammurapi. In it, he begs the ruler of nearby Cyprus to come to his aid:

> My father behold, the enemy's ships came [here]; my cities were burned, and they did evil things in my country. Does not my father know that all my troops and chariots are in the Land of Hatti, and all my ships are in the Land of Lukka?... Thus, the country is abandoned to itself. May my father know

it: the seven ships of the enemy that came here inflicted much damage upon us.[8]

No help arrived because the letter was never sent. It burned along with the rest of the city, its clay baked hard in the flames. The city was destroyed so utterly that it was never reoccupied. When excavating the ruins of Ugarit, archaeologists have found a layer of destruction that lies 2 metres thick in places, made of ash and broken brick. Roofs are caved in and scorched, and like Hattusha its streets are scattered with arrowheads. People buried their valuables in panic, and never returned to dig them up. Since most of Ugarit's forces were stationed elsewhere when the attack occurred, we can tell just how much it took them by surprise.

An earthenware statuette of two chariot riders, from Ugarit, ca. 1200–1150 BCE.

Across the region, it seems the Sea Peoples deployed the same tactics. They appeared without warning, wreaked havoc, sacked cities, and then disappeared over the horizon before anyone knew what had happened. These coastal communities had been menaced by pirates for centuries, but this was on a whole different scale. Other cities along the coast like Mersin, Tarsus and Ascalon suffered the same fate, and even those some way inland, like Hazor in the hills of Upper Galilee and the city of Yamhad on the site of the Syrian city of Aleppo.

The island of Cyprus, to whom the king of Ugarit had hoped to send his plea for help, didn't fare any better. On the Bronze Age site of Kokkinokremmos in the south of the island, archaeologists have found evidence that the whole town was abandoned in a hurry. The bronzesmith buried his tools in the courtyard of his workshop, the silversmith hid his silver between two slabs of a stone bench, while the goldsmith hid all his sheet gold in a pit. What happened to these artisans we may never know—but they never returned to retrieve their precious things.

For a long time, historians were content to attribute the collapse of many complex societies all at once to the Sea Peoples. These marauders themselves left no written sources, and precious few material traces have ever been conclusively connected to them. But, a little unusually, we do actually have a pretty good idea of what the Sea Peoples looked like. That's thanks to the sprawling low-relief carving that Pharaoh Ramesses III chose to adorn the outer wall of his mortuary temple at Medinet Habu, on the west bank of the Nile opposite Luxor in Upper Egypt.

An illustration of the different kinds of "Sea People" as shown in the Medinet Habu inscriptions.

The detailed carved relief shows a number of prisoners taken from the Sea Peoples: men wiry and tall and wearing kilts, with some sporting a distinctive kind of headdress that looks like a sheaf of feathers or reeds, fixed in place with a chinstrap; others wear skull caps, or horned helmets. These variations in their appearance point to a loose confederation of different peoples, choosing to sail under the same banner. While we don't know where they came from, some of the names of these peoples are known to us from inscriptions: the Danuna, the Tjekker, the Peleset, the Shardana and the Weshesh. They were seemingly a loose coalition, and no leaders or kings are ever mentioned.

Evidence suggests that at least some of the ethnic groups that made up the Sea Peoples weren't unfamiliar to the Egyptians. In fact, it seems some had sought employment in Egyptian courts and armies in the past, and there's some evidence that they had had diplomatic contact over perhaps as much as a few centuries before the collapse occurred. The Shardana people, who may have originated in Sardinia, had even supplied mercenaries to the pharaohs, and their distinctive pointed helmets can also be seen in a painting on the walls of the temple of Abu Simbel in Egypt's far south. But whoever they were, one thing is for certain: wherever the Sea Peoples went, destruction followed.

★★★

During the Bronze Age Collapse, we can effectively place the nations of the Eastern Mediterranean into two categories. First, there are those that cave completely under the pressures of the time and disappear, leaving only ruins behind. Into that group, we can place Mycenae, the Hittites, Ugarit, and others. In the second category are the civilizations that survive, albeit in a diminished and weakened form: these are the empires of Egypt and Assyria.

Assyria survived the coming onslaught by cutting its losses. It withdrew from all its less defensible territories and fell back to its imperial heartland between the Euphrates and Tigris rivers, recoiling like a tortoise into its shell. The example of Egypt is more interesting, and the man who is perhaps most responsible for its survival is the pharaoh of the time: Ramesses III.

Ramesses was a determined and tenacious ruler. Looking at the perfectly preserved mummy uncovered in the Valley of the Kings, it's easy to imagine his appearance in life: his high cheekbones and tall, narrow forehead give him a cerebral air, and inscriptions hint at him as a builder, a devotee to the gods and a statesman. Ramesses was the son of a usurper, a man named Setnakhte, who had seized the throne in a bloody civil war and begun the Twentieth Dynasty of Egypt. Setnakhte managed to rule for only four years before his death in 1186 BCE, when the crown passed to the young Ramesses, as the later inscriptions recount: 'The gods have appointed me to be king over Egypt…they decreed to me the kingdom while I was a child, and my reign is full of plenty.'[9]

This new Pharaoh must have felt a pressure to prove himself, perhaps reflected in the name he ruled under. The last pharaoh to hold the name Ramesses was Ramesses the Great, who had ruled ancient Egypt for sixty-seven years during the golden age of the New Kingdom, almost a century before. This new Ramesses clearly idolized this ancient king: not only did he name all his sons after his predecessor's sons, but also gave them the same positions in court.

Though we have only his own inscriptions to go by, it seems Ramesses III was a relatively benevolent ruler. He mentions planting trees to increase the shade along the harsh desert roads, and protecting the rights of women so that they didn't fear walking in the streets, as well as allowing soldiers to go home to their families during peacetime. He sent expeditions across the Red Sea to Yemen, where he discovered long-lost copper mines that boosted Egypt's wealth, and also brought back rare plants in pots to cultivate in his gardens. Under other circumstances, he might have been one of Egypt's great rulers.

When news of the Sea Peoples' attacks came to Ramesses, he would have been pharaoh for about eight years. He had already repelled two invasions from Libya, and must have been rising in confidence, but the news must have troubled him. He resolved that his kingdom would not share in the fate of its neighbours. Egypt couldn't react to the threat in the way the Assyrians had, by retreating inland and consolidating their defences. It had a long Mediterranean coast, making it vulnerable to invasion from the sea, and maritime trade was the backbone of its economy. Still, the ancient Egyptians had a poor reputation when it came to naval prowess. They were essentially a land-going power, and usually left the messy business of watery warfare to smaller powers like the Phoenicians. The Egyptians were used to dominating battlefields with vast assemblages of archers and swift units of horse-drawn chariots to sow panic and break the enemy lines. This required, of course, a large open battlefield.

Since members of Sea Peoples groups had served in Egyptian armies in the past, perhaps they knew this weakness. The Sea Peoples seem to have known that the best way to neutralize Egypt's tactics would be an attack on its very lifeblood. All of Egypt's great cities lay on the Nile, and if Egyptian resistance was broken on the river, they would fall one by one, leaving their riches open for the taking. Ramesses knew they would have to be stopped, and he chose as his battleground the lush, fertile Nile Delta. Red lotuses bloom here in the autumn and papyrus sedges grow along the banks. Back then, Nile crocodiles and hippopotamuses still ranged wild.

Ramesses would have to play to what strengths the Egyptian army still had in this challenging terrain. Informed by scouts of the Sea Peoples' approach, he decided to lay an ambush and give the Sea Peoples a surprise attack of their own, as he recounts in his Medinet Habu inscription:

> Now, it happened through this god, the lord of gods, that I was prepared and armed to trap them like wild fowl… I equipped my frontier in Zahi, prepared before them. The chiefs, the captains of infantry, the nobles, I caused to equip the harbour-mouths, like a strong wall, with warships, galleys and barges.[10]

As the enemy's ships amassed, Ramesses gathered archers on the banks, supported by spearmen and cavalry in their thousands, concealed in the reeds, all of them 'soldiers of all the choicest of Egypt, being like lions roaring upon the mountaintops'. Ramesses even remembers the 'horses…quivering in every limb, ready to crush the countries under their feet'. The tension must have been tremendous: all the soldiers of the Egyptian army holding their breath and waiting for that first sign of an enemy ship to come in from the sea.

The battle on the Nile Delta, as depicted on the north wall of the Medinet Habu mortuary temple.

Then, at last, a ship came around the bend in the river. After that came another, and another, until the whole seaborne might of the Sea Peoples was in sight. The Egyptians must have been able to hear the creak of 10,000 oars, the beating of the drums, the shouts of the helmsmen and soldiers. Then, once the Sea Peoples' ships were within range, Ramesses unleashed hell.

Arrows flew out of the reeds and rained down on the ships of the Sea Peoples. Panicked, the invaders attempted to land on the banks, but as they did, the Egyptian lancemen appeared out of the treeline and met them. While the enemy was held at bay, trapped and frantic on the river, the Egyptian navy sailed in and struck. They used grappling hooks to haul in the enemy ships. The chaos of this battle is encapsulated in the carvings at Medinet Habu. Men are shown impaled on spears, clambering onto the sides of ships, ducking arrows that whizz overhead. Boats overturn, spilling men into the river. Bodies float face down in the frothing water. In the brutal hand-to-hand struggle, the Sea Peoples were overwhelmed. Ramesses III's inscription recounts the fury of the battle:

> Those who reached my boundary…their heart and their soul are finished forever and ever. As for those who had assembled before them on the sea, the full flame was in their front, before the harbour-mouths, and a wall of metal upon the shore surrounded them. They were dragged, overturned, and laid low upon the beach; slain and made heaps from stern to bow of their galleys, while all their things were cast upon the water. [Thus] I turned back the waters to remember Egypt; when they [even] mention my name in their land, may it consume them [with fear].[11]

Ramesses's plan had worked. The Egyptians were the first people to turn back these sea-going invaders and stop their campaign of destruction. His inscription at Medinet Habu ends on the following triumphant note:

> Rejoice ye, O Egypt, to the height of heaven, for I am ruler of the South and North upon the throne of Atum... I have expelled your mourning, which was in your heart, and I have made you dwell in peace. Those whom I have overthrown shall not return.[12]

Some of the Sea Peoples seem to have landed in the region of Canaan too, and the Egyptians hunted them down and defeated them on land as well. But this victory alone would not save Egypt. The land of the pharaohs now stood alone in a devastated region. Virtually every land around them had been gutted and reduced to ash. Numerous established civilizations—the Mycenaeans, the Hittites, Ugarit, Babylon—had collapsed, and civil order had given way to chaos. The precarious trade routes on which they had all relied were now broken, and Egypt's economy went into a steep and unstoppable decline. By the end of the Late Bronze Age Collapse, Egypt was utterly diminished, a shadow of its former self.

As other enemies encroached on its borders, Egypt was able to fight them off, but its treasury became so depleted that it never fully recovered its imperial power. The first labour strike in recorded history happened during the twenty-ninth year of Ramesses III's reign, when Egypt could no longer provide food rations for its elite artisans constructing the King's tomb in the village of Deir el-Medina. 'Twenty days have elapsed in the month, and rations have not been given,'[13] complained one official. The lack of rations went on so long, that the workers eventually marched through the town, chanting: 'We're hungry...there is no more clothing, no more oil, no more fish, no more vegetables. Send (word) to the pharaoh...!'[14] If food was not reaching these crucial workers, we can only imagine the situation in the wider kingdom.

Ramesses III ruled for a total of thirty-one years, but he died in 1156 BCE, murdered by members of his own household. His death was followed by years of bickering among his heirs. Three of his sons would become king at different times, reigning as Ramesses IV, Ramesses VI and Ramesses VIII. Meanwhile, Egypt was increasingly beset by droughts, lack of seasonal floodwaters, famines, civil unrest and official corruption. As the power of the Pharaoh waned, that of the priests in Thebes grew—and the last pharaoh of the dynasty, Ramesses XI, had such a weak grasp on power that the priests essentially became the true rulers of the kingdom. The Egyptian Empire finally fractured less than eighty years after Ramesses III's reign, and never regained its former power.

★★★

Historians have long found the Sea Peoples a convenient culprit for the destruction that occurred across this region. But at other sites, the story is a little more complicated. The city state of Mycenae and all its satellite cities were certainly wiped out around the thirteenth century BCE, but it's not clear that this was the work of the Sea Peoples. Modern archaeologists credit this destruction to a more mundane source: the Mycenaeans' belligerent northern neighbours, the Dorians. It's thought that Mycenae was first weakened and distracted by Sea People attacks, before their neighbouring rivals smelled blood and moved in for the kill.

The Hittite capital of Hattusha, where we opened this story, is another example. It lies far inland in the mountains of Turkey, and it wasn't a likely target for coastal raiders. The more likely perpetrators are their long-term rivals, the Kaskians, the Phrygians or the Bryges. These invaders could have seen their opportunity when the Sea Peoples disrupted Mediterranean trade routes, caused shortages in the crucial tin supply and instigated a famine in Hittite lands. States of this era depended heavily on their allies to help them when they were threatened—but when numerous states found themselves under simultaneous threat, those alliances suddenly became ineffective, and everyone was left vulnerable.

Babylon in particular fell prey to the alliance problem. Babylon was one of the most ancient and powerful cities in the region, located about 100 kilometres south of modern Baghdad. It was ruled by a 500-year dynasty known as the Kassites. The Kassites had long depended on their allies in Assyria and the coastal regions to help defend it—but now those nations were busy defending themselves, and Babylon stood alone. To their north was the land of Elam, a hardy people who lived in the mountains of Southern Iran and had been causing trouble for the people of Mesopotamia since the Sumerian Age. The Elamite King Kutir-Nahhunte believed that the crown of Babylon belonged to him, as his father had before him. The previous king had threatened Babylon before, with fearsome rhetoric:

> Why I, who am a king, son of a king, seed of a king, scion of a king…why do I not sit on the throne of the land of Babylonia? I sent you a sincere proposal; you however have granted me no reply: you may climb up to heaven—but I'll pull you down by your hem; you may go down to hell—but I'll pull you up by your hair! I shall destroy your cities, demolish your fortresses, stop up your irrigation ditches, cut down your orchards…[15]

Kutir-Nahhunte led a successful invasion into Babylonia in the year 1158 BCE and went on to make good on what he had promised. None of Babylon's allies seemed able to help them. While Babylon burned, its last Kassite king was led to Elam in chains, along with a beloved statue of the Babylonian god Marduk.

So, although the Sea Peoples undoubtedly played a role in the collapse, we can see that the situation in this region wasn't always so straightforward. The archaeology of the end of the Bronze Age paints a picture of large and complex empires suddenly faltering when faced with smaller and less complex belligerents on their borders. It was a seismic shift in the way power was organized in the Eastern Mediterranean. It was long thought that part of this shift must have been the proliferation of iron weapons, which would in the centuries to come bring the age of bronze to an end. Iron had been in limited use since as early as 3000 BCE, and early people even worked the iron they found in meteorites—but iron is much harder to work than copper and tin, requiring more heat and thus more powerful furnaces. The knowledge of how to turn iron into steel, mixing it with the right proportion of carbon in the form of charcoal, would further transform it into a metal that was just as sharp and hard as bronze, but much cheaper and less dependent on fragile long-range supply networks.

In the second millennium BCE, only great nations with access to complex trade networks could forge bronze—but as steelmaking technologies proliferated, soon even tribal societies and tiny kingdoms could afford cutting-edge weaponry, smelted from what seemed like the very stones of the earth. Around this time, a new kind of sword referred to by archaeologists as the Naue Type II, or 'grip-tongue sword', arrived in the region from south-eastern Europe, first in bronze, but soon being wrought out of iron. It has been suggested that the effect may have been not dissimilar to the introduction of cheap assault rifles like the AK-47 in our own time, acting as a military leveller that allowed non-state actors to destabilize whole regions. However, more recent metallurgical archaeology has undermined this view, and most evidence shows that iron weapons were still a relative rarity in this region at the point that the crisis of the collapse was reaching its climax. The historian Robert Drews argues that 'the Catastrophe may somehow or other have contributed to the development of an ironworking technology. But it could not have been the other way around.'[16]

As a result, historians are left looking for other explanations. Some have even attempted to reconfigure the roles in this drama. They ask: what if the Sea Peoples weren't the villains? What if they weren't the perpetrators in the collapse of civilization, but another set of victims? This last theory offers us an intriguing opportunity to shift our perspectives completely.

***

Amid all the uncertainty, one thing we know for sure about the end of the thirteenth century BCE is that the climate of the Eastern Mediterranean underwent a sudden and lasting change. A study of fossilized pollen particles taken from sediments at the bottom of the Sea of Galilee has shown that a succession of severe droughts occurred over a 150-year period.

> The most striking feature in the entire Sea of Galilee pollen record appears at the end of the Late Bronze, between ~1250–1100 BCE; this time interval is characterized by the lowest arboreal vegetation percentages throughout the entire sequence... This event probably lasted slightly more than a century and is therefore a relatively prolonged event—the most pronounced dry episode during the Bronze and Iron Ages.[17]

During this time, formerly verdant lands became dry and arid, and more plants suited to desert landscapes flourished. Analysis of sediment cores and oxygen isotopes in mineral deposits in Israeli caves have all shown that the thirteenth and twelfth centuries BCE saw much less rain than the preceding centuries.

Alongside this scientific evidence, we can see marks of severe droughts and famines in the region's written records too. The Hittites in their dry, stony mountains were hit particularly hard. Letters from Ugarit tell of sending large quantities of grain up the hill roads to feed populous cities like Hattusha. In the mid-thirteenth century BCE, one Hittite queen sent a message to the Egyptian Pharaoh, asking him to send her a shipment of grain. Other tablets sent to the King of Ugarit discuss famine: 'Another thing, my lord: grain staples from you are not to be had! (The people of) the household of your servant will die of hunger! My lord, give grain staples to your servant!'[18]

There had been famines and droughts in the region before—they were simply a fact of life for people living in the precarious reality of the Bronze Age. But the climate change that occurred around this time was so severe and lasting that scientists have been prompted to search around for some explanation. One answer might lie nearly 4,000 kilometres to the north, over the stormy waters of the North Atlantic, on the snowy slopes of southern Iceland. This is a harsh tundra landscape over which the shadow of an enormous volcano looms. Its name is Hekla, and it is one of Iceland's most active volcanoes. In the ancient and medieval imagination, it was thought to be the gate to hell, and the prison where the traitor Judas was tormented. The Cistercian monk Herbert of Clairvaux wrote about the volcano in the twelfth century CE, that '[Mount Etna], The renowned fiery cauldron of Sicily, which men call Hell's chimney…that cauldron is affirmed to be like a small furnace compared to this enormous inferno.'[19]

Although an exact dating has not yet been possible, we know that some time in the region of 1200–1000 BCE, Hekla had its most cataclysmic eruption to date. Known as Hekla 3, this eruption threw nearly 7.5 cubic kilometres of volcanic rock into the atmosphere and covered the sky in a dark shroud of ash particles that persisted for years after the event. Studies looking at the growth rings of bog oaks in Ireland—trees half-fossilized in acidic marshy waters—have shown that for eighteen years after Hekla 3, the trees barely grew at all. Across the Atlantic in the United States, bristlecone pines, the oldest living trees on earth, provide similar evidence of this time of widespread darkness and cooling, which lasted about two decades.

Some Egyptologists and archaeologists have firmly dated this cataclysm to the time of the Bronze Age Collapse and point to it as a cause of the rapid and dramatic climate change. It is certainly a tempting theory that offers an explanation for a time of extreme drought, famine and unrest, as dark clouds may have blotted out the sun. One letter sent from the king of the kingdom of Amurru, a neighbour of Ugarit around modern Lebanon, cryptically blames the storm god Adad for the deaths of some notables: 'May all be well for you! May the gods protect you! Behold this matter which happened—how Adad killed (many) of my forces and nobles!'[20]

Others have proposed that a volcanic eruption in Sicily around 1300 BCE may have been to blame, or that the super volcano in Santorini, which had erupted devastatingly around 1600 BCE, may have resumed some activity. The cause may not even have been volcanic at all, and could have been due to variations in the sun's activity, or weather systems in the Atlantic depriving the Mediterranean of moisture. The reality then was much as it is today: the planet's climate system is fragile, interconnected and chaotic, and even relatively small changes in its equilibrium can have devastating effects. While these hypotheses are all subject to much lively debate and study, they do at least encourage us to re-evaluate our notion of the Sea Peoples as a marauding armada. Were the Sea Peoples, in fact, refugees themselves?

Imagine you are a citizen of an island in the Mediterranean, say Sardinia or Sicily. One year, the sky turns dim. The sun peeks through the grey haze, a pale white. There's drought too, and the crops won't grow. Starvation begins to set in on your island and chaos spreads; there are riots for food. Everywhere, people are saying that the gods are angry, that the world is dying. The next year at harvest time, it's the same story. And now waves of people begin to arrive, hungry people from the far north, where the sun is even dimmer, where the worst winters in living memory are ravaging the lands. What do you do? Do you stay and hope the sun comes back? Hope that the crops grow next year? Do you hope that your new, hungry neighbours are friendly? Or do you band together and do one of the things you do best—take to the sea?

You would start small, sailing from place to place, trying to find somewhere the gods haven't abandoned. But it's the same everywhere. Society is disintegrating in the wake of years-long droughts and famines, and wherever you go, more people join your ranks. As your number swells, you become powerful. You resort to theft. You steal from merchant vessels, and then small villages. You capture prisoners and gain even more new recruits. Your strength grows and grows, until you become an army of the sea. It seems no one can stand in your way. A roving band of refugee warriors, roaming the oceans in search of somewhere to call home.

For me, this makes sense of the mystery of the Sea Peoples—of how such a force of diverse peoples suddenly looms up seemingly from nowhere, with no direction or command structure. We can imagine the Sea Peoples as anarchic and opportunistic, probably changing leaders frequently, likely with a variety of opposing motivations and goals. Some would have wanted to find land to settle, others just to loot and burn. The centuries of drought had weakened many of the states they targeted, and softened them up for attack. When the Sea Peoples met their end in the shady shallows of the Nile Delta, they must have felt the utter hopelessness of their situation bear down on them. They were people without a land, who had wrought so much destruction on the lands of others.

We know that some of the Sea Peoples, at least, escaped elimination in the Egyptian marshes. One of the groups that made up their wandering army settled in the region of what is today Gaza, in the Southern Levant, and put down roots. They were known as the Peleset, whom the Hebrews later called the Peleshet, and we today call the Philistines. They would come to be remembered as one of the great rivals to the kingdoms of Israel and Judah, and gave their name to the later province of Palestine.

Whatever the truth of their origins, or what happened to cause the sudden shift in the region's climate, these first dominos to fall set off a series of cascading failures that passed through the societies of the Bronze Age. What happened next was what the historian Eric Cline describes as 'a perfect storm of calamities':

> This is what would have led to the rapid disintegration of one society after another, in part because of the fragmentation of the global economy and the breakdown of the interconnections upon which each civilization was dependent. In short, the flourishing cultures and peoples of the Bronze Age...were simply not able to survive the onslaught of so many different stressors all at the same time.[21]

The Bronze Age Collapse left the cities of the Eastern Mediterranean in ruins, its populations scattered, and whole cultures like the Mycenaean Greeks and the Hittites vanished for good. But even after this catastrophe, renewal came, and slowly people rebuilt from the rubble, like the first sprouts pushing through the ash of a recent forest fire. It's in the period following the Bronze Age Collapse that peoples like the Assyrians, Phoenicians, Greeks and even Romans sought the roots of their own civilizations, and found opportunities to rise. For those peoples, the Bronze Age

Collapse was not an end, but a beginning—and classical antiquity as we recognize it began to take form.

One Hittite text, which has come down to us in several fragments, seems to capture the spirit of this age, and it is known as the myth of Telepinu. It is a text that adheres to a poetic convention known as the 'vanishing god' myth, in which a certain deity is so offended by the misdeeds of humanity that he flies into a rage or a fit of sorrow and abandons his duties, leaving the world desolate. Telepinu is a god of farming and fertility, and perhaps also of the weather. The beginning of the text has been lost to us, so we don't know what it was that provoked his rage—but the poem describes its deadly consequences, as crops fail, animals cease to breed, ash and soot clog the air, and drought and famine beset the world.

> Thereupon soot beset the windows; smoke beset the house. The ashes lay crammed on the hearth… Off stalked Telepinu. Grain and…increase and abundance he took away from field and meadow. Off to the copses stalked Telepinu, and in a copse he buried himself… Forthwith the seed ceased to yield produce; forthwith oxen, sheep and men ceased to breed, while even those that had conceived did not bear. Hillsides were bare; trees were bare and put forth no new branches; pastures were bare; springs ran dry. A famine arose in the land; men and gods alike were about to perish of hunger.[22]

With all hope fading, gods and mortals alike perform a number of rituals to placate the rage of Telepinu and, little by little, he is soothed. Life returns to the ravaged land and the people are able to rebuild. Life, as it always does, goes on.

> So Telepinu returned to his house. He took thought for his land. The window said goodbye to soot; the house said goodbye to smoke. The shrines of the gods were restored to good state. The hearth said goodbye to the ashes that were piled upon it. He released the sheep which were in the fold; he released the oxen which were in the stall. Mother once again

nursed child; ewe nursed lamb; cow nursed calf… In the presence of Telepinu an evergreen was set up, and from it was hung the fleece of a sheep. Enwrapped in that fleece were the fat of a sheep, grain of corn, fruit of the vine, symbolizing increase of oxen and sheep, continuance of life and assurance of posterity.[23]

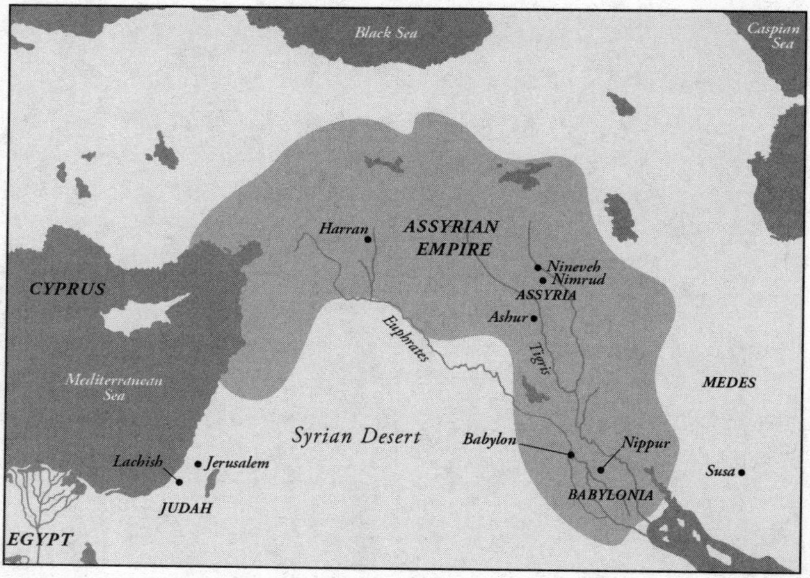
Black Sea
Caspian Sea
Harran
ASSYRIAN EMPIRE
Nineveh
Nimrud
ASSYRIA
CYPRUS
Ashur
Euphrates
Tigris
Mediterranean Sea
MEDES
Syrian Desert
Babylon
Nippur
Lachish
Jerusalem
Susa
BABYLONIA
JUDAH
EGYPT

3

Assyria

c. 2000 BCE–612 BCE

In the year 401 BCE, a Persian prince named Cyrus the Younger was fighting a bitter civil war against his brother for control of the imperial throne. To supplement his forces, he hired a mercenary army of mostly Greek soldiers: 10,000 spear-bearing hoplites who travelled the long road to Persia to fight on his behalf. Among them was the Greek writer and adventurer Xenophon, who later wrote about this expedition in his work *Anabasis*.

Xenophon and his companions met the enemy Persian army at the battle of Cunaxa, on the banks of the Euphrates. The Greek troops gave Cyrus value for his money, beating his brother's forces back and delivering a victory on their part of the field. But when the dust of the battle had cleared, they heard the bad news: Cyrus the Younger had been killed, apparently knocked from his horse by a young common soldier. His claim to the throne had died with him, and the war was over.

In the chaos of the aftermath, the general who led the Greeks had also been killed, and all of the other senior commanders were captured. The 10,000 mercenaries were now without a leader and stranded in the middle of a foreign land. Xenophon and the remainder of the Greeks knew that their only route home was to reach the Black Sea, which lay across the wide deserts of what is today Iraq. They were terrified, they had few supplies, and the enemy army was already pursuing them close behind.

Xenophon was one of the soldiers hastily elected to command, and he told his men to throw away everything they carried, shedding weight in order to outrun their enemies. In this way they pelted across the deserts and the fertile river lands dotted with date palms, following the Tigris River north. It was while fleeing in this manner that they stumbled upon something that must have made them stop in their tracks: the crumbling, deserted ruin of an enormous city, larger than anything Xenophon had seen back home in Greece. Later, he wrote about this discovery in *Anabasis*:

> They came upon a large deserted city, the name of which was Larissa: a place inhabited by the Medes in days of old; the breadth of its walls was twenty-five feet, and the height of them a hundred, and the circuit of the whole two *parasangs*. It was built of clay-bricks, supported on a stone basis twenty feet high... By the side of this city there was a stone pyramid in breadth a hundred feet, and in height two hundred feet; in it were many of the barbarians who had fled for refuge from the neighbouring villages.[1]

With the Persians in hot pursuit, Xenophon didn't have time to linger, and so the Greeks pressed ahead. Then, only a day or two later, they came across another ruin, this one even larger and more impressive, surrounded by another fortified wall.

> They marched one stage of six *parasangs* to a great deserted fortress... The basement was made of polished stone full of shells; fifty feet was the breadth of it, and fifty feet the height; and on this basement was reared a wall of brick, the breadth whereof was fifty feet and the height thereof four hundred; and the circuit of the wall was six *parasangs*.[2]

For days afterwards, Xenophon asked any local people they passed about these enormous constructions out there in the desert—but no one could tell him anything. Some thought they might have been built by the Medes, an ancient Iranian people who still occupied the area. Others told fantastical stories about the gods bringing down fire and thunder to destroy the ancient walls, killing everyone within.

Today, we know that these cities were the famed metropolises of Nimrud and Nineveh—the greatest cities of the Assyrian Empire—and it's thought that Xenophon, at the end of the fifth century BCE, was the first person to write an account of their ruins. At that time, the first stones of the Parthenon in Athens had been laid only fifty years earlier; the Colosseum in Rome would not be built for nearly 500 years—but by then, Nineveh had already been a ruin for more than two centuries. This city had flourished into a towering capital, home to hundreds of thousands of people, given birth to some of the ancient world's most beautiful art and architecture—and then all at once had fallen into dust.

Xenophon and his men eventually made it back to Greece, and he would survive to write his account. Today when we read about his experiences in *Anabasis*, some of the most affecting moments are when he must have looked out over the sand-blasted desert, at the grasses sprouting between the crumbling bricks of those abandoned cities, the hot wind battering his hair and tugging at his clothes, and wondered what in all the world could have happened here.

★★★

To us, the Assyrian Empire belongs to what feels like an impossibly distant past. But the citizens of Nineveh and Nimrud already considered themselves to be the inheritors of a long and fabled history. Since the invention of writing by the Sumerians around 3200 BCE, humans had been passing their knowledge down through the generations. As a result, the Assyrians held on to the memory of several of the kings of the Sumerian Age, revering them as semimythical heroes. Among these were the hero of the epic, Gilgamesh, and the Akkadian King Sargon the Great, who for the later Assyrians was about as distant in their past as we are from Julius Caesar. Like the Sumerians before them, the Assyrians saw the ruins of ancient cities scattering their landscape, and believed them to be the remnants left behind by a great flood that had once washed over the world.

Since the fall of the Neo-Sumerian Empire, the language of Akkadian had become the region's most widespread, and the Akkadian-speaking cities of the north were finally free to prosper under their own rule. One of these was the city of Ashur. Ashur was occupied from at least 2500 BCE, and it grew quickly, in part thanks to its natural advantages. It was nestled in a bend of the Tigris—about halfway between the modern cities of Tikrit and Mosul—and this watercourse sheltered it on its north and east sides, as well as making it a natural stop along the river trade route. As a consequence, the city soon became wealthy. Excavations show that by the second millennium, many of its dwellings were spacious mansions, and it became common for wealthy families to keep vaults beneath their floors to hide their many valuables—jewellery made of gold and polished brass, inlaid with semi-precious stones like carnelian, agate and lapis lazuli. Excavations have even uncovered dozens of private libraries and archives in the city, where texts written in cuneiform on clay tablets were stored—a clear indicator of a city overflowing with wealth.

The rich families of Ashur were also able to donate handsomely to religious institutions, and the city became home to no fewer than thirty-four temples to the various gods worshipped by all the people of Mesopotamia: the sun god Shamash and the moon god Sin, the storm god Adad, the water god Ea (once known as Enki), Ishtar the goddess of love and war, and the king of the gods, Enlil. We can imagine incantations washing out of the temple doors into the city streets, the priests competing for attention in the crowded city, the ringing of bells and banging of drums, the singing of hymns. Funeral processions may have floated past, chanting devotionals such as this one to the Babylonian god Marduk:

> The man who is departing in glory,
> May his soul shine radiant as brass!
> To that man, may the sun give life.
> And Marduk, eldest son of heaven,
> Grant him an abode of happiness.[3]

The temples also performed services for the sick. If you visited the temple of Ishtar with an ailment, you might hear something like this prayer being said over you by one of its priests:

> Bind the sick man to heaven, for from the earth he is being torn away! Of the brave man, who was so strong, his strength has departed. In his bodily frame he lies dangerously ill. But Ishtar, who in her dwelling is grieved for him, descends from her mountain, unvisited of men. To the door of the sick man she comes.[4]

Soon, like most cities of this time, Ashur developed a god of its own. In fact, the city virtually became a god. In the religious imagination of Mesopotamia, gods were closely associated with cities. Each city had a god in the way that every sports team has a mascot, and the god was believed to live in the highest chamber of the city's temple, often in a statue dedicated to them. If you visited another city on business, it was considered sensible to give an offering to the city's god while you were there, and if two cities went to war, it was thought that their gods were battling it out in the heavens, just as human armies were fighting down on earth. As a consequence, the more a city succeeded, the more power its god was presumed to have.

As the city of Ashur grew in importance, so the cult of the god Ashur was born. Grand temples were thrown up to this new deity, and as the city went from strength to strength, worship of Ashur rose to become the highest form of religious observance for its people.

Emblem of the god Ashur, from an Assyrian relief in Nimrud.

From what we can tell, this god rapidly took on new symbols and iconography: he became thought of as a robed man wearing a crown and holding a bow, often appearing in carvings at the centre of a winged disk, looking down on the world and the golden city over which he presided. As the confidence of the cult of Ashur grew, eventually Enlil's position as king of the gods, which he had held for a thousand years since the Sumerian Age, was in jeopardy. Over the next centuries, the god Ashur even took over Enlil's wife, the goddess Ninlil, and his sons Ninurta and Zababa. In a cuckoo-like displacement, Ashur, and not Enlil, was now the supreme god for this city's people. The people of the city of Ashur would soon become known as Ashurayeh. Today we call them Assyrians.

***

Like many of the powerful cities of this region, for the next millennium or so, the Assyrians of Ashur would make several attempts to found their own kingdom. Some of their earlier kings made impressive bids to build a larger empire, but the Eastern Mediterranean around this time was a crowded field. At various times, Ashur found itself butting up against the powerful empires of Babylon, the Mitanni and the Hittites, at times even being absorbed by them. All this would change as the Late Bronze Age Collapse swept over the Eastern Mediterranean, and like a great forest fire cleared away many of the region's former great powers. But in the period of desolation that followed the collapse, Assyria too was struggling. The historian Georges Roux summarizes its situation:

> towards the end of the tenth century BCE, Assyria was at her lowest ebb… Economic collapse was impending. She had lost all her possessions west of the Tigris, and her vital arteries, the great trade routes that ran through the mountain passes…were in foreign hands. Hostile highlanders occupied not only the heights of the Zagros, but the foothills down to the edge of the Tigris valley, while Aramaean tribes pitched their tents almost at the gates of Assur.[5]

By now, Assyria's territory consisted of little more than a strip of land along the Tigris, surrounded on all sides by determined enemies. But there were also things to be thankful for. For one thing,

Assyria's rivals were incapable of uniting, and this single fact would prove crucial for Assyrian survival. For much of history, its enemies hated each other as much as they hated the Assyrians. Having little in the way of natural boundaries or defences on the plains, Assyria relied on the fact that its enemies could be dealt with one by one. The powerful Assyrian army could march one way, then the other, smashing each enemy in turn.

The main cities of Assyria had also been able to continue their economic output throughout the crisis of the Bronze Age Collapse, and so had fared better than many rivals. Assyria still had chariots and horses and weapons; it had access to iron, and was beginning to use steel to forge powerful new weapons and armour. Their warriors had been trained by years of constant fighting and were now among the best in the world. And perhaps most importantly, the line of royal succession had supposedly not been broken for more than 200 years, meaning that the kings of Assyria drew on an ancient and unchallenged legitimacy among their people. No other state of the time could say the same. And to at least one Assyrian king, it must have seemed that if Assyria could only seize its opportunity, it could become a power unlike any seen before. That king was Tiglath-Pileser I.

Tiglath-Pileser ascended to the throne in 1114 BCE. He was the son of a remorseless ruler named Ashur-resha-ishi, who had named himself 'the avenger of Assyria' and the 'merciless hero of battle'. Tiglath-Pileser continued this ferocious reputation, and it's clear he was an energetic ruler and a skilful campaigner. One of his typically overflowing royal inscriptions describes him in the following manner:

> Unrivalled king of the universe, king of the four quarters, king of all princes, lord of lords...whose weapons the god Ashur has sharpened and whose name he has pronounced eternally for control of the four quarters...splendid flame which covers the hostile land like a rain storm...[6]

Tiglath-Pileser inherited an Assyria that was threatened on multiple fronts. In the north, climate shifts had been driving nomadic horsemen into the northern plains. The Mushku people of Syria had occupied certain Assyrian districts in the Upper Euphrates Valley for fifty years, while the Hittite people had also snatched some of its territories. And to the south lay the powerful city of Babylon, Assyria's ancient rival. Today, the Arabic name for the region of upper Mesopotamia still captures this feeling of isolation. They call it *Al-Jazīrah*—'the island'.

Tiglath-Pileser drove out first the Mushku, then the Hittites and Arameans. Everywhere he went, he placed a record of his victories. In one of the strong fortresses he built to solidify his conquests, he engraved the following message on a series of copper plates in the base of the walls:

> Altogether I conquered 42 lands and their rulers from the other side of the Lower Zab in distant mountainous regions to the other side of the Euphrates, people of Hatti, and the Upper Sea in the west.[7]

Tiglath-Pileser I loved to hunt, and he delighted in bringing back live specimens of animals from the faraway lands that he campaigned in:

> I killed ten strong bull elephants in the land Harran and the region of the River Habur, and four live elephants I captured. I brought the hides and tusks of the dead elephants along with the live elephants back to my city of Ashur.[8]

We can imagine the bustle of Ashur at this time: teams of construction labourers working day and night to build new palaces; exotic, never-before-seen animals in its pleasure gardens; while access to new trade routes brought new spices and fabrics to the city markets.

Tiglath-Pileser swept his Assyrian armies west, and conquered cities as he went. When he conquered the Hittite town of Pitru, he gained control of the highway to the Mediterranean. Assyria at this time was the only great power in this region with no access to a coastline, and we can see something of the wonder in the king's words when he boasts about going onboard a ship. The chronicles even record that he hunted and killed a sea creature known as a *nahiru*—perhaps a dolphin.

> I rode in boats of the people of Arvad and travelled successfully a distance of three double hours from the city Arvad, an island, to the city Samuru which is in the land Amurru. I killed at sea a nahiru, which is called a sea-horse.[9]

Tiglath-Pileser I died in 1076 BCE, having grown his kingdom into an empire that was all but unmatched in the region. As his own end grew near, he must have looked ahead to the dawning of a golden age for Assyria—and indeed the kings who followed were able to continue the empire's expansion—into Anatolia, Persia, Babylonia and the Levant. But the Assyrians were already sowing the seeds of their own destruction. For one thing, they were seen increasingly across the region as harsh, even cruel rulers. King Ashurnasirpal II, who ascended the throne in 883 BCE, was renowned for his remorselessness. Though he was by no means the first Assyrian king to do so, he made unprecedented use of terror tactics, torture, execution and mass deportations to drive fear into the hearts of his enemies. His inscriptions, above those of all the kings of Assyria, stand out for the delight they seem to take in the details of his campaign of terror:

> I burnt many captives… I captured many troops alive: from some I cut off their arms and hands; from others I cut off their noses, ears, and extremities. I gouged out the eyes of many troops. I made one pile of the living and one of heads. I hung their heads on trees around the city. I burnt their adolescent boys and girls. I razed, destroyed, burnt, and consumed the city.[10]

Whether because of these tactics or despite them, in the short term, Ashurnasirpal was an effective conqueror. But by the final years of the reign of his son Shalmaneser III, the people had had enough. Twenty-seven cities, including Ashur itself, rose up in rebellion.

In the long and bitter civil war that ensued, virtually all the people that Ashurnasirpal had conquered shook off Assyrian rule. Assyria's heavy-handed military domination of the region had made them hated. If they hoped to sustain a lasting empire, something would have to change—and the king who would eventually inherit this mess, who ruled as Tiglath-Pileser III, thought he knew what that something was. But it was not a softer and more diplomatic approach. He decided, in characteristic Assyrian fashion, that what the empire needed was an even more powerful army.

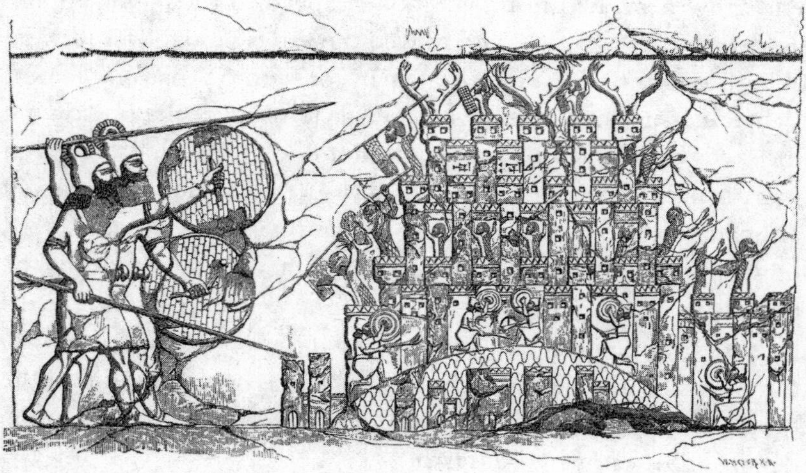

A typical Assyrian carving, showing the destruction of a rival city.

***

Up until the mid-eighth century BCE, the Assyrian army was much the same as any other Mesopotamian force, only a good deal larger. King Shalmaneser III once boasted a force of 120,000 men in his campaigns against Syria, at a time when the world population has been estimated at only 50 million people. If his inscriptions are to be believed, then around 0.25 per cent or one in every 400 of the global population was at that moment serving in the Assyrian army. Nevertheless, it was still a force mostly made up of peasant farmers, and this had long presented a problem. The empire could summon a horde of soldiers, plucked from their lands whenever the need arose, but when the autumn came around and the barley was golden in the fields, these armies of farmers had to march right back home and bring in the crops. Otherwise, the empire would go hungry.

Gathering this huge army from the fields was also an immensely time-consuming and difficult task. Rebellions could break out at any time of year, but if one occurred in some far corner of the empire, it couldn't be crushed until summertime. If the people of a rebellious city were clever, they could simply lock the gates and wait behind their walls for the armies of Assyria to go away—and in many cases that is exactly what they did.

But in the mid-eighth century BCE, the new King Tiglath-Pileser III embarked on a radical programme of reforming the Assyrian military, creating forces of elite armoured troops, cavalry and chariots. Meanwhile, conquered territories on the edges of the empire supplied the army's light infantry, who were considered expendable and often bore the brunt of the casualties. He also pioneered the use of a large engineering component to the fighting force. Soon Assyrian soldiers could build bridges and dig tunnels, construct fortifications and siege engines, as well as maintain the supply lines to keep the army going. Assyrian carvings show remarkably detailed scenes of the army crossing one of the great rivers—something they must have had to do multiple times a year. We see animal skins being inflated as buoyancy aids, chariots dismantled and turned into boats, rafts constructed to transport supplies and equipment.

Tiglath-Pileser III also increased production of iron and steel in the empire. Assyrian cities of this time must have become increasingly smoke-filled, the furnaces belching charcoal smoke, the sound of bellows and clanging hammers echoing off the buildings. The Assyrians entered a new era of iron mass production, using the metal to make knives, pins and chains, but also arrowheads, swords, spear blades, helmets and even iron scales that were sewn into soldiers' tunics for protection. The effect of these reforms was immediate. In 743 BCE, Tiglath-Pileser III marched north against the kingdom of Urartu and conquered it easily. Two years later, he marched west against the kingdom of Arpad.

The people of Arpad had fought the Assyrians before, and they knew what to do: simply close up their city gates and hold tight until the end of summer came. But as summer ended and autumn arrived, the people of Arpad must have realized that something was wrong. The Assyrians showed no sign of going home. In fact, it looked like they were settling in for a long stay. Tiglath-Pileser III laid siege to the city of Arpad for three years—something that would have been impossible with the old seasonal armies. When the city finally fell, he ordered it to be destroyed, and its inhabitants slaughtered.

In campaign after campaign, Tiglath-Pileser III conquered lands in Syria, and marched his new professional army down the Mediterranean coast, taking coastal cities all the way to Egypt. He invaded the Northern Hebrew Kingdom of Israel, destroyed their forces, installed a puppet king, and deported large numbers of Hebrew tribes to lands in Assyria. Perhaps most notably, he added one other remarkable new possession: Babylon, which had been the political and religious centre of southern Mesopotamia for more than a thousand years.

The division between Assyria and Babylonia was an ancient one. Once, Mesopotamia had been divided between Sumerians in the south and Akkadians in the north, but this had now evolved to become Babylonians in the south, and Assyrians in the north. It's a cultural division that still echoes today, since the distribution of the Sunni and Shia populations in modern Iraq roughly follows this same geographical divide.

Tiglath-Pileser III's conquest of Babylon shifted the balance of power in Mesopotamia, and it became one of the jewels in his crown. By 736 BCE, his empire encompassed almost the whole of the fertile crescent, and he controlled an unbroken corridor from the Persian Gulf to the Mediterranean that linked the trade routes of the Indian Ocean with those of North Africa and Europe. It was this empire and the formidable, seemingly unstoppable army it now commanded, that Tiglath-Pileser III would pass down to his younger son, who was to found the greatest dynasty of the Assyrians. His name was Sargon II, named after the ancient Akkadian hero, and his dynasty would become known as the Sargonid Kings. They would rule for three generations that would represent the highest point of the empire's achievements in war, art and literature. But they would also be the twilight of its age. With the last of these three generations, the empire would collapse in ash and flame.

***

The drama of the Sargonid Kings is one of the most remarkable family sagas to come down to us from the ancient world, and it truly begins with the son of Sargon, Sennacherib, who came to the throne in 705 BCE. Sargon II had been a respected and feared king, but for some reason, Sennacherib couldn't command quite the same level of respect. After only two years of his rule, several Assyrian vassals in the foothills to the east, in Syria and along the Mediterranean coast, all suddenly stopped paying their tribute. The Egyptians, always happy to throw sand in the face of the Assyrians, moved to back the rebels, and the young Sennacherib found himself plunged into a fight for the empire's survival.

The new king quickly gathered the imperial army and dealt with the rebels in the usual Assyrian way, rounding on them one by one. He marched east and subjugated the peoples of the Iranian lowlands, then he marched north and around the fertile crescent to the Mediterranean coast, to reconquer the rebellious kingdoms there. One of these campaigns is notable because we have accounts of it written both by the winners and the losers, in a level of detail almost unprecedented anywhere else in the eighth century BCE. These records have survived not only in the chronicles of Assyria, but also in the Bible. This was Sennacherib's campaign against the kingdom of Judah.

The kingdom of Judah was the second and more southerly of the region's two major Hebrew kingdoms, centred on the powerful city of Jerusalem. Its king at the time was called Hezekiah, an energetic ruler driven by religious fervour, as the Old Testament Book of Kings tells us:

> Hezekiah…did that which was right in the eyes of the Lord, according to all that David his father had done. He removed

> the high places, and broke the pillars; and he broke in pieces the brazen serpent that Moses had made; for unto those days the children of Israel did offer to it.[11]

Perhaps it was Hezekiah's religious devotion that led him to make the enormous gamble of defying the Assyrian Empire. Perhaps the recent rebellions in the empire had emboldened him, and he believed that it might be on the brink of collapse. Whatever his calculation, it backfired completely. He soon heard news that Sennacherib was marching on Judah with the full force of the Assyrian war machine.

Sennacherib first conquered the rebels of Ekron in Philistia, then Judah's fortified second city of Lachish—a victory recorded in a striking series of reliefs unearthed from the south-west palace at Nineveh—before making his way to Jerusalem. Hezekiah was ready. He had built a new wall around the city and dug an underground tunnel through solid stone that would bring in fresh water during any siege. But even so, the situation must have looked dire. The Judean king decided to negotiate.

> And Hezekiah king of Judah sent to the king of Assyria to Lachish, saying: 'I have offended; return from me; that which thou puttest on me will I bear.' And the king of Assyria appointed unto Hezekiah king of Judah three hundred talents of silver and thirty talents of gold.[12]

To pay the bounty, this devout king even stripped the gold from the temple in Jerusalem. However, Sennacherib was not appeased, and it looked as though all was lost for the defenders of Jerusalem. But then their luck turned. The Hebrew poets who wrote the Book of Kings recount King Hezekiah praying to his god to deliver him from the Assyrians, and this reply coming down to him:

> Hast thou not heard long ago how I have done it, and of ancient times that I have formed it? now have I brought it to pass, that thou shouldest be to lay waste fenced cities into ruinous heaps… And it came to pass that night, that the angel of

> the Lord went forth, and smote in the camp of the Assyrians a hundred fourscore and five thousand; and when men arose early in the morning, behold, they were all dead corpses. So Sennacherib king of Assyria departed, and went and returned, and dwelt at Nineveh.[13]

The most likely explanation is probably an outbreak of plague among the Assyrian army—a constant threat to any besieging force. The Assyrian sources are understandably quiet about what must have been an embarrassing defeat. The only inscription to mention this campaign focuses on the early victories won by the Assyrians, and on the massive tribute they exacted. Still, perhaps it was this embarrassment that led the recently conquered people of Babylon to desire their freedom.

Low-relief carving from the Central Palace in Nimrud, showing Assyrian troops attacking a besieged city using a battering ram on a siege ramp.

★★★

For centuries, Babylon had been a thorn in the side of the Assyrian kings. It was a proud and ancient city, and so powerful in its own right that it was exceptionally difficult to keep it in the empire. Various Assyrian kings tried different approaches to this problem. Some simply allowed a native Babylonian to rule the city and its surrounding territories, which kept the Babylonian people happy—but this often led to this Babylonian king declaring independence whenever the central power of Assyria was distracted or deployed elsewhere. Others tried imposing an Assyrian governor. This naturally enraged the Babylonians, who would rise up in rebellions and plots, and quite often toppled the Assyrian governor in favour of some Babylonian noble, who would then immediately declare independence. The third option was to keep the throne of Babylon in the family, crowning a brother or other relative. But this carried the ever-present risk that he would become overly ambitious and use the might of Babylon to seize the whole empire for himself. By 694 BCE this seemingly insoluble problem had become too much for King Sennacherib. For him, the conflict had become personal: the Babylonians were partially responsible for the death of one of his sons. After crushing his enemies in the north and along the Mediterranean coast, he marched east on a campaign to wreak his vengeance on the city and end the Babylonian problem for good.

In 689 BCE, the Assyrians embarked on a fifteen-month siege of Babylon, and when at last the city was defeated, Sennacherib razed and looted it, and even flooded its streets by bursting its canals and dams. Across the region, there was an outcry. Burning a Judean or Elamite city to the ground was one thing—but to do the same to the cultured, ancient and holy city of Babylon was too much. Sennacherib responded to this public relations disaster by trying to legitimize his actions. In a bizarre ritual, he hauled the statue of the Babylonian god Marduk back to Nineveh, where the god was put on trial. The statue of Marduk was eventually found guilty of whatever crimes he was accused of, but it's unlikely that this stunt did much to assuage the tide of public opinion.

Sennacherib's goal had been to destroy Babylon utterly, and he had succeeded. Its northern provinces were folded into the Assyrian Empire, while the city itself was left in ruins. But the obliteration of Babylon drained something from King Sennacherib. Afterwards, he no longer had any appetite for war, rarely going out on campaigns himself, and appointing generals to lead in his place. Instead of destruction, he dedicated the later years of his reign to building, primarily in the city of Nineveh, which he named his new capital.

Nineveh had been an important city in northern Mesopotamia for millennia, but when Sennacherib came to settle there, it was in a sorely neglected state. He renovated its palaces, and built new ones, decorating them with carvings of his early victories like the siege of Lachish. He constructed beautiful gardens, importing plants from across the empire and beyond. Cotton plants may have been brought from as far away as India. It has been suggested that the Hanging Gardens of Babylon, one of the Seven Wonders of the Ancient World, may in fact have been these gardens in Nineveh, which were designed to represent the empire in miniature form. 'I, Sennacherib...supplied Nineveh, together with its neighbourhood...gardens, vineyards, all kinds of products of the mountains,' he wrote. 'The fruits of all lands... I planted, letting out the waters where they did not reach the thirsty field, and reviving its vegetation.'[14]

By the end of Sennacherib's reign, Nineveh must have shone, a resplendent capital fit for the world's mightiest empire. But now the problem of succession was looming. Sennacherib had at least seven sons, but when the crown prince died in battle against the Elamites, he was left to choose a successor from those who remained. Finally, he decided to name the youngest, Esarhaddon, crown prince. Esarhaddon's inscriptions recount what happened next:

> A firm determination 'fell upon' my brothers. They forsook the gods and turned to deeds of violence, plotting evil. Evil words and deeds...they perpetrated against me. Unholy hostility they planned behind my back.[15]

Soon prince Esarhaddon was forced to flee Nineveh, after threats on his life. But the old King Sennacherib clearly missed the danger that was also growing against his own life. On the twentieth day of the tenth month of Tebet, in the year 681 BCE, the snubbed older sons fell upon their father while he prayed in one of Nineveh's temples, and killed him.

The death of Sennacherib sent shockwaves across the region, though Hebrew sources record it with some glee. Riding the tide of condemnation in Assyria, the crown prince Esarhaddon quickly gathered an army and marched out to meet his treacherous brothers in battle. The brothers' forces deserted *en masse*, unwilling to fight for the men who had murdered the old king. Esarhaddon marched on Nineveh facing virtually no resistance and seized the crown that was his birth right. 'I entered into Nineveh,' he wrote, 'my royal city, joyfully, and took my seat upon the throne of my father in safety.'[16]

Fresh from this victory, in 680 BCE, Esarhaddon announced the reconstruction of Babylon, taking pains to lay it out just as it had been before his father's rage had destroyed it: 'To its former dimensions I restored it and made it mountain high.'[17] Esarhaddon also expanded Assyria to its largest extent, invading Egypt and capturing it. But soon, the king's health began to fail. Frequent correspondence with physicians and exorcists shows that he cloistered himself away for long periods and suffered a variety of symptoms, including some that might suggest a period of depression. One letter from his chief physician seems to indicate that none of the usual treatments were working:

> As to what the king, my lord, wrote to me: 'I am feeling very sad; how did we act that I have become so depressed…?'—had it been curable, you would have given away half of your kingdom to have it cured! But what can we do? O king, my lord, it is something that cannot be done.[18]

With his health failing, under pressure to decide the succession, and determined not to repeat his father's mistakes, Esarhaddon opted for an optimistic course of action. He would name one of his younger sons, Ashurbanipal, King of Assyria, ruling the whole empire from Nineveh. And his eldest son, Shamash-shum-ukin, would be named King of Babylon, swearing an oath to the Assyrian Empire. His hope was that these two brothers would rule over the world's two greatest cities together, uniting them and ushering in a new age of peace and prosperity. It was a beautiful vision. But in fact, Esarhaddon's decision would begin the final chapter of the Assyrian age.

★★★

In 670 BCE in the city of Harran in northern Mesopotamia, a woman began speaking in tongues. Again and again, she ran through the streets and shouted out, for all to hear, a resounding and unmistakable message from the gods:

> A slave-girl of Bel-ahu-usur in a suburb of Harran; since the month of Sivan she is enraptured and speaks these prophecies about him: 'It is the word of Nusku: I will destroy the name and seed of Sennacherib!'[19]

Hearing of this prophecy from his network of spies, Esarhaddon ordered a crackdown across the empire. The homes of anyone found to be spreading this conspiracy were burned. Clearly shaken, Esarhaddon became obsessed with omens, and his court astrologers spent much of their time reassuring him. To ward off evil omens, he even undertook a number of times a ritual known as the 'substitute king', in which a commoner or some expendable member of the palace staff took the monarch's place for a hundred days. This commoner would sleep in the royal bed, wear the crown and royal garbs, and eat the king's food. During the allotted time, the actual king remained hidden, and was even renamed, sometimes given a common title like 'the farmer'. Meanwhile, the substitute absorbed whatever bad luck was headed the king's way, and at the end of the hundred days was put to death. The real monarch then returned to the throne, with the evil having passed him by.

However, even this ritual had no effect. While marching to Egypt in 669 BCE to suppress a rebellion in that new and restive province, Esarhaddon's health continued to worsen. His condition became critical as his army passed through the northern territories, and he died at Harran—the very same town where only a couple of years before the woman had run through the streets in ecstasies, foretelling his doom. Upon his death, his sons Ashurbanipal and Shamash-shum-ukin took up their thrones without any sign of turmoil, and the twin rule that he had planned began.

***

The reign of Ashurbanipal is without a doubt Assyria's golden age. The Assyrian Empire at this time was the largest the world had ever seen, and its capital, Nineveh, was probably the largest city on earth. King Ashurbanipal, meanwhile, is remarkable for the way he springs out of the historical sources as a fully formed character, subject to his own preoccupations and obsessions. For one thing, he was possibly the first literate Assyrian king. Up until his time, literacy wasn't considered a kingly attribute. Kings had servants and scribes to do their reading and writing for them, while they were expected to engage in manlier pursuits like hunting and fighting. But Ashurbanipal, as one of Esarhaddon's younger sons, hadn't always been intended for the throne. As such, he had been preparing for some kind of scholarly position in the temples when Esarhaddon's oldest son had died, and Ashurbanipal's career was rapidly rerouted. When he ascended to the throne, he was evidently proud of his ability to read, which he boasts about at length in his inscriptions.

> Nabu, the universal Scribe, made me a present of his wisdom… I learned the hidden treasure of all scribal knowledge, the signs of heaven and earth… I have studied the heavens with the learned masters of oil divination, I have solved the

> laborious problems of division and multiplication, which were not clear, I have read the artistic script of Sumer and the dark Akkadian, which is hard to master, taking pleasure in the reading of the stones from before the flood, being angered because I was addled by the beautiful script.[20]

Ashurbanipal's collection of clay tablets was unprecedented. It was the first attempt to create a universal library, a place where all the books ever written could be kept. He wrote to cities across the empire, instructing them to send him copies of every written work they had. Eventually, he amassed a collection of over 30,000 clay tablets. The library contained numerous observations of events and omens, texts detailing the behaviour of certain men, plants and animals, texts on the movements of the heavenly bodies, dictionaries of Sumerian, Akkadian and other languages, religious texts, rituals, fables, prayers and incantations, comical and satirical texts, and books of the ancient mythology and poetry of Mesopotamia. Most of the traditional Mesopotamian stories and tales known today, such as the *Epic of Gilgamesh*, have only survived because they were included in Ashurbanipal's library. But Ashurbanipal would not have the luxury of escaping into his books. Soon he had to deal with the very real challenges of running an empire.

Egypt was in a state of constant rebellion. In 667 BCE, Ashurbanipal marched the Assyrian army down the Nile as far south as Thebes and sacked numerous cities in the usual Assyrian fashion. This campaign crushed the insurgency, but as usual, it only created more resistance in the long run. Rebellions sprang up again the very next year, forcing him to march back to Egypt and stamp them out even harder. Despite his efforts, the Assyrians never succeeded in successfully integrating Egypt into their empire. Meanwhile, on the far side of the region, another people started to chafe at Assyrian rule: the Elamites, in the south of what is now Iran.

The Elamites had been instrumental in the fall of Sumerian society more than a millennium before, and since then had built a powerful and wealthy kingdom centred on their capital, Susa.

Ashurbanipal's father, Esarhaddon, had taken pains to coexist peacefully with the people of Elam, and even allowed outbursts of violence on their border to go unpunished, in the interest of peace. But Elam was now growing in confidence. Having little hope of defeating Assyria on the battlefield, they had settled for a similar tactic to the Egyptians in dealing with their powerful neighbour: supplying and arming rebel groups in Assyria, and causing as much trouble for them as they could without provoking an all-out war. But some time before 660 BCE, it's thought that the Elamite King Teumman made a secret pact with Ashurbanipal's brother, the King of Babylon, Shamash-shum-ukin.

For some time, Shamash-shum-ukin had been dissatisfied with his lot in life. In theory, he ruled over all the lands of Babylonia, but in practice most of the governors of the southern cities simply ignored him and considered Ashurbanipal their king. What was worse, Ashurbanipal would often dictate orders for him, and frequently meddled in the affairs of Babylon. Shamash-shum-ukin's pact with Teumman was simple: he would help the Elamites invade Assyria and topple Ashurbanipal—and in return, he would rule over Babylon as its only king. The Elamites were all too eager to accept. When the season of war came back around, their armies swept down from the mountains in a surprise attack on the Assyrians' southern territories.

The attack was not as successful as they might have hoped. Ashurbanipal repelled and pursued them, finally defeating Teumman for good at the Ulay River, close to Susa. One of Ashurbanipal's inscriptions boasts about this victory, which is also immortalized in a series of palace wall carvings:

> Like the onset of a terrible hurricane I overwhelmed Elam in its entirety. I cut off the head of Teumman, their King, the haughty one, who plotted evil. Countless of his warriors I slew… With their corpses I filled the plain about Susa… Their blood I let run down the Ulai [River]; its water I dyed red like wool.[21]

One striking image depicts Ashurbanipal relaxing in his gardens with his queen, surrounded by musicians and servants fanning him, bringing him drinks and food—and all the while, Teumman's severed head hangs in the branches of a nearby tree.

Ashurbanipal and his queen relax in their gardens, while on the far left the severed head of the Elamite king Teumman is visible.

It's not clear whether Ashurbanipal suspected his brother's hand in the Elamite surprise attack. Either way, one year later, Shamash-shum-ukin revealed his true intentions. He rose his armies in open rebellion against his brother and declared the lands of Babylonia to be independent, with some remnants of the Elamite army joining him. Ashurbanipal was wounded by the betrayal, with inscriptions cursing 'the faithless brother of mine',[22] and he responded by gathering the full might of his army and marching on Babylon just as his grandfather had done. This latest siege of Babylon went on for four years. Conditions quickly descended into horror as people starved and resorted to cannibalism: 'Famine laid hold upon them. They ate the flesh of their sons and daughters to stay their hunger, they gnawed leather.'[23] Finally, the city fell, and the Assyrian soldiers poured over its walls. Shamash-shum-ukin himself appears to have died in a fire. It's possible that when he saw that all was lost, he set fire to his own palace and stayed inside while it burned.

One year later, in 647 BCE, Ashurbanipal turned his attention to Elam, embarking on a war of extermination designed to wipe it out entirely. One Assyrian carving shows flames rising from Susa's towers and pouring out of its gate. Assyrian soldiers are carrying off all kinds of loot, while others steadily and meticulously demolish every building in the city with picks and hammers. Ashurbanipal was again unsparing in his destruction of the city:

> The zikkurat (temple tower) of Susa, which was built of enamelled bricks, I destroyed. Its pinnacles, which were of shining bronze, I broke down… For a distance of a month of twenty-five days' journey I devastated the provinces of Elam. Salt and *sihlu* [some prickly plant] I scattered over them… In a month of days I ravaged Elam to its farthest border. The noise of people, the tread of cattle and sheep, the glad shouts of rejoicing, I banished from its fields.[24]

The Assyrians had once more emerged victorious, their army undefeated, all challenges overcome, and now one of their oldest enemies utterly eradicated. The empire was at the height of its confidence.

***

Alongside all the trumpeting inscriptions and relief carvings of these military victories, it was in the final decade of his reign, perhaps around 640 BCE, that King Ashurbanipal commissioned the works of art that stand as perhaps the defining legacy of his entire civilization. These are the lion hunt reliefs of the north-west palace in Nineveh.

At this time, a breed known as the Asiatic lion roamed freely across the Middle East, North Africa and perhaps even parts of Europe. They were slightly smaller than their African counterparts, with a much shorter mane, and a distinctive fold of skin running down their bellies. The kings of Assyria had hunted lions for centuries, and the lion had come to represent all the dangers of the world that the king would need to triumph over. In the early years of the empire, lions were rounded up from the countryside and brought to the capital, but by the late period they were bred in captivity. These were hunted in more formalized and controlled performances, in full view of the city's inhabitants. The famed lion hunt reliefs portray one of these spectacles: the king in his chariot, armed with spear and bow; the lions in their cages, with a small person or child in a smaller cage above, tasked with opening the cage door; the soldiers penning in the lions with shields and spears, their trained dogs straining on their leashes.

A detail of the lion-hunt reliefs of Ashurbanipal, ca. 640 BCE.

These reliefs, currently on display at the British Museum in London, are among the most affecting pieces of art to come down to us from the pre-classical world. The details in the human figures—their fingernails and eyelashes—in the embroidered clothes and decorations of the king's chariot, are all realized to perfection. But while the humans are depicted formally, with little or no emotion on their faces, it's the lions that convey an almost human expressiveness and air of sorrow. It can be tempting, as a modern observer, to see in that sorrow a distillation of the mood that must have been enveloping the empire in its final years. The lion hunt reliefs were the last pieces of great art ever created in the Empire of Assyria.

★★★

There were multiple causes of the Assyrian collapse. One of these we've encountered in the preceding chapters: disrupted weather patterns leading to drought and crop failures. In fact, studies of stalagmite formations in caves in Iraq show that from about 675 BCE, the region was in the grip of another megadrought. This was not a deathblow for the empire, but it's clear that during these decades, the Assyrian state came under pressure from its environment, and was suddenly at an economic disadvantage to its rivals.

Far more pressing was the simple fact of how hated Assyria had become among its neighbours. The Assyrian Empire was the first true military superpower. Their armed forces were the most powerful in the region, a hammer that smashed all opposition, and this had been a major factor in their success as a society. But it would also become a liability. Their heavy-handed approach made them deeply unpopular, and their subject peoples only remained in the empire out of fear. Whenever they thought they had a chance, they would try to throw out their hated Assyrian rulers. The empire would then come down on these rebels even harder, in a vicious circle. Eventually, they were left with no other option but to do as Ashurbanipal did to Elam: to eradicate their enemies entirely. However, nature abhors a vacuum. Beyond the blackened and smoking lands of Elam to which Ashurbanipal had laid waste, another power had been waiting for their opportunity to expand—an opportunity that the Assyrians had dropped right into their laps. These people were the Medes.

The Medes spoke their own language and lived in the region of northern and western Iran then known as Medea. For centuries, their powerful rivals the Elamites had kept their ambitions in check—but suddenly, the Medes were at liberty to expand. They moved in to occupy Elam, and gathered what remained of its scattered and angry peoples under its banner. They also brought in several other peoples, including the Gutians, Manneans and Kassites. Soon they were a formidable force, all animated by a common cause: a burning hatred for the Assyrian Empire, and everything it stood for. All they needed was an opening—and this would come with the death of King Ashurbanipal.

★★★

For someone whose early life was so meticulously recorded, the final twelve years of Ashurbanipal's reign are a surprising mystery. We don't know how he died, or even how he spent the last decade of his life. Perhaps the king was struck down by physical illness. Or, like his father Esarhaddon, perhaps he fell prey to a family predilection for depression and paranoia. One inscription, possibly his final one, seems to represent a kind of lament, a wail of pain for the misfortunes that had befallen him. It stands out among all the boasting and bluster of the Assyrian kings as a true moment of vulnerability:

> I…have done good to god and man, to the dead and the living. Why is it that disease, heartache, distress and destruction are clinging to me? Enmity in the land, strife in the house, do not depart from my side. Disturbances, evil words, are continually arrayed against me. Distress of soul, distress of body have bowed my form. I spend my days sighing and lamenting (in oh's and ah's). On the day of the god of the city, on the days of the feast, I am disturbed. Death is making an end of me, is weighing me down. In anguish and grief I sit, lamenting day and night.[25]

Whatever the cause, in 639 BCE, the Assyrian chronicles, which had until then kept detailed records of his life and deeds, suddenly fall silent. For this period, virtually the only sources we have are the Bible and the writings of Herodotus, who compiled his histories 200 years later, and for whom Mesopotamia was a distant and mysterious land. But one thing we know for sure: after the death of Ashurbanipal, chaos reigned in Assyria and civil war seems once again to have split the empire.

From 616 BCE, a series of Babylonian chronicles tell the story of the final collapse of Assyrian society. In a surprise attack in the year 614 BCE, the Mede armies marched down through the foothills of the Zagros mountains and captured Ashur, former capital and birthplace of the Assyrian nation and the home of its god. The city burned, and its people were put to the sword. This was the first time in centuries that a city in the Assyrian heartlands had been captured and sacked, and a message had now been sent to all its enemies. The empire was weakened—and with enough of a push, perhaps it could even be toppled. One man heard this message loud and clear: a king of Babylon, who had big plans for the city he ruled. His name was Nabopolassar.

Nabopolassar is a curious character. We don't know anything about his origins, but he refers to himself in his inscriptions as '*mar la mammana*'—the son of a nobody. No other Mesopotamian king had ever described himself in this way, and we might guess that in the social upheaval following Ashurbanipal's destruction of the city, men were rising from the ranks of Babylon's common people to rule. When he heard of the Mede victory at Ashur, Nabopolassar must have been overjoyed. He gathered his armies and marched to the burning city as fast as he could to join them.

The Babylonian forces arrived too late for the fighting, but on the ruins of Ashur, they formalized their alliance: the Mede King Cyaxares married his daughter Amytis to the Babylonian prince Nabu-Kudurri-Usur II, who history would remember by his Hebrew name: Nebuchadnezzar. This situation had been the Assyrians' nightmare for centuries: its enemies now united against it in its moment of greatest weakness. For the rest of that year, the joint Mede and Babylonian forces pushed north up the Euphrates—but the Assyrian army was still formidable, and made them pay for every inch of land. It wasn't until 612 BCE that the Medes reached the walls of Assyria's capital, Nineveh. We can only imagine how that army must have felt, looking out at that city, with its towering ziggurat and glorious palaces. We can see evidence of the fierce battle that unfolded in the archaeological record. Excavations in Nineveh's south-eastern Halzi Gate have found the ground there littered with skeletons, lying one on top of another on the cobbled pavement. The bodies of horses also litter this gateway, along with countless iron spearheads and arrows, all of it left exactly as it was on the day the city fell.

The destruction was chronicled by Hebrew scholars of the time with understandable delight. One vivid account has survived in the Hebrew Bible, in a chapter known as the book of Nahum. Nahum almost certainly didn't witness these events, but he had a lively imagination. In his lines, we can almost hear the sound and fury of battle, as the Medes and Babylonians rampaged through the streets of Nineveh:

> The shield of his mighty men is made red, the valiant men are in scarlet: the chariots shall be with flaming torches in the day of his preparation, and the fir trees shall be terribly shaken.
>
> The chariots shall rage in the streets, they shall justle one against another in the broad ways: they shall seem like torches, they shall run like the lightnings.
>
> ...
>
> Woe to the bloody city! it is all full of lies and robbery.[26]

For Nahum, the destruction of Nineveh was a moral judgement on an empire that had wrought such deep suffering on others:

> O king of Assyria: thy nobles shall dwell in the dust: thy people is scattered upon the mountains, and no man gathereth them.
>
> There is no healing of thy bruise; thy wound is grievous: all that hear the bruit of thee shall clap the hands over thee: for upon whom hath not thy wickedness passed continually?[27]

By the end of that year, the three capitals of Assyria—Ashur the religious heart, Nineveh the administrative centre, and Nimrud, the military capital—lay in ruins. The Medes made no attempt to occupy them, and instead set about destroying them with the same viciousness that the Assyrians had once visited on the cities of Elam. Although Assyria's king had been killed, one general named Ashur-Uballit held out a determined resistance to the invaders, marshalling what remained of the Assyrian army around him. They shut themselves up in the town of Harran, and perhaps some of them would have remembered that this was the town where a century before a woman had prophesied doom for the Empire of Assyria, and where King Esarhaddon had met his end. In 610 BCE, the Mede armies finally marched on Harran and crushed what remained of the Assyrian resistance.

The ruins of Nineveh would have stood for some time as smoking heaps of blackened rubble. Slowly, grasses grew over them, and in summer the windblown sands rolled in. The city's walls and houses and the bodies lying in its streets were covered. Birds and wild foxes moved in, and hardy tamarisk trees sprouted along the corridors. The library of King Ashurbanipal was also buried, its clay tablets baked in the fires that had consumed the city. In a twist of fate, the destruction of the city is what ensured that this library would survive, the clay of many of its books baked and hardened as though in a kiln. The people who destroyed Nineveh defaced some of the carvings that lined the palace walls. They seem to have struck at the faces of the Assyrian kings and symbols of its vanished power, cracking the soft alabaster, but the lion hunt carvings, the lions with their sorrowful eyes, remained untouched.

Hundreds of years later, when Xenophon marched past with his 10,000 Greeks, fleeing from the Persian army, the people who lived in this region would not even remember who had built this city. They would say only that they thought it was the Medes, and that for some reason, the gods had punished them, and turned their cities into ruins.

In the 1850s, the Victorian archaeologist Austen Henry Layard visited Nineveh and wrote an account of these desolate remains:

> From the summit of an artificial eminence we looked down upon a broad plain, separated from us by the river. A line of lofty mounds bounded it to the east, and one of a pyramidical form rose high above the rest. Its position rendered its identification easy. This was the pyramid which Xenophon had described, and near which the ten thousand had encamped: the ruins around it were those which the Greek general saw twenty-two centuries before, and which were even then the remains of an ancient city.[28]

Layard was haunted by the beauty of these empty places, where the ruins hardly even bore the marks of human construction:

> Were the traveller to cross the Euphrates to seek for such ruins in Mesopotamia as he had left behind him in Asia Minor or Syria, his search would be in vain. The graceful column rising above the thick foliage of the myrtle, ilex, and oleander; the gradines of the amphitheatre covering a gentle slope, and overlooking the dark blue water of a lake—none of this can be found. All are replaced by the stern, shapeless mound rising like a hill from the scorched plain, the fragments of pottery, and the stupendous mass of brick-work occasionally laid bare by the winter rains… He is now at a loss to give any form to the rude heaps upon which he is gazing. Those of whose works they are the remains…have left no visible traces of their civilization, or of their arts: their influence has long since passed away.[29]

And like Xenophon two millennia before, Layard was struck by the immensity of what these ruins represented, their silent testimony to the yawning gulf of time that separates their age from ours:

> Desolation meets desolation. A feeling of awe succeeds to wonder. For there is nothing to relieve the mind, to lead to hope, or to tell of what has gone by. These huge mounds of

Assyria made a deeper impression upon me, gave rise to more serious thoughts, and more earnest reflection, than all the temples of Balbec, and the theatres of Ionia.[30]

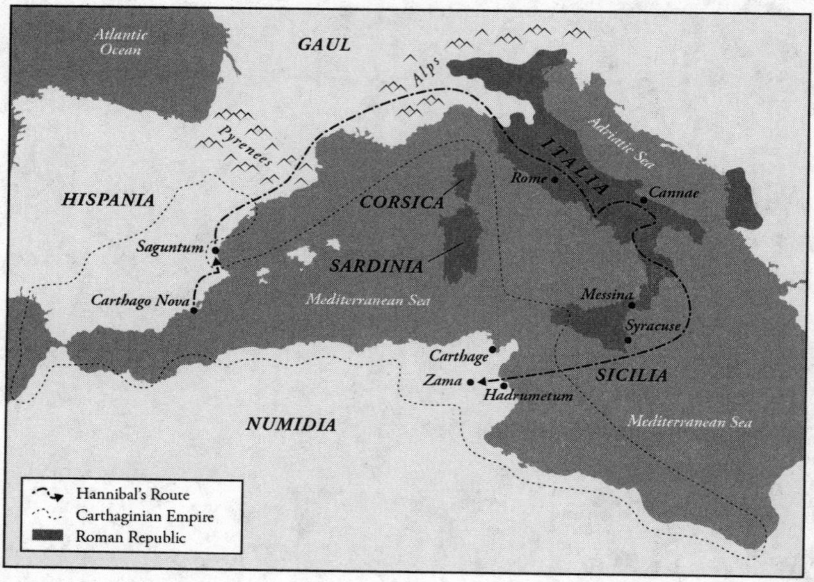
Atlantic Ocean
GAUL
Alps
Pyrenees
HISPANIA
CORSICA
SARDINIA
ITALIA
Adriatic Sea
Rome
Cannae
Saguntum
Carthago Nova
Mediterranean Sea
Messina
Syracuse
Carthage
Zama
Hadrumetum
SICILIA
NUMIDIA
Mediterranean Sea
Hannibal's Route
Carthaginian Empire
Roman Republic

4

Carthage

c. 800 BCE–146 BCE

During their reign as the apex predator of the Near East, the Assyrian Empire had long menaced the peoples of the Mediterranean coast. But one of those peoples would escape from under their thumb and forge an empire of their own, far over the sea. These were the series of city states that more than 4,000 years ago rose up on the stony shore of what is today Lebanon, overlooked by towering mountains covered in cedar forests. The largest of these cities were Tyre, Sidon and Byblos, and they were the birthplace of a culture that would one day be called 'Phoenician'.

The Phoenicians were given the name *Phoinike* by the Greeks, but it's unlikely that they would have used that word about themselves. They were united by a common Phoenician language, and by the worship of gods such as Baal Hammon, a heroic god named Melqart and his wife Astarte, but there's little to suggest a common identity, architecture or literature. Even the Greek word 'Phoenician' has a somewhat mysterious origin. In early literary works such as the *Iliad* and *Odyssey*, '*phoinix*' is also used to describe a particular shade of purple or crimson, and also a date palm, possibly due to the reddish colour of its ripe fruit—and so it has been suggested that the name comes from one of their earliest and most successful industries.

The Phoenicians of Tyre and other cities were among the first people to colour their clothes with a particular dye derived from the bodies of predatory sea snails known as the murex or rock snail. These snails produce their dye as a defence mechanism against predators, and depending on the species, can produce a vivid red or purple colour unlike anything else available in the ancient world. It could take more than 50 kilograms of snails to make a single gram of this dye, and as a result these fabrics were extremely expensive. In the ancient world, the colour purple soon became associated with wealth, and in turn, with royalty. This colour became known as 'Tyrian purple' after the city of Tyre, and later 'imperial purple', and it dyed the robes of the emperors of Assyria, Rome, and later Byzantium. So it's possible that *Phoinike* came to be used to describe these traders from the rocky coast of Lebanon—as the 'purple people'. With the dye industry booming, the Phoenicians ventured out on ever longer voyages out into the Mediterranean, driven by the need to procure more of these priceless snails.

Since as early as the third millennium BCE, Phoenician sailors from Byblos had developed ships with curved hulls, perfectly suited for travelling on the waves, along with techniques for waterproofing the hulls using bitumen or pitch. In the Book of Ezekiel in the Hebrew Bible, we find a poetic description of such a ship:

> They have made all thy ship boards of fir trees of Senir: they have taken cedars from Lebanon to make masts for thee.
>
> Of the oaks of Bashan have they made thine oars; the company of the Ashurites have made thy benches of ivory, brought out of the isles of Chittim.
>
> Fine linen with broidered work from Egypt was that which thou spreadest forth to be thy sail; blue and purple from the isles of Elishah was that which covered thee.[1]

The Phoenicians cultivated a reputation as able seafarers, and as uncompromising and shrewd traders, which earned them some degree of unpopularity. The *Odyssey*, written down in the eighth century, describes the Phoenicians as cunning and untrustworthy, the antithesis of the supposedly noble Greeks: 'Thither came Phoenicians, men famed for their ships, greedy knaves, bringing countless trinkets in their black ship.'[2]

The Mediterranean Sea on which the Phoenicians flourished had long been an insurmountable challenge to many of the region's powers. The Assyrians referred to it as *Id-Marrati*, or 'the Bitter River', which they believed to surround the whole earth, while the Egyptians referred to it as *Wadj-Wer*, or 'the Great Green'. These empires were river cultures, and were wary of the sea. For this reason, they were heavily reliant on commodities brought into the region by Phoenician sailors. Assyria thus offered the cities of Tyre and Sidon a degree of independence, so long as they ensured a constant flow of copper, tin, silver and other resources into Assyria, and acted as a navy-for-hire, providing their ships and sailors to the empire in times of war. Knowing what fate befell those who opposed Assyria, the Phoenicians had little choice but to accept. But Assyrian demand for metal was truly staggering, and meeting it would require a drastic expansion of the Phoenician trade network. As a result, the Phoenicians would buy their independence, and get rich at the same time.

The inscription of the Nora Stone, showing typical Phoenician writing.

At first, the Phoenicians set up simple trading posts at locations where they could find the most metal, such as Cyprus, with its stores of copper, and Sardinia, the Mediterranean's second largest island, rich in copper, iron, silver and lead. Phoenician settlers began arriving here in the middle of the ninth century BCE, and set up partnerships with the local people. These locals did the actual mining, while the Phoenicians simply turned up to buy the goods and take them away by ship. From Cyprus and Sardinia, Phoenician sailors pushed further west and set up the small colony of Utica in North Africa, and even reached southern Spain, where the mines practically overflowed with silver, iron and other metals. Archaeologists have found huge Phoenician furnaces in this region, designed for smelting metal ingots for transportation on an industrial scale.

Before long, the Phoenicians were sailing through the straits of Gibraltar, then known as the Pillars of Hercules, and out into the Atlantic Ocean, more than 4,000 kilometres from their homeland. The earliest piece of Phoenician writing found outside the Levant is an inscribed tablet known as the Nora Stone, unearthed in Sardinia, and apparently commemorating a Phoenician leader who may have died in conflict with the local people there.

'He fought with the Sardinians at Tarshish and he drove them out,' it reads. 'Among the Sardinians he is now at peace, and his army is at peace: Milkaton son of Shubna, general of king Pummay.'[3] But for the most part, the Phoenicians seem to have interacted with the people they met relatively peacefully, and most of all, profitably. And before long, Tyre, Sidon and Byblos found themselves at the far east of a trade network that sprawled ever westwards over the Mediterranean. Soon the centre of the Phoenicians' power would also shift in that direction, to a place where they could finally be free of the overbearing empires that constantly breathed down their necks. They would found a city there that would become one of the largest and wealthiest on Earth. That city would one day be known as Carthage.

***

Like so many aspects of our modern understanding of the Phoenicians, the name Carthage is itself a distortion, filtered through the accounts of others. In Latin, the city was known as *Carthago*, while the Greeks called it *Karkhēdōn*. But to its inhabitants, it was known as *Qart-Hadasht*, meaning 'the new city'.

Like many cities of its time, Carthage soon developed its own founding myth. It begins with a princess of Tyre named Elissa or Elishaya, who flees Tyre with a number of servants and temple women when her treacherous brother Pygmalion moves to seize her throne. This group of refugees sails along the coast of North Africa and comes ashore near the Phoenician colony of Utica, setting up camp on a hill known as Byrsa. The king who rules there, Iarbus, takes pity on them. But not too much pity. He offers to sell them a plot on the hill no bigger than an ox hide—but Elishaya is cunning, and cuts the hide into thin strips, lining them up to enclose the entire hill, a much larger area than the miserly king had intended. Iarbus has no choice but to give them the land he promised—and so Carthage is born.

From the hilltop of Byrsa, the city grows and grows, soon eclipsing King Iarbus's town of Utica. The miserly king becomes jealous, and demands that Elishaya marry him, so that he can absorb her flourishing town and everything she owns into his kingdom. If she refuses, he will burn the new city to the ground. Faced with this choice, Elishaya builds a pyre and climbs onto it, killing herself. This tragic but noble sacrifice has proven irresistible to generations of poets, and the Roman poet Virgil gives one rendition:

> Fluttered and fierce in her awful purpose, with bloodshot restless gaze, and spots on her quivering cheeks burning through the pallor of imminent death… [she] mounts in madness the high funeral pyre, and unsheathes the sword of Dardania… She sank on the pillow and spoke the last words of all:… 'Receive my spirit now, and release me from my distresses. I have lived and fulfilled Fortune's allotted course; and now shall I go a queenly phantom under the earth.'[4]

In honour of Elishaya's sacrifice, her people gave her the title of Dido, meaning female warrior or heroine, and this was the name by which she would later be known to Roman writers. This baroque tale of honour and tragedy has all the hallmarks of classical literature, and we can't assume that it bears any relationship to real events. Some details accord with what archaeology tells us:

the city was founded close to the older settlement of Utica, which it soon eclipsed in size. But perhaps the most important part of this founding myth is the hint it may give us about how the Carthaginians thought of themselves, and their place in the world: as a city of survivors who had found a refuge here on the North African coast; a city of sailors. They were resourceful and drove a hard bargain; they were clever, fond of outwitting their enemies, and they could always make a little go a long way. And, perhaps, that they would die before they gave up their freedom.

***

Regardless of its origins, it's clear from archaeology that the new colony city of Carthage grew quickly. This was partly thanks to its geography, which made it in many ways the perfect Phoenician settlement. Carthage was built in a small bay that itself belonged to a vast natural harbour, known today as the Gulf of Tunis. It stood on top of a series of sheer red cliffs that look down over the glittering blue waters of the Mediterranean, and it was also easily defended on its landward side, where a range of rocky hills, interspersed with lakes and saltwater lagoons, break the land into a series of narrow approaches.

Standing at the crucial halfway point between Tyre and the wealthy mines of Spain, it was also only about 200 kilometres by boat from Sicily, and about 300 kilometres from Sardinia, two crucial sites of Phoenician industry that were only growing in importance. Pottery found in even the earliest layers of Carthage's settlement shows a huge range of styles, coming from Greece, Italy, Spain and all the Phoenician colonies. Carthage also assimilated the existing population of North African peoples, and formed a hybrid culture that was part Phoenician and part African. This early archaeology paints a picture of a humble collection of mud-brick buildings lining the seashore, but within a century this outpost had exploded into a much more sophisticated and complex cityscape.

From the Greek writers, we learn that Carthage was a republic. It was ruled under a kind of oligarchic system, governed by a council of its wealthiest citizens. Aristotle, in his fourth-century BCE work *Politika*, or Politics, writes approvingly of the Carthaginian system of government and compares it to that of the Greek city state of Sparta:

> Many regulations at Carthage are good; and a proof of a well-regulated constitution is that the populace willingly remain faithful to the constitutional system, and that neither civil strife has arisen in any degree worth mentioning, nor yet a tyrant.[5]

But he also warns that the Carthaginian system put too much emphasis on the wealth of its rulers rather than their competence, and expresses concerns that this could lead to corruption.

> They think that the rulers should be chosen not only for their merit but also for their wealth, as it is not possible for a poor man to govern well or to have leisure for his duties... It is a bad thing that the greatest offices of state, the kingship and the generalship, should be for sale. For this law makes wealth more honored than worth, and renders the whole state avaricious; And it is probable that those who purchase their office will learn by degrees to make a profit out of it.[6]

Certain powerful families vied constantly for position, but there was no hereditary royalty in Carthage, and it's possible that here the myth of Elishaya or Dido played a role. Since the city was supposedly founded by a woman who had no children, no one could ever claim to be her true descendant, or to have an ancestral right to rule. Instead, the city was governed by a number of different semi-democratic bodies made up of wealthy citizens. One of these was called the tribunal of the one hundred and four, and another the council of elders, a kind of senate. The highest executive position was held simultaneously by two annually elected officers, who ruled on all civilian matters. The arrangement was complex and likely prone to corruption, but for the most part it seems to have worked.

While Carthage flourished, the Phoenician cities that had given birth to it began to flounder. Tyre and Sidon were still under the boot of Assyria, and around 670 BCE, the Assyrian King Esarhaddon forced them to embargo his enemies in Egypt, cutting off their most lucrative market. Soon, the surviving treaties show us that the King of Tyre was not even allowed to open messages without an Assyrian official present. As a result of these restrictions and the economic decline that followed them, it's likely that large numbers of Phoenicians fled to what was now the undisputed capital of the Phoenician world: the booming port city of Carthage. They brought their language, their knowledge, their gods and their gold with them. By the sixth century BCE, Carthage was one of the largest and wealthiest cities in the Mediterranean, and its sailors would soon embark on voyages of exploration that would not be matched for another 2,000 years.

The Phoenicians by this time had already sailed right to the end of the 'known world', through the Pillars of Hercules and out into the Atlantic Ocean—but their exploration didn't stop there. In fact, if ancient sources are to be believed, they may have been the first navigators to successfully circumnavigate Africa. Herodotus recounts one expedition that purportedly took place around 600 BCE, sponsored by a pharaoh of Egypt named Nechos:

> So, the Phoenicians set out from the Red Sea and sailed the southern sea; whenever autumn came they would put in and plant the land in whatever part of Libya they had reached, and there await the harvest; then, having gathered the crop, they sailed on, so that after two years had passed, it was in the third that they rounded the pillars of Heracles and came to Egypt. There they said (what some may believe, though I do not) that in sailing around Libya they had the sun on their right hand.[7]

Ironically, it is this detail that Herodotus finds unbelievable that has caused modern scholars to take the claim more seriously. The change in the position of the sun relative to the ship suggests that the voyage did indeed cross the Tropic of Cancer, and perhaps even the equator, causing the summer sun to appear in the north. If this story is true, then it means the Phoenicians may have rounded the southern tip of Africa more than 2,000 years before the Portuguese explorer Bartolomeu Dias in 1488.

More solidly attested voyages of Phoenician discovery would see an explorer named Hanno the Navigator sail perhaps as far south as Cameroon or Gabon. His voyage is recounted in a Greek text entitled the *Periplus of Hanno*, supposedly an accurate copy of an inscription that hung in the temple of Baal Hammon in Carthage. Hanno gives vivid descriptions of rivers of lava flowing into the ocean, possibly referring to the active volcano Mount Cameroon: 'We saw the land at night covered with flames. And in the midst there was one lofty fire, greater than the rest, which seemed to touch the stars.'[8] Hanno even writes about encountering gorillas, one of whose skins he took back with him to Carthage, where it was hung in a temple.

Another explorer, named Himilco, went in the opposite direction, sailing out into the Atlantic and north up the coast of Spain and France, and as far as the British Isles. There he saw whales in the Atlantic, and Celtic tribespeople sailing in coracles made of deerskin, a sight he found remarkable: 'They cleave the tempestuous sea, and the current of the Ocean abounding in monsters, with woven boats…from hides stitched together, and often travel through the immense sea in a skin.'[9] In 2019, a team of twenty modern sailors successfully piloted a replica of a single-masted Carthaginian merchant vessel across the Atlantic, departing from Carthage and landing in the Caribbean five months later, demonstrating that Phoenician ships had the ability to reach the Americas 2,000 years before Columbus.

***

As the population of Carthage grew, the city expanded. By 400 BCE, it may have reached a population of 400,000, and its walls had been rebuilt to a towering 15 metres high, with a triple line of ditches and defences on the landward side. The hill of Byrsa was now ringed not with ox-hide but with an imposing inner wall, looming over the rest of the city as a fortified citadel. Between there and the harbour stood the agora, the large open marketplace, where all manner of goods and foods could be bought. Archaeological studies of plant matter found in Carthage show that its citizens enjoyed a varied diet: wheat, barley and other grains, artichokes and cabbages, pulses and lentils, and fruits and nuts including pomegranates, grapes, figs, olives, peaches, plums, pistachios and almonds. They ate olive oil, plenty of fish—such as grey mullet, sea-perch and eels—and dolphins, as well as the meat of sheep, goats, pigs, chickens and occasionally dogs. The Carthaginians, like most people in the ancient world, were also obsessed with a pungent salty sauce known as garum, which was brewed from fermented fish entrails, and was probably similar to the fish sauce used in East Asian cuisine today. In the wreck of one Carthaginian ship, archaeologists have uncovered the remains of cannabis stalks, which may also have been enjoyed on land, possibly brewed into a tea. Wine was particularly beloved too, and especially a kind of sweet dessert wine made from sun-dried grapes.

A variety of animals would have been visible on the crowded city streets, including beasts of burden like oxen and horses, stray dogs and cats, and noisy caravans of donkeys arriving from the desert—the camel having not yet been introduced. A species of monkey known as the Barbary macaque is also native to this area, and Diodorus of Sicily records that Carthaginians kept these monkeys as apparently much-loved pets.

> In these cities many of the customs were very different from those current among us. For the apes lived in the same houses as the men, being regarded among them as gods, just as the dogs are among the Egyptians, and from the provisions laid up in the storerooms the beasts took their food without hindrance whenever they wished.[10]

And of course, in cavernous stables to the south of the city, were kept the animals that in many people's minds are most inseparably associated with Carthage: the elephants. The North African elephant is an extinct subspecies that lived north of the Sahara Desert. Carthaginian frescoes, coins and mosaics show that these animals had the swooping backs and large ears typical of the African elephants that roam the savannah—but they were considerably smaller, perhaps similar in size to another surviving subspecies, the African forest elephant. These reach a shoulder height of about 2.5 metres, though their heavy frames mean they weigh more than fifteen times the average horse. For this reason, these elephants were used by the Carthaginians as fearsome weapons of war.

In India and South East Asia it has always been common to use elephants as beasts of burden, to transport heavy loads for construction—but it's not clear whether the Carthaginians used their elephants in this manner, or whether these precious animals were only reserved for their power and prestige, to be used as living tanks on the battlefield, as the Roman historian Pliny the Elder describes:

> Elephants, when tamed, are employed in war, and carry into the ranks of the enemy towers filled with armed men; and on them, in a very great measure, depends the ultimate result of the battles... They tread under foot whole companies, and crush the men in their armour.[11]

As in India, these elephants may also have been used ceremonially in festivals and parades to carry kings and generals—as a living embodiment of the might of this new empire.

***

While Carthage didn't hesitate to go to war to defend its interests and protect its trade, it preferred diplomatic solutions to avoid fighting with its various Mediterranean neighbours. One such agreement was settled in 509 BCE with a minor city state in central Italy, in the region of Latium, whose people spoke a small Italic dialect called Latin. These people had just that year thrown off the rule of their Etruscan king, and brought in the rule of a pair of elected consuls drawn from the aristocracy, a system strikingly similar to, and perhaps even inspired by, the Carthaginian one. The name of this city was Rome.

The Romans at that time were one among several powers in

central Italy, facing rivals in the Etruscan kingdom and powerful tribal confederacies like the Samnites who were all fighting for dominance in central Italy. The Carthaginians seem to have taken note of this regional development and proceeded to sign a treaty with the new Roman Republic, the contents of which the Greek historian Polybius recalls:

> There shall be friendship between the Romans and their allies, and the Carthaginians and their allies, on these conditions: Neither the Romans nor their allies are to sail beyond the fair peninsula, unless driven by stress of weather or the fear of enemies... Carthage shall build no fort in Latium; and if they enter the district in arms, they shall not stay a night therein.[12]

The theme of the treaty was simple: you leave us alone, and we will leave you alone. And while Rome had clearly got their attention, it seems Carthage considered this new Italian republic to present little cause for concern.

★★★

Around 410 BCE, Carthage began minting its own silver coins, each stamped with the symbol of a palm tree—apparently a pun on the Greek word *Phoenike*. By promoting this symbol of Phoenician identity, Carthage was putting itself forward as the champion of the Phoenician people—the capital of the Phoenician world. Carthage now looked a lot like an empire. And like all empires, it soon found an increasing need to go to war.

It's often said that Carthage relied on mercenaries to fight its wars, but in fact, most of their soldiers were conscripted under the terms of treaties. Neighbouring Numidia to the west sent experienced cavalry and javelin throwers, while colonies on the island of Majorca sent slingers, and peasant spearmen with large round shields came from the fields of Libya. Celts from Spain made up some part of their forces, and sometimes even Greeks and Italians ended up fighting in these armies. There was only one group of people who hardly ever fought for Carthage, and that was the citizens of Carthage themselves.

The Carthaginian system relied largely on making life as comfortable as possible for the people of the capital. While its lower classes were sometimes drafted into the navy, few Carthaginian politicians ever risked the unpopular move of conscripting citizens to fight in the army. This was considered a job for other peoples. But soon, Carthage would find itself embroiled in a bitter struggle that would test this system to breaking point and threaten to bring the whole empire to the brink. These wars erupted over what was soon to become the most fought-over piece of land in the Mediterranean: Sicily.

A Punic coin bearing the mark of a palm tree.

***

Sicily is the largest island in the Mediterranean Sea, its landscape dominated by the active volcano Mount Etna, and separated from Italy by the narrow straits of Messina. At first, Carthage enjoyed an unrivalled position on the island, trading with the locals in the west, a short hop away from their capital in North Africa. But they soon came into conflict with another group of people that for much of this history were their greatest rivals on the sea and on land, a people who were also busy establishing colonies across the Mediterranean. These were the Greeks.

The Greeks, like the Phoenicians, were expert sailors, and had built a number of thriving colonies in southern Italy, in what is now Turkey, and around the Black Sea. From the eighth century BCE, Greek explorers and traders began expanding their interests into southern Italy and Sicily, an area that they would come to call *Megale Hellas*, or 'Greater Greece'. Greek settlers were in part inspired by the myth of their hero Herakles, whom the Romans would call Hercules. In some Greek colonies, this half-divine warrior was celebrated for slaying giants and mythical beasts, while in others his feats were more mundane. In southern Italy, for instance, he was remembered for banishing a plague of flies.

In one of the most dramatic episodes, during his tenth labour, Hercules is tasked with stealing the red cattle belonging to the ogre Geryon, who lived in Erythia in southern Spain. Since Geryon lived so far in the west, it was said, the hides of his cattle had been stained red by their proximity to the setting sun. After killing Geryon, Hercules takes his cattle and herds them all the way back home. 'Heracles then made his way from Celtica to Italy,' Diodorus of Sicily writes, 'and as he traversed the mountain pass through the Alps he made a highway out of the route, which was rough and almost impassable.'[13] This story of Hercules crossing the Alps was the dramatic pinnacle of a series of myths that would become known as the Heraclean Way, which were told to countless generations of Greek settlers, and then to the children of the Romans who followed them. As the Phoenician god Melqart became increasingly associated with Hercules, these stories were also told to the children of Carthage.

For several centuries, the Greek settlers in eastern Sicily maintained an uneasy peace with the Carthaginian settlements in the west. But as both powers required greater amounts of land to support their colonies, they found themselves on a collision course. By the late fifth century BCE, Sicily had erupted in warfare. For the citizens of Carthage, exempt as they were from serving in the army, the fighting must have seemed a long way from home, and they were content to let these wars simmer on for years. But the final episode of these conflicts, known as the Seventh Sicilian War, was to puncture this sense of invulnerability, and bring the war home to their shores in dramatic fashion. Their rival in this story was a king of Syracuse, a Greek city state on the south-eastern coast of Sicily, and his name was Agathocles.

Agathocles began life as a commoner in the Sicilian colonies, but entered the army and rose through its ranks, until he was able to enact a military coup and seize the throne of Syracuse in 317 BCE. From there, he set about subjugating cities all around him, and it wasn't long before the Carthaginians saw Agathocles as a serious threat. Carthage amassed a huge army, sailed for Sicily, and beat Agathocles back to Syracuse—where they laid siege. With his city surrounded, and no hope of reinforcements, Agathocles must have been desperate—but in a flash of inspiration, he decided on a truly daring course of action. He hatched a plan to break free of the siege by ship, set sail for Africa, and make a strike at the heart of his enemy: the city of Carthage itself.

When the Greek fleet set sail, the Carthaginians believed Agathocles to be fleeing. They chased him across the sea, pelting him with arrows, but he and his men were able to cross the sea and land on the beaches of Africa. Famously, he ordered his ships to be burned, to ensure that his men would have nowhere to run—and no choice but to fight. From the city walls of Carthage, the fires of the burning ships would have been visible on the horizon, and fear spread among its citizens. Carthage amassed a hurried army of citizen soldiers, hoping to overwhelm Agathocles with sheer numbers—but when they met the now desperate Greeks in battle, the inexperienced Carthaginians were sorely beaten, and fled back to the city. The result was pandemonium. The city had never been significantly threatened before, and there were now virtually no forces there to defend it. So great was the panic as Agathocles bore down on them that the Carthaginians seem to have turned in their desperation to an ancient rite that represents one of the darkest and most controversial aspects of their history: the ritual of child sacrifice.

These were violent times, when human life was cheap—but even so, this practice was mentioned with some revulsion by several ancient writers. The practice had begun as an authentic sacrifice of one's own beloved sons and daughters in hope of gaining the favour of the gods—but for a while now, wealthy Carthaginians had been running a macabre industry: a trade in other people's children for sacrifice. Plutarch paints a grisly portrait of these rituals:

> Those who had no children would buy little ones from poor people and cut their throats as if they were so many lambs or young birds; meanwhile the mother stood by without a tear or moan; but should she utter a single moan or let fall a sin-

> gle tear, she had to forfeit the money, and her child was sacrificed nevertheless; and the whole area before the statue was filled with a loud noise of flutes and drums so that the cries of wailing should not reach the ears of the people.[14]

For a long time, it was believed that these stories were exaggerations, Greek propaganda designed to demonize their Carthaginian enemies. But modern archaeological discoveries have more or less confirmed that child sacrifice did take place, at least at some times, and at least by some people in the city. Large collections of buried urns containing the cremated remains of children have been found in temple sites known as tophets. Some of these temples are large, with collections of cremation urns exceeding 2,000 in number. Masks and cymbals, incense burners and other paraphernalia suggest that the ceremonies were highly structured.

A Punic tophet at Carthage, where sacrificial victims were buried.

We should not get carried away with these findings: at most of these sites, analysis has shown that the majority of the child remains are of stillborn babies, or babies who died of natural causes. The relative lack of children's remains in any of the regular graveyards seems to show that the tophets were at least in part cremation sites for children who died naturally. But not all the remains seem to fit with normal patterns of child mortality, even in the ancient world. However the ritual had begun, at least in the later years of the city's existence, it clearly evolved into something darker and crueller.

With the army of Agathocles drawing near, and their last citizen defenders defeated in the field, the Carthaginians believed their gods were angry with them, as Diodorus recounts:

> They also alleged that Cronus had turned against them...as in former times they had been accustomed to sacrifice to this god the noblest of their sons, but more recently, secretly buying and nurturing children, they had sent these to the sacrifice. When they had given thought to these things and saw their enemy encamped before their walls, they were filled with superstitious dread, for they believed that they had neglected the honours of the gods that had been established by their fathers. In their zeal to make amends for their omission, they selected two hundred of the noblest children and sacrificed them publicly; and others who were under suspicion sacrificed themselves voluntarily, in number not less than three hundred.[15]

Agathocles rampaged around the countryside of Carthage for years, even capturing the city of Hadrumetum, but Carthage itself kept him at bay with its formidable triple-walled defences. The Greek king eventually ran out of steam, and limped back home to Sicily. All the same, he had left a lasting impression on the people of Carthage, laid waste to the countryside, terrified them so deeply that they had slaughtered hundreds of their own children, and likely left them on the brink of bankruptcy. A peace treaty in 307 BCE essentially returned the situation in Sicily to how it had been before the war.

The example of Agathocles, of a daring strike at the heart of your enemy right at the moment they least expect it, was one that later Carthaginian generals would remember. It was an episode that other powers in the region also paid particular attention to. Carthage had once been considered the region's major power, but a small Greek army had come within a hair's breadth of bringing it to its knees. Plutarch puts it bluntly in the mouth of one of his characters:

> For who could keep his hands off Libya, or Carthage, when that city got within his reach, a city which Agathocles, slipping stealthily out of Syracuse and crossing the sea with a few ships, narrowly missed taking?[16]

The next to take advantage of this perceived weakness was another Greek king named Pyrrhus.

★★★

Pyrrhus was the pugnacious King of Epirus, around what is today southern Albania. In his later life he styled himself as a hero of the Hellenic world, a defender of everything Greek—and right at that moment, the Greeks who most needed defending were the beleaguered colonies in southern Italy, in the region of *Megale Hellas*. These city states found themselves suddenly menaced by an emerging regional force—the rising city state of Rome. Throughout the fourth century BCE, this bizarre republic had been expanding, upsetting the established power balance in central Italy and ultimately absorbing all of Latium and the region of Campania—and were now extending their territory southward into southern Italy.

Carthage took notice of this, and penned another somewhat more anxious treaty with the Romans, asking them to promise not to found any cities in Africa. But on the whole they seem to have welcomed the rise of Rome as a potential ally against the hated Greeks. The Roman capital even had a district known as the *Vicus Africus*, or African quarter, suggesting that a population of Carthaginian merchants already lived and traded in the city. For Carthage, Rome was not so much an unwelcome rival as a new source of customers. But for the Greek states of southern Italy, Rome was a voracious new predator. Soon, many of them began sending out letters of distress to Pyrrhus, and the King of Epirus couldn't resist the call of this heroic struggle for the glory of Greece. He gathered an armada and a large army complete with twenty war elephants, and in 280 BCE he sailed to southern Italy in full force.

Pyrrhus defeated the Romans at Heraclea that year, and then at Ausculum the following spring, both at tremendous cost. He now expected them to cut their losses and admit defeat—but, slightly to the bemusement of Pyrrhus, Rome simply refused to surrender. This was something that would soon become a Roman hallmark. Some have argued that Rome's very nature as a citizen democracy contributed to its immense doggedness in warfare. Its leaders were politicians, in a state of constant competition for the support of the voting public, and any who signed a damaging peace treaty were likely to be eviscerated in public as a coward, or even a traitor. This meant that in wars with Rome's enemies, its senators would overwhelmingly vote to continue a war rather than admit defeat.

According to Plutarch, who was fond of inventing dialogue for his historical characters, Pyrrhus made the following quip after his third victory with Rome:

> We are told that Pyrrhus said to one who was congratulating him on his victory, 'If we are victorious in one more battle with the Romans, we shall be utterly ruined!' For he had lost a great part of the forces with which he came, and all his friends and generals except a few; moreover, he had no others whom he could summon from home, and he saw that his allies in Italy were becoming indifferent, while the army of the Romans, as if from a fountain gushing forth indoors, was easily and speedily filled up again.[17]

After this series of Pyrrhic victories, Pyrrhus soon realized that the conquest of Italy would elude him. He came within miles of Rome, but the tall Servian Wall surrounding the city meant that his beleaguered force had no hope of taking it. Still, he couldn't bear to return home empty handed. Instead, Pyrrhus headed to Sicily, with the aim of helping its Greek colonies in their fight against the Carthaginians. The Carthaginian response to Pyrrhus couldn't have been more different: they offered to pay him off generously to leave them alone, but Pyrrhus refused.

Still, Sicily too eventually defeated him. After finally being routed in southern Italy, he cut his losses and sailed for home with little to show for years of war. Plutarch imagines Pyrrhus, as he sails away, reflecting on the situation he has left behind:

> Pyrrhus looked back at the island and said to those about him: 'My friends, what a wrestling ground for Carthaginians and Romans we are leaving behind us!'[18]

That wrestling ground would be the arena for the next dramatic period of Mediterranean history. A conflict would soon unfold that would dwarf the Sicilian Wars for intensity and scale, would last for the next 130 years, would bring both powers to the brink of bankruptcy, and cost more than a million lives. This was the beginning of the Punic Wars.

★★★

The word Punic comes from Latin, and is a mutation of the Greek word *Phoenike*, or Phoenician. At this time, the Romans used it to describe the Phoenician superpower of Carthage, their rival across the sea. The historian Cassius Dio summarizes the situation, as Rome and Carthage slid towards war:

> The Carthaginians, who had long been powerful, and the Romans, who were now growing more rapidly stronger, kept viewing each other with jealousy; and they were led into war partly by the desire of continually acquiring more…and partly also by fear… It was a chance incident that broke their truce and plunged them into war.[19]

This chance incident would take place at a city called Messina. Standing on the north-eastern tip of Sicily at the narrowest crossing point between the island and mainland Italy, Messina was of immense strategic importance. Whoever controlled Messina controlled the crossing, and both Carthage and Rome were anxious about the city's future.

Sicily at this time had something of the Wild West about it: a lawless land where bandits and mercenaries roamed the countryside. One such band were a group of mostly southern Italians who called themselves the Mamertines, or the sons of Mars. They had been allowed into the walled town of Messina as refugees, but had betrayed its citizens and captured the city for themselves. Since then, they had spent twenty years running Messina as a kind of pirate fortress, a base to raid nearby towns and attack shipping. The trouble began in 265 BCE when Hiero, the latest Greek king of Syracuse, moved to finally bring these Mamertine pirates to justice. Facing execution for their crimes, the Mamertines played the only card left to them: trading on the strategic importance of their city. Hedging their bets, they sent out requests for help to both the big players in the region: Carthage and Rome. The Carthaginians came to their aid first, of course delighted to seize a town from the Greeks. This was just the latest move in the nearly two-centuries-long chess game on Sicily—but to the Romans, it was worrying. They began to fear that Carthage was plotting an invasion of the mainland, as Polybius recalls: 'The Romans, foreseeing this and viewing it as a necessity for themselves not to abandon Messene and thus allow the Carthaginians as it were to build a bridge for crossing over to Italy, debated the matter for long.'[20]

The Roman Senate was bitterly divided on what to do, with many expressing disgust at coming to the aid of these brigands. But eventually their fears won out. They voted to send a force to Messina to secure the crossing, led by a consul named Appius Claudius. The Romans crossed the straits stealthily, evading the Carthaginian navy, and when they arrived at Messina, the Italian Mamertine pirates ousted the Carthaginian general who had come to their aid and welcomed their fellow Italians into the town in his place. The Roman commander Appius then rounded on Syracuse, and its King Hiero surrendered. This was the end of the last independent Greek states of *Megale Hellas*, and the future of the Mediterranean would now be decided by either Carthage or Rome. Both sides marched to war.

In this conflict, the First Punic War, the Carthaginians treated Rome as a real threat: they drew up a large army of Celts, Iberians and others, and sent it to Sicily. Still, they maintained faith in their overall strategy, which had served them well in previous Sicilian wars. While the warships of Carthage commanded the waves, their trading empire would continue to fill their treasury with gold, and there would always be soldiers ready to fight for them. The Carthaginian navy benefitted from a thousand years of Phoenician shipbuilding and sailing, but their relatively unchallenged dominance of the sea had also made them complacent. Their primary weapons for fighting on the water were the heavy bronze rams fixed to the front of their ships. The Phoenician sailors would outmanoeuvre enemy ships with their superior sailing, and crash these rams into their sides, striking them in the hulls below the waterline.

The Romans knew they could not outmatch the Carthaginians at this difficult style of combat. They would need to bring the battles at sea into more familiar territory. To this end, they developed an ingenious new technology: a kind of boarding bridge that they called a *corvus* or 'crow'. These were raised like a drawbridge at the front of the ship, and could be dropped down onto the deck of an enemy vessel, where a metal spike on the underside drove into the boards, allowing the Roman legionaries to flood onboard. It was a brutally basic but surprisingly effective tactic.

The Carthaginian fleet was busy plundering at a place called Mylae, on the northern coast of Sicily, when they saw Roman sails on the horizon. Polybius recounts that the Carthaginians put to sea apparently not considering the engagement 'worth even the trouble of ranging their ships in any order'.[21] When they saw the 'crows' on the prows of the Roman vessels, they were perplexed—until they saw them in action. The Romans drew close, and their trap closed. Roman soldiers poured onto the Carthaginian vessels, and a slaughter began. The Carthaginians turned and fled, with the loss of fifty ships.

For Carthage, this was a disaster. A Roman invasion force now descended on the North African coast, and in response, Carthage sent out the entirety of its fleet to meet them on the open sea. Polybius records that more than 600 ships came together in the battle at Cape Ecnomus, probably involving at least 120,000 sailors, soldiers, rowers and marines. The enormous battlefield would have devolved into a chaos of clashing oars and rams, shouting men and the din of the *corvus* bridges thudding down into the decks. By the end of the day, the result was a decisive defeat for the Carthaginians. With their enemies scattered, the Romans successfully made the crossing into Africa, just as Agathocles once had. The Carthaginians had had enough, and asked the Romans for a peace treaty to sign. But the Roman demands were so punishing, that, even in their desperate state, they could not accept the terms. They fought on, and the Roman expeditionary force was beaten on the battlefield, and on the war went.

The First Punic War dragged on for twenty-three years, with most of the fighting taking place in and around Sicily. It finally ended with Carthaginian surrender in 241 BCE, and the signing of the Treaty of Lutatius. It was one of the longest continuous wars ever to take place in the ancient world, exhausting the men and resources of both Carthage and Rome. But Rome, as the victor, at least gained something from the years of carnage. Under the terms of the treaty, Carthage handed over all its remaining territory in Sicily, along with several groups of small islands nearby, and possibly Corsica too. It was also to pay a staggering 82 tonnes of silver in reparations over the next ten years. All of this meant that Carthage could no longer afford to pay its armies. In the same year that the treaty was signed, a large band of its former mercenaries, around 20,000 men or so, camped outside the city, refusing to budge until they got paid. When the Carthaginian senate still delayed payment, they mutinied and began looting and burning the countryside.

When this news reached some of the discontented and war-weary cities of Libya, they saw their chance to throw off Carthaginian rule entirely. Soon the empire was engulfed in a civil war that Polybius tells us went on for three years:

> [Carthage] had no store of provisions ready, and no expectation whatever of external assistance from friends or allies. They were indeed now thoroughly taught the difference between a foreign war, carried on beyond the seas, and a domestic insurrection.[22]

The man put in charge of restoring order in Carthage was a general named Hamilcar Barca. At enormous cost, he eventually crushed these rebels, but this internal conflict weakened the empire even further. At Carthage's moment of greatest weakness, Rome moved to capture Sardinia from them too, and the Carthaginians could do nothing to stop them.

The new balance of power in the Mediterranean was clear. If they were to reclaim any of the authority they had once had, the next generation of Carthaginian military leaders would need to produce a general of such genius that he could turn around the fortunes of this floundering empire. A general who could conduct a campaign so daring that it is still studied in military academies to this day. That man bore a name that in Phoenician meant 'by the grace of Baal', a man touched by the gods. His name was Hannibal.

★★★

Hannibal was the son of the general Hamilcar Barca. When the First Punic War ended, he was a boy of only six years old, and through much of his childhood, the fires of civil war burned all around him. Having lost the last of its profitable Mediterranean islands, Carthage's only economic hope was for its best general to expand its remaining colonies in Spain. Hamilcar soon departed for Spain, and took his young son Hannibal with him, to teach him the art of war, and to ensure that he passed on his hatred of Rome.

In Spain, Hamilcar succeeded in conquering numerous Celtic tribes, and built a new city that became known as 'New Carthage', now the southern Spanish city of Cartagena. As a boy, Hannibal might have visited the temple of Melqart or Hercules in Gades (now Cádiz), with a golden olive tree at its centre. He might have heard stories about Hercules too, and his legendary journey over the Alps, herding the cattle of Geryon the giant. Perhaps he would even have learned the history of the Greek Agathocles and his daring strike at his stronger enemy. And all the while, he must have dreamed of one day making his own mark on history.

When his father died, it fell to Hannibal to lead the Carthaginian armies in Spain. He inherited 60,000 battle-hardened troops and a stable of 200 war elephants. By the age of twenty-seven, Hannibal controlled more than half of the Iberian Peninsula, the wealthiest and most powerful province of the empire. The Roman poet Silius Italicus, in his first-century epic poem *Punica*, gives one later description of his character:

> By nature he was eager for action and faithless to his plighted word, a past master in cunning but a strayer from justice. Once armed, he had no respect for Heaven; he was brave for evil and despised the glory of peace; and a thirst for human blood burned in his inmost heart. Beyond all this, his youthful vigour longed to blot out…the shame of the last generation, and to drown the treaty of peace in the Sicilian Sea.[23]

His and his father's success in Spain restored the lifeblood of Carthage, and silver once again flowed through the empire. Hannibal soon felt increasingly confident about testing both the Carthaginian senate, and his hated enemy of Rome.

★★★

The location for the flashpoint that would spark the Second Punic War was the town of Saguntum, now Sagunto, just north of Valencia in southern Spain. Although Rome had allowed Carthage to exercise power south of the Ebro River, it had made clear that it would not tolerate a Carthaginian attack on Saguntum. But Hannibal was willing to call Rome's bluff. In 219 BCE, aged just twenty-eight, he led his army against Saguntum and put it under siege.

We can imagine that, back in Carthage, news of Hannibal's actions was met with both excitement and dismay. One of his opponents, a man named Hanno, is supposed to have delivered a blistering speech against him in the senate. 'It is Carthage against which Hannibal is now bringing up his pent-houses and towers,' the Roman historian Livy has him rage. 'It is the walls of Carthage he is battering with his rams. Saguntum's walls...will fall upon our heads, and the war we have entered upon with the Saguntines we must carry on against the Romans.'[24] But Hannibal also had plenty of supporters and even his strongest opponents knew that any move against him could ignite a civil war that would cost them the wealthy Spanish provinces on which their entire economy now rested.

The Romans too were paralyzed by indecision. For the eight months of the siege, they did nothing but complain. When Hannibal finally took Saguntum, they sent a delegation of ambassadors to Africa to demand that he be arrested and handed over for punishment. The clouds of war were once more gathering over the sea. The historian Appian describes this moment, as the Carthaginians chose the only option available to them:

> The chief of the embassy, pointing to the fold of his toga and smiling, said: 'Here, Carthaginians, I bring you peace or war, you may take whichever you choose.' The latter replied: 'You may give us whichever you like.' When the Romans offered war, they all cried out: 'We accept it.'[25]

During the civil wars of his childhood, Hannibal had learned never to let your homeland become a battlefield. And so he decided to take his war to Rome. He withdrew to his capital of New Carthage for the winter, to prepare and plan. With the Roman navy now in control of the seas, Hannibal would have to travel by land, a journey of about 1,500 kilometres. And at its end, a monumental problem loomed. The Italian Peninsula was a natural fortress, walled off by the snowy bastion of the Alps. To cross into Italy, Hannibal would need a radical solution. And it's here that those stories he heard as a child may have come back to him: stories of the hero Hercules herding his cattle directly over those peaks. The Romans believed that it was impossible to cross the Alps with an army, burdened by supplies, horses, oxen and elephants. It would be madness even to attempt it. For that reason, it was the last thing they would ever have expected.

★★★

When spring came, Hannibal set out. In the foothills of the Pyrenees, he faced vicious attacks from local clans, and it was only through the lavish distribution of gifts that the Gauls allowed him and his men to pass through France. At the wide river Rhône, one of France's largest rivers, his army crossed with difficulty, building rafts to ferry men, equipment and elephants across. Hannibal followed the Rhône north and reached the Alps in October. Winter was closing in, and the passes were choked with ice and snow. The later Roman writer Ammianus Marcellinus writes one account of these treacherous alpine roads:

> In these Cottian Alps…there rises a lofty ridge, which scarcely anyone can cross without danger. For as one comes from Gaul it falls off with sheer incline, terrible to look upon because of overhanging cliffs on either side…the spreading valleys, made treacherous by ice, sometimes swallow up the traveller.[26]

The march to the top of the pass took nine gruelling days, but the descent proved even more treacherous than the climb. On their way down, they found that a recent landslide had turned what was already a difficult road into an impassable precipice. Hannibal's solution to this problem has become one of the most famous episodes in the mythical retellings of his journey that emerged over the following centuries. The story goes that he ordered his men to gather large amounts of wood and build an enormous fire against the rock of the precipice. As the flames licked at the icy stone and the rock heated, the soldiers poured their rations of sour wine against the heated rock, causing its temperature to drop rapidly, and cracks to appear. With iron tools, they worked away at these cracks, until after four days of labour, steps could be cut into the rock. Whatever the truth of this episode, the purpose of telling this story was clear. Here was a new Hercules, it said—a man who has crossed the Alps with his war elephants, a man who achieves great labours wherever he goes, a man for whom the very rock of the mountain presents no obstacle.

Descending into the foothills, the men must have felt the lowland warmth wash over their skin with a sense of relief, as Livy recounts:

> Lower down one comes to valleys and sunny slopes and rivulets, and near them woods, and places that begin to be fitter for man's habitation. There the beasts were turned out to graze, and the men, exhausted with toiling at the road, were allowed to rest.[27]

Hannibal and his men stood and looked out over the lands of Italy below. They had caught the Romans completely by surprise.

***

The speed of Hannibal's attack stunned the Romans, as Polybius writes: 'Scarcely had the last rumour about the taking of Saguntum by the Carthaginians ceased to attract attention, than news came that Hannibal had arrived in Italy with his army.'[28]

To make matters worse, Hannibal was now recruiting allies from among the Gaulish clans in the Alpine foothills. In response, General Sempronius Longus led an army of more than 40,000 to intercept Hannibal's forces. In December 218 BCE, they met at the battle of Trebia, where Hannibal's powerful and determined forces utterly smashed the Roman army, killing at least 20,000 soldiers. From there, Hannibal marched south and crossed the Apennine mountains that run down the centre of Italy, and crushed another Roman army on the shore of Lake Trasimene, killing another 15,000 men and capturing 10,000 prisoners. After that, he seemed unstoppable. Smarting from their first two encounters on home soil, the Romans quickly opted to avoid meeting him in battle, trying instead to suffocate his army and cut off his supplies. They even resorted to a scorched-earth campaign, burning their own countryside in a desperate attempt to starve Hannibal's troops.

Hannibal kept pushing south, in the hope that the conquered

Greek cities of southern Italy would greet him as a Herculean liberator, and rise up against Roman rule. But the journey was hard: all but the largest of his elephants died in the Italian winter, and while riding through the marshes of central Italy, Hannibal caught an infection that caused the loss of one of his eyes. When he seized a large supply depot at the southern town of Cannae, the Roman senate realized that their strategy of suffocating him wouldn't work. They ordered an 86,000-strong army to be drawn up, the largest that had ever been raised in Roman history, and sent it to meet Hannibal at Cannae. Once again, Hannibal's tactical genius won the day. The defeat was so total that even elite members of Roman society were slaughtered on the battlefield.

When news of this staggering defeat reached Rome, the city went into a panic. Its citizens began seeing evil omens and portents everywhere. One senator was dispatched to Delphi to consult the oracle, and, as the Carthaginians had once done under threat from Agathocles, the Romans resorted to rituals of human sacrifice to appease their angry gods, as Livy describes:

> By the direction of the Books of Fate, some unusual sacrifices were offered; amongst others a Gaulish man and woman and a Greek man and woman were buried alive in the Cattle Market, in a place walled in with stone, which even before this time had been defiled with human victims, a sacrifice wholly alien to the Roman spirit.[29]

After the battle of Cannae, many of the old Greek cities of southern Italy joined Hannibal and rebelled against Rome. For the next decade, war raged all over the region. In 211 BCE, Hannibal even marched on Rome itself—but, just as Pyrrhus had before him, he found the imposing Servian Wall too great an obstacle. Rome now realized that the only way they could turn the tide of this war was to attack Carthage in return. They sent an army into Spain, led by a general named Publius Cornelius Scipio, who had been among the few survivors of the battle of Cannae. He attacked Carthage remorselessly, and met with great success.

In 209 BCE, in a devastating blow, Scipio captured the capital of

New Carthage. Three years later he defeated the last remaining Carthaginian army in Spain, essentially seizing the entire province and its abundant silver mines for Rome. Despite everything that Hannibal had achieved, the war was starting to turn in Rome's favour. In 205 BCE, with Hannibal still rampaging in Italy, the Romans gave Scipio command of the armies of Sicily and ordered him to set sail for Africa, bringing the war to the gates of Carthage itself. After a year of preparation, Scipio set sail in 204 BCE. Hannibal was forced to hurry back to Carthage and defend the city, as the Roman poet Silius Italicus renders it:

> Now that all her limbs were severed, Carthage depended entirely upon one man for support; and [only] the great name of Hannibal, even in his absence, kept the edifice of her greatness from falling in utter ruin. He alone remained... Without delay envoys sailed across the salt sea, to recall him and carry a message from his country: he was warned that, should he linger, he might find no city of Carthage standing.[30]

The limited number of ships available forced Hannibal to leave many of his new recruits and almost all of his horses behind in Italy. The final confrontation between Hannibal's forces and the Romans in Africa would come in October 202 BCE, at a place called Zama. Hannibal met Publius Scipio for the first time on the eve of the battle, and presented a dejected, weary face, as Polybius writes:

> Next day both commanders advanced from their camps, attended by a few horsemen. Presently they left these escorts and met in the intervening space by themselves, each accompanied by an interpreter. Hannibal was the first to speak, after the usual salutation. He said that 'He wished that the Romans had never coveted any possession outside Italy, nor the Carthaginians outside Libya.'[31]

Hannibal's forces included eighty elephants from the stables of Carthage. But events were starting to turn against them. One of

Carthage's most important allies, the kingdom of Numidia, which for centuries had provided its crucial shock cavalry, switched sides. Hannibal now found himself facing his own famous Numidian cavalrymen on the field. On top of this, the Romans had developed new tactics to neutralize Carthage's great strength: the fearsome war elephants. As the elephants charged, the Roman lines opened up to swallow them, and then pelted them with javelins. The animals panicked, stampeding back through the Carthaginian lines. In the chaos, the Numidian cavalry swung into the rear of the Carthaginian ranks, and Hannibal's army was driven from the field. He narrowly escaped with his life, and after retreating to the city of Hadrumetum with no forces left to fight, he bitterly advised the Carthaginian senate to sue for peace.

Carthage was once again decisively defeated. After seventeen long years of war, all of its overseas territories, in Spain and elsewhere, were stripped away. Carthage was ordered to pay about 375 tonnes of silver, nearly five times the amount they had paid after the First Punic War, and the treaty banned them from keeping any war elephants and restricted the size of their fleet to only ten ships, barely enough to even protect them from pirates. The rest of the Carthaginian navy was burned in its port. The Carthaginians were also restricted from declaring war anywhere outside Africa, and only in Africa if they got the permission of Rome first. They were now entirely subservient to Rome.

Hannibal lived as a wanted man for another twenty years after the battle of Zama. He went into exile in the East, fleeing to Tyre, and then to the Seleucid Empire and Armenia. The Greek writer Pausanias suggests that he died after having cut his finger on his drawn sword and developed septicaemia from the wound. Other more dramatic stories describe him taking poison when he finds his dwelling place surrounded by soldiers loyal to the Romans, come to capture him and take him back to Rome in chains.

★★★

The Second Punic War was over, and a fifty-year peace descended on the Mediterranean. During this time, despite its diminished situation, money still flowed into Carthage from across the seas, so much so that the Carthaginians offered to pay off the entirety of the reparations they owed to Rome just ten years after the end of the war, when the treaty had given them fifty years to pay. Some of the largest and grandest building projects in the city were constructed during these decades after the Second Punic War. For the people of Carthage, it must have been a time of renewed hope, as wounds began to heal.

But their situation had its downsides. Banned from declaring war without Roman permission, Carthage repeatedly found itself defenceless against ambitious rivals in North Africa, who coveted the wealthy lands they still held. One of these was the new Roman ally and treacherous King of Numidia, Massinissa, who had stabbed them in the back at the battle of Zama. Under the protection of Rome, he repeatedly moved to snatch away large swathes of their land. Each time this happened, the Carthaginians appealed to the Romans to allow them to defend themselves, but Rome consistently ruled in the Numidians' favour. In this way, Carthage was like a stricken whale, being eaten alive by sharks.

In 152 BCE, half a century after the end of the Second Punic War, the Numidian king seized a particularly valuable tract of farmland, and the Carthaginians were outraged. After stalling for some time, Rome finally agreed to send a delegation to Carthage to mediate this dispute. One of these diplomats was an irascible Roman senator by the name of Cato the Elder. Cato at this time was eighty-one years old, and had fought against the armies of Hannibal in Italy. As a result, he had fostered a lifelong hatred of the Carthaginians.

Arriving in Carthage, Cato expected to find a barbarian backwater, impoverished by two consecutive defeats at the hands of Rome. But what he found horrified him: Carthage seemed to be doing better than ever. In Plutarch's biography of Cato, he describes the old senator's reaction:

> The city was by no means in a poor and lowly state, as the Romans supposed, but rather teeming with vigorous fighting men, overflowing with enormous wealth, filled with arms of every sort and with military supplies, and [more than] a little emboldened by all this.[32]

Returning to Rome shaken by what he had seen, Cato now dedicated the final years of his life to a single cause. At every debate in the Roman senate, he ended each statement, whether on the price of grain or the wars in Gaul, whether on the appointment of new consuls or the response to a flood in the south, with a single phrase: '*Et ceterum censeo Carthaginem esse delendam*', or sometimes the snappier '*Carthago delenda est*'—'Furthermore, I believe Carthage must be destroyed.'

Many in the Roman Senate were starting to agree with him.

★★★

A year after Cato's visit, Carthaginian patience reached breaking point. The Numidians had gone too far, seizing yet another piece of wealthy land. Carthage sent an army of 50,000 men to seize back some of what the Numidians had taken, but their now weakened forces were decisively defeated. Still, to the Romans, this attempt had been a breach of their treaty, and enough of a pretext to go to war one final time and destroy their old rival for good.

In 149 BCE, a large Roman army landed in North Africa and prepared to march on the city of Carthage. The Carthaginians were distraught. They sent envoys to meet the Romans, who demanded that the city be demilitarized. The Carthaginians complied and came back with every piece of armour and weaponry they could find, offering their total surrender. In response, the Romans offered them peace—on one condition. But it was a condition so absurd that they must have known it would be rejected. They demanded that the Carthaginians abandon their city, so that it could be razed and moved 16 kilometres or so inland and away from the sea. For the seagoing Phoenicians of Carthage, complying with such a demand would have essentially ended their livelihoods for good.

The Carthaginians withdrew to their city, which was still a formidable fortress. Its triple line of defensive walls could withstand any assault, and it had complex cistern systems for gathering and storing rainwater. The Romans too settled in for a siege, but found it tougher going than they had expected. They controlled the seas, but swift Carthaginian sailors were still able to smuggle food into the harbour at night. The Romans tried again and again to storm the city, but each time they were fought back by the citizens, now fighting for their survival with every tool and improvised weapon they could find, as Appian recounts:

> All the sacred places, the temples, and every other unoccupied space, were turned into workshops, where men and women worked together day and night without pause, taking their food by turns on a fixed schedule. Each day they made 100 shields, 300 swords, 1,000 missiles for catapults, 500 darts and javelins, and as many catapults as they could. For strings to bend them the women cut off their hair for want of other fibers.[33]

The siege of Carthage went on for three years. In the year 147 BCE, command of the besieging army was given to a new consul, Scipio Aemilianus, who was the thirty-six-year-old adopted grandson of Publius Scipio, who had beaten Hannibal at the battle of Zama some fifty years earlier. With Aemilianus came his friend and official documenter of the expedition, the historian Polybius, who writes this part of his history as an eyewitness.

As the siege dragged on, the Romans eventually built a stone barrier in the mouth of the harbour, blocking any further attempts to resupply the city. Food became scarce. Still the defenders struggled on, but by spring 146 BCE, they were exhausted. Scipio Aemilianus finally breached the walls, and the legions poured in and began to massacre everyone they could find. The slaughter went on for six days, during which it's thought that 60,000 people were put to the sword. Scipio set his soldiers to work in shifts, so that they would not become tired of the killing, and on the seventh day, he gave orders to begin taking prisoners: a further 50,000 Carthaginians were rounded up and sold into slavery.

Carthage was burned to the ground and demolished brick by brick. Polybius, who accompanied Scipio throughout the entire siege, writes down that in the moment of his victory, Scipio is said to have wept, and recited lines from Homer's *Iliad*.

> Scipio, beholding this city, which had flourished 700 years from its foundation and had ruled over so many lands, islands, and seas…now come to its end in total destruction—Scipio, beholding this spectacle, is said to have shed tears and publicly lamented the fortune of the enemy. After meditating by himself a long time and reflecting on the rise and fall of cities, nations, and empires, as well as of individuals, upon the fate of Troy, that once proud city, upon that of the Assyrians, the Medes, and the Persians…either voluntarily or otherwise the words of the poet escaped his lips:—'The day shall come in which our sacred Troy and Priam, and the people over whom Spear-bearing Priam rules, shall perish all.'[34]

From its final victory in the Punic Wars, Rome emerged as the only superpower left in the Mediterranean. One by one, the scattered Greek kingdoms that remained were absorbed by the Roman Empire, and in the coming centuries, it would grow to encompass the entire shore of that sea, and would shape the entire course of European history. Carthage, by contrast, would become just a name, a coin that had lost its value, an emblem of an age that had passed into nothing. After the sacking of the city, the Romans ensured that the blackened ruins were emptied of all life, that no locals crept back to repopulate its ruins, and that never again would their great rival resurface in North Africa.

Some of the libraries and archives of Carthage, in which were kept their books of history and science, perhaps poetry and mythology, and records of the Phoenician voyages of discovery to the edges of the world, survived the burning of the city, and these were all taken by the Romans. Some were burned, while others were distributed among the Romans' African allies. As a result, virtually none have survived to the present day. Today, scarcely a few documents written by a Carthaginian can be read, and no works of literature or history. Their voices, just like their city, were erased, and for 2,000 years, their story has been told by others.

The territory of Carthage was absorbed into the new Roman province of Africa, with the city of Utica as its capital. For the next century, what remained of the ruins of Carthage were left to crumble into the sands, overgrown with scrub and weeds, washed with salt carried on the sea air, a home for wild dogs, gulls and crows. After a century of the city lying in ruins, Rome sent a party of 3,000 colonists to found a colony on the rubble. As they settled the area, the Punic ruins of Carthage were buried beneath a new Roman town that shared almost nothing of the city that had once stood there, except its name, and even the ruins of the city as they had once been were soon forgotten.

Around 1835, the British statesman Sir Grenville Temple visited the ruins of Carthage and recorded his disappointment upon finding how little remained, now just a scatter of lonely, melancholy ruins:

> Early on the morning following, I walked to the site of the great Carthage,—of that town, at the sound of whose name mighty Rome herself had so often trembled,—of Carthage, the mistress of powerful and brave armies, of numerous fleets and of the world's commerce, and to whom Africa, Spain, Sardinia, Corsica, Sicily, and Italy herself bowed in submission as to their sovereign.
>
> I was prepared to see but few vestiges of its former grandeur, it had so often suffered from the devastating effects of war, that I knew many could not exist; but my heart sunk within me when ascending one of its hills, [for] I beheld nothing more than a few scattered and shapeless masses of masonry. Its very name is now unknown to the present inhabitants.
>
> The scene that once was animated by the presence of nearly a million of warlike inhabitants is now buried in the silence of the grave; no living soul appearing, except occasionally a soldier going or returning from the fort, or the solitary and motionless figure of an Arab, watching his flocks from the summit of the fragment of some former palace or temple. Solitude and silence hold sway over the whole scene; a scene which impresses on the mind a feeling of melancholy, which I found difficult to shake off.[35]

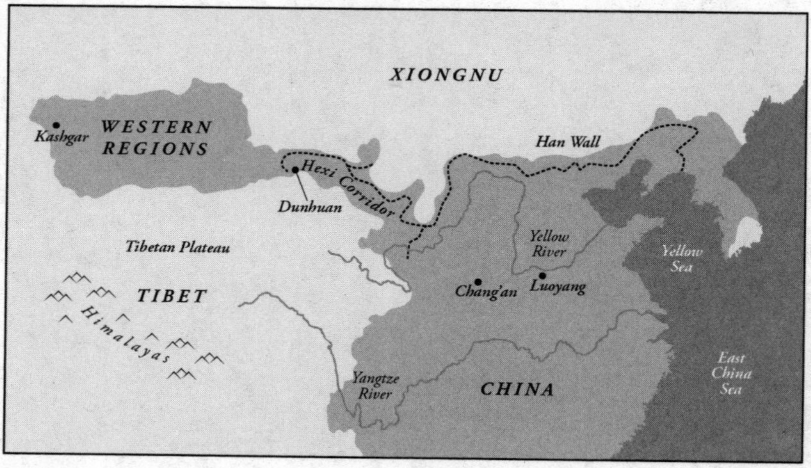
XIONGNU
Kashgar
WESTERN
REGIONS
Han Wall
Hexi Corridor
Dunhuan
Yellow
River
Tibetan Plateau
Yellow
Sea
Chang'an
Luoyang
TIBET
Himalayas
East
China
Sea
Yangtze
River
CHINA

5

Han China

202 BCE–220 CE

In the early years of the third century, around 207 CE, a Chinese poet by the name Cao Zhi made a journey back to the place of his birth: the city of Luoyang. At this time, the lands of China were in chaos, racked by a series of bitter civil wars. The armies of rival warlords were tearing its cities apart, and his journey through the mountains can't have been an easy one.

His hometown of Luoyang had once been a prosperous place. It had been the imperial capital of China for the last two centuries, when it was ruled by a dynasty known as the Han. For centuries, poets had written about Luoyang's leafy avenues full of blossom, leading to grand palaces and temples decorated with thousands of bronze statues. Cao Zhi knew that his home had suffered in the recent wars. Still, when he came over the crest of the Beimang Hills to the north, nothing could have prepared him for what he saw stretching out beneath him. The entire city was a blackened ruin. Later, he wrote a poem about what he saw:

In Lo-yang how still it is!
Palaces and houses all burnt to ashes.
Walls and fences all broken and gaping,
Thorns and brambles shooting up to the sky.
...
The fields are overgrown and will never be ploughed again.
I have been away such a long time
That I do not know which street is which.
How sad and ugly the empty moors are!
A thousand miles without the smoke of a chimney.
I think of the house I lived in all those years:
I am heart-tied and cannot speak.[1]

While it ruled China, the Han Dynasty had presided over a period of unprecedented prosperity and stability. But now the dream of Han China lay buried in the ruins of Luoyang.

★★★

The story of the Han Dynasty begins on the Central Plains of China. On its eastern edge, the high icy table of the Tibetan Plateau drops off into rolling mountains and valleys, and finally into an enormous stretch of wide, silty grasslands that stretch for nearly 2,000 kilometres to the Pacific Ocean in the east, and are criss-crossed by a number of enormous rivers. Among these, two of the most impressive are the Yellow River and the Yangtze.

The Yangtze is the longest river in Asia, and a relatively peaceful one. It has flowed along the same course for most of its history, by some estimates discharging into the sea at the same place for the last 11 million years. But north of the Yangtze is its sister, the far more changeable and deadly Yellow River. This waterway contains the highest amount of silt and sand of any river on earth, colouring it the distinctive yellow-brown that gives it its name. This silt gives the soil of the North China Plain an enormous fertility—but it also makes the river dangerous. As it flows, silt constantly builds up at its bottom, and when the riverbed rises too high, the Yellow River bursts its banks and floods vast areas of the surrounding countryside. In the most dramatic cases, it can change its course entirely, sometimes sweeping across the landscape for hundreds of kilometres and washing away everything in its path. Historically, this kind of devastating event has occurred about once every hundred years.

Humans likely arrived in China around 80,000 years ago, and hunter-gatherer activity has been verified in the region of these rivers for at least the last 27,000 years. Rice was first cultivated along the Yangtze around 8000 BCE, and the first true villages were founded in the fifth and fourth millennia. The Bronze Age, beginning here around 3000 BCE, brought the smelting of strong metal tools and weapons, and during these centuries a culture known as the Longshan domesticated the water buffalo and developed the plough and sophisticated irrigation techniques, while the Liangzhu culture in the Yangtze Delta carved immaculate objects from jade. Villages grew into towns, and towns into the first major cities. To the north lay the arid lands of the Gobi Desert, and beyond that, the wide grassy steppes of Mongolia and central Asia. To the west, the mountains, and the sea to the south and east, with dense tropical forests in the south. But within this fertile stretch of land, early civilizations flourished.

★★★

The first millennium BCE in China was a time of rapid change and feverish invention. The land's large population led to the swift development of a complex society, and advanced technologies soon followed. People learned to coat bronze in chromium oxide to increase its resistance to corrosion. Ironworking arrived in China by the year 1000 BCE, and within two centuries inventions like the blast furnace and bellows allowed the smelting of liquid cast iron, pre-dating its use in Europe by around two millennia. In agriculture, iron tools and mechanical devices like the multiple seed drill drove a productivity boom. The invention of sophisticated pulley systems and differential gears led to water-wheels and other mechanical devices that powered everything from flour mills to furnace bellows, as well as ingenious toys: one early emperor was buried with an entire water-powered mechanical orchestra that could play and sing through pipes and tubes. The crossbow was invented during this time too, and was in widespread use in Chinese armies, nearly 2,000 years before it became a fixture on European battlefields—including a repeat-action version, like an early machine-gun. One Chinese inventor even developed an early form of pinhole camera to view solar eclipses.

Upheaval followed hot on the heels of such rapid technological development. As in other parts of the world, the advancing technology of iron production meant that weapons and armour became cheap and easy to manufacture. The period that followed was known as 'The Warring States Period', and saw numerous feudal powers fighting and conquering one another. Soon, these had settled into seven large kingdoms, locked in constant competition. Among these was the kingdom of Qin, the furthest west, with its back to the Tibetan Plateau, 'well protected by mountains and girdled by the Yellow River'.[2]

Qin Shi Huang, the first emperor of China (nineteenth-century portrait).

The King of Qin, a man named Zheng, was an enthusiastic reformer, who revolutionized his kingdom's society and bureaucracy. He moved to undercut the power of aristocrats and landowners, to strengthen the central government and collect taxes directly from the peasantry. The Qin also took advantage of the latest military tactics, using small units of cavalry to mount guerrilla raids on supply lines and river crossings—and employed these to conquer the other six kingdoms of the plains. The early Han-era historian and court astrologer Sima Qian gives a vivid description of these days, and describes how the armies of Qin 'pressed the crumbling forces of its rivals, pursued those who had fled in defeat, and overwhelmed and slaughtered...until their shields floated upon a river of blood.'[3]

With much of China now under his rule, Zheng threw off the title of king, and in 221 BCE crowned himself the first emperor—and he would rule under the name Qin Shi Huang, or 'First Emperor of Qin'. Like the kings who had come before him, he held his new position through a kind of divine authority—what was called the *tianming*, or the 'Mandate of Heaven'. Qin's reign saw territorial expansion that grew the young Empire of China even further, but it was not without its troubles. He suffered three separate assassination attempts, and these filled him with paranoia, such that he built tunnels between his palaces in order to travel unseen, and became increasingly arbitrary and tyrannical, executing scholars who had disappointed him and burning books. He became terrified of death, and began trying to discover the secret that would allow him to live forever. The Emperor began drinking doses of the liquid heavy metal mercury, believing this would extend his life—but mercury is highly toxic. Prolonged exposure can affect the nervous system, causing depression, delirium and hallucinations. Despite all his efforts, the first emperor of China died in 210 BCE. For all its historical significance, the Qin Dynasty had barely lasted a decade.

The Emperor left very specific requests for his burial. He was interred in an enormous underground palace, an exact replica of the one he had lived in, populated with life-sized models of the courtiers and bureaucrats who had served him, fashioned with meticulous detail in terracotta. Outside the palace stood an army of thousands of terracotta soldiers, each with a slightly different face. Sima Qian describes the intricately constructed burial chamber:

> Craftsmen were ordered to make crossbows and arrows, rigged so they would immediately shoot down anyone attempting to break in. Mercury was used to fashion imitations of the hundred rivers, the Yellow River and the Yangtze, and the seas, constructed in such a way that they seemed to flow. Above were representations of the heavenly bodies, below, the features of the earth.[4]

At this point, the empire was a very new idea, a thin veneer over a still-divided land. Sima Qian tells us that while Qin flourished, 'its manifold laws and stern punishments caused the empire to tremble.' But when its power declined after the death of the first emperor, 'the people eyed it with hatred and the whole area within the seas rose up in revolt.'[5] China quickly fissured into eighteen kingdoms who once again began to war among themselves. It looked like the old chaos would return. But history had other plans.

During the years of unrest, it happened that a local sheriff from a small town in the state of Han was ordered to bring a group of slaves to the enormous construction site where Qin Shi Huang's tomb was being built. This man's name was Liu Bang. Along the way, some of these slaves escaped, and Liu Bang knew he would face punishment when he arrived. Instead, he decided to free the remaining slaves, and rebel against the empire rather than deliver them up. Many of the slaves he freed were so grateful that they took up arms and joined him.

Liu Bang and his followers soon entered the service of a rebel noble named Xiang Yu from the house of Chu. On the battlefield, he met with enormous success, and even managed to capture the Qin capital of Xianyang for the rebels. It was a decisive blow for the rebellion, and one from which the Qin Dynasty never recovered. When the Qin was finally defeated, the rebels divided what had once been its empire into eighteen kingdoms, and parcelled them out between them—with the Chu noble Xiang Yu taking the lion's share. But the commoner Liu Bang was snubbed. Despite having captured the Qin capital, Liu Bang was sent off to the remote Hanzhong region, and was given the title 'the King of Han'—while the rebel leader Xiang Yu declared himself 'Emperor of the Chu'. From his remote capital in the rocky Han River Valley, Liu Bang waited for his moment with the patience of a chess player—and in China to this day, the two sides of a chess board are referred to not as black and white, but as Chu and Han.

In 206 BCE, as the Chu found themselves faced with rebellions on all sides, Liu Bang made his move. He marched on Guanzhong and attacked the Chu. It would take four years of war, but in 202 BCE, Xiang Yu was killed in battle, and Liu Bang took up the throne that had once belonged to the Qin. Against all the odds, China was once more united under this unassuming commoner. On his coronation, Liu Bang took the name Han, after the province he had been gifted, and set up his court in the city of Chang'an. After his death, he would be given the name Han Gaozu—or 'high founder of the Han'. The age of the Han Dynasty had begun.

★★★

When the Han Dynasty came into possession of the newly united China in 206 BCE, it inherited not just the young empire, but also the empire's problems, as Sima Qian writes.

> The Han Dynasty…inherited the evils left by the Qin. The able-bodied men were all away with the army, while the old and underaged transported supplies for them. There was much hard work and little wealth. The Son of Heaven himself could not find four horses of the same colour to draw his carriage, [and] many of his generals were reduced to riding around in ox carts.[6]

The empire's economy was on its knees, with prices spiralling out of control. But easily the most pressing problem was the constant looming threat of China's fearsome neighbours to the north. These were the Xiongnu, who would be the greatest threat to imperial China throughout much of its early history.

Around 3500 BCE, the people of the Eurasian steppes had learned how to tame wild horses, and in the intervening millennia had developed a symbiotic relationship with those powerful animals. These people lived a nomadic lifestyle, travelling on horseback in large groups, without relying on agriculture. Ban Gu's *Book of Han* describes them as 'covetous for gain, human-faced but animal-hearted'.[7] From at least the fourth century BCE, these horseback raiders became a military nuisance to the settled societies of the Chinese plains. The *Records of the Grand Historian* gives a description of the Xiongnu people that emphasizes how different their values were:

> They move about in search of water and pasture and have no walled cities or fixed dwellings...they have no writing, and even promises and agreements are only verbal. The little boys start out by learning to ride sheep and shoot birds and rats with a bow and arrow... Thus all the young men are able to use a bow and act as armed cavalry in times of war. It is their custom to herd their flocks in times of peace...but in periods of crisis they take up arms and go off on plundering and marauding expeditions... If the battle is going well for them they will advance, but if not, they will retreat, for they do not consider it a disgrace to run away. Their only concern is self-advantage, and they know nothing of propriety or righteousness.[8]

The settled armies of the Chinese, despite all their technological advantages, found these nomadic hit-and-run armies incredibly difficult to fight. From as early as the seventh century BCE, they began building walls to defend the valleys and plains of the north. During his reign, Qin Shi Huang had ordered these scattered fragments to be joined together, closing any gaps. By the time he died, a single defensive barrier ran along much of the new empire's northern border. At the time that the new Han China rose from the ashes of Qin, the Xiongnu had banded together under the rule of a single ruler, a man who took the honorific title of Shanyu. This word would mutate over the centuries to become Khan, the title mostly famously associated with the fearsome Genghis Khan.

Under this emboldened Shanyu, Xiongnu horsemen had begun pushing at China's northern border, looting and burning cities.

Han Gaozu was a confident leader. He had defeated all his rivals in the civil war, and knew how to command his men—but he was about to find out that fighting the swift cavalry armies of the Xiongnu was a very different kind of challenge. He marched out to meet these northerners, but in the rocky mountain passes he walked into an ambush. Thousands of Xiongnu cavalry poured down the valley sides without warning, and tore into the Chinese army on all sides. The defeat was catastrophic.

From this point on, the first Han emperor abandoned the idea of a military solution to the barbarian problem. Instead, he pursued a policy of diplomacy and appeasement, paying staggering tributes to the Xiongnu in the form of silk, wine, rice and other kinds of food. The deal also entailed a more humiliating condition: the Han emperor was forced to send his eldest daughter to marry the Shanyu, and every time a new Shanyu came to power, he would be given a Chinese princess as a wife. In exchange, the Xiongnu agreed to stop their raids on the borders of the empire. An uneasy peace set in.

The next seventy years or so saw some measure of stability return, over the reigns of several emperors. The years around 130 BCE are recalled by Sima Qian as a time of wealth and plenty—even with the tributes paid to the Xiongnu:

> In the capital the strings of cash had been stacked up by the hundreds of millions until the cords that bound them had rotted away and they could no longer be counted. In the central granary of the government, new grain was heaped on top of the old until the building was full and the grain overflowed and piled up outside, where it spoiled and became unfit to eat.[9]

But, despite these surfeits, Han Gaozu's policy of appeasing the Xiongnu was no longer working. During the reign of the sixth Han emperor, Jing, more than 10,000 citizens living in the border regions were abducted and taken away to live as slaves to the Xiongnu. Large armies of horsemen were soon regularly raiding deep into the northern provinces, at one point even coming as close as 160 kilometres from the imperial capital. Many in the imperial court remembered the ambush and defeat of Han Gaozu, and, fearing the Xiongnu, preferred to continue the policy of appeasement. However, a small but vocal pro-war faction was forming at court, whose views were typified by the poet and politician Chia Yi:

> The situation of the empire may be described just like a person hanging upside down. The Son of Heaven is the head of the empire. The barbarians are the feet of the empire... Yet each year Han provides them with money, silk, floss and fabrics. And so the feet are put on top, and the head at the bottom.[10]

But it wasn't until the reign of an emperor named Wu that the pro-war coterie began to get people's attention.

***

In his later life, Emperor Wu cut an imposing figure. Traditional portraits show him with a furrowed brow, and a delicate moustache framing a thick black beard, built like a barrel and wrapped in swathes of imperial blue silk. But when he came to the throne in 141 BCE, Wu was only sixteen years old. What he lacked in age, he made up for in tenacity. He sat on the imperial throne until 87 BCE, a fifty-four-year reign that would remain an unbroken record in China for the next 1,800 years. Over this time, he led the Han through a period of rapid centralizing reform, reorganizing society around the principles of the ancient philosopher Confucius. He founded the Imperial University to train young scholars, and even developed a cultural organization known as 'the imperial music bureau'. But all of this would be useless if he couldn't solve the problem of the Xiongnu threat. In 133 BCE, Wu decided on a bold and aggressive new strategy, which would confront the Xiongnu head on. His plan was to lure the ruling Shanyu south with his army and into a carefully laid trap. With the fearsome army of the Shanyu out of the way, the forces of China would then march into their lands and end the threat forever. It was a risky plan, and it relied on total secrecy.

The bait would be a city called Mayi, a wealthy frontier town that acted as a trading post between China and the northern deserts. To help with the deception, the Chinese hired a local trader and smuggler to travel into the Xiongnu lands and ask for an audience with the Shanyu. We can imagine the Xiongnu ruler sitting on his throne in a large tent made of stretched yak skin, surrounded by crackling braziers. The smuggler told the Shanyu that he had killed the town magistrate of Mayi, and was willing to offer the whole city up to the Xiongnu Empire, if the Shanyu would only come and take it. The Shanyu was ecstatic, and immediately rode out to claim the city. It seemed like the Chinese plan was going perfectly.

But the further the Shanyu marched into Chinese lands, the more he felt that something wasn't right. His horsemen met with no resistance, not even from the border guards on the wall—and as he approached the city of Mayi, he noticed how empty the roads were. In the fields he saw herds of cattle with no herdsmen guarding them. The Shanyu ordered his men to halt. A captured Han soldier told them under interrogation what lurked nearby: the massed force of the empire, concealed and waiting for him to step into the jaws of their trap. The Shanyu ordered a hasty retreat, and with the ambush betrayed, the Han forces burst out of hiding and tried to follow him. But their 300,000 infantry and chariots could never keep pace with the Shanyu's horses, and he returned to his lands without losing a single man. In retaliation, the Shanyu ordered a devastating series of raids on Chinese border towns. Pillars of black smoke must have risen over the horizon for weeks, and, with its hand now revealed, Han China was forced to go to war.

Once again, they found that the armies of infantry and chariots—so effective in the river plains—were next to useless in the rocky terrain of the far north, and the infantry moved too slowly in the open deserts. Emperor Wu recognized that the horse was the weapon of this new age of warfare, and he made securing a reliable supply of trained warhorses a major focus of his government. He imported powerful new breeds of horse from Fergana in Uzbekistan, and developed large, armoured horse units to match their Xiongnu enemies in power and manoeuvrability. He would eventually maintain a supply of 300,000 horses, drawn from thirty-six pasture lands across China, and began loaning breeding horses to farmers for a period of three years, in exchange for an allocation of some of the foals. He even introduced a policy that allowed a family to excuse up to three of their male members from military service if they presented a single horse to the government.

The war for the north raged on for decades—but for a number of reasons, the Han slowly gained the upper hand. For one thing, the desert country beyond the wall had only a strategic importance to the Han, but it was crucial to the Xiongnu. Their nomadic empire was built out of trade, taxes and tribute paid to them by weaker kingdoms. As the war dragged on, they suffered a downturn in all three. In response, they increased the tax burden on the regions still under their control, and these populations grew resentful. Soon, more and more of the smaller clans in the Xiongnu coalition peeled away, and the trajectory of the war for the north became clear. It's at this point that a narrow strip of land between the Tibetan Plateau and the Gobi Desert began to play a crucial role in this story: the Hexi Corridor.

★★★

Today, the Hexi Corridor is the site of China's G30 highway. Looking at this long and lonely stretch of motorway, with cars zipping along it through the desert, it's hard to imagine that this was once a major battlefield in a war for the very existence of the Chinese state.

If you were a Chinese trader who wanted to make the lucrative journey to the west, you had a limited number of options. The towering Tibetan Plateau formed an impassable barrier along the whole western length of the empire, while to the south lay unmapped jungle. To the north was the desert, which spelled certain death for any traveller foolish enough to try to cross it. The only passage to the west was thus via a narrow, 1,000-kilometre stretch where the Tibetan Plateau finally drops off to the north, and looks out over the Gobi Desert. Waters running down from the hills here have created fertile oases between the mountains and the desert, providing fresh water and rest for travellers on this dangerous journey.

Anyone who controlled the Hexi Corridor controlled the flow of trade—and for centuries, the Xiongnu had grown rich from taxing all the goods that passed along it. Now the Han moved to seize it. The Xiongnu were masters of hit-and-run tactics, and would attack Chinese supply lines whenever they could—so, as they pushed along the Hexi Corridor, the Han did what they did best: they built walls. The Han extended the existing segments of their great wall so that it ran the whole length of the corridor, creating a fortified highway between the wall and the mountains, guarded by garrisoned forts. These sections of wall weren't the elegant snaking lines of stone that we imagine when we think of 'the Great Wall of China'—the most famous and frequently photographed sections today were built much later, by the Ming Dynasty. The Han walls were rough-and-ready earth constructions, built using frames of rose willow and rushes, filled with desert clay mixed with gravel and sand, compacted together and left to dry in the sun. But despite their hasty design, they were immensely effective. Many of them still stand in the barren sands, having weathered over 2,000 years exposed to the elements in the Gobi Desert. Goods and supplies could now flow along the Hexi Corridor to the soldiers fighting on the front, and the walls neutralized the Xiongnu's mobile tactics, choking their war machine. In the early decades of the first century BCE, the Xiongnu confederation truly splintered. Former members declared independence, and helped the Han Chinese carve up its territories. Finally, in 51 BCE, the Shanyu of the time formally surrendered. More than eighty years after Emperor Wu's failed ambush, the war against the Xiongnu had at last reached its end.

***

If you travelled down the Hexi corridor during this time, perhaps with a shipment of Chinese goods that you wanted to sell in the west, you would eventually reach the end of the Han fortifications, and pass through a wide portal known as the Yumen Pass, or Jade Gate. This was the crossing point from the lands of China out into the wide, unknown world. From there, you would see a desert of shifting sands stretching ahead of you. This is the Taklamakan Desert, which fills an enormous geographical feature known as the Tarim Basin. The region is easily visible from space: a great sandy eye in the centre of the Asian continent. Today, it is the province of Xinjiang, on China's border with Afghanistan, Kyrgyzstan, Tajikistan and Kashmir. But for the Chinese of the time, this wild area beyond their walls was known only as 'the western regions'.

Crossing the desert was very difficult, so trade caravans would skirt along its edges, in the shadow of the snowy mountains that rim the basin. All these caravans met on the far side of the desert in the city of Kashgar, where a famous stone tower stood. Here, Chinese merchants would trade their goods with merchants from the exotic lands to the west, who had travelled the dangerous mountain routes through Pakistan and Afghanistan. As the Han chased the Xiongnu out, they absorbed the sandblown cities clinging to the edge of this great desert. Soon, the western regions came under Han control, and for the first time, China was in charge of its own trade routes to the west.

By the end of the first century BCE, the territory of Han China had more than doubled, adding more than 4 million square kilometres. But Emperor Wu, in his old age, became plagued with the same kind of paranoia as Emperor Qin, nearly a hundred years before. He began doling out excessive punishments to members of the court who he believed were spreading rumours about him—and, like Qin, he began touring the country, talking to wise men and searching fruitlessly for the secret to eternal life. Whether he also started taking mercury pills is unknown, but he died in 87 BCE, at the age of sixty-nine, and was buried in a magnificent suit of jade armour in a crimson catalpa-wood and ivory coffin. Emperor Wu had turned the Empire of Han into one of the largest and most powerful empires on Earth. But he had also fallen prey to his predecessor's curse of paranoia and tyranny. He wasn't the first ruler of China to end this way, and as we'll see, he was also far from the last.

★★★

As is so often the case after the long rule of a successful king, Emperor Wu was followed by a series of inept successors. During this time, a powerful family known as the Wang clan came to amass huge power and wealth, and to take over the affairs of state. Of this family, one man—Wang Mang—rose above the rest.

Wang Mang was a Confucian scholar and a gifted speaker, who was immensely well liked among China's popular classes due to his populist promises. At one point, the imperial palace received a petition written on 500,000 rolls of bamboo, demanding that Wang Mang be given the highest political offices in the land. At the age of about fifty, buoyed up by popular support, he toppled the Emperor and seized the throne for himself. Wang Mang was the first non-Han emperor to rule China in 200 years. At the time, it must have seemed as if the Han Dynasty had ended for good, crippled by the corruption and mismanagement of its officials. But the rule of Wang Mang was an unmitigated disaster. Since he himself had usurped the throne, he was terrified of giving his advisors any power, and tried to make all the decisions of state himself, completely paralyzing the government. But his real undoing would come from one of China's deadliest and most unpredictable natural forces.

While Wang Mang was on the imperial throne, as it did every hundred years or so, the Yellow River changed its course, bursting its banks and washing away every town and village in its path. The new emperor was completely unprepared for this disaster. Peasants who had lost their homes in the floods felt that the Emperor had done nothing to help them, and it wasn't long before peasant revolts rose up around the country. The most powerful of these were known as 'The Red Eyebrows', since they painted their foreheads red when going into battle. The widespread chaos and loss of imperial control meant that the empire's borders began to fray. The Xiongnu, subdued for nearly a century, sensed weakness. They launched a surprise attack on the empire's outposts and captured the entire region of the Tarim Basin right up to the Jade Gate. From there, they poured around the great wall into the Hexi Corridor.

In just a matter of years, all of Emperor Wu's gains were undone. Meanwhile, the Red Eyebrow rebellion controlled large areas of the countryside in the central plains. Soon the nobles joined the peasants in revolt, and one wish was on all their lips: to topple Emperor Wang Mang and restore the dynasty of the Han.

Eventually, the citizens of the imperial capital of Chang'an rose up in the streets, overcame Wang Mang's palace guard and beheaded him. Wang's body was dismembered, and his head delivered to the temporary Han capital of Wancheng, to be hung on the city wall. There, the people's anger was so fierce that they dragged the head down and kicked it about the streets like a football. Chang'an was occupied by the Red Eyebrows, but before long, the food ran out, and the rebels began to riot and steal, despite their leaders' attempts to keep order. They burned palaces and other buildings and pillaged the city for days.

By 25 CE, the Han Dynasty was restored under Emperor Guangwu—but Chang'an was left a smoking ruin. As a result of the devastation, Guangwu decided that he would move his capital from Chang'an to Luoyang in the east. Because of this, these two phases of Han history are sometimes called the Western and the Eastern Han, or more simply the Former Han and the Later Han. Guangwu's reign was a new dawn for the empire, and another chance for the dream of a stable imperial China—but a number of challenges would soon emerge that would determine whether the lessons of the Former Han had been learned.

★★★

The new capital city of Luoyang was a beautiful place. The shallow Gu River flowed past its walls and diverted into an encircling moat, while the Luo River flowed 2 kilometres to the south, crossed by a floating bridge of boats. In the distance, the blue peaks of the Beimang Hills looked down on the city. Luoyang had been an important holy city for centuries. It was about a third of the size of Chang'an, but it enjoyed a better position, sitting at the crossing point of various major canals, as well as a sprawling road network of imperial highways. It was also further from the frontiers of the empire, making it more defensible than the former capital.

New palaces were built to accommodate the imperial court, and Guangwu transported the entire imperial library to Luoyang too, carrying the empire's collection of books and scrolls on 2,000 carts. A poem named 'Rhapsody on the Two Capitals', written by the poet and historian Ban Gu around 65 CE, celebrates the new Han emperor's achievement in transforming the old town into a true imperial city:

> He refurbished Luo City,
> Enhancing its imposing grandeur,
> Making resplendent its order and proportion.
> He made the Han capital shine through the empire
> Controlling all eight directions, it was their pivot.
> And then, within the imperial city
>   The palaces were glittering and bright;
>   The hall courtyards were divinely beautiful.[11]

By 36 CE, Guangwu had crushed the Red Eyebrows, as well as any lords still holding out in rebellion, and restored some measure of peace to the empire. Once the new capital was established, much of the first century in China was spent rebuilding. Impressive construction works also took place to control the rages of the Yellow River. But the empire was now a much-weakened power. Rebellions and uprisings had sapped its wealth, and the Xiongnu had resurged as a power in the north. The Chinese general Ban Chao was put in charge of reclaiming the Hexi Corridor and the western regions, and over the following decades he painstakingly beat the Xiongnu back, reclaiming the old crumbling walls as he went. By 91 CE, the Han Empire was once again in control.

This reopening of the western trade routes came at a crucial time in world history. In the decades since the Han had last controlled the Hexi Corridor, a new power had risen up, creating a stable, unified territory across central Asia. This was the Kushan Empire, covering much of Pakistan, Afghanistan and northern India. To the west of the Kushan Empire was the Parthian Empire, straddling Iran, much of the Middle East and modern Turkey. But, even further to the west, the Han had heard of an even greater power that rivalled their own, a mysterious empire of enormous wealth, centred on a vast inland sea.

This was the first time in history that just four large empires formed an unbroken chain from the Pacific Ocean to the Atlantic. Ban Chao recognized the potential that this unique moment in history could hold. In 97 CE, he dispatched one of his most trusted men, named Gan Ying, with instructions to journey as far west as he could, and to find out more about this faraway empire. Gan Ying set off to discover the truth about this power, which the Han Chinese knew by the name Daqin or 'Great Qin', though we know it by a more familiar name: Rome.

By the end of the first century, with its wars with Carthage a distant memory, the Roman Republic had given way to the Roman Empire, a confident, growing military power. It had conquered Judea, Egypt and Syria, and expanded into Arabia. When he returned some years later, Gan Ying wrote down everything he had learned about this exotic land:

> Its territory extends for several thousands of li. It has more than four hundred walled towns. There are several tens of smaller dependent kingdoms. The walls of the towns are made of stone. They have established postal relays at intervals, which are all plastered and whitewashed… They shave their heads, and their clothes are embroidered. They have screened coaches (for the women) and small white-roofed one-horse carts. When carriages come and go, drums are beaten and flags and standards are raised.[12]

He was particularly struck by the system for appointing Roman emperors, although it does seem that he acquired a sanitized version of the Romans' political system. 'Their kings are not permanent,' he wrote. 'They select and appoint the most worthy man. If there are unexpected calamities in the kingdom, he is unceremoniously rejected and replaced. The one who has been dismissed quietly accepts his demotion, and is not angry.'[13]

Sadly, Gan Ying never made it to the city of Rome. He reached the shore of a sea that may have been either the Mediterranean or the Persian Gulf, where some Parthian sailors discouraged him from going further. According to the *Book of Later Han*, they warned him that the journey could take up to two years, and that 'the vast ocean' caused travellers to 'get homesick, and some of them die'.[14] It's possible that the Parthians wanted to maintain control of the lucrative trade between Rome and China, and didn't want this Chinese ambassador cutting out the middlemen. But perhaps Gan Ying, tired of his journey and wanting to return to his family, simply made something up. After all, who back home would ever know?

Gan Ying was the first recorded man to travel the entire length of a route that would be of enormous importance for the history of the world. It became a highway connecting the East and the West, and would later spread inventions like gunpowder, paper, porcelain and the compass to the West—perhaps the greatest single engine of progress, driving cultural and technological exchange in every society it touched. But it was another Chinese commodity that would give the route its name: the Silk Road.

A natural protein fibre, produced by the larva of a particular kind of moth, silk had been harvested in China as early as 3600 BCE. Soft and shimmering and capable of holding resplendent colours, silk was costly in China, and in foreign lands was worth many times its weight in gold. During the period of the former Han Dynasty, Julius Caesar famously wore a silk cloak to the theatre and began a fashion craze among the Roman nobility. Queen Cleopatra was an avid collector of silk items, and silk has also been found in Viking graves and the tombs of the Egyptian pharaohs. The opening of the Silk Road would be one of Han China's enduring legacies. But for the Han, the storm clouds were already gathering. This time, the trouble would originate not in the barren wastes of the north, but in the very heart of the empire, in the imperial palace itself.

***

The imperial court of Han China was a place of elegance, refinement and beauty. But it was also a battleground. Anyone who had personal access to the emperor could use their influence to amass enormous personal power and wealth, and these were things that people were more than willing to kill for. The imperial palace was one of the most secure places on earth. Very few were ever permitted even to set foot in it, and no men could remain there after dark. There were, therefore, only two groups of people who had insider access to the emperor: the palace eunuchs, and the palace women.

Chinese artwork on a lacquered basketwork box showing noble figures, excavated from a Later Han tomb.

Eunuchs were typically castrated as a punishment for adultery, and due to their lack of reproductive capability were considered low risk to have around the royal family and their concubines. As a result, the Chinese emperors had employed them as servants for at least 3,000 years. But in the Later Han Dynasty, their use as palace attendants increased dramatically. Eventually the imperial court would be home to more than 2,000 eunuchs, working as fetchers and carriers, nurses, bodyguards, footmen, butlers and cooks. They were virtually the only men whom a cloistered young emperor would meet until he became an adult. Thanks to this privileged access to the inner court, the eunuchs eventually formed a kind of shadow government within the imperial palace.

The second faction was the palace women, and more specifically the empress dowagers. While her husband was alive, an empress enjoyed a supreme position in the royal court—but when he passed away, the dowager empress would need to be clever, and gather allies around her to maintain what power she could. An emperor could have a number of wives, so the court quickly became overpopulated with empress dowagers, each jockeying for position and influence. Empress dowagers were constantly poisoning other dowagers and their children, while eunuchs plotted against them and each other too. The emperors themselves were just chess pieces in this complex and deadly game. By the dawn of the second century CE, these emperors were increasingly chosen not for their skill or popularity, as in the past, but simply for how easy they would be to control. For this reason, they were very often children.

One extreme example is the fifth emperor of the Later Han Dynasty, Emperor Shang, who was crowned in 106 CE, at little more than 100 days old, thanks to the efforts of his mother, the dowager empress Deng Sui. Her older children had all died in mysterious circumstances, likely murdered by her rivals at court. At his coronation, the tiny baby would have been given the ancient legendary sword known as 'the sword that slew the snake', which had belonged to the first Han emperor, Han Gaozu, as well as the formal documents of accession written on fine paper, and the seal of state tied with its ribbon. Emperor Shang never reached his first birthday. His cause of death is unknown, but it is not hard to guess.

In the rare instances when an emperor reached adulthood, they were mostly kept from the business of ruling, encouraged instead to a life of indolence and pleasure. As the second century wore on, and weak young emperor followed weak young emperor, the power of these two warring factions only increased. But it wasn't until the reign of Emperor Ling, who came to the throne at the age of twelve, that the true disintegration of the Han Empire began.

Like many boy emperors before him, when he came of age, Ling was more inclined to spend time with his palace women than to run the state. He especially enjoyed creating role-playing scenarios to engage in with his consorts, as recorded in the *Book of Later Han*:

> The emperor ordered a market set up in the harem apartments and had all his women trade there. They robbed and fought one another, and the emperor dressed as a peddler, joined the crowd and drank wine and feasted with them.[15]

Ling was also financially reckless, and increased the burden of taxation on the people to fund his lavish lifestyle. Tax collectors were particularly hated among common people, and were frequently corrupt. Soon, peasant rebellions broke out. To fund the armies needed to put down these uprisings, the cash-strapped empire began selling minor titles and positions—but this further evidence of corruption only fanned the flames. Matters were made considerably worse when Emperor Ling started selling high political offices for money, severely damaging both the effectiveness and legitimacy of the Han civil service. Corruption now trickled down to every level, from the royal court to the lowest officials.

As a result, some peasant rebellions grew to be enormous. One of these was a religious insurgency known as the 'Yellow Turban Rebellion', stirred up by adherents to a sect of the relatively new Daoist religion. This group swept through the country, pillaging and raiding villages and, though it was ultimately crushed by the authorities, common people increasingly lost faith in the empire's ability to protect them. Villages and towns now banded together to form their own militias and small armies to defend themselves; local governors took on greater powers, and the central power of the empire began to falter.

As the decades passed and the simmering intrigue in the imperial court burned on, the rebellions got worse. Chief among these was the rebellion of the Qiang people, who lived in the mountainous regions of the Tibetan Plateau, in Liang province. This arid and rocky region in the north-west of China was the gateway to the Hexi Corridor, and the staging ground for caravans setting out for the western regions. The Qiang were a hardy people, who herded yak and cultivated narrow plains along creeks and mountain terraces. They built strong houses from granite fieldstones, as well as tall, narrow stone watchtowers in their fortress villages. By the middle of the second century, the rebellions by the Qiang had reached such a pitch that the empire was considering measures that we today would recognize as ethnic cleansing, with one general writing to the Emperor that 'the remnant enemy are reduced to ashes and are on the point of total destruction.'[16] Fan Ye, the compiler of the *Book of Later Han*, praised the army for making 'the valley quiet and the mountain vacant'.[17]

These cruel reprisals against ethnic minorities only hardened the hearts of the common people in the fringes of the empire. Before long, the state was locked in a number of rolling insurgencies in the west, which combined with the rebellions in the east to further sap its strength. Another result of these conflicts was the growing influence among the military of a company known as the Liang troops. These soldiers had spent their careers crushing the constant rebellions of the Qiang people. They were battle-hardened, remorseless and brutal in their methods. They became feared among both the peasantry and the imperial army—and they began to feel the power that came from that fear. One of the generals leading these Liang troops was a man named Dong Zhuo. He is remembered as a fearsome tyrant, a butcher and a sadist, and he would be the final nail in the coffin of the Empire of the Han.

★★★

When reading about the meteoric rise of Dong Zhuo, it's hard not to draw comparisons with the figure of Julius Caesar. Like Caesar, Dong Zhuo had spent his life fighting in the empire's periphery, earning the trust of his soldiers, and apprenticing in the ruthless application of power. He was born in the unforgiving landscape of Liang province, and as a boy he would have seen many Qiang rebellions put down with brutality. As a youth, he was strong and showed an immediate talent for violence, as well as horseback archery. In his early twenties, he joined one of the elite military units tasked with guarding the Emperor, and spent some months in the imperial capital, where he must have got his first taste of the power and prestige of the Emperor. But the counterinsurgency against the Qiang was becoming increasingly bloody. Less than a year into his time in the capital, in 166, his unit was sent back north. The campaign would have been bloody and ruthless: burning villages and doling out collective punishments to civilians. Dong Zhuo sufficiently impressed his superiors that he was rewarded with 9,000 rolls of fine silk—but, never one to miss an opportunity to increase his men's loyalty, he insisted that the reward should be shared with them.

For the decades that followed, Dong Zhuo crossed in and out of military life, becoming the governor and magistrate of different towns and counties. In the early 180s, when the Yellow Turban Rebellion sprang up, he was put in charge of a large army of the most feared Liang troops. In 185, with the yellow turbans crushed, Dong Zhuo was given the title 'the general who smashes the cowards'. His power had now grown such that he dreamed of even larger things. He returned to the rocky hills of Liang province, consolidating his hold over his fighting men, and exercising their brutality on the Qiang locals.

Perhaps noticing the growing danger represented by Dong Zhuo, the imperial government summoned him to the capital to take up office as the minister steward. This was a promotion, but also clearly designed to remove him from military command. Dong Zhuo refused, writing back to the Emperor that his soldiers would not allow him: 'My Huangzhong auxiliaries and the barbarians from the northwest have all come to me... They hold onto my carriage and refuse to let me leave. These Qiang and other non-Chinese have evil hearts and the nature of dogs. I cannot bring them under proper discipline, but I shall stay to keep them quiet.'[18]

As Emperor Ling lay dying and the power of the state faltered, the government tried again. But Dong Zhou once more declined.

> I have received your heavenly favour and held military command for ten years. My officers and men of every rank have long been close to me. They appreciate my generous care, and are always ready to obey my orders. I beg to take them with me to the north, to assist in the defence of the frontier.[19]

Although wrapped up in the deferential language of official correspondence, this was a clear affront to the imperial authority. Dong Zhuo had led his soldiers for years, out in the remote parts of the empire, and was the one in charge of paying and feeding them. They owed their loyalty not to the empire, with its weak succession of child kings, but to the man who rode ahead of them. And whatever he ordered them to do, they would carry out without question.

***

During the final years of the Emperor Ling's reign, the *Book of Later Han* records a number of strange omens:

> In the second month on the day *xinhai*, first of the month [7 Mar], there was an eclipse of the sun… On the day *jiwei* [15 Mar] there was an earthquake… In the sixth month on the day *dingchou* [31 Jul] a black emanation resembling a dragon, more than a hundred feet long, came down in the Eastern Court of the Hall of Gentle Virtue at a time when the emperor was present. In the autumn, in the seventh month on the day *renzi* [5 Aug], a dark rainbow appeared in the courtyard of the Rear Hall of the Jade Hall.[20]

The Emperor summoned wise men for advice on how to deal with these bad omens, but their response was not encouraging.

> They were asked how these omens and strange occurrences might be halted. [Counseller] Yang Ci replied… 'When Heaven sends a rainbow, all the world is angry and all within the seas is in confusion. A period of four hundred years of government is reaching its end. Now a gang of concubines and eunuchs have combined to dominate the court, and they cheat and deceive your celestial intelligence.'[21]

This advice naturally enraged the eunuchs, who arranged for these wise men to be assassinated. By this time, the eunuchs had outcompeted the empress dowagers for the reins of power, and were now despised by just about all the people of the empire. The secret wealth they had amassed was staggering, and everyone knew how easily they could manipulate the Emperor, as one story from the *Book of Later Han* colourfully illustrates:

> The eunuchs built great houses for themselves, rivalling the imperial palace. On one occasion the emperor wanted to climb the Observation Terrace in the Palace of Perpetual Peace, but the eunuchs were frighteneds he would see their mansions. They sent the harem official Shang Dan to say, 'The Son of Heaven must never climb high, for if he does so his people will be impoverished and scattered.' From this time on, the emperor never climbed a tower again.[22]

In 189, the wastrel Emperor Ling died, and was succeeded by a thirteen-year-old boy. It was at this moment that a group of military commanders saw their chance to rid the empire of the curse of these eunuch advisors. Among these commanders was the ruthless general Dong Zhuo. When he received the message asking him to become part of the plot, Dong Zhuo responded with glee: 'Though it is painful to burst an abscess, it is better than a malignant tumour. I now sound the bells and drums of punishment and march to Luoyang.'[23]

Dong Zhuo sets Luoyang ablaze in 191 CE (Qing dynasty illustration).

Dong Zhou arrived outside the capital in time to see flames rising over the city's southern palace. His co-conspirators had already struck, storming the city and slaughtering the eunuchs. Dong Zhuo swept into the capital of Luoyang and occupied it, but he was afraid that the combined force of the imperial armies could oust him. To make his forces seem stronger than they were, each night he ordered half of his men to leave the city in secret, and then return by daylight to great fanfare and in full view of his rivals' spies, making it appear that he was constantly receiving fresh reinforcements. Three days after his capture of Luoyang, Dong

Zhuo deposed the Emperor and set his even younger eight-year-old half-brother on the throne, crowning him as Emperor Xian. Dong Zhuo was now the true power in the empire. After the coronation of the new child emperor, Dong Zhuo forced his older brother to drink poison, then issued a chilling command to the royal court: 'Any person who seeks to impede the grand design will be dealt with by military law.'[24]

The corrupt rein of the eunuchs had been replaced with a military tyranny.

★★★

Dong Zhuo's actions caused outrage among the lords and nobles of the empire. A resistance was started by a man named Yuan Shao, who camped with his army on a crossing of the Yellow River, north of Luoyang. He was soon joined by his brother and other nobles from the previous regime. By the lunar new year of 190, their forces were swelling, and they posed a real threat to the usurper holed up in the capital. Dong Zhuo knew that he would not be able to hold Luoyang against an all-out assault, and as the rebel forces grew ever more powerful, their tents spreading across the plains, he made a drastic decision. He would flee west, back to the ancient capital of Chang'an, taking all his Liang soldiers and most of the capital's civilian population with him. As he left, he would burn Luoyang to the ground.

Dong Zhuo's men looted the city's palaces, temples, government offices and houses, stealing everything they could lay their hands on, and then they set their torches to the city. The great imperial libraries of Luoyang went up in flames. Some books were written on fine silk and were saved because the illiterate soldiers took them to use as screens, scarfs and umbrellas, but it's thought that more than ninety-six per cent of the empire's collection of books was destroyed in a matter of hours. It had once taken 2,000 carts to transport the empire's store of books from Chang'an to the new capital; the books that survived could barely fill seventy. The rebel lords encamped by the river crossing made their move too late. Reaching Luoyang, they found only a desolate ruin. No large buildings were still standing in the city, and the whole land was covered in ash. There was barely anywhere to shelter.

When Dong Zhuo reached the old capital of Chang'an, he set up an imperial court and attempted to govern what was left of the empire—but he was not in a strong position. Chang'an was more isolated than Luoyang, and the Qiang rebellions had erupted again, making those lands all but ungovernable. There was barely an economy to speak of either. Before torching Luoyang, he had melted down its famous bronze statues and turned them into coins, but since they were of poor quality and not properly marked, this resulted in the devaluation of all of China's copper currency, and the economy went into freefall. His rule now depended solely on the stores of treasure he had looted from the capital, and what he could plunder from the countryside. He became a pirate emperor, sending raiding parties into neighbouring provinces to bring back whatever they could steal. Meanwhile, half the country was up in arms against him. Those around him soon began to realize how untenable their situation was. Some accounts of this time paint a lurid picture of Dong Zhuo. They describe him holding macabre banquets where the main entertainment was the spectacle of prisoners of war being tortured to death, even boiled alive. It's said that while the other guests were put off their food, Dong Zhuo ate hungrily while his prisoners screamed. Some of these stories are likely later fabrications. But it's difficult to know for sure.

Soon, one of his bodyguards, a man named Lü Bu, decided that enough was enough. One morning, on 22 May 192, as Dong Zhuo set out to inspect his troops, Lü Bu and his co-conspirators drew daggers and stabbed him, before killing all of his family and supporters. Afterwards, Dong Zhuo's corpulent body was left in the street, and his killers supposedly put a lit candle wick in his belly button to mock him. He is said to have been so large at the time of his death that the candle burned for days on the fat of his stomach.

The villain of this chapter of Chinese history had been defeated, but the destruction he had caused could not be undone. The boy emperor, Xian, passed between the hands of the various warlords who fought for control of Chang'an after Dong Zhuo. Early in 195, a skirmish between two rival chieftains burned down its palace, and now both imperial capitals lay in ruins. Later that year, at the age of fourteen, Xian managed to escape with a select few attendants. They fled back across the country in disguise, travelling by ox cart, evading roaming bandits and the raiding parties of the warlords that were once again tearing China apart. When he finally reached his once beautiful home of Luoyang, the city had been a ruin for five years, and the streets would have been overgrown with weeds.

Xian and his attendants stayed in those soot-stained remains for a year. They managed to make some repairs to a small part of the imperial palace, rendering it habitable, kicking among the broken stones and heaps of ash. The Emperor's attendants foraged for wild grains among the skeletal buildings. Some of them starved, and others were killed by lawless people trying to eke out a living in the ruins. When a warlord named Cao Cao arrived and rescued the child emperor, this ruler of all the Chinese, the holder of the mandate of heaven, must have looked like any other soot-blackened orphan wandering the streets of the ruined city. Emperor Xian was treated fairly: he was made a duke and lived out his life in peace and comfort, dying peacefully at the age of fifty-three. Meanwhile, China was divided into three kingdoms, and a new age began. The fourteenth century writer Luo Guanzhong, in his historical epic known as *The Romance of the Three Kingdoms*, summarizes this period of Chinese history with the maxim: 'The empire, long divided, must unite; long united, must divide. Thus it has ever been.'[25]

***

Overlooking the city of Luoyang, in the Beimang Hills, lies a graveyard where for centuries the lords and emperors of the Han Dynasty had been laid to rest. Some time in the third century, the philosopher and poet Zhang Zai walked among those graves, and found them in a sorry and dilapidated state. Dong Zhuo's men had destroyed and looted many of the tombs decades before, while grave robbers during the years of chaos had seen to the rest. The walls of the mausoleums had crumbled, animals had made burrows between the fallen monuments, and children now played among the stones.

At Pei-mang how they rise to Heaven,
Those high mounds, four or five in the fields!
What men lie buried under these tombs?
All of them were Lords of the Han world.
…
When the dynasty was falling, tumult and disorder arose,
Thieves and robbers roamed like wild beasts.
…
The stones that were set in them, thieves have carried away.
The ancestral temples are hummocks in the ground:
The walls that went round them are all levelled flat.
Over everything the tangled thorns are growing:
A herd-boy pushes through them up the path.
Down in the thorns rabbits have made their burrows:
The weeds and thistles will never be cleared away.
Over the tombs the ploughshare will be driven
And peasants will have their fields and orchards there.
They that were once lords of a thousand hosts
Are now become the dust of the hills and ridges.[26]

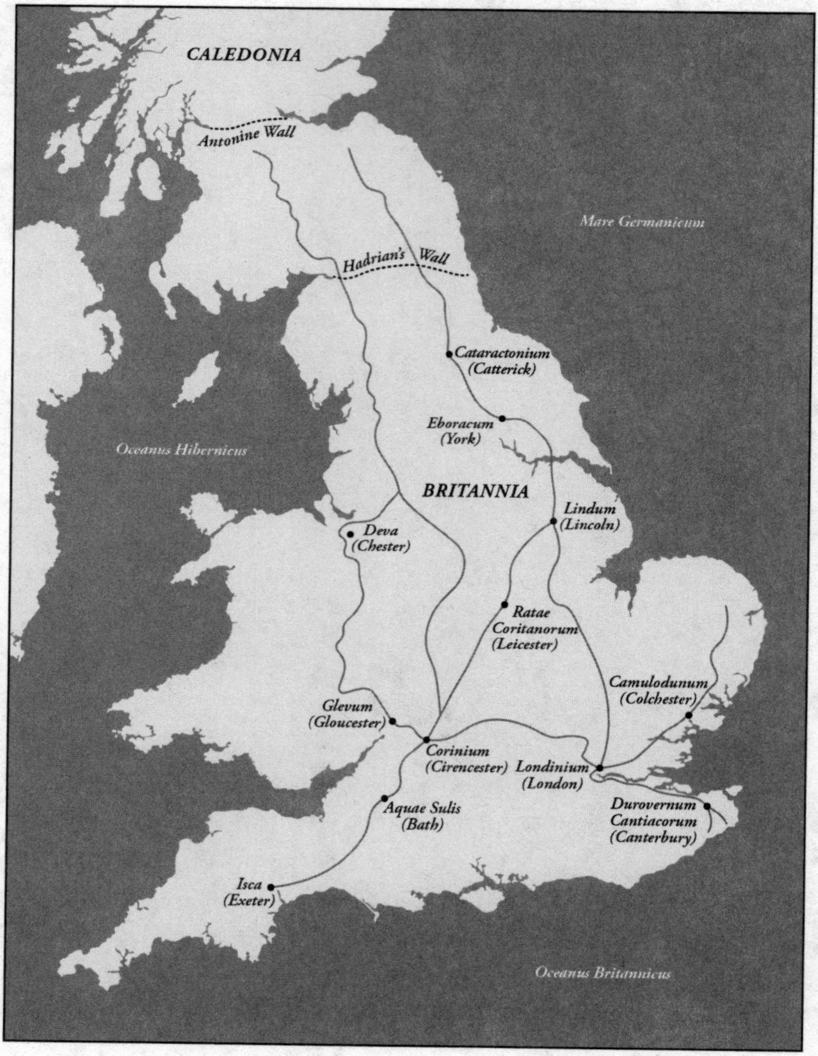

CALEDONIA
Antonine Wall
Mare Germanicum
Hadrian's Wall
Cataractonium
(Catterick)
Eboracum
(York)
Oceanus Hibernicus
BRITANNIA
Lindum
(Lincoln)
Deva
(Chester)
Ratae
Coritanorum
(Leicester)
Camulodunum
(Colchester)
Glevum
(Gloucester)
Corinium
(Cirencester)
Londinium
(London)
Durovernum
Cantiacorum
(Canterbury)
Aquae Sulis
(Bath)
Isca
(Exeter)
Oceanus Britannicus

6

Roman Britain

43–410

One day in the eighth or ninth century CE, an unknown British poet clambered through the rubble of an overgrown ruin. It was the crumbling remains of a long-abandoned bathhouse, now full of moss and waterweed, inhabited by frogs. They would later write a piece of poetry in Old English that gives us a glimpse into a lost and decaying world:

> Wonderous is this wall-stone,
> the fates have broken it,
> have burst the burgh-place.
> The work of giants perished,
> the roofs are fallen,
> the towers tottering,
> the hoar gate-towers despoil'd,
> rime on the lime,
> shatter'd the battlements,
> . . .
> There the baths were
> hot on the breast:
> Now all desolate.[1]

This poem, called simply 'The Ruin', has itself come down to us as something of a ruined object. It was published in a larger volume known as *The Exeter Book* or *Codex Exoniensis*—the largest and possibly oldest known manuscript of Old English literature—but it was damaged by fire at some point so that the words break off and cut out just like the shattered masonry it describes. Still, enough remains for us to picture the crumbling ruined building it describes. As you read these lines, you can almost feel the light falling through the broken roof and smell the stagnant water where luxurious baths once stood.

It's thought that the poem refers to the Roman British city of Bath. Bath was a spa town, visited since ancient times for its natural hot springs. It was once a shrine to the British mother goddess Sulis, and during the Roman occupation of Britain, it became a popular spa town known as *Aquae Sulis* or the 'waters of Sulis'. People came from far and wide to visit its thermal waters, and Bath thrived, the very image of a Roman city in the valley of the Avon River. But by the time the poetry of 'The Ruin' was written, Roman Britain was already a distant memory, remembered as a time of giants and legends.

"The Ruin" as it appears in *The Exeter Book*.

To get to the start of this story, we have to rewind back through the centuries, to the first century BCE, when the power and confidence of the Roman Republic was at its height. After conquering its rivals in Carthage and Greece, Rome captured swathes of territory across Europe, North Africa and Arabia. Its empire was huge and constantly expanding—but for the Romans, the ragged chalk coast of the British Isles was still the frontier of the known world. Roman sources describe Britain as a mysterious and frightening place, separated from the rest of Gaul by the surrounding *Oceanus*, the river-ocean that rimmed the entire world. Plutarch even suggests that some believed the island of Britain to be only a legend:

> The island was of incredible magnitude, and furnished much matter of dispute to multitudes of writers, some of whom averred that its name and story had been fabricated, since it never had existed and did not then exist.[2]

Although the crossing from mainland Europe to the British Isles is only 30 kilometres at its narrowest point, it's a body of water exposed to the harsh weather systems of the North Sea and North Atlantic, making it unpredictable. To the Roman historian Ammianus Marcellinus, it was 'a very narrow strait of the sea, which there rises and falls in a strange manner, being raised by violent tides, and then again sinking to a perfect level'.[3]

But the British archipelago, and its largest island of Great Britain, was not actually as remote as the Romans would have us believe. In fact, archaeology shows that there had long been a heavy traffic of trade passing back and forth between Britain and the mainland. By that time, this contact had been ongoing for at least 3,000 years. But when it came to expansion and conquest, for the Roman military this narrow stretch of water was still a considerable obstacle. By the mid-first century BCE, this treacherous crossing had already defeated the ambitions of several would-be invaders. While campaigning in Gaul, Julius Caesar invaded the British Isles twice. The first, in 55 BCE, met with ferocious organized resistance from local clans, and did little more than sink Roman life and treasure into the marshy lands of the Thames Valley. His second attempt, a year later, was on a much larger scale, and met with better success. But then he left, and the Romans would not land again in Britain for almost a century. After Caesar, Emperor Augustus planned three separate invasions that each fizzled out uselessly. In 40 CE, the mad Emperor Caligula even amassed a huge invasion force of 200,000 men on the Normandy coast—an attempt that might have been successful, had Caligula not supposedly ordered his men to give up the invasion and gather seashells from the Normandy beaches instead.

For the longest time, Britain was for the Romans an unobtainable prize, a land of mystery peopled by wild and unpredictable barbarians. 'Most of the inland inhabitants do not sow corn, but live on milk and flesh and are clad with skins,' Julius Caesar later wrote with palpable horror, having witnessed these unsavoury characters firsthand:

> All the Britons, indeed, dye themselves with woad, which occasions a bluish colour, and thereby have a more terrible appearance in battle. They wear their hair long, and have every part of their body shaved except their head and upper lip.[4]

Here again, we find traces of Roman exaggeration. Caesar was keen to paint the Britons as fierce and formidable opponents, as well as a wild people in need of the civilizing force of Rome. Still, while many Britons doubtless did rely on herding, there is also substantial evidence for crop-growing among the pre-Roman Britons. Archaeology even shows that some Iron Age Britons cast and distributed their own copper coins from at least 125 BCE, their faces stamped with images such as sheaves

A British Pre-Roman coin of the Corieltauvi clan of the British East Midlands, ca. mid-first century BCE.

of wheat and prancing ponies. And if woad was indeed used for body painting or tattooing, then it is another example of the connectedness of the island, since the plant is a non-native species likely introduced from Europe and cultivated for its striking indigo dye.

Neither was Britain a land of small, disorganized tribes—Julius Caesar had learned that twice, and would not soon forget it. Britain's kings ruled from fortified hilltop capitals, some of which were large and well-defended. Maiden Castle in Dorset is one example, defended by a quadruple line of ramparts and ditches, and a clear centre of industry. While culturally and linguistically diverse, Britain's people were also united by a shared religious belief presided over by religious figures known as Druids, a caste of Iron Age mullahs whose religion centred around veneration of one of Britain's most distinctive trees—the oak. 'The Druids—for that is the name they give to their magicians—held nothing more sacred than the mistletoe and the tree that bears it,' writes Pliny the Elder. 'It is the notion with them that everything that grows on it has been sent immediately from heaven, and that the mistletoe upon it is a proof that the tree has been selected by God himself.'[5] The word 'Druid' is even thought to derive from the proto-Celtic word *druwides*, meaning 'oak-knower'.

While the island's people were politically divided, some rulers did achieve considerable influence. From 9 CE, a king named Cunobelin of the Catuvellauni people ruled over a significant portion of south-eastern Britain from his capital at Verlamio just north of London. He printed his coins with the symbol of the wheatsheaf, and was clearly an admirer of the cultures of the mainland, giving himself the Latin title *rex*, or king. During his reign, imports of foreign luxury wares like wine, olive oil, the salty fish sauce garum and glassware and ceramics all increased dramatically. Some clans of the Britons even entered into alliances with the growing mainland empire, and essentially became Roman client states.

King Cunobelin would rule in the south-east for thirty years, but on his death, his kingdom fractured, and inter-tribal wars tore apart the countryside. On the other side of the sea, the Romans saw their opportunity. It was Emperor Claudius who finally enveloped the island into the Empire of Rome. His *casus belli* would come in the form of a British king named Verica, who had ruled a small Roman client state in what is now Sussex, and printed his coins with the symbol of the vine leaf—perhaps hinting at his Mediterranean allegiance. As Cunobelin's kingdom fell apart and war broke out across southern Britain, Verica fled to Rome and begged for protection from Emperor Claudius. For Rome, this was enough of a pretext to invade.

In 43 CE, Claudius successfully landed four legions, or around 20,000 men, on the British coast. The cautious emperor waited behind on the continent, perhaps wisely, considering the failures of his predecessors. He must have listened eagerly to every new report that came back to him, as his men landed in Kent, crossed its chalk downs and valleys, and attempted to cross the river Medway near Rochester. Here, an enormous mass of native British fighters awaited them. After a fierce two-day resistance, the British forces retreated to the banks of the Thames. The Romans followed, wading and swimming through the marshes of Essex, using their engineering expertise to build bridges across the swampy ground. After a final bloody confrontation, British resistance was crushed.

It wasn't until victory was all but assured that Emperor Claudius himself arrived on British shores. Famously, he brought with him a terrifying symbol of Roman power: a tamed war elephant, from the Roman province of Carthage. To the poor Britons witnessing the arrival of their conquerors, the sight of this animal, the crunch of its footfalls and the rattling of its mighty chains, must have ended any thought they had of successful resistance. In the decades that followed, Roman troops swept across the rest of country with ruthless efficiency, into Wales and the British Midlands, subduing peoples as they went. They were particularly keen to stamp out the cult of Druidism, which they viewed as a potential source of rebellion. At sites like Anglesey, these holy men were massacred. Tacitus, in his *Life of Agricola*, dramatizes a speech by a British chief, in which he decries the Romans as:

> robbers of the world...neither east nor west has satisfied them; alone of mankind they are equally covetous of poverty and

> wealth. Robbery, slaughter and plunder they falsely name empire; they make a desert and they call it peace.'[6]

By the year 90 CE, the north of England had been subdued. But when the Romans reached the rugged heath and forested hills of Caledonia (modern Scotland and Northumberland) they met their match. These lands were still covered in thick mats of primeval woodland dating back to the retreat of the glaciers, a landscape that the Romans called the *Silva Caledonia*, or 'Caledonian Forest'. This hostile geography, combined with the fierce warrior clans who lived there, meant that Roman advance would run out of steam before they reached the Scottish highlands. The writer Cassius Dio describes the northern clans who inhabited these lands as though they are something other than human:

> [These] tribes inhabit wild and waterless mountains and desolate and swampy plains, and possess neither walls, cities, nor tilled fields... They dwell in tents, naked and unshod... they are very fond of plundering... They can endure hunger and cold and any kind of hardship; for they plunge into the swamps and exist there for many days with only their heads above water, and in the forests they support themselves upon bark and roots.'[7]

Although these peoples gave themselves a variety of names—the Novantae, the Selgovae, the Votadini, the Venicones and the Caledonii—in the centuries that followed the Romans would come to know them collectively by the name 'Pict'. It comes from the same root as the English word picture—it means painted, perhaps indicating a culture of tattooing, or alluding to a kind of brilliant war paint they wore into battle. The Picts knew their hilly and heavily forested land well, and they were well-versed in what we today would call guerrilla warfare.

The Romans ceased their advance and declared the limit of their empire. They built forts along a jutting cliff that ran the breadth of the island, a shelf of igneous dolerite today known as the Great

Whin Sill that formed a natural barrier between the Roman lands and the lands of the Picts. One rare writing tablet, found in a rubbish heap in one of these forts and dated to the year 92 CE, complains that 'The Britons are unprotected by armour. There are very many cavalry. The cavalry do not use swords, nor do the *Brittunculi* mount to throw their javelins.'[8] The word 'Brittunculi' has never been seen in any other Roman source. With the Latin diminutive suffix-*culus*, it loosely translates to 'wretched little Britons', giving you a sense of how the Romans felt about their new subjects.

In 120 CE, Emperor Hadrian visited Britain, and was dismayed to find the Roman troops there still beset by rebellions and raids, exposed and vulnerable in this harsh land. He was, however, impressed with the natural fortification afforded by the ridge of volcanic stone they were camped on. He ordered this barrier to be made more fortified, with the construction of what would become the largest Roman artefact in the world: a mighty wall stretching 135 kilometres from coast to coast. This wall would be reinforced with eighty milecastles spaced at regular intervals, and supported by seventeen forts garrisoned by soldiers. The parapet was built to the height of 15 Roman feet or 4.4 metres—a little taller than a double-decker bus—and had a ditch dug on the defensive side to even further increase its imposing defences.

The Romans would make multiple attempts to push this border further north into Caledonia, but all of these attempts would ultimately fail. At one point, they even built another wall, known as the Antonine wall, 160 kilometres further to the north, at the narrowest point of the British Isles. This wall, spanning 63 kilometres from coast to coast, turned out to be useless. The land of Caledonia was ungovernable, and the Antonine wall was abandoned each time it was tried, its stones left to crumble into the peaty earth of the Scottish moors. But Hadrian's barrier stood. Roman cavalry led occasional scouting parties out into the lands between the two walls: they went to barter for truces, exchange hostages, and initiate trade. And the Romans knew when to spot a bargain too. Numerous hoards of Roman coins found north of Hadrian's Wall suggest that for at least some of the time, Rome was paying the Picts to hold back their attacks, and to remain in their rugged northern lands.

Meanwhile, South of this snaking line of stone, Roman Britain settled into a restive peace. There had been uprisings at first, the most famous and successful of which was led by the warrior Queen Boudicca of the Iceni people in 60 CE, only seventeen years after the conquest of southern Britain. She and her warriors had marched on the Roman capital of Colchester and burned it to the ground. Rome crushed this adventure brutally, and with it some of the last organized resistance to Roman rule. But the province of Britannia would never quite be pacified.

While perhaps not 'built in a day', Roman regional capitals like Londinium (London) and Camulodunum (Colchester) soon underwent an explosive frenzy of construction. Small fishing towns transformed in the space of only a few decades into bustling hubs of Roman commerce. Despite their colourful pantheon of gods, the real religion of the Romans was the religion of urbanism—the cult of the city—and they replicated the structure of Rome in every city they built. In London, Rome built an ornate forum—the remains of which have been found beneath modern-day Leadenhall Market and Lime Street—and a theatre, both enormous public buildings with marble fronts and tiled roofs, unlike anything the Britons had seen before. In southern Britain, luxurious villas went up as a new elite of Roman governors, civil servants and statesmen poured in. These residences were resplendent with mosaics and baths, even underfloor heating using the latest hypocaust technology. And each Roman city became a hub in the network of stone-paved roads along which imperial commodities moved.

Regular urban Britons could now enjoy incenses and perfumes from Greece and Arabia, amphoras of wine and red-gloss pottery from Gaul, olive oil from Spain, along with pepper and spices brought from as far away as India. In exchange, Britain supplied grain and precious metals to the Roman world: gold and silver, as well as lead and iron. Perhaps most importantly, the coastal hills of Cornwall and Devon were a rich source of tin, that rare metal crucial for bronzemaking, and which had flowed eastwards from Britain since the age of the Hittites, Ugarit and Mycenae. But

The first-century tombstone of a Roman soldier named Rufus Sita, found in Gloucester. The carving depicts him vanquishing an unruly native.

despite these benefits, Britannia was a costly possession. Records show that more resources were poured into the island than were ever taken out. Some at least must have realized that the empire couldn't fund this outpost forever.

Part of the cost of administering Britain was due to its countryside, a hotbed of rebellion. In the small villages of timber, turf-walled roundhouses that dotted the land, tribal loyalties held greater sway than any loyalty people felt to their Roman governors. Walled towns were thrown up across Britain, where foreign administrators poured in to enforce the new structure of imperial society. Tomb inscriptions from York show imperial officials coming from as far afield as France, Sardinia, Syria, Greece and North Africa. A cast of governors came and went too, usually staying for only three years or so—and none of them native to Britain. In fact, although we don't have complete records, there's no evidence of native Britons ever rising to the social rank of *equite* which would have been required to govern. This is a situation quite different from other Roman colonies like Gaul, where the Romans made some effort to bring Indigenous people on board with the imperial project. While some Britons might have felt the material benefits of Roman rule, it seems likely that they never truly felt part of the shared destiny that bound the rest of the empire together at its height.

Perhaps for this reason, it seemed rural Britain was only ever one step from anarchy. The threat of rebellion from within was coupled with raids by the Picts and the Maeatae on the walled northern border. The rich traffic of trade coming to and from Europe also created a boom in piracy, as seagoing raiders like the Saxons from the Germanic coast became increasingly bold, braving the stormy waters of the North Sea to harass shipping and even make incursions onto British shores. Even in the first century of Roman rule in Britain, the pressures that would eventually crush it like a can were bearing in on every side.

One of the key measures that archaeologists use to track the cycle of peace and war in the ancient world is the prevalence and location of buried coin hoards. When times were good, people felt secure enough to store their silver coins or gold jewellery in their home, or in the family vault or even in an early form of bank—but when times were bad, they couldn't risk that. They might bury their cash and other valuables as an extra precaution, or do so in a panic when the first plumes of black smoke appeared over the horizon. Once things settled down, they would return and dig the coins back up again—but if the unrest was serious enough, there might not be anyone left to retrieve them. This was bad news for their owners, but good news for archaeologists who wish to track a region's history of unrest. After the end of the Roman Republic in 27 CE, Rome had undergone nearly two centuries of constant steady expansion. The wars on its borders had been matched by a relative peace in the interior. But as the year 200 approached, the people of the empire were once again burying their gold in chilling numbers.

The Roman peace was shattering. Plague, brought from the East by soldiers returning from campaigns, had ravaged the population, at the height of the epidemic killing 2,000 people a day in the capital and decimating the imperial army. Trouble reigned in the political world too. Since the time of Julius Caesar and his successor Augustus, the Roman emperor had been a dictator with supreme power. Far from representing the popular will, the senate and judiciary were now merely agents of the emperor's command. Wherever absolute power exists, there are people who would risk everything to claim it—and so, against a backdrop of plague and famine, civil conflict erupted across Europe, over rival claims to the imperial crown. In these conflicts, it was quite often the generals stationed in Britannia, the empire's farthest and bleakest province, who heard the drums of war beat the loudest.

To understand why Britannia was such a source of trouble, you only have to look at the particular paradox that Roman Britain presented. Due to the various threats it faced both within and without, the administration required the constant presence of an enormous army to defend the territory and maintain order—as many as 40,000 soldiers, or about one eighth of the entire imperial army at its height. This meant that any one man put in charge of Britannia's defence force was automatically one of the empire's most powerful men. The paradox might not seem apparent at first, but this was one of the fatal flaws that led to the repeated humbling and final fall of Roman Britain.

One of the first characters in this story is a man named Clodius Albinus—one of the first generals to make what we might call the 'British mistake'. Born to an aristocratic noble family in the former Carthaginian city of Hadrumetum, Albinus had been given his name due to the extraordinary whiteness of his complexion. On his birth, his father wrote, 'A son was born to me on the seventh day before the Kalends of December, and so white was his body at birth that it was whiter than the linen clothes in which we wrapped him.'[9]

His striking appearance doesn't seem to have held him back. Albinus was eventually given a command in Gaul by Emperor Commodus, and after that was appointed governor of Britannia, where he stayed longer than many before him. The *Historia Augusta* recalls, 'He was tall of stature, with unkempt curly hair and a broad expanse of brow. His skin was wonderfully white… He had a womanish voice, almost as shrill as a eunuch's.'[10]

Albinus might have spent the rest of his life in Britannia, governing well and climbing the Roman social ladder, were it not for the events that were about to unleash blood and chaos across the wide expanse of the Western Roman Empire. The first of these key events was the death of Emperor Commodus in 192 CE. Widely reviled as a tyrant and a madman, Commodus died without an heir, leaving multiple claimants behind. As a result, the empire descended into a chaos that would cause the historian Cassius Dio to lament, 'our history now descends from a kingdom of gold to one of iron and rust'.[11] The name given to the following year, 193 CE, 'The Year of the Five Emperors', conveys an idea of the pandemonium. These claimants to the imperial throne fought and died, burning cities to the ground, slaughtering armies, until only two credible candidates emerged from the devastation. One of these was Albinus, the pale general stationed with his legions in Britain. The other claimant was the man sitting on the throne in Rome, the ruthless Emperor Septimius Severus.

Severus was also African, and had been born to a Punic father and a Roman mother in Leptis Magna, another former Carthaginian city on the coast of what is today Libya. He had long feared that Albinus would make a strike for the imperial throne, since as the historian Herodian recounts, 'the army in Britain…was large and very powerful, manned by excellent soldiers.'[12] Albinus had many supporters in the Roman senate, since he backed a return to some of the democratic ways of the old republic. After hearing of the death of Commodus, Albinus is supposed to have delivered the following speech in that piercing voice:

> If the senate of the Roman people but had its ancient power, and if this vast empire were not under the sway of a single man, it would never have come to pass that the destiny of the state should fall into the hands of a Vitellius, a Nero, or a Domitian… Now as for Commodus himself, how much better an emperor would he had been had he stood in awe of the senate!… Let the senate have rule, let the senate distribute the provinces and appoint us consuls.[13]

With senators sending secret messages of support to Albinus, the Emperor Severus became increasingly worried about the situation brewing in Britain. He even sent agents to the island with vials of poison, hoping that they would get an opportunity to slip some into Albinus's food—but the plot was uncovered. Albinus was stunned by the Emperor's attempt on his life, and rallied his forces to march on Rome. He knew he would have to act decisively, and he couldn't spare a single man. He took his three legions, every last soldier in Britain, and sailed for the mainland in 195 CE. Albinus was popular in Gaul and amassed a huge following, and after two years finally confronted Severus at the battle of Lugdunum, or present-day Lyon. What followed was an unimaginably bloody and drawn-out affair lasting more than two days and involving as many as 300,000 soldiers. At one point, Severus even believed his forces to be beaten, and began to flee the battlefield, casting off his imperial purple cloak so he would not be recognized. But at the last moment, a company of reserves swept into the battle, and turned the tide. The historian Herodian recounts the final decisive tipping point:

> Albinus's soldiers, thinking that the victory was theirs, now found themselves in disorder when this powerful and as yet uncommitted army suddenly attacked; after a brief resistance they broke and ran. When the rout became general, Severus' soldiers pursued and slaughtered the fugitives…[14]

When he realized that all was lost, that all his sacrifices had been for nothing, Albinus ran himself through with his own dagger. Severus wasn't magnanimous in victory. He rode his horse over Albinus's mangled body, and then paraded his head on a pike. He beheaded Albinus's family and purged his supporters in Rome, even throwing his headless body into the Rhône. The power of the emperor as supreme dictator remained, and the senate got quietly back into line.

Albinus had lost everything, but his dash for Rome also cost his province dearly. Over the long two years he had been at war, he had left Britannia completely undefended. Without a garrison to maintain the Roman order, the land descended into chaos. A huge part of Britain's economy at this time was driven by the constant presence of a Roman army, so when the soldiers departed, the people employed to supply them, to bake their bread, to sell them wine, to forge their swords and armour and repair their leather boots, all suddenly had no work and no way to support themselves. The economy collapsed, and local rebellions spread across the country, while outside forces raided and plundered with impunity. Picts from the north, Scottii from Ireland, and Jutes, Geats and Saxons from across the sea all ravaged the land that Albinus had left behind. Even ten years later, in 207, the situation remained so dire in Britain that the Roman statesman ordered to retake control of Britannia wrote that 'the barbarians there were in revolt and overrunning the country, looting and destroying virtually everything on the island.'[15]

So there is the British paradox: any force sufficiently large to occupy unruly Britain also presented an irresistible temptation to its commander. Any force that could hold Britain could also, in theory, take Rome. And so, the moment the imperial crown was up for grabs, Britain's governor would pile them all into ships and march on the eternal city, leaving Britain undefended. The victorious Emperor Severus, soon after trampling Albinus's body beneath the hooves of his horse, tried to ensure that never again would another challenger arise out of Britannia. He split the province in two, in an attempt to limit the power of any one local governor, and led a huge army into Scotland himself, hoping to drive back the northern attackers. But he didn't have Albinus's way with the natives. It seems this ill-conceived adventure achieved nothing, and Septimius Severus—by then a man of sixty-six—fell sick while campaigning in the foggy lands of Caledonia. He retreated to the city of Eboracum, or modern York, and there he died in the year 211 CE.

Roman rule ended in different parts of Britain at different times, and under different circumstances. After the time of Albinus came the fifty-year period known variously as 'the crisis of the third century' or 'the military anarchy', commonly dated to 235–284 CE. During this half century, no fewer than twenty-six claimants contested the imperial throne, and Roman authority across Western Europe collapsed. Incessant civil wars and rampant inflation crippled the economy, and Germanic raiders made incursions into Roman territory. It must have seemed as if a thousand pressures rained down on all sides. In all of this, despite Emperor Severus's measures, Britain remained a fertile staging ground for rebellion. In 260 CE, a Roman commander called Postumus staged an insurrection that carved Britain and Gaul away from the empire for ten years before they were retaken by Rome. A quarter of a century later in 286 CE, a Roman naval commander called Carausius, a common man who had risen through the ranks, declared himself emperor of Britain, and ruled for seven years before being overthrown. It wasn't all a history of failures either. In 306 CE, the man who would become known as Emperor Constantine the Great was crowned emperor in York. He successfully marched on Rome and spent the next twenty years fighting rival claimants in a series of bitter civil wars.

For much of the third century, Rome was at war with itself, and this period changed the empire forever. Rome's emperors were now military strongmen. Trade across the empire broke down, impoverishing the general population, while at the same time Rome's wealthy became an ultra-rich elite, far richer than they had ever been before. Meanwhile, the empire's enemies grew stronger and more organized, learning how to play to Rome's weaknesses. One event, remembered to history as 'The Great Barbarian Conspiracy' was to lay bare just how diminished the empire's power was.

It was the winter of 367 CE, and life for the Roman garrison at Hadrian's Wall was harsh. We can imagine cruel winds lashing the men stationed on the wall, snow on the ground, their breath visible in the freezing air. Letters they wrote at the time include complaints about the cold that bit at their feet, the lack of holidays and the stingy quantity of beer provided in their rations. But it's still hard to decipher exactly what was behind the decision these men took next. Perhaps it was down to hunger, cold or fear. Perhaps they were even bribed, since there was no shortage of Roman coin north of the wall. Whatever the reason, the soldiers tasked with defending the empire's northern border mutinied, and allowed a waiting army of Picts from Caledonia to cross the wall. This force swept down on the lands of northern England. Towns and villages burned, men and women were put to the sword. But before the Romans could send reinforcements to quash this invasion, something astonishing happened: waves of tribesmen of the fierce Attacotti from the outer isles, Scotti from Ireland, and Saxons from Germania landed on Britain's coasts. At the same time, parties of Franks and Saxons landed in northern Gaul. These didn't seem like random attacks, but coordinated raids, like nothing else the so-called barbarians had attempted before. They completely overwhelmed the Roman defences. Everywhere Roman towns burned, cities were sacked. Slaves escaped, and whole units of soldiers deserted in terror, some gathering together into bands that roamed the countryside, resorting to theft and murder to stay alive.

Writing around fifteen years later, the historian Ammianus Marcellinus paints a scene of pure chaos:

> Britain was reduced by the ravages of the united barbarians to the lowest extremity of distress; that Nectaridus, the count of the sea-coast, had been slain in battle, and the duke Fullofaudes had been taken prisoner by the enemy...at that time the Picts...and likewise the Attacotti, a very warlike people, and the Scots were all roving over different parts of the country and committing great ravages. While the Franks and the Saxons who are on the frontiers of the Gauls were ravaging their country wherever they could effect an entrance by sea or land, plundering and burning, and murdering all the prisoners they could take.[16]

For two years, chaos ruled in Northern Europe, until Rome sent its best general, Flavius Theodosius, to march on the roaming barbarian bands and restore order. Theodosius defeated some in battle and offered amnesty to others—but the damage was done. Rome's confidence in the face of the barbarian threat would never recover.

The empire's reduced ability to protect itself was only one factor of many in the collapse of Roman Britain. The economy had been in decline for decades, trade to other parts of the empire having been disrupted by the century of civil wars, by barbarian invasions and piracy. Pottery produced here reduced drastically in variety and decoration around this time. Iron production in the south plummeted. Around 350, the Roman sewers in Canterbury started clogging up, and no one bothered to clear them. A thick layer of silt began to build up in the public baths that everywhere stood as a symbol of Roman civilization. This decline seeped into every aspect of British life. As the fourth century entered its final decades, one man, an ambitious and hot-headed general called Magnus Maximus, would play a pivotal part in tipping the territory over into its final fall.

If Magnus Maximus had been a reader of history—if he had heard the story of that previous governor, Albinus, and his ill-fated march on Rome nearly two centuries earlier—he might have done things a little differently. Like Albinus, Maximus was a distinguished general. Hailing from the Gallaecian region of northern Spain, he had served in bitter campaigns in Africa and against Germanic tribes on the Danube River, as well as in the army of Flavius Theodosius, who had helped to restore order after the events of the Great Barbarian Conspiracy. He was also notable for being a devout Christian, a religion that had been outlawed in the empire only one lifetime before. Assigned to Britain in 380 CE, in Maximus's first year he faced down an army of Picts and Scots who had overrun Hadrian's Wall, emboldened by Rome's recent weakness in the face of outside attacks. After crushing this threat and returning the colony to some semblance of order, Maximus celebrated by building a huge church on London's Tower Hill.

But like other governors of Britannia before him, Maximus had ambitions greater than simply governing the empire's wettest and windiest dominion. For the last decade, he had watched from afar as an incredibly unpopular emperor, a young man named Gratian, sat on the Western imperial throne. Gratian loved to hunt, and bizarrely he spent all his time in the company of a band of Scythian archers. These were men from beyond the Danube, outside the bounds of the empire. To the Romans, they were barbarians. The young emperor loved the culture of these Scythians and even used to appear at court in the full traditional garb of a Scythian warrior: an ornately patterned overcoat and furs. People tolerated this eccentricity for a while, but in 378, Rome suffered a horrifying blow. By this time, the Roman Empire was effectively ruled by two emperors: Gratian in the West, and Valens in the East, who ruled from Constantinople. At the time, Valens was dealing with a rebellion of Goths and Huns. He brought a massive army of 30,000 men to crush a rebel force barely more than 10,000 strong—but these rebels stood and fought, and astonishingly, they won. Valens was killed along with 20,000 of his men, and his body was never recovered. The loss shook Rome to the core. Barbarian armies were now causing havoc across the Eastern territories, flouting the authority of Rome. Suddenly, the Western emperor's fondness for dressing up like a barbarian didn't seem quite so acceptable. Gratian's courtiers turned on him, and around the empire, other claimants to the throne sensed their chance and gathered their armies.

Once again, the British paradox came into play. The hot-headed Magnus Maximus, just like Albinus before him, commanded a large army in Britain—and he soon resolved to march on the mainland. Just like Albinus, he knew he couldn't spare a single man. He took the entire Roman garrison of Britannia, piled it onto a fleet of ships and set sail for Gaul in 383. Britain was once again left undefended. It's not known whether any of Maximus's advisors told him the story of Albinus, the pale-skinned Tunisian who was routed at Lugdunum. Did no one, on that creaking ship sailing to the continent, not one of them, mention to him what had happened when the last governor of Britain had tried to become emperor? Perhaps that is part of history's spell. It teaches us lessons even as it convinces us that these lessons don't apply to us—that we'll be the ones to break its endless chain. For Maximus, at least, nothing mattered to him except reaching Rome and seizing the purple cloak of the emperor for himself.

At first, Maximus seemed to be blessed. Everywhere he went, legions sent to fight him instead joined his cause. He met Emperor Gratian's army outside Lutetia (modern-day Paris), and Maximus's forces won the day. The young emperor fled with his Scythian bodyguards and was killed soon after, while Magnus Maximus declared himself emperor. But that was where his luck ran out. Before he'd even begun to rule, his support collapsed—and it did so in part because of the anarchy he'd left behind in Britannia. In his absence, raiders and pirates descended on the coastal communities and northern towns. The departure of the entire garrison once again caused an economic collapse, and Maximus had also taxed Britain brutally to pay for his war. Rebellions spread like a fire through dry heather. After suffering defeat in a series of civil wars, Maximus was captured and executed, and the senate even condemned him to *damnatio memoriae*—to have his name scrubbed from official histories.

Today, Magnus Maximus is still remembered in Wales in the myths of the *Mabinogion*, as the hero Macsen Wledig, who sailed across the sea on a quest, after having a dream one day while out hunting. The year of Maximus's departure, 383, is the last date ever to be found on a Roman coin in Wales. It's the last date too for any archaeological trace in the northern Pennine hills. In these places, that moment marked the end of Roman rule in Britain. The sixth-century British cleric St Gildas put it more bluntly, in his searing rant entitled *De Excidio et Conquestu Britanniae*, or *On the Ruin and Conquest of Britain*:

> After this, Britain is left deprived of all her soldiery and armed bands, of her cruel governors, and of the flower of her youth, who went with Maximus, but never again returned; and utterly ignorant as she was of the art of war, groaned in amazement for many years under the cruelty of two foreign nations—the Scots from the north-west, and the Picts from the north…like hungry and ravening wolves, rushing with greedy jaws upon the fold which is left without a shepherd.[17]

From this point, the British economy was in freefall. Entire industries collapsed almost overnight. Metal was no longer mined and smelted. British coffins stopped being sealed with nails, and the soles of boots were no longer studded with hobnails, showing how expensive iron had become. Pottery became a lost art. The suburbs emptied, as the urban economy unravelled thread by thread.

The astonishing thing is, Maximus was not even the last governor of Britain to make the 'British mistake'. This dishonour would fall to a common soldier called Constantine, who once and for all ended the Roman presence in Britain. Constantine was named after the great fourth-century emperor who had been crowned in York a hundred years before, but he would not enjoy the same reputation. In the aftermath of Maximus's departure, a bloody power struggle broke out in Britain, as rival factions within the Roman administration fought like dogs after a strip of meat. In the end, some kind of military coup installed this new governor. The historian Orosius, writing around 416 CE, can barely conceal his sneer: 'Constantine, a man from the lowest ranks of the soldiery, was chosen simply from confidence inspired by his name and without any other qualifications to recommend him.'[18] We can assume that Constantine, too, wasn't a reader of history. The moment he sensed weakness in Rome, he took all of his British legions and sailed for the continent. Completely overwhelmed by barbarian invasions and local infighting, the noble-born Emperor Honorius in Rome was forced to buy off this lowly soldier. He offered him the position of co-emperor, which he held for only a few years before an alliance of challengers chased him off the throne and killed him. Most of Constantine's soldiers never returned to their posts in Britannia.

For Rome, enough was enough. The province could no longer be sustained. The empire was so weakened that an army of Goths led by Alaric was now rampaging around Northern Italy, and even sacked Rome itself, the first time in 800 years that a foreign power had managed to do so. The collapse of the entire Roman Empire now seemed like a possibility. In 410, Emperor Honorius declared the end of the official Roman presence in Britain. He famously told the British, 'Look to your own defences.'

Doubtless for many who had suffered under the Roman occupation, their newfound freedom would come as a welcome relief.

But the turbulence that the sudden departure unleashed would have devastating and long-lasting consequences. Rome withdrew all remaining soldiers and administrators. They stopped collecting taxes in the province, which released some of the burden on its people, but they also stopped paying the administrators who ran its cities and ended the wages and supplies flowing to the local soldiers who had fought as auxiliaries in their legions. These men didn't go anywhere. Instead, they began to tax the population themselves, demanding money and goods in exchange for protection. These groups would ultimately grow into the basis of very early medieval society. These emerging warlords frequently fought their wars using the services of mercenary armies from the continent: Jutes from Denmark and Angles and Saxons from Northern Germany—men who brought their families and formed the first Anglo-Saxon kingdoms in Britain.

The people of Britain forgot Latin as an everyday language, and it survived only in the churches. They stopped writing for at least the next century, as far as we can tell. They forgot their Roman identities and adopted the cultures of the incoming peoples. We can see this in some places, where burials have been found that match those found in Germany and Norway, even though genetic testing shows the buried person to be British. And while all this went on, Britain's Roman infrastructure fell into ruins. Gradually, the opulent villas that had once dominated the countryside were abandoned and became dilapidated. Small estates fell first, some of them absorbed into the holdings of richer landowners—but the larger ones followed soon after. Mosaic floors cracked as roof beams collapsed, while private bathhouses became habitats for frogs and waterweed.

In the north, Hadrian's Wall was finally abandoned, seemingly in a hurry. At one of the best-preserved sites, an auxiliary fort called Vindolanda, archaeologists have found Roman cavalry swords simply abandoned, strewn on the ground. These are rare finds, since a sword was an expensive and precious object. Their owners would no more readily throw them away than a modern person might abandon their car. All kinds of objects pertaining to the daily lives of the soldiers have been found lying around too: bath sandals and writing tablets, pots and buckets and buckles. One day, it seems, everyone just got up and left.

After their departure, local people started using Hadrian's Wall as a quarry, taking its high-quality blocks of stone to build their houses and barns, even churches, so that the wall is now woven into the fabric of countless medieval buildings across the region. Near Carlisle, the medieval priory of Lanercost, for instance, was built using a large amount of material stolen from the wall, which runs just half a kilometre to the north. You can still see Roman inscriptions on some of the priory's stones, boasting about which legions had been stationed on that section of the wall. Meanwhile, tribal chieftains and local warlords, some of whom had been officers in the Roman army until recently, moved into the forts along the wall, and used them as private castles. In one fort, known as Birdoswald, it seems the descendants of the original garrison still lived there a century after the departure of Rome, building timber constructions inside its crumbling ruin. They probably received pay and supplies from people in the area in exchange for protection. Writing about similar garrisons on the German frontier, the Byzantine writer Procopius describes them clinging on to some of the traditions of their Roman past, even as their memories of the empire faded:

> Now other Roman soldiers, also, had been stationed at the frontiers of Gaul to serve as guards...having no means of returning to Rome, and at the same time being unwilling to yield to their enemy...handed down to their offspring all the customs of their fathers which were thus preserved... For even at the present day they are clearly recognized as belonging to the legions to which they were assigned when they served in ancient times, and they always carry their own standards when they enter battle, and always follow the customs of their fathers. And they preserve the dress of the Romans in every particular, even as regards their shoes.[19]

Large cities like London soon fell into disrepair. Trade at its port had been slowing over the past century, but now it stopped altogether. The large church built by Magnus Maximus on Tower Hill burned to the ground, and it seems people lacked either the knowledge, the resources or the will to rebuild it. The forum was dismantled and quarried for stone, the public bath was torn down, and the great basilica, once the largest building in north-west Europe, was also taken apart. People began to be buried inside the city limits too, something that the Roman authorities would never have allowed. Of the burials that have been excavated, studies show that four times more bodies bore wounds from stabbing and slicing weapons than in the preceding period.

London's population of nearly 30,000 people drifted away, back to a simpler existence in the countryside, to timber longhouses and roundhouses of thatch and wattle. In some places, the ancient hill forts of the pre-Roman Britons, which had lain empty for centuries, now burst back into life. Excavations at these sites have unearthed objects that seem to have been looted from the abandoned Roman towns and villas: dressed stone and glass and pottery. It seems that a cottage industry had grown up in scavenging the ruins of Roman towns and selling what could be found.

According to the historian Robin Fleming, the collapse of Roman society affected virtually every aspect of British life.

> When official political and economic links between Britain and the rest of the empire were severed, the production of a wide range of once-ubiquitous objects—mass-produced ceramics and glass, masonry buildings, freshly smelted iron billets, foodstuffs raised in market gardens, and many other things—went into steep decline. And within fifty years of 400, whole constellations of material objects had disappeared.[20]

People stopped eating stews, since there was no longer the industry to produce the large ceramic pots to cook them. Whole foodstuffs disappeared from the British diet—among them herbs like coriander and marjoram—and people foraged for wild foods instead. With no iron horseshoes being made, horses could no longer travel along the stone roads that the Romans had built without risking split hooves, and so these roads too fell into disrepair.

While London gradually emptied out, archaeological evidence shows that an enclave of the ultra-wealthy continued to live a somewhat Roman existence in a kind of gated community. They enjoyed the same wine and olive oil they always had, presumably imported at great expense. They denied the writing on the wall for as long as they could—but the decline was unstoppable. The rest of the city emptied, and nature crept back to reclaim its streets and alleys. By the end of the fourth century, everything south of the river Thames had been abandoned. Large pockets of London's urban fabric had turned into patches of overgrown wasteland, which leaves a distinct trace of compacted mulch in the archaeological record that historians refer to as 'dark earth'. People started growing wheat in the middle of the city. By the end of the fifth century, London was completely deserted. It was now an uninhabited ruin, a city of ghosts sinking into the marsh and mud of the river. One brooch with a Saxon design has been found on top of a pile of collapsed rooftiles in one abandoned bathhouse in Billingsgate, suggesting that people in the ages to come would visit the overgrown ruins, to wander and perhaps scavenge in the skeleton of the city.

In cities such as Bath, urban life continued in some form after the departure of Rome. While its temples crumbled and grand public buildings fell into disrepair, city authorities still managed basic repairs like re-cobbling the streets. But without their links to the Roman economy, the slow death of Britain's cities was all but assured. By the early fifth century, all of Britain's towns, large and small, simply ceased to exist. York, where Emperor Constantine the Great had been crowned, now stood empty and in ruins, reclaimed by the seasonal floods of the river Ouse. We know this because archaeologists have found the remains of water beetles, water voles, shrews and froghoppers inside the city, all animals that live exclusively in flooded and swampy ground and had been banished by the developments of the Roman era. The incoming Saxon people were obviously impressed by these Roman ruins, but also seem to have feared them as places of ghosts and curses. They rarely came near and built their own settlements at a considerable distance from them. At some sites like Caer Celemion in Hampshire, formerly a Roman *civitas* or regional capital named Calleva Atrebatum, there's some evidence that the wells of the decaying city were filled in to prevent people from returning. Ritual objects were also left behind, perhaps to ward off the curse that was believed to hang over those crumbling stones.

It's no coincidence that tales of giants form such a prominent part of British folklore. To understand why, you only have to picture the mighty temples and public buildings that were left behind in the wake of Roman rule. To the people of the early Middle Ages, who no longer knew how to build on such a scale, these constructions of bygone centuries must have seemed the work of a people of mythical proportions who had once walked England's rolling fields and primeval forests. It's this landscape that the poet of 'The Ruin' was trying to capture. The piece bears witness to a time when it felt that history was no longer moving forward, that tomorrow would be a more meagre time than today, and to a landscape strewn with monumental blocks of stone, the cavernous bathing halls and overgrown ruins slowly and unstoppably crumbling into the earth as the Classical Age finally passed into dust.

> There were bright buildings, many bathing-halls,
> Plenty of tall pinnacles, a great noise of people,
> Many a banqueting-hall full of revelry
> —Until Fate the mighty changed everything.
> Men fell dead all around; there came a time of pestilence;
> Death destroyed the whole host of the people.
> Their battlements became waste places,
> The citadel crumbled to pieces. Those who would have rebuilt it

Fell to earth in multitudes. Therefore these courts are dreary,
And this arch of red stone. The roof-work, strong and circular,
parts from its tiles, has fallen in ruins to the ground,
broken in to heaps; where once many a man,
glad of heart and bright with gold, splendidly arrayed,
proud and flushed with wine, shone in his armour.[21]

PART 2

THE MIDDLE AGE

In the lives of emperors there is a moment which follows pride in the boundless extension of the territories we have conquered, and the melancholy and relief of knowing we shall soon give up any thought of knowing and understanding them. There is a sense of emptiness that comes over us at evening, with the odor of the elephants after the rain and the sandalwood ashes growing cold in the braziers… It is the desperate moment when we discover that this empire, which had seemed to us the sum of all wonders, is an endless, formless ruin…that the triumph over enemy sovereigns has made us the heirs of their long undoing.

Italo Calvino, *Invisible Cities* (Translated by William Weaver)

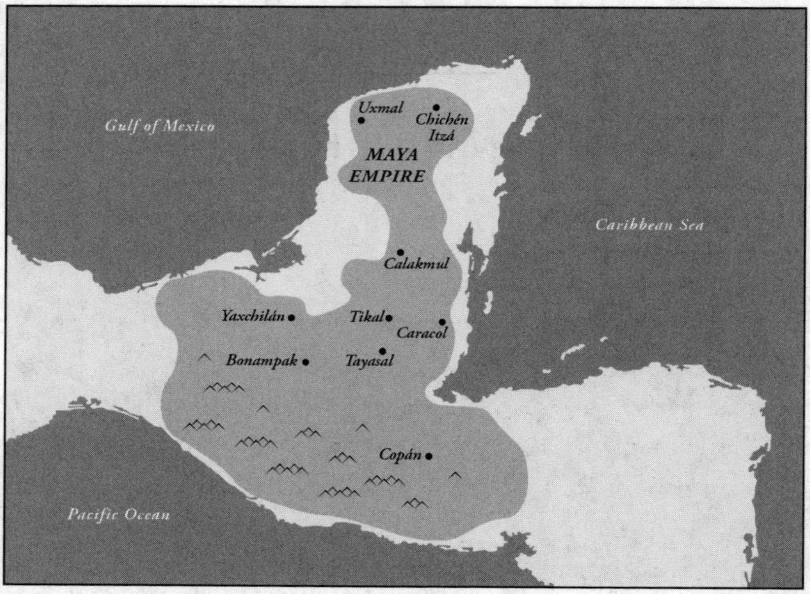
Gulf of Mexico
Uxmal
Chichén Itzá
MAYA EMPIRE
Caribbean Sea
Calakmul
Yaxchilán
Tikal
Caracol
Bonampak
Tayasal
Copán
Pacific Ocean

7

The Maya

c. 250–c. 950

In 1695, a Spanish monk named Andrés de Avendaño y Loyola and his men were fleeing, barefoot and starving, through the tropical forests of Central America. Avendaño had been part of a mission to convert the people of Tayasal, the last island stronghold of a once-mighty indigenous empire, the Petén Itzá kingdom. He had hoped to convince the king of Tayasal to convert to Christianity and accept Spanish control—but Avendaño had failed. The people of Tayasal had turned against the missionaries, and now he and his men were fleeing back to Spanish-controlled territory, in fear for their lives. It was hard going, through a hostile landscape riven with steep ravines, over rivers and densely forested hills. But then they came across something that stopped them in their tracks: an enormous pyramid of stone jutting out of the jungle canopy, tangled with roots and vines.

> Among these high hills which we passed over, there is a variety of old buildings…and though they were very high and my strength was little, I climbed up them (though with trouble). They were in the form of a convent, with the small cloisters and many living rooms all roofed over… It seemed to us that these buildings stood near a settlement…but it turned out to

> be the dream of a blind man, since we found ourselves, as we saw afterwards, very far from a settlement.[1]

Avendaño had observed Mayan people living in cities on the north coast of the Yucatán—but what he encountered here was something different. These were the ruins of a city larger than any he had seen in the New World—a city that rivalled the ancient capitals of the Old World in size, magnificence and grandeur. This was the great Mayan capital of Tikal. For seven centuries, this city had ruled a sprawling empire, conquered its enemies, written literature and raised monuments—and Tikal was just one of at least forty Mayan cities that had flourished in this region. But after that, archaeology tells a bleak story. In the mid-tenth century, more than 500 years before any European first set foot on the American continents, the complex web of Mayan civilization had come apart. The city of Tikal was abandoned, along with every single city in the Mayan lowlands. After this collapse, the forest swept in to reclaim them, and their imposing pyramids were left to crumble into the earth. Millions of people disappeared from the region, and the story of exactly how this happened remains one of history's great unanswered questions.

★★★

The Maya were not one people, but a loose collection of city states and kingdoms that clustered around the Yucatán Peninsula in the region of modern-day Guatemala, Belize, Honduras and southern Mexico. They shared a family of related languages and a cohesive culture that built stepped pyramids and carved stone monuments known as stelae. They cultivated maize, beans, peppers, squashes and cacao, from which they made a hot chocolate drink that was taken ceremonially from ornately patterned vases. They were a people of contradictions, who developed a mathematics capable of calculating dates in the millions of years, but never invented the wheel, the true arch or the pulley. They gave themselves colourful names that drew from the natural world around them: Lady Shark Fin, True Magician Jaguar, Double Bird, Smoke Serpent. Early written accounts of the Maya's appearance note the jade plugs they wore in their ears. They tattooed their skin with green ink, wore ornate headdresses and painted themselves with red and black paint. The Maya believed that time was circular, that history really did repeat itself, and that the future could literally be foretold by learning about the past. They worshipped a complex pantheon of gods, including the sun god, the god of maize and rain, the gods of the sky and the gods of the underworld, who lived in deep caves and hidden pools. Like the Aztecs, the Maya also famously played ball sports. One Spanish writer called Herrera wrote an account of a sport that he witnessed in central Mexico:

> The King took much delight in seeing sport at Ball, which the Spaniards have since prohibited, because of the Mischief that often happened at it... The ball was made of the gum of a tree that grows in hot countries. The balls made thereof, tho' hard and heavy to the hand, did bound and fly as well as our footballs.[2]

Even if we knew nothing else about the Maya's sophisticated society, the colossal ruins they left behind would be enough to prove their ingenuity—but when we acknowledge the environmental challenges they faced, we can't help but appreciate the monumental achievement their cities represent.

The Yucatán Peninsula is a shelf of karst limestone, soft and porous as a sponge. Over millions of years, rainwater has bored deep channels into this rock, and filled it with holes like Swiss cheese. There are barely any rivers here, since any rain that falls is immediately drained away into a twisting warren of underground sinkholes called *cenotes*. What's more, the Yucatán is a seasonal desert. Rain in this part of the world happens all at once and then not at all, with ninety per cent of rainfall occurring in the summer months, then dropping off and culminating in a four-month annual drought from January to May. For this reason, the Maya were constantly battling to preserve rainwater. To this end, they dug large tanks and plastered their bottoms to make them watertight.

To carry out all this physical labour, the Maya couldn't rely on animal help. In Afro-Eurasia, the domestication of beasts of burden like the horse, ox, camel and elephant helped multiply the labour potential of human workers. Even in the Andes, the Inca were able to use llamas to carry heavy weights across long distances—but in the Mayan lowlands, the only large animal was the reclusive tapir, which they sometimes hunted for food. All transportation was done on human backs, using the simple technology of a strap tied around the forehead.

Another challenge was the inefficiency of Mayan farming. Mayan staples like maize were very low in protein, and the harsh and humid environment meant that agriculture and food storage were a constant battle against the forces of tropical nature. The soil in Yucatán is very thin, sometimes only a few centimetres deep before you reach the karstic stone beneath, and it's easily washed away. For this reason, the early Maya relied on slash-and-burn techniques, hacking the forest away in patches and burning it in order to grow a few rounds of crops in the nutrient-rich layer of ash, before letting the jungle plants rush back in to reclaim the land—but soon they would have to develop new and ingenious methods of farming to feed their growing population.

For most of their history, the Maya were essentially a 'Stone Age' society. Copper working began in Mexico in the seventh century, long before contact with Europeans, but took several centuries to work its way down to the Mayan lowlands. The Maya never worked iron, or mixed copper with tin to make bronze. To cut and carve, they used blades made of the black volcanic glass obsidian, and hammers made of stone. Every one of their pyramids and temples was not only constructed without pack animals, but also ornately and intricately carved without metal tools. But despite these challenges, the Maya flourished—one of the only societies of comparative complexity ever to arise in such unfavourable conditions.

The Mayan world was essentially divided into two zones: the highlands in the south-west and the lowlands in the north-east. The highlands are a spine of rocky mountains rising to 1,000 metres in places, covered with pine forests that follow the line of the continental shelf. In those cool hills, the Maya found obsidian and jade, which they carved into tools and marvellous trinkets, and the highlands were also home to the quetzal, a bird with bright green feathers that they used to create the headdresses of their kings and priests. These high-value commodities led the Maya to build a number of trading posts in these hills, but there were few significant settlements in the highlands.

Looking down from one of these peaks, with your back to the Pacific Ocean, you would see ahead of you an undulating plain that stretches out towards the curve of the Atlantic coast, broken by bays and lagoons. These were the Mayan lowlands, and it's within this basin that the wealth of Mayan cities rose. This was a network of societies somewhat comparable to the Classical Greece of Sparta and Athens, or Renaissance Italy—different city states all sharing a common culture, but in constant rivalry, butting heads and locking horns. And just as in these other examples, a flowering of art, literature and discovery took place during the golden age of the Classic Maya Period.

The Pyramid of the Moon at Teotihuacán, Mexico

The largest and most powerful city throughout much of the Classic Period was Tikal. It's believed that Tikal may have housed as many as 90,000 people at its height, and the tallest of its limestone temples tower to a height of 64 metres, or more than twenty storeys. They were once ornamented with enormous masks of the jaguar sun god, plastered and painted a deep red using paint made of the blood-red mineral ore cinnabar that they collected from volcanic sources in the highlands. Tikal rose to such heights in the Mayan world through a fruitful partnership that it cultivated with a shadowy force to the north—a powerful society in central Mexico that exerted influence over much of what occurred in Yucatán. This was the city of Teotihuacán, which lay over 1,500 kilometres away in the Valley of Mexico.

CREDIT: WILLIAM R. COE.

Stele 31 at Tikal, showing the coronation of the Mayan king Sihyaj Chan K'awiil II, or "Storm Sky," supervised by Mexican warriors.

Teotihuacán was once the largest city in the pre-Columbian Americas, and the immense remains of its pyramids testify to its size and power. Cosmopolitan and multiethnic, it had a population estimated at 125,000 or more, which would have made it at least the sixth-largest city in the world at the time. Teotihuacán's success perhaps derives from its monopoly over a particular kind of green obsidian mined from nearby that was prized everywhere for its exceptional hardness and quality. Its wealth soon meant that the city commanded a powerful military, and crucial trade networks across the continent along which that green obsidian flowed. Like North American superpowers in our own day, Teotihuacán was also fond of intervening in the politics of its southern neighbours. In the early centuries of the first millennium, it began aggressively expanding its sphere of influence, extending its trade routes south into Mayan lands, and establishing embassies in faraway cities.

Archaeology shows that Tikal came under the influence of Teotihuacán in the fourth century. It's not clear whether this was a conquest, diplomatic arrangement or palace coup, but we know that a young ruler Yax Nuun Ahiin, known as 'Curl Nose', rose to power in Tikal with the help of this distant superpower. In his tomb, artefacts have been found carved from that tell-tale green obsidian that everywhere reveals the influence of Teotihuacán. His son, named Sihyaj Chan K'awiil or 'Storm Sky' would also inherit the throne with the support of Teotihuacán. One carving at Tikal known as Stele 31 shows this Mayan king being crowned, while Mexican soldiers carrying their distinctive dart throwers look on.

Under the influence of Teotihuacán, Tikal grew in wealth and power. While the Western Roman Empire collapsed on the other side of the Atlantic, Tikal expanded until it was the most powerful city in the Mayan world, its blood-red temples an unmistakable symbol of authority—and at its height it ruled over an empire of at least half a million people. We can tell that this was the case due to the inscriptions that the Maya left in stone. Virtually unique among the peoples of the Americas, the Maya were a literate culture. They had a rich and complex system of phonetic hieroglyphics, similar to those used in Egypt, made up of animal faces and human figures, and wrote on books

The *y ahaw* glyph.

made of bark paper or deer skin, using reed pens and conch shells as inkwells. They also painted writing onto pottery, on carved bone and shell, and on their plastered walls, as well as chipping lengthy inscriptions into the stones of their temples, ball courts and palaces.

One particularly useful hieroglyphic in the Mayan system is called '*y ahaw*'. It means 'his lord', and when it appears in the inscriptions of one city in reference to another, we know that this second city has been subjugated. Soon, Tikal's neighbours would begin using this glyph when referencing its kings. Following the progression of these inscriptions, we can see the influence of Tikal spreading year by year. Armed with weapons made of that green Teotihuacán obsidian, its armies brought city after city under its banner. For a while, it must have seemed that Tikal's imperial ambitions would lead to domination over all of the Mayan lowlands. That is, were it not for their great rival, the city of Calakmul.

Situated deep in the jungles of the Petén Basin region, Calakmul was a city with a distinctive character—and, like Tikal, it was building an empire. At every site that Calakmul conquered, they left a stone stele carved with their emblem: a snake head, which in the Mayan script makes the sound '*kaan*'. Its elites called themselves '*k'uhul kaanal ahaw*', or the lords of the snake. Calakmul was also somewhat unique for the emphasis it placed on the female line of its royalty. Whereas inscriptions in Tikal speak only about kings, those in Calakmul mention the joint rule of a king and queen.

In the early centuries of the Classic Period, Calakmul was outmatched by the might of Tikal, backed by its powerful benefactor in Teotihuacán. But these lords of the snake embarked on a remarkable centuries-long game of chess with their rivals. Following the progression of their snake symbols, we can watch as Calakmul worked to gather a network of allies, made up of the

The snake glyph of Calakmul.

small states that surrounded Tikal, threatening the great city's trade routes and supply lines, bleeding it of power. Over time, these snake emblems spread right across the Mayan world. Calakmul wrapped itself around Tikal and choked the life from its rival.

The strategy was a success. From the second half of the sixth century, Calakmul gained the upper hand, and would grow to become the largest city in the Mayan lowlands. Disastrously for Tikal, the distant power of Teotihuacán also collapsed during the sixth century under mysterious circumstances, the buildings of its elites burned and looted. Now Tikal was left all alone, without its benefactor, and surrounded by determined enemies. But it wasn't until the rule of one particular king, known as Double Bird, that Tikal's fortunes really took a turn for the worse.

***

We understand little about warfare in the Mayan world. From inscriptions, it seems the Maya often undertook low-level skirmishes and raids, and these small wars, known as 'axe wars', served a ceremonial and even symbolic function. They may have involved perhaps only a few hundred fighters, and their purpose was to capture prisoners for religious sacrifice, perhaps to decapitate an important noble, and presumably to bring back plunder to the capital. But occasionally, a different kind of war was undertaken that had a more brutal and all-encompassing nature. These wars are referred to in the inscriptions as 'star wars'—the name coming from a specific type of glyph used in the Maya script, which depicts a star showering the earth with fire. These kinds of conflict were rare in the Mayan world, but whenever they occurred they radically rebalanced power in the lowlands. These were wars of total conquest.

According to interpretations of certain difficult inscriptions, it appears that in 556 CE, the king of the red city of Tikal, Double Bird, embarked on an axe war against his former ally, the city of Caracol. Caracol had until recently been one of Tikal's vassal or client cities, likely supplying food and tribute, soldiers and workers. Double Bird's reasons for ordering the attack are unclear. It could have been punishment for some insult or failure to pay tribute, or because Tikal feared that it was falling under the influence of Calakmul and wanted to remind it who was in charge. Whatever the reason, Caracol's leaders didn't take this axe war in good humour. In retaliation, they announced the beginning of a true war—a star war—against their former masters in Tikal. We can assume that Calakmul gave every help it could to these insurgents. In 562, Tikal was overwhelmed, and its enemies swept into the city. The historian David Drew describes the scenes that must have taken place:

> Today we can reconstruct in outline what very probably happened. In 562 Tikal's enemies overran the city. They smashed and burnt monuments and shrines, uprooted stone stelae and broke them to pieces, discarding or burying the fragments... Archaeologists have found human bones, jade ornaments, caches of obsidian and fine pottery from temples and tombs on the North Acropolis scattered about and stuffed into nearby *chultunes* or underground storage chambers. The perpetrators of this iconoclasm set out to humiliate Tikal, to insult the memory of the royal dynasty they had defeated and very probably to take away in triumph some of its portable and holiest images.[3]

For the next century, Tikal's population stopped growing. No stone carvings or public monuments were erected. Its people were buried with only meagre possessions, and production of painted pottery ground to a halt. The fate of King Double Bird is unknown. He was probably taken back to Caracol or Calakmul and executed at the top of a pyramid. A new king was put in place in Tikal, known as Animal Skull, and although we know almost nothing about him, his tomb inscriptions show that he was not the son of Double Bird.

For the next century, Calakmul and not Tikal would rule the Yucatán. This Mayan rivalry would grind on for generations, with one side regaining the upper hand, only to lose it again. In the end, it wasn't war that caused the collapse of the Mayan world. At least, not entirely. To get to the root causes of this collapse, we need to look at the way that the complex, interconnected web of Mayan society arranged itself, the fatal flaws built into its structures, and the tensions and conflicts that would ultimately tear it apart.

★★★

One way that we can track the progress of the Mayan collapse is by looking at the number of inscriptions they left. When times were good, the Maya erected new temples, palaces and carved stelae. Around the year 500, as the Classic Mayan era just got started, the number of dated monuments was quite low. In the city of Copán, for instance, there were only ten built in the year 514. But as the years went by and Mayan society grew in strength and confidence, the number of monuments in Copán rose. It increased to twenty per year just a century later, and by 750 more than forty monuments were being consecrated every year. But then the collapse set in. After this, the number of dated monuments began to falter. Only fifty years later, in 800, only ten monuments were built. And by 900, the construction of new monuments had ended completely.

From 800 onward, all across the Mayan lowland, the signal of these inscriptions grows weak, falters and then dies out completely. Its cities fell silent one by one, like lights blinking out in the dark. The collapse first took hold in the south-west, along the Usamacinta River. At the city of Bonampak, the last dated inscription is from 792. The city of Yaxchilan stopped carving in 808, and from there, this wave of doom washed over the Mayan lowlands. The great snake city of Calakmul fell silent after 810, and Copán in 822. Tikal held out for another seventy years after the fall of its rival, but it too finally succumbed to the silence in 889. The last Classic Maya inscription of all, in the remote city of Toniná, comes in the year 909. Curiously, 'The royal record before the fall of these cities offers little hint of impending catastrophe', writes David Drew. 'No codices survive with prophecies of doom and there are few tell-tale signs of decline in Maya art, which remained vigorous until the end. All seems right with the world... Then communication is lost and silence descends.'[4]

As with many stories of collapse, the fall of the Classic Maya was not a tidy event with a clear single cause. The societies that populated the Mayan lowlands were fragile and interconnected things, interdependent on one another in complex systems of supply and tribute. All the environmental stresses discussed earlier meant that to succeed, Mayan society had to accommodate a number of stresses and imbalances. Of these, surely the most pressing was the capacity of the Maya to feed their booming population.

At their height, the population of some Mayan cities had grown to be as dense as 800 people per square kilometre. Today when we walk through the ruins of their spacious plazas and temples, it's hard to imagine that those overgrown terraces were once teeming with dense residential populations. But the urban populations were only the beginning. New research using LiDAR, a powerful laser scanning technology that can penetrate the tree cover over Mayan sites, has shown that settlement of the rural hinterlands was far more widespread, and far denser, than even the most outlandish previous estimates. It's now thought that in the eighth century, the whole area would have supported a population of perhaps as many as 15 million. To put this in perspective, England around the same time had little more than 1 million people. The Mayan lowlands at this time in history were one of the most densely populated areas on earth.

Thanks to the overgrown ruins of their temples, shaded beneath towering trees, we have a romantic idea of the Maya as a people who lived out their lives beneath the jungle canopy—but studies of pollen samples found in lake beds and swamps show that by the end of the eighth century, hardly any primary forest remained in the lowlands of the Yucatán. The Maya had cut down the trees not only in their cities, but between them as well. If you stood on top of one of the temples of Tikal or Calakmul around the year 800, rather than the thick forest canopy you see today, you would look out over houses and streets stretching out in every direction, and beyond that, people toiling in their fields.

Much has been made of this deforestation, with some historians blaming this tree loss on Mayan industries such as the burning of limestone to create lime mortar and stucco for the construction of their temples, leading to erosion and soil loss—but not all of this is fair, or in accordance with the latest evidence. The Maya used some timber for construction, for fuel, and for industrial processes like lime production, but the most crucial reason for deforestation was simply to clear land for farming. It was long thought that the Maya relied solely on slash-and-burn agriculture in the thin soil of Yucatán, but with the region's population estimates now revised significantly upward, it's clear that these methods would not have fed such a large number of people. The most recent aerial analysis has now shown that virtually the whole region was laced with networks of sophisticated terraces designed to capture water that runs down from the hills, and raised fields fed by dams and canals.

With no significant animal sources of food, and the population booming, ever more land would need to be cleared for crops. The extent to which this deforestation contributed to the end of the Classic Maya civilization has been extensively debated, with many arguing that its case has been overstated. The anthropologist Cameron McNeil points out that in many of the areas where they cleared primary forest the Maya seem to have cultivated orchards and plantations of crops like cacao, figs, star apples, tropical plums, cashews and avocados. He further argues that 'Although the ratio of upland herbs to trees indicates several episodes of heightened deforestation, none of these episodes correspond to the Late Classic Period (600–900 CE), the time of the collapse.' He goes on to conclude that 'The collapse of the ancient Maya cities may have numerous causes in common, but deforestation was not among them.'[5]

However, deforestation did significantly worsen one of the greatest threats that the Maya faced: that is, the droughts that would often rock this region. Droughts were a fact of life in the water-poor environment of the Yucatán. In the sixteenth century, one Spanish observer recorded a drought in which 'such a famine fell upon them that they were reduced to eating the bark of trees…nothing green was left.'[6] As we've seen, the most crucial role of Mayan infrastructure was to collect and store water to mitigate drought. But every system has its limits, and towards the end of the Classic Period, the Maya faced a series of devastating climate shocks.

From looking at sediment in the region, archaeologists have estimated that beginning in 760 CE, the Yucatán region suffered its worst drought in 7,000 years. Studies of soil layers have shown that around the mid-ninth century, so-called 'impenetrable clays' begin to appear that show a severe lack of moisture in the soil, and plants that usually grow on the shores of lakes and reservoirs were found only in the deepest parts of depressions—suggesting that these pools had shrunk to nothing. Stalagmites studied in the Northern Yucatán point to a sequence of four separate dry periods of ten to twenty years each during the so-called Terminal Classic Period of 800–950 CE, when rainfall reduced by as much as forty per cent.

The cause of these droughts is still much debated. Ice cores taken in Greenland show that levels of solar radiation around this time reached lows that hadn't been seen for millennia, and it's possible that this caused a harsh, dry cold to descend over the northern hemisphere, shifting fragile global weather systems. The archaeologist Richardson B. Gill has argued that 'a southward migration of the northern Yucatecan zone of aridity in the lowlands would have been devastating for the 95% of Maya cities that relied on dependable annual rainfall for their drinking water and for their crops.'[7]

In one surviving collection of Mayan texts and prophecies from the post-contact era, supposedly derived from a prophet (*chilam*) named Balam, you can almost hear the echoes of some authentic memory of what this time must have been like:

> When our rulers increased in numbers…then they introduced the drought. That which came was a drought, according to their words, when the hoofs [of the animals] burned, when the seashore burned, a sea of misery. So it was said on high, so it was said. Then the face of the sun was eaten; then the face of the sun was darkened; then its face was extinguished. They were terrified on high.[8]

Whatever the cause of this series of droughts—one thing we do know is that the loss of natural forest cover in this region would have greatly exacerbated them. Tree cover naturally increases the humidity of an environment—with pores in the leaves constantly releasing water through transpiration, as well as reducing evaporation by casting shade and slowing wind. Modern climate models estimate that deforested areas in Yucatán would have been much drier, and experienced rainfall reductions of up to twenty per cent.

The productive forces that had once led to Mayan prosperity now turned against them, and with a growing population to feed, they were helpless to stop it.

Coupled with drought appears to be the steady polluting of the Maya's water storage systems. Recent studies of ten of the old reservoirs of the city of Tikal have shown levels of chemical pollution that would have made them unsafe to drink—including levels of mercury beyond the toxic threshold. The Maya put great store in the deep red pigment derived from volcanic cinnabar, which they believed to contain *ch'ulel* or 'soul-force' due to its similarity in colour to blood. They painted their bodies with it, and the walls of their houses, and the towering temples of Tikal were all painted with this rich red dye. But cinnabar is made of mercury sulphide (HgS), a heavy metal compound that can have deleterious effects on human health. Researchers believe these chemicals may have gradually leached off the temple walls during rainfall, and entered the reservoirs. The so-called toxic effect threshold of mercury is one part per million—but studies at Tikal have shown that in places the level of mercury in its soil reached a staggering seventeen times this baseline. These levels can even pose a health risk to archaeologists excavating the site today. Studies at a wide range of Mayan sites have shown elevated levels of mercury at virtually all of them, and all of the highest mercury levels also appear in layers that date to the final years of the Classic Period, when the reservoirs would have shrunk during the droughts, and the concentrations of dangerous chemicals would have intensified.

Mercury sulphide is insoluble in water, and as a toxin has been estimated to be many times weaker than liquid mercury—but in sufficient dosage it still builds up in the body's tissues over time, causing a wide range of chronic neurological and psychological effects. 'Following long-term use of cinnabar, renal dysfunction may occur,' one study concludes, adding that 'studies of cinnabar suggest sedative and hypnotic effects'.[9] Since the drinking and cooking water for the Mayan kings and elite of Tikal was almost certainly drawn from these palace reservoirs, the leaders of the city were being steadily poisoned every time they sat down to eat and drink. This would have worsened their health, perhaps deteriorated their mental capacities, and compromised their ability to function in government. One late king named Dark Sun may even have suffered from metabolic syndrome related to chronic exposure: a carving on one of Tikal's temples depicts him with an enormous stomach unlike any other carving of a Mayan king—his obesity one possible side effect of mercury poisoning. In any other scenario, it would be easy for scientists to test the skeletal remains interred in Mayan tombs for increased mercury levels, but the question is complicated by the fact that the Maya used cinnabar in their burial rituals too. One grave of a royal woman has even been dubbed the 'Tomb of the Red Queen' due to the huge amounts of the pigment coating her skeleton and the objects buried with her—all of which would make extracting an uncontaminated sample very difficult.

Perhaps even more dangerous than cinnabar, genetic studies have also found traces of cyanobacteria (blue-green algae) known to produce deadly toxins in these same reservoirs. 'The main water sources for the site core of Tikal, especially the Temple and Palace Reservoirs, were seriously compromised as sources of drinking water by the end of the Late Classic Period,' one study's authors write. 'This period of reduced rainfall co-occurred with expanded Tikal populations when they were most reliant on water reserves.'[10]

The Maya closely associated the legitimacy of their rulers with the ability to provide clean drinking water. One Mayan symbol for royalty found carved on stone stelae and monuments was the waterlily—a flowering plant that can only flourish in clean water that is not too acidic and is not overgrown with algae. Healthy flowering waterlilies were a sign that everything in the city was going well, and the king was providing clean water for his people. But when the waterlilies began to die in Tikal's reservoirs, it would have been a frightening sign that would critically damage the legitimacy of the royal house.

One site that has been particularly well-studied in the context of the Mayan collapse is the city of Copán, in the uplands of what is now western Honduras. Copán was a small but densely populated city, built in a narrow, steep-sided river valley lined with pine forests. Its people loved sports—it had the largest ball court of any Classic Mayan city—and it used the emblem of the leaf-nosed bat on its inscriptions. For much of its history, it was a close ally of Tikal, and fought wars on its behalf. Copán was a trading post, perfectly positioned to profit from the obsidian, jade and quetzal feathers that flowed down from the hills—and from the mining of cinnabar from caves in the Copán valley. Copán was also seemingly an important site for either the production or importation of liquid mercury, refined from cinnabar ore. This was potentially used for ritual or medicinal purposes, but 'Substantially more liquid mercury has been found at the site of Copan…than at any other Maya site.'[11]

In the fertile alluvial silt of the valley floor, the locals grew in abundance their staples of maize, beans and chillis. From the fifth century onward, fuelled by this fertile soil and robust trade, the population of Copán boomed. By 800 CE, there may have been as many as 30,000 people living in this small area of only about 25 square kilometres in the valley. Between the years 650 and 750, construction of royal palaces and monuments was especially frenzied, and lesser nobles even began erecting their own palaces. This all points to a period of thriving economy—but the opulent lifestyle of the nobles had to be supported by the hard work of Copán's farmers. Analysis of skeletal remains from Copán paints a picture of inequality. From 650 onward, signs of disease and malnutrition among Copán's labouring residents increased. Their bones became porous and weak; their teeth showed increased stress lines. These signs of ill health appear in the graves of rich nobles and kings, too, but with far greater frequency in the graves of common people. As Copán grew through the fifth and sixth centuries, it expanded to fill the valley bottom. After the space ran out, people built their homes up the valley sides,

The glyph of Copán, featuring the leaf-nosed bat.

houses stacked on top of one another up the slopes and terraces trying to eke crops out of the meagre hillside farmland.

But you can't grow crops on a patch of soil endlessly. The Maya were responsible and knowledgeable farmers, and had spent more than 2,000 years coaxing crops out of the thin soil of the Yucatán. They must have understood that soil needs to be given long fallow periods to restore its essential nutrients and minerals. But, as the demands from the population increased, the rulers of these cities may have ordered their farmers to grow crops on the same soil again and again, with no fallow periods allowed. It would have been a short-sighted strategy that courted disaster in exchange for immediate gains. But at this point, the Maya may have had little choice.

When times were hard, the common people would blame their rulers. The Mayan system of rulership was based on an implicit promise: you support the king's lifestyle, and he will protect you; he will keep the gods happy, the rains falling and the crops growing. One part of the books of Chilam Balam of Chumayel called 'the interrogation of the chiefs' explicitly makes this connection between the king and the natural world:

> This is the first question which will be asked of them: he shall ask them for his food 'Bring the sun.' This is the word of the head-chief to them; thus it is said to the chiefs. 'Bring the sun, [my] son, bear it on the palm of your hand to my plate.'[12]

If the king was seen to break that promise, the people may have decided that he had to go. The Mayan warrior class, armed with throwing spears and obsidian-ridged wooden bats called *macuahuitl* and armoured only with padded cotton, must have maintained a shaky hold over a large and at times unruly population—and may have struggled to put down significant uprisings. One enigmatic inscription at Copán, dated to 820 CE, says only 'the founder's house has been destroyed',[13] suggesting that some form of dynastic change had occurred. The last sign of any king of Copán is in 822, with a single inscription by a ruler named U Cit Tok, perhaps some kind of usurper. He began the carving of a four-sided monument just as his predecessors had done—but it was never finished. One side shows him being crowned, but the next is only half-carved, and the remaining two sides are blank. It's as if the carver simply got up one day in the middle of his job and left. Whoever U Cit Tok was, it doesn't seem that he could muster enough support to keep the idea of a king alive. By 850, the royal palace of Copán was burned. A century later, in 950, there were still roughly 15,000 people living in the valley bottom, about half its previous population—but they continued to dwindle, and by the thirteenth century there is no sign of habitation at all. Pollen studies show that after this point the forests crept back to recover the ruins of Copán.

***

By the mid-800s, Tikal too was coming apart. Only one hundred years earlier, it had been at its height—all its most impressive blood-red temples and pyramids date from that time. But now its vital allies, at Uaxactun, Ixlu and Jimbal, were putting up stelae of their own, declaring their independence from the imperial capital. When food became scarce, the cities at the centre of the Mayan world—the cities of Tikal, Caracol and Calakmul—would have likely relied on their interconnected tributary networks to keep their citizens fed. As cities on the peripheries increasingly starved to feed their overlords, resentment must have reached a fever pitch. 'Then the rulers of the land were called,' writes the prophet Balam. 'Their blood flowed, and it was taken by the archers. They were terrified…'[14]

Tikal Temple I, as it appeared in 1896.

Instead of a centralized state, Tikal's domain was turning into a fractured mass of small kingdoms. What was worse, these minor kings often referred to themselves not only as independent, but as 'the Holy Lord of Tikal'—suggesting that it was now descending into civil war. By roughly 900, there was no longer a king in Tikal. The city fell into chaos, and the grand buildings were abandoned by the ruling class. Soon commoners moved in from the poorer districts to occupy the royal palace. It must have been a strange feeling for these Mayan peasants, to walk the palace halls and run their hands along its murals and carved stones. We can see the traces of their lives in a layer of what's called 'midden': shards of simple pottery and other rubbish that piled high in the corridors of once opulent apartments. These squatters also scratched graffiti into the plaster: images of temples and animals, caricatures of people they knew. For years afterwards, Mayan people would continue to revere the temples and holy places, and even the stone stelae of bygone kings, at times moving them to more convenient sites. However, it seems these people were not literate: some of the stelae bearing writing were re-erected upside down.

One by one, all the cities of the southern Mayan lowlands were abandoned. Survivors of this catastrophe moved northwards, and sought refuge in coastal settlements like Tulum and Chichén Itzá, where they formed flourishing hybrid cultures with northern peoples like the Toltecs. But the former heartlands of the Mayan world would never be reoccupied. The forests slowly grew back, and had only just recovered their old-growth density by the time the conquistadors arrived on these shores at the end of the fifteenth century.

★★★

In the early decades of the nineteenth century, the American writer, explorer and diplomat John Lloyd Stephens and his artist companion Frederick Catherwood hacked their way through the dense tropical forest of the Yucatán Peninsula. The pair had travelled for two weeks through the deep Guatemalan interior, following rumours that the ruins of an ancient city lay somewhere in the jungle. Their journey was difficult, beset by mosquitoes and the mud of the seasonal rains. But as they rounded a bend in the river, they came across a sight that few had laid eyes on over the last millennium: the top of a towering pyramid, just visible above the trees.

> We ascended by large stone steps, in some places perfect, and in others thrown down by trees which had grown up between the crevices...we followed our guide...through the thick forest, among half-buried fragments, to fourteen monuments... some in workmanship equal to the finest monuments of the Egyptians; one displaced from its pedestal by enormous roots; another locked in the close embrace of branches of trees, and almost lifted out of the earth; another hurled to the ground, and bound down by huge vines and creepers.[15]

At this time, it was commonly believed that only civilizations of the Old World like Greece and Rome had built cities of such magnitude and elegance. Many nineteenth-century historians simply refused to believe that these constructions were the work of the people who now lived a relatively simple existence in the flat plains of Yucatán and called themselves the Maya. Some proclaimed that ancient Egyptians, Indians, Chinese or Norse explorers must have somehow crossed the Atlantic from the Old World and built these towering pyramids, or perhaps even the mythical lost tribes of Israel, or the inhabitants of Atlantis.

A lithograph depiction of the Mayan city of Labna in Yucatán, by Frederick Catherwood, 1843.

Stephens and Catherwood would go on to explore more than forty Mayan sites around the Yucatán Peninsula, and the books that Stephens wrote about these explorations, illustrated with Catherwood's detailed lithographs, caused a global sensation. And the more they explored of the Yucatán, the more Stephens became convinced that these cities had been built up over centuries not by any visitors, but by an advanced society indigenous to the New World. '[These were] works of art,' he wrote, 'proving...that the people who once occupied the Continent of America were not savages.'

> We sat down on the very edge of the wall, and strove in vain to penetrate the mystery by which we were surrounded. Who were the people that built this city? In the ruined cities of Egypt, even in the long-lost Petra, the stranger knows the story of the people whose vestiges are around him. America, say historians, was peopled by savages; but savages never reared these structures, savages never carved these stones. We asked the Indians who made them, and their dull answer was '*Quien Sabe*?' 'Who knows?'[16]

Gradually, people began to accept that he was right, and the achievements of the ancient Mayan people were recognized. As they explored these ruined sites, Stephens wrote with haunting resonance about the ghostly melancholy of these ruins, silent beneath the shade of the forest canopy. In one memorable passage, he leaves us with the image of one statue,

> standing, with its altar before it, in a grove of trees which grew around it, seeming to shade and shroud it as a sacred thing; in the solemn stillness of the woods, it seemed a divinity mourning over a fallen people. The only sounds that disturbed the quiet of this buried city were the noise of monkeys moving among the tops of the trees...and, with the strange monuments around us, they seemed like wandering spirits of the departed race guarding the ruins of their former habitations.[17]

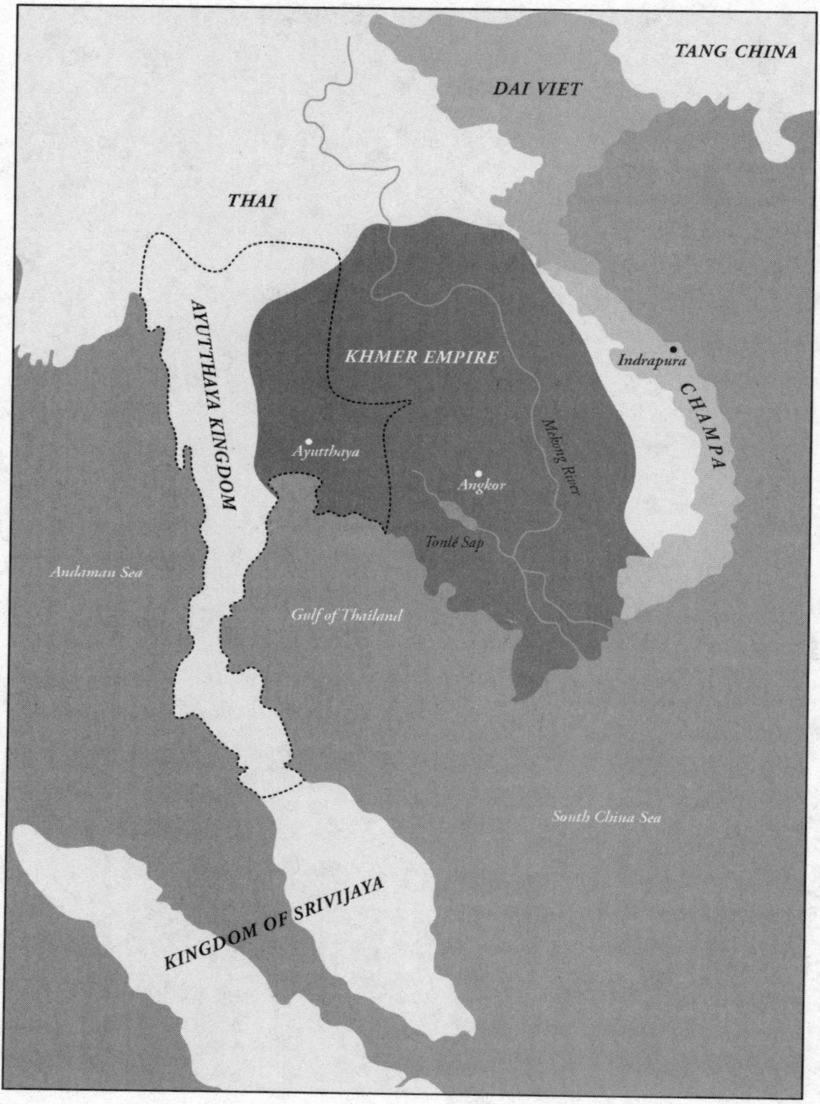
TANG CHINA
DAI VIET
THAI
AYUTTHAYA KINGDOM
KHMER EMPIRE
Indrapura
CHAMPA
Mekong River
Ayutthaya
Angkor
Tonlé Sap
Andaman Sea
Gulf of Thailand
South China Sea
KINGDOM OF SRIVIJAYA

8

The Khmer

802-1431

In the year 1913, the French writer and explorer George Groslier journeyed down the Mekong River in what is today Cambodia. Groslier was a painter, an architect, a photographer and a historian. He had spent time living among Cambodia's Khmer people, and learned their language—and his account of his travels gives one of the most vivid and evocative descriptions of the country:

The facade of the Western Gate of Angkor Wat, as depicted in 1866.

> It is low water, the river's time of great poetry, with the steep banks cut sheer in the fleshy red earth. All the trees there grow vigorously. There are teaks, with broad leaves of tender green; sugar palms and their fruit; bamboos like spurts of water, green and slender at bottom, tumbling up top with a delicate flourish; huge banyans sheltering pagodas; black mangos. There are bony-white cadavers of great trees, their twisted branches gesturing desperately at the passing waters.[1]

But of all the sights that Groslier saw, the one that most impressed him was the ruined temples of the ancient city of Angkor. 'I saw the great stone lotus rise above a sea of treetops,' he writes. 'I have just seen Angkor Wat, temple of the royal city.'[2]

> I had awaited the most advantageous hour, when the sun is low and about to vanish… The mass took on a grey-green hue so fine that the stone attained a vague transparency. The great bamboos to the sides were doubled in the still waters of the moats… Oxen passed by. And beyond all that, at the center of the immense horizontal line of galleries on the first foundations, above motionless palms and rising shadows, the staggering mass and its five conical towers bathed in sunlight.[3]

Of all the ruined sites of the world, few have captured the imaginations of travellers as completely as the remains of the Khmer Empire, a power that ruled a large part of South East Asia from the ninth to the fifteenth century, and covered much of Cambodia and Thailand, and parts of Vietnam and Laos. At the heart of this empire was the megacity of Angkor. Satellite imaging has revealed that during its peak in the eleventh to thirteenth centuries, this city covered an area of over 1,000 square kilometres, larger than New York City today, and its wider agricultural area is thought to have supported at least 1 million people, or 0.25 per cent of the world's population at that time. But by the middle of the fifteenth century, the entire city had been abandoned, left to crumble and be devoured by the voracious roots of banyans and silk cotton trees.

★★★

Since the first Western explorers encountered the ruins of Angkor at the end of the sixteenth century, its very existence—like the ruins of the Classic Maya—had upset Europe's notion of itself. Just as in Yucatán, many Western writers found themselves scrambling for an explanation for how such an impressive city could have been built in Cambodia—one of which was proposed by Marcello de Ribadeneyra in 1601:

> There are the ruins of an ancient city there which some say was built by Alexander the Great or the Romans, it is amazing that no one lives there now, it is inhabited by ferocious animals, and the local people say it was built by foreigners.[4]

One later writer even argued that this city must have been the work of the Roman Emperor Trajan, without explaining quite how he might have got there. In fact, virtually nobody in Europe gave credit to those who had actually built these temples: the people of Cambodia, who called themselves the Khmer.

The Khmer are one of the oldest ethnic groups of South East Asia. They arrived in the region over 4,000 years ago, probably from southern China, and were some of the earliest people in the world to use bronze, and to theorize the number zero in their mathematics. For much of their early history, the Khmer were ruled over by others. An empire known as Chenla had once ruled the lands of Cambodia, but following its collapse, the region broke up into a set of small Khmer kingdoms, which seem to have come under the sway of a foreign empire known in the inscriptions as Java—thought not to be the Indonesian island, but instead the Cham people of southern Vietnam. The Cham ran a powerful trading empire that could muster fleets of ships with dragon-headed prows to crush any resistance to their rule.

The beginning of the Khmer Empire is conventionally dated to the year 802 CE, when a revolutionary warrior led an uprising against the Cham, and crowned himself king of all the Khmer. He gave himself the name Jayavarman II, after the last king of

Chenla, a signal that he intended to restore the power and glory of the kings of old. Many of the remaining Khmer kingdoms still remained loyal to the Cham, and so in order to convince them to join him, Jayavarman devised an elaborate and mystical coronation rite. The most valuable inscription concerning this ritual is dated to 1052 CE, two centuries after his death, carved into the temple of Sdok Kak Thom in present-day Thailand:

> Then His Majesty Parameshvara (posthumous name for Jayavarman II) went to reign at Mahendraparvata… Then a Brahmin priest named Hiranyadarma, wise in *Siddhi* (magic power), came from Janapada, for His Majesty Parameshvara had invited him to conduct a ritual so that Kambujadesa (Cambodia) would not be dependent any more on Java and that he would be a sovereign *Chakravartin* (Universal King).[5]

This Hindu ceremony was known as the *Devarāja*, or god-king ritual. We don't know exactly what it involved, but from similar rituals in India, we can imagine perhaps an animal sacrifice, along with the burning of sacred kusha grass and incense, and the chanting of incantations in Sanskrit. However it was done, by the time the ritual was finished, Jayavarman had established himself not just as king of the Khmer, but as a kind of deity. When the remaining kingdoms of the Khmer heard that a god king had been crowned, their will to resist dissolved. Through a cunning programme of military campaigns, alliances, marriages and land grants, Jayavarman achieved the previously unthinkable: a unification of Cambodia that stretched from the northern border with China to the ocean in the south, with the old enemy of Champa pushed back into the east, and to the west a place identified by a stone inscription as 'the land of cardamoms and mangoes', likely Myanmar or east India.

His conquest complete, Jayavarman built a capital at a place he called Hariharalaya. He built the city on high ground, mirroring the cosmic image of Meru, the mountain home of the gods in Hindu belief. In view of the city, he built a vast reservoir, echoing the sea of milk that is supposed to surround Mount Meru. This construction must have been awe-inspiring for the people of the time, as he marshalled huge workforces to build embankments, drain swamps and dig ditches, and even diverted the course of the Siem Reap River—all testament to the king's divine status. But it would be Jayavarman's successors who would transform his kingdom into a true empire, and the grandeur of their constructions would reach heights that even he could never have imagined.

★★★

Much of our story will take place on the shores of a freshwater lake called Tonlé Sap, right in the centre of Cambodia. For most of the year, the lake drains into the Mekong River—but when the monsoon season begins in June, the Mekong suddenly swells into a raging torrent, and the river reverses its flow, filling the lake until it resembles an inland sea. Today, villages around this lake are famous for their houses perched on top of stilts that raise them three storeys into the air, clearing the monsoon waters, which can rise to up to 10 metres. But the challenges that the great lake presented to ancient people were offset by incredible benefits. Thanks to the mineral-rich sediment carried into the lake by the annual floods, Tonlé Sap has one of the highest concentrations of freshwater fish in the world, including enormous species like the Mekong giant catfish, which can grow to a length of 3 metres. One nineteenth-century European visitor to the lake wrote that 'The fish...are so incredibly abundant that when the water is high they are actually crushed under the boats, and the play of oars is frequently impeded by them.'[6]

The Khmer people also cultivated rice, first domesticated in the Yangtze River basin from marsh grasses that grow in swampy ground. Cultivation of this crop requires turning the landscape into a series of artificial wetlands, and for this reason the Khmer soon became experts in the control of water. Thanks to these natural resources and expertise, the nascent lakeshore kingdom would grow rapidly in size and grandeur. Every king who followed Jayavarman II would undertake the same ritual of the *Devarāja*, to crown themselves god king of Cambodia. For much of Angkor's history, its king was both the wielder of executive power and the centre of an opulent religious cult emanating from the temples of its capital.

The Hindu religion, originating in India, had a long history in South East Asia, and Cambodia at this time was what's known as an 'Indianized kingdom'—one influenced culturally, religiously and linguistically by the subcontinent. An ancient Khmer folktale tells the story of how the lands of Cambodia were founded by an Indian prince named Kaundinya, who is called by a mysterious voice to journey to the 'land of gold' where he would become king. When he reaches this land of gold, he is attacked by a fierce serpent woman named Nagisoma, who he defeats in single combat. Kaundinya spares her life, and she offers her hand in marriage. In celebration, Kaundinya throws his golden lance at the coast, and resolves there to build a city of gold, which he gives the name Kambuja—or, Cambodia.

The myth of Kaundinya illustrates the influence that Indian culture exerted on the lands of South East Asia. During the first millennium, peoples like the Khmer adopted India's hierarchical social structure based on caste, its Hindu myths and philosophies, and perhaps most importantly, the language of Sanskrit. Once a living language of North India, by this time Classical Sanskrit was no longer spoken by ordinary people, but had become a language of scholarship and religion, used among the elite of South East Asia just like Greek and Latin were once required learning among Europe's nobility. But it's important to note that while the elites of Angkor were enraptured with Sanskrit and Hinduism, many of the common people of Cambodia were not Hindu. They were either Buddhist, or followed their own ancient folk rituals that asked favours of the spirits who lived in the trees and the mountains. This division, between the culture of the wealthy Hindu nobles and the beliefs of the common people, would always form a stress line across Cambodian society.

★★★

The Khmer king who would build the first great city at the site of Angkor was a man named Yashovarman, who came to the throne in 889 CE. While we might take with a pinch of salt Yashovarman's own inscriptions, which refer to him as 'a lion man' who 'tore the enemy with the claws of his grandeur',[7] it is clear that he met with some success—and he certainly had a passion for building. In just the first year of his reign, he built over a hundred monasteries across the kingdom. He ruled for another twenty years, and during this time he built a whole new capital. Susceptible as ever to flattery, he named this city Yashodharapura, after himself, but today we know it by a name derived from the Sanskrit word *nagara*, meaning simply 'the city': Angkor.

In some traditions, Yashovarman went by another name: the Leper King. Leprosy, which can cause horrible deformities and skin lesions, was one of the most feared diseases right across the ancient world—and kings were just as vulnerable as anyone else. Today, a statue of the god Yama in Angkor has become a kind of shrine to Yashovarman. Eaten away by moss and discoloured by rain, in the popular imagination it has come to represent the harrowed flesh of the Leper King. Perhaps, as his symptoms worsened and he felt the certainty of his death draw closer, Yashovarman felt an ever greater need to leave his mark on the world—and this explains his mania for building. Whatever the truth of this legend, we know that from the foundations laid by Yashovarman, Angkor's empire grew and flourished until it was the most powerful in South East Asia.

There were a number of factors behind this success story. The first of these was the ruler's status as god king, which since the days of Jayavarman II had cemented his royal authority and allowed the peasants of Angkor to see service to their king as a kind of religious devotion. The second was the empire's efficient and decentralized tax system, which was administered through the religious establishment. Each village in the Khmer Empire had its own temple, which was both a religious building and an administrative centre. These temples were each run by a powerful family, who would collect taxes from the locals in order to support their own lands, to pay their labourers and soldiers—and to maintain their own luxurious lifestyles. Anything left over would be funnelled back to the royal treasury in Angkor. The status of these families depended on how much money they could send to the king, and so they competed bitterly, working as fast as they could to clear forest for new farmland and rice paddies, which soon covered the whole of the fertile central lowlands. This simple but effective system led to a swift expansion of the empire's economic capacity.

The final factor in the Khmer's success was their skill at water-management. As Angkor's numbers swelled, to deal with increased demand for rice, its people developed an ingenious system of water control that turned their capital into what has been called a 'hydraulic city'. If you were to fly over ancient Angkor at its height in the fourteenth century, you would see the land below etched out in remarkably regular lines, like a circuit board. These were the canals and inlets that allowed water to flow around the whole city in a circulatory system, inundating its fields and providing water for drinking, washing and bathing. The Khmer built complex junctions into their waterways, using canals with multiple bends when they wanted a steady flow of water, and long straight channels when they wanted a fast, direct flow into the reservoirs.

As water drained from the Kulen hills in the north, it was channelled into two enormous reservoirs, known as *barays*. These were the largest hand-dug reservoirs ever built, with the largest capable of holding 48 million cubic metres of water. The largest of these—the West Baray—is roughly the size of 2,000 football pitches. To this day, their distinctive pattern is one of the most readily visible human constructions from space. Instead of digging down to make these reservoirs, the ancient engineers heaped up enormous mounds of earth into banks—in places as much as 100 metres wide and 10 metres tall—and diverted rivers and canals to fill them. These reservoirs had a dual function: they acted as overflow tanks in the monsoon season, preventing the rice fields from flooding in an uncontrolled way, and they also allowed the Khmer to store water for the long months when little rain fell.

Angkor's water system was so vast and complex that many of its components are still a mystery to us—but it allowed the Khmer to harvest rice all year round. Soon, the city of Angkor boomed to unprecedented size. Angkor at its height was the world's largest pre-industrial city, with a population forty times larger than that of twelfth-century London. Like a modern city, Angkor was divided into a grid of regular city blocks, but every empty plot of land would also have been given over to farmland, which shared space with temples and administrative buildings. Much of this low-density city would have had the feel of an enormous village, where workers waded through the flooded rice fields back to their stilted houses, and water buffalo bathed in the canals. A traveller or pilgrim arriving at Angkor during the rainy season might have sheltered beneath the canopy of a roadside rest stop and warmed their hands by the fires, heard the chanting of monks in the temples nearby and the sound of bells, and smelled the incense and animals.

These three pillars—the divine power of the god king, taxation that incentivized growth, and their ingenious water management—supported the Khmer to build and flourish for over 400 years. But for each of Angkor's strengths, it had a corresponding weakness. Each of these pillars contained a fatal crack. First, while its king was powerful, his power depended on his religious status. Any shift in religion could undermine his royal authority. Second, while Angkor's tax system promoted growth, it also encouraged over-exploitation of the land, including deforestation, and fostered resentment among the exhausted and overtaxed peasants. And finally, the Khmer's greatest strength, their incredible skill at water management, also had the potential to become their greatest weakness. The water network that laced the city of Angkor and the whole of Cambodia at this time would have required a huge amount of labour-intensive maintenance—to repair damaged banks and inlets, and to clear the canals of accumulated silt. Angkor's water system was so complicated that under sufficient stress a single failure could cause a cascade effect, rippling through the whole network and bringing the world's largest city to its knees. All these factors would come into play as the Khmer Empire reached its height.

***

As so often happens throughout history, the rise of one empire begins with the fall of another. To the north of the Khmer, China's Tang Dynasty had presided over a golden age that lasted nearly 300 years. But around the time of the Leper King Yashovarman, the Tang Dynasty was entering a nosedive. Huge armies of bandits now ravaged China's countryside and sacked cities, smuggling valuable cargoes of salt and ambushing merchants. This period of chaos in China opened up an opportunity for the ambitious young empire of the Khmer. Kings like Yashovarman and his father expanded their territory inland, and the anarchy meant that merchants and traders looked to the golden towers of Angkor to provide security on the roads. By the twelfth century, the Khmer had come to dominate the lands of South East Asia, and the magnificence of their architectural works testified to their power. The most famous of all Khmer monuments today is the sprawling temple complex of Angkor Wat, literally 'City Temple', built by the Khmer King Suryavarman II in the early twelfth century. By some estimations, it is the largest religious structure ever built, four times larger than Vatican City. If the entire city of Angkor is taken into account, more stone was used in its construction than in all the pyramids of Egypt put together.

Angkor Wat was built out of as many as 10 million sandstone blocks, each weighing up to 1.5 tonnes, and these are held together without mortar, shaped so perfectly that the gaps between the stones are often invisible. Like most Khmer temples, Angkor Wat is designed to represent mythical Mount Meru: its 5-kilometre moat encloses three rectangular galleries, each raised above the next, and five towers designed to look like lotus buds about to bloom. What is also remarkable is the speed with which this edifice was thrown up. The medieval Khmer people built Angkor Wat in just under thirty-seven years, while the Normans took centuries to complete many of their cathedrals.

Despite his impressive constructions, King Suryavarman's reign was hardly a golden age. A low relief in the south gallery of Angkor Wat shows him riding into battle on the back of an elephant, and here he looks the perfect image of a warrior—his chest clad in armour, hordes of foot soldiers below, armed with spears and shields. This is obviously how the king wanted to be seen, but the reality was quite different. Suryavarman's appetite for warfare matched his architectural ambition, but he met with little luck on the battlefield. Throughout his reign, he had his sights set on the two coastal nations that made up the area of what is today Vietnam. One of these was Champa, which had once ruled over the disparate Khmer kingdoms—the other, the more northerly kingdom of Dai Viet.

King Suryavarman embarked on three separate invasions of these Vietnamese kingdoms, each resulting in failure. In one memorable instance in 1128, he led a huge army of 20,000 soldiers against the Viet people. This large force was decisively defeated, and the King only just made it back to Angkor alive. All this warmongering for little benefit must have drained the state coffers and caused instability and resentment in the kingdom. After Suryavarman's death, without an heir, increasingly inept rulers vied for control of the weakened Khmer state, and it was amid all of this that Angkor Wat was finally completed. Today its architectural grandeur has cemented his place in history as one of Cambodia's great kings—but it is a reputation that perhaps he did not entirely deserve.

★★★

Civil wars, rebellions and foreign invasions further weakened the Khmer state over the next thirty years, until its collapse must have seemed imminent. But in 1120, a prince was born who would change its fortunes for the better. This prince was one Jayavarman VII. From the various sculptures that depict him, we see a man with a broad, strong body and a large head covered with close-cropped hair. Unusually for a prince of Angkor, he was a devout Buddhist. His eyes are always closed in the statues, a half-smile of peaceful contemplation on his lips—but his broad jaw is also set in an expression of fierce determination.

Little is known about the childhood of Jayavarman. He was the son of King Dharanindravarman II, but for unknown reasons, when his father the king died in 1160, the young Buddhist prince went into exile—whether voluntarily or not—in the lands of Champa, that old enemy of the Khmer. This may have been connected to the fact that Jayavarman's brother soon claimed the crown. But this brother had little talent for ruling. He was soon ousted by a rebel leader named Tribhuvanāditya, who ruled the kingdom for ten years. This rebel was belligerent, and soon his insults drove the neighbouring kingdom of Champa to invade. In his exile, Prince Jayavarman must have observed the Cham armies leaving for war: the phalanxes of spearmen with their bright shields, the trumpeting of the war elephants, the long ships driven by oarsmen leaving the port of Vijaya. By this time, the Khmer Empire had been weakened by decades of infighting, and the Cham armies defeated it easily. The Cham burned the city of Angkor to the ground and executed the rebel chief Tribhuvanāditya. Now fifty years old, Jayavarman must have heard the news of his homeland's devastation with a heavy heart, and he resolved to return. When he arrived in Angkor in 1181, the desperate people greeted this Buddhist prince as their king, crowning him Jayavarman VII.

As he sat on the throne in the capital, Jayavarman must still have been able to smell the smoke in the air. Angkor's buildings were burned, and the bodies of its people still lay in the streets. The Cham armies were still rampaging through his land, burning villages and terrorizing the hungry people, who now looked to him for protection. Perhaps it was this newfound responsibility that brought Jayavarman's Buddhist pacifism to an end. He ordered a great army to be gathered, and drove the invaders from his lands. He now took revenge on the Cham people for the destruction of Angkor, and finally achieved what King Suryavarman had failed to do: seized the capital of Champa, and dethroned their king.

The Khmer Empire was now wider than it had ever been before, but when Jayavarman returned to his capital, he found it still in a state of destruction. He embarked on a building project that would have few equals in history, and would turn the capital of the

Khmer Empire into the envy of the world. This part of Angkor is known today as Angkor Thom, or 'the Great City'—a fortified complex combining palaces, administrative buildings and grand temples. This new citadel was an engineering marvel: a perfect square of mathematical precision, surrounded by a moat enclosing an area of 9 square kilometres.

Carvings in the Bayon temple in Angkor Thom give us a glimpse of the frenzy of construction work that went on. The city must have been wrapped in bamboo scaffolding as far as the eye could see, with the sounds of hammers and chisels knapping away at the stones, and the huffing of work elephants carrying their loads of stone through the streets. Workers lived mostly on a simple diet of rice and fermented fish paste, and used only ropes and manpower to heave enormous stone lintels and pillars into place. Jayavarman undertook an extensive public works programme too, building roads that connected every one of Cambodia's towns. The rebuilding project swelled the population of Angkor and supercharged the kingdom's economic growth.

Jayavarman was significant for one other reason. He was not the first Buddhist king of Cambodia, but he was the first to declare Buddhism the state religion, and from the moment of his coronation, he sought to convert Angkor's society from their Indianized Hindu culture to one that was entirely Buddhist. Before 1200, art in the temples of Angkor mostly portrayed scenes from the Hindu pantheon such as Vishnu reclining on a lotus leaf. Afterward, scenes from the Buddhist folktales, the *Jatakas*, and the life of the Buddha began to appear on the temples instead. Angkor Wat was slowly transformed into a centre of worship, not for the Hindu god Vishnu as it was designed, but for the Buddha. It amounted to a cultural revolution that pervaded every level of Khmer society.

Buddhism had always been a part of Angkor's society, but was often treated as a nuisance. Like Christianity in the Roman Empire, when a liberal and tolerant ruler held power, its followers could go about more or less unmolested—but it only took one ruler with a particular dislike for the religion for things to turn nasty. Now, just as Christianity had in Rome, Buddhists began to take over the culture that had once persecuted them. Buddhism succeeded in Cambodia because it was inclusive and universal in its outreach, a religion of the common people rather than the elites. Buddhist monks were recruited not only from noble and courtly circles, but also from among the peasant ranks. This inclusiveness was also reflected in its architecture. As part of his constructions at Angkor Thom, King Jayavarman VII built an enormous temple complex called the Bayon, and it was the first temple in Cambodia to be built without walls, emphasizing its openness to the public.

Wall carving from the reign of Jayavarman VII, late twelfth century at the Bayon temple in Angkor Thom, depicting the king mounting an elephant surrounded by soldiers and standard bearers.

However, the kingdom's conversion to Buddhism would have wide-reaching consequences that Jayavarman may not have anticipated. As a Buddhist, he renounced the title of god king, instead giving himself the humbler title 'the lord who looks down'—but he still retained the traditional religious power of the god kings who had come before him, and presided over the construction of both Hindu temples and Buddhist image houses. This was possible because Jayavarman was a Mahayana Buddhist, a branch of Buddhism that was highly malleable and adaptive. As it spread out of India into Cambodia, Tibet and China, it made accommodations with local customs and beliefs wherever it went. But in the century that followed Jayavarman's rule, the official religion would change from Buddhism to Hinduism and back again multiple times, depending on the beliefs of the ruler. This inconsistency seems to have led to widespread erosion of people's faith in the state religion. The common people must have asked themselves: 'Well, is the king a god or isn't he?'

Into this vacuum of trust swept a new, hardline branch of Buddhism imported from Sri Lanka, called Theravada. Theravada Buddhism was austere and uncompromising. Its monks lived in poverty, forbidden even to touch money. They wandered between villages on pilgrimages and lived only on what locals gave them to eat. For centuries, Khmer society had been a picture of feudal inequality. Khmer peasants paid taxes to the noble-run temples, worked the fields, and could be conscripted into work gangs whenever a new building project was underway. It's estimated that construction of the great reservoir of the West Baray, for instance, required the manpower of 200,000 peasants working for three years. Meanwhile, the king and his nobles, as well as the priests and holy men in the temples, used the peasants' taxes to fund lives of enormous luxury. The king's palace required the services of up to 4,000 palace women, while according to the inscriptions at just one medium-sized temple, it required a staff of nearly 13,000, including 600 dancers and 1,000 administrators.

It's not hard to see how this new ascetic Buddhism, whose priests lived in grass huts among the villagers rather than in golden temples, became so popular among Cambodia's common people—or how dangerous it would soon become for the authority of the crown. By 1295, only seventy years after Jayavarman VII's death, the spread of Theravada Buddhism had caused the monarch to lose virtually all religious supremacy. For the next rulers of the empire, this would spell disaster.

★★★

When Jayavarman VII died around the year 1220, he would have been close to one hundred years old. The pipes and conches, the drums and gongs and flutes that sounded at his funeral would have been audible from great distances. The people of Angkor were mourning their king, but they may as well have been mourning for their whole society. From this point on, all monumental religious building projects in Angkor came to an end. Soon, virtually all building projects ground to a halt. Over the next hundred years, the creation of stone inscriptions in the capital would slow until they eventually stopped altogether, and would not resume again until the mid-sixteenth century.

Frustratingly for historians, these stone inscriptions are more or less the only source for what was going on in this kingdom at this time. The Khmer were a literate and scholarly people, but their books were written on strips of dried palm leaf, which were so delicate and perishable that not a single Angkor-era paper text has survived to this day. With the end of stone inscriptions, we're left guessing as to exactly what happened in those years. The last recorded king of Angkor was Jayavarman IX, who reigned from 1327 to 1336, before he was supposedly killed by his head gardener, who married his daughter and took his place on the throne—just a hint of the kinds of chaos that seem to have engulfed the royal court. For the next 200 years, not even the name of one king has survived.

★★★

In 1296, the Mongol Emperor Timur Khan, who sat on the dragon throne of China, sent an embassy to the Khmer Empire. One member of this mission was a man named Zhou Daguan, who spent a year in Angkor during this period, and wrote a long report for the emperor on his return, which now stands as the only surviving eyewitness account of what life was like in the Khmer Empire. Zhou Daguan took detailed notes on everything he saw, from the 'stones…carved into the shape of elephants', to the clothing of the people, who 'all wear their hair wound up in a knot, and go naked to the waist, wrapped only in a cloth',[8] to the towering temples and the large numbers of monks he saw walking the streets. Despite the influence of the austere Theravada Buddhism, Zhou was also impressed by the magnificence that apparently still accompanied the Khmer King on his royal processions:

> Each time [the king] came out all his soldiers were gathered in front of him, with people bearing banners, musicians, and drummers following behind him. One contingent was made up of three to five hundred women of the palace. They wore clothes with a floral design and flowers in their coiled-up hair, and carried huge candles, alight even though it was daylight… All the ministers, officials, and relatives of the king were in front, riding elephants. Their red parasols, too many to number, were visible in the distance… Last came the king, standing on an elephant, the gold sword in his hand and the tusks of his elephant encased in gold.[9]

Aside from the remaining royal pomp, markers of decline were already beginning to show beneath the surface of Khmer society, and the signs of conflict. At one point, Zhou Daguan mentions that 'As a result of repeated wars with the Siamese the land has been completely laid to waste.'[10]

In the past century, the Khmer had suffered the rise of a number of powerful rivals in the region. A kind of early 'globalization' of commerce in South East Asia saw the rise of powerful coastal cities that began to eclipse the inland capital of Angkor as centres of trade. The Viet and Thai peoples had grown in strength and confidence, and were putting pressure on the Khmer. Around the start of the fourteenth century, three maritime city states on the lower Chao Phraya Valley in modern Thailand united to form a powerful confederacy. These would one day be known as the kingdom of Ayutthaya. By 1350, this new power had gained enough confidence to challenge the great powers of the region, including the now-weakened Khmer. In 1352, the Thai King Uthong was sufficiently emboldened to make a strike at the capital itself. He marched a large army into Cambodia and encircled Angkor.

The very features that made Angkor perfect for rice farming—its wide flat plains—made it a difficult city to defend in times of war. Some historians have also argued that the extensive system of roads built by Jayavarman VII, which had boosted the empire's economy in previous centuries, now worked against it, allowing its enemies to march across the territory at speed. Angkor fell in that first siege, and then for a period passed between Thai control and rebel Khmer kings. This chaos roiled for nearly a century, until the final decisive conflict in 1431, when the armies of Ayutthaya once again marched on Angkor, surrounded it and laid siege. The Thai armies cut off the city's supplies on both the land and the canals. We can imagine the drums of war beating, and the trumpeting of the elephants, the smoke rising from the siege camps as Angkor was slowly throttled of life. After seven long months, the city fell, and the Thai forces sacked it completely. Statues from Angkor have been found decorating the Thai capital of Ayutthaya, suggesting an organized campaign to despoil the city. A Khmer prince soon chased away these Thai usurpers, but after this humiliation, Khmer kings could no longer rule from Angkor. They moved the king and his court south to a more defensible location, near where the Cambodian capital Phnom Penh is today. It was the end of the golden era of the Khmer Empire.

★★★

Despite its loss of status, Angkor had recovered from the destruction of war in the past—and historians have struggled to explain why the city was abandoned in the years that followed. Some have argued that only a cataclysm like an earthquake or the arrival of bubonic plague can account for the city's ruin—but the archaeological record shows no signs of these disasters, and suggests that Angkor's decline was not a thunderclap. New scientific evidence, including analysis of sediment cores, shows that land use in the centre of the city had reduced gradually for more than a hundred years before its collapse. It's now thought that at least part of the story of the city's downturn may have been caused by shifts in the region's climate, and the global transition from the Medieval Warm Period to the Little Ice Age.

Looking at the enormous canals to the south of Angkor, we see that around this time they became filled with a large amount of coarse-grained sand. This suggests a period of torrential rainfall and flooding, during which large silt deposits were swept down from the hills. But, around the same time, the exit channels that usually drained water from the large reservoirs were deliberately blocked to conserve water. Some were narrowed, while others were turned into inlets to increase the water flowing into the lakes. This seems to point to a period of drought, when the citizens were fighting to keep the reservoir levels high. The answer to this apparent paradox came in the recent publication of a study into the widths of tree rings in Cambodia, covering a period of nearly a thousand years. Tree rings are wider in periods of heavy rainfall, and thinner in years of low rainfall—and the study shows that after around 1350, monsoon rainfall in South East Asia became incredibly variable. A twenty-five-year period of severe droughts occurred from 1330 to 1375, and again from 1400 to 1425. Between these extreme dry periods, the rain fell in a deluge. 'On a planetary scale, the climate was fluctuating far more intensely in the period from the mid-fourteenth to the early-mid-sixteenth century,' writes the historian Roland Fletcher.

> By the thirteenth century...the infrastructure of Greater Angkor was huge, ageing and intractable. Some parts of the water network were between 300 and 500 years old. In addition, the network was profoundly complex, convoluted and full of redundancies and old superseded features.[11]

The Khmer were well prepared for droughts that lasted one or two years—but a nearly thirty-year drought would have caused immense damage to this primarily agricultural economy. Desperate to irrigate their fields, the people would rush to adapt the drainage canals, running long, straight channels from the hills directly to the city, so that more water could flow into their reservoirs and fields. Then the drought would come to an end, not with the usual monsoon rains, but with an unexpected deluge. The emergency inlets that had increased water flow during the drought would now become the city's downfall. Water would rush down them in greater volumes than the system was designed to withstand, and the reservoir would fill to bursting. The Khmer may have attempted to drain their reservoirs, but it would do no good. It must have been a terrifying sight as the water poured over the banks, turning streets into rivers and sweeping away the fragile wooden houses. The people of Angkor would once again work to re-engineer their water system, blocking the new inlet canals and widening the outlets to drain the reservoir, using a staggering amount of manpower and energy. But just when they had finished, the drought would return. This repeated cycle of drought and flood was a stress that Angkor's water system simply couldn't withstand.

One bridge leading into the temple complex of Angkor Thom tells a chilling story. The bridge appears to have been hastily constructed out of building material recycled from nearby temples, with little of the refinement of nearby constructions. The fact that the Khmer people had to hastily construct this bridge shows that something had gone terribly wrong with their water control system. And the fact that they had to reuse stones from some of their most sacred and revered buildings shows that the situation was desperate. Judging by the damage done to the bridge, it seems that the Siem Reap River, which was supposed to run under it, carved a way around it, causing its entire eastern end to collapse.

Angkor is an example of what's called a cascading systems failure. As Angkor diminished in relevance as an administrative and religious centre, fewer resources would have been spent maintaining its water system, and the cycle of drought and flooding would finally have broken it completely. As larger parts of the city flooded, sewage and sanitation systems would have failed, and diseases like dysentery and cholera, and malaria from mosquitoes thriving in stagnant water, would have spread among the flooded streets. More people would have left, leaving even fewer people to maintain its remaining systems. The onerous maintenance of the water system meant that Angkor essentially had a minimum possible population. Below that, the system would have failed utterly, the city would have flooded permanently, and life there would have become unliveable.

Someone entering the city of Angkor in the latter half of the fifteenth century—a scavenger or a pilgrim to one of its faded temples, or just a fisherman on his way to the lake—would likely have found streets still flooded by the bursting of the city's great waterworks, overgrown with lilies and lotuses, and covered by the shade of the jungle canopy. 'It is half-light and half-darkness, a greenish twilight,' wrote one visitor, Malcolm MacDonald, in the 1950s. 'A lifeless, haunted sort of illumination such as might glimmer in a ghostly underworld.'[12]

Soon after its abandonment, the seeds of the banyan and silk cotton trees would fall on the abandoned temples and palaces of Angkor. The control of these voracious plants must have represented much of the effort of maintaining these buildings in the previous centuries—but now they ran rampant. Their seedlings would sprout and put down their hanging roots like bunches of hair, which would then swell and harden into woody trunks. The banyans enveloped the temples and palaces, crushing stone walls beneath their weight, driving roots between stones and plucking apart the walls of temples, cracking stone pillars like twigs.

Today, the ruins of Angkor remind us of the dangers of the challenges our own societies face. They remind us of the threat that growing inequality poses to social cohesion, and the dangers posed by an increasingly variable and unpredictable global climate. We may hope that our existing systems are robust enough to withstand whatever climate change throws at us in the next century. But, as the example of Angkor shows, this is something we may not be able to take for granted. In the tenth-century temple of Phimeanakas in Angkor, now crumbled and moss-covered in the midst of the forest, one inscription in Sanskrit and Khmer called the 'Hymn to the Tree of Awakening' leaves us with a haunting prayer:

> King of the forest, endowed with blessings,
> you give refuge to all, O giver of fruits!
> Neither lightning bolts nor axe blades,
> neither gusts of wind nor pious flames,
> neither rogue kings nor angry elephants:
> may none drag you down to destruction.
> Blinking eyes, twitching brows,
> nightmares, unsettling thoughts:
> O sacred fig, appease them all,
> be they human or divine.[13]

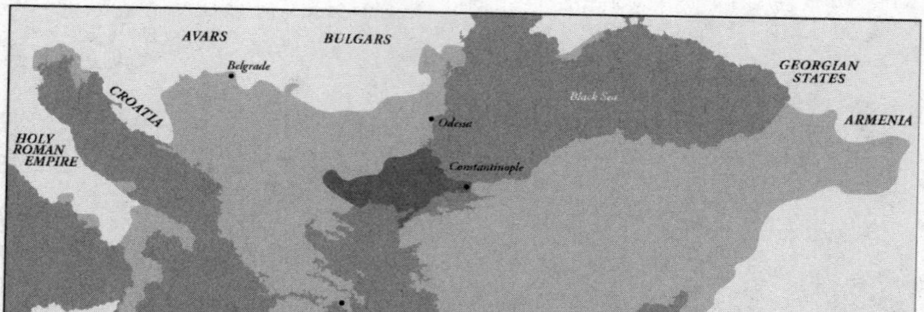
AVARS
BULGARS
Belgrade
GEORGIAN STATES
CROATIA
Black Sea
Odessa
ARMENIA
HOLY ROMAN EMPIRE
Constantinople
Athens
Nicosia
Byzantine Empire ~1030
Byzantine Empire ~1355
Mediterranean Sea

9

Byzantium

395–1453

The story of the Byzantine Empire is a bridge that spans a great gulf of human history, from the Classical era to the dawn of the early modern world. In many ways it is the defining story of the Middle Ages. It began with an unassuming Greek colony on the Bosphorus named Byzantion, supposedly founded by a prince of Megara named Byzas. Around 667 BCE, the oracle at Delphi told Byzas to set sail from his home and settle in 'the land opposite the city of the blind'. As he sailed through the Bosphorus Strait on his way into the Black Sea, Byzas sighted a Greek colony on the Asian side called Chalcedon—but he saw immediately that the European side was a much better place to settle, a defensible position with a large natural harbour. The settlers of Chalcedon had been blind to miss this perfect spot. Prince Byzas landed, opposite the 'city of the blind', and named his new city Byzantion, after himself. Over the centuries, this city would wear many other names: Nova Roma, Constantinople, Dersaadet, Konstantiniyye, Stamboul—and today we know it as Istanbul.

The advantages that Byzas had seen in the location were indeed formidable. It stood at the narrowest point of the Bosphorus Strait, a natural crossing point that controlled all shipping traffic between the Black Sea and the Mediterranean, as well as land-based trade ferried between the continents. What was more, the swift currents that flowed through the narrow channel would make it difficult for any army to attack by sea. The harbour was a long sliver of river estuary, sheltered from the currents and large enough to hold thousands of ships, that would come to be known as the Golden Horn, thanks either to the enormous wealth that would flow through it in the centuries to come, or to the rich yellow light that would often blaze on its surface as the sun set over the sea. Byzantion was established as a perfect wedge shape nestled between the Golden Horn and the Sea of Marmara, and any attackers who wanted to take the city had only a single approach by land. It was the perfect spot to build a fortress that would become virtually unassailable.

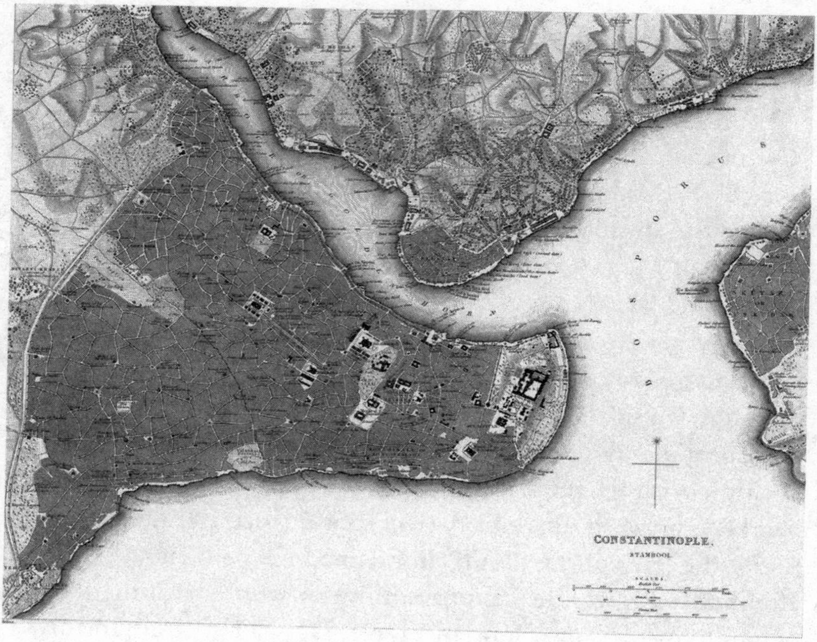

A map of Constantinople/Stamboul in 1840.

Byzantion's importance would only grow during the late Roman period, as the power of Europe's largest empire faltered. By the end of the third century, this vast Mediterranean power could no longer be ruled from the city that had given birth to it. Rome was crippled by corruption, and its people increasingly suffered from a disease that they believed was caused by bad air, or *mal aria* in Latin, which we know today as malaria. In 285, Emperor Diocletian split the empire into two administrative regions, with western Europe and western North Africa comprising the Western Empire, with its capital at Mediolanum—or modern Milan—and the wealthier eastern regions of Greece, Turkey, Syria, the Levant and Egypt forming the Eastern Empire. In the hope of ending the divisions and civil wars that had racked the empire, each half would be governed by two rulers apiece, in a system known as the tetrarchy, or rule of four. But the tetrarchy soon fell apart, and another devastating civil war raged. Emperor Constantine—crowned in the British city of York—fought with his rivals Maxentius and Licinius over who would rule. During this twenty-year conflict, Constantine made a remarkable conversion to the young Eastern religion of Christianity. When he emerged victorious and united the whole empire once more, he decided to construct a new capital in the East. He considered various options, but in 330 CE he settled on the small trading city of Byzantion, which sat at the point where Europe and Asia meet.

Like the ancient explorer Byzas, Constantine saw his own reflection in this golden city. He renamed Byzantion after himself, calling it Kōnstantinoupolis, and it was also known informally as *Nova Roma*, or 'New Rome'. Constantine immediately began an enormous building project, with the goal of turning Constantinople into a worthy imperial capital. He laid out a new central square, naming it the Augustaeum, with a senate-house in a grand basilica on the east side and the Great Palace of the Emperor to the south. Nearby was the Hippodrome for chariot-races, its track 450 metres long, with stands for up to 100,000 spectators. The approach to this racetrack was adorned with a 32-metre obelisk, exactly the same height as the one that stood in the Circus Maximus in Rome—a clear statement that Constantinople was every bit the equal of the eternal city. Constantine also built an imposing city wall running between the Golden Horn and the Sea of Marmara. The city would grow fast, and by the beginning of the fifth century it was already spilling out beyond Constantine's walls, and a new series of defences would soon have to be built. Today, we can trace the success of the city in the advancing rings of its walls, growing outwards like the rings of a tree—but these walls also testify to the increasingly dangerous world that surrounded the young capital.

In the West, Rome's power was faltering. Civil wars like the rebellion of Magnus Maximus had bled the empire white, and emptied its treasuries, and far-flung provinces like Britannia were throwing off its rule. What's more, in 410 CE, two years into his reign, the Eastern Emperor Theodosius received news of an unthinkable tragedy. An army of Goths led by the general Alaric had laid siege to the city of Rome three times, and on the third had burst over its walls and sacked the city. While no longer the empire's capital, this was still an act that shocked the world. 'A barbarian storm, of which prophecies long ago spoke, fell upon Rome,' wrote Bishop Palladius in 420, 'and it did not even spare the bronze statues in the Forum. Plundering with barbarian madness, it destroyed everything. Thus Rome, beautified for 1200 years, became a ruin.'[1] Starving and desperate refugees fled across the Mediterranean to Africa. St Jerome, a Western native now living in Bethlehem, lamented:

> Who would believe that Rome, built up by the conquest of the whole world, had collapsed, that the mother of nations had become also their tomb; that the shores of the whole East, of Egypt, of Africa, which once belonged to the imperial city, were filled with the hosts of her menservants and maidservants.[2]

Theodosius was determined that Constantinople would not follow the fate of Rome. He ordered the construction of a series of walls around the city that were among the most imposing defensive structures ever built: a ring of three concentric walls, each taller than the last, with an enormous moat before them which could be flooded on demand. The innermost wall was almost 5 metres thick and included ninety-six towers, each 20 metres tall. The city gate was built of marble, topped with a magnificent sculpture of a chariot pulled by four elephants. These walls were so formidable that they would not be breached for a thousand years, and it would take a complete revolution in military technology to do it.

***

Despite the administrative division between east and west, most Romans of the time didn't consider the empire to have been split. The terms Western and Eastern Roman Empire were coined in modern times to describe these two political entities, but for much of their shared history, the Romans of both halves of the empire went on viewing it as a single entity. Still, there were significant divisions between them. The overwhelming culture of the Eastern Empire was Greek, and throughout its history Greek was the language of its administrators and city-dwellers, while the Western Romans spoke Latin. But the people of the Byzantine Empire seldom referred to themselves as Greek, and even the term Byzantine is a much later invention. Until the end of their history, right through the Middle Ages, the people referred to themselves as Romans, and their lands as 'Rhomania'. Byzantine rulers were in fact greatly offended whenever their rivals in the Holy Roman Empire tried to diminish their claims by referring to them as 'Emperor of the Greeks'.

While it was no longer the capital of the Western Empire, at the end of the fourth century, Rome had still been its symbolic heart, an economic powerhouse, and the home of an immensely rich aristocracy. But with the destruction of the fifth century, its position wavered. A second sacking of the city by the Vandals in 455 once again halved the population, and by this time Rome's influence extended no further than the borders of the Italian Peninsula. Wealth no longer flowed to it from the rest of its empire, and the complex economic web it had spun began to unravel. A revolt by Germanic mercenary troops known as the Heruli finally toppled this vestige, and the remnants of the Roman army were defeated at the Battle of Ravenna in 476. The emperor was forced to resign, and the Western Roman Empire vanished as a political entity entirely. Writing from the East, St Jerome encapsulates what must have been the fear and uncertainty of that time: 'What is safe if Rome perishes?'[3]

Throughout this period of Western crisis, Constantinople flourished. It continued to grow in size and importance, becoming the undisputed capital and centre of the Mediterranean world. Throughout the whole period of Rome's collapse, the East was seen as a safe haven, and received an influx of refugees. This was the beginning of the city's role as a sanctuary to the destitute, the city that the poet Niketas Choniates would later refer to as the 'beloved refuge of strangers, queen of the queens of cities, song of songs and splendor of splendors'.[4] The eastern half of the empire weathered the tremors of the fifth century well. It endured Hun and Ostrogoth invasions, and was plagued by Vandal pirates, but suffered no permanent damage. In the east, the frontier with the Persian Sassanids held.

For Constantinople, the closest call came in early 447, when the strongest earthquake in living memory ravaged the area, collapsing a section of the Theodosian Walls at the exact moment that an army of Huns led by Attila was marching towards the city. The walls, which had taken nine years to build, would have to be repaired in only a few months. The man in charge of this near-impossible task, a prefect called Constantinus, knew that the city had one great untapped resource: its immense spirit of competition.

In Constantinople, chariot racing held people's fanatic devotion the same way that sports teams do today. Four teams raced in the sands of the Hippodrome—the reds, whites, greens and blues—and bitter rivalries existed between their supporters. Riots and even deaths were not uncommon at the racecourse when rival gangs met. With Attila's hordes descending on the city, and the walls in ruins, Constantinus went down to the Hippodrome, raised his hands and made a simple announcement: each team's fans would be given a section of wall to rebuild, and they had to gather as many of their supporters to help as they could. The declaration of a competition was clear and irresistible, and more than 16,000 fans gathered to repair the city walls. We can imagine the frenzy of activity as these masses climbed the scaffolding with stone, brick and mortar, singing their team songs and jeering at their rivals as, together, they rebuilt their fallen walls.

We can imagine the look on the face of Attila when he arrived at the gates of Constantinople and found not the earthquake-crumbled ruin that his scouts had promised, but a triple line of defensive walls, their limestone glistening white in the sun: the strongest fortification in the known world. The Huns, unable to take the city, were happy to be paid off, and Constantinople was saved. The Eastern Empire's success and survival was such that in the sixth century, one man would go on a crusade to recover the fragmented lands it had once governed, and even recapture Rome itself. His name was Justinian.

***

Justinian inherited the Byzantine throne from his uncle Justin in 527 CE. Quite remarkably, Justin had begun his life as a swineherd in Dardania, a mountainous region in the Balkans. He had come to Constantinople as a refugee, before rising through the ranks of the palace guard, eventually becoming a senator, then commander of the palace guard, and then emperor. After this he brought his young nephew, the boy Justinian, to the capital to be educated. After his uncle's death, Justinian became emperor in turn, and set about the job of ruling with unmatched energy. He became known as the 'emperor who never sleeps', but contemporary sources also indicate that he had a controversial character. He caused a scandal by marrying Theodora, a lower-class courtesan with a lascivious reputation. The sixth-century historian Procopius of Caesarea even wrote one damning text, entitled *Anecdota*, a tell-all purporting to reveal the true Justinian and Theodora—a text that has come to be known as *The Secret History*. Here, Procopius portrays Justinian as cruel, incompetent, and petty:

> He carried out an indefinite number of murders to accomplish these ends. For in his eagerness to gather all men into one belief as to Christ, he kept destroying the rest of mankind in senseless fashion, and that too while acting with a pretence of piety. For it did not seem to him murder if the victims chanced to be not of his own creed.[5]

Procopius even goes so far as to claim that Justinian and his wife were possessed by evil spirits, and wandered the halls at night without their heads. In the early days of his reign, Justinian resolved to renovate the city and ordered plans to be drawn up for a new church that would rival the now dilapidated St Peter's tomb in Rome, bringing marbles from all over the empire for its construction. The result was one of the world's most remarkable buildings. Its dome rises 55 metres, with a span of 30 metres. The church of St Sophia or Hagia Sophia, is still one of Istanbul's most recognizable landmarks.

Justinian was also determined to increase the economic potential of his empire, which led him to commit what is perhaps history's first act of corporate espionage. For centuries, silk had been the sole preserve of Chinese craftsmen, and its manufacture was a jealously guarded secret. But in 551, two Byzantine monks who had been preaching in India journeyed on to China, where they observed the technologies and intricate methods used in the raising of silkworms and the production of silk. Back in Constantinople, Justinian offered the monks a fortune if they were able to smuggle some of these mysterious worms back to the capital. The monks set out again for China, this time carrying hollow bamboo canes with hidden compartments inside. There, they convinced others to smuggle the silkworms out for them, brought them home and eventually established a breeding population. Their actions began a Byzantine trade in silk, with silk factories setting up in Constantinople, Beirut, Antioch and Thebes. They quickly established a monopoly on silk in Europe, and this formed one of the bases for their economy throughout the medieval period, swelling the empire's wealth. This is just one example of the exchange of technologies that took place along these routes.

But Justinian had even greater ambitions. He wanted to recover all the lands of the Western Roman Empire, a project he called *renovatio imperii*: the Restoration of the Empire. Justinian's army, headed by a general named Belisarius, marched across North Africa, and conquered the Vandals who occupied it in only nine months. Then they set their sights on Italy, where an Ostrogoth king still ruled. Belisarius swept through Italy and laid siege to the city of Rome for a year, finally marching through its gates and taking it in 536. From his throne in Constantinople, Justinian watched as the lands of old Rome fell once more under his banner. When Belisarius marched into Rome, he would have seen its grandeur much faded. Earthquakes had damaged many of its buildings, but its aqueducts were still running, and its baths still functioned. A threadbare population had begun to reclaim some of their importance in the region, if nothing like the total dominion they had once exercised.

For Justinian and Belisarius, Rome was the ultimate symbol of the revitalized empire, and they would not give it up for anything. The years that followed saw a series of long and costly wars against the Ostrogoths—and, while they succeeded in reclaiming Rome, the Byzantines also did immense damage to the eternal city. In these wars, as much as ninety per cent of Rome's citizens either died or fled, leaving a population of perhaps only 30,000 people. Of the thirteen aqueducts that had once carried water directly into the city, only two remained in operation. Ironically, if there had ever been hope of rebuilding Rome to the glory of its ancient past, then the Byzantines under Justinian had ended that hope forever.

The conquests of Justinian, though remarkable, were short-lived. The Byzantine Empire simply didn't have the resources to maintain such a large empire for any length of time. The Gothic wars drained its wealth and distracted its military forces. Meanwhile, the 540s brought the first known outbreak of bubonic plague in west Eurasian history: the so-called 'Plague of Justinian'. This pandemic would kill anywhere between 25–100 million people over the next two centuries. Justinian is even reported to have contracted the disease, although he was one of the approximately half of all people who recovered. The plague weakened the Byzantine Empire at a critical point and, in 568, the Germanic people called the Lombards invaded Northern Italy, defeated the small Byzantine army left there, and established their own kingdom. The dream of resurrecting the ancient empire was dead.

Justinian died in 565, leaving no children. He had inherited an imperial treasury of 29 million gold coins, but his wars had all but bankrupted the state. Even his architectural legacy, the Hagia Sophia, had seen its dome collapse in 558 after being weakened by an earthquake the year before—an event that must have seemed to some like God's judgement on an emperor whose lofty ambitions had fallen so short.

Soon, cracks would begin to show in the empire too. In the east, Byzantium was under pressure from the powerful Sassanids—a Persian empire that ruled from the city of Ctesiphon near modern Baghdad. Wars with this rival sometimes dragged on for decades, weakening both empires, and usually resulting in bitter, costly stalemates. In Europe, they would also be pressed by the Bulgarian Empire and other rivals. Byzantium's position at the crossroads of continents gave it unique advantages, but also presented this obvious challenge: the empire had frontiers in Europe and in Asia, and enemies in both the east and west felt emboldened to attack while its back was turned. In the early seventh century, for example, the emperor-general Heraclius had great successes in Asia, routing experienced Persian generals and recovering large amounts of territory—but he soon had to give it all up and march back to Constantinople to repel an army of Avars advancing on the capital from Europe. For the empire, wolves were always approaching from both directions—and soon a new rival would arise out of an unlikely quarter: the seemingly empty desert sands of Arabia.

★★★

In Arabia in the early 600s, a warrior visionary known to history as Muhammad rose to topple the established powers of the region, and gathered a powerful military force around him. After his death in 632, the successors of Muhammad spread out of the Arabian Peninsula, and swept into the lands of both the Sassanids and the Byzantines, both weakened by their constant wars with one another. To the shock of the world, the Arab advance from the south resulted in the disintegration of the Sassanid Empire.

For the Byzantines, this came as a complete surprise. In 634, the Arabs defeated a Byzantine force sent into Syria, and captured Damascus. The holy city of Jerusalem followed soon after in 637, a disaster for the Christian Byzantines that would remain a sore point for many centuries to come. The Arabs quickly swallowed up Byzantine territories in Asia Minor, before taking Egypt—the former breadbasket of the empire. Muslim forces next set their ambitions to the sea, and built a navy strong enough to raid the islands of Cyprus and Rhodes, and to destroy 500 Byzantine ships on the sea. The former Roman province of Carthage fell around 647. By 674, the Muslims even felt bold enough to make a strike at the great city of Constantinople itself.

The Arab attack was daring, but it was also methodical. Their fleet began by capturing port towns along the coast, and then setting up a blockade of Constantinople, attempting to stifle the city. 'In this year in March, a rainbow appeared in the sky, and all mankind shuddered,' wrote the eighth-century abbot and chronicler Theophanes the Confessor. 'Everyone said it was the end of the world. In this year the deniers of Christ readied a great expedition.'[6] But the Byzantines had one more trick up their sleeve: a mysterious superweapon of terrifying power. The secrets of this substance were guarded so closely that even today there is lively debate over its composition. It would be named after the Greek Byzantines who developed it, and so it would be known as Greek fire.

Incendiary weapons had been used in warfare for centuries before—but Greek fire was different. It was developed by a man named Kallinikos, who had fled the Arab conquests and come to Constantinople, that 'refuge of strangers'. Greek fire was an extremely inflammable substance, possibly based on petroleum, that set even the surface of the sea ablaze. Water could not douse the flames, and by some accounts even made them more intense. The substance was dispensed in liquid form, often through siphons or copper piping, and its use was accompanied with smoke, and the sounds of thunder.

Greek fire took the Muslim fleet by surprise, and their ships burned in the waters of the sea of Marmara. Their defeat at sea was coupled with a Byzantine victory on land, and the Arab forces were repelled, having suffered enormous losses. Growing division in the Muslim lands soon forced them to attend to their own affairs, and a peace deal was struck. Against all the odds, Byzantium had survived once again.

★★★

Over the next centuries, storm after storm would rage against the city of Constantinople, but it always held. Its powerful walls, its natural defences and the ingenious invention of Greek fire kept it safe. For this reason, Byzantium as a successor state to the Roman Empire survived into the height of the Middle Ages, and became the undisputed centre of the medieval world. For the Byzantine people, their capital was a constant source of pride. They called it 'the eye of the world', or 'the reigning city'. Its banner, with the Byzantine crescent moon, would have fluttered and snapped over its rooftops and countless churches and icon houses. Visitors would have wandered down narrow streets between buildings of orange-brown bricks still manufactured with Roman methods. Bronze church bells would have rung out among the calling of sea birds and the clatter of wooden window shutters. Dozens of languages were heard on its streets, as one tenth-century knight, Bartolf of Nangis, recorded:

> In this city are Greeks, Bulgarians, Alans, Comans, Pigmaticans, Italians, Venetians, Romanians, Dacians, English, Amalfitans, even Turks; many heathen peoples, Jews and proselytes, Cretans and Arabs and people of all nations come together here.[7]

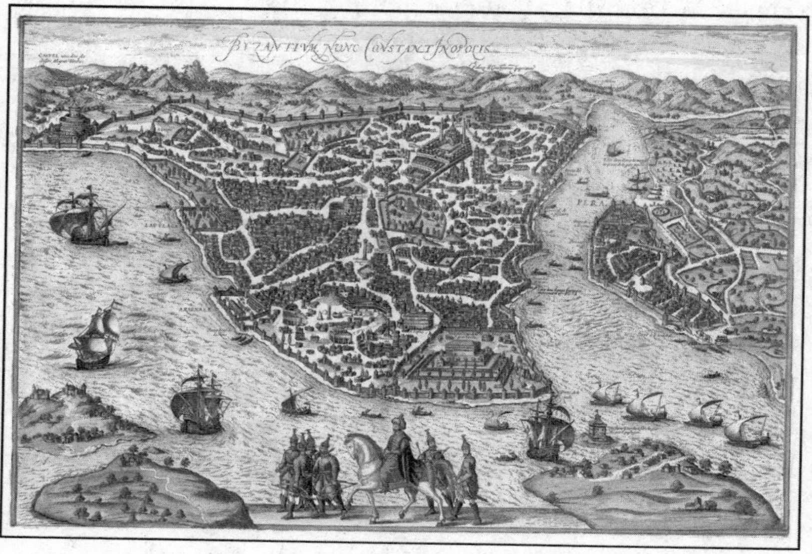

Woodcut of Constantinople in the early Ottoman Period by Giovanni Andreas Vavassore, ca. 1535.

Behind studded iron doors, large houses enclosed courtyards, with stables, cattle sheds, chicken coops and storerooms. Many wealthier homes were also centrally heated, using a hypocaust system inherited from the ancient Romans, although most relied on the heat given off by charcoal braziers. The kitchens usually contained a low hearth with a square pipe forming a chimney above. During the day, the skyline must have been fogged with woodsmoke from these chimneys. Many houses even had sewage systems that led out to sea.

Performers would have plied their trades in the streets: acrobats, jugglers and fire eaters. A bishop of Cremona, visiting in 949, describes one of these performances:

> A man carried on his head, without using his hands, a wooden pole twenty-four feet or more long. Then two boys appeared, who went up the pole, did various tricks on it, and then came down head first, keeping the pole all the time as steady as though it were rooted in the earth, which filled me with great astonishment and admiration.[8]

But of course, being poor in Constantinople was a pretty miserable existence. From the fifth century onward, skyscraper blocks of flats, of five to nine storeys, were built to serve as tenements for working people, just like in a modern city. These quarters were usually little better than slums. 'Constantinople is a city of extremes,' wrote Odo of Deuil, a visitor who passed through in 1147. 'She surpasses other cities in wealth, and she surpasses them in vice. [She] is squalid and fetid and in many places afflicted by permanent darkness, for the wealthy overshadow the streets with buildings and leave these dirty, dark places to the poor.'[9]

Constantinople was famous for its spice markets and perfumeries. 'Each market has gates which are closed upon it at night,' one visitor wrote. 'The majority of the artisans and salespeople in them are women.'[10] Another extract from the *Book of the Eparch*, an 895

CE handbook of city guild regulations, gives a sense of the heady aromas of these markets:

> Let them sell: Pepper, spikenard, cinnamon, aloes wood, amber, musk, incense, myrrh, balsam, indigo, sweet-smelling herbs, mint...in short any article which is used for perfumery or for dyeing. Let their counters stand...above the bronze portico, so that the sweet perfume may waft upwards... [and] permeate the vestibule of the imperial palace. Anyone contravening these rules shall be flogged, shaved and banished.[11]

On the days when imperial processions and religious ceremonies were held, the unpleasant smells of the medieval city were masked with wreaths of rosemary and pine chips, with rose petals and marjoram. But above all, visitors to the city were awestruck by its sheer size and magnificence. At half a million people, it was the largest city that Europeans would ever see. In the mid-tenth century, the poet Konstantinos of Rhodes wrote about the effect it had:

> After a long and wearisome journey, the traveller sees from a distance towers rising high into the air and, like strong giants in stride, columns that rise up to the highest point, and tall houses and temples whose vast roofs reach to the heights. Who would not become instantly filled with joy? And when he reaches the wall and draws near to the gates, who does not greet the city, lower his neck, kneel to the ground, and grasp the famous earth?[12]

But over the centuries, the world around Constantinople had changed. In Western Europe, the post-Roman era had given way to the Middle Ages, and the continent now comprised a patchwork of kingdoms whose people seemed crude to the sophisticated Byzantines. In Western Europe, a feudal system now dictated that the lords and ladies of the land were born into their right to rule. There it was impossible for peasants to rise above their stations—but in

Byzantium, there was no legal status given to nobles. Great families could fall, and others, such as Justinian's, could rise out of nowhere. Over its history, four emperors of Byzantium were women.

In the intervening years, the ancient capital of Rome had risen once again—not as an imperial power, but as the centre of Roman Catholicism and the seat of the Pope. Though the people of Western Europe spoke many different languages, they were united by their relationship to this Latin church. The differences in translation between the Greek and Latin religious texts naturally led to disagreement between the branches of Christianity, some of them exceedingly bitter. In 1054, an event known as the East-West schism tore the Christian world down the middle. All Latin churches in Constantinople were shut down, and excommunications were fired like volleys of arrows from one side of Europe to another. This rift only grew wider as time went on.

Having discovered how costly wars could be, the Byzantine Empire now preferred where possible not to fight. In the centuries following the rise of Islam, it became exceptional at projecting what we might call 'soft power'. Foreign kings were allowed to compete for the hands of Byzantine princesses, and to be given honorific titles of the empire. Many sent their young princes to be educated among the empire's sophisticated aristocracy. The Byzantines were expert at creating extravagant ceremonies that impressed and overwhelmed the ambassadors of foreign powers. The historian Anthony Kaldellis recounts the visit of one delegation from Asia Minor in the year 946 CE:

> The reception hall and its surroundings were decked out with silk hangings, laurel wreaths and flowers, and silver chains, and the hall was covered with Persian carpets and sprinkled with rose water. The entire court, thousands of people, stood in a prescribed order in full ceremonial regalia, acclamations were chanted to the accompaniment of organs, and the emperor sat on a throne that was imagined to be a replica of that of the Old Testament king Solomon. It was flanked

> by mechanical moving animals, including roaring lions and warbling birds, and could be lifted up into the air while the envoys were prostrate on the floor.[13]

All this theatre served to impress and terrify foreign delegations. It projected one simple message: you have arrived in the capital of the empire, the New Rome, the eye of the world. And, of course, when soft power failed, there was always the Byzantine army.

In the mid-tenth century, this was a formidable force of roughly 140,000 soldiers, or about five per cent of all adult males in the empire. To supplement this, the Byzantines also employed foreign mercenaries, usually small units of specialized soldiers from neighbouring lands. But easily the Byzantine's most powerful military asset was their capital, the unconquerable city of Constantinople. Over the centuries, they had increased its siege defences even further and constructed several hundred enormous underground water cisterns, so that they would never go thirsty during even the longest sieges. Just as impressive were the three open-air cisterns built near the Theodosian walls, which held a combined 600,000 cubic metres of water. Today, one of these vast cisterns houses a football stadium.

The Byzantines also cast an enormous iron chain, its links as thick as a man's arm, that could be winched across the entrance to the estuary of the golden horn, barring entry to the port. Time and again, the Byzantines would fall back to the defences of their city, and there no attacker was able to defeat them. But through the eleventh century, a new threat was rising that would ultimately force the empire into a difficult and painful compromise, and lead, in the coming centuries, to the ruin and waste of their great capital. This threat came in the form of the Seljuk Turks.

***

From their homeland near the Aral Sea, the Turks had built an empire that stretched across mainland Persia and the Middle East, capturing Baghdad and much of the Eastern Mediterranean coast.

In 1071, the Byzantine Emperor Romanos IV Diogenes considered them enough of a threat to march an army of 40,000 soldiers—comprising Byzantine troops and a large contingent of mercenaries, including Turkic soldiers—into Asia, to meet them at a place called Manzikert in what is now Armenia. The battle was a disaster: half of Romanos's troops deserted, and he became the first Roman emperor to be captured in battle in 900 years. While casualties of the battle itself were not enormous, this was a devastating blow to the empire's morale. When Emperor Romanos ransomed himself at the price of 1.5 million gold pieces, the surrender of several cities and the betrothal of his daughter to a Turkish prince, the embarrassment proved too much for his subjects. He was toppled from power and blinded, later dying from an infection related to his wounds.

The thirty-year period of civil war and court machinations that followed damaged the Byzantine state far more than their battlefield loss. As Byzantine armies destroyed one another, the Turks happily seized more of their cities, further depriving the empire of the economic base it needed to rebuild. In only a few years, the Byzantines had lost their heartlands in Asia, and their enemies on all sides were emboldened. The historian Anna Komnene, who was the daughter of Emperor Alexios, wrote the following mournful appraisal only a few decades after the battle:

> The fortunes of the Roman Empire had sunk to their lowest ebb. For the armies of the East were dispersed in all directions, because the Turks had over-spread, and gained command of, countries between the Black Sea and the Hellespont, and the Aegean Sea and the Mediterranean.[14]

Another eleventh-century Byzantine historian, Michael Attaleiates, strikes an even more moribund note, writing 'We were pressed on all sides by the bonds of death!'[15] For centuries now, despite their differences, Western Europe had relied on the Byzantines to hold back the ambitions of the various Muslim empires that had risen and fallen in Asia—but it was becoming increasingly clear that they couldn't hold out on their own forever. If Byzantium was to remain as a bulwark at the gates of Europe, it would need some radical help. Into this situation strode a militant and ambitious pope named Urban II.

Urban was a French noble, who had a vision of a new kind of aggressive, expansionist Christianity. For centuries, European pilgrims had travelled to Jerusalem, often passing through Byzantium, crossing the Bosphorus at Constantinople, before heading into Syria and down the coast of the Levant. But Urban had a vision of what he called an 'armed pilgrimage', a mighty flexing of the military muscles of Western Europe, which would spread fire and death in its wake. Soon, he would get his opportunity.

★★★

The eleventh-century Byzantine Emperor Alexios I Komnenos feared for the future of his empire. In 1093, he was desperate enough to send out a dramatic series of requests for help, 'heavy with lamentation and full of weeping, begging with tears for the aid of the entire Christian people',[16] as one Byzantine source has it. Alexios even turned to some of the empire's bitterest rivals, the Roman Catholic Church and the Pope, who the Byzantines diminutively referred to as 'the bishop of Rome'. Alexios had expected perhaps a few regiments of well-equipped Western knights to bolster his beleaguered armies—but he got much, much more than he bargained for.

On 27 November 1095, the Pope called together the Council of Clermont, and urged all those present to take up arms under the sign of the Cross. Urban declared that they would finally recover Jerusalem and the East from the Muslim powers. He also made the bold promise that all those who went to war on his behalf would be forgiven all their sins. To the sin-obsessed people of medieval Europe, this offer seemed too good to be true. The response was enormous. Anna Komnene gives one description of the arrival of this horde in her chronicle the *Alexiad*:

> After him came another innumerable, heterogeneous crowd, collected from nearly all the Frankish countries, together with their leaders, kings, dukes, counts and even bishops... One might have likened them to the stars of heaven or the sand poured out along the edge of the sea.[17]

This army is thought to have contained more than 100,000 people, a migration made up largely of mobs of poor peasants, who had marched across the continent, gathering new recruits and looting in every town they passed through. They had only got as far as the Rhineland when they ran out of provisions, and whipped up in righteous fury, attacked the sizeable Jewish population who lived there, massacring their villages and stealing their food and livestock. But eventually they did reach the fabled walls of Constantinople.

When Emperor Alexios saw this horde gathered outside his city, his blood must have run cold. One particularly unruly group led by a man named Peter the Hermit even began looting and burning Byzantine villages near the capital, and Byzantine troops had to be dispatched to restore order. Alexios must have wondered whether it might be wiser to take his chances with the Turks rather than this rabble of Latins. But he decided to make his deal with the devil. He allowed this crusader army to cross the Bosphorus, and march into the Holy Land. The crusaders, despite their general lack of experience, equipment and discipline, did well. They took the city of Nicaea in June 1097, and Antioch a year after that. Jerusalem was taken by assault on 7 July 1099, with the crusaders massacring the city's defenders.

For the next 200 years, there would be some form of crusader presence in the eastern Mediterranean and Levant. We shouldn't doubt the crusaders' religious convictions, but these also aligned conveniently with economic and strategic considerations. Just as it had been in the days of Ugarit and the Phoenicians, this stretch of coast was a crucial gateway through which trade goods entered the Mediterranean from the Silk Road. Here the Latins set up small crusader kingdoms, a kind of early prototype of the settler states that would later characterize European colonialism—and wealth flowed back to Europe through the old Phoenician ports of Acre and Jaffa.

Emperor Alexios had bet on the crusades—and for a period of about two centuries, the gamble paid off. Two subsequent crusader armies passed through Constantinople on their way to the Holy Land, and from 1100 onward, the five emperors of the Komnenos Dynasty presided over a century-long restoration of the military, territorial, economic and political position of the Byzantine Empire, while their Muslim rivals were busy fighting the constant influx of Latin armies. But the empire was on borrowed time. As the power of the crusades demonstrated, Western Europe was no longer a distant backwater; it had become a world of its own, with its own tensions, conflicts and interests. Alexios's deal had unleashed dark forces that would ultimately spiral out of control. This would come to a head during perhaps the most disgraceful campaign ever conducted by a crusading army in the east: the Fourth Crusade.

★★★

The goal of the Fourth Crusade was similar to those that had come before it: to recapture the Muslim-controlled city of Jerusalem, which had been retaken in 1187 by the Ayyubid dynasty of Saladin. Crusades had always been chaotic, poorly organized affairs, run as a kind of directed anarchy. But the Fourth Crusade set a new standard for chaos. The crusaders gathered in Venice in 1200 CE, but when they arrived, they found they didn't have enough money to pay for their transport onward to the Holy Land. The Venetians, seeing an opportunity, asked the crusaders if they would attack one of their rivals, the Catholic city of Zara in modern Croatia, then held by the Christian nation of Hungary. The crusaders, deciding that anything was justified if it ultimately ended with the recapture of Jerusalem, besieged Zara, sacked it and burned it to the ground. This act of violence against their fellow Christians shocked Europe, and Pope Innocent III issued an order of excommunication for the whole crusader army, excoriating their actions in fiery terms:

> To the counts, barons, and all the crusaders without greeting… Behold your gold has turned into base metal and your silver has almost completely rusted since, departing from the purity of your plan and turning aside from the path onto the impassable road, you have withdrawn your hand from the plough and looked backward with Lot's wife. For when you should have hastened to the land flowing with milk and honey, you turned away, going astray in the direction of the desert.[18]

The army leaders, perhaps wisely, chose not to pass news of their excommunication down to their men. But while many viewed this ungovernable force as a danger and a disgrace to Christendom, others saw in it an opportunity.

Alexios IV Angelos was a bitter man. He was the son of a Byzantine emperor, but his father had been deposed in a coup, and now he lived in exile with his brother-in-law, the King of Germany. Alexios had been told all his life that the people of Constantinople waited in anxious anticipation of his return, and he had long been scheming to make this happen. When he heard news of the failing Fourth Crusade, still heavily in debt to the Venetians, running out of money, and now wintering in the ruined city of Zara, he saw his chance.

Alexios offered the leaders of the crusade a simple deal: you take the city of Constantinople and put me on its throne, and I will open the treasuries of Byzantium, pay off your debts, and fund the rest of your crusade to Jerusalem. The leaders of the crusade jumped at the opportunity—but even on their journey to the city, they detected signs that Alexios's promises couldn't be relied upon, as one crusader leader, Count Hugh of Saint-Pol, recalls:

> Sailing from there, then, through the strait, we passed by the Arm of Saint George...one league from Constantinople. There, we were stunned, very much astonished, that none of the friends or family of the young man, who was with us, or any messenger of theirs came to him, who might tell him about the situation in the city.[19]

When the Fourth Crusade arrived at Constantinople on 23 June 1203, the metropolis had a population of approximately half a million. It was defended by a force of 15,000 soldiers, including 5,000 of the famed Varangian guard, Norse warriors who defended the kings of Byzantium. 'All those who had never seen Constantinople before gazed very intently upon the city,' wrote one crusader, Geoffrey of Villehardouin. 'There was indeed no man so brave and daring that his flesh did not shudder at the sight.'[20]

When they arrived, they found that the great defensive chain had been drawn across the Golden Horn, blocking access to the port. One side of this chain terminated in the tower of Galata, across the Golden Horn from the city—and so they determined to seize this tower and break the chain. They landed, charging their horses directly out of their transport ships, and beat back the tower's defenders—mercenary troops of English, Danish and Italian origin. On 6 July, the largest ship in the crusaders' fleet, the *Aquila*, smashed through the chain, and the port was opened to their fleet.

Next, the crusaders turned their attention to the city walls. On 17 July, they sailed into the Golden Horn and drew their ships up below the sea walls. They swarmed up the masts, scrambling across catwalks to reach the top. Other ships landed on the shoreline, and the crusaders used picks and shovels to hack away at a gateway that the defenders had hurriedly bricked up. The defenders sent the first assault packing, but the next day, the crusaders were successful. The Byzantine Emperor fled the city, and Alexios and his crusader friends swept in—not to the celebrations of its citizens as he had hoped, but to the jeers of all the people of Constantinople, sounding down to him from the walls.

Attack of the Crusaders on Constantinople—miniature in a Venetian manuscript, ca. 1330.

The crusaders sailed into the port of Constantinople, and Alexios Angelos was crowned Emperor of the Romans on 1 August 1203. Sir Hugh, writing to the Pope and trying his best to make his conquest of Constantinople look like it had been a good idea, reassured him of Angelos's promises:

> Our new emperor, with everything that he had promised us fully and completely rendered, bound himself to us by oath to cross the sea with us in next March's voyage, accompanied by ten thousand soldiers, and to provide food for one year to the entire army of the Lord.[21]

The actual situation was much different. When the previous emperor fled the city, he had taken with him more than 1,000 pounds of gold and some priceless jewels, leaving the imperial treasury drastically depleted. Clearly getting a little nervous about his new friends, Alexios gave leave for the Latin soldiers to take any priceless works of Byzantine art that they could find in the city's churches, outraging the city's people. These artefacts were destroyed and their gold melted down—but even then, Angelos barely made a dent in the sum he had promised the Latin warriors.

Riots broke out in the city, and, frustrated by their inability to fight with Muslims in the holy land, the crusaders began destroying Constantinople's mosques instead. But the city had not earned its reputation as 'the refuge of strangers' for nothing: its residents came out in force to protect their Muslim neighbours. In retaliation, the crusaders set the city ablaze, and the riots soon spiralled into a full-blown revolution against the new emperor Alexios. He was swiftly overthrown by a rebel leader named Doukas, and strangled in early February 1204.

The crusaders demanded that this new Emperor Doukas honour the debt that had been promised to them. When he refused, they embarked on a campaign of revenge and destruction that saw the city ravaged over three days of blood and fire. The crusaders systematically violated the city's holy sanctuaries, destroying or stealing all they could lay hands on. Thousands of Constantinople's civilian population were massacred. The famous bronze horses from the Hippodrome were torn down and sent back to adorn the facade of St Mark's Basilica in Venice, where they remain to this day. Other statues were melted down to make bronze coins, about which Niketas Choniates quips: 'Thus great things were exchanged for small ones.'[22]

Declaring a victory for Christendom, the crusaders selected a new emperor from among their own ranks, and divided the territory of the Byzantine Empire into various new crusader states. What followed was a period of Latin rule in Constantinople which lasted for the next sixty years or so—but the Latins soon found that governing this large and fractious empire was no easy matter. They lost one territory after another, until what was now called the Latin Empire was reduced to no more than the city of Constantinople. The last Latin emperor was Baldwin II, a man who would become known as 'Baldwin the Broke' due to his incessant money problems. He was even forced to sell some of the city's priceless Christian relics to keep the state running, including the supposed crown of thorns from Jesus's crucifixion. He was eventually ousted from his throne by a Byzantine lord, and much of modern Greece and the Asian territories returned to the empire. But it was now a much-diminished throne, and Constantinople a much-diminished city.

Over the decades since its sack, the population of Constantinople had barely recovered. By the end of the reign of Baldwin the Broke, the city was little more than a cluster of villages inside the ancient walls, separated by overgrown wasteland, fields and crumbling ruins. Even in the still-populated parts of the city, Constantinople must have been an eerie place. A century later, it would contain no more than 35,000 people, barely a tenth of the number it had been built to house. Its wide avenues and spice markets, its fairs and perfumeries, must have been virtually empty, silent and cold, as packs of dogs wandered through the lonely streets. The fourteenth century brought crop failures, and the devastating famine of 1315, followed quickly by an even greater disaster, one that would spread to every corner of Europe: the Black Death. The Greek writer Nikephoros Gregoras, wrote about the horrifying effects of this disease on Constantinople around 1346:

> It lasted for that whole year, passing through and destroying... the continental coast, towns as well as country areas... The prominent signs of this disease, signs indicating early death, were tumorous outgrowths at the roots of thighs and arms and simultaneously bleeding ulcerations, which, sometimes the same day, carried the infected rapidly out of this present life.[23]

By the fourteenth century, the Byzantine Empire had begun to look remarkably like its Western twin, nearly a thousand years before. The plague exacerbated its economic problems, and destructive civil wars broke out that fatally drained the empire's manpower and resources. In 1343, the empress dowager known as Anna of Savoy even took the drastic measure of pawning the empire's crown jewels to the Venetians in exchange for funds to fight her wars. The emperors now ruled under a shoddy construction of gilded leather and cut glass—a sad symbol of how far the fortunes of the empire had slumped.

Perhaps luckily for the Byzantines, their rivals were also suffering. While it mostly avoided the ravages of the plague, the Seljuk Empire was shattered by the arrival of the Mongol armies of Genghis Khan, and its territories were divided into a number of small Mongol client states, known as *beyliks*. But with the withdrawal of the Mongols, one of these states would soon expand to absorb the others, and regather some of the power that the Seljuks had once held. This state was led by a Turkish tribal leader named Osman, who would give his name to this new rising power. It would become known as the Ottoman, and its rise would spell the true end of Byzantium.

***

The Ottoman rise to power in Anatolia is wreathed in legend, and it can be difficult to separate fact from fiction—but it's clear they had great diplomatic skill, and the ability to raise large numbers of troops. Within ninety years of the first establishment of the Ottoman Beylik, the Byzantine Empire had once again lost all its Asian territories to this new power, which now extended its ambitions across the Hellespont, and onto the shores of Europe. In 1354, a powerful earthquake struck, and the Byzantine fortress at Gallipoli—on the European side of the waters—was all but destroyed. The Ottoman Sultan chose his moment to strike, crossing the water and seizing the area, quickly fortifying it. This was the Ottomans' first foothold in Europe, and their presence would only grow as the fourteenth and fifteenth centuries wore on. Soon, they would form a pincer around the city of Constantinople, and only its formidable walls stood between it and capture.

Sultan Mehmed II The Conqueror by a follower of Gentile Bellini, early sixteenth century.

Aghast, the western Latin powers put together a number of crusades in an attempt to halt the Ottoman conquests in Europe. In exchange for this help, the Eastern Church was forced to submit to the authority of the Pope. While some thought this a temporary measure to stave off the Muslim immediate threat, others saw it as a kind of cultural suicide. In response, one Byzantine admiral named Loukas Notaras is even supposed to have thundered: 'I would rather see a Turkish turban in the midst of the City than the Latin mitre!'[24] To many, it must have seemed that Byzantium had now pawned away not just its relics, its crown jewels and its famous works of art, but also its soul.

To add insult to injury, this spiritual compromise achieved very little. The Crusade of Nicopolis in 1396 was utterly routed by Ottoman forces. Half a century later, the Crusade of Varna met with an even more crushing defeat. These efforts distracted the Ottomans for some time, but their abject failures discouraged Western kings from sending any more aid to the dying Empire of Byzantium. The man who would finally topple the empire that had lasted for a thousand years was born in 1432. He was an Ottoman king known to history as Mehmed the Conqueror.

★★★

Mehmed had inherited an empire that held territory across much of what is today Turkey, as well as in Greece and Bulgaria—but Constantinople was the one territory in the midst of all this land that he couldn't yet lay claim to. At the age of twenty-one, in 1453, Mehmed decided to take his chances. But Constantinople, although reduced, was still a formidable target. It was guarded by only about 10,000 soldiers, but its triple line of land walls, built nearly a thousand years before, had never been breached.

Mehmed's first step was to cut off the city, and take control of the Bosphorus. But he knew that to bring down those walls, his armies would need a weapon of a size and power that the world had never before seen. To help him in this task, he hired the services of a radical Hungarian engineer named Orban. Mehmed asked Orban if he could build a cannon that would bring down the walls of Constantinople. Orban replied, 'I have examined the walls of the city in great detail. I can shatter to dust not only these walls with the stones from my gun, but the very walls of Babylon itself.'[25] The young sultan was impressed, and gave Orban everything he asked for. Three months later, he completed a cannon called Basilica, at the time the largest gun ever built. It was over 10 metres long, and weighed so much that it had to be dragged to the walls of Constantinople by a team of sixty oxen and 400 men, along with seventy smaller guns, which edged towards the city at a rate of only 4 kilometres a day. Slowly, Constantinople's death drew near.

When the Sultan arrived at the city on 2 April 1453—the Monday after Easter—he began the siege with a fearsome bombardment. Basilica was horrifically inaccurate—but when it landed a hit, the destruction it caused was immense. Iron cannonballs had yet to be developed, and so the cannon hurled smooth balls of marble or granite, each weighing three quarters of a tonne, a distance of more than a mile at the walls of Constantinople. Due to the immense amount of explosive used, the cannon had to be cooled with olive oil between shots. We can imagine the sweating Ottoman workmen toiling around this bronze monster, the air wavering above its superheated sides, the sizzle of oil and the sharp smell of gunpowder as each enormous plume of smoke burst from its gaping mouth.

The bombardment went on for forty-eight days, with repeated attempts by the Turks to storm the city—but even under this fearsome assault, the walls held. The siege of Constantinople is one of those historical events that has passed into legend, and its details are familiar to anyone with knowledge of military history: the fighting on the water; the defenders waiting for Venetian reinforcements that never came; the Turkish sappers digging tunnels under the walls, which the Byzantines always discovered; Sultan Mehmed's daring surprise plan to carry his boats over land on wooden rollers and into the waters of the Golden Horn past its long chain. During the siege, prayers were held daily in the Hagia Sophia, the austere chanting of the Byzantine monks soaring out over the imprisoned city. Cannon fire would have rolled outside the city like a thunderstorm, interspersed by the firecracker sounds of the smaller guns popping in the distance. The psychological toll of the bombardment must have been immense. As the mood inside the city darkened and food grew short, panic set in among its inhabitants. Nicolò Barbaro, a Venetian visiting Constantinople at the time, remembered the appearance of ominous signs in the sky overhead on 22 May:

> At the first hour after sunset the moon rose, being at this time at the full, so that it should have risen in the form of a com-

> plete circle; but it rose as if it were no more than a three-day moon, with only a little of it showing... The moon stayed in this form for about four hours... When we Christians and the pagans had seen this marvellous sign, the Emperor of Constantinople was greatly afraid, and so were all his nobles, because the Greeks had a prophecy which said that Constantinople would never fall until the full moon should give a sign.[26]

Barbaro notes the increasing panic among the commanders of the army too:

> Zuan Zustignan, that Genoese of Genoa, decided to abandon his post, and fled to his ship, which was lying at the boom... and as he fled, he went through the city crying, 'The Turks have got into the city!'... When the people heard their captain's words, that the Turks had got into the city, they all began to take flight, and all abandoned their posts at once and went rushing towards the harbour in the hope of escaping in the ships and the galleys.[27]

Finally, the time came. The Turkish soldiers, the elite Janissaries of the Ottoman Sultan, burst over the walls. Barbaro recalls the sound and fury:

> After being driven back from the barbicans the Turks again fired their great cannon, and the pagans like hounds came on behind the smoke of the cannon, raging and pressing on each other like wild beasts, so that in the space of a quarter of an hour there were more than thirty thousand Turks inside the barbicans, with such cries that it seemed a very inferno, and the shouting was heard as far away as Anatolia.[28]

Just like the soldiers of the Fourth Crusade 200 years before, the Ottomans rampaged through the city, and the bloodshed was tremendous—although with the city's reduced population, the casualties were much lower than before. It's said that when the Sultan

Mehmed stepped into the smoking ruins of the ancient Palace of Boukoleon, built by Emperor Theodosius in the fifth century, he uttered two lines by the famous Persian poet Saadi Shirazi, who had himself seen the devastation of the Mongol invasions:

> The spider weaves the curtains in the palace of the Caesars;
> The owl calls the watches in the towers of Afrasiab.[29]

The Byzantine Empire had lasted for 1,123 years and 18 days. But now the great liturgy that had echoed from the dome of the Hagia Sophia fell silent.

★★★

For many of the city's beleaguered inhabitants, its conquest was a trauma from which they could never successfully heal. The painful truth of history was converted into legend. One story concerned the priests who had been preaching in the Hagia Sophia when the city fell: instead of being massacred, the legend says, they had in fact melted into the south wall of the sanctuary, and when the city was back in Christian hands, they would return and take up their service at the point when they had been interrupted. Another story holds that rather than perishing in battle, the last emperor was turned into marble by an angel, and waits in a cave below the Golden Horn to one day return in triumph. Niketas Choniates, upon seeing the devastation of the city, wrote the following lament:

> As we left the city behind… I threw myself, just as I was, on the ground and reproached the walls… 'If what you were built to protect is no more, for what purpose do you still stand?… What shall become of us? Whither shall we go? What consolation shall we find in our nakedness, torn from thy bosom as from a mother's womb?'[30]

As its people told these stories, Mehmed the Conqueror moved his imperial capital to Constantinople, and a great cultural shift took place. Turkish people now settled in large numbers in Byzantium—

but the city would leave just as indelible a mark on its conquerors. Indeed, Mehmed II would long claim that the Ottoman Empire was a continuation of the Roman Empire, not an end to it. He gave himself the title of Caesar, and allowed the Byzantine Church to continue functioning. In his palace he collected a library which included works in Greek, Persian and Latin, and gathered Greek scholars at his court. He even invited a Venetian painter to come and paint his portrait.

Byzantium left its mark, too, on the religion of Islam. The crescent moon had been the symbol of the Byzantine Empire since as early as 670 BCE, in honour of the Greeks' patron goddess Artemis, the hunter. After the capture of Constantinople, Mehmed adopted it for his own banner, changing it slightly into a waxing moon, as it had been on the day of the city's conquest. This crescent would become the official standard of the Ottoman Empire, and by the twentieth century had become recognized internationally as the official symbol of Islam.

As Constantinople fell, the city that had once accepted refugees from all corners of the world now sent its own people streaming across Europe—and wherever they went, Byzantine refugees brought with them the ancient learnings of the Greeks, of Demosthenes and Xenophon, Thucydides, the dialogues of Plato, Aeschylus and Homer, and the works of Polybius, Appian and Cassius Dio. In 1488, some thirty years after the fall of Constantinople, Dimitrios Chalkokondylis published the first Greek book to be printed in Florence: a printed edition of the *Iliad* and *Odyssey*. Many of the classical sources referred to in this book have only survived because they were copied down in the libraries of Byzantium. Edward Gibbon once summarized the seismic effect this had on European learning:

> The restoration of the Greek letters in Italy was prosecuted by a series of emigrants who were destitute of fortune and endowed with learning...the natives of Thessalonica and Constantinople escaped to a land of freedom, curiosity and wealth, and taught their native language in the schools of Florence and Rome.[31]

These refugees would tutor scholars like the humanist philosopher Marsilio Ficino and the Italian poet Poliziano in Florence. The Medici family of Italy became patrons of one Byzantine lecturer, establishing the Platonic Academy of Florence. The fall of Byzantium sowed the seeds of what would become the European Renaissance, and as one age ended, another began.

The Fall of Byzantium disrupted long-established trade routes that joined Europe to Asia along the Silk Road, forcing European traders to search for new routes to the markets of the East, and develop maritime technologies. Within forty years of the siege of Constantinople, European explorers rounded the southernmost cape of Africa, opening up the sea route to India, and just a few years later their desire to find a western route to Asia would lead to the discovery of the Americas. Christopher Colombus had been inspired to undertake his voyage in part because of the ancient Greek text known as the *Geographia*, written by the philosopher Claudius Ptolemy, which had been preserved in the libraries of Byzantium and brought to Western Europe after its fall.

Byzantium would also continue to welcome the tired and huddled masses of the world to shelter behind its walls. In 1492, the same year that Colombus discovered Hispaniola, European antisemitism reached fever pitch, and the Jews of Spain were expelled by the royal Alhambra Decree. Sultan Bayezid II, the eldest son of Mehmed the Conqueror, dispatched the Ottoman navy to escort the Jews safely to his lands, where they could settle. For another generation at least, the city of Constantinople would earn the title that once emblazoned its name in the European imagination: 'refuge of strangers, queen of the queens of cities'.

For the longest time, the memory of Byzantium has been buried, not only beneath the streets of modern Istanbul, but in the study of history, too. The eighteenth-century writer Montesquieu described the Byzantine Empire as 'a tragic epilogue to the glory of Rome',[32] and European Enlightenment thinkers overwhelmingly shared this view, seeing it as a relic of the past, unchanging and static, that had played little part in the history of Europe.

The modern Turkish author Orhan Pamuk, in his 2005 memoir *Istanbul: Memories and the City*, writes about how the memory of Byzantium has been lost:

> Like most Istanbul Turks, I had little interest in Byzantium as a child. I associated the word with spooky, bearded, black-robed Greek Orthodox priests... To me, these were remnants of an age so distant that there was little need to know about it. As for the Byzantines, they had vanished into thin air, or so I'd been led to believe. No one had told me that it was their grandchildren's grandchildren's grandchildren who now ran the shoe stores, patisseries and haberdashery shops of Beyoğlu.[33]

Today, the ruins of the Theodosian walls of Constantinople still trace their battered and crumbling route from the Sea of Marmara to the Golden Horn, through the modern city of Istanbul. These walls serve as a testament to the power of the people who turned the remnants of Rome into a flourishing and stable empire, a well-spring of art and culture, and a repository of the knowledge of the ancients that would pass its wealth on to the generations that came after. They stand as a symbol of the empire that never truly died, but lives on today, ingrained in the fabric of the cultures of both East and West, Christian and Muslim, and reaching back down the ages—from the time of the ancients to the dawn of a new world.

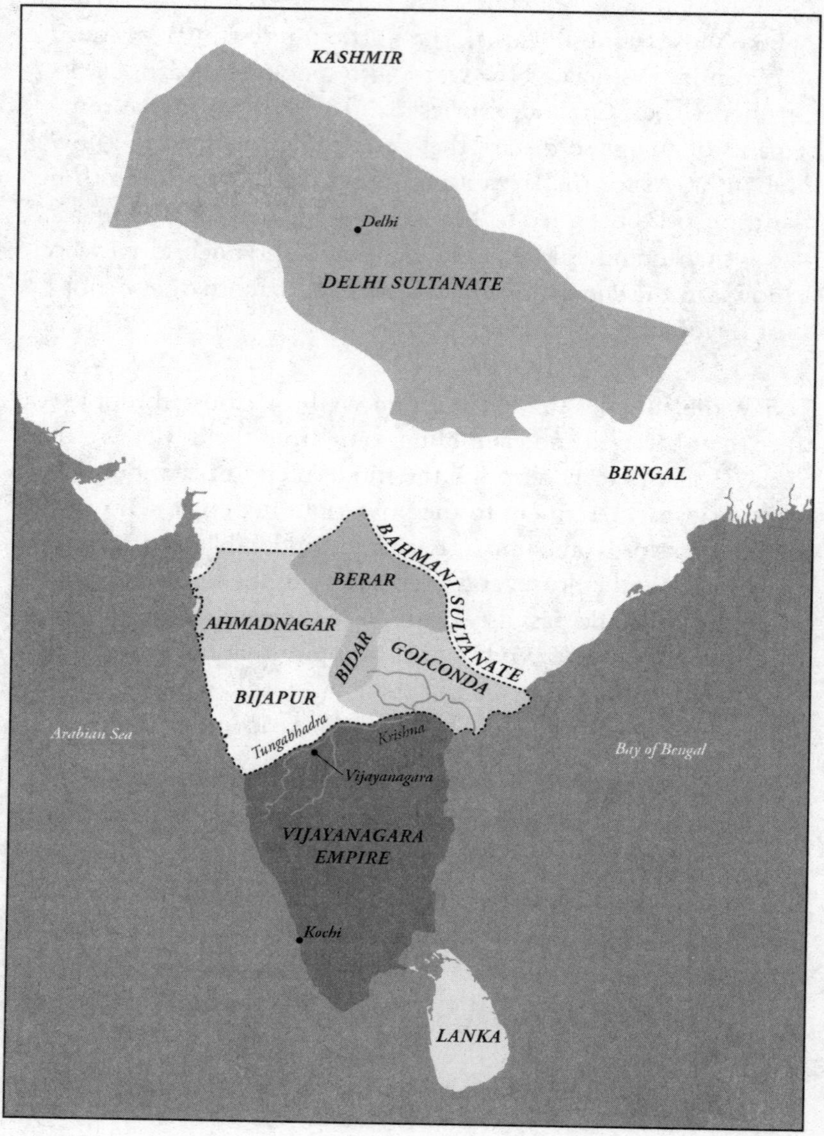

KASHMIR
Delhi
DELHI SULTANATE
BENGAL
BAHMANI SULTANATE
BERAR
AHMADNAGAR
BIDAR
GOLCONDA
BIJAPUR
Arabian Sea
Tungabhadra
Krishna
Vijayanagara
Bay of Bengal
VIJAYANAGARA EMPIRE
Kochi
LANKA

10

Vijayanagara

1336–1646

Today, the lands of India are united in a single modern nation—but it is perhaps one of the most diverse nation states on earth, and certainly the largest with so many different cultures within its borders. The citizens of Tamil Nadu, Karnataka, Maharashtra, and all the twenty-eight states of modern India, are as different from one another as those of France, Germany and Italy. They vary in their traditional dress, diet, ritual observances, and in the twenty-two major languages spoken across the subcontinent. But perhaps the most marked differences from region to region are in the realm of religion.

Today, the word 'Hinduism' is applied clumsily to the great variety of religious traditions that originate in India, and take as their starting point the ancient Sanskrit texts of the Vedas, first recorded in writing around 3,500 years ago. Many Hindus refer to their religion as *Sanātana Dharma*—the eternal way, or the eternal duty—but Indian religion was never united or systematized under a central authority. Though many people now consider these diverse traditions, sects and orders to be a single religion, in the past they were seen as significantly different, and hostility has often existed between them.

In very simple terms, Hindus believe in one god, named Brahman, who is refracted into many different aspects, the way a beam of white light refracted through a prism can be shown to contain many colours. The ancient text the *Maitri Upanishad* explains this concept, in which each living being also contains a spark of this original god:

> Verily, that One became threefold…eightfold, elevenfold, twelvefold, into an infinite number of parts… [He] has entered into and moves among created beings; He became the overlord of created beings. That is the soul within and without—yea, within and without![1]

Although Brahman can manifest in many ways, most Hindus predominantly worship one of two manifestations of this supreme power: Shiva and Vishnu. In Hinduism, Shiva is both the creator and the destroyer, a beautiful and fearsome god who represents the primal energy of the universe. He is often depicted as a dancer, pirouetting the universe from creation to destruction and back, on and on into eternity. Shiva embodies the idea that life and death are part of the same process: a beautiful mushroom might spring out of the decay of a fallen oak; the flesh of a gazelle gives life to the lion; the fall of one civilization gives rise to another.

Vishnu, on the other hand, is the preserver: the one who holds things together, if only for a time. Whenever the need arises, he appears on earth in human form, embodied as great mythical heroes like Rama and Krishna, and ensures that the world retains its balance. The tales of these heroes are told in a vast collection of texts, and the greatest of these is known today as the *Mahabharata*, or 'Epic of India'. The *Mahabharata* has similarities in theme and scope with Homer's epics, and with ancient compendiums of history and myth such as the Bible. It tells the story of how the lands of north India were divided in two by a war between two great powers, and ends in a great, world-ending battle, after which the age of heroes and giants comes to a close—and our age, the final age of man, begins. At around 1.8 million words, the *Mahabharata* is perhaps the longest piece of literature ever written—roughly ten times the length of the *Iliad* and *Odyssey* combined—and it forms a chaotic and magnificent tapestry of myth and legend that has few equals.

In the past, India has often been depicted by historians as a kind of geographical fortress, sealed off on every side by the mountains and sea—but in fact, this is far from the case. The seas that might appear to hem it in were actually busy highways, with constant trade and traffic connecting India to the Persian Gulf and Red Sea on one side, and Cambodia, Sri Lanka, Indonesia and China on the other. Indian pepper and cinnamon flavoured the meals eaten by faraway Roman senators, and an Indian bronze Buddha figurine has even been found in a ninth-century Viking grave on the small Swedish island of Helgo. In the north-west, the mountains of Pakistan and Afghanistan were a formidable boundary, but a number of routes like the Khyber and Bolan passes cut through their rugged cliffs, and allowed Alexander the Great to march his large army into the Punjab in the fourth century BCE. He would be followed by many other would-be conquerors down the ages. And while the Himalayas were the most impenetrable boundary of all, that didn't stop Indian Buddhism from spreading across them into Tibet, and onward, reaching as far north as Japan.

However, as the world entered the second half of the first millennium, India's contact with the outside led to a new religion entering the diverse mix of Indian belief. The younger faith of Islam would bring both conquest and culture. It would create a rift that split the subcontinent in two, but would also connect it to the capital cities of the wider world and bring a new age of prosperity and advancement. The arrival of Islam to India heralded a time of paradoxes, contrasts and ironies—and chief among these was that it spurred the rise of one of the greatest Hindu empires on the Indian Peninsula: the Empire of Vijayanagara.

***

The history of Islam in India is long and complex. According to traditional claims, it arrived on the shores of the subcontinent during the life of the prophet Muhammad, brought by traders who arrived by sea from the Persian Gulf—but while in the south Islam arrived along these trade routes, the arrival of Islam in the north was a much less peaceful affair. As we have seen, the Muslim empire emerged swiftly, recreating the conquests of Alexander, and rising to become a major power within twenty years of the prophet Muhammad's death—clear proof, for its devotees, of the divine nature of Islam's revelations. But like Alexander's empire after his death, its territory soon broke apart into separate kingdoms. Each of these was ruled over by sultans—a word derived from the Arabic *sultah*: 'power' or 'authority'—and now stretched across the Middle East, North Africa and Central Asia.

For a few centuries, the sultanates did not progress beyond the boundary of the Indus River in the north—but in the early 1190s a warlord called Muhammad Ghori invaded from the Ghor region of Afghanistan and captured the regional capital of Delhi—establishing his own Muslim kingdom there. By the year 1300, the Delhi Sultanate had established a lasting power that stretched from the Indus Valley to the Bay of Bengal, from the foothills of the Himalayas to the arid plateau of the Deccan in central India. This power was Sunni Islamic, culturally a blend of Turkic and Persian traditions, and in its more stable moments, its rulers dreamed of expanding ever further into the south, and eventually raising their banner over the entire subcontinent. These dreams would finally be realized by perhaps the most complex and controversial figure to ever rule India—a man named Muhammad bin Tughluq.

Muhammad bin Tughluq was a mercurial ruler. On one hand, he was an intellectual, a lover of poetry, an expert in the Quran and Islamic law, who could speak Persian, Arabic, Turkish and Sanskrit. Like all the sultans of Delhi, he was Muslim, but was mostly tolerant of other religions, and was the only sultan recorded to take part in his people's Hindu festivals. On the other hand, all that erudition could not disguise his darker side.

His court scholars record that he came to the throne after the death of his father and his brother, the crown prince, in a freak accident, when a pavilion that they were sitting under collapsed. 'A thunderbolt from the sky descended upon the earth,' writes one scholar named Barani, 'and the roof under which the sultan was seated fell down, crushing him and five or six other persons so that they died.'[2] However, the traveller Ibn Battuta was visiting Delhi at the time, and records quite a different version of events—that, in fact, the pavilion had been rigged to collapse:

> The scheme was that whenever the elephants would tread on one side of it, the whole building would fall in ruins... And the elephants were led up from one direction as was planned. And when they walked on that side, the pavilion fell in on the Sultan and his son Mahmud. Muhammad bin Tughluq gave orders to fetch axes and mattocks in order to dig for them, but he made a sign to delay, and in consequence they were not brought out until after sunset. They cleared away the ruins, and found the sultan dead, with his back bent over his son to protect him.[3]

As with many rulers who come to power through treachery, Muhammad bin Tughluq spent his reign in a state of deep paranoia. He doled out extremely harsh punishments, often executing those who displeased him—and this cruel streak earned him the epithet 'Muhammad *Khuni*', or 'Muhammad the Bloody'. One chronicler, the Persian scholar Firishta, who settled in India in the sixteenth century, wondered at how 'So little did he hesitate to spill the blood of God's creatures that...one might have supposed his object was to exterminate the human species altogether.'[4] Another report by the Portuguese writer and traveller Fernão Nuniz even recounts a popular story about how he once declared war on the sun, after it had the temerity to shine into his eye.

Despite this arbitrary ruler, by this time, the power of the Delhi Sultanate was seemingly unstoppable. It continued to grow, swallowing up a South Indian people known as the Kakatiyas, and other surrounding Hindu kingdoms. By the 1350s, the sultanate stretched for thousands of kilometres, forming a belt across India from sea to sea, nearly encompassing the entire peninsula. The threat must have put all the Hindu rulers of South India on high alert. But the mad Sultan Muhammad bin Tughluq died in 1351, and after his death, the Sultanate of Delhi began to disintegrate. Many of its newly conquered lands rose up in rebellion. Opportunist enemies to the north soon got word of the anarchy, and in 1398 the Turko-Mongolian warlord Timur descended on Delhi and put it to the sword. Timur had no intention of staying in India; he simply gathered up loot, women and slaves as he passed through, and returned to his capital of Samarkand, in modern Uzbekistan. But like the sacking of Rome, his destruction of Delhi tore the heart out of an already struggling empire.

Into this terrain of blood and fire, two brothers would rise from obscure beginnings, and transform this region. They would move the centre of Indian power from the Muslim north to the Hindu south, and build a city that would stand among the greatest in the medieval world. They were known as the Sangama brothers, and their names were Bukka and Harihara.

★★★

The exact origins of the Sangama brothers are wreathed in mystery. Many historians believe it's likely that Harihara and Bukka were commanders of the southern Hoysala Empire, stationed on the Tungabhadra River, in what is now the state of Karnataka, with orders to repel any Muslim incursions from the north. Other myths recount how they were captured and held as prisoners of war by the Delhi Sultanate. Whatever the case, it's clear that as the Delhi Sultanate collapsed, Harihara and Bukka raised a considerable army, which included large cohorts of Muslim mercenaries—possibly former sultanate soldiers who were no longer getting paid—and fought to establish an independent Hindu state in South India. The historian Robert Sewell recounts one legend about Harihara:

> During his reign this chief was one day hunting amongst the mountains south of the river when a hare, instead of fleeing from his dogs, flew at them and bit them. The king, astonished at this marvel, was returning homewards lost in meditation, when he met on the river-bank the sage…named Vidyaranya or 'Forest of Learning,'…who advised the chief to found a city on the spot.[5]

This fable offers an illuminating image of how the young power of Vijayanagara would come to see itself: as the hunted rabbit who turned round and learned how to bite. With this force, the brothers set out to capture the areas that the disintegrating Delhi Sultanate had left unguarded. Within a few decades, they would absorb a large and wealthy portion of South India. At their former post, an unassuming village on the rocky banks of the Tungabhadra River, they laid the foundations of a city that would announce the arrival of this new and confident power. They named it Vijayanagara, from the Sanskrit *vijaya*, meaning victory, and *nagara*, meaning city: the city of victory.

Vijayanagara was a city of soaring temples and wide avenues, with sophisticated urban planning—and it was also a formidable fortress. The surrounding landscape is dominated by huge granite boulders, heaped up into impassable hills that provide excellent natural defences, while the torrential Tungabhadra River protected it on the north side, almost impossible for an army to ford. The brothers enhanced these natural defences by fortifying the passes between the hills with strong gates and towers. These massive walls, which can still be traced in the landscape, enclosed an area of more than 650 square kilometres. An ambassador for the Timurid ruler of Persia, a man named Abd al-Razzaq Samarqandi, visited in the early 1440s. 'It is built in such a manner that seven citadels and the same number of walls enclose each other,' he wrote. 'The seventh fortress which is placed in the centre of the other occupies an area ten times larger than the marketplace of the city of Herat.'[6] These ramparts were manned by soldiers who surveyed the broad roads that ran in and out of the city. Between the concentric rings of walls were areas filled with obstructive boulders known as 'horse stones', designed to guarantee that any attacking army would have a difficult time advancing, while the soldiers of Vijayanagara rained arrows down on their heads.

Looking at the wider region around Vijayanagara, it's not hard to see why they considered these defences essential. Across the region, a number of Muslim kingdoms had emerged from the fragments of the Delhi Sultanate, and of these the most powerful was the Bahmani Sultanate. According to tradition, the Bahmani Sultanate was founded by an army commander named Zafar Khan, who had served under the erratic Sultan Muhammad bin Tughluq before declaring independence in 1347. It quickly grew into an impressive dominion in the heart of South India that would last for the next 170 years. And for the people of Vijayanagara, it represented a constant looming threat on their border.

***

Nationalist historians in India and in the West have often framed the conflict between these two medieval kingdoms in cultural terms, imagining the kingdom of Vijayanagara as a bastion, defending Hindu culture against Islamic invaders—but there's little evidence that the rulers or citizens of Vijayanagara thought this way. One inscription from the time of the Sangama brothers depicts the Bahmani sultans as just one of their enemies, with the others being rival Hindu kingdoms:

> When his sword began to dance on the battlefield, the faces of the Turushkas (Turks) shrivelled up, Konkana Sankaparya was filled with fear, the Andhras ran into caves, the Gurjaras lost the use of their limbs on every road, the Kambojas' courage was broken, the Kalingas suffered defeat.[7]

Here there is no hint that the Bahmanis were any more despicable to the kings of Vijayanagara than the many Hindu kings with whom they fought equally long and bitter wars. Indeed, the idea of a unified Hindu identity simply didn't exist in the fourteenth century. In fact, conflict between the Bahmani sultans and Vijayanagara most often arose over practical and economic matters, like access to resources, supply lines and trade routes. One bitter issue of contention was a fertile tract of land between them, rich in iron, gold and diamonds, known as the Raichur Doab. Other conflicts would break out over wealthy port towns on the east and west coasts, which controlled trade with the Muslim world and were a crucial conduit for the most important military resource of the time: warhorses imported from Arabia, Persia and Central Asia.

Thanks to their close trade and cultural links to the rest of the Muslim world, the Bahmanis were always better supplied with horses, and so their sultan would became known as *Ashvapati*, the 'lord of horses', while the kings of Vijayanagara were known by the title *Narapati*, the 'lord of men'—alluding to their armies of massed infantry. The kings of the Gajapatis in the east, with their vast stables of elephants, became known as the 'lords of elephants', completing the triangle.

In the early days, Vijayanagara's infantry force was no match for the horsepower of the Bahmani sultans—and the tradition of learning across the Muslim world also gave the Bahmanis a technological advantage. One of the first sultans, Muhammad Shah Bahmani, was an early adopter of the new technology of gunpowder weaponry, which had reached India from China via the Mongols. At this time, it was used mostly to create exploding projectiles to be fired from catapults, and occasionally crude rockets—but soon the sound of cannon fire would ring out over the battlefields of medieval India, and the Bahmani sultans' head-start with this technology would put them in a strong position in the coming centuries.

For these reasons, although it was the larger and often wealthier kingdom, Vijayanagara frequently found itself on the losing side of wars with its Muslim neighbour. These were not, however, wars of conquest. The two kingdoms would fight over a sea port, a strip of land or a certain fort—but when the result became clear, the loser would sue for peace, pay an enormous sum of money to the victor, often hand over a daughter in marriage, and return home. There was never any suggestion that one side would conquer and consume the other. Still, the Bahmanis were of growing concern to the kings of Vijayanagara.

Despite the danger of its northern rival, from the mid-fourteenth century, the city of Vijayanagara grew steadily from the centre of a wealthy kingdom into a great world capital. It would soon house as many as 300,000 people, at a time when Paris, the largest city in Europe, had little more than 200,000 inhabitants. By 1500, with the Cambodian city of Angkor now depopulated, Vijayanagara was probably the world's second-largest city after Beijing—and it was probably India's richest.

An 1868 photograph of Hampi by Edmund Lyon, showing the ruins of the Hampi bazaar, and the distinctive granite boulder landscape.

Vijayanagara was truly a city of stone: all its palaces and stables, its towers and walls, even the ordinary houses were carved out of solid blocks of granite cut from the surrounding terrain. 'The city of Bidjanagar simply has no equal in the world,' wrote Abd al-Razzaq. 'It is such that the pupil of the eye has never seen a place like it, and the ear of intelligence has never been informed that there existed anything to equal it in the whole world.'[8] In the early sixteenth century, the Portuguese traveller Domingo Paes also visited:

> The size of the city cannot all be seen from any one spot, but I climbed a hill whence I could see a great part of it; I could not see it all because it lies between several ranges of hills. What I saw from thence seemed to me as large as Rome and very beautiful to the sight.[9]

Vijayanagara was divided into several districts, each with a unique character. In an area known today as the sacred centre, the Virupaksha temple still soars out of the ruins of the city. The streets here would have been full of the sounds of chanted hymns and clanging temple bells, incense smoke and the pleas of the faithful as they came to pray, to be healed, to be closer to the gods. Further south lay what's been termed the urban core, a large walled area that contained both houses and markets, as well as workshops, rest houses and other places of business. There were temples for Jains here, as well as Hindu followers of both Vishnu and Shiva, and one area with a mosque. The Portuguese traveller Duarte Barbosa, arriving in Vijayanagara around 1501, gave the following description of this district:

> The folk here are ever in such numbers that the streets and places cannot contain them. There is a great traffic and an endless number of merchants and wealthy men... The King allows such freedom that every man may come and go and live according to his creed, without suffering any annoyance and without inquiry whether he is Christian, 'Jew,' Moor or Heathen.[10]

Barbosa pays particular attention to the smells that wafted from the spice markets: 'Here also is used vermillion, saffron, rosewater, great store of opium, sanders-wood, aloes-wood, camphor musk...and scented materials. Likewise much pepper is used here and everywhere throughout the kingdom, which they bring hither from Malabar.'[11]

We can imagine scenes of family life, children running in the streets, woodsmoke billowing overhead. Men gathered to play games of chance and strategy on street corners, while chewing betel nuts and leaves, which are still chewed across India for their mild stimulant effect. The day of an average citizen of Vijayanagara would have started with a visit to a local bath house. Men and women had separate bathing places, which were available at different times of the day. After bathing, families would go to their local temple to give offerings and receive blessings for the day ahead. Shopkeepers in this part of the city and everywhere else would have needed to be constantly alert to the mischief of the monkeys—the red-faced rhesus macaques, and the silvery Hanuman langurs—huge troops of which still live in the region. Now, as then, these animals love nothing better than to drop down from shop awnings and steal food from anyone who has let down their guard.

Krishna Temple tank and shrine, photographed in 1856 by colonial photographer Alexander Greenlaw.

From outside the city walls, lines of bullock carts, laden with local produce like rice, millet, squashes and other vegetables, would have snaked through the lacework of surrounding towns, roads and fields, heading for market. Towering over it all was the royal centre, an area of monumental palaces and mansions that were home to the wealthy elite. While they were Hindu, it's clear these elites had great admiration for their Muslim rivals to the north. The architecture of their homes clearly displays a blend of South Indian and Islamic styles. Some wall paintings in Vijayanagara even depict the court wearing Muslim fashions for formal events: tall caps and flowing gowns. On one hand, the rulers of Vijayanagara clearly modelled themselves on the South Indian empires of the past, like the Chalukyas, the Pandyas and the Cholas—but they also evinced a radical and forward-looking desire for new influences, from the Muslim world and beyond. After all, in the fast-moving world of medieval India, kingdoms that fell behind didn't last long.

Soon one king in particular would come to power who was determined to modernize and hybridize Vijayanagara, and end the days of paying tribute to the powerful Muslim kingdoms to the north. His name was Deva Raya II.

★★★

Deva Raya II was a boy when he came to the throne as the *raya* (ruler) of Vijayanagara in 1432. Abd al-Razzaq, who visited some ten years later, describes the young king:

> The king was dressed in a robe of green satin, around his neck he wore a collar, composed of pearls... He was of an olive colour, of a spare body, and rather tall. He was exceedingly young, for there was only some slight down upon his cheeks, and none upon his chin. His whole appearance was very prepossessing.[12]

Aspiring to turn his empire from a defensive, inward-looking kingdom into a modern state, Deva Raya sent out word to the Muslim world that Vijayanagara's doors were open. He welcomed talented Muslims into his court, and enlisted as many as 200 Muslim officers into his army, giving them homes and even building a mosque in Vijayanagara. 'He also commanded that no one should molest them in exercise of their religion,' writes Firishta, 'and moreover, he ordered a Koran to be placed before his throne on a rich desk, so that the faithful might perform the ceremony of obeisance in his presence without sinning against their laws.'[13]

Vijayanagara would soon have a thriving Muslim quarter. Some carvings on the great temples show Muslims taking part in the daily life of the city: Arab horse handlers taking care of their steeds, and beturbaned Muslim riders rearing up on these imported horses. To these Muslim mercenaries would soon be added units of Muslim gunners, trained in the use of muskets. Deva Raya II also engaged in large infrastructure projects, digging vast networks of irrigation canals that expanded the agricultural potential of the land around the city, allowing the metropolis to boom to an even greater size.

In 1443, Abd al-Razzaq, despite having arrived from the wealthy Silk Road city of Samarkand, was struck by the resplendence of the citizens of Vijayanagara:

> All the inhabitants of the country, whether high or low, even down to the artificers of the bazar, wear jewels and gilt ornaments in their ears and around their necks, arms, wrists, and fingers… The king has many elephants in the country, but the large ones are specially reserved for the palace. The king has a white elephant, exceedingly large, with here and there as many as thirty spots of colour. Every morning this animal is brought into the presence of the monarch; for to cast eye upon him is thought a favourable omen.[14]

He even gives a bashful account of the city's apparently thriving red light district, reporting that 'The splendour of those houses, the beauty of the heart-ravishers, their blandishments and ogles, are beyond all description. It is best to be brief on the matter.'[15]

When al-Razzaq was brought in to meet the nineteen-year-old king, Deva Raya bombarded his visitor with questions about the Muslim powers of the world—how many horsemen the King of Persia had under his command, what his great nobles were like, and how they behaved, what the great cities of Herat and Shiraz were like, and so on—clearly showing his curiosity and admiration for the Muslim world.

But things at court were not always plain sailing, and the king sat at the top of a fragile hierarchy packed with jealous rivals. While Abd al-Razzaq was staying in the city, Deva Raya II was the target of one particularly dramatic assassination attempt by one of his brothers, which shows how dangerous ruling Vijayanagara could be:

> This unnatural brother…drew forth the poignard, and wounded him several times severely, so that the monarch fell down behind the throne; and the perfidious wretch, be-

> lieving that he was dead, left one of his myrmidons behind to cut off the king's head. He himself rushed out to the portico of the palace, and exclaimed, 'I have killed the king, his brothers, the nobles, the ministers, and the other chiefs, and I am now your king.'[16]

But he had not counted on Deva Raya's resilience. As the soldier approached to decapitate him, the King fought back in dramatic fashion:

> But when the bravo advanced to fulfil his murderous orders, the king, seizing the seat behind which he had fallen, dealt with it such a blow upon the breast of the villain, that he felled him to the ground…and ran out of the chamber by the way of the female apartments. While his brother, seated at the head of the tribunal of justice, was inviting the people to recognize him as their sovereign, the king himself came forward and exclaimed, 'Behold, I am alive and safe, seize the assassin.' The multitude immediately bore him down, and slew him.[17]

Deva Raya II did eventually die in 1446. He had left his kingdom a larger, wealthier and more outward-looking place than he had found it—but the period that followed was one of chaos and dissolution. Deva Raya's son is said mysteriously to have died of a broken heart, perhaps a euphemism for poison, while his grandson who next took the throne was murdered by his own son, who would go on to be killed by his own younger brother.

Observing the chaos among the royal family, soon the commanders of the military hungered for power themselves. One of these, a general named Saluva Narasimha, seized the throne in a military coup in 1485, and ended the Sangama Dynasty that had ruled since the founding of Vijayanagara 150 years earlier. Saluva Narasimha was a poet and self-styled expert in lovemaking, but he didn't seem to care much for the boring business of ruling the kingdom. He spent much of his reign writing a long book of detailed erotic instruction, and died only a few years after taking the throne.

During the reigns of the hapless kings that followed, in 1498, a small fleet of four Portuguese ships, captained by the explorer Vasco de Gama, arrived in South India—the first European to ever successfully complete this journey by sea, and he returned with cinnamon and pepper, silk and jewels. For the first time, Europeans had circumvented the Silk Road, and a new system of global trade would supercharge their economies in the centuries to come. The Portuguese would soon set up a trading post at Goa, on India's west coast, and for centuries to come Europeans would continually increase their presence and influence in India. The King of Vijayanagara at the time offered one of his daughters in marriage to King Manuel of Portugal, in exchange for sending a Portuguese princess to marry him, so that 'two kings would be allied for the purpose of joint actions on land and sea… [that] the blood of the two royal houses would mingle'.[18] The Portuguese declined the offer. But other than this, the appearance of these foreigners excited little attention in the court of Vijayanagara.

The time of upheaval was put to an end with the reign of the most famous of the emperors of South India. He was a ruler named Krishnadeva Raya—the last great king of Vijayanagara.

★★★

Krishnadeva was never meant to be king. He was the son of a lower-ranking queen than his two brothers, and so they both got a shot at ruling before he did. But they catastrophically mismanaged the kingdom, and faced constant rebellions and uprisings. When Krishnadeva's brother lay on his death bed, he was determined that his own infant grandson should take the throne. He ordered that his brother should be blinded, which under Indian law would disqualify him from ruling. According to legend, the King's servants brought him the eyes of a recently slaughtered goat, and told him that his wishes had been carried out. The King died satisfied that his line was secure, and Krishnadeva took the throne as Krishnadeva Raya. Domingo Paes described the new king as 'of medium height, and of fair complexion and good figure, rather fat than thin; he has on his face signs of small-pox,' and praised him as 'a great ruler and a man of much justice, but subject to sudden fits of rage.'[19] Paes also records that the King was what we might think of as a fitness fanatic:

> This king is accustomed every day to drink a *quartilho* (three-quarter pint) of oil of sesamum before daylight, and anoints himself all over with the said oil; he covers his loins with a small cloth, and takes in his arms great weights made of earthenware, and then, taking a sword, he exercises himself with it till he has sweated out all the oil, and then he wrestles with one of his wrestlers. After this labour, he mounts a horse and gallops about the plain in one direction and another till dawn, for he does all this before daybreak.[20]

Krishnadeva Raya showed a similar energetic attitude to his rule. One of his first acts was to bring the troublesome elephant lords of the nearby Gajapati kingdom back under his control, seizing important forts along the way. This victory must have boosted his reputation at home, and fed what was apparently an enormous ego. 'Overcome by his glory,' gushes one royal inscription, 'the sun sinks into the western ocean as if quite unable to endure the distress of mind.'[21] But Krishnadeva was also an eminently practical man. He published a series of political maxims in his work *Amuktamalyada* that contained advice for how a kingdom should be ruled:

> A King should improve the harbours of his country and so encourage its commerce... Make the merchants of distant foreign countries who import elephants and good horses attached to yourself by providing them with daily audience, presents and allowing decent profits. Then those articles will never go to your enemies.[22]

The Virupaksha Temple tower (gopura) as it appeared in 1856.

Under Krishnadeva, the Vijayanagara Empire nearly doubled in size. To mark his accession, in 1510 he ordered the construction of a grand gateway tower, known as a *gopura*, to adorn the temple to the god Virupaksha. This remarkable structure was built on mathematical principles, using a fractal design in which individual elements of the tower resemble the whole. This gives the tower a mesmerizing shape and represents the infinite repetition of universes that lies at the heart of Hindu cosmology.

This was a true golden age in South India—a time of peace, stability and prosperity. But it was not to last. In little more than fifty years, this vast city would be destroyed, emptied of its population and left to crumble into the earth. And this dramatic downfall began with what, at the time, must have felt like a brilliant victory: the collapse of their longstanding rival, the Bahmani Sultanate.

***

Like Vijayanagara, the Bahmani Sultanate had for decades been enthusiastically importing people from across the Muslim world:

soldiers, architects, artists, holy men and scholars. They had helped to transform it into a world centre of culture and innovation—but this policy also had its costs. The Indian Bahmanis felt increasingly resentful of the newcomers, mostly Persian-speaking Iranians who they referred to as 'The Westerners'. Towards the end of the fifteenth century, this anger turned mutinous. When the enraged ruler of the city of Ahmednagar rebelled in 1490, the other regions soon followed.

By 1518, nine years into Krishnadeva Raya's reign, the Bahmani Sultanate had fractured into five individual kingdoms, all fighting among themselves. The power of the Bahmani sultans had evaporated in a matter of years, and Vijayanagara was now all but unchallenged in the south of India. For Krishnadeva Raya, now in his late forties and nearly a decade into his reign, this chaos presented an obvious opportunity. That rich triangle of land known as the Raichur Doab, with its fertile farmland and mineral wealth, was now in the hands of Ismail Adil Shah, the Sultan of Bijapur. In 1520, Krishnadeva Raya marched an army of 100,000 soldiers across the Tungabhadra River and laid siege to the fort of Raichur.

This conquest would not be as easy as Krishnadeva hoped. The kings of Vijayanagara had not taken advantage of the developing technology of the cannon as their Bahmani rivals had, and they also lacked effective siege equipment. The Hindus resorted to old-fashioned tactics, hacking away at the fort walls with pickaxes and hammers. The defenders meanwhile, well-stocked with cannons, rained down fire and death from the walls. It seemed like the siege would last forever, until Krishnadeva got word that the Sultan of Bijapur himself was marching an army towards him, equipped with nearly a thousand of the latest powerful cannons imported from Persia. Perhaps feeling a tremble of apprehension, Krishnadeva lifted the siege and went out to meet the Sultan in battle. When the two armies met, the Sultan ordered his cannoneers to fire all their guns at once, in a devastating volley. His hope was that the psychological impact of the massive bombardment would break the will of the Vijayanagara soldiers—and he was right: a thousand cannonballs tore through the Vijayanagara ranks, forcing them to retreat.

It looked like all was lost for Vijayanagara. But, as the Portuguese witness Fernão Nuniz recalls, Krishnadeva Raya refused to admit defeat. He rallied his generals and elite cavalry around him and gave them a stunning and quite ruthless order:

> 'Who ranges himself with me?' he cried.... Then he took a ring from his finger and gave it to one of his pages, so that he might show it to his queens in token of his death. Then he mounted a horse and moved forward with all his remaining divisions, commanding to slay without mercy every man of those who had fled.[23]

Krishnadeva and his generals managed to make them turn and run in the opposite direction, towards the Bahmani forces. The pure crushing weight of these bodies, backed by as many as 27,000 horses, turned the tide back on the Muslim soldiers. The Sultan's cannons, having all fired at once, had to reload all at the same time, and they were unable to summon another volley before they were overrun. Krishnadeva's forces drove them into the Krishna River, where a massacre began. The rabbit had once again turned and bitten its pursuer.

Krishnadeva Raya now besieged the fort of Raichur, with the support of a company of Portuguese mercenaries who had brought with them the latest arquebuses. This type of long-barrelled gun achieved an astonishing degree of accuracy for early firearms—so much so that one of these Portuguese snipers was apparently able to kill the fort's commander when he raised his head above the rampart, with either a very skilful or a very lucky shot:

> The captain of the city seeing the dismay that had spread amongst his people, began to turn them back with encouraging words... And he, wishing to see for himself where the Portuguese were, reached over with his body in front one of the embrasures and was killed with a *musquet*-shot that struck him in the middle of his fore-head.[24]

THE SUMERIANS

The marshes of southern Iraq preserve a sense of the landscape in which the Sumerian cities arose. **Photo Credit: Gustavo Olgiati**

The standard of Ur—war side (top) and peace side (bottom), c. 2600 BCE.

The Ziggurat of Ur as it appears today. Much of the visible brickwork dates from ill-advised reconstruction efforts under Saddam Hussein.
Photo Credit: Khezez

THE LATE BRONZE AGE COLLAPSE

The ruins of Ugarit. An ancient port city in northern Syria in the outskirts of modern Latakia, Ugarit grew to impressive wealth, until it was dismantled during the Late Bronze Age Collapse. **Photo Credit: Alen Ištoković**

The mortuary temple of Ramesses III at Medinet Habu, where his battle with the Sea Peoples is memorialized. **Photo Credit: Asta**

THE ASSYRIANS

Artist's impression of the city of Nineveh, from *The Monuments of Nineveh* by Sir Austen Henry Layard, 1853.

The Lion Hunt of Ashurbanipal, showing the style of Assyrian palace carvings at their most developed. By 612 BCE, perhaps as little as twenty-five years after these were made, the empire had fallen apart and Nineveh had been sacked and burned. **Photo Credit: Carole Raddato**

CARTHAGE

View across the bay of Tunis from the hill of Byrsa. In the foreground are Punic ruins. **Photo Credit: Mourad Ben Abdallah**

The Punic port of Carthage, still visible in the landscape of the Tunisian capital, Tunis. The circular port, or 'cothon,' was home to Carthage's formidable navy, while the longer rectangular port in the foreground was for docking civilian vessels. **Photo Credit: Citizen59**

HAN CHINA

The ruins of an ancient watchtower from China's Han Dynasty (202 BCE–220 CE) in Dunhuang, Gansu Province, China. The tower was part of the old line of rammed-earth fortifications that once stretched along the Hexi Corridor. **Photo Credit: The Real Bear**

A mural from a Han-era tomb in Luoyang, showing typical dress of the period. **Photo Credit: Gary Todd**

ROMAN BRITAIN

A stretch of Hadrian's Wall about one mile west of the Roman fort near Housesteads. **Photo Credit: Steven Fruitsmaak**

The extensively reconstructed Roman Baths in Bath, England.
The darker lower sections of the pillars show the extent of the Roman remains. **Photo Credit: Travel Bild**

THE MAYA

The Pyramid of the Sun in Teotihuacán, in central Mexico. Evidence shows that the people of Teotihuacán exerted significant influence over the Mayan city of Tikal before apparently collapsing. **Photo Credit: Maciej Cisowski**

The temples of Tikal, visible over the forest canopy. **Photo Credit: USAID Biodiversity & Forestry**

THE KHMER

TOP:
Ta Prohm Temple, Angkor, Cambodia. The temple's stele records that the site was once home to more than 12,500 people. After the fall of the Khmer Empire in the fifteenth century, the temple was abandoned and has become host to vast strangler figs and silk-cotton trees.
Photo Credit: James Wheeler

BOTTOM:
Angkor Wat, the crowning glory of the city of Angkor.
Photo Credit: Max Mishin

BYZANTIUM

The Hagia Sophia in Istanbul. The current structure was built by the Byzantine emperor Justinian I as the Christian cathedral of Constantinople for the Byzantine Empire between 532 and 537 CE. **Photo Credit: Shutterstock**

The partially reconstructed Theodosian Walls of Constantinople, showing their three-layered defences. **Photo Credit: Shutterstock**

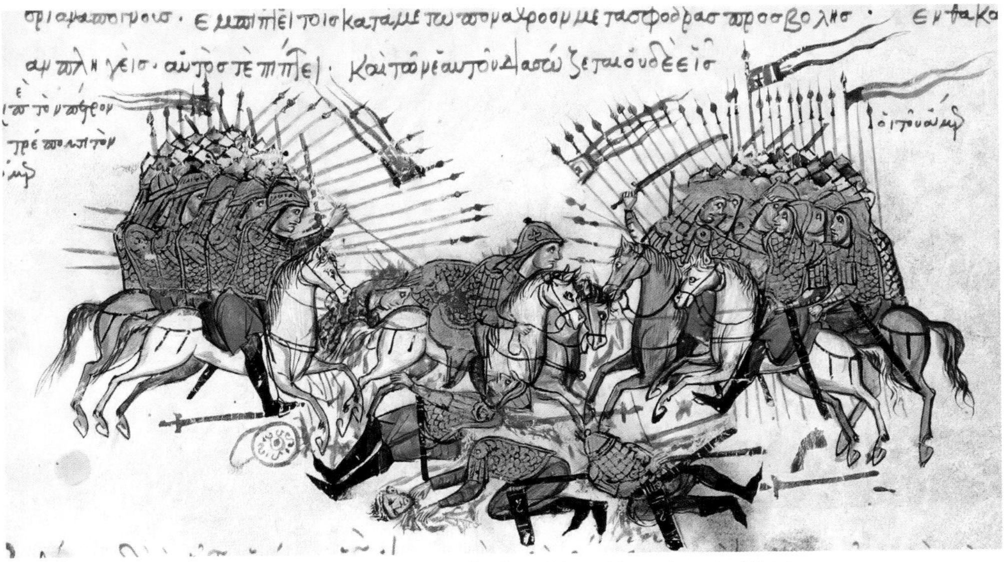

Clash between Byzantines and Arabs at the Battle of Lalakaon (863) and defeat of Amer, the emir of Malatya.
Chronicle of John Skylitzes, cod. Vitr. 26–2, fol. 73va, Madrid National Library.

The medieval Galata Tower, a watchtower in the Genoese colony
in Constantinople with the Hagia Sophia and Blue Mosque in the distance. **Photo Credit: Shutterstock**

The gopura (temple tower) of one of Hampi's temples, with the distinctive rubble landscape visible behind it.
Photo Credit: T. Veerababu

SONGHAI

The Great Mosque of Djenné in Mali, the largest mud-brick building in the world. **Photo Credit: Ralf Steinberger**

The Dogon village of Songo, in the mountainous border region of Bandiagara in Mali, West Africa. **Photo Credit: Shutterstock**

THE AZTECS

The remains of the Templo Mayor (Great Temple) of Tenochtitlan, excavated from beneath modern-day Mexico City. The temple was built in subsequent layers like a Russian doll, and the vestiges of former temples can be seen within its structure.
Photo Credit: Arterra Picture Library

A modern CGI reconstruction of how the city of Tenochtitlan may have looked. **Photo Credit: Thomas Kole—A Portrait of Tenochtitlan project**

THE INCA

The site of Machu Picchu, showing habitations, streets, and terraces for cultivation. **Photo Credit: Beto Huaman Moreano**

The zigzagging walls of the Inca fortress of Sacsayhuamán, which overlooks the capital of Cusco. **Photo Credit: José Solis Cruz**

EASTER ISLAND

Ahu Tongariki, Rapa Nui. The largest of the ahu platforms found on the island, Ahu Tongariki houses fifteen moai statues. While the statues were all toppled at some point, they were re-erected in the twentieth century. **Photo Credit: Shutterstock**

Two of the buried 'stone heads' situated beneath the Rano Raraku quarry. Although they have bodies, these moai have been buried up to their necks in the run-off from the quarry. **Photo Credit: Lachcim Kejarko**

Raichur fort surrendered soon after. These rich, contested lands now belonged to Vijayanagara. But Krishnadeva Raya's victory caused a ripple of concern among the kingdoms of the region, especially those that had once been part of the Bahmani Sultanate. A number of diplomats were dispatched from neighbouring kingdoms to urge the king not to try to expand his empire further. If he ignored their warnings, they said, the kingdoms would be forced to unite against him. With our gift of hindsight, we know that Krishnadeva should have taken this threat very seriously—but instead he sent each of them the same reply: 'I pray you do not take the trouble to come hither, for I will myself go to seek ye if ye dare to await me in your lands;—and this I send you for answer.'[25] In fact, Krishnadeva was so emboldened that he decided to do what no king of Vijayanagara had dreamed of before. That was to march north and seize the Sultan's capital city of Bijapur itself.

★★★

Bijapur was one of the largest and wealthiest cities in the lands that had once been part of the Bahmani Sultanate. It was a centre of culture, trade and commerce, as well as of learning and scholarship, and contained a number of lavish gardens and water pavilions. Fernão Nuniz travelled with Krishnadeva Raya as he embarked on this campaign far into enemy territory, and recalls catching sight of Bijapur as Krishnadeva's armies approached: 'It has numbers of beautiful houses built according to our own fashion, with many gardens and bowers made of grape-vines, and pomegranates, and oranges and lemons, and all other kinds of garden produce.'[26]

Meanwhile, seeing Krishnadeva's army on the horizon, the Sultan of Bijapur did the only thing he could: he fled the city and went into hiding. Krishnadeva entered the city with little resistance, and decided to stay there until the Sultan handed himself over and consented to kiss the foot of Krishnadeva Raya. As it turned out, this was a long time. During their stay in the city, to keep themselves warm and fed, Krishnadeva Raya's soldiers demolished its beautiful buildings for firewood, and they drank its reservoirs dry:

> The city was left almost in ruins—not that the King had commanded it to be destroyed, but that his troops, in order to make fires for cooking, had torn down so many houses that it was a great grief to see. The Sultan Adil Shah sent to ask the King what wrong the houses had done that he had commanded to destroy them; for there remained no other houses standing save only the palaces, where the King Krishnadeva was staying. The King sent answer that it was not he who had done it, but that he could not control his people.[27]

Eventually, the drinking water supply exhausted, Krishnadeva was forced to leave. He had not captured the Sultan of Bijapur, but he had certainly made his point. Vijayanagara was without doubt the strongest power in South India. The destruction of Bijapur was a stinging reminder to the sultans in the region that if they continued fighting among themselves, a greater enemy to the south would swallow them up, one by one.

★★★

Krishnadeva Raya died on 17 October 1529. His eldest son had been poisoned as a child—a victim of palace intrigue—and his next son was too young to be considered. So on the king's death, the crown passed to his feckless younger brother Achyuta. Nuniz remembers him as 'a man of very little honesty' who 'gave himself over to vice and tyranny'.[28] With the credibility of the crown so compromised, a number of opportunists fancied their chances at seizing the throne. Chief among these was a divisive and ruthless social climber named Rama Raya.

Rama Raya began his career as a courtier in the kingdom of Golconda, to the north of Vijayanagara. But he had a keen nose for opportunity, and during the reign of Krishnadeva, he made his way south to the Hindu court to serve him. Rama Raya's mother was the daughter of a chieftain in the east, affording him enough social standing to marry one of the King's daughters—and as the now son-in-law to Krishnadeva Raya, the ambitious Rama Raya worked to increase his power and influence in the court. When the feckless Achyuta died after ruling for thirteen years, Rama Raya raised a successful rebellion and placed a young boy, a distant nephew of Krishnadeva, on the throne. As the boy's regent, Rama Raya, then aged around fifty-seven, became the true power behind the throne. When this young king reached adulthood, and suggested that he might now be old enough to take over the reins of the state, Rama Raya had him imprisoned. The boy king would now appear only once a year to the crowds, while Rama Raya acted as emperor. By 1562, even these annual appearances were stopped, and Rama Raya was the unchallenged head of state.

One of the great composers of this time was a man named Kanaka Dasa, who lived through this period. One of his famous songs describes how many of the citizens of Vijayanagara must have felt, as the kingdom descended into corruption over the twenty-three years of Rama Raya's regime:

> Where did truth and duty go? The noble can't survive anymore,
> thieves and habitual adulterers strike it rich, the rest are poor.
> ...
> No one pays the soldiers, no helping rains shower the earth.
> Those with food and clothes are corrupted by bribery.
> ...
> Worshippers of Shiva are clashing with the Vishnu devotees.
> Great offerings are made to the most horrific violent gods.
> Who could list all the wrongs of the time?[29]

Rama Raya's devious plotting was not restricted to matters in his own court. The sultans of the Deccan often asked for Vijayanagara's help in their wars against one another, and Rama Raya happily allied himself first with one, then another, with the hope of thereby weakening them all, and often breaking his promises not to destroy mosques or unnecessarily hurt Muslim civilians. One of these sultans, Husain Nizam Shah I of the Sultanate of Ahmadnagar, grew to particularly hate Rama Raya. Firishta recalls one meeting between them, when the King of Vijayanagara openly insulted his guest:

> At the time of the meeting, Ramraj [Rama Raya] showed great vanity and loftiness and remained seated, and had Husain Nizam Shah kiss his hand in this manner. Husain Nizam Shah was furious at the improper behaviour of Ramraj, and in order to reproach the Raja, he at once, in that very company, called for water and washed his hands. On seeing this, Ramraj was enraged and said in the Kannadi language, 'If this man were not my guest, I would instantly cut him to bits with my sword.'[30]

The final straw apparently came when Rama Raya sent Husain a long and insulting list of demands for tribute. According to a Muslim poet named Hasan Shauqi, this included camels from Kabul, ambergris, aloes, musk, a large silver bell, a golden flute, weapons such as maces and Bahmani daggers, jade pitchers, ruby cups, diamond cubes, and—most insulting of all—the foot bracelets of the Sultan's wife. Finally, he demanded that Husain stop eating beef, and convert to worshipping Shiva. If he refused, the poet relates the following threat allegedly delivered by Rama Raya.

> I'll spare neither Turk nor Turkish bow,
> I'll spare neither rich nor poor,
> I won't spare a single scholar or holy man,
> Neither aged nor youth,
> Neither young man or old.[31]

Whether this episode is true, or just one of Shauqi's many poetic flourishes, what is certain is that Husain had had enough. He put aside his differences with the other sultans of South India, and they united against Rama Raya. The sultans sealed their tentative alliance with marriages, even exchanging forts as part of the dowries, in order to settle the territorial disputes that had divided them. Through Rama Raya's arrogance, Vijayanagara had united its enemies against it, and they were now all marching south, hungry for revenge.

The year was 1565, and Rama Raya was now well into his

eighties. Still, when he heard of the combined forces of the sultans marching south, he was determined to ride out with his great army and lead it to victory. He had good reason to be confident. Despite their alliance, the sultans of the Deccan were still no match for Vijayanagara. According to records, Rama Raya marched out with 70,000 cavalry, and more than 500,000 foot soldiers—the entire army of Vijayanagara brought to bear for a final, decisive battle for the future of South India. It's not clear how many soldiers the sultans brought to the battle, but it's clear that the odds didn't look good. They were not only outnumbered, but had also lost the advantage in firepower that their ancestors had enjoyed. In the more than forty years since the armies of Krishnadeva had scraped a victory at Raichur, Vijayanagara had truly joined the gunpowder age. Some sources say that Rama Raya marched to meet the sultans with a thousand cannons, while others put the number at more than 2,000. After a few skirmishes, the two armies finally met on 23 January 1565, on the plains that stretch alongside the Krishna River. Today, this confrontation is remembered by the name of a fortified town about 25 kilometres to the north: Talikota.

The armies of the sultans had also learned lessons from their defeat forty years earlier. They now had decades of experience in using cannons on the battlefield, and their tactics had evolved. They had brought with them gunners from Turkestan—then considered the best in the world. This time, instead of arranging their cannons in a single line that fired all at once, they were placed in three staggered lines, creating an almost continuous blanket of fire. When the battle began, the forces of Vijayanagara unleashed a barrage. Firishta recounts how 'Both armies being in motion soon came to battle, and the infidels began the attack by vast flights of rockets and rapid discharges of artillery.'[32] But the superior firepower of the sultans gained the upper hand. One source named Rafi' al-Din Shirazi describes how the Muslims packed their cannons with copper coins, in one of the first uses of what would become known as 'grapeshot'. These superheated coins would have torn into the Vijayanagara soldiers.

Rama Raya was carried around the battlefield in a palanquin. At one point, he's said to have sat on a throne, surrounded with piles of jewels and coins, handing them out to anyone who would charge into the heat of the battle. Despite the sultans' powerful guns, it seemed that once again the overwhelming numbers of Vijayanagara would win the day. Firishta writes that 'the Sultans began to despair of victory, and even to prepare for retreat.'[33] But then something happened to turn the tide completely.

According to Firishta, one of the Sultan's elephants stampeded into the lines of Rama Raya's men, right towards the King of Vijayanagara—and in the path of the raging animal, his palanquin bearers fled, abandoning their king to be captured. Rama Raya was brought to Husain and beheaded. Firishta recounts how the head was 'placed on the point of a long spear, that his death might be thus announced to the enemy.' After this, 'when they saw their chief destroyed, [they] fled in the utmost disorder from the field, and were pursued by the allies with such success, that the river was dyed red with their blood.'[34] Those who were able, with horses and elephants, fled the battlefield, while a huge number of foot soldiers were left behind to be massacred. The historian Mirza Ibrahim al-Zubairi, in his work *Basatin al-Salatin*, recalls how the sultans paused to rest and nurse the sick and wounded. 'Then they turned toward Vijayanagar.'[35]

***

We can imagine the scenes as the frightened people of Vijayanagara watched the columns of the wounded and battle-stained soldiers winding down the road without their leaders, telling stories of the defeat. But they knew what to expect. When the armies of the sultans arrived, the leaders of Vijayanagara would have to admit defeat, and agree to pay up an enormous sum in reparations. Some of Rama Raya's brothers managed to escape the battlefield and make it back to the city. They were now the assumed leaders of the empire, and might have been expected to begin amassing a tribute payment to buy off the Muslim victors. Instead, the brothers gathered up all the treasure they could find, piled it into ox carts and fled, leaving the city to its fate. Vijayanagara was now without an army, without leaders, and, crucially, without any money to pay off its enemies. When the sultans' armies arrived, and found that the city's treasuries had been emptied, they began a campaign of looting. Over the next days and weeks, they stripped Vijayanagara of any wealth it had left. The Muslim poet Shauqi, unsurprisingly, describes this event in triumphant terms:

> The Shah ordered the plunder of the city,
> The order was given to both noble and commoner,
> They then rendered the city desolate,
> They harassed and killed.
> Both open and hidden wealth were revealed,
> Treasure was brought up from beneath the ground.[36]

Another Muslim scholar, al-Zubairi, claimed that

> they razed the lofty buildings and temples to the ground. The work of destruction was carried out with a vengeance... During the confusion and disorder following the Muslim invasion, the citizens out of fear lurked in their houses, cellars, wells, and reservoirs. Those that were well to-do betook themselves to the neighbouring mountains and caverns with their family and chattels... The Muslim army remained at Vijayanagar for about six months. To a distance of twenty leagues round the city everything was burnt and reduced to ashes.[37]

With the sacking of the city, its empire fractured. 'The city itself was so destroyed, that it is now totally in ruins and uninhabited,' wrote Firishta. 'The country has been seized on by the tributary chiefs, each of whom hath assumed an independent power in his own district.'[38]

But the archaeological evidence suggests that the destruction was not as thorough as some of these accounts claim. In fact, fire damage has been observed only in the central temple and royal districts. Buildings such as the main palace complex and audience hall were burned, as well as others that represented the royal authority of the state. But in the residential parts of the city, the houses and markets, the destruction was much less pronounced, and there is no evidence of a wholesale burning of the city, or of an enormous massacre. Still, the city does seem to have undergone a dramatic reduction in its population. The Italian merchant Cesare Federici, who visited and wrote an account two years afterwards, reports:

> The foure kings of the Moores entred The sacking of the city Bezeneger with great triumph, & there they remained sixe moneths, searching under houses & in all places for money & other things that were hidden, and then they departed to their owne kingdomes, because they were not able to maintaine such a kingdome as that was, so farre distant from their owne countrey…the city of Bezeneger is not altogether destroyed, yet the houses stand still, but empty, and there is dwelling in them nothing, as is reported, but Tygers and other wilde beasts.[39]

With their leaders gone, their administration collapsed, and the entire empire fragmenting, the people of Vijayanagara could not maintain their city. Bit by bit, the stone buildings that had survived the invading army were dismantled, or simply left to the vines and wild dogs. The great city of victory became a ghost town, and eventually even its grand name was dropped in favour of the name of one of its smaller districts: Hampi. Birds soon made their homes in the temple roofs: Indian robins, large grey babblers, blue rock thrushes, quails and the rare yellow-throated bulbul. Grasses, and later banana and coconut palms and frangipanis would sprout in the streets and yards, lifting the flagstones with their roots. Monkeys and bats would colonize the broken staircases and roof vaults.

In the year 1800, a Scottish captain by the name of Colin Mackenzie was travelling in the south of India, when he visited the ruined city of Vijayanagara, by then largely abandoned for more than 200 years. Mackenzie's visit to the ruins is recorded in a journal he kept at the time, which has never been published, but which survives in the British Library. In his neat, curling cursive, Mackenzie records what it was like to wander through the overgrown ruins of this great city, as his guides told him what they could about its history:

> South and half southwest of Anagoondy are still remaining many great ruins of the ancient city: palaces, pagodas, droogs and fortifications, to which the people give the name of Allputtoon, or 'the ruined city'. The Palaces with the grand stables for elephants and horses are there to be seen. Westward…a line of basins and cups cut out of fine black stones and placed on each side of a water conduit. They say that here was formerly the king's garden.[40]

Here and there, families of monkeys would have clambered over great boulders, chattering and chasing one another. Mackenzie climbed up onto the rocky granite hills nearby, and from there sketched the first comprehensive map of the site. He was not a man given over to poetry, and he let his maps and sketches do the talking. But beside his map, he does describe in terse form the sights that he saw as he explored the ruins.

The Garuda Temple, Maha Mandapa and Eastern Gopura of the Vitthala Temple complex in Hampi/Vijayanagara, by Alexander Greenlaw, 1856.

Only a few decades later, in the 1850s, another East India Company officer, one Colonel Alexander Greenlaw, would visit the ruined site with an early camera, and would take photographs of the ruins in their undisturbed condition. In them, we can see the carved edifices overgrown with mosses, growths of cactus-like euphorbia and grasses, their ornate cupolas strangled by vines. We can see the beautiful bathing houses spilling over with waterweeds, the halls of long-dead kings now silent and shaded beneath cracking roofs. In his journal, Mackenzie describes the sight of the city, now sunken beneath the earth:

> This place is now almost ruined, but its remains are still very magnificent and curious. The houses of the inhabitants are entirely destroyed, and the ruins now form high banks and eminences under which are buried many great houses whose terraces are level with or sunk below the soil. Many of these we see in passing among the inner ruins.[41]

★★★

After the fall of their capital, the fugitive kings of Vijayanagara continued to rule in a much-diminished form for several decades, shifting their courts to their remaining territories in southern Andhra. In their grandeur and ceremony, their processions and festivals, they attempted to recreate past splendours—but they now ruled over a tiny portion of what they once had. By the dawn of the seventeenth century, that power too evaporated, and the last of Vijayanagara's lords disappeared into obscurity. With the economic heart ripped out of the empire, towns and villages around the city of Vijayanagara and on the nearby coasts also went into decline. The dance of Shiva went on, and another empire passed into ruins.

In 1626, little more than sixty years after the battle of Talikota, the British East India Company built its first fortified port near the coastal town of Pulicat. This town was once the gateway by sea to the Vijayanagara Empire, but in the decades since its collapse, the town had fallen on hard times. The fort the British built was shoddy and indefensible, and the trading company abandoned it after only six years—but two years later, the British tried again, a little further to the south, at a small fishing village called Madraspatnam. It's said that the site was chosen because the head of the company factory, Francis Day, had fallen in love with a Tamil girl who lived nearby. At this time, the land was ruled by one of the lords left over from the fragmented and scattered Vijayanagara Empire. He was more than happy to grant a lease to that small and humble parcel to this foreign company in exchange for a share of their takings. This was the first true foothold of the British East India Company in India, a foothold that would grow into colonial domination of the entire landmass—and it came out of the weakness and dissolution of the Empire of Vijayanagara. Around the globe, the new age would bring about an unprecedented collision of human societies. Some would survive this contact, while others would crumble entirely.

PART 3

WORLDS COLLIDE

The old is dying and the new cannot be born;
in this interregnum a great variety of morbid symptoms appear.

Antonio Gramsci, *Prison Notebooks*
(Translated by Quintin Hoare and Geoffrey Nowell-Smith)

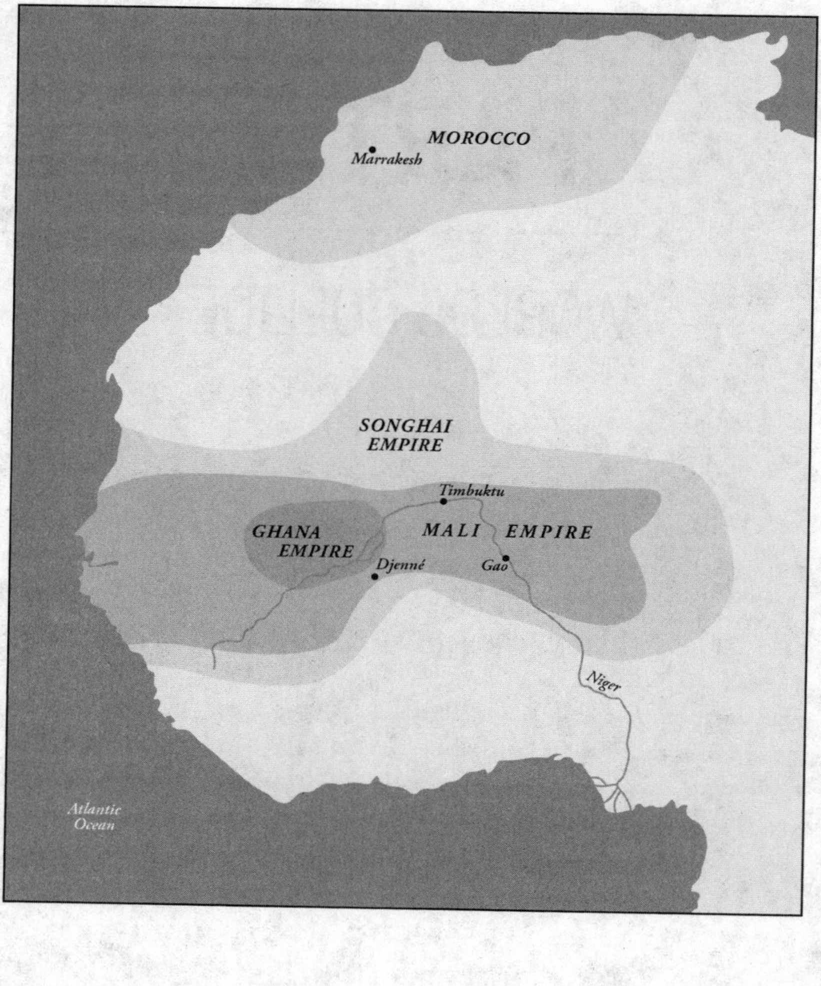
MOROCCO
Marrakesh
SONGHAI
EMPIRE
Timbuktu
GHANA
EMPIRE
MALI EMPIRE
Djenné
Gao
Niger
Atlantic
Ocean

11

Songhai

1460–1591

The Sahara Desert is a vast expanse of sand dunes, rock plateaus and salt flats that covers an area totalling 9 million square kilometres, or around thirty per cent of the African continent. Much of this chapter's story will take place in a landscape just to the south of this desert, known today as the Sahel. The word derives from the Arabic word for 'shore', because people have always thought of it as the 'coast' of this great sand sea. The Sahel is a zone of transition, neither the desert to the north, nor the verdant savannah to the south: for most of its 5,000-kilometre length, it is a flat landscape of semi-arid grasslands and steppes, broken by thorn scrublands and patches of acacia trees. But there are also spots of incredible richness—and one source of these is the West African watercourse known as the Niger River.

The name Niger is thought to derive from the Berber phrase *ger-n-ger*, meaning 'river of rivers'—and it runs from the highlands of south-eastern Guinea over 4,000 kilometres across West Africa, in a sweeping sickle shape. At its widest point, the Niger is nearly a kilometre across, and in its annual spate it turns the desert green across a huge area—in fact, its cultivation zone is more than five times the size of the Nile's. The medieval West African chronicle known as the *Tarikh al-Fattash* paints a glowing picture of the wealth and beauty of this region: 'Malli encompasses a region of four hundred towns and...its soil is extremely rich. Among the kingdoms of the sovereigns of the world, only the lands of Syria surpass it in beauty. Its inhabitants are rich and live very well.'[1]

According to oral tradition, the story of human settlement along the Niger River begins with a people known as the Sorko. They built settlements along the riverbank, and fashioned boats from African mahogany. They were soon joined by the Gao, skilled hunters who knew how to bring down the hippopotamus and crocodiles that lived there, and then by the Doh people, who had adapted to a life growing crops in the rich floodplains. Finally, hardy people from the north, who rode horses and called themselves the Songhai, moved into the region. From the beginning, this was a blended society that survived by unifying elements into a successful whole, and which would forever use the Niger River as its lifeblood.

Down the centuries, a number of great empires rose up in this region. First, the Empire of Ghana rose up on the fringes of the Sahara Desert around the eighth century. Its people were regional pioneers of ironworking, and by 1000 CE had conquered a number of their neighbours and begun to build a true empire. Part of their success was in harnessing the power of a new animal import into the region. Until around the fourth century, horses were the main mode of transportation in West Africa—but while strong and fast on hard ground, they are poorly suited to the harsh environment of the desert. 'That desert is haunted by demons,' wrote the fourteenth-century writer Ibn Battuta. 'If [a man] be alone, they make sport of him and disorder his mind, so that he loses his way and perishes. For there is no visible road or track in these parts—nothing but sand blown hither and thither by the wind.'[2]

Then a remarkable new resource began arriving from Arabia: an animal with large, flat feet, and a fat-storing hump that made it perfectly adapted for survival in the heat—the camel. Immensely resilient and strong, camels were able to carry weights of up to 150 kilograms, and enabled large-scale trade across the desert. The economy of West Africa was now linked with the Mediterranean. Soon huge caravans of camels criss-crossed the desert, piled high with goods and luxuries, as well as supplies for the gruelling weeks-long journey. According to Ibn Battuta, the average caravan contained 1,000 camels, but the largest had as many 12,000. On these new routes, the kingdoms of West Africa transported ivory, spices, wheat and exotic animals to Europe, as well as a steady trade in slaves.

By the end of the first millennium, the enslavement of Christians by Christians had more or less ended in Europe, but the keeping of non-Christian slaves persisted. Prisoners captured during wars between Muslim and Christian countries were often kept as slaves by both sides. However, for both Muslims and Christians, sub-Saharan Africa was the source of a seemingly infinite supply of forced labourers. These enslaved people were transported across the desert under horrendous conditions, to be sold in the markets of North Africa, the Byzantine Empire, Venice or the Iberian Peninsula. Some were forced to work as labourers and domestic servants, others to fight as soldiers in medieval armies. Slavery was a cruel fact of life at this time—but the resource that truly defined West Africa's trade was not people, or even ivory or spices, but gold. West Africa is remarkably rich in this rare metal, and until the exploitation of the Americas in the sixteenth century was the world's top producer. So much gold left this region during the Middle Ages that Europeans and Arabs believed that it must be home to a single monumental mine, a mountain of gold that was being kept a secret by African kings—perhaps even the legendary mines of King Solomon.

In fact, the majority of West Africa's gold wasn't mined but panned on the banks of the Senegal and Niger rivers. During the long dry season, when agriculture was impossible, many farmers would hang up their farm tools and go prospecting for gold instead. The tenth-century Iranian geographer Ibn al-Faqih must have heard some version of this process, which he relates in his geography text *Kitab al-Buldan*, or *The Book of Lands*: 'In Africa, gold grows in the sand, like carrots do, and is picked at sunrise.'[3] These part-time prospectors would sell their tiny amounts of gold to the trading caravans that passed through, which would then travel north and exchange it with North African traders, in return for salt and exotic Mediterranean goods. Soon a veritable river of gold flowed north across the desert, and the early kingdoms of West Africa became extremely wealthy. One man would come to embody this enormous wealth in the European imagination, and became West Africa's most famous medieval king—Mansa Musa, the wealthiest man in the world.

★★★

Musa was the king, or *mansa*, of the Empire of Mali. The Ghana Empire, which had dominated West Africa for five hundred years, went into decline at some point during the thirteenth century. Its power weakened, its client states demanded independence, and finally one of its own conquered subjects eclipsed it in power, snapping up its old dominions and seizing control of the lucrative Saharan trade routes. This rising power would become known as Mali, and it further embraced the system of trans-Saharan trade.

Cultures also travelled along these trade routes too, and soon West Africa was introduced to the young religion of Islam. For the early kings of Mali, conversion to Islam was an entry point into the Mediterranean world, a way to gain acceptance and influence—but religion would always form a fracture that ran the length of West African society. The people living in the farms and villages, who worked the land and herded the cattle, followed eclectic cults that worshipped their ancestors, alongside the ancient spirits of nature, and the magic that lived in the mountains and the forests. The Muslim chronicles record these worshippers with distaste: 'an unbelieving people who worship idols among trees and stones; they make sacrifices to them and pray to them for their needs… Among these people are diviners and sorcerers'.[4]

But in the cities, Islam would become the primary religion. Becoming a Muslim didn't just help you to trade with foreigners—it could also shield you from the increasingly bold slave-taking raiders who came down from the Sahara. As in the Christian world, under Islamic law it was illegal for a Muslim to enslave another Muslim, and this prohibition was taken very seriously. Kingdoms that converted to Islam also enjoyed a measure of protection from invasion by other Muslim states. By the time Mansa Musa took the throne, Mali had been a Muslim Empire for more than a hundred years.

The medieval Catalan Atlas contains a depiction of this king of Mali, holding a gold coin and wearing a gold crown. It records that 'This black Lord is called Musse Melly and is the sovereign of the land of the black people of Gineva (Ghana). This king is the richest and noblest of all these lands due to the abundance of gold that is extracted from his lands.'[5]

Mansa Musa, the King of Mali, as depicted in the Catalan Atlas, sheet 6. III.11.

Mansa Musa's journey to become the King of Mali is probably one of the strangest stories of royal inheritance in history. The year was 1312, and Musa was an elite member of the Mali court, serving an eccentric old king thought to have been Mansa Muhammad ibn Qu. Towards the end of his reign, this old King Muhammad became convinced that it would be possible to sail far enough across the Atlantic Ocean that he might 'reach the other side'. The Arab historian Shihab al-Umari spoke to Mansa Musa in person, and recounts the King's version of what happened next:

> The king who was my predecessor did not believe that it was impossible to discover the furthest limit of the Atlantic Ocean and wished vehemently to do so. So he equipped 200 ships filled with men and the same number equipped with gold, water, and provisions enough to last them for years, and said to the man deputed to lead them: 'Do not return until you reach the end of it or your provisions and water give out.' They departed and a long time passed before anyone came back. Then one ship returned.[6]

This vessel brought back tales of a great whirlpool that had sucked the rest of the fleet down beneath the waves. But the Mansa Muhammad was not deterred—and he apparently decided that if you want a job done, you should do it yourself:

> Then that sultan got ready 2,000 ships, 1,000 for himself and the men whom he took with him and 1,000 for water and provisions. He left me to deputize for him and embarked on the Atlantic Ocean with his men. That was the last we saw of him and all those who were with him, and so I became king in my own right.[7]

This story has long fascinated historians of West Africa, since of course Muhammad would be proven right by history. Other lands really did lie beyond the ocean. While there is no evidence that the journey was successful, it would not be impossible—in 1970 the experimental archaeologist Thor Heyerdahl sailed from Morocco to Barbados in a simple reed boat named *Ra II* in only fifty-seven days. But there are also any number of reasons why Mansa Musa would want to lie about the death of his predecessor.

However he came to power, Musa was clearly keenly aware of his image. The *Tarikh al-Fattash* remembers him as 'virtuous, pious, and devout', and even that 'he freed one slave during each day of his rule'.[8] In 1324, he began a famous pilgrimage to Mecca, accompanied by a caravan of 60,000 men in brocades and silks, and eighty camels each carrying 130 kilograms of gold—what today would be more than 300 million dollars. In every city he stopped at, Mansa Musa is reported to have handed out this gold in huge amounts to the poor—but in doing so, he inadvertently left economic chaos in his wake. In Cairo, Medina and Mecca, the sudden influx of gold caused enormous inflation which devastated their economies for years to come. On his way home, perhaps a little bashful, Musa loaned back all the gold he could find in Egypt, in an attempt to stabilize the price. It was the first and last time in history that one man has controlled the price of the world's gold.

But the Empire of Mali, while incredibly wealthy, wasn't destined to last. It soon followed in Ghana's footsteps, and one of its client states, which was just beginning to flex its muscles, soon took its place as one of the largest African empires in history: the kingdom of Songhai.

★★★

There are essentially three groups of sources about the history of this region of West Africa, and they can often give wildly divergent versions of events. The first are the Arab travellers and historians who occasionally crossed the Sahara and wrote about what they saw. One of these is the traveller Ibn Battuta, a sort of Berber Marco Polo who travelled around much of the known world, and crossed the Sahara to explore the kingdoms of West Africa during the time of the Mali Empire. The second source of information is the storytelling of West Africa itself. This region is home to a unique tradition of folklore, presided over by a caste of mystics and holy men known as the griots. The griots were repositories of oral tradition, and their stories were often not written down until the nineteenth century. As in all folkloric traditions, their tales naturally diverge and mutate over time, and differ greatly between regions, and they often mix historical detail with fantastical elements. Still, studies of this folklore have been used comparatively to corroborate or strengthen other sources. The final source is a kind of mixture of these two traditions: the scribes of Timbuktu. The city of Timbuktu was home to a serious scholarly tradition, where learned people were trained. The scribes of Timbuktu were genuinely interested in recording history, and were connected to an international network of intellectuals that stretched from the palaces of Delhi through the libraries of Baghdad and Alexandria, to the mosques and synagogues of Córdoba in Spain. Two of the most prominent works by these scribes are the *Tarikh al-Fattash*, probably by either Mahmud Kati or his grandson, and the *Tarikh al-Sudan* by Abd al-Rahman al-Sadi. These are known collectively as 'the Timbuktu Chronicles'.

Although many of the scholarly families of Timbuktu traced their lineage back to Arab Muslims who had emigrated into the area, many of them were also West African, and were steeped in the ancient griot traditions. For this reason, their histories are at times also cross-pollinated with tales of magic, prophecies and dream visions, with which they had a complicated relationship. At one point, Kati even apologizes that 'Most of the tales we recounted here are almost certainly not true. We ask forgiveness from God the most high.'[9] Both the Timbuktu Chronicles were political documents, written on the orders of kings, and they often cast these rulers in the most flattering light. But if we apply their accounts cautiously, and in relation to other sources, they offer useful insights.

The earliest mention of the kingdom of Songhai appears in the writing of the ninth-century scholar Ahmad al-Ya'qubi. He describes a small riverside power centred around the trading city of Gao, where the expanse of the Sahara met the green floodplain of the Niger. Just outside of Gao, a great sand dune known as 'the rose dune' looms over the skyline, and since ancient times it has been thought to be the home of sorcerers. Despite Islam being officially adopted by the royal court of Songhai as early as 1019, Gao would always retain this deep-seated cultural connection to these old ways. The city was a cosmopolitan marketplace where kola nuts, gold, ivory, slaves, spices, palm oil and precious woods were traded for salt, textiles, weapons, horses and copper. As well as gold, trade here was sometimes conducted with cowries, the shells of a type of sea snail that served as currency. Cowries served much the same purpose as gold: they were beautiful enough to be universally desired, and rare enough to be safe repositories of value.

By 1325, the wealth of the city of Gao had swollen to such a degree that Mansa Musa, the King of Mali and richest man in the world, desired to seize it. Musa's army was powerful. If accounts are to be believed, Mali at this time had an army of 100,000 soldiers, including 10,000 horsemen, drawn from the aristocracy just like European knights. Ironworking as a craft had been perfected in the Empire of Ghana so that now whole clans among Mali's Mandinke people were given over to it, responsible for creating the spearheads, swords and arrows used by the imperial army. Mali's soldiers wore leather helmets, and iron chainmail imported from Arabia. They also incorporated specialist fighters from the different territories that made up the empire. Oral historians recount the use of poison bowmen from the Sankarani River in the south, fire archers from Wagadou to the north, and heavy cavalry from the northern state of Mema.

Faced with this force, Gao was soon folded into the Empire of Mali, and it did well as part of this greater power. Ibn Battuta visited Gao nearly three decades later, in 1353. In his writings, Battuta is often quite withering about Africa. He was scandalized by many of the customs of Mali's people, and at one point he rudely turns up his nose at the food offered to him by a local chief, commenting bitterly that 'there was no good to be hoped for from these people, and I made up my mind to travel [back to Morocco] at once.'[10] So it's telling that Gao, and particularly its cuisine, impressed him.

> I went from there to Gawgaw, which is a large city on the Nile (Niger), and one of the finest towns of the Negrolands. It is also one of their best-provisioned towns, with rich in plenty, milk, and fish, and there is a species of cucumber there called *inání* which has no equal.[11]

While the Mali Empire met with initial success, it also suffered from deep structural flaws. One of the greatest challenges most societies faced before the modern age was that of royal succession. Uncertainty around who should become king caused civil wars that routinely brought countries to their knees, destroyed industries and decimated populations—and in many ways they represented a greater danger than any plague, earthquake or famine. In Europe, kings were occupied with the pressing need to sire a son to ensure the smooth succession upon their deaths—but in West Africa, the problem was usually not too few sons, but too many. West African kings usually had multiple wives, with four allowed under medieval laws, and so heirs tended to abound. The chronicles record one later king, Askia Muhammad bearing thirty-seven sons, while the oral tradition places the number of his children at closer to 500. These large families meant that any new king usually had countless brothers and uncles who all fancied a shot at the throne. Few succession laws existed, and those that did were often so elaborate that there were many possible interpretations. This dynamic would characterize much of the history of medieval West Africa: during the long reigns of its great kings, its society would flourish—but their deaths nearly always led to disaster.

Mansa Musa died in 1337 and was succeeded by his son Maghan, who ruled for only four years before one of his uncles killed him and took the throne. Such an illegitimate act outraged the lords of the kingdom, and they each brought forth their contesting claims. A succession crisis followed, during which no king ruled for more than a few years, and which destroyed the unity of the empire. Mali's strong, united army splintered into factions loyal to the rival claimants. Sensing weakness in the once-united empire, horsemen from the land of Mossi to the south of the Niger began raiding around the city of Timbuktu. Soon, one of Mali's distant vassals, the coastal kingdom of Jolof, declared independence—and when Mali failed to respond, other vassals saw their chance.

Mali had always been a single-ethnicity project. While it ruled over a large variety of regions and ethnicities, its rulers and elites were all drawn from a people known as the Mande, who used the empire to project their power over other groups. It ruled through force and at times cruelty—and at the first sign of trouble, these groups would seek to throw off the yoke of Mande rule and claim their independence. One of these vassals was the wealthy trade city of Gao, the home of the Songhai people. They soon declared independence, and seized large territories in the east, perhaps banding together other elements of the resistance against Mali. Yet another succession crisis rocked the Mali Empire, and caused it to lose access to the northern trade routes. With those, Mali also lost the ability to import horses—the region's most crucial strategic resource.

Out of all the chaos, the young Songhai kingdom saw an opportunity to rise from the old empire's ashes, and it was fully established by the 1430s. The next century saw the continuing decline of Mali, and the rise of Songhai. By the second half of the fifteenth century, this new kingdom was poised to become one of Africa's great powers, and one man—a ruthless and fearsome military leader—was about to take full advantage of the opportunity that this age of chaos had created. His name was Sunni Ali.

★★★

Sunni Ali took the throne of Songhai in 1464, and ruled from his capital of Gao. His reign would mark an unprecedented expansion of his small kingdom, extending it further than the Mali Empire ever had. Ali is remembered very differently by the two sides of Songhai society. In the oral tradition of the African griots, he is 'Ali Ber', or 'Ali the great', a strong, wise man who commanded the powers of magic, the first ever emperor of the Songhai. But in the chronicles written by Muslim scholars, he is remembered as a cruel and tyrannical ruler. The *Tarikh al-Fattash* reserves particular condemnation for him.

> The tyrant, the debauched, the cursed, the oppressor, the Shī 'Ali, the last king of this dynasty, who was a model of shameful conduct… 'Ali was always victorious, pillaging every land on which he fixed his choice.[12]

From the moment he took power, Ali went to war—and he was determined to modernize and reorganize his military. Having seen the Mali Empire collapse after losing its access to the trade in horses, Ali resolved to begin the large-scale breeding of horses in Africa. He also introduced iron breastplates for his cavalry to wear beneath their tunics—no doubt a burden in the West African heat, but a military advantage over their rivals. Sunni Ali also pioneered the use of a river navy, and the Songhai soon commanded a fleet of 400 boats that could transport troops and supplies up and down the Niger River at rapid speeds. The *Tarikh al-Sudan* recalls the remarkable success that Sunni Ali enjoyed: 'He reigned for 28 years. He waged 32 wars, and won every one. He was always the conqueror, never the conquered.'[13]

Ali would become famous for his extreme ruthlessness, of which the chronicles give us some sense. He reserved a particular hatred for the nomadic pastoral Fulbe people, and when they rebelled against their Songhai conquerors, Sunni Ali had them executed *en masse*, so that, according to the chronicles, their remaining population could fit beneath the shade of a single tree. The chronicles even attribute to him actions that sound almost cartoonishly villainous: 'His heart was so hard that he once threw a baby into a mortar and forced the mother to grind it, even while the baby was still alive. The flesh was then fed to the horses.'[14]

It's certainly possible that Ali was as bloodthirsty as the Timbuktu Chronicles say—but it's worth remembering that these texts were political tools written after Ali's death, on the order of kings who were trying to legitimize their own line of succession. At times, Sunni Ali did understand the value of mercy, if somewhat arbitrarily. He often overturned death sentences that he had only recently handed down, and he also spared the lives of those useful to him. Conquered peoples were ordered to join his army, swelling its numbers until the Songhai kingdom commanded a force of 40,000 infantry and 10,000 cavalry.

One thing that clearly defined Ali was a hatred of the scholars of Timbuktu. It's possible that he viewed these scholarly communities as the source of the rumours about his lack of piety that circulated at the time—including reports that he scandalously left all five of his daily prayers for the evening, knew no Quran verses by heart, and declined to bow when he prayed. Al-Sadi writes that Ali 'hated' the scholars for their 'elitism'.[15] Whatever the reason, in 1468, Ali gathered his forces and marched on perhaps the greatest prize in all of West Africa: the great capital of scholars, the heart of learning, the library city of Timbuktu.

***

In the European imagination, Timbuktu has become a metaphor for remoteness. When we say 'all the way to Timbuktu', we mean a place as far away as it is possible to get. But in the Middle Ages, Timbuktu was the centre of a thriving desert culture. Timbuktu had become a permanent trading settlement around 1100, and, under the stewardship of the Mali Empire, had grown to house a population of well over 100,000 (double its population today). At its height it was home to Arab, Italian and Jewish merchants, and thanks to the practice of taxing around a tenth of all the goods that passed through it, it became vastly wealthy, leading in turn to a flourishing of culture, and above all literacy.

Timbuktu has the perfect climate for producing and storing books. Books here were written on sheepskin, tree bark, and even papers imported from Italy, and the dry desert air meant their pages never warped or cracked. Books were written in African languages like Songhai and Fulani, but also in Arabic, and some were beautifully illuminated with gold leaf. Timbuktu's people saw these books as symbols of wealth and power—and so an active trade in literature began with the rest of the Islamic world. Over the centuries, they collected hundreds of thousands of manuscripts. Gao was the administrative heart of West Africa, but Timbuktu was its intellectual centre, its brain.

Sunni Ali made no secret about his intentions for the city. When he arrived in full force, he sent a messenger into Timbuktu ahead of his army to deliver a chilling warning to its defenders. The *Tarikh al-Fattash* describes the scene:

> Unsheathing a sword and brandishing it by the hilt, he added: 'This is the sword of the King. I have been ordered to cut the throat of anyone who stays the night in this town.'... In a blink of the eye, all the town's inhabitants fled. Some did not even take their supper that night, while others forgot to bring blankets for sleeping.[16]

Having taken the city with barely any resistance, Ali put any who remained to the sword, and burned the town. The *Tarikh al-Sudan* recounts how 'Sunni Ali entered Timbuktu, committed gross iniquity, burned and destroyed the town, and brutally tortured many people there.'[17] Luckily, many of the scholars and wealthy families who fled had taken their collections of books with them, while others managed to hide their books in secret places in their houses. Over the remaining twenty-four years of his reign, Ali embarked on no fewer than five purges of the city, attacking its noble families, destroying its books and expelling its scholars. People must have cried out for some alternative to this tyrant—and if the chronicles are to be believed, that alternative was already gathering power. His name was Askia Muhammad.

Muhammad had no legitimate claim to the throne, but he was a nobleman and a warrior who held a position known as the Tondi-Farma—the lord of the mountains. This title meant that he was in control of the red sandstone bluffs to the south, along the rocky cliffs of what is now the modern border with Burkina Faso—a tough region, full of mountain bandits. It was one of the most highly militarized borders in the empire, so Askia Muhammad had a large and battle-hardened army at his disposal. Muhammad was also frequently at odds with King Sunni Ali. The chronicles never make clear the nature of these disagreements, but he was even imprisoned and sentenced to death on a number of occasions, but 'as he was wise and prudent, the tyrant never did him any harm'.[18] Askia Muhammad was clearly rebellious, but also apparently indispensable, and he was steadily positioning himself as an alternative to the tyrant king. Soon enough, he would get his chance.

Sunni Ali died in November 1492, in mysterious circumstances. In the *Tarikh al-Fattash*, he is struck down by God as a punishment for abusing a holy man, but in the *Tarikh al-Sudan*, Ali drowns when a flash flood washes into his camp near the village of Kuna. Of course, flash floods were a deadly fact of life on the medieval Niger, just as they are today—but the village of Kuna was also in the mountainous territory controlled by Askia Muhammad. Perhaps after being sentenced to death by Sunni Ali multiple times,

Muhammad finally decided to put an end to the erratic king's rule. The *Tarikh al-Fattash* mentions that Ali's soldiers buried him before anyone else had even learned of his death—perhaps because he had wounds on his body that they wanted to conceal.

Ali was succeeded by his son Baru, who was determined to crush the threat that Askia Muhammad posed to his rule. Baru gathered his forces, and marched out to meet Muhammad at a place called Anfao. 'The battle was so violent and the fighting so bloody,' Kati writes, 'that everyone believed that his final hour had come… But God (May He be praised!) granted victory to the Askia Muhammad.'[19] Askia Muhammad was now the Emperor of Songhai. He would be one of the great kings of West Africa, a hero remembered in epics and song. But already around the world, wheels were beginning to turn that would seal the fate of West Africa for centuries to come.

★★★

The death of the tyrannical king Sunni Ali, in November 1492, came at a historical tipping point. Around the world at this time, big things were underway. One month before, England's King Henry VII had laid siege to the French port of Boulogne, forcing the French king to sue for peace and pay 50,000 crowns in annual tribute. An enormous meteorite weighing over 150 kilograms landed in a fireball outside the walled town of Ensisheim in the Alsace region of France. And on the other side of the world, in the islands of the Caribbean, only days before Sunni Ali died, a European explorer named Christopher Columbus first set foot in the New World. The battle of Anfao in 1493, when Askia Muhammad won the day outside the walls of Gao, came just a few months before Columbus's second voyage—and in the history of the African continent, this discovery would begin one of its bleakest chapters.

It's not recorded whether news of these developments reached the new king of Songhai, Askia Muhammad—but he had quite enough to be occupying him at home. He had inherited a Songhai territory that had never been larger, now comprising a broad diversity of ethnic groups, including the Fulbe, Soninke, Tuareg, Dogon, Bambara and Bozo—but it had also suffered greatly from decades of civil war and attacks from its aggressive neighbours. In response to ongoing attacks on the weakened empire, Muhammad sought to reform the army, expanding its powerful cavalry and moving away from the use of slave soldiers and conscripts to become a true professional standing army. He also embarked on a series of campaigns that would expand the boundaries of the Songhai Empire until it was the largest contiguous empire that sub-Saharan Africa had ever seen. He announced a legally sanctioned *jihad* against the Mossi people to the south, before marching north against the Turaged people, and seizing the Saharan salt mines of Taghaza, where the salt was so abundant that the houses were built out of salt bricks.

While he shared something of Ali's military skill, Muhammad's character stood in stark contrast to his predecessor. Whereas Ali had lived only for war, Muhammad was also a diplomat and an administrator. He sought to reconcile the differences in his empire, making peace with the persecuted scribes and scholars in Timbuktu, bringing banished families back from exile, and even maintaining personal friendships with some of them. The *Tarikh al-Sudan* records approvingly that: 'He strove to establish the community of Islam and improve people's lot. He befriended the scholars, and sought counsel from them over the appointments and dismissals he made.'[20]

While the histories don't mention Sunni Ali doing a single thing outside of his borders—apart from a fleeting mention in one Egyptian chronicle—Askia Muhammad brought in a new age of diplomacy, forging connections that reached right across the Muslim world. He even made a pilgrimage to Mecca, in imitation of the legendary Mansa Musa. Perhaps most crucially, in a symbolic act, he invited a leader from each of the empire's ethnic groups to join him on this journey, including people like the Fulbe who had been massacred under Sunni Ali. This effort, more than anything, was the true source of Askia Muhammad's success: he began to forge a state that crossed ethnic boundaries, incorporated all the different peoples within its borders, and inspired loyalty in them that subsumed their original ethnicity. It was a very modern kind of state.

Muhammad also united the two sides of the empire—its heart

in Gao and its brain in Timbuktu—bringing the Muslims of Timbuktu over to his side, while never renouncing the ancient magic of his ancestors. In this way, he fused together an empire that looked like it might truly last. Muhammad's reign saw the establishment of standardized trade measures and regulations, as well as an organized tax system. He began policing trade routes, divided the empire into states, and appointed ministers who took care of finance, justice, agriculture and other areas of government. His reforms ushered in an age of virtually unprecedented peace and prosperity.

The tomb of Muhammad I Askia in Gao, Mali, photographed by Walter Mittelholzer, ca. 1930.

But this golden age would come to an end. As he neared seventy, Askia Muhammad became blind and began relying on a powerful vizier to act for him. According to West African law, his blindness would have disqualified him from ruling, but he was reluctant to pass the crown to any of his thirty-seven sons. These sons soon grew impatient, and eventually one of them, a man named Musa, grew tired of waiting. Musa is remembered in the chronicles as an impudent and stupid boy, spoiled by a life of royal luxury. 'No one more despicable or vile…ever occupied the throne of the Songhay,'[21] spits the *Tarikh al-Fattash*. He moved to seize his father's crown, banishing the old man Askia Muhammad to an island in the middle of the Niger River, referred to as a place infested with mosquitoes and toads. Musa's usurpation naturally enraged Askia

Muhammad's other sons, many of whom probably thought they had a better claim. Musa lost power in 1531 after only a two-year reign, during which he killed more than thirty of his rival brothers and cousins. The Songhai Empire, like Ghana and Mali before it, had few clear laws of succession. While Askia Muhammad made many legal reforms during his reign, in this area it seems no one had mustered the political will to enact change.

The next twenty years saw almost constant bloodshed, as various claimants to the throne fought for supremacy. The civil wars disrupted the trade hubs of Djenné, Timbuktu and Gao, and the country's wealth ran dry. West African armies lived and died by their supply of horses, and each warring prince needed a steady supply to replenish his army. These were usually imported across the desert from Europe at great expense—but with all the disruption and chaos, increasingly only one resource remained in abundance in West Africa: its people.

★★★

In the early fifteenth century, Portuguese explorers had begun to conduct expeditions to explore beyond the Saharan coast of Africa, in hope of finding a sea route to Asia, and of finding the source of the lucrative trans-Saharan gold trade. They settled the island of Madeira in 1419, and the Azores in 1432, and used these as bases for further exploration. While the routes of their voyages were similar, the Portuguese would not have been aware of the earlier voyages of Carthaginian explorers like Hanno, since the document of his 'Periplus' was at that time in the Byzantine libraries of Constantinople, and would not reach Western Europe until the city's fall some decades later.

As voyage after voyage returned with little profit from West Africa, the Portuguese royalty almost lost interest in exploration—but that all changed in 1471, when the merchant and explorer Fernão Gomes reached present-day Ghana, on what would soon become known for obvious reasons as 'the Gold Coast'. Here, he discovered the booming overland trade in gold, all of it passing through the Songhai lands. Keen to get a piece of this action, Gomes established his own trading post there, which became known as 'Elmina'—the mine—due to the immense amount of gold it procured. In 1482, King João II of Portugal ordered a fortified factory to be built at Elmina, to extract ever greater amounts by sea. This had the effect of undercutting the economy of the Songhai Empire, circumventing their previous monopoly on the transport of gold. And meanwhile, the Europeans also began the extraction of slaves.

Slavery was intertwined with European exploration of Africa from the beginning. At first, Portuguese crews would seize their own slaves from coastal settlements and in the Canary Islands, carrying them off to be sold and forced to labour in the Iberian Peninsula or elsewhere in the Mediterranean—but these raids soon met with increasingly organized African resistance. The chronicler de Zurara recounts one such event in 1446, when a raiding ship was surrounded and attacked by African vessels, who managed to kill most of the crew. Ultimately, the Europeans decided that it was less costly to let locals do their dirty work for them. Like elsewhere in the world, slaves had always been taken in warfare in Africa, as a way of profiting from the taking of prisoners of war. However, wars were never started purely for the purpose of capturing slaves. This all changed, as the unifying Songhai Empire fragmented, and the overseas market for slaves grew.

The failure of political control in West Africa's largest empire coincided with the establishment of the European trading posts by the Portuguese at São Tomé and São Salvador, and the development of plantation farming in the Caribbean, when demands for enslaved African labour began to exponentially increase. This was the beginning of the transatlantic slave trade. Within twenty years of Askia Muhammad's death, barely fifty years after the conquistadors made landfall in the Americas, as many as 250,000 Africans had already been kidnapped and transported to the New World. By the time the slave trade was abolished in the nineteenth century, the number would exceed 12 million, of which nearly 2 million died on the voyage. 'The African continent was bled of its human resources via all possible routes,' writes Congolese historian Elikia M'bokolo.

> Across the Sahara, through the Red Sea, from the Indian Ocean ports and across the Atlantic. At least ten centuries of slavery for the benefit of the Muslim countries (from the ninth to the nineteenth). Then more than four centuries (from the end of the fifteenth to the nineteenth) of a regular slave trade to build the Americas and the prosperity of the Christian states of Europe.[22]

The loss of Africa's manpower would critically undermine its economies. Eventually, the bloodletting in Songhai did come to an end, when a man named Askia Daoud came to its throne in 1549. A shrewd operator, his ability to stabilize the nation led to a brief renaissance, and he even embarked on public works, including the foundation of public libraries. For this reason, he is often referred to as Songhai's second greatest king, after Askia Muhammad. Askia Daoud undertook a number of campaigns to stamp down insurgencies that had arisen in the twenty years of unrest since Muhammad's death, and sent his cavalry up into the mountains to put a stop to bandit raids there, with some success. But if he had any hopes of expanding his borders further, they would have been frustrated by a failed campaign against the Mossi in which several of his commanders were killed.

During Daoud's thirty-four-year reign, Songhai's agriculture suffered from droughts and famines, and in response it seems that the majority of citizen farming was replaced with slave plantations. Slavery in Songhai was a complex institution that varied over time, and slaves held a similar position to the serfs that were still held across Europe. Their freedoms were doubtless restricted, but this was not the chattel slavery of the Atlantic trade. Slaves in Songhai could get married, own property and land, and even own slaves themselves, and their children were not born into slavery. There are even stories of royal slaves attaining great power and wealth in Songhai, going on to command political influence in the capital after the deaths of their masters. But during Askia Daoud's reign, the empire became a true slave state. Songhai would soon be a land where plantations of slave rice farmers supported whole villages of slaves, and a slave army, all presided over by a slave bureaucracy.

Towards the end of Daoud's life, things got even worse. In 1582, a great plague killed many in Timbuktu. With Daoud's death came another period of chaotic civil war in which it has been estimated that half of the imperial army were lost—and this was accompanied by further drought, followed by famine and inflation. A strong Songhai state at the height of its power might have been able to ride out these challenges—but with rival princes and commanders fighting over the throne, and their position in the gold trade lost, there was no energy left to help Songhai's people. Its largely slave-based agriculture began to collapse. At this moment, the man who would be Songhai's final, doomed king ascended to the throne: a man named Askia Ishaq II, in whose hands the empire would finally disintegrate.

★★★

Unfortunately for Songhai, the unrest in their lands coincided with the rising of another star in the region: the kingdom of Morocco. For many years now, Morocco had been growing in strength and confidence. In 1549, a new dynasty known as the Saadi had seized control of the country, and in 1578 caused enormous upset by decisively defeating a Portuguese invasion force at the battle of Alcácer Quibir, even killing the Portuguese King Sebastian and expelling Portugal from some of its North African trading posts. The victorious campaign had emptied the Moroccan treasuries, but left their confidence at an all-time high—so much so that the Moroccan Sultan Ahmad al-Mansur even angered the Ottoman Empire by declaring himself Caliph, the pre-eminent leader of the Muslim world. This ambitious but cash-strapped sultan now turned his gaze southwards. One of the prizes that the Moroccans most coveted was the salt mines of Taghaza—but they too had seen declining returns in the gold trade since the Portuguese maritime trade began, and doubtless wanted to seize control of these precious metals at their source. By now, news of the internal divisions in Songhai had reached beyond its borders, apparently carried by a slave who had escaped from the salt mines at Taghaza and fled to the court of the Sultan, 'informing him of the weakness of Songhay's leadership and providing intelligence about them concerning their desperate circumstances, their depraved natures, and their enfeebled power, urging him to take the land from their hands.'[23]

With dreams of an empire that spanned the Sahara, the Sultan seized his chance, and ordered the preparation of an invasion force. The man he chose to lead this force was a blue-eyed Spaniard who went by the name Judar Pasha, who had been captured as a boy by Moroccan slave-raiders, castrated and brought up in the service of the Sultan. Judar had no small task ahead of him. To invade Songhai, he and his men would have to cross the desert with all their equipment. What's more, the Sultan had given him few resources: he had barely more than 4,000 men, including just 500 light cavalry, to face the army of tens of thousands that guarded the borders of Songhai. But they had something that, in all their years of civil war, the kings of Songhai had neglected: gunpowder.

After the guns of Mehmed the Conqueror had ground the walls of Constantinople to dust in 1453, the power of this new technology had become obvious. By the late fifteenth century, gunpowder weapons had evolved from enormous siege cannon into handheld devices, now with triggered matchlock mechanisms that did away with the need to light a fuse. Around 1520, towards the end of Askia Muhammad's reign, the musket had transformed the tactics of European battlefields. Some African powers like Borno and other states on the Gold Coast would recognize the power of these new weapons and begin importing them—but the rulers of Songhai, perpetually occupied with putting down rival challengers and *coups d'état*, fell behind in these crucial decades.

The Sultan Ahmad al-Mansur had spent seventeen years in the now-Ottoman capital as a boy, and was much impressed with their embrace of the new technology. When Judar Pasha left Marrakesh on 16 October 1590, the majority of his 4,000 men were musketeers, and he also brought with him eight English cannons and 14 tonnes of gunpowder and shot, travelling with 10,000 camels and 1,000 packhorses. They reached the edge of the Sahara on 22 December 1590 and from there began the perilous journey across the desert. After three trudging months on the road, his forces arrived on the banks of the Niger in February 1591, dusty and beleaguered, and only enough of them to fill a large theatre. From there, they marched on the Songhai capital of Gao. They were intercepted by the Songhai imperial army in the cattle pastures near a place called Tondibi.

Estimates vary, but the defence force gathered by the Songhai King Askia Ishaq likely topped 40,000 men, outnumbering the Moroccans ten to one. The ground would have shaken with the force of the pounding feet and hooves, the cavalry accompanied by a substantial troupe of drummers and other musicians, tens of thousands of archers and infantry, spears clattering overhead as they marched. The Songhai campaign didn't get off to a great start. They had heard about the new weapons that the Moroccans had brought with them, and planned to neutralize them by sending a stampede of a thousand cattle towards the Moroccan lines, hoping to soak up some of their musket fire, and to panic the foreigners into retreating. But this tactic didn't quite go as planned. The *Tarikh al-Fattash* records how 'when the cows heard the sound of the rifles, they became frantic. They stampeded back towards the soldiers of the askiya, crushing a great many of them.'[24]

King Askia Ishaq ordered his soldiers forward, while one of his generals pleaded with him to stop: 'Do not rush to your death, do not order your brothers to be killed, and do not cause all of the Songhay to perish at a single place and time!'[25] But the Askia did not listen. The Songhai infantry advanced, and fared little better than the cattle. Moroccan muskets let off puffs of smoke in the distance. Pellets of lead and iron would have whizzed through the air, passing right through armour and flesh, mowing down dozens in a single volley. Panicking, King Ishaq sent in his cavalry to try to break the lines of musketeers, but the horses also panicked, and the riders were slaughtered. As the Moroccans finally advanced, drawing swords for close combat, only the Songhai rearguard remained. One Spanish source even records that they bent their knees to the ground and tied them into position, so that they could maintain their spear line even as the strength of their muscles failed. But it was a doomed effort. The Songhai force was utterly crushed, and Judar Pasha's men descended on the helpless city of Gao. They sacked it and burned its buildings, before moving on to the richer trading centres of Timbuktu and Djenné, as the *Tarikh al-Sudan* remembers:

> It is beyond our powers to fully describe all the misery and losses that were suffered at Timbuktu when the Moroccans took occupation of this town... The Moroccans even tore off the doors of the houses and cut down the town's trees.[26]

Horrified by the defeat, the Songhai generals deposed Ishaq, and the central power of the state collapsed. Morocco attempted to occupy the Songhai lands, but the challenges of maintaining an empire on both sides of the Sahara proved too great. Still, they looted everything they could. The wealth of Timbuktu, Gao and Djenné was systematically stripped, and huge quantities of gold dust were shipped across the desert. When Judar Pasha returned to Morocco in 1599, nine years after setting out with his army, his caravan included thirty camel-loads of gold as payment for his services.

The fall of imperial Songhai, only eight years after the death of perhaps its second greatest king, sent splinters running right across the empire, just as had happened to Ghana and Mali. Soon, where a single nation had existed, now countless small states and nations reasserted their freedoms and separate borders. West Africa cracked like an egg. Non-Muslims began raiding in Muslim lands, and there was no longer any hope of unified resistance to the spreading influence of European colonialism. Predatory European traders set up slave trading posts all along the African coast, profiting from the chaos, and the full horror of the transatlantic slave trade reached new heights, draining the manpower of Africa on an industrial scale. Its economy and society destroyed, Timbuktu in turn lost its position as a centre of learning. The author of one of the chronicles, Al-Sadi, would lament in his preface to his chronicle, 'I have witnessed the ruin of learning, and its utter collapse.'[27]

Many of his fellow scholars were kidnapped and enslaved, transported across the Atlantic to the New World, where they laboured in horrendous conditions to enrich colonial economies. Enslaved Africans would play a part in the colonization and conquest of the Americas, making up much of the earliest expeditions into the New World. Some would even gain their freedom, like the Black conquistador Juan Garrido—born in West Africa around 1480 during the reign of Askia Daoud—who accompanied Hernán Cortés on his conquest of Mexico. But most of those transported would never see a life outside of servitude.

The thirteenth-century Great Mosque of Djenné as it appeared in 1906, in ruins. The building has since been reconstructed.

Timbuktu would also never reclaim its former glory. As the years drew on, the great city's libraries gathered dust. Over the centuries, their manuscripts became precious heirlooms, and the city's noble families hid them away in private collections, often protecting them at great personal risk against raiders and invading armies—a tradition that continued into the present day, when in 2012 the city's residents helped to protect its literary heritage as the town was occupied by the West African branch of *al-Qaida*. It's thanks to the efforts of these families of book lovers that the two great Timbuktu Chronicles have survived, and today we can read the stories of the Askias of Songhai. The *Tarikh al-Fattash* levels its final blistering verdict on the society of Songhai:

> What caused the ruin of the state of Songhay and compelled God to throw it into disorder, what brought divine punishment down upon its citizens—which they had mocked up until this point—was their failure to observe the laws of God, the iniquity of the slaves, as well as the pride and arrogance of the great ones… We belong to God: it is to him that we should return.[28]

Like Timbuktu, the capital city of Gao slowly shrank into obscurity. Sycamore trees and silk cottons put down roots into the cracks in its walls. Soon only about 300 modest houses would cluster here, surrounded by the ruins of the city's former glory, overgrown with thorns and bushes. The fractured states of West Africa would eventually be folded into the sea-going empires of European nations: the French, British, German and Portuguese, who dismantled their industries, extracted their resources and their people, and grew richer on them.

In 1858, the German traveller and writer Heinrich Barth set out on a journey across the Sahara Desert, determined to reach its far edge and the fabled city of Timbuktu. It took him three years to complete his circuitous 20,000-kilometre journey, but even still, he was always on the lookout for more sights, and on the return leg he heard rumours of something that only a handful of living Europeans had ever seen: a great ruined city lost in the African brush, a city that had once commanded West Africa's greatest empire. His guides called this city Gógó.

> As soon as I had made out that Gógó was the place which for several centuries had been the capital of a strong and mighty empire in this region, I felt a more ardent desire to visit it than I had to reach Timbúktu… I was fully aware that Timbúktu had never been more than a provincial town… Gawó or Gógó had been the centre of a great national movement, from whence powerful and successful princes, such as the great Mohammed el Háj A'skia, spread their conquests.[29]

Barth set out along the Niger River with his guides, but on arrival at the site he was much disappointed to find only a small collection of houses, with heaps of overgrown rubble where the ancient city had once stood:

> This once busy locality, which, according to the unanimous statements of former writers was the most splendid city…is now the desolate abode of a small and miserable population. Just opposite my tent, towards the south, lay the ruined massive tower, the last remains of the principal mosque…of the capital. All around the wide open area where we were encamped, was woven a rich corona of vegetation… The eastern tower is in ruins, but the western one is still tolerably well preserved. It rises in seven terraces, which gradually decrease in diameter. The inhabitants still offer their prayers in this sacred space…although they have not sufficient energy to repair the whole.[30]

Gao, Niger, as photographed in 1930–31 by Walter Mittelholzer.

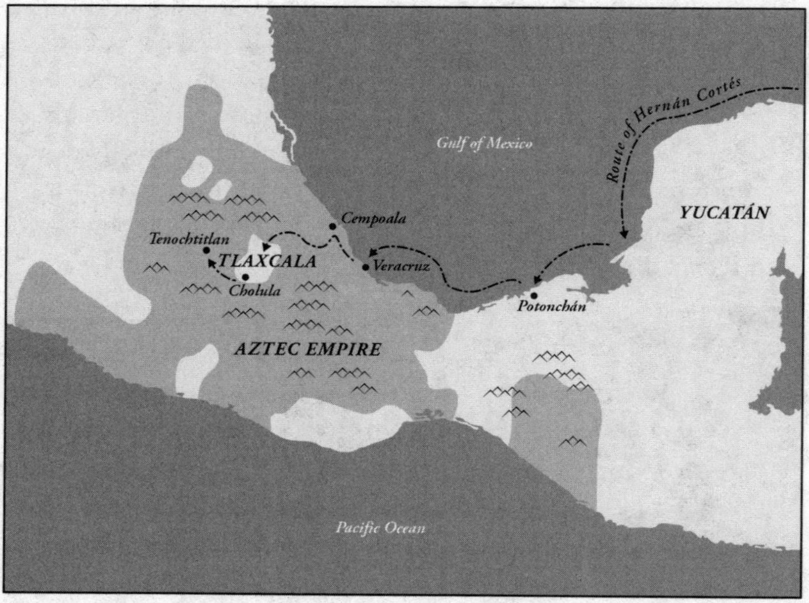

Gulf of Mexico
Route of Hernán Cortés
YUCATÁN
Cempoala
Tenochtitlan
TLAXCALA
Veracruz
Cholula
Potonchán
AZTEC EMPIRE
Pacific Ocean

12

The Aztecs

c. 1325–1521

On the night of 21 February 1978 in the centre of Mexico City, a group of workmen from the city's electric company were digging through the asphalt at the corner of República de Guatemala and República de Argentina Street. At first, it seemed like just another job. But then, just over 2 metres down, their diggers struck something. It was an enormous piece of carved stone, decorated with intricate patterns. Archaeologists soon descended on the area, and as they excavated further, they found that the stone was a disc, over 3 metres in diameter. On its surface was carved the image of a female deity, naked and decapitated, her disembodied head adorned with a crown of feathers, surrounded by snakes and skulls.

This was a depiction of a God named Coyolxauhqui, who had been worshipped by the Indigenous people of Mexico, and it soon became clear that the disc stood at the base of an enormous pyramid. This was the main temple of a city that had been completely erased beneath the streets of the modern metropolis—a city that had once been called Tenochtitlan. It was the heart of a powerful society, known today as the Aztec Empire. The fall of their civilization, one of the most remarkable and bloody stories in human history, would mark the turning point in the European conquest of the American mainland, as the two long-separated sides of the world met for the first time.

Archaeologists of the Mexican Instituto Nacional de Antropología e Historia working to excavate the Coyolxāuhqui Stone after its discovery.

★★★

The Atlantic Ocean is the youngest of the world's five oceans. It began to form during the late Jurassic period, approximately 150 million years ago, following the break-up of the supercontinent Pangaea that had once united much of the world's landmass. When the Atlantic first started to rip this continent in two from north to south, dinosaurs still roamed the earth. This ocean would grow by 3 centimetres a year as the tectonic plates pulled apart at the Mid-Atlantic Ridge, and the Americas were gradually torn away. The Atlantic Ocean was already around 2,500 kilometres wide by the time the dinosaurs were wiped out by the Chicxulub asteroid impact about 66 million years ago, which struck the earth just off the coast of Yucatán in southern Mexico. The ocean kept growing as the planet's large animal life recovered from that catastrophe, and all modern mammals diverged from our small rat-sized ancestors. Since the earliest known fossils of *Homo sapiens* entered the archaeological record around 300,000 years ago, the ocean has grown by 9 kilometres. Today, the Atlantic stands at 4,800 kilometres wide in places, with its narrowest point at about 2,800 kilometres near the equator—and across this great gulf of time, it has formed a barrier between the Americas and the continental landmass of Afro-Eurasia.

How and when humans arrived in the Americas is a question that is being constantly updated and revised as new evidence emerges, and just as in Europe, the story is likely one of multiple waves of settlement that left varying impacts. New evidence of fossil footprints in White Sands National Park in New Mexico suggests that humans were present in the Americas from at least 20,000 years ago, and the most comprehensive mitogenomic DNA studies have shown that the people of the Americas arrived from north-east Asia in the region of Siberia, and diverged from those populations 'between 24,900 and 18,400 years ago'.[1] These populations either crossed a land bridge in the region of the Bering Strait, exposed by the low sea levels of the last ice age, or travelled along the Pacific coast in canoes. From there, they occupied the entire continent.

Much of this story will take place in a landscape known as the Valley of Mexico—a highlands plateau in central Mexico, sandwiched between two great ranges of mountains and volcanoes. Archaeology suggests that the earliest humans arrived here around 12,000 years ago, when the valley floor was still covered with a great body of water, 80 kilometres long and 40 kilometres wide: Lake Texcoco. The earliest people found vast herds of mammoths roaming the pine forests bordering the great lake, and hunted them, fished and set up simple communities. Agriculture began around the lake about 7,000 years ago, and by 1200 BCE, a number of large villages coalesced. To the north, the lands of the Chihuahuan Desert were tough and arid, and so over time countless migrating peoples and nomadic groups travelled south into the valley.

As we saw in Chapter 7 on the Maya, the great society of Teotihuacán had once grown up in the Valley of Mexico, and they were followed by the Toltecs, who reached prominence from 950 to 1150 CE. By 1300, the dozens of settlements around the lake had grown into powerful city states in their own right, each with a tall pyramid-shaped temple at its heart, booming markets and sophisticated methods of farming. A thick traffic of canoes criss-crossed the lake, bringing trade between the markets of these cities. At this time, a people known as the Tepanecs had gained a hegemony over the valley, ruling a network of allies and client states from their city of Azcapotzalco, which rose on the western bank of the lake. At least forty other cities paid tribute to them and sent soldiers to fight in their armies.

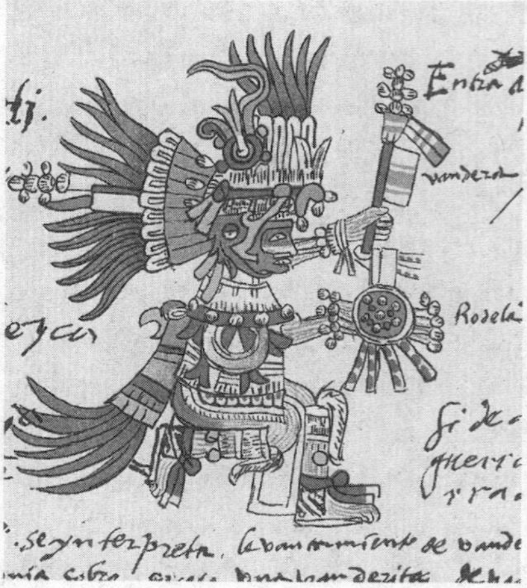

Representation of the Aztec/Mexica god Huītzilōpōchtli, from the recto of folio 5 of the sixteenth-century *Codex Telleriano-Remensis.*

It was around this time that a new band of migrants arrived in the valley, claiming to have fled from a land called Aztlan. They had been wandering in the deserts for many years, searching for a new place to call home. They called themselves the Mexica—but today, they have become known by a name derived from their mythical homeland: the Aztecs. We can imagine how these weary desert travellers must have felt when they crested the hills and saw the wide, green Valley of Mexico, the cities scattered around the lake, glittering like jewels. They would give it the name Meztliapan, or 'the Lake of the Moon', but they would struggle to find a home there. The steady flow of people migrating south meant that nearly all the land in the valley had already been claimed.

The Aztecs were a rough bunch. They didn't wear the embroidered clothes of the city-dwellers, or have their sophisticated manners, and their years in the wilderness had made them tough. They worshipped a fierce, warlike God named Huitzilopochtli, whose name meant 'hummingbird of the south', and followed rites of blood sacrifice with apparent enthusiasm. According to myth, their god Huitzilopochtli reassured them: 'I will lead thee to the place to which thou art to go; I will appear in the guise of a white eagle…when I arrive there, I will alight and there thou wilt see me; so presently make my temple.'[2]

According to the myth, it was around the year 1325 that they finally saw their sign: a white eagle with a snake held in its beak, perched on a cactus on an inhospitable strip of marshland lying some way off the western shore of Lake Texcoco. This was now the only uninhabited land left in the valley. The Aztecs built canoes and paddled out to this lonely stretch. There, they built a small number of huts and a reed altar to their god Huitzilopochtli. The Mexica named this humble settlement after one of their legendary kings, a man named Tenoch, who had led them through the desert. This was the birth of Tenochtitlan. 'Now we have reached our promised land,' the god Huitzilopochtli tells them, 'here you must keep guard and wait, and the four corners of the earth you must conquer.'[3]

Over the years that followed, the Mexica set about the task of improving their meagre sandbank. They built artificial islands out in the lake, driving tall stakes into the shallow lake bed, then piling earth within them. Over the years, these new islands spread out from the original centre in a chaotic pattern, connected by bridges and canals. The people of Tenochtitlan also created island gardens called *chinampas*, on which they grew all kinds of crops, from maize, beans and squashes to tomatoes, chilli peppers and flowers. The farmers paddled between these gardens in their canoes, carrying sprouting plants and tools, bringing back the crops in baskets.

Remarkably, this island city grew at enormous speed. By 1450, little over a century since the traditional date given to its founding, it housed as many as 200,000 people. By this time, Tenochtitlan would have looked something like an enormous Venice, a lattice of canals and waterways, joined to the mainland by three stone causeways to the north, south and west. 'The city spreads making circles of emerald,' one Mexica poet would write, 'scattering splendours like feather of quetzal… In her there is coming and going of barges.'[4]

Fed by mountain springs, Lake Texcoco was unusually salty, and the Mexica had to build dams that separated the salty lake water from the drinkable fresh water that ran into it. Salt production became another key local industry. 'They take the lake water, which is salty, and lead it through ditches into depressions where they thicken it,' wrote the Spaniard Pedro Mártir de Anglería. 'Once thickened, they boil it, and then form it into balls and loaves which they take to markets or fairs.'[5] As well as farming, the Mexica would have fished and hunted wild birds and deer. They also ate several species of insect, including one they called the *axayácatl*, a kind of marsh fly. Francisco Hernández de Toledo relates how the Mexica prepared this food:

> The *axayácatl* is a small, lacustrine fly…collected with nets from the lake in such great quantities that great numbers of them are cut up and mixed together to form little balls, which are sold in the markets throughout the year; the indians cook them in salty water wrapped up in maize husks, and prepared in this way they comprise a good food, abundant and agreeable.[6]

The rough bunch of Mexica warriors who had first arrived in the valley were now a sophisticated and settled people. With a central role in the canoe-based trade of the lake, they now enjoyed all the comforts of settled society: 'fine emeralds, the stones of much value, the gold and silver, the fine feathers…the fine cocoa which has come from afar'.[7] They had also successfully adopted the Toltec and Teotihuacán traditions of pyramid building and stone carving. They welcomed craftsmen and engineers from all the other cities of the valley, and in 1418, the Mexica began the construction of a vast series of aqueducts, stretching for 4 kilometres across the lake to bring drinking water into the heart of the city from the freshwater springs at Chapultepec. After the first aqueducts were damaged by a flood, they would be replaced with a more durable set of aqueducts built from stone. An enormous dam was also built to protect the city from seasonal flooding.

Tenochtitlan was divided into a number of key districts. In the north there was Cuepopan, or 'the place where flowers bloom', and in the west Moyotlan, 'the place of the gnats'. To the east was Atzcoalco, 'the place of the herons'. The small marshy island where the Mexica had first settled was now the grand temple district of Teopan, or 'the place of the gods'. Here, the majority of palaces, temples and schools for noble children were found. In place of the small reed shrine that had once stood there, an enormous pyramid now rose at the head of a grand courtyard, measuring half a square kilometre. The great stone disc with the image of the moon goddess Coyolxauhqui, which would one day be uncovered by a group of Mexico City electrical workers, now formed the base of the steps leading up to the pyramid.

Tenochtitlan was a place of pleasure and luxury. It had a botanical garden and even a zoo, which Spanish visitors later found remarkable, since nothing of the kind yet existed in Europe. Drinking alcohol was strictly forbidden in Mexica society, but people surreptitiously drank *pulque*, a particular kind of milky alcohol drink brewed from the agave plant. If you walked the streets of Tenochtitlan, you might also see groups of people eating hallucinogenic mushrooms, or drinking them brewed into a tea. These were used especially among poets and priests, for whom they took on a religious significance, as one piece of oral poetry records:

> I have drunk fungus wine and my heart weeps.
> On earth I have only pain.
> ...
> It matters nothing...
> we are all together
> precious jewels of the god, strung on a thread;
> ...
> we are all together
> jewels of his necklace.[8]

One of the most remarkable of the city's sights could be found in its northern part. Here, in the district of Tlatelolco, a great market was held. This city in the lake had now become the crossroads of trade in the region, with boats coming from all the lakeside cities to sell their produce here. An enormous, colourful variety of food—including sweet potatoes, manioc, sapote, guavas, avocados, plums, acacia beans, tortilla flatbreads, turkey meat and eggs, fish and other goods—were brought from all over the valley and beyond. The Aztecs loved riddles, and while the market-goers mingled, they may have laughed and exchanged new ones they'd heard that week. Some examples of these Aztec puzzles were written down by the Spanish friar Bernardino de Sahagún in the sixteenth century:

> What 'thing and thing' goes through a valley and carries its guts dragging?—This is the needle and its thread.
>
> ...
>
> What 'thing and thing' is ten stones that someone has on his back?—These are the fingers and their nails.
>
> ...
>
> What 'thing and thing' is a mirror in a house made of pine branches?—This is the eye with its lashes.[9]

But the darker side of Tenochtitlan would have been immediately apparent to any visitor. Arriving at the market of Tlatelolco, it would have been hard to ignore the imposing pyramids that rose from the district of Teopan—and at the head of these was the one that today is known as the Templo Mayor, or Great Temple. At the top of the 114 steep steps of this pyramid, peaking at a height of 60 metres, were two shrines—one painted blue, the other a deep, dark red. The blue-painted shrine was dedicated to the god Tlaloc, whose name meant 'wine of the earth'. He was the god of rain and fertility, the god of life. But the great red temple was dedicated to the fearsome hummingbird-god and patron of the Mexica, Huitzilopochtli. The steps leading down from both shrines would have been darkened by a cascade of dried blood.

The Aztecs believed that Huitzilopochtli took the form of the sun, and every day chased his siblings, the moon and stars, across the sky. They believed that if he ran out of energy for this chase, the world would end—and there was only one way to keep him moving. In the Aztec view, every living being had a fragment of the sun lodged in their heart, which was why the body gave off warmth and life. They believed that cutting out the heart of a sacrificial subject and burning it in offering to Huitzilopochtli gave him the energy he needed to continue his chase. For the purpose of sacrifice, the Aztecs bred several animals: dogs, eagles, jaguars and deer. The cult of the god Quetzalcoatl even required the sacrifice of butterflies and hummingbirds. But the Aztecs are most infamous for their sacrifice of humans.

As we've seen, humans were sacrificed for religious purposes in various societies around the world, and throughout Mesoamerican history. In Mexica society, this was done in a wide variety of ways, but the most common was for a sacrificial victim to be brought to the top of one of the pyramids in Tenochtitlan, where a priest would plunge an obsidian dagger into the victim's chest to remove the heart. The still-pulsating heart was placed in a bowl and burned, allowing its energy to return to the sun. Meanwhile, the body was thrown down the steps of the pyramid, dismembered and fed to the animals in the city zoo.

It's impossible to know the full extent of this bloodthirsty practice before contact with Europeans. Sacrificial victims were usually prisoners of war, captured during battle with rival states. Warfare in the Aztec world was a highly ritualized affair, fought with wooden clubs and obsidian spears, and Aztec soldiers were generally not aiming to kill their enemy on the battlefield. Their main goal was to capture men and bring them back to Tenochtitlan to be sacrificed. For a pubescent boy, capturing his first enemy for sacrifice was considered a rite of passage. After taking two prisoners, he would be allowed to wear sandals into battle, and would be rewarded with a feathered cloak. At four captives, he would be given a jaguar skin to wear into battle. Jaguar warriors held a similar position to European knights, and climbing this ladder was the only way that a commoner could enter the nobility. Eventually, he could be promoted to the rank of 'eagle warrior'—the military elite of the Mexica—and would go into battle wearing a beaked helmet and resplendent feathers. This system has led some to argue that while a grisly spectacle, Aztec sacrifice did little more than relocate the casualties of conflict. While an Old World battle might have seen tens of thousands killed on the battlefield, an Aztec conflict produced relatively few battlefield casualties, with the associated killing taking place publicly, in the heart of their cities.

A model of Tenochtitlán's Templo Mayor, or Great Temple, in the Aztec (Mexica) Gallery, INAH, National Museum of Anthropology, Mexico City.

It is impossible to say how the ordinary Mexica felt about the practice of sacrifice, but their feelings were doubtless varied and complex. Spectators may have watched with a mixture of fear and fascination, as European peasants once spectated our own grisly, drawn-out public executions of traitors and heretics. Many may have revelled in the bloody spectacle, while others turned away. While we can never really know the answer to this question, one thing is for sure: the practice of human sacrifice was about to increase sharply thanks to a dramatic change in the political landscape of the Valley of Mexico.

★★★

The dramas of the Aztec kings can be pieced together from various sources. Chief among them are the Spanish friars Diego Durán and Bernardino de Sahagún, who both worked closely with Indigenous Mexica to write down long accounts of their history during the sixteenth century, resulting in large compendia of Nahua mythology, language and culture—the Durán and Florentine Codices. Other sources include the part-Nahua historians Fernando Ixtlilxóchitl and Chimalpahin Quauhtlehuanitzin, who wrote down what could still be gleaned from oral culture around the start of the seventeenth century.

At the time our story begins, around the year 1420, the Tepanec people still ruled over much of the valley of Mexico, and the island city of Tenochtitlan was under their thumb. The Tepanecs had a powerful army, supplied with warriors by more than forty cities. Their capital city of Azcapotzalco had apparently got its name ('anthill') due to its huge population, and it controlled the shore of the lake right where the great causeways of Tenochtitlan met the land. As a result, they essentially controlled all traffic in and out, taxing the island city heavily and exacting tribute from it.

One factor in the Tepanecs' success was the long reign of their current king, Tezozomoc. According to accounts, by 1420 Tezozomoc was already over a hundred years old. He had ruled in Azcapotzalco for more than fifty years, and had held on to power with a combination of military might and targeted assassinations. 'The tyrant Teçoçomoc...had himself proclaimed emperor, granting many favours to his allies and confederates,' writes Fernando Ixtlilxóchitl. 'However, most of the lords of the remote provinces were increasingly rebellious...'[10]

At one point, fearful of the rising power of Tenochtitlan, this king attempted to devastate them with a demand for increased tribute: 'O people of Azcapotzalco, you have seen how...the Aztecs are rising, becoming proud, they are trying to get ahead of us. Lest they rise more...let us order them to pay double the usual tribute.'[11] The King was astonished when the wealthy Mexica fulfilled his demands—but their resentment was clearly rising.

While the tyrant Tezozomoc ruled, the Tepanecs were able to suppress this resistance around the lake. But in 1426, King Tezozomoc died. 'The body of Teçoçomoc was burned,' Ixtlilxóchitl recounts, 'and his ashes placed in the main temple of Azcapotzalco.'[12] His death led to a succession crisis when one of his sons named

Maxtla seized the Tepanec throne. As the Tepanecs devolved into civil war, the subjugated cities of the lake saw their chance, and soon rose up in rebellion. At the heart of this resistance was the city of Tenochtitlan.

At this time, the king of the island city was a man named Itzcoatl—'obsidian serpent'. He formed an alliance with a young exiled prince named Nezahualcóyotl from the city of Texcoco on the other side of the lake, a boy with a Hamlet-like story whose father had been killed by Tezozomoc, and who would become famous for his poetry. Together, the two kings of Tenochtitlan and Texcoco gathered a huge army of lakeside peoples. The war that followed raged on for two years. At first the Tepanecs besieged Tenochtitlan, hoping to take out the island city and thereby destroy the resistance—but the lake city was exceptionally well-placed to withstand a siege. The Tepanecs could only cut off the supplies arriving by land, and a steady stream of goods and reinforcements would have easily passed in and out of the city by canoe. The city held out until King Itzcoatl arrived with his enormous army of allied cities, and sent the besieging army packing.

The Tepanecs' retreat quickly turned into a rout, and the combined armies of Itzcoatl and Nezahualcóyotl marched on their capital of Azcapotzalco in the year 1428. 'All of the Mexica lords assailed Maxtla's men relentlessly until they were broken and defeated,' Ixtlilxóchitl writes. 'They were forced to flee, and many died as they were being pursued. Nezahualcoyotzin's forces entered the city and destroyed and razed it, tearing down the temples and the largest houses.'[13] The usurper Maxtla was dragged back to Tenochtitlan, and killed at the top of its great temple. The era of Tepanec rule was over, and now a new power ruled in the valley. This new power, formed from the alliance between Nezahualcóyotl's Texcoco, Itzcoatl's Tenochtitlan, and the junior partner of Tlacopan, would become known as the 'Triple Alliance'. Together, these three cities would rule over the Valley of Mexico, and form the foundation of what would one day come to be known as the Aztec Empire.

***

With his Tepanec enemies crushed, King Itzcoatl settled down to the business of ruling. Helping him in his task was his nephew, a Machiavellian figure known as Tlacaelel. Tlacaelel was the kingdom's *cihuacóatl*—the highest political position below the king. In fact, he would hold this position through the reign of four subsequent kings, apparently declining the crown multiple times. During this tenure, he acted as a reformer and modernizer, improving the Aztec state's administration and taxation. He also had a quite modern understanding of the importance of propaganda, and destroyed any historical texts in the library of Tenochtitlan that undermined his king's legitimacy, as remembered in the Florentine Codex.

> Once they used to keep a record of their history,
> but it was burned at the time
> when Itzcoatl reigned in Mexico.
> It was agreed, and the nobles of Mexico said:
> it is not fitting that all the people
> should know the paintings.
> The common serfs
> will be led astray
> and the earth will be made crooked,
> because in the documents are many lies.[14]

Tenochtitlan soon eclipsed the other parties of the Triple Alliance, and Tlacaelel had the ambition of establishing it as an imperial power to surpass anything the Tepanecs had achieved. To do this, he enacted various religious reforms in the empire. The god Huitzilopochtli—the god of war and the sun—had always been the patron god of the Mexica, but worship of this deity soon rose to supplant all others. The power of the military increased, and human sacrifices became a daily affair in the empire, reaching an industrial scale. It was the dawn of a new militaristic age in Mexico. During the time of Tlacaelel, the Aztec Empire sent armies marching out beyond the volcanic sierras to conquer even farther territories. 'He was the beginning and foundation of this edifice,' writes the Nahua chronicler Chimalpahin. 'This man had the spirit and daring to...succeed in making lords of the Mexica people and republic, mistress and subduer of the greater and best part of all the New World.'[15]

The empire was a network of tribute that saw wealth flow from subjugated peoples into the city of Tenochtitlan. After conquering the city of Chalco, its people gave the following profession of subjugation:

> O Mexica... Now that we shall be your vassals we can serve you by providing you with wood for your buildings, stone, loads of earth, carved canoes, laborers to till your lands and masons for your works, brave spirited soldiers for your wars, and foodstuffs and campaigns.[16]

The administration of this empire was conducted over a network of well-maintained roads. With no horses, messages were carried by a relay system of runners stationed at 4-kilometre intervals, allowing communication along the whole length of the empire in only a day or two. Aztec rule was uncompromising and violent. In the villages they conquered, their soldiers and tax collectors were hated, their squashing of any resistance brutal. 'Tenochtitlan was a beautiful parasite,' writes the historian Inga Clendinnen, 'feeding on the lives and labour of other peoples and casting its shadow over all their arrangements.'[17]

There was one people, the Tlaxcalans, who lived just over the mountains to the east in the Valley of Tlaxcala, whom the Aztecs treated with unmatched cruelty. The Tlaxcalans remained independent, but they were at a constant state of war with the Aztec Empire. The Aztecs blockaded them, so that no luxury goods such as salt or fine textiles could be brought into their lands. They were kept as a captive, besieged population, and forced to compete each year in ritualized battles known as 'flower wars', so called because 'flower' in the Nahuatl language was associated with notions of poetic or noble deeds. For these events, the Mexica war bands dressed in their most extravagant clothes, carrying shields hung with feathers and embroidered with heraldic symbols, in orange cloaks and red hats, wearing masks, tassels and jangling bells. 'In the midst of the plain they are beautifying themselves in the image of gilded birds,' wrote one Mexica poet. 'They make glory out of the beautiful songs, the beautiful flowers.'[18]

But the stakes in the flower wars were very real. Warriors would have carried spears, obsidian daggers, and heavy bladed *macuahuitl*, and with these weapons they would beat their enemies into submission and drag them back to Tenochtitlan where their blood would stain the steps of the Great Temple. After a flower war, the skulls of the captured prisoners were displayed as grisly trophies on enormous racks called *tzompantli* in the city of Tenochtitlan, some of which have been excavated by archaeology. The largest ever found contained over 650 skulls.

When the shadowy chief advisor Tlacaelel died, aged ninety, the island city of Tenochtitlan presided over an empire that stretched from the Atlantic to the Pacific Ocean. It governed the lives of as many as 6 million people—but like the Tepanec Empire before them, like the Assyrians and Carthaginians on the other side of the world, many of its subjects harboured a bitter hatred for the Mexica. Some, like the Tlaxcala, would have taken any opportunity to throw off their yoke.

Around this time, the Florentine Codex recounts that a great omen appeared in the sky over Mexico: a comet of dazzling brilliance, 'like a flame, a tongue of fire, as if it were showering the light of the dawn. It appeared as if it were piercing the heavens.'[19] This comet would be remembered as a harbinger of doom. In little over thirty years, the people of Tenochtitlan would encounter another power that would outmatch them in military force, in ruthlessness, and at times in cruelty—an alien power from across the great sea that would bring about the end of the Aztec age.

As we saw earlier, Stone Age humans had likely crossed into the Americas by 20,000 years ago, during the last ice age. When the planet's climate warmed and sea levels rose, the North Pacific crept in to separate Asia and the Americas. The world's humans were then separated into two populations—one on each of the world's large landmasses. One day, those populations would meet again, and the developments they had made during the intervening millennia were to determine which would survive the encounter. For a number of reasons, the people who settled in the smaller landmass, the continents of the Americas, were at an inherent disadvantage.

A depiction of the fiery comet that was supposed to have presaged the arrival of the Spanish, from the first page of the *Durán Codex*.

For one thing, the Old World landmass is more than double the size of the Americas, and its population was much larger. The people of the Americas had simply arrived in their lands later than other humans. We evolved as a species in Africa between 800–300,000 years ago, and at some point in the last 200,000 years or so began to migrate out of Africa, following the River Nile and crossing the Red Sea, and on to the rest of the world. We reached southern Asia and China by about 80,000 years ago, and most of Europe by 30,000 years ago, pushing out species of archaic humans who lived there. This means that modern humans had already settled in virtually the whole Afro-Eurasian landmass for tens of thousands of years before they ever set foot in the Americas. By the fifth century CE, while the Empire of Teotihuacán had only just reached its height and was interfering with the Mayan city of Tikal, the Old World had already seen millennia pass that had seen the rise and fall of the Sumerian, Egyptian, Assyrian, Babylonian, Persian and Roman empires. By the year 1200, a century before the Mexica had even arrived in the Valley of Mexico, China alone had surpassed 140 million people—probably more than double the population of the entire Americas.

This head-start alone may have proven decisive—but the Old World enjoyed numerous other advantages that would compound the technological discrepancy. One of these was in animal life. There were only two animals in the Aztec world that could be domesticated—turkeys and dogs—but in the Old World, livestock like goats, cattle and pigs contributed greatly to the amount of protein available to the population, with powerful animals like the ox, camel and elephant also being useful as pack and draft animals. In the Old World, horses also provided human societies with an enormous amount of muscle power, and allowed speedy communication and travel across long distances, as well as spurring the development of accompanying technologies like the wheel. Many of the peoples of the Americas were perfectly aware of how to construct a wheel, and in fact there are numerous examples of Mexica children's toys with perfectly engineered wheels—but without draft animals to pull carts, the wheel didn't save much work, and was never applied to larger vehicles. Instead, like the Maya, the Aztecs carried things with leather straps fitted onto their foreheads, which tied up large numbers in manual labour.

The north-south orientation of the Americas also means that travel between its large societies required crossing various climate bands, and made the establishment of long-range trade networks more difficult. In the Old World, the east-west trade route of the Silk Road allowed convoys of pack animals to transfer goods between distant lands while remaining within a relatively consistent climate, and technologies and innovations would travel along these roads too. This meant that if something was invented in China or India, it would only be a matter of years before it would be available in Europe, and vice versa. Meanwhile, innovations in the

Americas—like the complex alphabet of the Maya, or the bronze-working of the Inca—didn't travel far beyond their borders.

The exponential curve in the development of technology meant that small head-starts could compound into significant discrepancies, and we can see these advantages play out in real time. While bronze-making began in India and the Near East around 3300 BCE, experimentation with bronze work was only just getting started in Mexico when Tenochtitlan was at its height in the fourteenth century. High-carbon steel was invented in South India in the sixth century BCE, and soon spread around the Old World. It would never be struck upon in the Americas. When the Toltec Empire declined in the Valley of Mexico in the twelfth century, the people of China had already invented gunpowder, and a magnetic compass for use at sea. By the time the Aztec emperors Itzcoatl and Nezahualcóyotl were born, the first handheld cannons had been invented in north-eastern China, and naval artillery had been used for the first time in Korea. By the height of their reigns, the arquebus had already been developed in Spain. While Tlacaelel was advising the kings of Tenochtitlan and reforming the Aztec state, the Ottoman Sultan Mehmed the Conqueror used his enormous bronze cannons to tear down the walls of Constantinople.

One technology above all others would prove to be the decisive factor in the coming collision of worlds—and that was the ocean-going caravel, and its larger successor, the carrack. Until the 1400s, Old World sailors had been largely restricted to sailing around coasts—but developments in naval technology would soon produce large, durable ships with as many as six sails and capacious holds, well-suited for long ocean-going expeditions. A complex system of rigging allowed for greater control and more sophisticated sailing techniques, and lateen sails meant that even the slightest gust of wind could be caught. With this new ship, regular voyages would soon take place between Europe and India, all around the coast of Africa, and eventually to China. In the final decades of the fifteenth century, the European countries that looked out over the Atlantic Ocean—England, France, Castile and Portugal—began to wonder if there existed a shortcut to these lucrative markets—a shortcut across the great gulf of the Atlantic itself. In 1492, only five years after the death of Tlacaelel in Tenochtitlan, a carrack called the *Santa María* set sail, supported by two smaller caravels. On board was a man who in his native Genoese was known as Cristoffa Corombo; in Spanish, Cristóbal Colón; in Italian as Cristoforo Colombo; and in English as Christopher Columbus. The collision of worlds was underway.

★★★

There were two principal actors in the great drama that is about to unfold. The first is the most wealthy and powerful man in the world—at least, as far as he knows. He is the King of the Aztecs, Moctezuma II. Like many Mexica of his time, Moctezuma had dark, wavy hair, an aquiline nose, and a large forehead. His name meant 'lord frowns in anger', but witnesses recall that his voice was eloquent, courteous and diplomatic, though he often spoke so quietly that the movements of his lips could barely be seen. Moctezuma was the ninth *tlatoani* or king of Tenochtitlan, and came to power in 1502 at the age of thirty-five, when the empire was at the height of its power and confidence.

An anonymous eighteenth-century portrait of Hernán Cortés, based on the painting sent by Cortés himself to sixteenth-century historian Paulo Giovio.

For his coronation, Moctezuma first went into a spiritual retreat, fasting and praying in the temples, and then emerging to a raucous ceremony with music, dancing, feasts and the arrival of visiting nobility from all over the Aztec lands. After the coronation, it was traditional to go to war. Moctezuma crushed a number of rebellions, and brought many captives back to Tenochtitlan to be sacrificed, alongside a heap of tribute and spoils. The blood would have run down the steps of the temple for days. Moctezuma would have worn a headdress made of shimmering green quetzal feathers, and we can imagine the cheering of the crowds as the new emperor raised his hands, and all the lands of the Aztecs bowed down beneath him.

To find the second actor, we must travel nearly 9,000 kilometres to the east. In 1502, as Emperor Moctezuma donned his headdress and climbed the steps of the Great Temple to be crowned, a sickly, irritable boy of seventeen was sitting at home in the village of Medellín, in western Spain. This boy's name was Hernán Cortés. He was born a hidalgo: a class of people with noble ancestry who didn't own any land, and whose sons therefore had little to inherit. 'He was a source of trouble to his parents as well as to himself,' writes his sixteenth-century biographer Francisco López de Gómara, 'for he was restless, haughty, mischievous, and given to quarrelling.'[20] He was a womanizer, and loved to gamble, a habit that never left him.

Columbus had landed in the Caribbean when Cortés was only seven years old, and by the time Cortés reached eighteen, the Florentine explorer Amerigo Vespucci had suggested that the lands discovered by Columbus were not the edge of Asia, as had previously been thought, but an entirely new landmass—one that would eventually be named after him. The relatively new technology of the printing press had spread this idea all over Europe. When deciding whether to travel to the New World, or go to fight in Italy as a mercenary, de Gómara writes that Cortés 'decided on the Indies…because it struck him as the more promising on account of the quantity of gold that was being brought from there.'[21]

Cortés set sail in 1504 at the age of nineteen, arriving two months later on the island of Hispaniola, where Columbus had first landed in the New World. Columbus actually went to his grave insisting that he had reached Asia as he had hoped to, and had not discovered a new continent—an ironic detail considering this is the achievement we remember him for. Nevertheless, his colonization of Hispaniola had set the pattern for the settlement of the New World. The native population had been enslaved and worked to death extracting gold for the settlers, before being all but wiped out by European diseases to which they had no immunity. Partly as a result of the loss of this native workforce, enslaved Africans would begin to be transported from 1501.

Cortés must have stepped off the ship into a steamy nightmare, full of the sick and dying, a place where some laboured in chains, and others got filthy rich. But it's clear he appreciated the opportunities this New World could offer. He stayed in Hispaniola for six years, working as a notary and learning the law, before joining an expedition in 1511 led by a man named Diego Velázquez de Cuéllar, to conquer the neighbouring island of Cuba and repeat there what had been done in Hispaniola. The native population was massacred, cut down from over 100,000 people to barely more than 20,000 in only the first few years, and again to 2,000 quickly after that. Cortés was the clerk to the treasurer of the expedition, responsible for noting down profits acquired, and ensuring that the Spanish crown got its *quinto real* or 'royal fifth'—the twenty per cent tax it levied on all loot taken in the New World. When the invasion of Cuba was complete, Velázquez became its first governor, and he was sufficiently impressed with Cortés's bookkeeping and legal knowledge that he appointed him as personal secretary, gifting him a large estate, including gold mines, and many more enslaved people to work for him. But it's clear that the ambitious Cortés was beginning to grate on Governor Velázquez.

In 1517, an expedition led by one Francisco Hernández de Córdoba explored the coast of Mexico for the first time, and met Mayan people living on the north coast of the Yucatán peninsula. At this time, no one was sure what the large landmass to the east was. Some believed it was just another large island, while others continued to maintain, as Columbus always had, that it was the mainland of Asia. But Córdoba's expedition was ill-fated. They were attacked by local Maya, and fifty Spaniards were killed, with the expedition leader later dying of his wounds. The Córdoba expedition was followed in 1518 by another, led by the Spaniard Juan de Grijalva. This time, the Spaniards went with greater protection, arming their ships with small culverin cannons. Cortés doesn't seem to have paid much attention to these expeditions, perhaps occupied with his work—but when Juan de Grijalva failed to return from his voyage, and one search party sent to look for him also didn't return, a second rescue mission was put together. Cortés was chosen to lead this expedition. He wasn't the obvious choice: he had never led an army, or commanded any kind of military post. But, crucially, he had agreed to finance half the expedition himself. Velázquez was, as de Gómara records, 'somewhat stingy, and had little stomach for spending'.[22] But the governor's orders were clear: this was not a true invasion of Mexico. That he hoped to lead himself in the coming years.

Despite his inexperience, in just one month, Cortés was able to gather 300 men and six ships, ready for his rescue mission. But before they could set off, disaster struck, from Cortés's perspective—the men they were supposedly setting out to find sailed back into port. They brought back incredible stories of cities of tall pyramids and paved streets, and recounted meeting a delegation from a powerful king who was said to live there, named Moctezuma. With its *raison d'être* vanished, and becoming increasingly nervous that Cortés was about to get all the glory of new discoveries, Governor Velázquez withdrew his support for the voyage, and even explicitly forbade Cortés from setting sail. Now with a half-provisioned expedition, and a great deal of his own money already spent, something rebelled in Cortés. With dreams of gold and conquest in his mind, 'Cortés decided to leave at once, and proclaimed he was going on his own authority'.[23] He set sail on 18 November 1518, telling his men, 'I offer you great rewards, although they will be wrapped about with great hardships… I shall make you in a very short time the richest of all men who have crossed the seas'. It's said that the governor hurried down to the docks to try to stop him, but arrived to find the ships already asea.

Stopping at ports along the Cuban coast, Cortés's force swelled to around 630 men, including crossbowmen and musketeers, sailing in eleven ships. Few of them were soldiers or had any military experience—most were merchants and traders. They brought along a number of Indigenous women, a few dozen African men, some enslaved, and others like the conquistador Juan Garrido apparently freedmen. They packed the ships with thirteen horses, a few cannons, and dogs trained for war. The invasion of Mexico had begun.

***

The Grijalva expedition the previous year had caused quite a stir in Moctezuma's court. One morning, lookouts guarding the coast had sighted the Spanish ships in the distance, their tall white sails emblazoned with red crosses. The watchmen immediately paddled out on their canoes to investigate. They were led aboard the Spanish ships, where they made a sign of respect, as the Florentine Codex records: 'They entered the boats…and when they had drawn near to the Spaniards, then before them they performed the earth-eating ceremony at the prows of the boats'.[24] The Spaniards exchanged gifts of beads and textiles with them, and left with a promise that they would soon return.

This small group of Mexica returned to the capital, obviously a little shaken by their encounter: 'day by day, night by night they travelled in order to come to warn Moctezuma, in order to come to tell him exactly of its circumstances'.[25] When they arrived, they were summoned to report to the King himself. These lowly watchmen from the coast would have come before the Emperor barefoot, and would have bowed their heads when they spoke to him. Meeting his eyes would have been strictly forbidden. They gave their king the beads that the Spanish had given them, and then, as clearly as they could, they told him what they had seen. Moctezuma was clearly troubled by what he heard. Strange rumours must have been spreading around the region for years now. In 1512, a canoe of native Jamaicans had landed in Moctezuma's lands, apparently refugees from some terrible destruction that was being wrought there. A strange chest had even washed up on the shores of the Gulf of Mexico, and been brought to Tenochtitlan for inspection, where it was found to contain several suits of bizarre clothes.

Moctezuma was a cautious and pragmatic ruler, and his first instinct was always to seek out more information before acting. 'No one shall speak anything [of this],' he told the men. 'No one shall let it escape his lips. No one shall let any of it out. No one shall loose a word of it.'[26] He told them to return to the coast and establish a permanent watch there, in case the strangers in their large ships returned. But the days passed, and nothing more happened. The Aztec new year soon came around. One of Moctezuma's favourite palace women bore him a new son. He watched performances of jugglers and dancing dwarves. Poets from Texcoco came to his palace and recited poetry on life's fleeting nature, the flowery deaths of warriors, and the sorrow of loss. 'What are you thinking? Why so serious, friend?' one such Mexica poem goes. 'Do the flowers not please you, singer?... The butterfly comes and goes like a flower; let us suck honey from the flowers, from the clusters in our hands.'[27]

Life in Tenochtitlan went on. But then, as the year drew to a close, more large ships were sighted on the horizon. Moctezuma ordered a delegation to go and meet these strangers, and find out what they wanted.

***

Cortés and his eleven ships had quickly made the short crossing from Cuba to Mexico, and sailed for several weeks past overgrown sandbars and white sand beaches lapped by sapphire blue waters. Unknown to Cortés and his men, in mid-March of 1519, they passed over the exact spot where, 66 million years earlier, the Chicxulub asteroid had impacted the earth and wiped out the dinosaurs. Travelling at an average rate of 4 knots, or about 7 kilometres an hour, it would have taken the ships an entire day and night to cross the vast ring of its crater, invisible beneath the waves.

One day, a lookout shouted that there was a canoe paddling out to meet them. Inside the canoe was a man dressed and tattooed in the style of a Mayan peasant, but they were astonished to hear him shout out in Spanish: 'Gentlemen, are you Christians? Whose subjects are you?'[28] This was Gerónimo de Aguilar, who had been shipwrecked eight years earlier when trying to sail for Cuba. He had lived as a slave among the Maya before managing to escape, and had kept himself sane through those long years by obsessively keeping track of what weekday it was back in Europe. To his distress, he discovered that it was Sunday, when he had thought it to be a Wednesday. During his captivity, Aguilar had learned a little of the Yucatec Maya language of his captors, and, seeing how useful he could be, Cortés enlisted him for his voyage, promising to take him back to Cuba when the mission was done.

Needing to restock their water supply, Cortés's expedition stopped off at a large Mayan town named Potonchán near the mouth of the Tabasco River. The locals came out to meet them armed, until 'the whole river bank appeared to be covered with Indian warriors carrying all the different arms which they use, and blowing trumpets and shells and sounding drums,'[29] wrote one of Cortés's men, Bernal Díaz del Castillo. These Mayan people tried to drive the Spaniards away by force. 'They boldly began to let fly arrows at us, and made signals with their drums,' Bernal Díaz writes, 'and like valiant men they surrounded us with their canoes.'[30]

When Cortés let off his guns, the Maya panicked, and the horsemen got ashore and rode down 400 villagers. The Mayan chief of Potonchán offered a formal surrender, and handed over large amounts of gold and a group of twenty enslaved women as part of his tribute. One of these women would be christened Marina, but to the Indigenous people of the region, she would come to be known with fear and reverence by the name Malintzin—the *tzin* suffix in Nahuatl acting as a sign of respect and submission. This woman had been enslaved from the Nahua-speaking borderlands of Coatzacoalcos, before being sold to the lord of Potonchán. She had likely lived a rough life of abuse and servitude—but her experience meant that she now spoke both Mayan and Nahuatl. Her utility was immediately apparent. 'Cortés took her aside with Aguilar,' writes de Gómara, 'and promised her more than her liberty if she would establish friendship between him and the men of her country… [as] his interpreter and secretary.'[31] Between Malintzin and Aguilar, who spoke Mayan and Spanish, Cortés was now able to communicate in virtually any language in the region. He could now make any people he encountered understand his demands. And, perhaps more importantly, he could lie.

***

From the beginning, Cortés knew that he was on a potentially illegal mission. He had defied the Cuban Governor Diego de Velázquez, to whom some of the men aboard his ships were still somewhat loyal. For this reason, one of his first acts was to scuttle ten of his eleven ships, ensuring that no one could sneak away and inform Velázquez of his whereabouts. 'He arranged with several of the sailing masters to have them holed, beyond the possibility of pumping or plugging them,'[32] de Gómara recounts. Future historians would embellish this story with the more dramatic burning of these ships, a part of the Cortés myth that evokes the classical Agathocles, the tyrant of Syracuse who had once burned his ships on the beaches of Carthage.

The eleventh ship, Cortés sent back to Spain with a letter to the King of Spain and Holy Roman Emperor Charles V—the first of five that he would write—and a collection of golden artefacts looted from nearby villages. This was clearly designed to go over Velázquez's head, and legitimize the mission with an appeal to a higher authority. With the same aim in mind, Cortés put his legal knowledge to work and immediately founded a new town, which he called Vera Cruz, or 'the True Cross'. It wasn't much of a town—likely a few tents and other temporary shelters huddled on the sandbanks—but Cortés furnished it with all the legal necessities, including a municipal council made up of several of his sunburned soldiers. In a legal sense, Cortés could now claim to be the governor of the new town, placing him on equal authority with Velázquez, and empowering him to act on behalf of the King.

Only a few days later, a group of Mexica men in fine feathers and cloaks arrived at Vera Cruz, and announced that they were messengers of Emperor Moctezuma. They brought gifts of gold and incense, as well as food. Others were hidden among the trees overlooking the beach—Moctezuma's finest court painters, sent with their brushes and paints to record everything they saw. Cortés made sure to give the Mexica a demonstration of his gunpowder weaponry, as the Florentine Codex records: 'They then shot the great Lombard gun. And the messengers…indeed fainted away and swooned; they each fell; each one, swaying, fell.'[33]

Cortés claimed that he was an ambassador sent by his king, who ruled the greater part of the world. He even ventured that some of his men were suffering from a disease of the heart, and that only the precious metal gold could be used as a treatment. He asked whether Emperor Moctezuma could help him and his men in getting some. The ambassador from Tenochtitlan, not sensing the danger, said that Moctezuma had a lot more gold in his capital of Tenochtitlan. Probably from that moment, the fate of the empire was sealed. Cortés decided then and there that he would journey to Tenochtitlan and take the land for himself. He ordered his men to prepare to march.

★★★

In the palace of Moctezuma, the Emperor's angry words echoed down the halls. He had summoned his chief soothsayers and magicians and was taking out all of his frustration on them. Part of their job was to predict the future by all the known means: by taking hallucinogenic mushrooms and gazing into obsidian mirrors, by casting kernels of grain onto the pages of holy books, and tying and untying knots. But now they had all failed to predict the astonishing arrival of these bizarre foreigners. The priest Diego Durán later wrote down recollections of those who were there:

> Motecuhzoma, furious, cried, 'It is your position, then, to be deceivers, tricksters, to pretend to be men of science and forecast that which will take place in the future, deceiving everyone by saying that you know what will happen in the world, that you see what is within the hills, in the center of the earth... But everything is a lie, it is all pretense.'[34]

When his rage abated, Moctezuma must have pored over the images that his painters brought back to him: the ships with white sails, the men in their iron clothes, and perhaps most strangely, the creatures they rode on, apparently a kind of tall deer with no horns. He must have blanched as the ambassadors described the demonstration of the foreigners' weapons.

> Especially did it cause him to faint away when he heard how the gun, at command discharged; how it resounded as if it

> thundered when it went off… Fire went showering forth; sparks went blazing forth. And its smoke smelled very foul… And when the shot struck a mountain, it was as if it were destroyed, dissolved. And a tree was pulverized; it was as if it vanished; it was as if someone blew it away.[35]

Moctezuma is often caricatured as a weak and indecisive emperor, hamstrung by superstition, but that's not entirely fair. Later European writers delighted in sharing stories of how the Aztecs believed them to be some kind of god, perhaps even Quetzalcoatl himself—but none of this is held up by evidence. If the Mexica ever mistook the Spanish for gods, it's clear they quickly assessed the reality of the situation: that these were men from a different place, whose weapons were more powerful than their own. In those first days, Moctezuma actually took a number of decisive measures. First, he sent out messengers to all the cities of Mexico, to find out what was known about these strangers. Next he ordered spies to every town and village between Tenochtitlan and the coast, to report back immediately if the Spanish tried to move inland. He created a 'war room' in Tenochtitlan where people could constantly update him on the Spaniards' movements, and even commanded his magicians to place hexes on the foreigners. But despite these measures, the uncertainty began to take its toll:

> [Moctezuma] enjoyed no sleep, no food. No one spoke more to him. Whatsoever he did, it was as if he were in torment. Ofttimes it was as if he sighed, became weak, felt weak. No longer did he enjoy what tasted good, what gave one contentment.[36]

The Spaniards' advantage wasn't simply in guns, steel and horses, but also in information. To Moctezuma, they were a complete mystery. He didn't know what they wanted. They didn't have a city that could be besieged, or wives and children that could be captured for leverage. They had no known weaknesses, making it very difficult to devise a strategy against them. But on the Spanish side, things were rather different. 'The comparatively quick and widespread communication channels available to the Spanish gave them a geopolitical perspective throughout the events that the Aztecs, for all their intelligence, even brilliance, simply lacked,'[37] writes historian Camilla Townsend. In the days after landing in Mexico, Cortés had already sent letters to Spain, requesting reinforcements and providing information about the new lands. His letters were soon printed and distributed around European cities, inspiring others to follow in his footsteps. Cortés also benefitted from years of experience of similar conquests in the Caribbean, where all the elements of his strategy had already been extensively tested—the finding of interpreters, the gathering of information, the taking of hostages and the recruitment of native allies. In fact, in only a few days, Cortés had learned all the information he needed. He knew that Moctezuma was the most powerful emperor in the region, who ruled from a city called Tenochtitlan, and possessed a great deal of gold. Even more important: he had learned that this Moctezuma had enemies.

The key to his strategy would be to find allies among the people who hated the Aztecs the most. These, he soon learned, were the besieged and terrorized people of Tlaxcala. On 8 August 1519, Cortés set out towards Tenochtitlan, with the intention of passing through the Tlaxcala Valley and making contact with these great enemies of the Mexica. He knew that the road to the coast would be his lifeline for supplies and reinforcements, and so he left almost half of his company in Vera Cruz, taking with him 300 foot soldiers and fifteen horsemen.

The Valley of Mexico lay about 400 kilometres from the coast. The first stretch of the journey was flat, hot and tropical, with dense forests dotted with Aztec plantations of maize and other crops. Then, the great snow-capped volcanoes rose up ahead of them. Everywhere they went, villages gave them supplies of maize and gold, even additional local slaves whom they used to haul their guns. They crossed a cold, bleak salt flat where water became scarce, and they soon ran out of food. 'God knows how much my people suffered from thirst and hunger,' wrote Cortés, 'and especially from a hail and rainstorm that hit us there.'[38] Bernal

Díaz remembers, 'There was a great scarcity of food and a wind came down from the snowy hills on one side of us which made us shiver.'[39] But eventually they managed to reach the Tlaxcala lands.

Cortés expected to be welcomed with open arms—but years of conflict had clearly put the Tlaxcalans on the defensive. 'Their country had often been entered by craft and cunning and then laid waste, and they thought that this was another attempt to do so,'[40] Bernal Díaz writes. 'As we marched on, two armies of warriors approached to give us battle. They numbered six thousand men and they came on us with loud shouts and the din of drums and trumpets, as they shot their arrows and hurled their darts.'[41]

For the next two days, the Tlaxcalans clashed with the Spanish, sending ever greater numbers of troops to meet them until, according to Cortés, 150,000 soldiers were ranged against them—presumably the entire army of the Tlaxcalans. All the while, Cortés tried to make signs of peace, and begged them through interpreters to stop their attack.

The Tlaxcalans fell on the Spanish lines and nearly surrounded them, but the glass blades of their *macuahuitl* shattered against the steel armour of the Europeans. The Spanish steel swords sliced their cotton armour, while crossbow bolts and gunshots tore through their ranks and spread terror. The Spanish horsemen repeatedly charged with their lances. 'In this engagement, one soldier was killed, and sixty were wounded,' Bernal Díaz writes, 'and all the horses were wounded as well.'[42]

The Tlaxcalans eventually grew dispirited and withdrew. Cortés and his men descended on nearby Tlaxcalan villages, slaughtering everyone they could find. 'I burnt more than ten villages, in one of which there were more than three thousand houses,' Cortés wrote. 'The inhabitants fought with us, although there was no one there to help them.'[43] With the devastation of their lands threatened, the Tlaxcalans relented and sued for peace. 'The following day messengers arrived from the chieftains,' Cortés wrote back to the Spanish King, 'saying that they wished to be vassals of Your Highness and my friends; and they begged me to forgive them for what they had done.' Cortés now had the allies he needed.

***

The defeat of the Tlaxcalan army by little more than 300 foreign soldiers sent ripples throughout the Aztec world, as Bernal Díaz recalls:

> Terror fell on the whole country at learning how, being so few in number and the Tlaxcalans in such great force, we had conquered them... So that now Montezuma, the great Prince of Mexico, powerful as he was, was in fear of our going to his city, and sent five chieftains, men of much importance, to our camp at Tlaxcala to bid us welcome, and say that he was rejoiced at our great victory against so many squadrons of warriors.[44]

Moctezuma's messengers told Cortés that the Aztec emperor would be delighted to welcome him to Tenochtitlan. However, it was better if he didn't come: the roads were bad, unfortunately, and supplies of food in Tenochtitlan had been very low recently. They were only thinking of the Spanish and their comfort, they said. Cortés lied, insisting his king had ordered him to go to Tenochtitlan. The Mexica warned him also never to trust the Tlaxcalans, for it was in their nature to be traitors. 'When I saw the discord and animosity between these two peoples I was not a little pleased,' Cortés wrote, 'for it seemed to further my purpose considerably... And I remember that one of the Gospels says, "*Omne regnum in se ipsum divisum desolabitur*".'[45]—a kingdom divided cannot stand.

***

Cortés's expedition stayed in the capital of Tlaxcala for a few weeks, and he ordered his men to be on their best behaviour, not to take anything that wasn't offered to them or enter the temple district of the city. Its citizens soon warmed to the Spanish, even showing them some of their precious relics: giant bones, presumably of mammoths. 'They said that...in times past there had lived among them men and women of giant size with huge bones... So that we could see how huge and tall these people had been they brought us a leg bone of one of them which was very thick and the height of a man,'[46] Bernal Díaz writes.

It's clear that the Tlaxcalans began to see a rare opportunity in these strange guests, to change their fortunes for the better. They told Cortés that the nearby city of Cholula was a great ally of Moctezuma, and that attacking it would significantly weaken him. In reality, the Cholulans weren't particularly close to the Mexica, but they were a powerful rival of the Tlaxcalans. Alarmed at the thought of the nearby threat and urged on by the Tlaxcalans, Cortés marched to Cholula, alongside a large number of Tlaxcalan warriors. It was a wealthy city with many tall towers, and it once held the world's largest pyramid by volume. When the Spanish and their allies arrived, the Cholulans met them peacefully, but Cortés unleashed a tidal wave of violence. The Florentine Codex records 'the stabbing, the slaying, the beating of the people. The Cholulan had suspected nothing; neither with arrows nor with shields had he contended against the Spaniards.'[47] The massacre went on for two days. The whole city burned, and the Spaniards destroyed a temple to the god Quetzalcoatl, the primary god of Cholula. This was a clear message to Moctezuma. The city of Tenochtitlan now lay only 80 kilometres away, beyond a wall of soaring volcanoes. Cortés's ultimate destination was drawing near.

★★★

When Moctezuma heard of the sacking of the powerful city of Cholula and the destruction of the temple by only a couple of hundred Spaniards, he was inconsolable, as the Florentine Codex recalls:

> All which had come to pass, they gave, told, related all the account to Moctezuma… It was just as if the earth moved; just as if the earth rebelled; just as if all revolved before one's eyes. There was terror.[48]

Moctezuma had a spy in every village, and with each report that came in, he knew the Spaniards were drawing closer, along with thousands of Tlaxcalan warriors, and other peoples who had joined their ranks. In a desperate attempt, Moctezuma even sent one of his servants dressed in royal garbs with as much gold as he could carry, hoping that if he gave them what they wanted—gold, and a meeting with him—they would turn back. But the Spaniards saw through the disguise. Next, he ordered the roads to be blocked with cactuses and other thorned plants like agave, but the Spaniards easily overcame these obstacles, and panic descended in Moctezuma's court. The magicians that Moctezuma had sent to slow down the foreigners reported that their spells had had no effect. Even worse, some of them had experienced visions in which they saw the whole Aztec Empire, all its temples and palaces, houses and towers, going up in flames.

★★★

Finally, Cortés and his men passed through the mountains and saw the Valley of Mexico stretching out before them. They would have seen the wide blue waters of Lake Texcoco, the white clutter of dozens of cities ringing its bank, the grasslands striated with fields of corn, beans, chilli peppers and cotton, smoke rising from the chimneys. And in the middle of the lake, the glittering jewel of Tenochtitlan. Many of the conquistadors were speechless. Others, like Francisco de Aguilar, would later gush about what they saw: 'Castellated fortresses, splendid monuments… Royal dwelling places! Glorious heights! How marvellous it was to gaze on them.'[49]

As they approached the causeway, out on the middle of the bridge, the Spanish saw a figure standing in a crown of green quetzal feathers, surrounded on either side by warriors wearing jaguar skins and eagle feathers. Emperor Moctezuma had come out to meet them. Tenochtitlan was guarded by the vast army of the Aztec Empire. It's quite possible, at this point, that they could have overwhelmed the Spanish, as the Tlaxcalans nearly had. But Moctezuma knew that if he tried and failed to defeat the Spanish in full view of his citizens, his kingship, and likely his life, would be over. So he had decided to finally meet this foreigner and see what he wanted. The Florentine Codex recounts the sight the Spaniards made: 'Their iron lances, their halberds seemed to glisten, and their iron swords were wavy, like a water [course]... Some came all in iron; they came turned into iron; they came gleaming... Hence they were dreaded.'[50]

Neither Cortés nor Moctezuma were much given to flowery words. According to the Florentine Codex, the following exchange is all they said at first:

> Then [Cortés] said to Moctezuma: 'Is this not thou? Art thou not he? Art thou Moctezuma?'
> Moctezuma replied: 'Indeed yes; I am he.'
> Thereupon he arose; he arose to meet him face to face.[51]

Moctezuma extended his courtesy to the Spaniards, and they were shown into the city and given lodgings in a former royal apartment while he worked out what they wanted. The palace, wrote Francisco de Aguilar, 'was a wonder to behold. There were innumerable rooms inside, antechambers, splendid halls, mattresses of large cloaks, pillows of leather and tree fibre, good eiderdowns, and admirable white fur robes.'[52]

When the Spanish arrived in their opulent lodgings, they began firing off their guns and cannons in celebration. The sounds resounded around the city streets, and the locals hid in fear. 'Fear prevailed. It was as if everyone had swallowed his heart. Even before it had grown dark, there was terror, there was astonishment, there was apprehension, there was a stunning of the people.'[53] As Cortés and his men went to sleep that night in the palace, they would have heard the soft blowing of conch shells echoing from the temples at midnight. The beating of drums would have announced the arrival of the dawn.

★★★

Cortés and his men spent the next few days in the city of Tenochtitlan. They saw the towering, bloodstained temples and the market of Tlatelolco. 'Some of the soldiers among us who had been in many parts of the world,' Bernal Díaz wrote, 'in Constantinople, and all over Italy, and in Rome, said that so large a market place and so full of people, and so well regulated and arranged, they had never beheld before.'[54]

Moctezuma, increasingly feeling that he was losing control of his kingdom, gave up much of his treasury to the Spaniards. He handed over ornately decorated gold jewellery, headbands and chestplates, statues and other incomparable works of art, most of which they immediately melted down into gold bricks—but none of this seemed to satisfy them. It seemed as if they were waiting for something—and Moctezuma would soon find out what that was.

Not long after Cortés's arrival in Tenochtitlan, news arrived from Vera Cruz that six of Cortés's men had been killed in a quarrel with some local Mexica. This was a relatively minor trifle—but Cortés welcomed it as a pretext to move against Moctezuma and take the Aztec emperor himself as a hostage. He swept into the throne room and told Moctezuma to go with the Spanish to their lodgings, for his own protection. Cortés warned the Emperor not to make a noise or cry out in any way, telling him: 'order your people not to be angry or make a disturbance, and bear in mind that if any ill befalls us, you will pay for it with your life'.[55] The Emperor realized what was happening, and he must have gone pale. He pleaded with the Spaniards to reconsider. 'My person is not such as can be made a prisoner of,' he told them. 'Even if I would like it, my people would not suffer it.'[56]

But suffer it they did. That night, Cortés arrested seventeen Mexica lords who he said had plotted the attacks. He had them burned alive in the courtyard of the great temple, using piles of arrows and wooden *macuahuitl* from the Tenochtitlan armoury as kindling. Moctezuma was brought to watch, with chains on his feet. 'If before this he was scared,' Bernal Díaz recounts, 'he was then much more so.'[57] It's said the Mexica watched the executions in complete silence. It would have been clear to everyone, even the common people in the street, that from this moment on, Cortés was the true power in the Aztec Empire.

Moctezuma, for the most part, bore his imprisonment with dignity but resignation. He continued the usual business of governing his empire—he met his lords and watched jugglers and poets as usual—but everywhere he went, Spanish guards went with him.

He must have felt a sense of abject misery and fear. But then in April 1520, a messenger managed to slip the Aztec emperor a secret note that represented a glimmer of hope. It was a painting of nineteen Spanish ships, off the coast of Mexico. To Moctezuma, the meaning was clear: another group of Spaniards were arriving, and they were not friends of Cortés.

***

Diego de Velázquez, the Governor of Cuba, had spent the six months since Cortés's departure stewing in his bitterness. He had confiscated much of Cortés's property in Cuba, but this had done little to sate his appetite for revenge. When he heard that Cortés had sent news and chests full of gold directly to the King, bypassing him completely, Velázquez exploded. He ordered one of his lieutenants named Pánfilo de Narváez to sail to Mexico with 900 men, apprehend Cortés and drag him back to Cuba in chains.

With the use of couriers and secret notes, Moctezuma was able to communicate with Narváez as he sailed up the Mexican coast. Narváez told Moctezuma that Cortés and his men did not, in fact, have the support of the Spanish crown. 'Narvaez sent to tell Montezuma many abusive and many uncivil things about Cortés and all of us,' remembers Bernal Díaz, 'such as that we were bad men and thieves who had fled from Castile without the permission of our Lord and King.'[58] Moctezuma sent Narváez food and gold, and begged him to come and help—but all the while, he played the model prisoner. He and Cortés even played a Mexica game of marbles called *Totoloque*, although Moctezuma politely complained that the Spaniard cheated when he kept score, 'in that he always marked one point too many'.[59] But as time went on, Moctezuma grew terrified that his double dealings would be discovered. He went to Cortés and came clean, hoping that the news would spur the Spaniards to pack up and flee. He urged him to leave Tenochtitlan while there was still time.

Cortés was in a bind. 'I dared not leave the city,' he wrote, 'for fear that once I had done so the inhabitants would rebel and I would lose all the gold, the jewels, and even the city itself; for once that was lost the whole country would be lost also.'[60] He would now have to march back to the coast and face Narváez, leaving enough of his men behind to hold the Emperor prisoner. His force would be dangerously split, and everything he had won now lay in the balance.

★★★

At the start of May, Cortés and as many as 250 of his men set off on their march back to the coast. Cortés sent a messenger to the Tlaxcalans, asking them for 4,000 men to help him fight Narváez—but this development had clearly shaken their confidence in their new ally. They sent Cortés twenty turkeys as a gift instead. On the coast, Narváez had landed and set camp at a place called Cempoala, at the top of one of the town's temples, and waited for Cortés's army to arrive. Narváez outnumbered Cortés three to one, and was confident of success. But Cortés had been in Mexico for over a year at that point, and had learned how best to fight in the landscape. While Narváez slept, Cortés and his men crept through the night, a torrential rain covering their movements. They climbed the pyramid stealthily and ambushed the guards, setting the temple on fire as they went. In the skirmish that followed, Narváez lost his right eye, and surrendered. His soldiers were mercenaries with no particular loyalty, and when Cortés dazzled them with stories of mountains of gold waiting back in Tenochtitlan, they agreed to join him. Far from defeating Cortés, Velázquez had delivered him fresh reinforcements. More powerful than ever, he now set his sights on returning to Tenochtitlan. But in his absence, events in the city had taken a dark turn.

The man that Cortés had left in charge was named Pedro de Alvarado. Alvarado was a harsh man with a red beard, flamboyant and quick to anger—perhaps the worst person to command such a precarious situation. Cortés had left him only about a hundred men, and a crowd of Tlaxcala allies of doubtful loyalty, and with these he had to keep his grasp on a city of perhaps 200,000. The situation would come to a head as an annual Mexica ceremony neared—an event known as the festival of Toxcatl.

The Toxcatl ceremony involved the sacrifice of a young man, chosen from among the people for his good looks and charm. For the last year, he had lived as an embodiment of the god Tezcatlipoca, being showered with every luxury—but now his time had come, and he would be sacrificed. Before he left, Cortés had given Moctezuma permission to hold the festival, on condition that there would be no human sacrifice that year. But, with Cortés gone, the Mexica sensed weakness and division in the foreigners. They stopped providing the Spaniards with food, and some collaborating Mexica turned up dead. Alvarado feared that the Mexica were preparing to scale the palace walls, or tunnel under them, to rescue the captive Moctezuma. The Spaniards began to feel increasingly under siege.

On the third night of the festival, the Mexica sang sacred songs and dressed in feathered headdresses and bright embroidered clothes. 'There was singing,' the Florentine Codex recalls, 'the singing resounded like waves breaking.'[61] As the ceremony went on, it became obvious that the Mexica were going to ignore Cortés's orders and carry out the sacrifice anyway. Alvarado, enraged at their disobedience, ordered his men into the sacred precinct, dressed for war. Other armoured soldiers guarded the exits. As the festival reached its climax, and the drums crashed and flutes shrieked, Alvarado commanded the Spanish to fall upon the gathered Mexica, and a slaughter began. The Mexica memories of this event recorded in the Florentine Codex are full of gruesome, specific details that read like the authentic memories of trauma:

> Thereupon they surrounded the dancers. Thereupon they went among the drums. Then they struck the drummer's arms; they severed both his hands; then they struck his neck. Far off did his neck [and head] go to fall... Of some they slashed open their backs: then their entrails gushed out. Of some they cut their heads to pieces; they absolutely pulverized their heads...and when in vain one would run, he would only drag his intestines like something raw as he tried to escape.[62]

The Spaniards began to loot and burn the temples in a frenzy of destruction, and the Mexica realized that this was their chance to regain their freedom. The drums beat, and an Aztec priest is said to have bellowed out, 'Brave warriors, O Mexicans, hasten here! Already they have died, they have perished, they have been annihilated, O Mexicans, O brave warriors!'[63]

Illustration from the *Durán Codex*, showing the massacre at the Tōxcatl festival.

Commoners grabbed their weapons, and warriors flooded the street. The Spanish were forced to retreat to the palace, where they settled in for a siege, with a number of their Tlaxcalan allies and the Emperor as their hostage, waiting for Cortés to return.

***

After twenty-three days, Cortés returned to the shores of Lake Texcoco, his forces swelled by Narváez's men. He now commanded about 1,000 Spaniards and many thousands of reassured Tlaxcalan warriors who had joined him on his return journey. Cortés found Alvarado and his men holed up in the palace, on the edge of starvation. The city was in open revolt, and the crowds came out every day to batter on the palace doors. Cortés ordered Moctezuma to go out onto the terrace of the palace and appeal for calm. Seventeen years earlier, a similar crowd had cheered his glorious coronation. But now the Mexica met their emperor with utter silence. Moctezuma called out that it would be better to surrender to the Spanish, that it was impossible to fight them. One source, the Codex Ramírez, recalls an Aztec warrior shouting back to Moctezuma:

> What is that which is being said by that scoundrel of a Montezuma, whore of the Spaniards? Does he think that he can call to us, with his woman-like soul, to fight for the empire which he has abandoned out of fright...?[64]

It wasn't long before the first stones began to rain down on the King, and as soon as the first one landed, his authority vanished. Soon, the whole crowd was pelting him. Moctezuma was struck several times before the Spanish were able to rescue him. It's said he refused any treatment for his wounds, and died on the morning of 30 June 1520. Some Mexica sources refute the claim that Moctezuma was killed in this way, and say that the Spanish simply knifed him once their situation in the city became untenable. Either way, they were quick to burn the body, as the Florentine Codex records:

> Thereupon they placed him on a pile of wood... Thereupon they kindled it, they set fire to it. Thereupon the fire crackled, seeming to flare up, to send up many tongues of flame... And Moctezuma's body seemed to lie sizzling, and it smelled foul as it burned.[65]

★★★

Cortés knew that he could not stay in the city. His power over the Mexica people had evaporated. He hatched a plan to slip out of the palace and across the western causeway while the Mexica slept. His men packed all the gold they could carry into their bags, and muffled the hooves of their horses. 'It was somewhat dark and cloudy and rainy,' remembers Bernal Díaz. Everything went to plan at first. But as they crept through the narrow streets, a woman by the docks spotted them and shouted out a warning, and soon 'the voices, trumpets, cries and whistles of the Mexicans began to sound'.[66]

On open ground, the Spanish horses and cannons were unbeatable—but in the narrow streets, on the islands broken by bridges and canals, the Aztecs knew exactly how to fight. They massed around the Spanish in war canoes and on the rooftops, pelting them with arrows and stones, while warriors ran them down from the rear. 'Two of the horses slipped and fell into the lake,' writes Bernal Díaz, 'the lake was full of canoes so that we could do nothing.'[67] The Mexica's hatred was now such that they abandoned their usual battle practice of taking captives, instead killing the Spaniards with a sharp blow to the back of the head, a punishment usually reserved for petty criminals. The bodies of the dead on both sides choked up the canals, and legend has it that some of the Spanish, weighted down with stolen gold, sank to the bottom of the lake. The retreat became a rout. A reasonable estimate for the number of Spanish killed on this night is around 600. Thousands of their Tlaxcalan allies were killed too. But just over 400 Spaniards, Cortés among them, managed to fight their way across the causeway to safety. They managed to fight off the pursuing Aztec forces at the Battle of Otumba, where once again their horsemen were in their element on the open ground. From there, they fled back to the safety of Tlaxcala.

Aztec warriors pursue retreating Spanish conquistadors after The Night of Sorrows, as depicted in the *Florentine Codex*, book XII, folio 51.

Tenochtitlan had delivered the most crushing defeat ever inflicted on European colonists in the New World. The Spanish would call it the *Noche Triste*: the night of sorrows. The Mexica must have been elated, but their emperor now lay dead, and multiple tributary cities were openly denying the authority of Tenochtitlan. The fabric of the Aztec Empire was fraying.

Cortés was by this point a man possessed. Many of his men begged him to march back to the coast where they could fortify Vera Cruz and prepare for a counterattack, but he refused. 'On no account would I go across the mountains to the coast,' he wrote. 'I told them that I would not abandon this land.'[68] At Tlaxcala, he spent the next six months gathering an army of tens of thousands of native allies, to add to his remaining Spaniards, and at the head of this army he marched to Tenochtitlan just after Christmas of 1520.

When the Spaniards reached the lake, they now marched at the head of an army of as many as 200,000 native allies who had all come to take part in the final destruction of Tenochtitlan. At the lakeshore, they cut down pine trees to build twelve ships of a kind known as brigantines, which they loaded with cannons and musketeers. Cortés first blocked all the main causeways leading to Tenochtitlan, and with his ships blockaded any attempts to resupply it by water. Tenochtitlan was now truly under siege.

The Mexica were not only besieged and encircled from without—they were now also coming under attack from an invisible enemy. When the expedition of Pánfilo de Narváez had arrived in Mexico to arrest Cortés, he had brought with him some enslaved African men, and one of these, named Francisco de Eguía, was apparently infected with smallpox. When they had stayed the night in Cempoala, he had spread this disease to an Indigenous family before dying, and from there the fates of millions in the New World were sealed.

'There spread over the people a great destruction of men,' the Florentine Codex records. 'Some it indeed covered [with pustules]; they were spread everywhere, on one's face, on one's head, on one's breast, etc. There was indeed perishing; many indeed died of it.'[69] Bernal Díaz writes that 'the whole country was stricken and filled with it, from which there was great mortality, for according to what the Indians said they had never had such a disease.'[70]

In the Old World, after millennia of exposure to smallpox, the disease still killed a third of all the people it infected, usually in childhood—but in the New World, it combined with other diseases like measles to tear through populations, in places killing nine out of every ten people. This critically weakened the Aztecs, and harrowed their leadership. Moctezuma's successor, a man named Cuitláhuac, even died of smallpox during the siege.

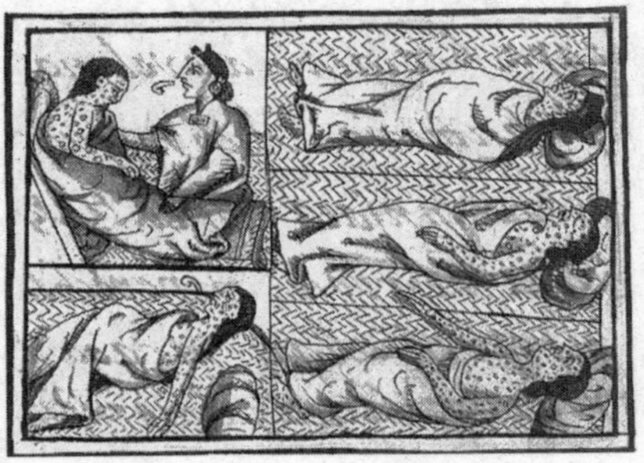

An Aztec illustration depicting the effects of smallpox on the infected, from the *Florentine Codex*.

After many weeks, Cortés finally advanced into the starved city across its three causeways. The fighting was bitter, going street to street, fighting for each house and bridge at a time, with heavy losses. The Mexica began to use sacrifices as a weapon of terror, in full view of the Spanish armies. 'On some high towers which are there [they] sacrificed them naked,' Cortés remembers, 'opening their chests and tearing out their hearts as an offering to the idols. The Spaniards…recognized those who were being sacrificed as Christians by their white naked bodies.'[71] At night, the Mexica beat their war drums incessantly, so that Bernal Díaz grew to hate 'the cursed drum, which I again declare had the most accursed sound and the most dismal that it was possible to invent.'[72] The resilience of the Aztecs took Cortés by surprise, and he soon resorted to extreme methods. He had wanted to hand the city of Tenochtitlan over to his king as a pristine prize, but now he ordered the Spanish to demolish every district they came to and use the rubble to fill in the canals and waterways.

Just as the Spanish adapted their tactics, the Mexica learned to make evasive manoeuvres in their canoes to escape from gunfire, and even lured some of Cortés's brigantines onto submerged sandbanks, then boarding and killing their commanders. At night, the city's defenders snuck out and cleared the rubble from the canals. But as the months of grinding battle wore on, famine and disease weakened the Mexica. They ate wood and leather, even bricks crushed into powder. When the Spanish reached the city centre, they located the well that the Mexica had been drinking from and destroyed it, forcing them to drink the salty lake water instead. The Aztecs had no new supplies, no new soldiers and no relief. Meanwhile, a steady flow of supplies came from the coast to Cortés. The result of the battle must have become clear. The final stand took place in the great market of Tlatelolco, where the Mexica were surrounded and utterly destroyed. They finally surrendered on 13 August 1521. Some years later, an Aztec poet wrote the following bitter lament about the fall of the city.

> Broken spears lie in the roads;
> we have torn our hair in our grief.
> The houses are roofless now, and their walls
> are red with blood.
>
> Worms are swarming in the streets and plazas,
> and the walls are spattered with gore.
> The water has turned red, as if it were dyed,
> and when we drink of it,
> it has the taste of brine.
>
> We have pounded our hands in despair
>   against the adobe walls,
> for our inheritance, our city, is lost and dead.
> The shields of our warriors were its defense,
> but they could not save it.[73]

The Spanish stood victorious over the smoking ruins of Tenochtitlan. Hernán Cortés and his small group of soldiers had, within two years, brought down an empire. But not everyone was satisfied with their takings. 'All of us captains and soldiers were somewhat thoughtful,' remembers Bernal Díaz, 'when we saw how little gold there was and how poor and unjust were our shares.'[74]

The victory had come at great cost. Humiliated by his failure to capture the city intact, Cortés soon set about erasing all trace of Tenochtitlan. He enslaved vast numbers of Mexica, and put them to work demolishing their own city—all its houses and palaces and temples—and building European-style buildings on the ruins. He even changed Tenochtitlan's name, renaming it Mexico because it was an easier word for the Spanish to pronounce. The Franciscan friar Toribio de Benavente Motolinía, who arrived there four years later, described the hellish scenes:

> The seventh plague was the construction of the great City of Mexico, which, during the early years used more people than in the construction of Jerusalem. The crowds of labourers were so numerous that one could hardly move in the streets and causeways, although they are very wide. Many died from being crushed by beams, or falling from high places, or in tearing down old buildings for new ones.[75]

After the empire collapsed, the Spanish did their best to eradicate Aztec culture, burning all the Mexica books they could find, so that today only sixteen books written by pre-contact Aztecs have survived. During the siege, the Spanish had destroyed the Aztec dams and methods for water control, and so in its early years Mexico City was prone to destructive floods. To remedy this, in the 1600s the great Lake Texcoco was drained, in the hope that fertile farmlands would be revealed beneath the water—but all that took its place were stagnant salt flats. Across these, the new Mexico City would expand at an enormous rate. Today, it is one of the largest cities in North America, with more than 20 million people living in its wider metropolitan area. The entire lakebed was paved over, and the enormous expanse of Lake Texcoco simply ceased to exist. Today, Mexico City is still beset with floods and subsidence caused by the ghost of this vanished lake.

Diego Velázquez, the governor of Cuba and Cortés's nemesis, was dismissed as governor in 1521, when his abuse of Indigenous labour became too embarrassing for the crown—but he was restored to office two years later. He died unexpectedly one year after that at the age of fifty-nine, and on his death was considered the richest Spaniard in the Americas. Pánfilo de Narváez, the captain who had been sent to arrest Cortés, was released from captivity after two years, and sent back to Spain missing one eye. He returned to adventuring in the Americas several years later in 1527, and led a disastrous expedition to Florida: hurricanes, shipwrecks and disease meant that of the 600 men he set sail with, only four made it home. Narváez himself was drowned. Malintzin, the enslaved woman that had accompanied Cortés on his conquest and acted as his translator, would go on to give birth to Cortés's son. She later married one of his soldiers, who she followed to Spain. She was warmly received there at the Spanish court, and became a Spanish lady of high society.

The story of Cortés's destruction of the Aztec Empire would become legendary in Europe, and the publication of his letters in the years that followed caused a sensation. The myth of the handful of conquistadors toppling an empire began to be exaggerated, and the contribution of hundreds of thousands of Tlaxcalan warriors forgotten. 'The kingdoms and lines of…the Assyrians, Medes, and Persians, ended, but their names and renown live on in the histories,' gushes de Gómara. 'The Conquest of Mexico and the conversion of the peoples of New Spain can and should be included in the histories of the world… Long live, then, the name and memory of him who conquered so vast a land.'[76]

Cortés would spend the rest of his life chasing after the feeling of glory that he must have felt at the fall of Tenochtitlan, but he would never recapture it. He returned to Spain several times, but his fame and popularity threatened the Castilian nobility, and he was sidelined at court. On one possibly apocryphal occasion, he even tried to talk to the Spanish King by jumping aboard his carriage. The King didn't even recognize him, and asked who he thought he was. Cortés is supposed to have replied indignantly, 'I am Hernan Cortés, who has given you more kingdoms than all the towns bequeathed to you by your ancestors!'[77]

Cortés died of dysentery in Seville on 2 December 1547. He

was sixty-two years old, embittered and alone. Perhaps fittingly for such a restless, dissatisfied character, his remains were moved eight times in the following decades, first around Spain and then overseas to Mexico. In the nineteenth century, the rising swell of pride in Indigenous Mexican identity meant that Cortés became a figure of hatred, and the marker on his tomb was hidden for fear it would be destroyed. Finally, his bones were moved to Jesús Nazareno Church in Mexico City, next to the Pino Suárez subway station. His burial place is marked only by an orange plaque bearing his name and dates, and today he receives few visitors. We could hardly put it better than a Mexica poet, whose words come down to us—persistently, defiantly—through the centuries:

Friends, let us still rejoice.
O friends, be not sad.
It is true the earth is nobody's possession:
none shall remain upon it!
. . .
Only a brief moment we wander intoxicated
beside thee, at thy side, O Giver of Life.
It is only a place where we know one another, on earth.
None shall remain upon it!
Feathers of quetzal are torn;
paintings, they are destroyed;
flowers, they wither:
everything goes to His Home.[78]

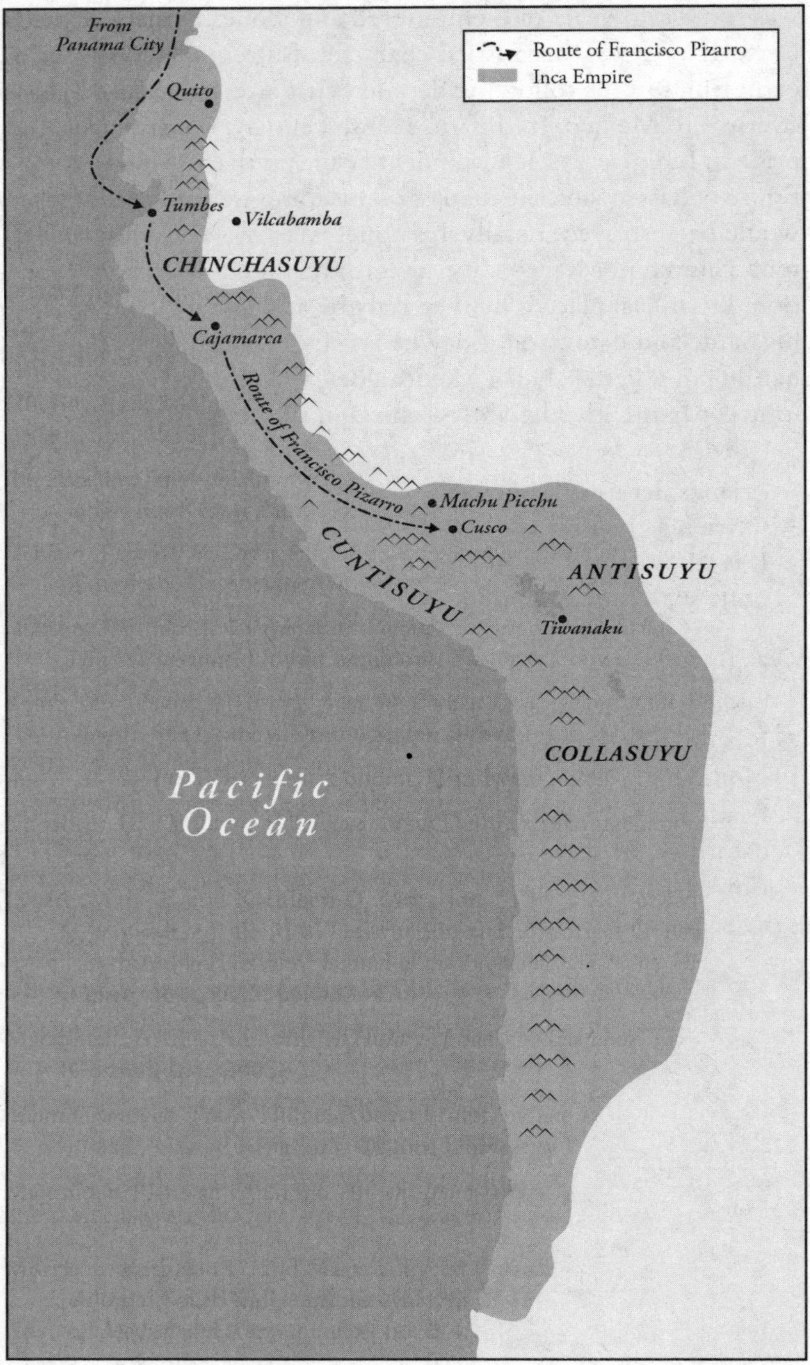
Route of Francisco Pizarro
Inca Empire
From Panama City
Quito
Tumbes
Vilcabamba
CHINCHASUYU
Cajamarca
Route of Francisco Pizarro
Machu Picchu
Cusco
CUNTISUYU
ANTISUYU
Tiwanaku
COLLASUYU
Pacific Ocean

13

The Inca

c. 1200–1533

The Andes mountains are the longest continental mountain range in the world. They stretch more than 7,000 kilometres across South America, from north to south, about a sixth of the way around the circumference of the earth. These are also the world's tallest mountains outside of the Himalayas, with the highest peaks towering up to nearly 6,700 metres or 22,000 feet—roughly two thirds the cruising altitude of an airliner. Since their formation 6–10 million years ago, this geological rampart has had a dramatic effect on the circulation of the earth's atmosphere, giving rise to some of the planet's most extreme landscapes. To the east, they act as a wall to the continent's rainclouds, pooling and gathering them, resulting in the vast jungle rainforest of the Amazon—but the land on the Pacific side of the mountains couldn't be more different. In fact, the desert that has formed there, known as the Atacama, is one of the driest places on earth. Some weather stations set up there in modern times have never detected any rain. Still, across this desert, about forty rivers do flow down from the mountains, forming rich oases—and for at least the last 10,000 years, humans have made their home here. Many common crops, including avocados, peanuts and pineapples, were domesticated and farmed in these valleys, which receive virtually no rainfall. In these desert lands, several early societies rose up like the Moche and the Nazca—but it's in the mountains themselves that the greatest civilization of South America would emerge.

★★★

The Andes mountains are among the most hostile environments on earth. Among their high craggy peaks of sandstone, limestone and granite, less than two per cent of the land is suitable for growing food. Even at the bottom of the valleys, it is rare to find any fertile soil. The mountains above about 4,800 metres are capped with snow and ice all year round, and the snows creep much lower in the winter months. Their narrow gorges are home to quick-flowing rivers, and can only be crossed at certain points where it's possible to build bridges. For this reason, many of the early myths of the Andean peoples relate the journeys of migratory groups looking for a suitable place to live.

In the Inca conception of their own history, their story began with a small band of highlanders who migrated to a place called Cusco, a warm valley in the highlands of southern Peru, likely around 1200 CE. This valley is around 40 kilometres long, fertile and watered by the Huatanay River, and it's easy to see why these weary travellers would have stopped there. Their mythical leader, Manco Cápac, is supposed to have led them there using the guidance of a golden staff, and the advice of the sun. The Inca creation myth, recorded in the sixteenth century by the chronicler Juan de Betanzos, describes the scenes that these first migrants would have seen upon their arrival.

> In the place which is called today the great city of Cuzco… there was a small town of about thirty small, humble straw houses… The rest of the area around this town was a marsh of sedge with sharp-edged leaves.[1]

Tradition holds that these people had come from a place called

Tiwanaku. Tiwanaku was a grand city founded around 100 CE on the shore of Lake Titicaca, to the south of Cusco in what is now western Bolivia. In the city of Tiwanaku, the art of Andean stone-carving reached its earliest heights. In fact, it's here that the Inca creator god Viracocha is supposed to have carved humanity out of the very stone of the mountain itself. 'During this time of total night, they say that a lord emerged from a lake in this land of Peru,' goes the Inca creation myth.

> He went from there to a place near the lake where today there is a town called Tiahuanaco… There, they say that he suddenly made the sun and day, and ordered the sun to follow the course that it follows… He made some people from stone, as a kind of model of those that he would produce later… together with a chieftain to govern and rule over them, and many women, some pregnant and others delivered…[2]

A 1920 photograph showing children seated before the Gate of the Sun at the site of Tiwanaku, Bolivia.

Wandering the stone-littered landscape of Tiwanaku today, where pieces of carved volcanic andesite still litter the ground, and cracked statues of human and animal faces peer out of the walls, it's not hard to see where the Inca got this idea. The city went into decline and suffered a dramatic depopulation around the year 1000, and any Inca who visited it in the centuries that followed would have found it a ruin, which to them must have felt like the abandoned workshop of a great mason who had only just put down his hammer.

The Inca were also heavily influenced by a people known as the Wari. The Wari were a desert culture, but between the year 540 to 650, while Europe reeled from the collapse of the Roman Empire in the West, the Wari expanded across the hostile mountains of the Andes. Their buildings were not as refined as those of Tiwanaku, often built out of rough, uncut fieldstones, using mud for mortar—but this unfussiness allowed them to build on a much larger scale. Their city walls were often as far as 12 metres or four storeys high, and their aqueducts could run for as much as 40 kilometres across the landscape.

The Wari were experts at water control, and marshalled enormous work gangs to build reservoirs and channels that cut through the dry coastal plains and transformed the landscape of the low Andes. They also developed ingenious terraces for growing food, designed to hold fertile soil and absorb and disperse the heat of the sun. On these terraces, lowland crops like tomatoes, squashes and pumpkins, even types of tobacco, were grown for the first time in the high Andes. The compendium of indigenous knowledge known as the Huarochirí manuscript remembers the Wari somewhat uncharitably: 'In very ancient times…when a great number of people had filled the land, they lived really miserably, scratching and digging the rock faces and ledges to make terraced fields.'[3] But the Wari were successful. Their empire was centralized and organized, with trade routes that extended throughout the mountains and allowed coca leaves, tobacco and bright feathers to pass west out of the jungle, while maize, seashells and dried fish passed east from the coast. But for reasons we can never entirely know, around the year 1000, this early empire rapidly came apart. By the year 1100, all of the major Wari centres were abandoned and never reoccupied.

The city of Cusco found itself at the location where the influence of Tiwanaku and the Wari overlapped, and so it inherited something of a hybrid culture, benefitting from both predecessors' achievements. The Wari had introduced the idea of an empire that would unite the territories of the Andes—but with their collapse, what followed was centuries of fragmentation and warfare in the mountains, as rival states competed to fill the power vacuum. From these wars, the Inca would rise. They would model themselves both culturally and politically on the Wari, even dressing their nobles in woven tunics descended from Wari traditional dress. They built their imperial capital at Cusco, and modelled it after the Wari cities. All of this was designed to send a message to the people living among the high mountain passes: the days of chaos were coming to an end; the heirs of the old empire had arrived to bring order once more, and these heirs were the people of the Inca.

The Inca would soon embark on a rapid expansion that would see them grow to become the greatest empire ever seen in South America, in what may have been as little as fifty to eighty years. According to tradition, this would be thanks to one great king, a conqueror of unmatched skill and energy—a kind of Andean Alexander. His name means 'he who overturns space and time': Pachacuti Inca Yupanqui.

***

Pachacuti was born in Cusco, in the palace of Cusicancha. As he grew up, he would have looked out over the hills as the sun washed the grassy valley sides, and watched birds fly over the yellow thatched rooftops of the city. As a boy, it's recorded that he learned history, laws and language from his teacher named Micuymana, and in later life he would become a revered poet.

Pachacuti was not intended for the throne—that was reserved for his older brother Urco—but some time in the early fifteenth century, a people known as the Chanka invaded the lands of Cusco.

Pachacuti's father, the king, fled along with the crown prince Urco, believing the city to be lost. Pachacuti stayed behind and, according to the story, rallied the disheartened Inca soldiers around him before leading them against the invaders. It's said that Pachacuti fought so fiercely, even the stones of the mountains rose up to fight the invaders, and he was given the title 'the earth shaker'. Reading between the lines, it's possible that the Chanka army may have been caught up in one of the frequent earthquakes and landslides that rock this region. Whatever the cause, Pachacuti's victory was so celebrated that, around 1438, his father had little choice but to name him his successor.

From the moment he became king, Pachacuti embarked on a series of grand construction projects, rebuilding Cusco after the war with the Chanka, and turning it into a city that would be the envy of the entire region. Meanwhile, he led the Inca army in a series of victories that stretched their land even further. Part of Pachacuti's success was that wherever he conquered, he also built. He constructed irrigation channels and cultivated terraces in every territory he expanded into. During his reign, the Inca road system expanded dramatically, until it stretched more than 5,000 kilometres from Ecuador to Chile, allowing the army to travel quickly to wherever it was needed. Pachacuti understood the importance of intelligence, and relied heavily on a network of spies and informants who would infiltrate neighbouring states and bring back reports on their power and wealth. Pedro Cieza de León, a Spanish-Jewish conquistador who collected Inca recollections, describes how this king would attempt to win over the rulers of these kingdoms:

> They always arranged matters…so that things should be pleasantly and not harshly ordered… They marched from Cuzco with their army and warlike materials, until they were near the region they intended to conquer. Then they collected very complete information touching the power of the enemy… The Inca sent special messengers to the enemy to say that

> he desired to have them as allies and relations, so that, with joyful hearts and willing minds they ought to come forth to receive him in their province, and give him obedience as in the other provinces; and that they might do this of their own accord he sent presents to the native chiefs.[4]

Most of the neighbouring rulers seem to have accepted, and were peacefully folded into the empire—but the offer wasn't without an implicit threat. Refusal to accept Inca rule resulted in an invasion, and rulers who resisted were executed without exception.

The Inca army at this time was a powerful force. The Inca and other Andean cultures had the most advanced metallurgy of the American continents, and made tools and weapons from copper and bronze. Their weapons were spears launched using spear throwers, arrows and javelins, slings, as well as clubs and maces made from the hard black wood of the chonta palm, with blunt or spiked metal heads. Any commoner could be conscripted as part of the system of organized labour, and at times the army could exceed 140,000 men. The Inca had no iron or steel, and no real technological advantage over other Andean cultures—so they often relied simply on sheer force of numbers to overwhelm their opponents. This huge army would march into battle to the beating of drums, the blowing of trumpets made of wood, conch shells or horn, and it's not hard to see why many Andean kingdoms elected to bend the knee rather than face it in battle.

The logistical network that supported this army was no less impressive. Inca soldiers marched along immaculately maintained highways through the mountains, lined with barrack-like shelters called *tambos*, and fed from the well-supplied storehouses. 'Throughout all the royal roads,' writes Cieza de León, 'there were built, from half-league to half-league, small houses, well roofed with wood and straw… [that] lined the roads at regular intervals.'[5] Thanks to these highways, the Inca army was able to move faster, gain speedier information, and amass a greater force than any of their rivals.

A typical Inca *qullqa* storehouse, in Ollantaytambo, southern Peru—about seventy kilometres northwest of Cusco.

Once the Inca had taken control of a town, whether peacefully or by force, they would always build a large, fortified storehouse called a *qullqa*. These storehouses were always built high up the valley sides, to take advantage of the mountain winds to keep food dry—but they also acted as a highly visible symbol to the people in the valleys below. In one region alone, there were nearly 3,000 of these storehouses, with a combined capacity of 170,000 cubic metres, or nearly seventy Olympic-size swimming pools. These the Inca would fill with food—naturally freeze-dried potatoes and corn, beans, dried meats and other long-lasting foods—as well as clothing, blankets and shawls, even sandals, which would then be distributed to the population. It would have been clear to everyone in the new Inca province which side their bread was now buttered.

Religious belief in this region was incredibly diverse, and, like the Romans, the Inca practised an inclusive attitude that allowed them to incorporate a diverse range of people into their empire. In territories they conquered, local religions and cults were allowed to continue, and where possible were folded into the existing mythos of the Inca. When they conquered the people of Huarochirí province, for instance, they happily took on their god Maca Uisa, with an added mythos about how he had helped to defeat some rebellious peoples. 'Maca Uisa reduced all those villages to eroded chasms by flashing lightning and pouring down more rain, and washing them away in a mudslide,' records the Huarachirí manuscript. 'From that time onward, the Inca revered Paria Caca even more, and gave him fifty of their retainers.'[6] Of course, the Inca god Viracocha never lost his place at the top of this increasingly crowded pantheon.

Machu Picchu, Peru—an exceptionally well-preserved Inca outpost, displaying typical construction of houses, terraces and public buildings.

One of the most remarkable constructions of this period is the outpost that would one day be known as Machu Picchu, perched on a mountain ridge rising half a kilometre above the valley floor, with steep cliffs plunging down on either side. It's not clear exactly what this town was designed for. It was never self-sufficient, and relied on constant supplies being ferried up to it from the rest of the empire, meaning that it must have had a specific purpose. Some believe it may have been a royal retreat, chosen for the beauty of its location, while others argue that it was a plantation or trading post for coca leaves, a high value crop that the Inca chewed and brewed into tea for medicinal purposes and for a mild narcotic effect. More than a hundred steps of white granite connect the town's temples and houses, its water reservoirs, terraces, and its sun temple. It must have been a magnificent sight, with its thatched rooftops gleaming bright in the sun, while herds of llama trekked up the narrow mountain roads to supply it with the necessities of life, and the clouds rolled over its grassy slopes.

★★★

'Inca' was the Quechua word for 'lord', and around this time it began to refer to the empire's ruling ethnic group too. The king who reigned in Cusco was now known as the Sapa Inca, or 'the Lord without Equal'. By the end of the reign of Pachacuti, the city of Cusco had become the heart of an entity known as Tahuantinsuyu. In Quechua this means 'four regions together', and has been translated as something like 'the land of the four quarters'. This was now a stable imperial state, ruling over four provincial governments with strong leaders: Chinchasuyu in the north-west, Antisuyu in the north-east, Kuntisuyu in the south-west and Qullasuyu in the south-east. The roads leading to each of these four provinces all met at a crossroads in the central plaza of the city of Cusco, where the babble of dozens of languages would have been heard on the streets.

The imperial capital of Cusco was a strange city. There were no markets or squares, no workshops or places of business. Foreigners and commoners were forbidden to stay in the city overnight, and it was home purely to the temples and priests, as well as the king in his palace. On the hill overlooking Cusco, the Inca built a powerful fortress named Sacsayhuamán, a citadel of zigzagging stone walls built from enormous blocks of andesite. At the heart of this forbidden city was the no less impressive Coricancha, or 'golden enclosure', which the Spanish would later refer to as the temple of the sun. This was the spiritual and ceremonial heart of the empire. Cieza de León recounted the magnificence of the Coricancha's appearance, based on the evidence given to him by Cusco's surviving Inca princes and the few remaining eyewitnesses who had seen the temple in its glory days:

> The stone is somewhat black in colour, rough, yet excellently cut. There are many doors and their arches are of a fine construction; at mid height of the walls runs a band of gold, of some seventeen inches in width and two in depth. The doors and arches are also embossed with sheets of this metal... In one of these houses, the grandest of all, was the figure of the sun, of great size and made of gold, and encased with precious stones.[7]

From its seat at Cusco, the Inca Empire would grow to become truly vast: at around 2 million square kilometres at its height, it was about the size of the Western Roman Empire. It was nearly ten times the size of its nearest American rival, the Aztec Empire, and ruled over twice the number of people—up to 12 million. The Inca domain stretched from north to south for around 4,000 kilometres, or a tenth of the way around the globe.

The Inca were deeply suspicious of the Amazon to the east, and the cloud forest foothills that descend into it, known as 'the eyebrow of the jungle'. In Quechua they called this region *rupa-rupa*, meaning 'hot-hot', and while the Inca tended to keep well clear of the rainforest's shady depths, they were clearly fascinated by the place: the jaguars, snakes and tropical birds of the jungle appear constantly in Inca art. These forests were a source of brightly coloured feathers that the Inca wove into their clothing for decoration, and they were also where widely traded luxury crops like tobacco and coca plants could be grown.

The Inca economy is one of the most intriguing aspects of their society. Andean cultures had always exhibited a large amount of reciprocity, since the rugged landscape demanded large amounts of people come together to cut stone, dig channels and aqueducts in the rock, or build houses, and this led to a remarkably communalized labour system. To the extent that we can fit its structure into modern definitions, many have described it as an example of state socialism, or even communism.

As far as we can tell, the idea of private property didn't exist in Inca society, and they progressed on the basis of shared ownership of assets, resources and the means of production. When an Inca couple got married, they were given a house and a plot of land by the state, which they would use to produce enough food for themselves. The state provided seeds and tools, as well as a pair of llamas for transportation, wool and manure. In return, the family would give any surplus to the common storehouse, and they would agree to perform a public service known as *mit'a* whenever called upon—perhaps to labour on a construction project for part of the year, or work in a particular workshop making cloth or pottery, work as a message-runner, or to fight in the army. Other than food and water, cloth was perhaps the most important resource in the Andes. For clothing and containers to store food, Andean society required millions of metres of thread, the bulk of which was made by women, who would have gone about the streets with their drop spindles, devices that allowed them to spin while walking around and taking care of their other duties.

While the system had socialist aspects, it was certainly not an egalitarian paradise, and nobles and officials with more than a hundred subordinates were exempt from the labour tax. The hierarchy of society was rigidly enforced, and peasants had little power. The authorities even conducted inspections of people's houses, to ensure that commoners did not own any gold or silver, have any valuable clothing, or keep more than ten animals. This entire system of organized labour was centrally planned from Cusco, and quite remarkably operated without a single word ever being written down.

The Inca never developed a written language, and so kept no written records—but they recorded information in a remarkable system known as *quipu*. This used rope knots of different sizes, positions and colours to represent different information, and could be decoded by people initiated in this art, who were known as a *quipucamayoc*. 'They count by certain knots on cords, and so record what each chief has brought,' wrote one early eyewitness, Hernando Pizarro. 'When they had to bring us loads of fuel, maize, chicha, or meat, they took off knots or made knots on some other part; so that those who have charge of the stores keep an exact account.'[8]

All the information on how many taxpayers there were, who had been born and died, the number of able-bodied men available for military service, the quantities of cloth and food and animals—all this was recorded in the *quipu*, and with a kind of counting table known as a *yupana*. 'They count on boards. They count by numbers from one hundred thousand, ten thousand, one hundred, ten, until they reach one,' wrote the Indigenous historian Felipe Guamán Poma de Ayala. 'They keep track of everything that happens in this kingdom, celebrations, Sundays, months and years. In each city, town and village of Indians there were accountants and treasurers.'[9] It has also been speculated that the *quipu* may have been used as a memory aid to help in the recitation of epic poetry—but we may never know, as the system has never been deciphered in modern times, and the knowledge of how to interpret the *quipu* has been lost.

Illustration of a trained *quipucamayoc* and a yupana counting table (bottom left) by Poma de Ayala.

With its sprawling territory, its well-oiled, centrally coordinated economy, and its state-of-the-art road network, by the turn of the sixteenth century the Inca Empire was at the height of its power and confidence—but events were brewing in the wider world that would soon bring them into contact with powers far outside their past experience, and which would ultimately lead to the wholesale collapse and disintegration of their society.

★★★

The Sapa Inca Huayna Capac, drawn by Poma de Ayala.

The name of the Inca Emperor Huayna Capac meant 'the young mighty one'. He had come to power at the age of twenty-five, in 1493. Just one year earlier, Christopher Columbus had first set foot in the Caribbean, and was at that time back in Europe, preparing for his second voyage. Emperor Huayna Capac was a conqueror by nature. During the nearly three decades of his long reign, the Inca army was constantly on the move, and the empire doubled in size, expanding into present-day Chile and Argentina. For much of his reign, he was hell-bent on subjugating the tropical northern territory of what is now Ecuador and Colombia, where tribal peoples had long resisted Inca expansion. These wars in the jungle were a bitter quagmire. The terrain was difficult, and the Inca soldiers were not used to the climate. During this time, constant warfare must have become a daily fact of life in the empire.

In the year 1515, while staying in his northern capital of Tumipampa and preparing for another campaign, Huayna Capac heard rumours of some unusual strangers who had arrived by boat. 'News reached him that some strange people, of a type that was quite unknown, were cruising in a ship along the coasts of his empire and had wanted to know what country this was,' remembers the chronicler Inca Garcilaso de la Vega. 'This naturally aroused the entire attention of the king, who immediately made enquiries as to who these people were and from where they came.'[10]

Huayna Capac was deeply troubled by this appearance. 'He surrounded himself with a permanently powerful army, chosen among the veterans of his conquests, and he had countless offerings and sacrifices made to the sun.'[11] But the strangers had left, and no further word was heard from them. 'Three or four years having passed and no disturbing events having occurred, people grew less anxious and, little by little the Empire recovered its former calm,' writes de la Vega.

When the city of Tenochtitlan was besieged and destroyed far away in Mexico in 1521, Huayna Capac was twenty-eight years into his reign. By then, he may have all but forgotten about that disturbing appearance of those foreigners six years earlier. But still, there were troubling rumours coming from the north—rumours of a wave of destruction passing over the land. Whole villages were being wiped out, laid low by some mysterious plague. Perhaps Huayna Capac dismissed these rumours at first. That is, until he developed a fever the likes of which the Inca had never encountered before.

'One day, as Huayna Capac was coming out of a lake in which he had just bathed, near Quito,' writes the chronicler, 'he was suddenly seized with a sensation of chill, which was followed by one of intense heat.'[12] This was likely smallpox, which struck some Indigenous Americans with such speed that they never developed pustules. His condition rapidly deteriorated, and in 1527, the Sapa Inca Huayna Capac died in the north, more than a thousand miles from home. On his deathbed, he is supposed to have uttered a prophecy of doom:

> Our father the sun has revealed to me that after the reign of twelve Incas, his own children, there will appear in our country an unknown race of men who will subdue our Empire. I think that the people who came recently to our own shores are the ones referred to… These people will return shortly after I have left you, and that they will accomplish what our father the sun predicted they would.[13]

Whether or not these were actually his dying words, they certainly show the apocalyptic mood that would soon sink in among the snowy peaks and deep valleys of the Andean mountains. Within a few weeks, the Emperor's mummified body began its 2,000-kilometre journey south to Cusco. His lords carried him on a throne, bound tightly in white cloth. The procession travelled on the great Chinchasuyo road that separated the coastal plains and the towering mountains above, a caravan of lords and warriors, porters and llamas, slowly climbing up through the terraced roads and canyon valleys.

When the Emperor's retinue arrived in Cusco, they found the city devastated. While they had been away, the plague had reached the capital and killed countless citizens, along with many lords and officials. The Inca's sophisticated road system—one great engine of their progress—had now become a conduit for disease. Bodies must have piled up in the streets, with hardly enough people left to carry them away. Before the people of the Andes had even set eyes on a European, the contact of the two worlds had unleashed chaos. On his deathbed, Huayna Capac had named his oldest son his successor—but before this prince could take the throne, he died of the same disease that had killed his father. With no clear successor, the empire now teetered on the brink of civil war. In the traditional capital of Cusco, one of Huayna Capac's sons called Huáscar declared himself the rightful ruler. But in the rebellious northern region of Quito, another of his sons was in charge of a sizeable army. That man's name was Atahualpa.

***

'Atahualpa was a man of some thirty years of age,' wrote the chronicler Francisco López de Xerez, 'of fine appearance and disposition, somewhat stocky, his face imposing, beautiful and ferocious, his eyes bloodshot.'[14] He was a tenacious battlefield commander, whose troops had been hardened by long years fighting his father's jungle war in the north. 'Warlike, ambitious and daring,' writes the historian W. H. Prescott, 'he was constantly engaged in enterprises for the enlargement of his own territory… His restless spirit excited some alarm at the court of Cusco.'[15]

It wasn't long before Atahualpa defied his brother Huáscar's claim to the throne and declared himself ruler of the north. For two years, both brothers eyed each other suspiciously across their borders—but in 1529, war broke out, and Atahualpa marched south to seize the entire empire for himself. The civil war that followed lasted for three years. During this time, Spanish sources portray Atahualpa as ruthless in the prosecution of his campaign. Juan de Betanzos, who was married to an Inca princess, wrote that Atahualpa buried some rebel chiefs alive, while with others 'he ordered that their hearts be pulled out while they were alive. He said he wanted to see the colour of the hearts of evil men.'[16]

A seventeenth-century illustration of the Sapa Inca Atahualpa.

In 1532, Atahualpa forced his brother back to his final stronghold of Cusco, before finally defeating him. He imprisoned Huáscar, and purged any members of the royal court who may have had stronger claims to the throne than his own. His victory was total. Atahualpa was now well on his way to becoming the thirteenth Sapa Inca, the next in a line of kings that stretched back a hundred years to the reign of Pachacuti. His land may have lain in ruins, his people may have been ravaged by disease and war, but the entire world now seemed to bow down before him.

***

Playing opposite Atahualpa in this drama is a man named Francisco Pizarro. Pizarro was born in 1478 in Extremadura in south-eastern Spain, then part of the kingdom of Castile. There is no official record of Pizarro's birth, suggesting he may have been illegitimate, and he began his life herding pigs in the dusty town of Trujillo. After an early career as a mercenary, in 1502 he sailed to Hispaniola, where he earned a considerable fortune as a slaver, plantation owner and trader.

In the New World, Pizarro achieved a wealth and status that would have been impossible in Spain, where the entrenched class system would have always treated him as a peasant. He seems to have fostered no desire to ever return to his homeland, and instead spent his days surrounded by all the trappings of wealth in the New World. Still, Pizarro dreamed of one day making his name as an adventurer. In 1513, he joined the explorer Vasco Núñez de Balboa and sailed to modern-day Panama. The Spaniards didn't know it yet, but this was the thinnest point of the American landmass, where only 50 kilometres of land separates the Atlantic Ocean from the Pacific. It's at this crossing point between the oceans that the destiny of Pizarro, and the fate of the Inca, would be sealed.

A seventeenth-century portrait of Pizarro.

Balboa and Pizarro set about the settlement of Panama with the usual destruction and enslavement of Indigenous people that accompanied all European settlement in the New World. One local chief called Comogre decided to cooperate, and offered to pay them off in both gold and information. It was from him that the Spaniards first heard of the existence of another ocean to the west. 'I am told that the other sea is very good for canoe navigation,' Comogre told them, 'for that it is always smooth, and never rough like the sea on this side.'[17] In one version of events, Comogre's son, angry that the Spanish kept demanding gold, is said to have burst out: 'If you are so hungry for gold that you leave your lands to cause strife in those of others, I shall show you a province where you can quell this hunger.'[18]

Legends of a mythical city of gold lying just beyond the horizon were a common motif in the Spanish exploration and settlement of the Americas—and it's not hard to see how this piece of folklore emerged. Whenever local people discovered the Spanish obsession with the precious metal, they would often assure them that there was plenty of gold just over the next hill, if only they would pack up and leave them in peace. We don't know whether Comogre and his son really knew about the Inca and their temples of gold high in the Andes, or whether they were just trying to move the Spanish on—but the result was the same. Balboa organized an expedition to cross the isthmus of Panama, and reach what he called 'the other sea'.

Pizarro was made a captain of this expedition, which hacked its way through the jungle, the conquistadors boiling in their armour, beset by mosquitoes and flies. Finally, they heard the sound of waves, and crested a low rise to see a beach, and beyond it a boundless blue ocean stretching to the horizon. They had arrived at the cutting edge of the continental plate, which for the last 150 million years had been forging westwards into the Pacific—and Balboa would be remembered as the first native of the Old World to reach it. But the life of a conquistador was violent and pitiless. Pizarro had been Balboa's friend for many years, but when the opportunity came to betray him in the years that followed, he didn't hesitate. In one of the routine power struggles that took place here at the edge of the world, Pizarro was ordered to arrest Balboa by his rival the governor of Panama, and the explorer was later executed. For his services in this matter, Pizarro was given a swampy bit of land to call his own, and this is where he might have stayed for the remainder of his life. That is, if it wasn't for the news that would soon come trickling down the coast from Mexico, of the incredible exploits of one of his distant cousins—a fellow Castilian Spaniard named Hernán Cortés.

★★★

At this time, Cortés was considered a hero in the Castilian court—his fall from grace some way in the future—and with the printing of two of his letters in Seville in 1522 and 1523, his conquest of Tenochtitlan would become legendary. Cortés was seven years younger than Pizarro, and through his mother he was his second cousin once removed. Pizarro openly admired his overachieving relative, and must have dreamed of emulating some of his success. Both Cortés and Pizarro had grown up in Extremadura, and both had set sail to explore the New World, living in Hispaniola at the same time—but there the similarities end. Cortés had had a legal education and worked as a notary and treasurer. While we may not always trust his account of events, the five letters he wrote during the conquest of Mexico speak to us out of history with a commanding voice, explaining his motivations, his desires and his fears, replete with biblical quotations and classical allusions. Pizarro is more of an enigma. He was born to a poor family, and could neither read nor write. For this reason, we learn of him and his motivations only through those who accompanied him.

The fame and wealth that Cortés won for himself in Mexico reignited Pizarro's lust for adventure. By this time he was in middle age. 'He was tall and spare, having a good face and a thin beard,' wrote another of his cousins, Pedro Pizarro:

> It was his custom whenever anyone asked him for anything always to say No...in order that he might not fail to keep his word. And, though he said no, he always did in the end what was asked of him, if there were not reason against it.[19]

Pizarro joined a company heading along Panama's Pacific coast, determined to find out the truth about the rumoured cities of gold that were supposed to lie to the south. While Cortés's expedition had been a relatively amateur affair, with few professional soldiers, Pizarro's was even more of a rough bunch. He had about a hundred men, none of them soldiers, and many of whom had signed up to escape debts or avoid jail time. They had enough money for only two ships, and they set sail in November 1524. The expedition crept along the coast for more than a year, dogged by bad weather and worse luck. Running out of supplies, the men were forced to eat raw shellfish and wild berries that made them ill. But then, in 1526, they came across something they had never seen before in the Americas: a native boat with a sail.

Drawing nearer, they found a raft carrying twenty Indigenous people, as well as a variety of jewellery and cloth, belts, necklaces and pins of gold and silver, inlaid with gems. The sailors' clothes were finely embroidered, decorated with patterns of birds, flowers and animals. When the Spaniards asked greedily where these goods came from, they were told that it had all come from a wealthy land called Peru that lay to the south. The news lit a fire under Pizarro—but his men were tired of the expedition, and the governor of Panama had ordered them home. Nevertheless, Pizarro shared something of Cortés's passion for dramatics, and in this instance his words passed into legend and idiom. He drew a line in the sand with his sword and announced:

> Friends and comrades! On that side are toil, hunger, nakedness, the drenching storm, desertion, and death; on this side, ease and pleasure. There lies Peru with all its riches; here, Panama and its poverty. Choose, each man, what best becomes a brave Spaniard. For my part, I go south.[20]

Most of Pizarro's men were not won over by this piece of oratory. Only thirteen of them stepped over the line in the sand—but it was enough for his journey to continue. In 1528, Pizarro and his skeleton crew reached the Inca town of Tumbes, today located on the border between Ecuador and Peru. Here, finally, was evidence of the wealthy empire they had been promised. Tumbes was a thriving port city and hub of the salt trade, with a strong fortress and a fine temple, well supplied with water from several aqueducts that fed into fountains and public baths. The people of Tumbes received Pizarro and his men politely, and sent out balsa rafts with food for the new arrivals. 'When the natives of the mainland saw the ship approaching on the sea,' writes Cieza de León, 'they were astounded because they were seeing something they had never seen or heard about.'[21] The people of Tumbes even gave Pizarro two boys, who he took with him back to Panama, and taught to speak Spanish—these he would use as translators throughout the following years. Cieza de León writes that the people of Tumbes dispatched a messenger to the Inca King Huayna Capac, informing him of the Spaniards' arrival—'But they say that when the news arrived, [Huayna Capac] was already dead.'[22]

Encouraged, and reeling from his discovery, Pizarro sailed further up the coast, and everywhere he saw small towns and picturesque coastal hamlets where the people told him that they were part of a great empire, whose glittering gold capital lay far up in the high mountains. Pizarro saw the enormous networks of aqueducts that made even the coastal deserts bloom, and the well-maintained roads linking the settlements, and felt that he had evidence enough to confirm the rumours. But his tiny force had no hope of making anything of it. He returned to Panama and prepared for another voyage.

***

The arrival of the Spanish at Tumbes caused a ripple of consternation in the Inca lands, already in the throes of civil war and racked by plague. 'After Huayna Capac had died, people scrambled for political power,' records the Huarochirí manuscript, 'each saying to their others, "Me first! Me first!" It was while they were carrying on this way that the Spanish Vira Cochas [lords] appeared.'[23]

One later Inca ruler named Titu Cusi, who had been a boy at the time of the invasion, recounted his memories of that time to a Spanish missionary. In the resulting document, looking back from a distance of forty years, Titu Cusi relates the words of his father—one of Atahualpa's brothers—as he hears about the Spanish arrival:

> 'How dare those people intrude into my country without my authorization and permission? Who are these people and what are their ways?' The messengers answered, 'Lord...they claim to have come by the wind. They are bearded people,

> very beautiful and white. They eat out of silver plates. Even their sheep, who carry them, are large and wear silver shoes.'[24]

Titu Cusi even captures what it was like to see the Spaniards reading for the first time:

> We have witnessed with our own eyes that they talk to white cloths by themselves and that they call some of us by our names without having been informed by anyone and only looking into the sheets, which they hold in front of them.[25]

As in the conquest of Mexico, Inca sources recall the appearance of portents before the arrival of the Spaniards. An eagle had been attacked by condors above the main square of Cusco, and many had reported seeing a blood-red circle enveloping the moon. 'There followed earthquakes of such unusual violence that great rocks were shattered in pieces and mountains collapsed,' attests Inca Garcilaso de la Vega. 'The sea became furious, overflowed its shores, invading the land, while numerous comets streaked the heavens, sowing terror in their wake.'[26] No one knew what the arrival of the foreigners could mean.

★★★

When Pizarro arrived back in Panama, many were astonished, having assumed his expedition lost at sea. But no one was particularly interested in his discoveries, and the governor of Panama refused him permission for any more expeditions. Pizarro was frustrated. The temptation of the faraway empire, along with all its gold and glory, began to possess him. We can imagine him lying awake at night in the hot Panama air, listening to the whining of mosquitoes overhead and the cackling of spider monkeys in the trees outside his cabin, all the while thinking about the glory and gold that might await him, far away on the shores of the other sea. In 1528, he decided to sail back home for the first time, with the intention of gaining an audience with the most powerful man in Europe—the

King of Spain, Archduke of Austria and Holy Roman Emperor—Charles V and his queen, Isabella.

When he stepped off the ship, Pizarro must have found Spain much changed. He had left it as a wealthy late medieval kingdom, but in the last three decades, the newly united state had become the bustling hub of a colonial empire. Its ports had swollen with the wealth coming in on its treasure ships, and now enormous thousand-tonne galleons carrying hundreds of cannons would have towered over the roofs. By then used to frontier life, he must have found the opulence of the royal court in Toledo staggering. Pizarro managed to secure an audience, perhaps helped by the presence of his then-popular cousin Cortés at court, and when he came before the royal couple, he offered up gold and jewels, exotic birds and embroidered cloth, even the fleece of a llama, along with a newly drawn map of Peru.

Charles and Isabella must have looked at these treasures hungrily. The capture of Mexico only eight years before and the establishment of the colony of New Spain had brought them enormous riches—and now this commoner was offering to conquer another indigenous empire and bring back perhaps even more treasure. On 26 July 1529, Queen Isabella signed a charter called the Capitulación de Toledo, authorizing Pizarro to invade Peru, 'to conquer, discover, pacify and populate the coast of the South Sea of said Land'.[27] Without the Inca having the slightest knowledge of it, with the stroke of a pen ten thousand kilometres away, their land had been renamed 'New Castile'—and Pizarro had been named its governor. The Queen also made Pizarro a knight of the Order of Santiago, Spain's highest order of merit, and gave him several Dominican friars to take with him, to underscore the notion that he was on a religious mission. They gave him provisions to buy artillery in Panama, twenty-five horses from Jamaica, and thirty African slaves—but other than this, the monarchy offered no direct financial support. For the crown, Pizarro's expedition was low risk and potentially very high reward.

By January 1530, Pizarro had returned to Panama and prepared his expedition. He brought with him as an assistant his fifteen-year-old cousin Pedro, who would later write one of the most important eyewitness accounts of the invasion. Pizarro had his usual run of bad luck on the voyage: strong headwinds blowing up the Pacific coast stopped his progress for nearly two weeks, and storms ravaged the ships. Still, he must have barely been able to contain himself as they sailed past Colombia and Ecuador, sharing tales of the bustling town of Tumbes that awaited them. But when they finally sighted Tumbes, Pizarro was astonished to find the city abandoned—a ghost town. 'The town of Tumbez was destroyed,' wrote the conquistador Francisco López de Xerez. 'It seemed to have been an important place, judging from some edifices it contained... The natives say that these edifices were abandoned by reason of a great pestilence, and by reason of the war.'[28]

Pizarro was distraught. He made camp in the ruins and lingered there for a few months, trying to gather information about what had happened from some locals hiding nearby. The people of Tumbes were now frightened and suspicious, and when some local chiefs plotted to attack his men, Pizarro had them burned alive. Soon terror of the newcomers spread among the nearby peoples. Over the course of his conquest of Peru, Pizarro—like Cortés—used these terror tactics constantly, and burned dozens, perhaps hundreds, of local chiefs.

Pizarro must have known that his situation was precarious, and his soldiers expected more than to simply set up camp in the ashen ruins of Tumbes. Soon his promises of gold would have to be fulfilled. Finally, he resolved to march up into the hills and find this fabled city of gold. Pizarro set out on 16 May 1532 with a company of 187 men, made up of 102 foot soldiers, sixty-two horsemen, three artillery operators with cannons, and twenty crossbowmen. Ahead of them lay a journey of more than 2,000 kilometres across deserts and over snow-capped mountains.

***

It's not clear why Atahualpa allowed Pizarro to found his settlement on the coast, or to march unhindered into the hills. With his powerful army, 'he could have killed all the Spaniards who were going up [into the mountains] or at least the greater portion of them,' reflected Pedro Pizarro, 'and those who escaped would have turned in a rout and would have been slain upon the road.'[29] But Atahualpa did nothing. As in Mexico, some chroniclers at the time explained this inaction with claims that the Inca believed the Spanish to be gods—but these accounts were often intended to flatter the Europeans, and can't entirely be trusted. If there was initial confusion about the foreigners' divinity among the people of Peru, it's an idea that they quickly dispensed with, as Cieza de León recalls:

> As these Spaniards were so free from all restraint, and held the honor of the people so lightly...and how shamelessly and without the fear of God they violated the *mamaconas* [virgins]... [the Inca] began to say that such people were not sons of God, but that they were worse than *Supais*, which is their name of Devil.[30]

The most likely answer is that Atahualpa was simply too busy to deal with the Spanish. He had just won a bitter civil war by the skin of his teeth, with his brother imprisoned and currently being transported to face judgement—and he must have been focused on securing his shaky grip on the empire. When Pizarro began his march up into the hills, Atahualpa was just then in the middle of a march of his own, a triumphal procession back to Cusco, where he intended to destroy the last remaining noble families loyal to Huáscar, strip Cusco of its wealth, drag the treasure back to his home of Quito, and declare himself Emperor of the Inca.

The arrival of this small group of foreigners was certainly a curiosity for him, but there's no indication he considered their tiny force to be a threat. Titu Cusi recalls that Atahualpa was more interested in hunting the Europeans' horses, which he believed to be a new kind of llama. Atahualpa agreed to meet with the Spanish, and sent an envoy of guides with instructions to lead them to the small town of Cajamarca, where, as part of his victory tour, he was already scheduled to conduct a coming-of-age ritual in which he presented ceremonial weapons to local youths. Agreeing to meet the Spaniards was a show of good faith, but Atahualpa also wanted to give them a show of force. In the heart of his empire, faced with the full might of his army, any aggression by these mysterious foreigners could be swiftly crushed. It seems Atahualpa quite reasonably expected to make Pizarro his subject, and if that didn't work, to kill him. But things would not go according to his plan.

★★★

Pizarro and his men travelled slowly along the Inca roads, passing inland through the desert forests of the Amotape hills and stopping at Inca towns and storehouses. They were supported by a team of enslaved men and women from Africa and central America, and by some local soldiers and porters that they had either convinced or forced to follow them. On their way they were impressed with the paved roads, and saw the desert landscape watered by extensive irrigation systems, with crops and animals in abundance. As they climbed higher into the mountains they marvelled at the sophisticated bridges that crossed the tumultuous mountain rivers. They also learned more about the lands ahead, sometimes through torturing locals, or from minor lords who hated Atahualpa and wanted to see him fall. They found out that this King Atahualpa had a vast army, and heard about the recent violent civil war. They even saw the bodies of men hanging by their feet at the entrance of one town, executed as a punishment for backing the losing side. Despite all these warnings, Pizarro decided he would meet this Inca king and take him prisoner. In this plan, Pizarro was clearly imitating the example of Cortés and his legendary capture of Moctezuma—but Cortés hadn't invented this tactic, and the taking of native hostages was extremely common among the early colonists of the Americas. Pizarro himself likely had a long history of kidnap and ransom during his time in Nicaragua and Panama—and if this King Atahualpa was as rich as Pizarro had heard, then he could expect his ransom to be truly enormous.

The journey into the high mountains was hard. 'It was so steep that, in places, they had to ascend by steps,' writes Xerez. 'The cold is so great on these mountains that some of the horses, accustomed to the warmth of the valleys, were frost-bitten.'[31] Beyond 2,500 metres, altitude sickness would have set in. At one point, food and supplies arrived for the Spanish from Atahualpa, along with his wishes that they should come to meet him soon. Finally, the Spanish found their way to the wide valley where the town of Cajamarca stood.

Surrounded by green hills, the valley bottom was marshy, fed by the waters of three rivers. On the hills surrounding the town, Pizarro and his men saw the encamped army of Emperor Atahualpa: as many as 80,000 battle-hardened men. These tough Inca soldiers must have looked with curiosity but also a little derision at the ragtag group of Spanish adventurers, filthy from their weeks on the road, pink in the face and out of breath in the mountain air, many of them covered in boils from tropical diseases. 'The Governor arrived at this town of Caha-marca on Friday, the 15th of November, 1532, at the hour of vespers,' writes Xerez. 'In the middle of the town there is a great open space, surrounded by walls and houses. The Governor occupied this position, and sent a messenger to Atabaliba [Atahualpa], to announce his arrival.'[32]

Atahualpa was still in seclusion as part of his ritual, and didn't hurry out to meet the Spanish—a clear reminder about who was in charge. Meanwhile, Pizarro ordered his artillerymen to set up their cannons on the ceremonial plaza in the middle of the city. The encamped Inca army watched, somewhat perplexed, but did nothing to intervene. That night, a storm came in over the hills, bringing rain and hail. The hailstones must have plinked and plonked on the helmets of the Spanish soldiers as they encamped among the temple stones, and gazed at the lights of the Inca camp, stretching across the hills for many miles.

In the morning, they went to meet with Atahualpa. At first, the Sapa Inca showed little interest in the Spaniards, and even feigned boredom. He complained that they had treated some of his people poorly on the coast, burning people alive and abusing priestesses in the temples. Pizarro denied the accusations, and promised that he wanted to swear loyalty to Atahualpa and fight on his behalf. While initially suspicious, the Inca Emperor soon warmed to this idea, and suggested that they should go together and crush a local chief who was defying him. Pizarro happily agreed, saying that the job would take only ten Spanish horsemen—to which boast Atahualpa laughed in disbelief. To seal the deal, they drank maize beer together from golden cups that Pizarro must have noticed with some interest. They arranged to meet again in the grand plaza of Cajamarca the following day. 'The Spaniards spent the whole night on guard,' writes Pedro Pizarro, 'with a fair measure of fear.'[33]

As the sun rose, Pizarro prepared his ambush. He hid his cavalry inside the great halls that surrounded the plaza, while his artillery pieces were loaded and waiting to fire. But Atahualpa was in no hurry. Pizarro and his men waited, and waited. Finally, as the afternoon grew late, they heard the sound of the vast Inca army drawing near. The Spanish soldiers were terrified. 'Many of the Spaniards made water without knowing it out of sheer terror,'[34] remembers one. Pizarro spoke urgently to his men, 'saying to them all that they must be of good courage, and make fortresses of their hearts,' writes Xerez. 'He told them that, at the moment of attacking, they must come out with desperate fury and break through the enemy.'[35]

For his part, Atahualpa made a number of bad decisions. He had originally planned to enter the city with a troop of well-armed elite soldiers, but his meeting with Pizarro the previous day seems to have set his mind completely at ease. At the last minute, he elected to march into Cajamarca with only his ceremonial troops and servants, most of whom were unarmed. Xerez recalls the colourful scene that unfolded before the waiting Spanish as the Inca King entered the courtyard, resplendent in full ceremonial dress.

> First came a squadron of Indians dressed in a livery of different colours, like a chessboard... Next came three squadrons in different dresses, dancing and singing. Then came a number of men with armour, large metal plates, and crowns of gold and silver. Among them was Atabaliba in a litter lined with plumes of macaws' feathers, of many colours, and adorned with plates of gold and silver.[36]

The Inca army behind them was also arranged for a ceremony, rather than battle—stretched out in a long column along the road. Many of them would not even have realized that something was wrong before it was too late.

When Atahualpa and his ceremonial guard entered the plaza, Pizarro gave the order to attack. The cannons went off with a terrifying crack, and cannonballs would have whizzed into the Inca lines, smashing bodies to pulp as they went. His gunners fired into the Inca procession, and then the cavalry hiding in the temples came charging out, their bridles hung with bells to create maximum noise and confusion. The Spanish horses, guns and cannon were three weapons that the Inca had never even imagined, and the effect of being attacked with all three at once must have frozen them in their tracks.

> On seeing the horses charge, many of the Indians who were in the open space fled, and such was the force with which they ran that they broke down part of the wall surrounding the square, and many fell over each other. The horsemen rode them down, killing and wounding, and following in pursuit. The infantry made so good an assault upon those that remained that in a short time most of them were put to the sword.[37]

The Spanish slaughtered as many as 7,000 Inca over the following two hours, as the sun set red over the city. 'They started killing them with the horses, the swords or guns, like one kills sheep, without anyone being able to resist them,'[38] remembered the Inca noble Titu Cusi. As darkness fell, Atahualpa himself was captured, and Pizarro ordered his men to fall back into the temple with their captive. We can only imagine the rage and disbelief the Emperor must have felt: to have fought for so long against his brother, only to have this bolt from the blue strike him down. Xerez captures some of the Emperor's mood in his account:

> The Governor went to his lodging, with his prisoner Atabaliba despoiled of his robes, which the Spaniards had torn off in pulling him out of the litter… When Atabaliba was dressed, he made him sit near him, and soothed his rage and agitation at finding himself so quickly fallen from his high estate.[39]

As the dust of battle settled, Atahualpa's shock gave way to the kind of calculations we might expect of this experienced senior statesman—and it's clear he soon began to consider how to turn the situation to his advantage. While the Spaniards kept him in captivity, he regaled them with tales of the wealth of the Inca Empire, and especially emphasized Cusco as the jewel in its crown, urging them to march there and loot it. In fact, he himself had been intending to march to Cusco and destroy it. He conveniently neglected to mention his own city of Quito, where he had been intending to move his imperial court. Xerez recounts the glorious promises that Atahualpa made to the Spanish.

> Atabaliba said: 'I will give gold enough to fill a room twenty-two feet long and seventeen wide, up to a white line which is halfway up the wall.' The height would be that of a man's stature and a half. He said that, up to that mark, he would fill the room with different kinds of golden vessels, such as jars, pots, vases, besides lumps and other pieces. As for silver, he said he would fill the whole chamber with it twice over. He undertook to do this in two months.[40]

The Spanish were all too eager to accept, and decided to stay in Cajamarca and await the Emperor's bounty. To their astonishment, Atahualpa made good on his promise. Over the next ten days, gold flooded into the town of Cajamarca from all over the empire, until the room was filled with a glittering pile of ornaments. The Inca 'brought many vases, jars, and pots of gold, and much silver, and he said that more was on the road,' writes Xerez. 'The Governor ordered it all to be put in the house where Atahualpa had his guards, until he had accomplished what he had promised.'[41]

This offer by Atahualpa is often portrayed as a desperate bid by a terrified man—but given the hand he was dealt, it was actually a remarkably clever move. In a short time, he had deduced the Spaniards' weakness—their obsession with gold. The thing that Atahualpa feared most was that his brother Huáscar would escape from his imprisonment and seize the empire while he was thus inconvenienced. Filling a room of that size with gold would take many weeks, giving him the time to send word to his men to dispose of his imprisoned brother and any other nobles who could still oppose him. Atahualpa also knew his mountain kingdom well. The Spanish didn't know that the rainy season was just beginning in the Andes, and even a short delay meant that they would soon face increased snowfall and mudslides that would isolate them from their coastal supply lines. Detaining them in the relatively unimportant town of Cajamarca would slow their march on the power centres of Quito or Cusco, and when they did finally make a move, the weight of the gold would slow them down and potentially expose them to ambush.

From his captivity, Atahualpa was able to spread the news across the entire empire in a matter of days. As soon as the Inca soldiers transporting his brother Huáscar heard what was happening, they summarily executed their prisoner on the road. Atahualpa was now the only remaining prince with a strong claim to the throne, meaning that Pizarro would need him alive. In just a matter of days, the Sapa Inca had turned a bad situation significantly in his favour. And the best part of the deal was that the gold that poured into Cajamarca every day didn't even belong to him. His treasury in Quito remained untouched, while he directed the Spanish to exactly where to find the gold of his political rivals: his dead brother Huáscar and the noble families who had opposed him in the civil war. Atahualpa was buying his freedom, while at the same time diminishing his own rivals in the kingdom. It was the work not of a desperate man, but of a shrewd political operator. The Spanish were now a weapon that the Sapa Inca could aim at will, with just a few words in the right ears.

Unfortunately for Atahualpa, others would soon learn this same lesson. In the weeks that followed, his great rivals, the lords of Cusco, worked to spread rumours among the Spanish, who were becoming increasingly paranoid. 'During these nights the Governor and his Captains never slept,'[42] remembers Xerez. Nerves were beginning to fray. These lords of Cusco convinced Pizarro that Atahualpa had an army of 200,000 marching their way, along with a horde of 30,000 cannibals ravenous for European flesh. Apparently fearing losing control of the situation, on 26 July 1533 Pizarro made the rash decision to execute Atahualpa, as Xerez recalls:

> His sentence was that, for the treason he had committed, he should die by burning, unless he became a Christian... They brought out Atabaliba to execution; and, when he came into the square, he said he would become a Christian. The Governor was informed, and ordered him to be baptized. The Governor then ordered that he should not be burned, but that he should be fastened to a pole in the open space and strangled. This was done, and the body was left until the morning of the next day... He died with great fortitude, and without shewing any feeling.[43]

'Without delay, he had my uncle Atahuallpa brought out of prison into the open,' remembers the Inca Titu Cusi, 'and, without any resistance, garrotted him on a pole in the middle of the square.'[44]

The Spanish never made any attempt to fortify the city against an attack or prepare for battle against the massive army that was supposedly heading their way—suggesting that they had never really believed the threat. They dug a grave for Atahualpa, the last true emperor of the Inca, and left him to the worms.

★★★

After the death of Atahualpa, the Spanish installed the first of many puppet emperors, one of Atahualpa's brothers named Túpac Huallpa—but he died of imported diseases in only a matter of months. Next, they crowned another brother, Manco Inca Yupanqui. He was the father of the later ruler Titu Cusi, and was loyal to the Spanish for a time—but when he saw his opening, he rebelled. He laid siege to the Spanish in Cusco in 1536, attacked the new capital of Lima, and fled to the remote jungles of Vilcabamba, where he founded a rebel state. This was the last fortress of the free Inca, and it would hold out against the Spanish here for a further three decades.

Several puppet emperors would follow in Cusco, but none lasted very long. Many were assassinated by their own people, who looked on them as collaborators. Others escaped into the mountains and became rebel chiefs. In fact, for the next half century, the Spanish continually fought Inca insurgencies, struggling to pacify a land that they had long since declared conquered. Meanwhile, hardship spread. In 1616, the Quechuan nobleman Felipe Guamán Poma de Ayala authored a remarkable text known as his *Letter to a King*, which he sent to the King of Spain, Philip III. In it, he recounts the abuses and injustices of the colonialists, accompanied with illustrations he drew himself—and denounces the hardship inflicted on his people. It amounts to one of the first full-throated denunciations of the colonial system ever written by one of its subjects.

> Just imagine that our people were to arrive in Spain and start confiscating property, sleeping with the women and girls, chastising the men and treating everybody like pigs! What would the Spaniards do then? Even if they tried to endure their lot with resignation, they would still be liable to be arrested, tied to a pillar and flogged. And if they rebelled and attempted to kill their persecutors, they would certainly go to their death on the gallows.[45]

It is unlikely that the Spanish King ever read it. The document made its way to Denmark, where it lay undiscovered until the early twentieth century.

***

Francisco Pizarro had dreamed of surpassing Cortés in the glory of conquest, and by many measures, he had succeeded. Pizarro had destroyed an empire ten times the size of the Aztec Empire, using only about a third of the manpower, and he and his men were now rich beyond their wildest imaginings. 'When in ancient or modern times has so great an enterprise been undertaken by so few against so many odds,' revelled Xerez, 'and to so varied a climate and seas, and at such great distances, conquer the unknown?'[46]

But Pizarro's days of glory would be short-lived. In the ten years that he ruled Peru, he presided over a greedy and corrupt regime that brought about the steady collapse and disintegration of Andean society. Much of the population was reduced to the level of serfs, and the Spanish systematically stripped the temples and palaces of the Inca, reusing the stones to build their own mansions and churches. The golden temple of the Coricancha in Cusco was stripped of its gold and demolished, and the Convent of Santo Domingo would later be constructed over its ruins.

Despite the destruction, repression and suffering inflicted on them, the people of the Andes fought to keep their culture and history alive. One example of this is the remarkable document, known only as the Huarochirí manuscript, which attempted to record all that the surviving people of Huarochirí Province remembered about the myths, religious notions and traditions of their people. Although it was compiled seventy years after the invasion, and under the direction of a Spanish cleric who believed the Inca gods to be devils, it stands as one of the principal sources of information about pre-contact Peru. Its unnamed authors introduce it as follows:

> If the ancestors of the people called Indians had known writing in earlier times, then the lives they lived would not have faded from view. As the mighty past of the Spanish Vira Cochas is visible until now, so too, would theirs be. But since things are as they are, and since nothing has been written until now, I set forth here the lives of the ancestors of the Huaro Cheri people, who all descended from one forefather: what faith they held, how they live until now, those things and more; Village by village, it will all be written down: how they lived from their dawning age onward.[47]

As news of Pizarro's conquest spread, Spaniards from across the colonial Americas began to flock to Peru. In 1534, a large fleet of twelve ships arrived, led by Pedro de Alvarado, Cortés's captain who had slaughtered the people of Tenochtitlan as they celebrated their festival of Toxcatl. In the more than a decade since, he had developed a reputation for even greater cruelty. He arrived in Peru with a full party of settlers, slaves and weapons, prepared to colonize this new land. He was among the first to follow Pizarro, but he would be far from the last. Before long, Pizarro came into conflict with these new arrivals, and 'New Castile' was plunged into civil war, which further devastated the land and what remained of the Inca cities. The reign of the conquistadors in Peru was not the enlightened rule of the glorious Christian knights that they imagined themselves to be, but more like rival mafias fighting over territory.

Fresh waves of smallpox fell upon northern Peru in the 1530s, and would be followed by others in the decades that followed, as well as epidemics of measles. 'They died by scores and hundreds,' wrote one witness. 'Villages were depopulated. Corpses were scattered over the fields or piled up in the houses or huts. The price of food rose to such an extent that many persons found it beyond their reach. They escaped the foul disease, but only to be wasted by famine.'[48]

Despite these hardships, the free Inca of Vilcabamba soon learned to bridge the technological divide with the Spaniards. They acquired modern weapons, including arquebuses, artillery and crossbows, and learned how to use them to great effect in guerrilla raids. By the 1540s the rebel king Manco Inca was recorded to be skilled enough to ride a horse into battle. But these adaptations were not enough. On 24 June 1572, a Spanish army led by veteran conquistador Martín Hurtado de Arbieto made a final advance on the Inca's remote jungle capital. The city fell, and the last Inca king, Túpac Amaru, was captured and sentenced to be beheaded at the age of twenty-eight.

On the day of his execution, 24 September 1572, a scaffold was erected in front of the main cathedral in the central square of Cusco, draped in black cloth. As many as 15,000 people came to Cusco's central square to watch. 'It was only possible to push through the streets and squares with the greatest of difficulty,' wrote one chronicler. 'And since there was no room left to stand, the Indians climbed the walls and roofs of the houses.'[49] 'If an orange had been thrown down,' wrote the soldier Baltasar de Ocampo, 'it could not have reached the ground anywhere, so closely were the people packed.'[50] He recounts that when Túpac Amaru mounted the scaffold, the entire crowd let out a bloodcurdling wail of mourning.

> The whole crowd of natives raised such a cry of grief that it seemed as if the day of judgment had come... When the Inca beheld the scene, he only raised his right hand on high and let it fall. With a lordly mind he alone remained calm, and all the noise was followed by a silence so profound that no living soul moved, either among those who were in the square or among those at a distance.[51]

Then he spoke these final words in Quechua: 'Creator of the world, behold how my enemies spill my blood.'[52] With him, the Inca line came to an end.

***

Pizarro lived a violent life, and he died a violent death. He was sixty-three years old in June 1541, when a group of armed men burst into his palace. They were loyal to the son of a rival conquistador whom Pizarro had once had garrotted, and who had sworn revenge against him. Pizarro managed to kill two of his attackers and wound a third, before being stabbed in the throat, and then falling to the floor, where they flocked around him and struck him again and again. One might wonder whether in those moments he thought about the Inca Emperor Atahualpa, and the look in his eyes as he had been strangled against that pole in Cajamarca. Perhaps then he would have understood what that look meant—to have gained everything you had ever fought for, only to have it snatched away.

The fates of other conquistadors were hardly more glamorous. One who returned home, a man named Mansio Serra de Leguizamón, would famously gamble away much of the gold he had acquired in Peru, including a golden image of the sun looted from the Coricancha temple of Cusco, 'made of a gold plaque...composed of a round face, prolonged by rays and flames,' according to the chronicler de la Vega. Leguizamón 'was a great gambler and he had no sooner acquired this treasure than he gambled and lost it in one night.'[53]

As the Inca Empire fractured and collapsed, only those rare places that the Spaniards couldn't reach were preserved. One of these was the cloud outpost of Machu Picchu, whose location would be lost until the early twentieth century. Some time in the 1530s, the Inca Empire simply left it behind to crumble into the hillside. As the cloud rolled in over the hills day after day, mosses and lichens and creepers would grow over the walls, until the immaculate terraces were completely covered.

The site of Vilcabamba, the last fortress of the Inca, was also abandoned and forgotten. Today, its location is known as Espíritu Pampa, or the plain of ghosts. On 2 July 1964, the American explorer and archaeologist Gene Savoy was the first to travel to the site and correctly identify it. Savoy writes about the melancholy ruins, crumbling in the green twilight of the forest:

> Watching the first sunlight fall upon these ancient walls after a lapse of several centuries is a memorable experience. The white granite blocks, covered by thin layers of delicate lichen, take on a ghostly appearance. An ominous quiet falls over the jungle… For the first time I realize what we have found. We are in the heart of an ancient Inca city. Is this Manco's Vilcabamba—the lost city of the Incas?… For four hundred years they have remained in the realm of legend. Some even doubted they existed. But I always knew they were there, somewhere, awaiting discovery.[54]

But if he had hoped for ornate stone architecture like that of Machu Picchu or Cusco, he was disappointed:

> Some would expect to find cyclopean walls covered with sheets of gold, or finely cut stone of the classic Cuzco style. Old Vilcabamba wasn't this at all. She was old and worn. The walls of her buildings were toppled, covered with thick, de-

> caying vegetable matter: their foundations under tons of slide and ooze… Four centuries of wild jungle had twisted that part which remained. But she had not lost her dignity. One could easily see she had been a great metropolis, a colossus of the jungle. A wave of melancholy swept over me.[55]

At the sight of these lonely ruins, we could be reminded of the prayers written by the first great Inca King, Pachacuti Inca Yupanqui—his songs for the prosperity and wellbeing of his people, written in an age when the people of the mountains still determined their own future, and the sun still shone on the Inca.

> O Lord
> fortunate, happy, victorious Wiracocha,
> merciful and compassionate toward the people:
> Before you stand your servants and the poor
> to whom you have given life and put in their places:
> Let them be happy and blessed
> with their children and descendants;
> let them not fall into veiled dangers
> along the lonely road;
> …
> You who order,
> who fulfill what you have decreed,
> let them increase.
> So the people do not suffer and,
> not suffering, believe in you.
> Let it not frost
> let it not hail,
> preserve all things in peace.[56]

Anakena Beach
Mount Terevaka
RAPA NUI
Rano
Raraku
Crater
Ahu Tongariki
Hanga Roa
Rano
Kau
Crater
South Pacific Ocean
MOTU NUI

14

Easter Island

c. 1150–1838

Captain Jacob Roggeveen had been at sea for 247 days. He had set sail from the Netherlands the year before with three ships—*Arend*, *Thienhoven*, *Afrikaansche Galey*—and 223 hands, and had reached the Falkland Islands by 30 December. From there, they rounded Cape Horn in wild seas, docked in Chile for a time, and then sailed west, out into the next great uncharted frontier for colonial exploration: the South Pacific. He and his crew were searching for a hypothetical continent known as 'Terra Australis', which was believed to lie in the southern seas somewhere south of Australia. But so far, their hopes had been in vain.

'We have now come about 500 miles to the Westward of Copayapo, situated on the coast of Chile,' he wrote in his journal on 2 April 1722, 'and yet not come in sight of the unknown Southland (according to existing accounts of it), for the discovery of which our Expedition and Voyage is specially undertaken.'[1] Ahead of them lay nothing but flat, open sea. 'Breeze unsteady, with calms,' he writes, 'also thick weather and showers. Saw a turtle, floating weed, and birds.'[2] Then one day, they sighted a scrap of land breaking the line of the horizon. It was Easter Day, 1722.

'There was great rejoicing among the people,' wrote Roggeveen, 'and every one hoped that this low land might prove to be a foretoken of the coastline of the unknown Southern continent.' As the Dutch mariners got closer, they saw smoke rising from villages along the coast, 'from which we concluded that there were people dwelling on the same'. It soon became clear that this was not the tip of a continent, but just a small island, a dot in the middle of the ocean. Still, the Dutch were curious. It was a seemingly barren land, the slopes covered in rough grass, and 'from its outward appearance it suggested no other idea than that of an extraordinarily sparse and meagre vegetation.'[3]

'The weather was very variable, with thunder, sheet lightning and showers,' remembers Roggeveen. 'The wind unsteady from the North West, and occasional calms.'[4] When the *Arend* and *Thienhoven* drew near to the shore, the island's inhabitants came out to the ships on canoes, greeting the Dutch crew with friendly astonishment. Roggeveen went ashore, and what he found there amazed him. Along the beach was a line of enormous stone statues with their backs to the sea. They were carved from black volcanic stone, some of them standing 10 metres high and topped with crowns of red sandstone.

> These stone figures caused us to be filled with wonder, for we could not understand how it was possible that people who are destitute of heavy or thick timber, and also of stout cordage, out of which to construct gear, had been able to erect them; nevertheless some of these statues were a good 30 feet in height and broad in proportion.[5]

Roggeveen and his men didn't stay long. After a few days, they sailed away from the island and on across the Pacific, in search of a continent that would never materialize. But the remarkable sight of those stone statues stayed with them, a source of wonder and puzzlement. Roggeveen even began to imagine how productive this island could one day be, if Europeans were able to make a permanent settlement. 'This place,' he mused, 'as far as its rich soil and good climate are concerned, is such that it might be made into an earthly Paradise, if it were properly worked and cultivated.'[6]

Unknown to him, the century that followed would see unimaginable devastation rain down on this island, and every one of its remarkable stone statues would be toppled, and left to lie windswept and forlorn on these grassy hills.

***

The Pacific Ocean is vast. It covers one third of the earth's total surface area—larger than the landmass of all its continents combined. Across this expanse of blue sea are scattered more than 30,000 islands of varying size. Easter Island is at the eastern corner of an area called the Polynesian triangle, an expanse of water nearly the size of Asia, dotted with more than a thousand small volcanic islands averaging only about 30–40 square kilometres each. Easter Island itself is a loosely triangular shape, made up of three extinct volcanoes at each of its points. It is small—only about 24 kilometres from end to end—and it is more than 2,000 kilometres from the nearest inhabited island.

'With its bleak grass-grown surface, its wild rocks and restless ocean, it recalls some of the Scilly Isles or the coast of Cornwall,' wrote the archaeologist Katherine Routledge when she visited in 1913.

> From every part are seen marvellous views of rolling country; everywhere is the wind of heaven; around and above all are boundless sea and sky, infinite space and a great silence. The dweller there is ever listening for he knows not what, feeling unconsciously that he is in the antechamber to something yet more vast which is just beyond his ken.[7]

The people who have lived on Easter Island for centuries call it by the name '*Te pito o te henua*', which means either 'land's end' or 'navel of the world' depending on translation, and today's Polynesians call the island Rapa Nui. The Polynesians who first settled the island arrived from the west, having left the mainland of the Asian continent some time before 3000 BCE and gradually island-hopped all the way across the ocean. In Polynesian mythology, this ancient homeland is remembered as Havaiki, or Hiva.

These hardy sailors were some of the most successful ocean-going settlers in history. They built sophisticated, sturdy canoes with two hulls, double masts and sails, making them both stable and fast, and capable of covering great distances. The spirit of this age is captured in one traditional Polynesian fisherman's prayer.

O mighty being—
moving freely in the broken fragments of the rainbow,
Go before me upon this day!
May you become a support ever lifting our ship
high above the wind-tossed crests of the surging seas,
As we sail upon our double-hulled vessel
over the wide ways of the ocean,
So that we sink not beneath the hurrying waves.[8]

These early settlers navigated the oceans without any physical navigation devices or written notes. They could determine their location using only the stars—and memorized these astral positions, and those of islands and sea routes, with unwritten stories and songs. They also used natural cues to help them navigate, including the flight paths of sea birds like the black, white and brown tern. This ancient Polynesian sailors' song shows the importance that these birds held in Polynesian culture.

Mine is the migrating bird
winging afar over remote oceans,

Ever pointing out the sea road of the Black-heron—
the dark cloud in the sky of night.

It is the road of the winds
coursed by the Sea Kings to unknown lands![9]

Storms in the Pacific could be deadly to these early explorers, but when a severe typhoon struck, they had a survival method that seems unthinkable to a modern sailor. They would purposely flood their canoes, the wooden hulls providing enough buoyancy to stay afloat, while the part-submerged boat could survive being buffeted about in the gale-force winds without overturning. The sailors would climb inside the flooded hulls, keeping their heads above water, and wait for the storm to pass. 'Torrents of driving rain fall from the cloven skies, into the storm tossed heavens below,' goes one traditional song. 'A deluge descends from the sundered skies into the raging gale below!'[10]

There is even some evidence that Polynesian sailors reached the coast of South America, probably in the region of modern Colombia. These explorers may have returned with the sweet potato, which would become a favourite Polynesian crop (although it may have also arrived naturally), and brought with them traces of South American DNA that entered their gene pool from about the year 1200, three centuries before Columbus would reach the landmass from the other side. One recent genomic study concluded: 'We find conclusive evidence for prehistoric contact of Polynesian individuals with Native American individuals (around 1200 CE) contemporaneous with the settlement of remote Oceania.'[11]

There is some debate about exactly when these intrepid Polynesian adventurers arrived on Easter Island. For a long time, it was assumed that settlers had arrived some time in the fourth to fifth centuries, around the same time that Hawaii was settled—but today most researchers believe that Rapa Nui wasn't settled until around 1200 CE. An ancient piece of Rapa Nui folklore credits the settlement of the island to a Polynesian king called Hotu Matu'a, who is led to the island by the dream vision of a prophet named Hau Maka. 'The dream soul of Hau Maka continued her journey and went ashore,'[12] goes the story. The soul travels around the island, naming each part of it in turn—and when Hau Maka wakes, he goes to tell his king what he has seen: 'Hau Maka went to tell the king about the dream. When he arrived there, he told his dream. He described the dream in detail, including all lands his dream soul had seen.'[13]

Amazed by the story, the King organizes a great expedition to find this island and settle there. 'When you speak to the young men,' the King says, 'tell them that these orders are from me, the orders of King Matua. Tell them that they have only one year to finish building the canoe and to launch it.'[14] The Rapa Nui settlers packed their canoes with everything that was required for the traditional Polynesian lifestyle. They brought their staple foods: bananas, a root vegetable called taro, sweet potatoes and sugarcane, as well as chickens and another food staple—the Polynesian rat. They also brought saplings of the paper mulberry tree, the fibres of which they used to create textiles.

The settlement of the Polynesian islands was the final chapter of the journey of at least 100,000 years and 30,000 kilometres that had taken humanity out of Africa, through Asia and on to the Americas—the last of humanity's great migrations. Easter Island was the final and most remote stop along this journey, and so in some ways humanity's restless journey ended on these shores. One Polynesian sailors' song gives voice to a lookout on one of these vessels, sighting land in the distance: 'Now the far cries of land birds are heard as they swoop into the troughs of the waves upon the horizon. Ha! Now they settle upon a low-lying reef… Now they come to rest upon the land rising above the ocean's rim!'[15]

Hotu Matu'a and his settlers arrived on Easter Island at Anakena, a white coral sand beach on the north of the island. The landscape they would have seen when they disembarked was very different from the one we see today. Far from the bare grassy slopes first spied by Roggeveen in the eighteenth century, the island was then covered by a thick forest of tropical palm trees. If you dig down into the island's soil, you can still see the hollows left by the roots of these trees. Studies of these root moulds, as well as pollen analysis, show that when humans arrived on Rapa Nui, the island was home to more than twenty-one tree species, some of which were large, including at least three which grew up to 15 metres or more. One species, now extinct, known as *Paschalococos disperta*, or the Easter Island palm, may have been one of the largest palm species in the world, its bulbous trunk capable of reaching more than 25 metres tall and a metre thick. These settlers were farmers, and they soon began to clear the forest, using slash-and-burn agriculture in order to plant their crops.

The sand of Anakena beach, the site of that first settlement, is particularly good at preserving bone and human remains, and skeletons examined here have given scientists excellent insights into the lives of the ancient Rapa Nui islanders. For instance, we know that, as well as crops, around half of their nutrition came from marine animals including dolphins, seals, fish and sea turtles. These turtles were caught by hand by divers who would swim into the inky depths at night, and whom Polynesian culture revered as heroes. They carved their fishhooks from bone, made ropes from the fibres of the Hau tree, and cooked in earth ovens known as *umu*. 'When you build your earth oven,' advises one traditional Polynesian song, 'be sure that the heap of stones glows with the intense heat of the fire which you have built; Make yourself over into an assiduous and capable workman, O my son!'[16] They were ingenious and drew on inherited knowledge contained in the songs of their ancestors, and they spread quickly across the small landmass until the whole of Rapa Nui was fully populated with as many as 4,000 people, and its forest cover was cleared.

★★★

Ever since the story of Easter Island entered into the popular imagination in the Western world, one particular narrative has dominated. It began with European explorers from as early as 1786, was propagated by Victorian and twentieth-century anthropologists, and finally popularized by authors such as the scientist Jared Diamond in his 2005 book *Collapse*. In this narrative, the inhabitants of Easter Island were the architects of their own demise. Their population boomed until the island could no longer support their numbers. They cut down their trees for firewood, construction material, and supposedly to use as scaffolds and rollers in the monomaniacal pursuit of transporting their large numbers of enormous statues. The loss of trees destroyed the fertility of the island's soil, and productivity collapsed. Along with the collapse of the island's ecology, the complex and centralized society that had carved the hundreds of stone statues began to fall apart. Starvation ran rampant, and this led to a period of violent civil war, and even cannibalism. Shortly before the arrival of the Europeans in 1722, this story goes, the whole of Rapa Nui society had come apart, and only a few hundred survivors were left. 'In just a few centuries,' Diamond writes, 'the people of Easter Island wiped out their forest, drove their plants and animals to extinction, and saw their complex society spiral into chaos.'[17] The archaeologists Paul Bahn and John Flenley go even further, viewing the island's deforestation as an indictment of the entire human race: 'The person who felled the last tree could see that it was the last tree. But he (or she) still felled it. This is what is so worrying. Humankind's covetousness is boundless. Its selfishness appears to be genetically inborn.'[18]

In the latter half of the twentieth century, as we became increasingly concerned about our own industrial society's destructive impact on our environment, the story of Easter Island gained widespread appeal as a cautionary tale. The island in the middle of the ocean seemed like a perfect microcosm of our planet suspended in the void of space, while the stone statues were allowed to become emblems of human folly, our pride and our desire always to build bigger and better than our neighbours. But this narrative rests on some questionable assumptions. The first of these is that the island was deforested due to the greed of its inhabitants and their maniacal obsession with statue-building. Second, that the loss of the forest led to societal collapse. Third, that the society collapsed at all, at least before contact with the outside world. As we will see, none of these are supported by the evidence.

★★★

As soon as they arrived, the Rapa Nui islanders began carving the monuments that would one day make them famous around the world. Stone statues are common on islands across the Polynesian world—but no other island can compete with the size or the incredible number of the Easter Island statues, which its people call *moai*. The statues are known for their large, broad noses and strong chins, their brooding brows and deep eye slits. The Easter Islanders called them *aringa ora ata tepuna*, that is, 'the living faces of the holy ancestors'—and more than a thousand of them have been documented around the island.

Of these, 288 *moai* stand along the coastline, on monolithic stone platforms called *ahu*. These *ahu* are themselves impressive undertakings, built of enormous stones, cut and assembled so precisely that not even a razor blade can fit in the gaps. The *moai* stand with their backs to the sea, their deep-set, expressive eyes staring inland over the fields and hills of Rapa Nui. Almost all of the statues are carved from tuff, a stone formed from volcanic ash which is slowly compacted into solid rock—although fourteen have been found carved from the harder basalt. Tuff is relatively soft and easy to carve, and has been used for construction since ancient times; it can be seen in buildings such as Rome's Colosseum.

Most of the *moai* were carved in a quarry on the outer cliff edge of the Rano Raraku crater, a volcanic caldera on the lower slopes of Ma'unga Terevaka, the island's largest extinct volcano. The crater is 700 metres across, formed of ash and pieces of volcanic tuff thrown up in an ancient explosion, ringed by cliffs 160 metres high. The islanders chipped the *moai* directly from the bedrock here with a hard basalt chisel known as a *toki*, and hundreds of these tools can be found littered around the quarry, their marks everywhere in the rock walls.

One fascinating aspect of this quarry is that there are many incomplete *moai* abandoned here: 397 in total, or nearly half of the island's total *moai* population. Some *moai* were left in the cliffs, half excavated—usually because the stoneworkers discovered a seam of hard rock that would have been virtually too difficult to carve away with their stone tools. Others have obvious flaws or cracks, while some have fallen over during the difficult act of raising them. Other *moai* were simply too ambitious in size. The largest of these, nicknamed 'El Gigante', is nearly 22 metres tall, the size of a seven-storey building, and

El Gigante, the largest *moai* ever carved.

was left lying on its back, still ensconced in the rock face and staring forever up at the sky. This enormous statue would weigh an estimated 270 tonnes if fully carved out, and it's hard to imagine how the islanders ever intended to move it. It's been speculated that some of the larger *moai* may have been intended to stay in the rock face, perhaps keeping guard over the quarry. Some of them seem to be peacefully sleeping in the grottos carved out of the cliff wall, like the reclining Buddhas of South East Asia, or the tomb effigies of Europe in the Middle Ages—but it's hard to say with any certainty what the islanders intended for them.

The work would doubtless have been slow and painstaking—it's thought that an entire statue could take up to a year for a team of twelve people to carve—but it also may have carried a great deal of status. While these workers were carving a *moai*, they weren't labouring in the fields or conducting all manner of other useful tasks—and so their community was investing in their work. Before the carving could even begin, there would have likely been ceremonies and rites that had to take place, chants and incantations designed to summon the protective spirit of the ancestor to inhabit the stone. Many traditional Rapa Nui working songs survive today, and we can imagine the workers singing while they spent long days chipping at the cliff. 'Chipping! *Chipping*!' cries one traditional Polynesian carving song. 'Your hand slips—when the rock is very hard... Dubbing away! *Dubbing away*! Oh! Chipping! Chipping!'[19] One surviving Rapa Nui folksong even derives its rhythm from the striking together of two stones, which evokes the sounds of the *toki* tools knapping away at the statue.

After much arduous work, the whole outline of the *moai* would be carved out, until it was only attached to the bedrock by a narrow keel along its back. The carvers would then gather up stones and earth underneath to support the *moai* while they chipped away the final spine of stone. It must have been an incredible moment when that stone umbilical cord was cut, and the great statue broke free of its stony slumber. The *moai* would then have been edged clear of the quarry by large teams and slid down the grassy slope of the volcano. This was one of the most dangerous parts of a *moai*'s journey, and a number of cracked and abandoned statues stand on the slope, looking like an army of stone wanderers marching down from the volcano. These abandoned statues, buried up to their necks in the refuse from the quarry, form some of the most iconic images of Easter Island today, even though these 'stone heads' actually have bodies buried beneath the earth. Once the *moai* reached the bottom of the hill, the workers would raise it up to a standing position so they could finish carving its back, using soft pumice to wear it smooth and add surface details. Then they would prepare to transport it into its final resting place.

A 1914 photograph of an unfinished *moai*, showing the basalt keel that remained to be carved along the length of its back.

We don't know for sure how the ancient islanders moved these vast statues. This question obsessed early visitors to the island, who couldn't see how a people without metal tools, pulleys or wheels could transport hundreds of them up to 20 kilometres over the island's undulating terrain. The largest successfully transported *moai*, nicknamed Paro, was nearly 12 metres tall including his crown, and at 82 tonnes weighed more than a Boeing 737 aircraft. When asked by early visitors how their ancestors had moved these statues, the islanders would simply reply, 'they walked, and some fell by the way'.[20] Foreign visitors assumed this must be a piece of local folklore, a kind of magical thinking that imagined the statues to be the living spirits of the ancestors. Early archaeologists thought that the *moai* were moved horizontally, perhaps on a wooden sledge, or using logs as rollers, but recent research has cast doubt on this theory—and now the idea that the *moai* had 'walked' has gained greater traction.

In the 1980s, researchers Pavel Pavel and Thor Heyerdahl conducted experiments on concrete replicas and even one abandoned *moai*, to see if they could have been moved upright with what they evocatively dubbed 'the refrigerator method', and their results were promising. 'They worked together rhythmically, easily and without strain,' wrote Heyerdahl. 'In this manner the experimental image wriggled forward as if it were "walking".' At first they were afraid that the *moai* might topple forward, Heyerdahl writes, 'but Pavel reassured us that the design of the *moai* was so ingenious that the colossus would have to tilt almost sixty degrees before it would fall.'[21] One elderly islander watching the experiment even volunteered an old piece of the Rapa Nui language: 'When the *moai* started to move, the old islanders used the verb *neke-neke*...to inch forward by moving the body, due to disabled legs or the absence thereof.'[22]

Littered across Easter Island are the sad shapes of statues that broke during their transportation. These figures have become known as 'road *moai*'. Interestingly, none of the road *moai* have eyes. It seems that the islanders waited to carve these until the statues were in place on their platforms, fitting them with white coral and obsidian pupils, so that they could truly 'come alive'. This practice has echoes of similar traditions that we can find in Sri Lanka, where the eyes of a temple statue of the Buddha are always the last thing to be painted in a ritual known as *netra maṅgalaya*. 'There was a special *pirit* or protective chant of passages from the Dhamma that accompanied the act,' wrote one witness of the practice. 'What's more, certain artists specialized in the task, and they alone, must be employed.'[23] While the Buddha's eyes are painted, the artist does not look directly at the statue as a sign of respect, and paints over their shoulder using a mirror. Some form of ritual likely also accompanied the carving of the *moai* eyes too.

The road *moai* also contain a number of crucial clues about how the statues were transported. In recent years, a team of archaeologists led by veteran Rapa Nui researchers Terry Hunt and Carl Lipo conducted a comprehensive study on the positions and locations of each road *moai*. They discovered that when road *moai* were found on uphill paths, they usually lay on their backs. And when the cracked statues were abandoned on downhill paths, they usually lay on their fronts. On flat ground, it was more like fifty-fifty. This suggests that the statues were not dragged horizontally on wooden rollers, but were indeed transported upright as Pavel and Heyerdahl believed.

Once this detail had been noticed, other curiosities about the road *moai* fell into place. They had bulkier lower halves and rounder bellies than their upright cousins, which had puzzled researchers for a long time—but Hunt and Lipo's theory made sense of these features. The islanders designed the *moai* in two phases: in the first transportation phase, the *moai* were bottom-heavy, like a bowling pin, and once in place on the platforms, they were carved into their more slender and elegant final shape. Lipo and Hunt proposed that the statues were raised upright and rocked back and forth by teams of islanders with three ropes—one on either side, and a third stabilizing the statue from behind—so that the statues would have appeared to 'walk' across the ground. In 2012, they even put their theory into practice, using a 5-tonne replica of some of the smaller *moai* on the island. Their team was able to successfully transport the *moai* nearly 100 metres in just forty minutes, and with a team of only eighteen people.

If this is indeed how the statues were moved, it must have been an incredible sight. There would have likely been a huge amount of communal ceremonial activity around the walking of these statues too, with people coming from all over the island to watch, sing and dance and perform rites—and with the largest *moai* weighing more than 80 tonnes, the thundering of its movements must have made the ground shake. During the weeks that it took to transport one of these statues, it must have felt like a god really had come down to Earth.

The question over how the *moai* were moved has great implications for the traditional narrative of Easter Island's ecocide. If Lipo and Hunt are correct and the statues were walked into place, then the islanders wouldn't have needed trees to move them, and the part of the collapse narrative relating to the *moai* comes into question. 'Walking the moai did not require vast amounts of timber for wooden sleds, rollers, or sliders,' they conclude. 'It was not a reckless mania for moai that exhausted the island's forest and tipped the ecological scales toward catastrophe.'[24] So what did happen to Easter Island's trees?

Undoubtedly much of the forest was cut down by humans—but they didn't do this unconsciously or foolishly. They did it for the same reason that people in Iceland or England cut down much of their forests: because they were farmers. The Rapa Nui, like all Polynesians, farmed energy-rich foods like sweet potatoes, taro and sugar cane, which were vastly more productive than whatever food they could have gathered from the forest. So much of the deforestation was controlled and conscious, and improved the quality of people's lives. It's also clear from the earliest Dutch accounts that the Rapa Nui didn't 'cut down the last tree'. In fact, one of Roggeveen's crewmembers, Carl Friedrich Behrens, writes that 'all the country is under cultivation and we saw in the distance whole tracts of woodland.'[25]

This loss of biodiversity did present several significant challenges. With reduced tree cover, the ocean winds and storms threatened to blow away the topsoil, and salt spray from the sea effectively salted the earth in coastal regions—but the islanders reacted to these challenges with ingenuity. Archaeologists have found evidence of areas where the Rapa Nui planted and cultivated groves of palm trees, probably for their materials. One of the Dutch officers on Roggeveen's voyage reported on the wide variety of uses the islanders had for palm leaves, which must have come from somewhere—and Roggeveen himself witnessed groves of fruit trees. 'It was now deemed advisable to go to the other side of the Island,' he wrote, 'whereto the King or Head Chief invited us, as being the principal place of their plantations and fruit-trees, for all the things they brought to us of that kind were fetched from that quarter.'[26]

The Rapa Nui began farming using a technique known as rock mulching, which has arisen in other cultures that farm in water-poor places. This involves laying rock beds which prevent the soil from washing or blowing away, also reducing the amount of water evaporated by the sun. These rock gardens also increase the amount of nutrients available to the growing plants, as the rainwater flows over the rocks and carries minerals to the roots. There's strong evidence that the Rapa Nui people also cultivated crops underground. Easter Island has one of the largest systems of volcanic caves in the world, and the islanders' relationship with the caves goes back to the first known moment of their history. When their original founder, Hotu Matu'a, first disembarked on Anakena beach, the myth describes him lodging in one of these caves. 'They went on land, sat down, stretched out, and dried in the sun,' goes the story. 'They went on land, turned around, and climbed up together to the cave Pu Pakakina. There they stayed.'[27] Some of these caves can stretch for 3 or 4 kilometres and are present beneath more than thirty per cent of the island's territory. As the forests of Rapa Nui retreated, its people started cultivating sizeable gardens in the parts of the caves that received light. Here, they could grow sweet potato, yam and taro, sheltered from the Pacific winds.

Above ground, they also sheltered crops using circular rock walls called *manavai* that could be up to 2 metres tall, and also reduced the amount of water run-off and concentrated nutrients in the soil. Archaeologists have identified over 2,500 of these circular rock gardens around the island, although it's likely that this is only a fraction of the original number. Studies have shown that even today, with no active maintenance being done on them, these rings of stones are still operating as designed by the ancient gardeners: levels of phosphorus and potassium—crucial minerals for plants—are much higher inside the *manavai* than in the soil outside.

With their rock gardening techniques, the Rapa Nui were able to make the land much more productive after the forest was cleared than it was before. Far from the barren landscape they had anticipated from afar, when Roggeveen and Behrens got ashore, they both describe the islanders bringing them various foods, all wrapped in palm leaves: 'women as well as children brought palm branches, red and white streamers, and various kinds of fruits, Indian figs, large nuts, sugar-cane, roots, fowls—alive, boiled, and roast.'[28] In fact, studies done on the skeletons of islanders from around the time of contact show that they suffered less from malnutrition than the average European. They happily fed the sailors, and didn't make any attempt to beg for food from the newcomers. They were much more interested in the Europeans' hats, and one brave islander even climbed through a porthole on Roggeveen's ship to steal a tablecloth. In fact, it was the Europeans, suffering from malnutrition after weeks at sea, who begged the islanders for food, giving them linens in exchange for sixty chickens and thirty bunches of bananas. Decades later in 1786, sources from a French expedition likewise described a land that appeared to be flourishing, contrary to the reports they had heard from others:

> Instead of meeting with men exhausted by famine... I found, on the contrary, a considerable population, with more beauty and grace than I afterwards met in any other island; and a soil, which, with very little labour, furnished excellent provisions, and in an abundance more than sufficient for the consumption of the inhabitants.[29]

A key part of the starvation narrative is the assumption that the island descended into a period of brutal conflict once resources ran scarce. But if resources were actually abundant, can we also question this assumption? The folklore of the islanders does record a period of warfare, during which two ethnic groups on the island were supposed to have clashed. These were known as the *Hanau epe*, either 'stout people' or 'long-ears', and *Hanau momoko*, meaning either 'thin people' or 'short-ears'. But there is little evidence of organized warfare on the island, and this piece of oral folklore may simply be a legend. Much more reliable is the archaeological record.

The evidence of a sustained conflict is usually hard to miss. For example, on Fiji—another Pacific island, 7,000 kilometres from

Rapa Nui—archaeologists have found the remains of hilltop forts and fortified towns. 'Tahitians constructed massive war canoes for interisland raids,' write Lipo and Hunt, 'and Hawaiian chiefdoms battled each other in long-standing wars involving hundreds of warriors with fearsome battle clubs.'[30] The signs of war include increased number of weapons, increased building of defensive structures, and skeletal remains that bear the marks of violence.

Like the Maya and the Aztecs, the islanders of Rapa Nui made blades called *mata'a* from the black volcanic glass obsidian. Some researchers long contended that the profusion of these blades on the island points to mass production of weaponry—but studies of the blades themselves have found that their edges were mostly covered in vegetable matter: sweet potato and taro. 'Morphometric analysis shows...that *mata'a* were not specifically designed for interpersonal violence but were general purpose tools that may have been used for peaceful tasks.'[31] These *mata'a* were found in the highest concentrations around the islanders' rock gardens, where they were most likely used for everyday tasks like food preparation.

In a historical zone of conflict, archaeologists would expect to see skeletons missing their heads, for instance, or skulls with arrowheads inside, or broken, fractured or damaged bones bearing weapon marks—but studies of remains on Easter Island have shown that the islanders led a remarkably peaceful existence. Only 2.5 per cent of the skeletons studied have been found to have suffered any trauma, and almost all of these injuries were non-lethal. 'The people had, to judge by appearances, no weapons,' wrote Behrens in 1722, 'although, as I remarked, they relied in case of need on their gods or idols which stand erected all along the sea shore in great numbers, before which they fall down and invoke them.'[32]

In the search for defensive structures, archaeologists have also been frustrated. The Pacific island of Rapa Iti, five times smaller than Easter Island, has no fewer than fourteen hilltop fortresses, with watchtowers and walls, ditches and wooden palisade fences. Here we find weapons and human remains bearing the marks of violence. On Easter Island, no such strong evidence exists. In fact, Rapa Nui was 'notable for its lack of violence'.[33]

So, another of our popular assumptions about Easter Island

crumbles. We are left having to explain how Rapa Nui's culture could possibly have been less violent than many other comparable societies, and certainly less violent than life in any European city of the time. We may never fully explain this. Some have speculated that the small size of the island, with close family connections between communities, made conflict risky and difficult to countenance. Some historians have argued that the erection of the *moai* themselves may have helped prevent conflict, by allowing the island's communities to compete for dominance and status in a non-violent way.

Another bonding practice may have emerged in the remarkable ritual known as the 'birdman competition'. The later history of the island is dominated by the cult of a mysterious shapeshifter known as the *tangata manu*, or birdman. This ceremonial figure, with a human body and the head and wings of a bird, is depicted in cave paintings.

Each year, the men of Rapa Nui took part in a test of strength and daring that called on them to become the human embodiment of the birdman for that year. The contestants who competed to become the birdman had a simple enough task. Off the southwest coast of Rapa Nui, on a tiny islet, a rocky outcrop known as Motu Nui is home to several species of birds including the sooty or black tern. These were imbued with both practical and mystical importance for Polynesian sailors, and it's not hard to see how they also assumed a powerful religious significance.

The birdman contest took place during the laying season. Young men would swim out to Motu Nui, a distance of about a kilometre, through choppy, shark-filled seas and powerful currents. They carried with them a few days' supplies under their arm, wrapped in a bundle of reeds called a *pora*. They then had to climb ashore and scramble up through the flocks of cackling sea birds and search through their nests, looking for the first egg of the season. Sometimes they would have to remain on the island for days before they found one. But once they claimed their precious prize, they had to swim with it all the way back to Rapa Nui and climb the sheer 300-metre cliff of the volcano Ranu Kao. 'The men of the celebrating clan carried them to the mainland, swimming with them in baskets bound round the forehead,' writes Katherine Routledge. 'They were then taken in procession round the island.'[34] Each year, the first man to complete this triathlon event would be crowned that year's birdman. We might speculate that allowing warrior-age men to battle it out in this test of strength, agility and stamina every year may have played a role in reducing violence and feuds on the island. The evidence therefore suggests that there was no starvation and no widespread warfare on Easter Island. This might leave us asking: where did we even get the idea that their society had collapsed?

***

'There exists in the midst of the great ocean, in a region where nobody goes, a mysterious and isolated island,' wrote the nineteenth-century French seafarer and artist Pierre Loti. 'The island is planted with monstrous great statues, the work of I don't know what race, today degenerate or vanished; its great remains an enigma.'[35]

Confusion about who had built the statues of Easter Island was one of the consistent themes of European exploration of the island. It was considered a mystery: 'How could a (seemingly) Stone Age society of cave dwellers have produced stonework to rival the majesty of the pyramids of Giza...on a solitary island so incredibly remote?'[36] We've encountered this kind of thinking a number of times over the course of this book. Whether it's assuming that the city of Angkor was built by the Roman Emperor Trajan, or that the Mayan pyramids of Tikal were built by the citizens of Atlantis, European explorers have often struggled to believe that the Indigenous people of non-European lands were capable of complex and impressive constructions. Only a so-called advanced civilization could have built these things, this kind of circular thinking goes, and the people living here don't look like an 'advanced' civilization. In fact, what appeared to early European visitors to be an enigma wasn't anything of the sort: the stone statues of Easter Island hadn't been built by some vanished ancient culture, but by the people who lived there still, and seemed to those Europeans to be so simple.

But in fact, a collapse *would* occur on Rapa Nui—only it wasn't because they cut down the trees. There is one event in its history that I believe encapsulates the complete destruction that ultimately descended on Easter Island: the toppling, in just a few years, of every one of its standing statues.

For centuries, the islanders had loved and revered the *moai* that their ancestors had spent generations carving and transporting. In 1722, Roggeveen recounted what he saw of the islanders' devotion to these statues:

> They kindle fire in front of certain remarkably tall stone figures they set up; and, thereafter squatting on their heels with heads bowed down, they bring the palms of their hands together and alternately raise and lower them.[37]

On 15 November 1770, forty-eight years after the first European visit, two Spanish ships landed and spent five days on the island, performing a very thorough survey of its coast. They re-christened it Isla de San Carlos, and claimed it on behalf of King Charles III of Spain. They also ceremoniously erected three wooden crosses and a Spanish flag on a hill. At that moment, it seems that all the island's 200 erected statues were still standing. But just four years later, the British explorer Captain James Cook sailed past the island and found a much different situation. Cook's diary entry for 17 March 1774 gives his account of the impoverished state of the island:

> This is undoubtedly the same Island as was seen by Roggewein in Apl 1722 altho' the descriptions given of it by the authors of that voyage do's by no means correspond with it now... No Nation will ever contend for the honour of the discovery of Easter Island as there is hardly an Island in this sea which affords less refreshments and conveniences for Shipping [sic] than it does;—Nature has hardly provided it with any thing fit for man to eat or drink, and as the Natives are but few and may be supposed to plant no more than sufficient for themselves.[38]

According to Cook, the population at this time only numbered 600 or 700. He also noted that the islanders now carried weapons when approaching foreign visitors: wooden clubs and spears topped with obsidian points. But the final tragic detail was the fact that in the four years since the Spanish expedition, virtually all the standing *moai* on the island had been toppled.

> On the East side of the Island near the Sea, they met with three Platforms of Stone work, or rather the ruins of them: on each had stood four of those large Statues, but they were all fallen down from two of them and also one from the third; every one except one were broken by the fall and otherways defaced.[39]

By 1838, every single coastal *moai* had been taken down. Now the only standing statues were those abandoned on the slopes below Rano Raraku. What happened to cause the islanders to take up weapons? What reduced their population so drastically? And what made them so dramatically turn against their gods? The answer may lie in the very event that opened this chapter: the arrival of three Dutch sails on the horizon, on Easter Day, 1722.

A 1797 illustration depicting the French explorer La Pérouse investigating the *moai*.

At the sight of the enormous ships dropping anchor some way off the coast, the islanders must have felt how we would feel if a vast alien spaceship were to one day materialize over one of our cities: a mix of fear and wonder, a sense that the world would never quite be the same again. They selected one of their number as an envoy, and in my view it's not unlikely that he would have been the winner of the most recent birdman competition—the island's champion and protector. This man got in his canoe and rowed out to meet the strange vessels. When he approached, he saw that there were men on board, and he waved to them. The Dutch Captain Roggeveen wrote about this incredible encounter:

> This hapless creature seemed to be very glad to behold us, and showed the greatest wonder at the build of our Ship. He took special notice of the tautness of our spars, the stoutness of our rigging and running gear, the sails, the guns—which he felt all over with minute attention—and with everything else that he saw. When the image of his own features was displayed before him in a mirror, he started suddenly back and then looked towards the back of the glass, apparently in the expectation of discovering there the cause of the apparition. After we had sufficiently beguiled ourselves with him, and he with us, we started him off again in his canoe towards the shore.[40]

But when the Dutchmen get ashore, Behrens paints a darker picture. It's clear from his and Roggeveen's accounts that the Europeans were nervous when they stepped ashore. They had heard stories of violent encounters with Pacific Islanders, and despite their guns and cannons, they were afraid of the Rapa Nui. The natural curiosity and boldness of the islanders made matters worse. When the Dutch got ashore, the Rapa Nui pressed around them, grabbing at their hats and clothes, and even touching the guns they carried. It's not clear which Dutchman shot first, but soon a burst of fire tore into the crowd. Behrens recounts what happened next, as he recognized a familiar face among the murdered islanders:

> Many of them were shot at this juncture; and among the slain lay the man who had been with us before, at which we were much grieved. In order to obtain possession of the bodies they congregated in great numbers, bringing with them presents of various kinds of fruits and vegetables, in order that we might the more readily surrender to them their slain. The consternation of these people was by no means abated: even their children's children in that place will, in times to come, be able to recount the story of it.[41]

Just as Behrens writes, the story of this violent encounter must indeed have reverberated through the history of the Rapa Nui. We can assume it would have rocked their sense of the world. The islanders didn't carry weapons, instead relying on their gods to protect them. We can only imagine what would happen to this belief system when multiple islanders were killed with these mysterious weapons—when the killers then walked around the island, even approaching the supposedly protective statues, before sailing away. How could the Rapa Nui's belief in the protective power of the *moai* survive this encounter? Worse, the Europeans' bullets were not their deadliest legacy. Just as in other encounters in the Americas, the Europeans had brought their usual stowaways: viruses and bacteria to which the islanders' immune systems had never been exposed. On other, better-observed Polynesian islands, the reduction in population after first European contact was as much as ninety per cent. On Rapa Nui, the Dutch sailors' close contact with the islanders, along with the linens that they traded for food, would have been vectors of disease transmission.

It's possible that after Roggeveen's initial contact, the population of the island may have crashed to only a few hundred. The population would only just have recovered by the time that, forty-eight years later, the Spaniards arrived and delivered a whole new dose of invisible death to the islanders. The causes of this epidemic would have been incomprehensible to the Rapa Nui—and in fact, the Europeans of the time knew little more. They believed illnesses were caused by miasmas, or bad night air, those being the day's prevailing theories. As whole families sickened and died, the

Rapa Nui must have again believed that the *moai* had failed them or, worse, turned against them. And, one by one, they began to bring them down.

★★★

One remarkable fact about Easter Island is that it may be one of the few places on earth where writing was independently invented—alongside only Sumerian cuneiform, Chinese characters, Mayan glyphs and perhaps Egyptian hieroglyphics and the Indus Valley. A script called *rongo-rongo* has been found on just a few dozen surviving wooden objects and tablets, usually carved with a shark's tooth, or a piece of obsidian. These tablets were all plundered by private collectors in the late nineteenth century, and are now scattered in museums and private collections around the world. Today, none remain on Easter Island. Every modern attempt to decipher *rongo-rongo* has failed, and the script stands as one of the great mysteries of Rapa Nui. The island legends state that Hotu Matu'a brought the wooden tablets with him when he landed on Rapa Nui, but this seems unlikely: there is no known tradition of writing anywhere else in Polynesia.

It's been argued that *rongo-rongo* writing could be a more modern invention—that the islanders saw Europeans reading and writing and were inspired to create their own script. If this were the case, then the written language of *rongo-rongo* would have emerged, flourished and fallen into oblivion, all within a span of less than a hundred years. However, one of the symbols shows, clearly and unambiguously, the distinctive bulbous shape of a jubaea palm tree, a species that went extinct on the island at least seventy years before European contact, showing that *rongo-rongo* was developed during a time when these monster palms still grew over Rapa Nui.

In 1864, a French churchman, Eugène Eyraud, arrived on the island, and described seeing quantities of these writing tablets, although the islanders no longer valued them as repositories of knowledge.

> In every hut one finds wooden tablets or sticks covered in several sorts of hieroglyphic characters: They are depictions

> of animals unknown on the island, which the natives draw with sharp stones. Each figure has its own name; but the scant attention they pay to these tablets leads me to think that these characters, remnants of some primitive writing, are now for them a habitual practice which they keep without seeking its meaning.[42]

Other European visitors in the later nineteenth century reported seeing islanders using the tablets as reels for their fishing lines, and as tools for fire-starting—and by this time, none could agree on how to read them. Whatever knowledge was held on the *rongo-rongo* tablets, it had been lost. The reason for this can be found in the tragic final stage of Rapa Nui's collapse.

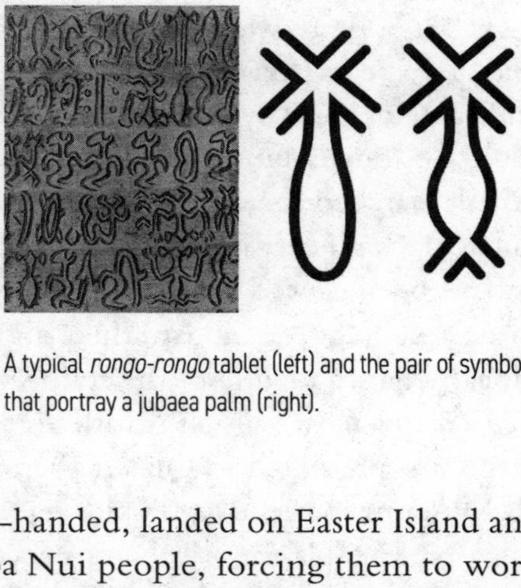

A typical *rongo-rongo* tablet (left) and the pair of symbols that portray a jubaea palm (right).

By 1789, maps were being printed that showed exactly where Easter Island was. In the nineteenth century, the island became a common stopover for ships who wanted to pick up food and other supplies—but as time went by, the visits became more sinister in intent. In 1805, a crew of American sealers, finding themselves short-handed, landed on Easter Island and kidnapped twenty-two Rapa Nui people, forcing them to work on their ship, and keeping them in shackles below deck. This was the beginning of increasingly organized slave-taking raids against the island, and traffic to the South Pacific was only to increase as North Atlantic whale populations were hunted towards extinction, and whalers increasingly ventured into the southern seas.

Soon the Rapa Nui were understandably hostile to any foreigner who tried to land there. When a Russian expedition tried to land in 1816, the Rapa Nui pelted the sailors with stones. The slave raids reached their peak in the 1860s, when large, heavily armed expeditions began arriving from Peru. They would scour the island, rounding up everyone they could find. More than 1,500 Rapa Nui people were captured in these raids, and only a few who managed to hide were spared. The Rapa Nui people were transported to Peru and put to work on plantations or as domestic servants. Eventually, after a public outcry, the Peruvian government was forced to repatriate them, though this only led to further tragedy. Some of the dozen or so islanders who had survived enslavement and the voyage home were infected with smallpox, and before long this spread through the remaining island population. This would be the final death knell for the island's distinctive and beautiful culture. Among those taken as slaves were every single one of the priestly class, the only people who could read the *rongorongo* script. The continuity of songs, myths and tales that had for centuries carried the folk memory of Rapa Nui was lost.

By 1866, there were just 111 adult islanders living on Easter Island. Two years later, when the HMS *Topaze*, a fifty-one-gun British frigate of the Royal Navy, landed on Easter Island, the islanders could no longer summon the energy even to throw stones. The British searched the island until they found the most exquisite example of a *moai* ever carved—one of the only fourteen *moai* known to have been carved from hard basalt. They put ropes around the statue and dragged it aboard their ship. When a British sailor asked a local what the name of the statue was, they replied that he was *Hoa Hakananai'a*, which translates to: 'our stolen friend'.[43] The statue was presented to Queen Victoria, and remains in the British Museum to this day, despite repeated requests by the modern Rapa Nui people for it to be returned.

In 1888, Easter Island was annexed by Chile. It was leased to the Williamson-Balfour Company, a machinery importer and operator of several flour mills, which turned the whole island into a sheep ranch. Capitalism had arrived on Easter Island. The remaining Rapa Nui were cleared off their lands and moved to the town of Hanga Roa on the west coast, where they were ordered to build a 3-metre stone wall around the town, beyond which they were forbidden to set foot. Cut off from their traditional agriculture, the only way for the Rapa Nui to survive was to work as labourers on the sheep ranch. They were now effectively indentured servants on their own island. Rapa Nui's hillsides were grazed by sheep for more than sixty years—and this, more than anything the Rapa Nui had done, destroyed the last remaining trees and stripped the island of its topsoil. One American visitor to the island, a company man named William Thomson, recounted the damage that intensive sheep farming had done to the island's ecology:

> In other parts of the island may be seen, in places in considerable numbers, a hardwood tree, called by the natives *toromiro.* These must have flourished well at one time, but are now all, or nearly all, dead and decaying by reason of being stripped of their bark by the flocks of sheep which roam at will all over the island.[44]

Looking at the evidence, a new narrative emerges, and we see that the mystery of Easter Island isn't a mystery at all. Rapa Nui was not the site of an ecological suicide, but rather of a genocide. And, to add insult to injury, they would go on to be used as a cautionary tale by the very industrialized society that had destroyed them. The truth is that the islanders didn't foolishly damage their environment and bring about their own downfall; in fact, they made their island garden flourish. Through ingenuity, they built a unique and remarkable visual culture and maintained the peace among their communities. So when we reach for Easter Island as a fable, we should be very careful about our reasons. As we face the challenges of our own time, perhaps we should be asking not what warning we might take from the fate of Easter Island, but what its people might have to teach us. Or, as one Polynesian proverb says, '*O te puoe te muhumuhu no te ta'ata ana'e iho 'o tei 'ite i te fa'aro'o*—The seashell sings for him alone who knows how to listen.'[45]

When she visited in 1913, Katherine Routledge would become the first to complete a full survey of Easter Island's remains. She and her team conducted extensive excavations, unearthing more than thirty *moai* statues, and they also managed to document a number of the myths and oral histories of the islanders, by visiting tribal elders in a leper colony situated north of the now-walled town of Hanga Roa. Over her stay on the island, Routledge was moved by the windswept ruins of the fallen *moai* that still scattered the grassy hills of this land that had lost its faith in its gods. 'In Easter Island the past is the present,' she wrote. 'It is impossible to escape from it.'

> The shadows of the departed builders still possess the land. Voluntarily or involuntarily the sojourner must hold commune with those old workers; for the whole air vibrates with a vast purpose and energy which has been and is no more. What was it? Why was it? The great works are now in ruins, of many comparatively little remains; but the impression infinitely exceeded anything which had been anticipated, and every day, as the power to see increased, brought with it a greater sense of wonder and marvel. 'If we were to tell people at home these things,' said our Sailingmaster, after being shown the prostrate images on the great burial place of Tongariki, 'they would not believe us.'[46]

"The New Zealander," a woodcut by Gustave Doré that appeared as the final plate in *London: A Pilgrimage* by Douglas Jerrold and Gustave Doré, 1872

EPILOGUE

> 'I like to think how easily Nature will absorb London as she absorbed the mastodon, setting her spiders to spin the winding-sheet and her worms to fill in the grave, and her grass to cover it pitifully up, adding flowers—as an unknown hand added them to the grave of Nero.'
>
> Edward Thomas, *The South Country* (1909)

In 1872, the French illustrator Gustave Doré published his collection *London: A Pilgrimage*, containing scenes of life in the capital during the late nineteenth century. London was then the centre of a global empire that had superseded the Spanish, Portuguese, Dutch and French empires to become the largest in the world, had conquered India and claimed dominion over a third of the world's population. But the final plate of the book was an image titled 'The New Zealander'. It imagines a foreign visitor in the distant future gazing at the ruins of London, just as Europeans of the time contemplated the crumbling remains of Athens and Rome. Strewn out before this antipodean wanderer lies the cracked dome of St Paul's Cathedral, the pillars of the Commercial Wharf overgrown with willows.

By the time Doré engraved this image, the trope of the New

Zealander was an old one. In 1819, Percy Bysshe Shelley wrote about a 'transatlantic commentator' arriving in the city,

> when London shall be an habitation of bitterns; when St. Paul's and Westminster Abbey shall stand, shapeless and nameless ruins, in the midst of an unpeopled marsh. When the piers of Waterloo Bridge shall become the nuclei of islets of reeds and osiers, and cast the jagged shadows of their broken arches on the solitary stream.[1]

It was the writer Thomas Babington Macaulay who moved this traveller to the southern hemisphere, imagining in 1840 a time 'when some traveller from New Zealand shall, in the midst of a vast solitude, take his stand on a broken arch of London Bridge to sketch the ruins of St. Paul's'.[2] The trope became so overused in the following decades that by 1865 the satirical magazine *Punch* would declare that the New Zealander 'can no longer be suffered to impede the traffic over London Bridge. Much wanted at the present time in his own country. May return when London is in ruins.'[3]

Since people first encountered the ruins of past societies, we have felt a sense of trepidation. Like Scipio watching Carthage in flames, we have always wondered: what will become of us?

It is not possible to make confident pronouncements about the future, and history has always made fools of those who try. There are numerous low-probability scenarios for the collapse of modern industrial society. We know that in the context of deep time, supervolcanoes and extinction-level asteroid impacts are an eventual certainty—but the odds stand against either occurring any time soon. We have so far managed to keep the planet's nuclear arsenal in its silos, although that danger remains ever-present. A pandemic that combines high mortality with high transmission rates is a constant threat, and we could even concern ourselves with the more fanciful ideas of rogue AIs and other futuristic spectres that for now belong to the realm of Hollywood. Many of these scenarios are plausible, and their risks should not be overlooked. But the challenges of the next century will be utterly defined by one threat: global warming.

The modern industrialized age has brought marvels. It brought the eradication of the horror of smallpox, saw humans walk on the surface of our moon, and created machines that can speak and to some extent think. It has lifted countless millions out of poverty. It is an engine that we built, and it is very good at what it does—but it is also changing our planet in alarming and extremely rapid ways.

In 1896, the Swedish chemist Svante Arrhenius calculated the effects on the planet's temperature of an atmospheric gas that he called 'carbonic acid'—which we know today as carbon dioxide (CO2). 'If the quantity of carbonic acid in the air should sink to one-half its present percentage, the temperature would fall by about 4°,' he later wrote. 'On the other hand, any doubling of the percentage of carbon dioxide in the air would raise the temperature of the earth's surface by 4°; and if the carbon dioxide were increased fourfold, the temperature would rise by 8°.'[4] Today, anyone with a handle on basic physics and chemistry can repeat Arrhenius's calculations, and find the same answer—an answer that has now been more or less corroborated by the world's most powerful computerized climate models.

To Arrhenius, this was an idle calculation—and in fact may have felt reassuring, given that many people at the time were concerned about the speculated return of the Ice Age. But now more than a century later, we are living in the world that Arrhenius foresaw. Since the dawn of the industrial revolution, we have burned an estimated half a trillion tonnes of carbon, essentially transferring hundreds of gigatonnes of the earth's crust into the atmosphere. As a result, 'Since records began in 1850, seventeen of the eighteen hottest years have occurred, all since 2000.'[5] A number of 'tipping points' have also been identified, which speed up and amplify the effects caused by CO2 and the even more potent greenhouse gas methane, meaning that the changes we have seen are in the more severe range of what was predicted in previous decades. In other words, we are now living in what was previously considered the 'worst-case scenario'.

One of these tipping points is the melting of the Arctic sea ice, which currently reflects up to eighty per cent of the sunlight that falls on it back into space, thus cooling the planet. We have now experienced multiple years when the Arctic has seen temperatures 20°C higher than average, with record low ice levels, and the sea is projected to have its first ice-free summer as early as the 2030s, 'irrespective of emission scenarios'. After that, 'Extended occurrences of an ice-free Arctic in the early summer months are projected later in the century.'[6] With the reflective power of the ice cap gone, the energy of the sunlight will be absorbed by the sea instead. The feedback effect of all global ice and snow loss has been calculated to add fifty per cent to the global warming effect.

This process is to some extent already locked in. 'We are not far from the moment when the feedbacks will themselves be driving the change,' writes polar scientist Peter Wadhams. 'That is, we will not need to add more CO2 to the atmosphere at all, but will get the warming anyway.'[7] Even if all global carbon emissions stopped overnight, the earth would continue to warm into the late twenty-first century—but other than a five per cent drop during the Covid pandemic, global carbon emissions have grown every year, and continue to grow. Many fossil fuel-producing countries are actually expanding their industries, a move that the author of one UN report has called 'insanity'.[8] There is no sense in becoming excessively maudlin about the subject, or listing off each way that we are passing into a very dangerous era for our planet. 'You already know enough,' Sven Lindqvist once wrote. 'So do I. It is not knowledge we lack. What is missing is the courage to understand what we know and to draw conclusions.'[9]

In April 2023, the SpaceX rocket *Starship* exploded in the skies above the Gulf of Mexico on its maiden test flight. The company would later attract some mockery by describing this as 'a rapid unscheduled disassembly',[10] conjuring to the imagination the possibility of a mid-air disassembly that might have been conducted in a more orderly manner. But this is actually the paradox we face. We must disassemble the rocket even as it flies. We must keep it flying even as we disassemble it. We have built a machine that will destroy the world as we know it, and we depend on it to live.

Even with drastically reduced emissions, the next century will see the delayed effects of the carbon we have already emitted, which will include: increased natural disasters; sea-level rise inundating areas where hundreds of millions of people currently live; the flooding of major cities; reductions in staple crop yields and breadbasket failure; 'dustbowlification' and the expansion of deserts; climate refugees fleeing areas affected; an increase in conflicts—just to name a few. These threats combine to create what one UN body has called a 'dangerous tendency for the world to move towards a global collapse scenario.'[11]

It is possible that our technological ingenuity will save us, as it has before. It was once feared that the earth's population would exceed the planet's ability to provide food in the twentieth century—but the 'Green Revolution' in agricultural technology saw food production continue to outpace population growth, averting disaster. It is not inconceivable that a new revolution in energy production or moonshot technologies like planetary-scale carbon capture or orbital mirrors might avert our predicament, but these technologies still belong to the world of the future and are nowhere near implementation. As Wile E. Coyote always finds out in the end, you cannot keep running over the cliff forever. Eventually, you will have to look down. Whether we like it or not, these changes are on their way—and their effect on our societies will be profound.

As we have seen throughout this book, the collapse of a society is rarely simple. Climate collapse is likely to be 'an extended process that starts small and plays out over the course of a century or more',[12] and it will happen unevenly around the globe. In a coup for Thomas Babington Macaulay, one study rated New Zealand as the best place on earth to survive a global collapse, followed by other island nations, 'Iceland, the UK, Tasmania and Ireland'.[13] In other places, walls are already being built between the wealthy world of the former colonial empires and the parts of the world likely to suffer the most from climate change. From the West Bank and Gaza to the US southern border, from the Saudi border with Yemen to the Australian coastal defences and the EU's eastern and Mediterranean fronts, 'No continent has been spared from the reinforcement and fortification of borders, which has come to define the beginning of the twenty-first century.'[14] Most border walls in the world were constructed in the last two decades. A new international order is taking place based on these walls: inside them, life is protected and valued—outside, life is considered cheap. The IEP estimates that '1.2 billion people could be displaced globally by 2050'.[15] The Fragile States Index 2023 listed 56 countries in their 'high warning' category or higher, and climate pressure has been implicated in recent conflicts in Syria, Mali and Libya, among others. To put a dark spin on William Gibson's famous quote: 'The future is already here—it's just not very evenly distributed.'[16]

Like the people of the Bronze Age, or the Maya city states, the interconnected nature of our global economy means that a crisis in one part of the world is soon felt everywhere. We in the West produce our textiles in Bangladesh, our semiconductors in Taiwan, our phones and computers in China, all transported through crucial trade chokepoints like the Panama and Suez canals. We do not have the luxury of building our walls and cowering behind them, or of disappearing into denial or its equally disempowering cousin 'doomerism'. It is time to accept the changes and challenges of the next century, while also fighting with everything we have to save as many lives as possible. It is not a matter of abandoning hope, but changing it: 'In abandoning hope that one way of life will continue, we open up a space for alternative hopes.'[17]

The imagery of societal collapse has long been populated by a figure now as tired-out as Macaulay's New Zealander: the rugged survivor loping across the hellscape with shotgun and nuclear family of dependants in tow. It is an image of individualist survival that has more in common with the genre of the American Western than any observed reality—and in fact we know that during crises people tend to bind together. The collapse of our modern society—in whole or in part—would likely see many of the world's evils return to places from which they have been mostly banished, but it is only through building communities that humans can survive, and have any hope of preserving the values that we know must endure. If a time of privation and violence really does lie ahead, everyone must ask themselves: what can we preserve? But also: what can we leave behind?

If we are unable to save ourselves, then what might the future hold for a post-collapse world? Here, we wander into the realm of science fiction. But as we have seen throughout this book, humans have an immense resilience, and so long as the planet's climate eventually stabilizes, humanity will not go extinct. However, our large cities may be unsustainable in a society of reduced complexity, population and resources. Like the ruins of Nineveh, Carthage or Angkor, they will be left to nature. The transformation of even a large city like London would be swift. Within a decade or more, fast-growing imported pests like Japanese knotweed and Chinese buddleia would sweep through the city and burst through the cracks that open in our unmaintained streets. Native rosebay willowherb, or fireweed, would spread among the ruins, just as it once did among the bomb sites of the Blitz. The writer Robert Macfarlane describes this steady triumph of nature over concrete.

> The water in the city's outdoor swimming pools has thickened with leaf debris, which mulches darkly down; the first stage in the creation of tiny fens. Blackthorn marches from the hedges, suckering rapidly along, and elm works out in small thickets, keeping its head low (for Dutch Elm disease is still present). A soil cap deepens on the tarmac, low in nutrients and therefore highly bio-diverse, on which clover, grass, and wildflowers including orchids thrive... Owl populations boom, enjoying the availability of nest-sites in the ruins and the surge in mice numbers.[18]

Strays will abound, and soon packs of wild dogs will become the most dangerous predators. Buildings will slowly be covered in sheets of ivy and elder, and sycamores will sprout from walls, cracking the bricks with their roots and binding them. Our skyscrapers and large buildings of metal and concrete will lose their windows eventually, and vegetation will drape down their sides. Alan Weisman describes the sensory experience of the abandoned city of Varosha, in the demilitarized buffer zone of Cyprus.

> The honeycombed facades of empty hotels, 10 stories of shattered sliding glass doors opening to seaview balconies now exposed to the elements, had become giant pigeon roosts.

> Pigeon droppings coated everything. Carob rats nested in hotel rooms, living off Yaffa oranges and lemons from former citrus groves.[19]

Once water infiltrates a building, it can become uninhabitable in a season, and structural damage follows soon after. Eventually, perhaps after a century or more, the steel structures of our great towers will rust and soften, and they will fall. Without continued maintenance on the Thames Barrier that currently protects London from rising sea levels, more than 130 square kilometres of the city would flood. After this, the city would become a series of seasonally inundated wetlands broken by the crumbling rows of houses and apartment blocks, populated by an amalgam of ancient native species: marsh marigold, woundwort, horsetail, all joined by exotic fugitives from the city's botanical gardens.

An abandoned steelworks in 2020 France, now overgrown with vegetation.

Eking out a living among these ruins of a vanished world will be difficult. But in many ways the lives of the people who come after our industrial society may be better than the peoples who came before it. On a warmer planet, tropical diseases like malaria may spread further north, but smallpox has already been eradicated, and other afflictions like leprosy have been cleared from much of the world. If some degree of medical knowledge can be preserved, then future people will understand germ theory, and know to boil water, disinfect wounds, and quarantine the sick. Unlike our ancient ancestors, their crops will be descended from our highly cultivated modern variants, and their livestock from high-yield modern breeds. And with the tangerine glow of streetlights gone from the night sky, they will once more see the stars.

Most of the easily reachable iron, copper and tin was mined long ago, and so the people of the coming centuries will likely need to extract these materials from the ruins of the fallen world. Just as the scavengers of post-Roman Britain once picked through their abandoned cities, so people may clamber through the leaning, unstable skyscrapers, along streets now turned into forests, hung with vines and creepers. They will strip their steel rebar, copper piping, and aluminium facades, so that the scrap can be melted down and beaten into knives, hammers, weapons and other objects. They will gather trinkets of plastic and glass to sell on, artefacts whose original use will be forgotten, but are still cherished. In coastal cities, they may paddle between the inundated buildings in canoes, and like the Mayan peasants who once inhabited the abandoned palaces of their kings, perhaps they will wonder at the strange markings painted on the cracked roads they now sail over, still visible on the rusting road signs that rise out of the water, and written in long-dead neon over these cities of ghosts.

How will they remember us? Like the delicate paper that the Carthaginians and Khmer wrote on, the *rongo-rongo* of the Rapa Nui, or the *quipu* of the Inca, our digital world will leave few footprints. Virtually all our writing, our video, our music and film, exists only in the context of the continuance of an electric grid, servers and computer screens. New solid-state drives may last a long time, but whether anyone will be able to read them is another matter—and our paper books will not last long unless they are copied down. Future people may end up knowing less about us than about the Sumerians and Assyrians, who had the sense to write things down on durable clay, or the Mayans who wrote on stone. Perhaps, like the ancient Greeks who wandered among the walls of Mycenae, or the Britons gazing at the Roman ruins, they will invent myths of a race of giants who built those now incomprehensible totems of concrete and steel. Perhaps, like the Medes who lived around the ashen remains of Nineveh, or the Hebrew poets who saw ruins like the Ziggurat of Ur, they will spin stories of a people who had angered the gods with their pride, and had a terrible judgement brought down upon them and their fallen towers. Perhaps they, like many ancient peoples, will tell tales of a great flood that drowned the whole world, and brought about the birth of a new one.

With virtually all the easily available fossil fuels already burned, the world would not be able to restart the industrial revolution—at least not in the same way as before. After an unknown number of years—perhaps thousands, perhaps only hundreds—its peoples might rebuild and achieve a level of technological sophistication comparable to the eighteenth century. If electricity is rediscovered, it will necessarily be generated by wind and water rather than the easier burning of coal, and we can fancifully imagine a gradual technological revolution similar to our own—but this time based from the beginning on renewable power. Their world would be built not on an economy of extraction and exploitation, but one of reuse and repurposing. While we have attempted to engineer green policy into our societies *post hoc* in a desperate attempt to avert disaster, their sustainability will be born out of necessity—ingrained from the beginning into the DNA of their economies, and perhaps also in their mentalities. This distant world, perhaps thousands of years in our future, will have risen out of much death and suffering. But it will be a world that might finally have some hope of lasting. We will not live to see it, but there are people who will. And one day, perhaps one of them will tell our story.

★ ★ ★ ★ ★

ACKNOWLEDGEMENTS

There are too many intellectual debts in this book to name, although the sources section of each chapter gives some hint as to the work of the historians and researchers who have made this book possible. I would like specifically to thank professor of Greek and Roman history Dr Michael J. Taylor, Assyriologist Eleanor Bennett, Deccan historian Manu Pillai and the Byzantinist Peter Sandham for their help and advice with some of the ancient chapters. I would like to thank my PhD supervisors Petra Rau and Rebecca Stott for their intellectual guidance and early encouragement. I would like to thank my researchers Brian Stolk, Joe Macdonald and Ciarán Falvey for their work in the archives. Special thanks go to the University of East Anglia Library, British Library and Robert Sainsbury Library and Sainsbury Research Unit (SRU) for their help with access to their invaluable collections. Special thanks go to my editor Rowan Cope, who helped to wrestle this manuscript into its current shape, as well as editors Alba Ziegler-Bailey and David Bamford for their tireless work. Thanks as always to my agents Eve White and Ludo Cinelli for their constant support.

The book is utterly indebted to the work of the historians who have made it possible, especially: Samuel Noah Kramer, Jerald Jack Starr, Gwendolyn Leick, Georges Roux, Harriet Crawford, Eric Cline, Robert Drews, Guy Middleton, Michael Wood, Eckart Frahm, Karen Radner, Adrian Goldsworthy, Richard Miles, Peter Frankopan, Rafe De Crespigny, Michael Lowe, John E. Hill, Robin Fleming, Guy de la Bédoyère, Francis Pryor, Stuart Laycock, Michael D. Coe, David Drew, Heather McKillop, David Webster, AnnCorinne Freter, Charles Higham, Christopher Pym, Kenneth So, Robert Browning, Andrew Dalby, Anthony Kaldellis, John Julius Norwich, Manu Pillai, William Dalrymple, Robert Sewell, Michael Gomez, Nehemia Levtzion, Elikia M'bokolo, John Hunwick, Christopher Wise, Hugh Thomas, Inga Clendinnen, Alfonso Caso, Miguel León-Portilla, James Lockhart, Barbara E. Mundy, Irene Nicholson, Matthew Restall, Michael E. Smith, Tzvetan Todorov, Camilla Townsend, Brian Bauer, R. Alan Covey, John Curl, John Hemming, Kim MacQuarrie, Gordon F. McEwan, William H. Prescott, Irene Silverblatt, Stuart Stirling, Carl Lipo, Terry Hunt, Dan Bendrups, Robert Langdon, Katherine Routledge, John Francis Stimson, Rupert Read, Jem Bendell, David Skilton, Sven Lindqvist, Daniel Steel, Peter Wadhams, Joseph Tainter, Robert Macfarlane and Alan Weisman. Special thanks to the work of the Electronic Text Corpus of Sumerian Literature (ETCSL), run by Dr Jeremy Black, Dr Graham Cunningham, Dr Gábor Zólyomi and Dr Eleanor Robson. Also thank to the Perseus Digital Library at Tufts University, run by Gregory Crane, Marie-Claire Beaulieu, Bridget Almas, Alison Babeu, Frederik Baumgardt, Tim Buckingham, Lisa Cerrato and Anna Krohn. Many thanks to the University of East Anglia, and the Arts and Humanities Research Council (AHRC) for funding my PhD. Thank you to all the readers and listeners who have sent in their support, their comments and corrections, their kind words, and their constant encouragement. Without them, none of this would have been possible.

NOTES

PART I
1. The Sumerians

1 Della Valle, Pietro, p. 261

2 *Ibid.*

3 Rice 2002, p. 134

4 Maspero 1880, vol. 3, p. 16

5 Barjamovic 2019, p. 124

6 Kramer 1981, p. 94

7 *The Sumerian King List* (ETCSL t.2.1.1), 1–39

8 *Inana and Enki* (ETCSL t.1.3.1), 10–17

9 *Ibid.*

10 Benjamin, p. 258

11 *Enmerkar and the lord of Aratta* (ETCSL t.1.8.2.3), 500–514

12 *The Epic of Gilgamesh*, Tablet XI (Translation by William Muss-Arnolt)

13 *Ibid.*, Tablet I

14 *Ibid.*, Tablet XI

15 Stele of the Vultures (CDLI P222399) (Translation by Jerald Jack Starr)

16 King 2020, p. 190

17 *Ibid.*, p. 194

18 *The Legend of Sargon*, in Rogers 1912, p. 136

19 *Ibid.*

20 *Ibid.*

21 Kramer 1971, p. 324

22 Rogers 1912, pp. 203–204

23 *The Sumerian King List* (ETCSL t.2.1.1), 266–296

24 The *Esagila Chronicle / Weidner Chronicle* (Translation by Alan Millard)

25 Oppenheim 1967, pp. 71–72

26 *The Ancient Near East: An Anthology*, pp. 419–420

27 *The Cursing of Agade* (ETCSL t.2.1.5), 272–280

28 *The Death of Ur-Namma* (ETCSL t.2.4.1.1), 31–51

29 *The Marriage of Martu* (ETCSL t.1.7.1), 126–141

30 *The Lament for Sumer and Urim* (ETCSL t.2.2.3), 27–37

31 *The Lament for Urim* (ETCSL t.2.2.2), 230–240

32 Loftus 1857, p. 163

33 *The Epic of Gilgamesh*, Tablet X (Translation by William Muss-Arnolt)

2. The Late Bronze Age Collapse

1 Drews 1993, pp. 4–8

2 Pausanias, 2.25.8

3 Homerus, *Iliad*, 4:513–521 (Translation by Edward Earl of Derby, pp. 93–94)

4 Bryce 2005, p. 370

5 Cline 2021, p. 39

6 Carol Bell, quoted in Cline 2021, p. xvi

7 Breasted 1906, pp. 37–38 § 64

8 Nougayrol *et al.*, pp. 87–90

9 Breasted, *op. cit.*, p. 39 § 67

10 *Ibid.*, p. 38 § 65

11 *Ibid.*, p. 39 § 67

12 *Ibid.*, p. 39 § 67

13 O. Berlin P.10633, quoted in Edgerton 1951, p. 137

14 *The Turin Strike Papyrus*, recto 1, l.2 and 2, ll. 2–5 quoted in Wilkinson 2013, pp. 358–359

15 Potts, 7.6. VAT 17020

16 Drews 2020, p. 76

17 Finkelstein *et al.*, p. 160

18 RSO 23:184–85, no. 107, ll. 14′–20′ (Translation by Yoram Cohen)

19 Herbert of Clairvaux, *Liber De Miraculis*, quoted in Thorarinsson 1970

20 RSO 23:95–96, no. 45 (Translation by Yoram Cohen)
21 Cline 2021, p. 188
22 Gaster 1961, pp. 302–303
23 *Ibid.*, pp. 312–315

3. Assyria

1 Xenophon, *Anabasis*, 3.4.8–10 (Translation by Rex Warner)
2 *Ibid.*, 3.4.11–13
3 Talbot 1873, p. 134
4 *Ibid.*, p. 135
5 Roux 1992, p. 282
6 Frahm, Eckart, *A Companion to Assyria*, p. 3
7 Odarico 1994, p. 74
8 Grayson *et al.*, 1991, 'Tiglath-pileser' A.0.87.1. p. 26
9 *Ibid.*, Tiglath-Pileser A.0.83. p. 37
10 *Ibid.*, Ashurnasirpal II A.0.101.1. p. 201
11 The Bible, 2 Kings 18:3–4
12 *Ibid.*, 2 Kings 18:14
13 *Ibid.*, 2 Kings 18:25–36
14 Luckenbill 1926, Sennacherib 333. p. 150
15 *Ibid.*, Esarhaddon 501. p. 200
16 *Ibid.*, Esarhaddon 506. p. 202
17 *Ibid.*, Esarhaddon 654. p. 247
18 Radner 2015, p. 50
19 *State Archives of Assyria Online*, SAA 16, 059
20 Luckenbill 1926, Assurbanipal 986. pp. 378–379
21 *Ibid.*, 787. pp. 299–300
22 *Ibid.*, 926. pp. 358–359
23 *Ibid.*, 794. p. 303
24 *Ibid.*, 810–811. pp. 309–311
25 *Ibid.*, 984. pp. 377–378
26 The Bible, Nahum 2:3–3:1
27 *Ibid.*, 3:18–19
28 Layard, 1852, p. 3
29 *Ibid.*, pp. 4–5
30 *Ibid.*

4. Carthage

1 The Bible, Ezekial 27:5–7

2 Homer, *Odyssey*, 15.415

3 Cross 1972, 'An Interpretation of the Nora Stone'

4 Virgil, *Aeneid*, Book 4, 636–667, p. 90

5 Aristotle, *Politics*, 2.1272b

6 *Ibid.*, 2.1273a.20

7 Herodotus 4.42.3–4

8 *Periplus of Hanno the Navigator*, 16 (Translation by Wilfred H. Schoff, p. 5)

9 Avienus, *Ora Maritima* § 80 (Translation by Ralph B. Morley)

10 Diodorus Siculus, *The Library of History*, Book 20, 58.4–5

11 Pliny the Elder, *Natural History*, Book VIII, 9

12 Polybius, *Histories*, 3.22.4–13 (Translation by Evelyn S. Shuckburgh)

13 Diodorus, Book 4, 19.3

14 Plutarch, *Moralia*, De Superstitione 13

15 Diodorus, Book 20, 14.4–7

16 Plutarch, *Pyrrhus*, 14.5

17 *Ibid.*, 21.9–10

18 *Ibid.*, 23.6

19 Cassius Dio, Fragments of Book 11.43

20 Polybius, *Histories*, 1.10.9

21 *Ibid.*, 1.23

22 *Ibid.*, 1.71.8

23 Silius Italicus, *Punica*, Book 1:56–69 (Translation by James Duff)

24 Livy 21.10.10 (Translation by F. G. Moore)

25 Appian, *The Foreign Wars*, Book 6, 3.13

26 Ammianus Marcellinus, 15.10.3–5 (Translation by John C. Rolfe, vol. 1, p. 183)

27 Livy 21.37.5

28 Polybius, *Histories*, Book 3 Summary: Approach of Scipio

29 Livy 22.57.6

30 Silius Italicus, *Punica*, Book 17:149–200

31 Polybius, *Histories*, 15.6

32 Plutarch, *Life of Marcus Cato*, 26.2

33 Appian, *The Foreign Wars*, 13.93

34 *Ibid.*, 19.132

35 Temple 1835, vol. 1, pp. 91–93

5. Han China

1 'The Ruins of Lo-Yong' (Translation by Arthur Waley), in *A Hundred and Seventy Chinese Poems*, p. 86

2 Sima Qian, Book 6 (Translation by Watson Burton, in *Qin Dynasty*, p. 75)

3 *Ibid.*, p. 79

4 *Ibid.*, p. 63

5 *Ibid.*, p. 77

6 Sima Qian, Book 30 (Translation by Watson Burton, in *Han Dynasty II*, p. 61)

7 Quoted in Waldron 1990, p. 41

8 Sima Qian, Book 110 (Translation by Watson Burton, in *Han Dynasty II*, p. 129)

9 *Ibid.*, Book 30, p. 63

10 Quoted in Wang 2013, p. 218

11 Quoted in Rafe de Crespigny 2016, p. 69

12 *Hou Hanshu* 88:11 (Translation by John Hill)

13 *Ibid.*

14 *Ibid.*, 88:10

15 *Zizhi Tongjian* 58, Guanghe 4: 181 (Translation by Rafe de Crespigny in *Emperor Huan and Emperor Ling*, pp. 336–337)

16 *Hou Hanshu* 66, quoted in de Crespigny 2016, p. 371

17 *Hou Hanshu* 87, quoted in Tse 2018

18 *Hou Hanshu* 72, quoted in de Crespigny 2016, p. 452

19 *Ibid.*, p. 452–453

20 *Zizhi Tongjian* 57, Guanghe 1: 178 (Translation by Rafe de Crespigny in *Emperor Huan and Emperor Ling*, pp. 294–296)

21 *Ibid.*, p. 297

22 *Zizhi Tongjian* 58, Zhongping 1: 184, p. 353

23 *Hou Hanshou* 72, quoted in de Crespigny 2016, p. 455

24 *Ibid.*, p. 457

25 Luo Guanzhong (Translation by Moss Roberts, p. 3)

26 *The Desecration of the Han Tombs* (Translation by Arthur Waley), in *A Hundred and Seventy Chinese Poems*, pp. 97–98

6. Roman Britain

1 *Codex Exoniensis*, pp. 476–478 (Translation by Benjamin Thorpe)

2 Plutarch, *Life of Caesar*, Chapter 23:2

3 Ammianus Marcellinus, Book 27, 8:6 (Translation by Charles D. Yonge, p. 454)

4 Julius Caesar, *Gallic Wars*, Book 5, Chapter 14

5 Pliny the Elder, Book 16:95 (Translation by John Bostock)

6 Tacitus, *Agricola*, 30.4, quoted in Morley 2010

7 Cassius Dio, *Epitome of Book* 77, pp. 262–264

8 Vindolanda Tablet 164 (Tab.Vindol. 164) (Translation by Alan Bowman)

9 *Historia Augusta*, 'The Life of Clodius Albinus', Chapter 4:6, pp. 467–469

10 *Ibid.*, Chapter 13:1, p. 487

11 Cassius Dio, *Epitome of Book 72*, Book 72, Chapter 35:4

12 Herodian, 2.15.1 (Translation by Edward Echols)

13 *Historia Augusta*, 'The Life of Clodius Albinus', Chapter 13:5, pp. 467–469

14 Herodian, 3.7.6

15 Herodian, 3.14.1

16 Ammianus Marcellinus, Book 27, 8:1–5, p. 453–454

17 Gildas, *De Excidio*, Chapter 14–16 (Translation by J. A. Giles, p. 13)

18 Orosius, Book 7, Chapter 40:4

19 Procopius, Book 1, Chapter 12:16–19

20 Fleming 2021, p. 33

21 'The Ruin', 21–37, pp. 199–201 (Translation by Israel Gollancz)

PART II
7. The Maya

1 Avendaño y Loyola (Translation by Philip Ainsworth Means, p. 167)

2 Herrera, quoted in Stephens 1843, vol. 2, p. 305

3 Drew 1999, p. 227

4 *Ibid.*, p. 343

5 McNeil 2009

6 Diego de Landa (Translation by Alfred Marston Tozzer, p. 185)

7 Gill 2007, p. 285

8 *The Book of Chilam Balam of Chumayel*, Book 2:12 (Translation by Ralph Roys, p. 76)

9 Jie Liu *et al.*, p. 1

10 Lentz *et al.* 2020, p. 4

11 Gorokhovich *et al.* 2020

12 *The Book of Chilam Balam of Chumayel*, Book 9:29, p. 89

13 Stuart 1993, pp. 344–346

14 *The Book of Chilam Balam of Chumayel*, Book 2:12, pp. 76–77

15 Stephens 1841, vol. 1, p. 102

16 *Ibid.*, p. 104

17 *Ibid.*, p. 103

8. The Khmer

1 Groslier 1913, p. 1

2 *Ibid.*, pp. 31–32

3 *Ibid.*, p. 32

4 Higham 2003, p. 2

5 K.235, 'Sdok Kak Thom stele' (1052 CE), quoted in James St Julian 2014

6 Henri Mouhot 1864, p. 21

7 Bergaigne, *Inscriptions Sanscrites*, p. 322, quoted in Chandler 1992, p. 40

8 Zhou Daguan, Chapter 2:3 (Translation by Peter Harris, pp. 34–35)

9 *Ibid.*, Chapter 38–40, p. 51

10 *Ibid.*, Chapter 40:34, p. 50

11 Fletcher 2018, pp. 246–247

12 MacDonald 1987, p. 113

13 *Hymn to the Tree of Awakening* (Translation by Trent Walker, in Stewart *et al.* (eds.) 2022, pp. 6–7)

9. Byzantium

1 Palladius, *The Lausiac History*, 54 (Translation by Walter Emil Kaegi, p. 156)

2 Wace 1912, pp. 499–500

3 Smylie 1996, p. 7

4 Niketas Choniates, *Historia*, 591 (Translation by Harry J. Magoulias, p. 325)

5 Procopius, *Anecdota*, Chapter 13:7 (Translation by Henry Bronson Dewing, p. 159)

6 Theophanes 353 (Translation by Harry Turtledove, p. 52)

7 Bartolf of Nangis, *History of the Franks who stormed Jerusalem*, quoted in Dalby 2010

8 Liudprand of Cremona, Chapter 9 (Translation by F. A. Wright)

9 Odo of Deuil, *Expedition of Louis VII* (Translation by V. G. Berry)

10 Ibn Battuta, *Travels*, pp. 506–508 (Translation by H. A. R. Gibb)

11 *The Book of the Eparch* (Translation by E. H. Freshfield)

12 Konstantinos of Rhodes, *On Constantinople*, 319–349 quoted in Kaldellis 2017, p. 5

13 Kaldellis 2017, p. 10, after Konstantinos VII, *Book of Ceremonies* 2.15 (Translation by Ann Moffatt)

14 Anna Comnena, *The Alexiad* (Translation by E. A. Dawes, p. 13)

15 Michael Attaleiates, *History*, p. 198

16 Shepard 2005: 298

17 Anna Comnena, *The Alexiad* (Translation by E. A. Dawes, pp. 262–263)

18 Andrea 2000, p. 41

19 *Ibid.*, p. 190

20 Geoffrey of Villehardouin pp. 58–59, quoted in Philips 2005, p. 144

21 Andrea 2000, p. 200

22 Niketas Choniates, *Historia*, 649, (Translation by Harry J. Magoulias, p. 358)

23 Benedictow 2021, p. 143

24 Przemyslav 2022, p. 101

25 Crowley 2009, pp. 90–91

26 Barbaro (Translation by John Melville-Jones)

27 *Ibid.*

28 *Ibid.*

29 Teule 1999, p. 51

30 Niketas Choniates, *Historia*, 592 (Translation by Harry J. Magoulias, p. 326)

31 Gibbon, vol. 7, pp. 129–30

32 Browning 1992, p. xi

33 Pamuk 2005 (Translation by Maureen Freely, p. 218)

10. Vijayanagara

1 *Maitri Upanishad*. (Translation by Robert Ernest Hume, p. 424)

2 Ziauddin Barani, *Tarikh-i-Firoz Shahi*, p. 235

3 Ibn Battuta (Translation by H. A. R. Gibb, p. 196)

4 Firishta (Translation by John Briggs, vol. 1, p. 412)

5 Sewell 1900, p. 19

6 *Ibid.*, p. 88

7 Rao, *Mysore Gazetteer*, vol. 2, p. 1467, quoted in Pillai 2018, pp. 75–76

8 Sewell 1900, p. 88

9 *Narrative of Paes*, in Sewell 1900, p. 256

10 Barbosa 1918, p. 202

11 *Ibid.*, p. 203

12 Samarqandi, *Matla'u-s Sa'dain*, in Sir Henry Miers Elliot (ed.) 1872, p. 113

13 Firishta, quoted in Sherwani 1985, pp. 236–237

14 Samarqandi, *op. cit.*, p. 109

15 *Ibid.*, p. 111

16 *Ibid.*, p. 116

17 *Ibid.*

18 Subrahmanyam 2012, p. 13

19 *Narrative of Paes*, in Sewell 1900, pp. 246–247

20 *Ibid.*, pp. 249–250

21 Mandya Taluq 55, 1534 (Translation in Rice 1894, *Epigraphia Carnatica*, p. 44)

22 Sarasvati 1925, pp. 70–72

23 *Chronicle of Fernão Nunis*, in Sewell 1900, p. 338

24 *Ibid.*, p. 345

25 *Ibid.*, p. 349

26 *Ibid.*, p. 353

27 *Ibid.*, p. 354

28 *Ibid.*, p. 367

29 Kanakadasara Kirtanegalu (Translation by William J. Jackson in *Vijayanagara Voices*, p. 198)

30 Firishta, quoted in Subrahmanyam 2012, p. 80

31 *Fath-Nama-i Nizam Shah* by Hasan Shauqi, quoted in Subrahmanyam 2012, p. 85

32 Firishta (Translation by John Briggs, vol 3., p. 129)

33 *Ibid.*

34 *Ibid.*, p. 130

35 *Basatin al-Salatin* of Mirza Ibrahim al-Zubairi (Translation in Basu 2000, p. 254)

36 *Fath-Nama-i Nizam Shah* by Hasan Shauqi (Translation in Subrahmanyam 2012, p. 89)

37 Lycett 2013, p. 434

38 Firishta, *op. cit.*, vol 3., p. 131

39 Cesare Federici, quoted in Hakluyt, Richard 1589, p. 383

40 Colin Mackenzie, 1800 (British Library MSS Eur Mack Gen 10–11)

41 *Ibid.*

PART III
11. Songhai

1 Timbuktī, *Tarikh al-Fattash* (Translation by Christopher Wise, p. 74)
2 Ibn Battuta, *Travels* (Translation by H. A. R. Gibb, p. 319)
3 Wright 2007, p. 19
4 Al-Maghili, quoted in Gomez 2019, p. 201
5 *The Catalan Atlas*, quoted in Fauvelle 2021, p. 192
6 Levtzion & Hopkins 2000, pp. 268–269
7 *Ibid.*
8 Timbuktī, *Tarikh al-Fattash*, pp. 63–64
9 *Ibid.*, p. 85
10 Ibn Battuta, *op. cit.*, p. 320
11 *Ibid.*, p. 334
12 Timbuktī, *Tarikh al-Fattash*, p. 87
13 *Tarikh al-Sudan*, quoted in De Villiers 2012, p. 102
14 Timbuktī, *Tarikh al-Fattash*, pp. 87–88
15 Sa'dī, *Tarikh al-Sudan* (Translation by John Hunwick, p. 94)
16 Timbuktī, *Tarikh al-Fattash*, p. 99
17 *Tarikh al-Sudan*, quoted in *The Cambridge History of Africa*, vol. 5, p. 421
18 Sa'dī, *Tarikh al-Sudan*, pp. 96–97
19 Timbuktī, *Tarikh al-Fattash*, p. 105
20 Sa'dī, *Tarikh al-Sudan*, p. 103
21 Timbuktī, *Tarikh al-Fattash*, p. 155
22 Elikia M'bokolo in *Le Monde diplomatique*, 2 April 1998
23 Timbuktī, *Tarikh al-Fattash*, pp. 186–187
24 *Ibid.*, p. 255
25 *Ibid.*
26 Sa'dī, *Tarikh al-Sudan*, pp. 271–272
27 *Tarikh al-Sudan*, quoted in Davidson 2014, p. 153
28 Timbuktī, *Tarikh al-Fattash*, p. 262
29 Barth 1858, vol. 5, p. 215
30 *Ibid.*, p. 216

12. The Aztecs

1 Potter *et al.* 2018
2 Caso 1958, p. 92

3 Nicholson 1959, p. 51

4 *Ibid.*, p. 24

5 Pedro Mártir de Anglería, quoted in Parson 2001, p. 161

6 Francisco Hernández de Toledo (Translation in Staller and Carrasco 2009, p. 125)

7 Nicholson 1959, p. 51

8 *Ibid.*, p. 186

9 Sahagún, *The Florentine Codex*, Book 6, Chapter 42 (In Kingsborough 1831, p. 178, my translation)

10 Ixtlilxóchitl, *History of the Chichimeca Nation*, p. 81

11 Diego Durán, *The History of the Indies of New Spain* (Translation by Doris Heyden, pp. 54–55)

12 Ixtlilxóchitl, *History of the Chichimeca Nation*, p. 87

13 *Ibid.*, p. 119

14 León Portilla, quoted in Nicholson 1959, p. 25

15 Chimalpahin Quauhtlehuanitzin, *Codex Chimalpahin*, 1:49, quoted Schroeder 2016

16 Diego Durán, *op. cit.*, p. 147

17 Clendinnen 2014, p. 11

18 Nicholson 1959, p. 47

19 Sahagún, *The Florentine Codex*, Book 8, Chapter 6 (Translation by Arthur Anderson and Charles Dibble, p. 17)

20 López de Gómara, p. 8 (Translation by Lesley Byrd Simpson)

21 *Ibid.*

22 *Ibid.*, p. 19

23 *Ibid.*, p. 21

24 Sahagún, *The Florentine Codex*, Book 12, Chapter 2 (Translation by Arthur Anderson and Charles Dibble, p. 5)

25 *Ibid.*, p. 6

26 *Ibid.*, pp. 6–7

27 Nicholson 1959, p. 141

28 Thomas 1994, p. 163

29 Bernal Díaz del Castillo, p. 98

30 *Ibid.*

31 López de Gómara, p. 56 (Translation by Lesley Byrd Simpson)

32 *Ibid.*, p. 90

33 Sahagún, *The Florentine Codex*, Book 12, Chapter 5 (Translation by Arthur Anderson and Charles Dibble, p. 16)

34 Diego Durán, quoted in Townsend 2003, p. 667
35 Sahagún, *The Florentine Codex*, Book 12, Chapter 7, p. 19
36 *Ibid.*, Book 12, Chapter 6, p. 17
37 Townsend 2003, p. 680
38 Cortés, *Letters from Mexico*, p. 55
39 Bernal Díaz del Castillo, p. 177
40 *Ibid.*, p. 184
41 *Ibid.*, p. 188
42 *Ibid.*, p. 196
43 Cortés, *Letters from Mexico*, p. 60
44 Bernal Díaz del Castillo, p. 211
45 Cortés, *Letters from Mexico*, pp. 69–70
46 Bernal Díaz del Castillo, p. 229
47 Sahagún, *The Florentine Codex*, Book 12, Chapter 11, p. 29
48 *Ibid.*, p. 30
49 Thomas 1994, p. 277
50 Sahagún, *The Florentine Codex*, Book 12, Chapter 11, p. 30
51 *Ibid.*, Book 12, Chapter 16, p. 44
52 Thomas 1994, p. 280
53 Sahagún, *The Florentine Codex*, Book 12, Chapter 17, p. 47
54 Bernal Díaz del Castillo, p. 302
55 López de Gómara, p. 170
56 *Ibid.*
57 Bernal Díaz del Castillo, p. 319
58 *Ibid.*, p. 351
59 *Ibid.*, pp. 323–324
60 Cortés, *Letters from Mexico*, p. 118
61 Sahagún, *The Florentine Codex*, Book 12, Chapter 20, p. 55
62 *Ibid.*
63 *Ibid.*, p. 56
64 Codex Ramírez 147, quoted in Thomas 1993, p. 401
65 Sahagún, *The Florentine Codex*, Book 12, Chapter 23, pp. 65–66
66 Bernal Díaz del Castillo, p. 421
67 *Ibid.*, p. 422
68 Cortés, *Letters from Mexico*, p. 145
69 Sahagún, *The Florentine Codex*, Book 12, Chapter 29, p. 83

70 Bernal Díaz del Castillo, p. 399
71 Cortés, *Letters from Mexico*, p. 241
72 Bernal Díaz del Castillo, p. 575
73 León-Portilla 1992, p. 137
74 Carrasco 2008, p. 313
75 Motolinía 1973, pp. 41–42
76 López de Gómara, p. 4
77 Neale-Silva 1938, p. 69
78 Nicholson 1959, pp. 184–185

13. The Inca

1 Betanzos, p. 13
2 *Ibid.*, p. 7
3 *Huarochirí Manuscript* 1:3–5, pp. 43–44
4 Cieza de León 1883, pp. 47–48 (Translation by Sir Clements Robert Markham)
5 *Ibid.*, p. 64
6 *Huarochirí Manuscript* 23:296–297, p. 115
7 Quoted in Stirling 2005, p. 69
8 Hernando Pizarro 1533, p. 122
9 Guamán Poma de Ayala 2010, *The First New Chronicle*, p. 289
10 Vega 1966, p. 339
11 *Ibid.*, p. 341
12 *Ibid.*, p. 342
13 *Ibid.*, p. 343
14 Quoted in Stirling 2005, p. 41
15 Prescott 1847, p. 142
16 Betanzos, p. 201
17 Andagoya 1865, p. xii
18 Arredondo 2019, p. 33
19 Pedro Pizarro, vol. 2, p. 339 (Translation by Philip Ainsworth Means)
20 Prescott 1847, p. 114
21 Cieza de León 1999 (Translation by Alexandra Parma Cook and Noble David Cook, p. 107)
22 *Ibid.*, p. 113
23 *Huarochirí Manuscript* 14:197, p. 90
24 Titu Cusi Yupanqui 2011 (Translation by Ralph Bauer, p. 64)

25 *Ibid.*

26 Vega 1966, p. 340

27 Covey 2020, p. 185

28 Xerez 1872, p. 19

29 Pedro Pizarro, vol. 1, p. 173

30 Cieza de León 1883, pp. 9–10

31 Xerez, p. 37

32 *Ibid.*, p. 44

33 Pedro Pizarro, vol. 1, p. 177

34 *Ibid.*, pp. 179–180

35 Xerez, p. 52

36 *Ibid.*, p. 53

37 *Ibid.*, p. 55

38 Titu Cusi Yupanqui, p. 62

39 Xerez, p. 56

40 *Ibid.*, p. 65

41 *Ibid.*, p. 69

42 *Ibid.*, p. 101

43 *Ibid.*, pp. 101–103

44 Titu Cusi Yupanqui, p. 69

45 Guamán Poma de Ayala, *Letter to a King*, p. 141

46 Restall 2021, p. 1

47 *Huarochirí Manuscript* 1:1–13, pp. 41–42

48 Moses 1914, vol. 1, p. 385

49 MacQuarrie 2007, p. 375

50 Ocampo 1897, p. 226

51 *Ibid.*, pp. 226–227

52 *Ibid.*, p. 230

53 Vega 1966, p. 115

54 Savoy, pp. 119–120

55 *Ibid.*, p. 120.

56 Translation by John Curl, in Curl 2001, pp. 133–135

14. Easter Island

1 Roggeveen 1908, p. 4

2 *Ibid.*, p. 6

3 *Ibid.*, p. 10
4 *Ibid.*, p. 8
5 *Ibid.*, pp. 15–16
6 *Ibid.*, p. 21
7 Routledge 1919, p. 133
8 Stimson 1957, p. 33
9 *Ibid.*, p. 73
10 *Ibid.*, p. 75
11 Ioannidis *et al.* 2020, p. 1
12 Barthel 1978, p. 28
13 *Ibid.*, p. 31
14 *Ibid.*, p. 54
15 Stimson, p. 76
16 *Ibid.*, p. 26
17 Diamond 1995
18 Bahn and Flenley 1992, p. 214, quoted in Middleton 2017, p. 321
19 Stimson 1957, p. 28
20 Routledge 1919, p. 193
21 Heyerdahl 1989, p. 226, quoted in Lipo and Hunt 2011, p. 79
22 *Ibid.*, p. 227
23 Bullis 1992
24 Hunt and Lipo 2011, p. 92
25 Behrens, p. 137
26 Roggeveen, p. 19
27 Barthel, p. 60
28 Behrens, p. 134
29 Quoted in Heyerdahl and Ferdon 1961, p. 57
30 Hunt and Lipo 2011, p. 93
31 Lipo and Hunt 2016, p. 1
32 Behrens, p. 136
33 *Ibid.*, p. 94
34 Routledge 1919, p. 265
35 Quoted in Trachtman 2002
36 Bendrups 2019
37 Roggeveen, p. 15
38 Cook 2017, p. 348

39 *Ibid.*, p. 344
40 Roggeveen, p. 8
41 Behrens, p. 134
42 Fischer 1997, p. 12
43 Capek, p. 12
44 Thomson 1889, p. 456, quoted in Hunt and Lipo 2011
45 Stimson, p. i
46 Routledge 1919, p. 165

Epilogue

1 Shelley, *Peter Bell the Third*, quoted in Goldsmith 1993, p. 214
2 Macaulay, vol. 4, p. 99
3 'A Proclamation', *Punch*, 1865
4 Arrhenius, p. 53
5 Bendell and Read, p. 77
6 Kim 2023, p. 5
7 Wadhams 2016, p. 108
8 Carrington 2023
9 Lindqvist, p. 2
10 Victor and Chang 2023
11 United Nations Office for Disaster Risk Reduction 2022, p. 51
12 Steel *et al.*, p. 2
13 Carrington 2021
14 Vallet 2023
15 IEP, *Ecological Threat Register 2020*, p. 3
16 William Gibson, quoted in Rosenberg 1992
17 Lynch 2017, quoted in Bendell and Read, p. 61
18 Macfarlane 2014, pp. 125–126
19 Weisman, p. 95

SOURCES

PART I
1. The Sumerians

Al-Zahery, Nadia, Maria Pala, Vincenza Battaglia, *et al.* 'In search of the genetic footprints of Sumerians: a survey of Y-chromosome and mtDNA variation in the Marsh Arabs of Iraq.' BMC Evol Biol 11, 288 (2011).

Barjamovic, Gojko, *et al.* 'Food in Ancient Mesopotamia. Cooking the Yale Babylonian Culinary Recipes.' *Ancient Mesopotamia Speaks: Highlights from the Yale Babylonian Collection*, edited by A. Lassen, E. Frahm and K. Wagensonner. United States, Yale Peabody Museum of Natural History, 2019, pp. 108–125.

Benjamin, Walter. 'These on the Concept of History.' In *Illuminations*. 1955. Ed. Hannah Arendt. New York, Harcourt, Brace & World, 1968.

Black, Jeremy, *et al.*, editors. *The Literature of Ancient Sumer.* Oxford University Press, 2004.

Bottéro, Jean. *Everyday Life in Ancient Mesopotamia.* Trans. Antonia Nevill. United States, John Hopkins UP, 2001.

Burstein, Stanley Mayer. *The Babyloniaca of Berossus.* United States, Undena Publications, 1978.

Cooper, Jerrold S. *Sumerian and Akkadian in Sumer and Akkad.* Orientalia Nova Series, vol. 42, 1973, pp. 239–246.

Crawford, Harriet. *Sumer and the Sumerians.* 1991. 2nd ed. Cambridge University Press, 2004.

———— editor. *The Sumerian World.* London, Taylor & Francis, 2013.

———— *Ur: City of the Moon God*. United Kingdom, Bloomsbury, 2015.

Cullen, H. M., *et al*. 'Climate change and the collapse of the Akkadian empire: Evidence from the deep sea.' *Geology*, April 2000, vol. 28, no. 4, pp. 379–382.

Della Valle, Pietro. *The travels of Sig. Pietro della Valle, a noble Roman, into East-India and Arabia Deserta*. Trans. George Havers. London, J. Macock and Henry Herringman, 1665. Early English Books Online Text Creation Partnership, University of Michigan Library: https://quod.lib.umich.edu/e/eebo/A65012.

Enmerkar and the lord of Aratta (ETCSL t.1.8.2.3). *The Electronic Text Corpus of Sumerian Literature* (etcsl.orinst.ox.ac.uk/cgi-bin/etcsl.cgi?text=t.1.8.2.3). Oxford, 1998.

ETCSL (The Electronic Text Corpus of Sumerian Literature). Edited by J. A. Black, G. Cunningham, E. Fluckiger-Hawker, E. Robson and G. Zólyomi. (etcsl.orinst.ox.ac.uk). Oxford, 1998.

Fagan, Brian M. *The Long Summer: How Climate Changed Civilization*. United Kingdom, Granta Books, 2005.

Graeber, David, and David Wengrow. *The Dawn of Everything: A New History of Humanity*. United Kingdom, Penguin Books Limited, 2021.

Inana and Enki (ETCSL t.1.3.1). *The Electronic Text Corpus of Sumerian Literature* (etcsl.orinst.ox.ac.uk/cgi-bin/etcsl.cgi?text=t.1.3.1). Oxford, 1998.

Jack Starr, Jerald. *Translations of the Stele of the Vultures and the Eannatum Boulder*. Sumerian Shakespeare. http://sumerianshakespeare.com/38801.html.

Jacobsen T. and R. M. Adams. 'Salt and Silt in Ancient Mesopotamian Agriculture: Progressive changes in soil salinity and sedimentation contributed to the breakup of past civilisations.' *Science* 128(3334), Nov. 21 1958, pp. 1251–1258.

King, Leonard W. *A History of Sumer and Akkad*. Outlook Verlag, 2020.

Kramer, Samuel Noah. *The Sumerians: Their History, Culture, and Character*. 1963. United States, University of Chicago Press, 1971.

———— *History Begins at Sumer: Thirty-Nine Firsts in Recorded History*. 1956. 2nd ed. United States, University of Pennsylvania Press, 1981.

Lambeck, Kurt. 'Shoreline reconstructions for the Persian Gulf since the last glacial maximum.' *Earth and Planetary Science Letters*, vol. 142, iss. 1–2, 1996, pp. 43–57.

Lees, G. M. and N. L. Falcon. 'The Geographical History of the Mesopotamian Plains.' *The Geographical Journal*, vol. 118, no. 1, 1952, pp. 24–39.

Leick, Gwendolyn. *Mesopotamia: The Invention of the City*. Allen Lane, 2001.

Liverani, Mario. *The Ancient Near East: History, Society and Economy*. United Kingdom, Routledge, 2013.

Loftus, William Kennett. *Travels and Researches in Chaldæa and Susiana: With an Account of Excavations at Warka, the 'Erech' of Nimrod, and Shúsh, 'Shushan the Palace' of Esther, in 1849–52*. United Kingdom, James Nisbet and Company, 1857.

Maeda, Tohru. 'Royal Inscriptions of Lugalzagesi and Sargon.' *Orient* 40:3–30, 2005.

Marsden, B. G. 'Orbit Determination and Evolution of Comet C/1995 O1 (Hale-Bopp).' *Earth, Moon, and Planets* 79 (1), 1997, pp. 3–15.

Maspero, Gaston. *History of Egypt, Chaldea, Syria, Babylonia, and Assyria*, vol. 3. 1880.

McIntosh, Jane. *Mesopotamia and the Rise of Civilization: History, Documents, and Key Questions*. United States, ABC-CLIO, 2017.

Millard, Alan. 'The Weidner Chronicle (1.138)' in *Context of Scripture*, vol. 1. Ed. W. W. Hallo & K. L. Younger. Leiden, Brill, 1997.

Mithen, Steven. *Thirst: For Water and Power in the Ancient World*. Harvard University Press, 2012.

Oppenheim, A. Leo. *Letters from Mesopotamia: Official, Business, and Private Letters on Clay Tablets from Two Millennia*. United States, University of Chicago Press, 1967.

Ravinell, Alberto and Whitney Green. *The Storm-God in the Ancient Near East*. Eisenbrauns, 2003.

Rice, Michael. *The Archaeology of the Arabian Gulf*. 1994. United Kingdom, Taylor & Francis, 2002.

Rogers, Robert William. *Cuneiform Parallels to the Old Testament*. Oxford University Press, 1912.

Roux, Georges. *Ancient Iraq*. 1964. 3rd ed. United Kingdom, Penguin Books, 1992.

Silver, Minna. 'Climate Change, the Mardu Wall, and the Fall of Ur in Fortune and Misfortune in the Ancient Near East.' In: *Fortune and Misfortune in the Ancient Near East: Proceedings of the 60th Rencontre Assyriologique Internationale Warsaw*, July 2014, pp. 21–25.

Sołtysiak, Arkadiusz. 'Physical anthropology and the "Sumerian problem".' *Studies in Historical Anthropology*, vol. 4:2004[2006], pp. 145–158.

Taylor, J. E. 'Notes on the Ruins of Muqeyer.' *Journal of the Royal Asiatic Society of Great Britain and Ireland*, vol. 15, 1855, pp. 260–276.

The Ancient Near East: An Anthology of Texts and Pictures. United Kingdom, Princeton University Press, 2011.

The Context of Scripture: Canonical Compositions from the Biblical World. Eds. K. Lawson Younger, William W. Hallo. Netherlands, Brill, 1997.

The Cursing of Agade (ETCSL t.2.1.5). *The Electronic Text Corpus of Sumerian Literature* (etcsl.orinst.ox.ac.uk/cgi-bin/etcsl.cgi?text=t.2.1.5). Oxford, 1998.

The Death of Ur-Namma (ETCSL t.2.4.1.1). *The Electronic Text Corpus of Sumerian Literature* (etcsl.orinst.ox.ac.uk/cgi-bin/etcsl.cgi?text=t.2.4.1.1). Oxford, 1998.

The Epic of Gilgamesh. Trans. William Muss-Arnolt. New York, D. Appleton and Co., 1901.

The Lament for Sumer and Urim (ETCSL t.2.2.3). *The Electronic Text Corpus of Sumerian Literature* (etcsl.orinst.ox.ac.uk/cgi-bin/etcsl.cgi?text=t.2.2.3). Oxford, 1998.

The Lament for Urim (ETCSL t.2.2.2). *The Electronic Text Corpus of Sumerian Literature* (etcsl.orinst.ox.ac.uk/cgi-bin/etcsl.cgi?text=t.2.2.2). Oxford, 1998.

The Literature of Ancient Sumer. Ed. Jeremy Black. Italy, Oxford University Press, 2004.

The Marriage of Martu (ECTSL t.1.7.1). *The Electronic Text Corpus of Sumerian Literature* (etcsl.orinst.ox.ac.uk/cgi-bin/etcsl.cgi?text=t.1.7.1). Oxford, 1998.

The Sumerian King List (ETCSL t.2.1.1). *The Electronic Text Corpus of Sumerian Literature* (etcsl.orinst.ox.ac.uk/cgi-bin/etcsl.cgi?text=t.2.1.1). Oxford, 1998.

Toynbee, Arnold J. *A Study of History*. London, Bobbs-Merrill Company Incorporated, 1934.

——————— *A Study of History: Abridgement of Volumes I-VI*. Kiribati, Oxford University Press, 1947.

Wolkstein, Diane and Samuel Noah Kramer. *Inanna: Queen of Heaven and Earth: Her Stories and Hymns from Sumer*. United Kingdom, HarperCollins, 1983.

Ziskind, Jonathan R. 'The Sumerian Problem.' *The History Teacher*, vol. 5, no. 2, 1972, pp. 34–41.

2. The Late Bronze Age Collapse

Astour, Michael C. 'New Evidence on the Last Days of Ugarit.' *American Journal of Archaeology*, vol. 69, no. 3, 1965, pp. 253–258.

Baker, Andy, *et al.* 'The Hekla 3 volcanic eruption recorded in a Scottish speleothem?' *The Holocene* 5 (3), 1995, pp. 336–342.

Bell, Carol. 'The merchants of Ugarit: oligarchs of the Late Bronze Age trade in metals?' *Eastern Mediterranean Metallurgy and Metalwork*, 180, 2012.

Berger, Daniel, *et al.* 'Isotope systematics and chemical composition of tin ingots from Mochlos (Crete) and other Late Bronze Age sites in the eastern Mediterranean Sea: An ultimate key to tin provenance?' *PLoS One*. 2019 Jun 26; 14(6):e0218326.

Bietak, Manfred. 'Minoan Presence in the Pharaonic Naval Base of "Peru-Nefer".' *British School at Athens Studies*, vol. 18, 2010, pp. 11–24.

Breasted, James. H. *Ancient Records of Egypt: Historical Documents from the Earliest Times to the Persian Conquest*, vol 4, 1906.

Bryce, Trevor. *The Kingdom of the Hittites*. United Kingdom, Oxford University Press, 2005.

———— *The Trojans and their Neighbours*. London; New York, Taylor & Francis, 2006.

———— *Warriors of Anatolia: A Concise History of the Hittites*. United Kingdom, Bloomsbury Publishing, 2018.

Cline, Eric H. *1177 B.C.: The Year Civilization Collapsed: Revised and Updated Edition*. United Kingdom, Princeton University Press, 2021.

Cohen, Yoram. 'The "Hunger Years" and the "Sea Peoples": Preliminary Observations on the Recently Published Letters from the "House of Urtenu".' *Archive at Ugarit*. 2021, SBL: Atlanta.

Collins, Billie Jean. *The Hittites and Their World*. United States, SBL Press, 2007.

Cornelius, Izak. 'The Battle of the Nile—Circa 1190 B.C.' *Military History Journal*, vol. 7., no. 4, 1987, pp. 141–145.

Drake, Brandon L. 'The influence of climatic change on the Late Bronze Age Collapse and the Greek Dark Ages.' *Journal of Archaeological Science* 39 (6), 2012, pp. 1866–1870.

Drews, Robert. *The End of the Bronze Age: Changes in Warfare and the Ca-*

tastrophe Ca. 1200 B.C. 3rd ed. United Kingdom, Princeton University Press, 1993.

————— 'Medinet Habu: Oxcarts, Ships, and Migration Theories.' *Journal of Near Eastern Studies*, vol. 59, no. 3 (July 2000), pp. 161–190.

Edgerton, William F. 'The Strikes in Ramses III's Twenty-Ninth Year.' *Journal of Near Eastern Studies*, vol. 10, no. 3, 1951, pp. 137–145.

Finkelstein, Israel, *et al*. 'Climate and the Late Bronze Collapse: New Evidence from the Southern Levant.' *Tel Aviv* 40 (2013), pp. 149–175.

Gaster, Theodor Herzl. *Thespis: Ritual, Myth, and Drama in the Ancient Near East*. Garden City, NY, Doubleday, 1961.

Grattan J. and D. Gilbertson (2000). 'Prehistoric "settlement crisis", environmental changes in the British Isles, and volcanic eruptions in Iceland: An exploration of plausible linkages.' *Volcanic Hazards and Disasters in Human Antiquity*, edited by Floyd W. McCoy and Grant Heiken. GSA Special Paper. vol. 345. Boulder, CO, Geological Society of America.

Homerus. *The Iliad, Rendered into English Blank Verse*. Trans. Edward Earl of Derby. 2 vols. London, John Murray, 1867.

Jablonka, Peter. 'Troy in regional and international context.' *The Oxford Handbook of Ancient Anatolia*, edited by Sharon Steadman and Gregory McMahon. Oxford University Press, 2011.

Jung, Reinhard and Mathias Mehofer. 'A sword of Naue II type from Ugarit and the Historical Significance of Italian type Weaponry in the Eastern Mediterranean.' *Aegean Archaeology*, 8, 2008, pp. 111–136.

Karageorghis, Vassos and James David Muhly, editors. *Cyprus at the Close of the Late Bronze Age*. Cyprus, A. G. Leventis Foundation, 1984.

Kilani, Marwan. *Byblos in the Late Bronze Age*. Leiden, Brill, 2019.

Lewartowski, Kazimierz. *The Decline of the Mycenaean Civilization: An Archaeological Study of Events in the Greek Mainland*. Poland, Zaklad Narodowy, 1989.

Manning, Stuart W., Cindy Kocik, Brita Lorentzen, *et al*. 'Severe multiyear drought coincident with Hittite collapse around 1198–1196 BC.' *Nature*, 614, 2023, pp. 719–724.

Middleton, Guy D., editor. *Collapse and Transformation: The Late Bronze Age to Early Iron Age in the Aegean*. United Kingdom, Oxbow Books, 2020.

Nougayrol, Jean, Emmanuel Laroche and Charles Virolleaud. *Ugaritica. V: nouveaux textes accadiens, hourrites et ugaritiques des archives et bibliothèques privées d'Ugarit*. New York, Stony Brook University, 1968.

Paulette, Tate. 'Domination and Resilience in Bronze Age Mesopotamia.' *Surviving Sudden Environmental Change: Answers from Archaeology*, edited by Jago Cooper and Payson Sheets. United States, University Press of Colorado, 2012, pp. 167–96.

Pausanias. *Pausanias' Description of Greece with an English Translation by W. H. S. Jones, Litt.D., and H. A. Ormerod, M.A.*, in four volumes. Cambridge, MA, Harvard University Press; London, William Heinemann Ltd., 1918.

Potts, Daniel T. *The archaeology of Elam: formation and transformation of an ancient Iranian State.* Cambridge University Press, 1999.

Pritchard, James B. (ed.). *Ancient Near Eastern Texts Relating to the Old Testament with Supplement.* United States, Princeton University Press, 1978.

Pulak, Cemal. 'The Uluburun Shipwreck: An Overview.' *The International Journal of Nautical Archaeology*, vol. 27, iss. 3, 1998, pp. 188–224.

Quinn, Josephine. 'Your Own Ships Did This!: Review of 1177 BC: The Year Civilisation Collapsed, by Eric Cline.' *London Review of Books*, vol. 38, no. 4, 18 February 2016.

Ramesses III. 'Medinet Habu inscription of Ramesses III's eighth year (1178 BCE).' Trans. John A. Wilson in Pritchard, J. B. (ed.) In: *Ancient Near Eastern Texts relating to the Old Testament*, 3rd ed., United States, Princeton University Press, 1969.

Snodgrass, Anthony. 'Cyprus and the Beginnings of Iron Technology in the Eastern Mediterranean.' *Early Metallurgy in Cyprus, 4000–500 B.C.*, edited by J. D. Muhly, R. Maddin and V. Karageorghis. Nicosia, Pierides Foundation, 1982, pp. 289–295.

Tainter, Joseph. *The Collapse of Complex Societies.* United Kingdom, Cambridge University Press, 1988.

Taylour, William. *The Mycenaeans.* United Kingdom, Thames and Hudson, 1983.

Thorarinsson, Sigurdur. *Hekla, A Notorious Volcano.* Trans. Jóhann Hannesson, Pétur Karlsson. Reykjavík, Almenna Bókafélagið, 1970.

Voskos, Ioannis, and A. Bernard Knapp. 'Cyprus at the End of the Late Bronze Age: Crisis and Colonization or Continuity and Hybridization?' *American Journal of Archaeology*, vol. 112, no. 4, 2008, pp. 659–684.

Weiss, Harvey, editor. *Megadrought and Collapse: From Early Agriculture to Angkor.* United States, Oxford University Press, 2017.

Wilkinson, Toby. *The Rise and Fall of Ancient Egypt*. United Kingdom, Bloomsbury Publishing, 2010.

Wilson, John Albert and William Franklin Edgerton, editors. *Historical Records of Ramesses III.: The Texts in Medinet Habu Volumes I and II.* United States, University of Chicago Press, 1936.

Wood, Michael. *In Search of The Trojan War.* United Kingdom, Ebury Publishing, 2015.

Wyatt, Nick. *Religious texts from Ugarit*. United Kingdom, Bloomsbury Academic, 2002.

Yon, Marguerite. *The City of Ugarit at Tell Ras Shamra.* United States, Pennsylvania State University Press, 2006.

Yurco, Frank J. 'End of the Late Bronze Age and Other Crisis Periods: A Volcanic Cause.' *Gold of Praise: Studies on Ancient Egypt in Honor of Edward F. Wente*, edited by Emily Teeter and John Larson. *Studies in Ancient Oriental Civilization*, vol. 58. United States, Oriental Institute of the Univ. of Chicago, 1999, pp. 456–458.

3. Assyria

Black, J. A., G. Cunningham, E. Fluckiger-Hawker, E. Robson, and G. Zólyomi, *The Electronic Text Corpus of Sumerian Literature* (etcsl.orinst.ox.ac.uk). Oxford, 1998.

Cole, Steven W. and Peter Machinist. *Letters From Priests to the Kings Esarhaddon and Assurbanipal.* 1998.

Cotterell, Arthur. *The First Great Powers: Babylon and Assyria.* United Kingdom, Hurst & Co., 2019.

Davis, Andrew R. *Reconstructing the Temple: The Royal Rhetoric of Temple Renovation in the Ancient Near East and Israel.* United States, Oxford University Press, 2019.

de Odorico, Marco. 'Compositional and Editorial Processes of Annalistic and Summary Texts of Tiglath-pileser I.' *State Archives of Assyria Bulletin*, 8, 1994, pp. 67–112.

Esarhaddon and Erle Leichty. *The Royal Inscriptions of Esarhaddon, King of Assyria (680–669 BC).* United States, Penn State University Press, 2011.

Evans, Paul S. 'The Invasion of Sennacherib in the Book of Kings: A Source-Critical and Rhetorical Study of 2 Kings 18–19.' *The Journal of Theological Studies*, vol. 62, iss. 2, October 2011, pp. 666–669.

Feldman, Marian H. 'Assur Tomb 45 and the Birth of the Assyrian Empire.' *Bulletin of the American Schools of Oriental Research*, no. 343, 2006, pp. 21–43.

Foster, Benjamin Read. *Before the Muses: An Anthology of Akkadian Literature*. United States, Pennsylvania State University Press, 2005.

Frahm, Eckart (ed.). *A Companion to Assyria*. United Kingdom, John Wiley & Sons, Incorporated, 2017.

————— *Assyria: The Rise and Fall of the World's First Empire*. United States, Basic Books, 2023.

Grayson, Albert Kirk, *et al*. *Assyrian Rulers of the Early First Millennium bc, I (1114–859 bc)*. Toronto, University of Toronto Press, 1991.

————— *Assyrian rulers of the third and second millennia* BCE *(to 1115* BC*)*. Buffalo, University of Toronto Press, 1987.

de Jong, Matthijs. *Isaiah among the Ancient Near Eastern Prophets: A Comparative Study of the Earliest Stages of the Isaiah Tradition and the Neo-Assyrian Prophecies*. Netherlands, Brill, 2007.

Layard, Austen Henry. *A Popular Account of Discoveries at Nineveh*. United Kingdom, John Murray, 1852.

Luckenbill, Daniel David. *Ancient Records of Assyria and Babylonia*. 2 vols. United States, Greenwood Press, 1926.

Luukko, Mikko, and Greta van Buylaere. *The Political Correspondence of Esarhaddon*. Finland, Helsinki University Press, 2002.

Maspero, Sir Gaston Camille Charles. *Life in ancient Egypt and Assyria*. London, Chapman and Hall, 1892.

————— *The Struggle of the Nations: Egypt, Syria and Assyria*. United Kingdom, Appleton, 1897.

Michel, Cécile. *Economy, Society, and Daily Life in the Old Assyrian Period*. 2017.

Oded, Bustanay. 'The Phoenician Cities and the Assyrian Empire in the Time of Tiglath-Pileser III.' *Zeitschrift Des Deutschen Palästina-Vereins* (1953–), vol. 90, no. 1, 1974, pp. 38–49.

Oppenheim, A. Leo. *Ancient Mesopotamia: Portrait of a Dead Civilisation*. 1964. United States, University of Chicago Press, revised 1977.

————— *Letters from Mesopotamia*. Chicago, University of Chicago Press, 1967.

Parpola, Simo. 'Letters from Assyrian and Babylonian Scholars.' *State Archives of Assyria*, 10, 1993.

Radner, Karen. *Ancient Assyria: A Very Short Introduction*. United Kingdom, Oxford University Press, 2015.

———— 'Economy, Society, and Daily Life in the Neo-Assyrian Period.' In: Eckart Frahm (ed.). *A Companion to Assyria*. Wiley, 2017.

———— 'The Trials of Esarhaddon: The Conspiracy of 670 BC.' *ISIMU: Revista sobre Oriente Próximo y Egipto en la antigüedad*, 6, 2003, pp. 165–183.

Ragozin, Zénaïde. *The Rise and Fall of the Assyrian Empire*. Germany, Ozymandias Press, 2018.

Reade, J. 'Xenophon's Route Through Babylonia and Assyria.' *Iraq*, 77, 2015, pp. 173–202.

Roux, Georges. *Ancient Iraq*. United Kingdom, Penguin Books, 1992.

Simo Parpola. *Letters from Assyrian and Babylonian Scholars (State Archives of Assyria, 10)*, 1993.

Sinha, Ashish, *et al*. 'Role of climate in the rise and fall of the Neo-Assyrian Empire.' *Science Advances*, vol. 5,11 eaax6656, 13 November 2019.

Sołtysiak, A. 'Drought and the fall of Assyria: quite another story.' *Climatic Change*, 136, 2016, pp. 389–394.

State Archives of Assyria Online, SAA 16, 059. oracc.museum.upenn.edu/saao/P313533. Accessed 10 November 2022.

Talbot, Henry F. 'Assyrian Sacred Poetry.' In: *Records of the past: Being English translations of the Assyrian and Egyptian Monuments*. Society of Biblical Archæology (London, England), vol 3, 1873.

The Bible: Authorised King James Version. 1611. Ed. Robert Carroll and Stephen Prickett, Oxford University Press, 2008.

Wise Bauer, Susan. *The History of the Ancient World: From the Earliest Accounts to the Fall of Rome*. United States, W. W. Norton, 2007.

Xenophon. *Anabasis*. In: *The Persian Expedition*. Trans. Rex Warner. New York, Penguin Books, 1949.

Yamada, Shigeo. *The Construction of the Assyrian Empire: A Historical Study of the Inscriptions of Shalmanesar III Relating to His Campaigns in the West*. Germany, Brill, 2000.

4. Carthage

Ammianus Marcellinus. *Ammianus Marcellinus, with an English Translation*. Trans. John C. Rolfe. 3 vols. United States, Harvard University Press; London, William Heinemann, Ltd., 1935–1940.

Appian. *The Foreign Wars.* Trans. Horace White. New York, The Macmillan Company, 1899.

Aristotle. *Politics.* In: *Aristotle in 23 Volumes*, vol. 21. Trans. H. Rackham. London, William Heinemann Ltd., 1944.

Avienus. *Ora Maritima.* Trans. Ralph B. Morley. Aikaterini Laskaridi Foundation, 1992. *ToposText.* topostext.org/work/751. Accessed 7 August 2023.

Barceló, Pedro. 'The Perception of Carthage in Classical Greek Historiography.' *Acta Classica*, vol. 37, 1994, pp. 1–14.

Cassius Dio. *Dio's Roman History. Cassius Dio Cocceianus.* Trans. Earnest Cary. Herbert Baldwin Foster. William Heinemann, Harvard University Press. London; New York, 1914.

Charles, Michael B. 'Carthage and the Indian Elephant.' *L'Antiquité Classique*, vol. 83, 2014, pp. 115–127.

Charles-Picard, Gilbert and Collette. *Daily Life in Carthage at the Time of Hannibal.* Hassell Street Press, 1961.

Craig, Matthew. 'Ancient Carthage in Today's Sunshine.' *Current History (1916–1940)*, vol. 16, no. 6, 1922, pp. 1040–1045.

Cross, F. M. 'An Interpretation of the Nora Stone,' *Bulletin of the American Schools of Oriental Research*, 208 (December 1972:16).

de Prorok, Count Byron Khun. 'Ancient Trade Routes from Carthage into the Sahara.' *Geographical Review*, vol. 15, no. 2, 1925, pp. 190–205.

DeWitt, Norman J. 'Rome and the "Road of Hercules".' *Transactions and Proceedings of the American Philological Association*, vol. 72, 1941, pp. 59–69.

Feeney, Denis. 'Carthage and Rome: Introduction.' *Classical Philology*, vol. 112, no. 3, 2017, pp. 301–311.

Goldsworthy, Adrian. *The Fall of Carthage: The Punic Wars 265–146bc.* 2000. United Kingdom, Orion Books, 2006.

Hanno the Navigator. *The Periplus of Hanno: A Voyage of Discovery Down the West African Coast.* Trans. Wilfred H. Schoff. Philadelphia Commercial Museum, 1912.

Herodotus. *Herodotus, with an English translation by A. D. Godley.* Cambridge, Harvard University Press, 1920.

Homer. *The Odyssey with an English Translation by A. T. Murray, PH.D. in two volumes.* London, William Heinemann, Ltd., 1919.

Hoyos, Dexter. *Mastering the West: Rome and Carthage at War.* United States, Oxford University Press, 2015.

———— *Hannibal's Dynasty: Power and Politics in the Western Mediterranean, 247–183* BCE. Kiribati, Routledge, 2003.

———— *Truceless War: Carthage's Fight for Survival, 241 to 237* BCE (History of Warfare). Boston, Brill, 2007.

Livy. *Books XXI—XXII with an English Translation.* Trans. F. G. Moore. ('Loeb Classical Library') London, William Heinemann, Ltd., 1929.

Miles, Richard. *Carthage Must Be Destroyed: The Rise and Fall of an Ancient Civilisation.* United Kingdom, Penguin Books, 2011.

Oded, Bustanay. 'The Phoenician Cities and the Assyrian Empire in the Time of Tiglath-Pileser III.' *Zeitschrift Des Deutschen Palästina-Vereins* (1953–), vol. 90, no. 1, 1974, pp. 38–49.

Plutarch. *Moralia.* Trans. Frank Cole Babbitt. ('Loeb Classical Library') London, William Heinemann Ltd., 1928.

———— *Life of Marcus Cato.* From: *Plutarch's Lives* with an English Translation by Bernadotte Perrin. ('Loeb Classical Library') London, William Heinemann Ltd., 1914.

———— *Life of Pyrrhus.* From: *Plutarch's Lives* with an English Translation by Bernadotte Perrin. ('Loeb Classical Library') London, William Heinemann Ltd., 1920.

Polybius. *Histories.* Trans. Evelyn S. Shuckburgh. London, New York, Macmillan, 1889.

Quinn, Josephine. *In Search of the Phoenicians.* United Kingdom, Princeton University Press, 2019.

Ridley, R. T. 'To Be Taken with a Pinch of Salt: The Destruction of Carthage.' *Classical Philology,* vol. 81, no. 2, 1986, pp. 140–146.

Silius Italicus. *Punica.* Trans. James Duff. United States, University of Toronto, 1927.

Steinby, Christa. 'War at Sea in the Second Punic War.' *Ancient Society,* vol. 34, 2004, pp. 77–114.

Temple, Grenville. *Excursions in the Mediterranean: Algiers and Tunis.* 2 vols. London, Saunders and Otley, 1835.

The Bible: Authorised King James Version. 1611. Ed. Robert Carroll and Stephen Prickett. United Kingdom, Oxford University Press, 2008.

Virgil. *Aeneid.* Trans. J. W. Mackail. London, Macmillan & Co. 1885.

Wolters, Edward J. 'Carthage and Its People.' *The Classical Journal*, vol. 47, no. 5, 1952, pp. 191–204.

5. Han China

Ban Gu. *The History of The Former Han Dynasty by Pan Ku*, vol. 2, *First Division, The Imperial Annals Chapters VI–X*. Trans. Homer H. Dubs, P'an Lo-chi and Jen T'ai. Baltimore, Waverly Press, Inc., 1944.

Bielenstein, Hans. *The Restoration of the Han Dynasty*. Stockholm, 1953.

Chin, Tamara. 'Defamiliarizing the Foreigner: Sima Qian's Ethnography and Han-Xiongnu Marriage Diplomacy.' *Harvard Journal of Asiatic Studies*, vol. 70, no. 2 (December 2010).

Chun-shu Chang. *The Rise of the Chinese Empire: Nation, State, and Imperialism in Early China, ca. 1600 b.c.–a.d.* 8. University of Michigan Press, 2007.

Creel, Herrlee G. 'The Role of the Horse in Chinese History.' *The American Historical Review*, vol. 70, no. 3, 1965, pp. 647–672.

de Crespigny, Rafe. *Emperor Huan and Emperor Ling: Being the Chronicle of Later Han for the years 157 to 189* AD *as recorded in Chapters 54 to 59 of the Zizhi tongjian of Sima Guang*. 1989. Trans. Rafe de Crespigny. Internet Edition 2018.

——————— *Fire over Luoyang: A History of the Later Han Dynasty 23–220* AD. Leiden, Brill, 2016.

Di Cosmo, Nicola. 'Han Frontiers: Toward an Integrated View.' *Journal of the American Oriental Society*, vol. 129, no. 2, 2009, pp. 199–214.

Duan Qingbo. 'Scientific Studies of High Level of Mercury in Qin Shihuangdi's Tomb.' 2007. In Jane Porter (ed.). *The First Emperor: China's Terracotta Army*. Harvard University Press. pp. 202–207.

Frankopan, Peter. *The Silk Roads: A New History of the World*. London, Bloomsbury, 2015.

Hardy, Grant R. and Anne Behnke Kinney. *The Establishment of the Han Empire and Imperial China*. United Kingdom, Bloomsbury Academic, 2005.

Hill, John E. 'The Western Regions according to the Hou Hanshu.' The Xiyu juan "Chapter on the Western Regions" from *Hou Hanshu* 88, 2003.

———————and Ye Fan. *Through the jade gate to Rome: a study of the silk routes during the Later Han Dynasty*. 2009.

Jing Liu. *Foundations of Chinese Civilization: The Yellow Emperor to the Han Dynasty (2697 BCE–220 CE)*. United States, Stone Bridge Press, 2016.

Kelley, Charles Fabens. 'Art of the Han Dynasty.' *Bulletin of the Art Institute of Chicago* (1907–1951), vol. 35, no. 7, 1941, pp. 114–116.

Kroll, Paul W. *Reading Medieval Chinese Poetry: Text, Context, and Culture*. Lediden, Brill, 2014.

LaFleur, Robert André. *China*. United Kingdom, Bloomsbury Academic, 2010.

Lewis, Mark Edward. *The Early Chinese Empires: Qin and Han*. United Kingdom, Harvard University Press, 2010.

Loewe, Michael. *Everyday life in early Imperial China during the Han period*. United States, Hackett Publishing Company, 1968.

———— *Faith, myth, and reason in Han China*. United States, Hackett Publishing Company, 2005.

Luo Guanzhong. *Three Kingdoms: A Historical Novel*. Trans. Moss Roberts. United States, University of California Press, 2020.

Richter, Antje. *Letters and Epistolary Culture in Early Medieval China*. United States, University of Washington Press, 2013.

Sima Qian. *Records of the Grand Historian of China: Qin Dynasty*. 1961. Trans. Burton Watson. Columbia University Press, and Research Centre for Translation, Chinese University of Hong Kong, 1993.

———— *Records of the Grand Historian of China: Han Dynasty II*. 1961. Trans. Burton Watson. Columbia University Press, and Research Centre for Translation, Chinese University of Hong Kong, 1993.

Thorne, T. P. M. *'Yellow Sky': Crisis for the Han Dynasty*. United Kingdom, PaMat Publishing, 2015.

Tse, Wicky W. K. *The Collapse of China's Later Han Dynasty, 25–220 CE: The Northwest Borderlands and the Edge of Empire*. United Kingdom, Taylor & Francis, 2018.

Waldron, Arthur. *The Great Wall of China: From History to Myth*. New York, Cambridge University Press, 1900.

Waley, Arthur. *A Hundred and Seventy Chinese Poems*. United Kingdom, Constable & Co., 1923.

Wang Yü-ch'üan. 'An Outline of The Central Government of The Former Han Dynasty.' *Harvard Journal of Asiatic Studies*, vol. 12, no. 1/2, 1949, pp. 134–187.

Wei Qian and Xing Huang. 'Invention of cast iron smelting in early China: Archaeological survey and numerical simulation.' *Advances in Archaeomaterials*, vol. 2, Issue 1, 2021, pp. 4–14.

Yuan-kang Wang. 'Explaining the Tribute System: Power, Confucianism, and War in Medieval East Asia.' *Journal of East Asian Studies*, vol. 13, no. 2, 2013, pp. 207–232.

Yu Ying-Shih. *Trade and Expansion in Han China: A Study in the Structure of Sino-Barbarian Economic Relations*. United States, University of California Press, 1967.

Yutang Sun and Ma Yong. 'The Western Regions under the Hsiung-Nu and the Han.' *History of Civilizations of Central Asia*, edited by Ahmad Hasan Dani, Baij Nath Puri, János Harmatta, vol. 2. France, Unesco, 1992.

6. Roman Britain

Ammianus Marcellinus. *The Roman History of Ammianus Marcellinus*. Trans. Charles D. Yonge. London, George Bell and Sons, Ltd., 1894.

Bédoyère, Guy de la. *Roman Britain: A New History*. United Kingdom, Thames and Hudson Limited, 2010.

———— *Real Lives of Roman Britain*. United Kingdom, Yale University Press, 2015.

———— *Roman Towns in Britain*. United Kingdom, Tempus, 2003.

Birley, Anthony. *Septimius Severus: The African Emperor*. 1971. New ed. United Kingdom, Taylor & Francis, 2002.

———— *The People of Roman Britain*. United Kingdom, University of California Press, 1980.

Bowman, Alan and David Thomas. *The Vindolanda Writing Tablets (Tabulae Vindolandenses II)*. London, British Museum Press, 1994.

Breeze, David J. 'Auxiliaries, Legionaries, and the Operation of Hadrian's Wall.' *Bulletin of the Institute of Classical Studies*. Supplement, no. 81, 2003, pp. 147–151.

Carlson, David R. 'Bede on Roman Britain's End.' *Latomus*, vol. 73, no. 1, 2014, pp. 188–199.

Cassius Dio. *Roman History, Volume IX: Books 71–80*. Trans. Earnest Cary, Herbert B. Foster. ('Loeb Classical Library') Cambridge, MA, Harvard University Press, 1927.

Codex Exoniensis: A collection of Anglo-Saxon poetry, from a manuscript in the li-

brary of the dean and chapter of Exeter. Trans. Benjamin Thorpe. United Kingdom, The Society of Antiquaries of London, 1842.

Collingwood, R. G. 'The Roman Evacuation of Britain.' *The Journal of Roman Studies*, vol. 12, 1922, pp. 74–98.

Cunliffe, Barry. *Iron Age Communities in Britain: An Account of England, Scotland and Wales from the Seventh Century bc Until the Roman Conquest.* United Kingdom, Taylor & Francis, 2004.

Dobson, B., and J. C. Mann. 'The Roman Army in Britain and Britons in the Roman Army.' *Britannia*, vol. 4, 1973, pp. 191–205.

Dumayne-Peaty, Lisa. 'The Effect of the Roman Occupation on the Environment of Hadrian's Wall: A Pollen Diagram from Fozy Moss, Northumbria.' *Britannia*, vol. 25, 1994, pp. 217–224.

Dyson, Stephen L. 'Native Revolts in the Roman Empire.' *Historia: Zeitschrift Für Alte Geschichte*, vol. 20, no. 2/3, 1971, pp. 239–274.

Fleming, Robin. *Britain After Rome: The Fall and Rise, 400–1070.* United Kingdom, Allen Lane, 2010.

———— *The Material Fall of Roman Britain, 300–525* CE. United States, University of Pennsylvania Press, Inc., 2021.

Gambash, Gil. 'To Rule a Ferocious Province: Roman Policy and the Aftermath of the Boudican Revolt.' *Britannia*, vol. 43, 2012, pp. 1–15.

Gardner, Andrew. 'Thinking about Roman Imperialism: Postcolonialism, Globalisation and Beyond?' *Britannia*, vol. 44, 2013, pp. 1–25.

Gildas. *De Excidio et Conquestu Britanniae.* From: *The works of Gildas and Nennius, Translated from the Latin.* Trans. J. A. Giles. United Kingdom, 1841.

Graham, A. J. 'The Division of Britain.' *The Journal of Roman Studies*, vol. 56, 1966, pp. 92–107.

Harper, Kyle. 'The Environmental Fall of the Roman Empire.' *Daedalus*, vol. 145, no. 2, 2016, pp. 101–111.

———— *The Fate of Rome: Climate, Disease, and the End of an Empire.* United Kingdom, Princeton University Press, 2017.

Heather, Peter. 'The Late Roman Imperial Centre and Its Northwest Frontier.' *Social Dynamics in the Northwest Frontiers of the Late Roman Empire: Beyond Transformation or Decline*, edited by Nico Roymans *et al.* Amsterdam University Press, 2017, pp. 11–38.

Herodian. *Herodian of Antioch's History of the Roman Empire.* Trans. Edward C. Echols. University of California Press; Cambridge University Press, 1961.

Historia Augusta, Volume I: Hadrian. Aelius. Antoninus Pius. Marcus Aurelius. L. Verus. Avidius Cassius. Commodus. Pertinax. Didius Julianus. Septimius Severus. Pescennius Niger. Clodius Albinus. Trans. David Magie. ('Loeb Classical Library') Cambridge, MA, Harvard University Press, 1921.

Jackson, Ralph and Richard Hobbs. *Roman Britain: Life at the Edge of Empire.* United Kingdom, British Museum Press, 2010.

Jones, Michael E. *The End of Roman Britain.* Greece, Cornell University Press, 1998.

Julius Caesar. *Caesar's Gallic War.* Trans. W. A. McDevitte and W. S. Bohn. 1st ed. Harper's New Classical Library. New York, Harper & Brothers, 1869.

Laycock, Stuart. *Britannia—The Failed State: Tribal Conflicts and the End of Roman Britain.* United Kingdom, History Press, 2012.

Moore, Alison Jane, Louise Revell and Martin Millett, editors. *The Oxford Handbook of Roman Britain.* United Kingdom, Oxford University Press, 2016.

Morley, Neville. '"They Make a Desert and Call It Peace": The Nature of Roman Rule.' *The Roman Empire: Roots of Imperialism.* United Kingdom, Pluto Press, 2010, pp. 38–69.

Opper, Thorsten. *Hadrian: Empire and Conflict.* United States, Harvard University Press, 2008.

Orosius. *Seven Books of History Against the Pagans: The Apology of Paulus Orosius.* Trans. Irving Woodworth Raymond. New York, Columbia University Press, 1936.

Pearson, Andrew. 'Piracy in Late Roman Britain: A Perspective from the Viking Age.' *Britannia*, vol. 37, 2006, pp. 337–353.

Pliny the Elder. *The Natural History.* Trans. John Bostock and Henry T. Riley. London, Taylor and Francis, 1855.

Plutarch. *Life of Caesar.* From: *Plutarch's Lives.* With an English Trans. Bernadotte Perrin. ('Loeb Classical Library') Cambridge, MA. Harvard University Press; London, William Heinemann Ltd., 1920.

Procopius. *History of the Wars, Volume III: Books 5–6.15. (Gothic War).* Trans. by H. B. Dewing. ('Loeb Classical Library') Cambridge, MA, Harvard University Press, 1916.

Pryor, Francis. *Britain ad: A Quest for Arthur, England and the Anglo-Saxons.* United Kingdom, Harper Perennial, 2005.

———— *Britain bc: Life in Britain and Ireland Before the Romans.* United Kingdom, Harper Perennial, 2004.

Russell, Miles and Stuart Laycock. *UnRoman Britain: Exposing the Great Myth of Britannia.* United Kingdom, History Press, 2011.

Salway, Peter. *The Frontier People of Roman Britain.* Kiribati, Cambridge University Press, 1965.

Sargent, Andrew. 'The North-South Divide Revisited: Thoughts on the Character of Roman Britain.' *Britannia*, vol. 33, 2002, pp. 219–226.

Shanzer, Danuta and Ralph W. Mathisen, editors. *Romans, Barbarians, and the Transformation of the Roman World: Cultural Interaction and the Creation of Identity in Late Antiquity.* United Kingdom, Taylor & Francis, 2016.

Tibbs, Andrew. *Beyond the Empire: A Guide to the Roman Remains in Scotland.* United Kingdom, Robert Hale Non Fiction, 2019.

'The Ruin'. In: *The Exeter Book Part II: Poems IX–XXXII.* vol 2. Trans. Israel Gollancz. Ed. W. S. Mackie. London, Oxford University Press, 1934.

Wood, Ian. 'The Fall of the Western Empire and the End of Roman Britain.' *Britannia*, vol. 18, 1987, pp. 251–262.

Woods, David. 'Caligula's Seashells.' *Greece & Rome*, vol. 47, no. 1, 2000, pp. 80–87.

PART II
7. The Maya

Adams, Richard E. W. 'Introduction to a Survey of the Native Prehistoric Cultures of Mesoamerica.' *The Cambridge History of the Native Peoples of the Americas*, edited by Richard E. W. Adams, Murdo J. Macleod, vol. 2: Mesoamerica, part 1. United Kingdom, Cambridge University Press, 2000.

Andrews, E. Wyllys and William L. Fash. 'Issues in Copán Archaeology.' *Copán: The History of an Ancient Maya Kingdom*, edited by E. Wyllys Andrews and William L. Fash. Santa Fe, NM; Oxford, School of American Research Press and James Currey Ltd, 2005, pp. 395–425.

Avendaño y Loyola, Andrés de. *The Second Entrada of Padre Avendaño.* Trans. Philip Ainsworth Means. In: *History of the Spanish conquest of Yucatan and of the Itzas.* Peabody Museum of American Archaeology and Ethnology, Harvard University, 1917.

Braswell, Geoffrey E. 1997. 'La cronología y la estructura del colapso en Copan, Honduras.' In *Los Investigadores de la Cultura Maya*, 5, vol. 1, pp. 262–273. Universidad Autónoma de Campeche, Campeche, Mexico.

Carballo, D. M. 'Implements of State Power: Weaponry and Martially Themed Obsidian Production Near the Moon Pyramid, Teotihuacan.' *Ancient Mesoamerica*, 18 (1), 2007, pp. 173–190.

Clynes, Tom. 'Exclusive: Laser Scans Reveal Maya "Megalopolis" below Guatemalan Jungle.' *National Geographic*, Feb. 2018, www.nationalgeographic.com/history/article/maya-laser-lidar-guatemala-pacunam. Accessed 19 September 2023.

Coe, Michael D. *Breaking the Maya Code*. United Kingdom, Penguin Books, 1994.

Cook, Benjamin, *et al*. 'Pre-Columbian Deforestation as an Amplifier of Drought in Mesoamerica.' *Geophysical Research Letters*, 2012. 39. 16706.

———— 'Environmental Legacy of Pre-Columbian Maya Mercury.' *Frontiers in Environmental Science*, 10, 2022.

———— 'Soil and slaughter: A geoarchaeological record of the ancient Maya from Cancuén, Guatemala.' *Journal of Archaeological Science: Reports*, 15, 2017, pp. 330–343.

Culbert, T. Patrick. *The Classic Maya Collapse*. Albuquerque, University of New Mexico Press, 1973.

Demarest, Arthur. *Ancient Maya: The Rise and Fall of a Rainforest Civilization*. United Kingdom, Cambridge University Press, 2004.

Diamond, Jared. *Collapse: How Societies Choose to Fail or Survive*. United Kingdom, Penguin Books, 2005.

Drew, David. *The Lost Chronicles of the Maya Kings*. 1999. United Kingdom, Phoenix, 2000.

Fash, William L. and Ricardo Agurcia Fasquelle. 'Contributions and Controversies in the Archaeology and History of Copán.' *Copán: The History of an Ancient Maya Kingdom*, edited by E. Wyllys Andrews, William L. Fash. United States, School of American Research Press, 2005, pp. 3–32.

———— 'Political Decentralization, Dynastic Collapse, and the Early Postclassic in the Urban Center of Copán, Honduras.' *The Terminal Classic in the Maya lowlands: Collapse, Transition, and Transformation*, edited by Arthur A. Demarest, Prudence M. Rice and Don S. Rice. Boulder, University Press of Colorado, 2005, pp. 260–287.

Fedick, Scott L. 'The Maya Forest: Destroyed or cultivated by the ancient

Maya?' *Proceedings of the National Academy of Sciences*, vol. 107, no. 3, 8 Jan. 2010, pp. 953–954.

Gause, E., 'A Critique: Jared Diamond's Collapse Put in Perspective.' *Papers from the Institute of Archaeology*, 24(1), 2014, Art. 16.

Gill, Richardson B. 'Drought and the Maya Collapse.' *Ancient Mesoamerica*, vol. 18, no. 2, 2007, pp. 283–302.

——— *The Great Maya Droughts: Water, Life, and Death*. Albuquerque, University of New Mexico Press, 2000.

Gorokhovich, Yuri, *et al.* 'Mercury source in Copan (Honduras): Local mining or trade?' *Journal of Archaeological Science: Reports*, vol. 33, 2020.

Graham, Ian. *The Art of Maya Hieroglyphic Writing.* Cambridge, Peabody Museum Press, 1971.

Hammond, Norman. 'The Maya Lowlands: Pioneer Farmers to Merchant Princes.' *The Cambridge History of the Native Peoples of the Americas*, edited by Richard E. W. Adams and Murdo J. Macleod, vol. 2: Mesoamerica, part 1. United Kingdom, Cambridge University Press, 2000, pp. 197–249.

Haug, Gerald H., *et al.* 'Climate and the collapse of Maya civilization.' *Science*, 299.5613, 2003, pp. 1731–1735.

Hodell, David A., Jason H. Curtis and Mark Brenner. 'Possible role of climate in the collapse of Classic Maya civilization.' *Nature*, 375.6530, 1995, pp. 391–394.

——— Mark Brenner and Jason H. Curtis. 'Terminal Classic drought in the northern Maya lowlands inferred from multiple sediment cores in Lake Chichancanab (Mexico).' *Quaternary Science Reviews*, 24.12–13, 2005, pp. 1413–1427.

Jie Liu, *et al.* 'Mercury in traditional medicines: is cinnabar toxicologically similar to common mercurials?' *Experimental Biology and Medicine (Maywood)*, vol. 233, no. 7, 2008, pp. 810-817.

Kennett, Douglas J., *et al.* 'Development and Disintegration of Maya Political Systems in Response to Climate Change.' *Science*, 338, 2012, pp. 788–791.

——— Marilyn Masson, Carlos Peraza Lope, *et al.* 'Drought-Induced Civil Conflict Among the Ancient Maya.' *Nature Communications*, 13, Art. 3911, 2022.

Landa, Diego de. *Landa's Relación de Las Cosas de Yucatán: A Translation.* Trans. Alfred Marston Tozzer. United States, Kraus, 1966.

Lentz, David L., Trinity. L. Hamilton, Nicholas. P. Dunning, *et al.* 'Molecular genetic and geochemical assays reveal severe contamination of drinking water reservoirs at the ancient Maya city of Tikal.' *Scientific Reports*, 10, 10316, 2020.

——— *et al.* 'Paleoecological Studies at the Ancient Maya Center of Yaxnohcah Using Analyses of Pollen, Environmental DNA, and Plant Macroremains.' *Frontiers in Ecology and Evolution*, vol. 10, 2022.

Lucero, Lisa J. 'The Collapse of the Classic Maya: A Case for the Role of Water Control.' *American Anthropologist*, vol. 104, no. 3, 2002, pp. 814–26.

Manahan, T. Kam. 'The Way Things Fall Apart: Social Organization and the Classic Maya Collapse of Copan.' *Ancient Mesoamerica*, vol. 15, no. 1, 2004, pp. 107–125.

Martin, Simon and Nikolai Grube. *Chronicle of the Maya Kings and Queens: Deciphering the Dynasties of the Ancient Maya*. London and New York, Thames & Hudson, 2000.

McAnany, Patricia A., *et al.* 'Bellicose Rulers and Climatological Peril? Retrofitting Twenty-First-Century Woes on Eighth-Century Maya Society.' *Questioning Collapse: Human Resilience, Ecological Vulnerability, and the Aftermath of Empire*, edited by P. A. McAnany and N. Yoffee. Cambridge, Cambridge University Press, 2010, pp. 142–175.

McKillop, Heather. *Ancient Maya: New Perspectives*. United Kingdom, W. W. Norton, 2006.

McNeil, Cameron L., *et al.* 'Evidence disputing deforestation as the cause for the collapse of the ancient Maya polity of Copan, Honduras.' *Proceedings of the National Academy of Sciences*, vol. 107, no. 3, 14 Dec. 2009, pp. 1017–1022.

Medina-Elizalde, Martín, *et al.* 'High resolution stalagmite climate record from the Yucatán Peninsula spanning the Maya terminal classic period.' *Earth and Planetary Science Letters*, vol. 298, iss. 1–2, 2010, pp. 255–262.

Paine, Richard R. and AnnCorinne Freter. 'Environmental Degradation and The Classic Maya Collapse at Copan, Honduras (A.D. 600–1250): Evidence from Studies of Household Survival.' *Ancient Mesoamerica*, vol. 7, no. 1, 1996, pp. 37–47.

Popol Vuh: The Definitive Edition of the Mayan Book of the Dawn of Life and the Glories of Gods and Kings. Trans. Dennis Tedlock. United States, Simon and Schuster, 1985.

Salisbury, David, Mimi Koumenalis and Barbara Moffett, 'Newly revealed hieroglyphs tell story of superpower conflict in the Maya world.' In *Exploration: The Online Research Journal of Vanderbilt University*, 19 September 2002.

Schele, Linda and David Freidel. *A Forest of Kings: The Untold Story of the Ancient Maya*. United States, HarperCollins, 1992.

Sharer, Robert J. and Loa P. Traxler. *The Ancient Maya (6th, fully revised ed.)*. 1946. Stanford, CA, Stanford University Press, 2006

Shen, Helen. 'Drought hastened Maya decline.' *Nature*, 08 Nov. 2012. nature.com/articles/nature.2012.11780. Accessed 13 August 2021.

Stephens, John L. *Incidents of Travel in Central America, Chiapas, and Yucatán*. New York, Harper & Brothers, 1841.

———— *Incidents of travel in Yucatán*. New York, Harper & Brothers, 1843.

Stuart, David. 1993. 'Historical Inscriptions and the Maya Collapse.' *Lowland Maya Civilization in the Eighth Century A.D.*, edited by Jeremy A. Sabloff and John S. Henderson. United States, Dumbarton Oaks Research Library and Collection, 1989, pp. 321–354.

Tedlock, Dennis. *2000 Years of Mayan Literature*. 1st ed. United States, University of California Press, 2010.

The Ancient Maya of Mexico: Reinterpreting the Past of the Northern Maya Lowlands. Ed. Geoffrey E. Braswell. United Kingdom, Taylor & Francis, 2014.

The Book of Chilam Balam of Chumayel. Trans. Ralph Loveland Roys. United States, Library of Alexandria, 1933.

Valdés, Juan Antonio and Federico Fahsen. 'Disaster in Sight: The Terminal Classic at Tikal and Uaxactun.' *The Terminal Classic in the Maya lowlands: Collapse, transition, and transformation*, edited by Arthur A. Demarest, Prudence M. Rice, Don S. Rice. United States, University Press of Colorado, 2005, pp. 162–194.

Webster, David, *et al. Copán: The Rise and Fall of an Ancient Maya Kingdom*. United States, Wadsworth/Thomson Learning, 2007.

———— and AnnCorinne Freter. 'Settlement History and the Classic Collapse at Copan: A Redefined Chronological Perspective.' *Latin American Antiquity*, vol. 1, no. 1, 1990, pp. 66–85.

———— *The Fall of the Ancient Maya: Solving the Mystery of the Maya Collapse*. New York, Thames and Hudson, 2002.

———— *The Population of Tikal: Implications for Maya Demography*. United Kingdom, Archaeopress Publishing Limited, 2018.

8. The Khmer

Aeusrivongse, Nidhi. 'The Devarāja Cult and Khmer Kingship at Angkor.' *Explorations in Early Southeast Asian History: The Origins of Southeast Asian Statecraft*, edited by Kenneth R. Hall and John K. Whitmore. United States, University of Michigan Press, 1976, pp. 107–148.

Behnke, Alison. *Angkor Wat*. United States, Twenty-First Century Books, 2008.

Bergaigne, Abel Henri Joseph. *Inscriptions sanscrites de Campa et du Cambodge*. Paris, Imprimerie Nationale, 1893.

Briggs, Lawrence Palmer. *The Ancient Khmer Empire*. United States, American Philosophical Society, 1951.

Chandler, David. *A History of Cambodia*. Boulder, Westview Press, 1992.

Coedès, George and Pierre Dupont, 'Les stales de Sdok Kak Thorn, Phnom Sandak et Prah Vihar.' *BEFEO*, 43, 1943–46, pp. 63–64.

Coe, Michael D, and Damian Evans. *Angkor and the Khmer Civilization*. United Kingdom, Thames & Hudson, 2018.

DiBiasio, Jame. *The Story of Angkor*. Thailand, Silkworm Books, 2013.

Diskul, M. C. Subhadradis. 'Ancient Kingship in Mainland Southeast Asia.' In A. L. Basham (ed.). *Kingship In Asia and Early America*. Colegio de Mexico, 1981, pp. 143–160.

Fletcher, R. 'Angkor, food production, water management and climate change: The trajectory of urbanism in SE Asia to the mid-second millennium CE.' *Water and Society from Ancient Times to the Present: Resilience, Decline, and Revival*, edited by Federica Sulas, Innocent Pikirayi. Oxford, Routledge, 2018, pp. 238–258.

Groslier, George. *A l'ombre d'Angkor; notes et impressions sur les temples inconnus de l'ancien Cambodge*. Paris, A. Challamel, 1913. Trans. Pedro Rodríguez: *In the Shadow of Angkor: Unknown Temples of Ancient Cambodia*. United States, DatASIA, 2014.

Hall, Kenneth R. 'Temples as Economic Centers in Early Cambodia.' *Maritime Trade and State Development in Early Southeast Asia*. University of Hawai'i Press, 1985, pp. 148–182.

Hawken, Scott. 'Designs of Kings and Farmers: Landscape Systems of the

Greater Angkor Urban Complex.' *Asian Perspectives*, vol. 52, no. 2, 2013, pp. 347–367.

Henley, David. 'Ages of Commerce in Southeast Asian History.' *Environment, Trade and Society in Southeast Asia: A Longue Durée Perspective*, edited by David Henley and Henk Schulte Nordholt. Netherlands, Brill, 2015, pp. 120–132.

Higham, Charles F. *The Civilization of Angkor.* United States, University of California Press, 2001.

——— 'The Origins of the Civilisation of Angkor.' *Proceedings of the British Academy*, vol. 121, 2002 Lectures. United Kingdom, OUP/British Academy, 2003, pp. 41–90.

Jacques, Claude and Philippe Lafond. *The Khmer Empire: Cities and Sanctuaries from the 5th to the 13th Century.* Thailand, River Books, 2007.

Mabbett, Ian W. *Angkor: Celestial Temples of the Khmer Empire.* United Kingdom, Abbeville Press Publishers, 2002.

MacDonald, Malcolm. *Angkor and the Khmers.* Singapore, Oxford University Press, 1987.

McCurry, Steve. *Sanctuary: The Temples of Angkor.* London, Phaidon Press, 2002.

Mouhot, Henri. *Travels in the Central Parts of Indo-China (Siam), Cambodia, and Laos, During the Years 1858, 1859, and 1860*, vol 2. United Kingdom, Murray, 1864.

Osborne, Milton. *The Mekong: Turbulent Past, Uncertain Future.* United States, Grove Atlantic, 2007.

Pym, Christopher. *The Ancient Civilization of Angkor.* United Kingdom, New American Library, 1968.

Rooney, Dawn and Peter Danford. *Angkor: An Introduction to the Temples.* Hong Kong, Odyssey, 1999.

Sisowath, Chanto, *et al.* 'Globalization and Generational Change: The Evolution of Cambodia's Social Structure.' *Fairness, Globalization, and Public Institutions: East Asia and Beyond*, University of Hawai'i Press, 2006, pp. 300–311.

Smith, Robert. *The Kings of Angkor.* Independently published, 2019.

So, Kenneth T. *The Khmer Kings and the History of Cambodia.* Bangkok, Thailand, DatAsia Press, 2017.

Stargardt, Janice. 'Water for the State or Water for the People?: Wittfogel in South and Southeast Asia in the First Millennium.' *Water Societies and Technologies from the Past and Present*, edited by Yijie Zhuang and Mark Altaweel. UCL Press, 2018, pp. 256–268.

Stewart, Frank, *et al.*, editors. *Out of the Shadows of Angkor: Cambodian Poetry, Prose, and Performance Through the Ages*. University of Hawaii Press, 2022.

St Julian, James. 'Jayavarman II, the "Devaraja" cult and the formation of the Khmer Empire.' *Teaching History*, vol. 48, iss. 1, 2014, pp. 17–24.

Sutherland, Heather. 'Geography as Destiny?: The Role of Water in Southeast Asian History.' In: Peter Boomgaard (ed.). *A World of Water: Rain, Rivers and Seas in Southeast Asian Histories*. Netherlands, Brill, 2007, pp. 27–70.

9. Byzantium

Andrea, Alfred J., editor. *The Capture of Constantinople: The 'Hystoria Constantinopolitana' of Gunther of Pairis*. United States, University of Pennsylvania Press, 1997.

Andrea, Alfred J. and Brett E. Whale. *Contemporary Sources for the Fourth Crusade: Revised Edition*, Netherlands, Brill, 2008.

Anna Comnena (Komnene). *The Alexiad*. Ed. and trans. Elizabeth A. Dawes. London, Routledge, Kegan Paul, 1928.

Attaleiates, Michael. *History*. Ed. and trans. A. Kaldellis and D. Krallis. Washington, DC, 2012.

Barbaro, Nicolò. *Diary of the Siege of Constantinople 1453*. Trans. John Melville-Jones. New York, 1969.

Bartsocas, Christos. S. 'Two Fourteenth Century Greek Descriptions of the "Black Death".' *Journal of the History of Medicine and Allied Sciences*, vol. 21, no. 4, 1966, pp. 394–400.

Benedictow, Ole Jørgen. *The Complete History of the Black Death*. United Kingdom, Boydell Press, 2021.

The Book of the Eparch. Trans. E. H. Freshfield. Ed. I. Dujcev. London, Variorum Reprints, 1970.

Browning, Robert. *The Byzantine Empire (Revised Edition)*. 1980. New ed. The Catholic University of America Press, 1992.

Cameron, Averil. *Byzantine Matters*. United States, Princeton University Press, 2014.

Choniates, Niketas. *Chronicle*. Trans. Harry J. Magoulias. In: O *City of Byz-*

antium: Annals of Niketas Choniatēs. Detroit, Wayne State University Press, 1984.

Congourdeau, Marie-Hélène. 'Black Death in Constantinople (1343–1466).' *Medicina Nei Secoli*, 11, 1999, pp. 377–389.

Crowley, Roger. *Constantinople: The Last Great Siege, 1453*. United Kingdom, Faber & Faber, 2005.

Dalby, Andrew. *Tastes of Byzantium: The Cuisine of a Legendary Empire*. 2003. New ed. Bloomsbury USA, 2010.

Dalby, Andrew and Rachel Dalby. *Gifts of the Gods: A History of Food in Greece*. United Kingdom, Reaktion Books, 2017.

Gautier, Théophile. *Constantinople of To-day*. Trans. Robert Howe Gould. London, David Bogue, 1854.

Geoffrey of Villehardouin. *The Conquest of Constantinople*. Trans. M. R. B. Shaw. In: *Chronicles of the Crusades*. United Kingdom, Penguin Classics, 1963.

Gibbon, Edward. *The History of the Decline and Fall of the Roman Empire*. Ed. J. B. Bury. London, Methuen, 1926, 2nd ed., 7 vols.

Halsall, Paul. *Medieval Sourcebook: Niketas Choniates: The Sack of Constantinople (1204)*.

Hunt, Patrick. 'Late Roman Silk: Smuggling and Espionage in the 6th Century CE.' *Great Events in History*, vol. 2. United States, Salem Press, 2004.

Ibn Battuta. *The Travels of Ibn Battuta: AD 1325–1354*. Trans. H. A. R. Gibb. Cambridge, Taylor & Francis, 1958.

Kaegi, Walter Emil. *Byzantium and the Decline of the Roman Empire*. 1992. New ed. United States, Princeton University Press, 2000.

Kaldellis, Anthony. 'A Byzantine Argument for the Equivalence of All Religions: Michael Attaleiates on Ancient and Modern Romans.' *International Journal of the Classical Tradition*, vol. 14, no. 1/2, 2007, pp. 1–22.

———— *Byzantium Unbound*. (Past Imperfect) United Kingdom, Arc Humanities Press, 2019.

———— *Streams of Gold, Rivers of Blood: The Rise and Fall of Byzantium, 955 a.d. to the First Crusade*. United States, Oxford University Press, 2017.

———— *The Byzantine Republic*. United States, Harvard University Press, 2015.

Kermeli, Eugenia. 'Osman I'. *Encyclopedia of the Ottoman Empire*, edited by Gábor Ágoston and Bruce Masters. United States, Infobase Publishing, 2009.

Kitromilides, Paschalis M. 'The Byzantine Legacy in Early Modern Political Thought.' *The Cambridge Intellectual History of Byzantium*, edited by Anthony Kaldellis and Niketas Siniossoglou. United Kingdom, Cambridge University Press, 2017, pp. 653–668.

Konstantinos of Rhodes. *On Constantinople*. In: *Constantine of Rhodes, On Constantinople and the Church of the Holy Apostles*. Trans. Ioannis Vassis. Ed. Liz James. United Kingdom, Routledge, 2016.

Laiou, Angeliki E. and Cécile Morrisson. *The Byzantine Economy*. United Kingdom, Cambridge University Press, 2007.

Littman, Robert and M. Littman. 'Galen and the Antonine Plague.' *American Journal of Philology*, 94, 1973, pp. 243–255.

Liudprand of Cremona. *The Embassy to Constantinople and Other Writings*. Trans. F. A. Wright. In: *The Works of Liudprand of Cremona*. London; New York, George Routledge & Sons, 1930.

Luttwak, Edward. *The Grand Strategy of the Byzantine Empire*. United Kingdom, Harvard University Press, 2009.

Marciniak, Przemysław. 'Constantinople as a (Unwilling) Multireligious Space (33–1453).' In: *Geographies of Encounter: The Making and Unmaking of Multi-Religious Spaces*. Switzerland, Springer International Publishing, 2022, pp. 99–112.

Mayr-Harting, Henry. 'Liudprand of Cremona's Account of His Legation to Constantinople (968) and Ottonian Imperial Strategy.' *The English Historical Review*, vol. 116, no. 467, 2001, pp. 539–556.

Nicolle, David and Christa Hook. *Constantinople 1453: The End of Byzantium*. Oxford, Osprey Military, 2000.

——————— *The Fourth Crusade 1202–04: The Betrayal of Byzantium*. United Kingdom, Bloomsbury, 2011.

Norwich, John Julius. *A Short History of Byzantium*. United Kingdom, Penguin Books, 1998.

Odo of Deuil. *Expedition of Louis VII*. Trans. V. G. Berry. New York, Columbia University Press, 1948.

Pamuk, Orhan. *Istanbul: Memories and the City*. Trans. Maureen Freely. United Kingdom, Faber & Faber, 2005.

Phillips, Jonathan. *The Crusades, 1095–1204*. United Kingdom, Taylor & Francis, 2014.

———— *The Fourth Crusade and the Sack of Constantinople*. United Kingdom, Pimlico, 2005.

Procopius. *The Anecdota or Secret History*. Trans. Henry Bronson Dewing, vol. 6. ('Loeb Classical Library') Cambridge, MA, Harvard University Press, 1935.

Raoult, Didier. *Paleomicrobiology: Past Human Infections*. Germany, Springer Berlin Heidelberg, 2008.

Rautman, Marcus Louis. *Daily Life in the Byzantine Empire*. London, Bloomsbury Academic, 2006.

Rodgers, Kelly. *The Byzantine Empire: A Society That Shaped the World*. United States, Teacher Created Materials, 2012.

Sarris, Peter. *Empires of Faith: The Fall of Rome to the Rise of Islam, 500–700*. United Kingdom, Oxford University Press, 2012.

Shepard, Jonathan. 'Cross-purposes: Alexius Comnenus and the First Crusade.' In *The First Crusade: Origins and Impact*. Ed. Jonathan Phillips. United Kingdom and United States, Manchester University Press, 1997.

Shepard, Jonathan. '"How St. James the Persian's head was brought to Cormery". A relic collector around the time of the First Crusade.' *Zwischen Polis, Provinz und Peripherie. Beiträge zur Byzantinischen Geschichte und Kultur,* edited by L. M. Hoffmann and A. Monchizadeh. Wiesbaden, Harassowitz Verlag, 2005, pp. 287–335.

Smylie, James H. *A Brief History of the Presbyterians*. United Kingdom, Presbyterian Publishing Corporation, 1996.

Talbot Rice, Tamara. *Everyday Life in Byzantium*. London, B.T. Batsford, 1967.

Teule, Herman G. B. and Krijna Nelly Ciggaar, editors. *East and West in the Crusader States: Context, Contacts, Confrontations II: Acta of the Congress Held at Hernen Castle in May 1997*. Belgium, Peeters, 1999.

Theophanes. *The Chronicle of Theophanes*. Trans. Harry Turtledove. United States, University of Pennsylvania Press, 1982.

Tougher, Shaun, editor. *The Emperor in the Byzantine World: Papers from the Forty-Seventh Spring Symposium of Byzantine Studies*. United Kingdom, Taylor & Francis, 2019.

Tsiamis, Costas, *et al*. 'Epidemic waves of the Black Death in the Byzantine Empire (1347–1453 AD).' *Le Infezioni in Medicina*, vol. 19, 3, 2011, pp. 194–201.

Vescia, Monique. *The Rise and Fall of the Byzantine Empire*. United States, Rosen Publishing, 2016.

Wace, Henry and Philip Schaff. *Nicene and Post-Nicene Fathers of the Christian Church*. New York, Charles Scribner's Sons, 1912.

Ward-Perkins, Bryan. 'Old and New Rome Compared: The Rise of Constantinople.' *Two Romes: Rome and Constantinople in Late Antiquity*, edited by Gavin Kelly and Lucy Grig. United Kingdom, Oxford University Press, 2012.

Williams, Stephen and J. G. P. Friell. *The Rome That Did Not Fall: The Survival of the East in the Fifth Century*. United Kingdom, Routledge, 1999.

10. Vijayanagara

Ahmed, Fouzia Farooq. *Muslim Rule in Medieval India: Power and Religion in the Delhi Sultanate*. United Kingdom, Bloomsbury Publishing, 2016.

Allchin, Bridget and Frank Raymond Allchin. *The Birth of Indian Civilization: India and Pakistan Before 500 B.C.* India, Penguin Books India, 1993.

Asher, Catherine B. and Cynthia Talbot. *India Before Europe*. 2006. 2nd ed. United Kingdom, Cambridge University Press, 2022.

Barani, Ziauddin. *Tarikh-i-Firoz Shahi*. In Elliot, Henry M. *The History of India, as Told by Its Own Historians: The Muhammadan Period*, vol. 3. United Kingdom, Trübner, 1871.

Barbosa, Duarte. *The Book of Duarte Barbosa, An Account of the Countries Bordering on the Indian Ocean and Their Inhabitants: Written by Duarte Barbosa, and Completed about the Year 1518 a.d.* Ed. Mansel Longworth Dames. vol. 1. United Kingdom, Hakluyt Society, 1918.

Barron, E. J., *et al.* 'Paleogeography, 180 million years ago to the present.' *Eclogae Geologicae Helvetiae*, 74 (2), 1981, pp. 443–470.

Basu, K. K. 'The Battle of Tālikōta: Before and After (from Muslim Sources).' In *Vijayanagara: History and Legacy*, ed. S. Krishnaswami Aiyangar. New Delhi: Aryan Books International, 2000, pp. 245–254.

Dalrymple, William. *The Anarchy: The East India Company, Corporate Violence, and the Pillage of an Empire*. India, Bloomsbury USA, 2019.

Eaton, Richard M. '"Kiss My Foot", Said the King: Firearms, Diplomacy, and the Battle for Raichur, 1520.' *Modern Asian Studies*, vol. 43, no. 1, 2009, pp. 289–313.

Elliot, Sir Henry Miers, and John Dowson. *The History of India, as Told by Its Own Historians*. 7 vols. London, Trübner, 1871.

Firishta, Muhammad Qāsim Hindū-Šāh Astarābādī. *Tarikh-i-Firishta*. Trans. John Briggs, in *Tarikh-i-Firishta, or, History of the rise of the Mahomedan power in India, till the year A.D. 1612*, vol. 1. United Kingdom, Longman, Rees, Orme, Brown, And Green, 1829.

Hakluyt, Richard. *The Principal Navigations, Voyages, Traffiques & Discoveries of the English Nation: Made by Sea Or Over-land to the Remote and Farthest Distant Quarters of the Earth at Any Time Within the Compasse of These 1600 Yeeres*. 1589. Reprint. United Kingdom, J. MacLehose and Sons, 1903.

Husain, Āghā Mahdī. *The Rise and Fall of Muhammad Bin Tughluq*. India, Luzac, 1938.

Ibn Battuta. *Travels in Africa and Asia*. Trans. H. A. R. Gibb. London, Routledge and Kegan Paul, 1929.

Jackson, Peter. *The Delhi Sultanate: A Political and Military History*. United Kingdom, Cambridge University Press, 2003.

Jackson, William J. *Vijayanagara Voices: Exploring South Indian History and Hindu Literature*. United Kingdom, Taylor & Francis, 2016.

Keay, John. *India: A History: from the Earliest Civilisations to the Boom of the Twenty-first Century*. United States, Grove Press, 2010.

————— *India Discovered*. London, Windward, 1984.

Kodad, S. B. *The Battle of Talikota*. New Delhi, Sri Ramachandra Publication, 1986.

Lycett, Mark T. and Kathleen D. Morrison. 'The "Fall" of Vijayanagara Reconsidered: Political Destruction and Historical Construction in South Indian History.' *Journal of the Economic and Social History of the Orient*, 56.3, 2013, pp. 433–470.

Macdonell, Arthur Anthony. *A History of Sanskrit Literature*. United States, Cosimo, Inc., 2005.

Maitri Upanishad. Trans. Hume, Robert Ernest, in *The Thirteen Principal Upanishads*. United Kingdom, Oxford University Press, 1921.

Majumdar, Ramesh Chandra. *Ancient India*. 1952. India, Motilal Banarsidass, 2018.

Morrison, Kathleen D. and Mark T. Lycett. 'Inscriptions as Artifacts: Precolonial South India and the Analysis of Texts.' *Journal of Archaeological Method and Theory*, vol. 4, no. 3/4, Springer, 1997, pp. 215–237.

——— 'The "Fall" of Vijayanagara Reconsidered: Political Destruction and Historical Construction in South Indian History.' *Journal of the Economic and Social History of the Orient*, 56.3, 2013, pp. 433–470.

Nilakanta Sastri, Kallidaikurichi Aiyah. *A History of South India from Prehistoric Times to the Fall of Vijayanagar.* India, Oxford University Press, 1976.

Nizami, Khaliq Ahmad. *Some Aspects of Religion and Politics in India During the Thirteenth Century.* India, Idarah-i Adabiyat-i Delli, 1974.

Paes, Domingos, and Fernão Nunes. *The Vijayanagar Empire: Chronicles of Paes and Nuniz.* India, Asian Educational Services, 1991.

Panikkar, Kavalam Madhava. *A Survey of Indian History.* India, Meridian Books, 1947.

Pillai, Manu S. *Rebel Sultans: The Deccan from Khilji to Shivaji.* New Delhi, Juggernaut, 2018.

Rao, C. Hayavadana. *Mysore Gazetteer*, vol. 2, part 3. Bangalore, Government of Mysore, 1930.

Ramanujan, S. R. *Vijayanagara: The Never to be Forgotten Empire.* India, Notion Press, 2019.

Ray, Aniruddha. 'The Rise and Fall of Vijayanagar: An Alternative Hypothesis to "Hindu Nationalism" Thesis.' *Proceedings of the Indian History Congress*, vol. 64, 2003, pp. 420–433.

Reddy, Srinivas. *The Giver of the Worn Garland: Krishnadevaraya's Amuktamalyada.* India, Penguin Books, 2010.

Rice, Benjamin Lewis. *Epigraphia Carnatica.* India, Mysore Government Central Press, 1894.

Ridgeon, Lloyd V. J., editor. *Major World Religions: From Their Origins to the Present.* United Kingdom, Routledge Curzon, 2003.

Samarqandi, Abd al-Razzaq. 'Narrative of the Journey of Abd-Er-Razzaq.' In R. H. Major (ed.). *India in the Fifteenth Century being a Collection of Narratives of Voyages to India.* New Delhi, Deep Publications, 1974.

——— *Matla'u-s Sa'dain.* In Elliot, Henry M. *The History of India, as Told by Its Own Historians: The Muhammadan Period*, vol. 4. United Kingdom, Trübner, 1871.

Sarasvati, Rangasvami. 'Political Maxims of the Emperor Poet, Krishnadevaraya.' *Journal of Indian History*, no. 4(3), 1925.

Sewell, Robert. *A Forgotten Empire (Vijayanagar): A Contribution to the History of India.* 1900. Reprint. India, Asian Educational Services, 2000.

Sharma, Ram Sharan. *Indian Feudalism, C. ad 300–1200*. India, Macmillan India, 2009.

Sherwani, Haroon Khan. *The Bahmanis of the Deccan*. India, Munshiram Manoharlal, 1985.

Stoker, Valerie. *Polemics and Patronage in the City of Victory: Vyasatirtha, Hindu Sectarianism, and the Sixteenth-Century Vijayanagara Court*. United States, University of California Press, 2016.

Subrahmanyam, Sanjay. *Courtly Encounters: Translating Courtliness and Violence in Early Modern Eurasia*. Germany, Harvard University Press, 2012.

Verghese, Anila. *Archaeology, Art and Religion: New Perspectives on Vijayanagara*. Oxford University Press, 2000.

PART III
11. Songhai

Adu-Boahen, Kwabena. 'The Impact of European Presence on Slavery in the Sixteenth to Eighteenth-century Gold Coast.' *Transactions of the Historical Society of Ghana*, no. 14, 2012, pp. 165–199.

Barth, Heinrich. *Travels and Discoveries in North and Central Africa, 1849–1855, Vol. 5*. London, Longman, Brown, Green, Longman & Roberts, 1858.

Boxer, Charles Ralph. *The Portuguese Seaborne Empire 1415–1825*. London, Hutchinson, 1969.

Conrad, David. *Empires of Medieval West Africa: Ghana, Mali, and Songhay*. United States, Infobase Publishing, 2010.

Cooley, William Desborough. *The Negroland of the Arabs Examined and Explained*. London, J. Arrowsmith, 1966.

Cory, Stephen. 'The Man Who Would Be Caliph: A Sixteenth-Century Sultan's Bid for an African Empire.' *The International Journal of African Historical Studies*, vol. 42, no. 2, 2009, pp. 179–200.

da Costa, Emilia Viotti. 'The Portuguese-African Slave Trade: A Lesson in Colonialism.' *Latin American Perspectives*, vol. 12, no. 1, 1985, pp. 41–61.

Davidson, Basil. *West Africa Before the Colonial Era: A History to 1850*. United Kingdom, Taylor & Francis, 2014.

De Villiers, Marq, and Sheila Hirtle. *Timbuktu: The Sahara's Fabled City of Gold*. Canada, McClelland & Stewart, 2012.

Elbl, Ivana. 'Cross-Cultural Trade and Diplomacy: Portuguese Relations with West Africa, 1441–1521.' *Journal of World History*, vol. 3, no. 2, 1992, pp. 165–204.

———— 'The Volume of the Early Atlantic Slave Trade, 1450–1521.' *The Journal of African History*, vol. 38, no. 1, 1997, pp. 31–75.

Ewa, Ibiang Oden. 'Pre-colonial West Africa: the Fall of Songhai Empire Revisited.' *Journal of the Historical Society of Nigeria*, vol. 26, 2017, pp. 1–24.

Fage, J. D. 'Slavery and the Slave Trade in the Context of West African History.' *The Journal of African History*, vol. 10. no 3, 1969.

Fauvelle, François-Xavier. *The Golden Rhinoceros: Histories of the African Middle Ages*. United Kingdom, Princeton University Press, 2021.

Ferro, Mark. *Colonization: A Global History*. London, Routledge, 1997.

Frank, Andre Gunder. *ReORIENT: Global Economy in the Asian Age*. United Kingdom, University of California Press, 1998.

Gewald, Jan Bart. 'Gold—The True Motor of West African History: An Overview of the Importance of Gold in West Africa and its Relations with the Wider World.' In *Worlds of Debt: Interdisciplinary Perspectives on Gold Mining in West Africa*. Netherlands, Rozenberg Publishers, 2010.

Goldfarb, Richard J., *et al.* 'West Africa: The World's Premier Paleoproterozoic Gold Province.' *Economic Geology*, 112 (1), 2017, pp. 123–143.

Gomez, Michael. *African Dominion: A New History of Empire in Early and Medieval West Africa*. United States, Princeton University Press, 2019.

———— 'Timbuktu under Imperial Songhay: A Reconsideration of Autonomy.' *The Journal of African History*, vol. 31, no. 1, 1990, pp. 5–24.

Goodwin, A. J. H. 'The Medieval Empire of Ghana.' *The South African Archaeological Bulletin*, vol. 12, no. 47, 1957, pp. 108–112.

Green, Hilary. *International Trade in the Middle Ages*. United Kingdom, Amberley Publishing, 2022.

Hale, Thomas. *Griots and Griottes: Masters of Words and Music*. United States, Indiana University Press, 2007.

Ibn Battuta. *Travels*. Trans. H. A. R. Gibb. *The Travels of Ibn Battuta:* AD *1325–1354*. Cambridge: Taylor & Francis, 1958.

Inikori, Joseph, editor. *Forced Migration: The Impact of the Export Slave Trade on African Societies*. New York, Oxford University Press, 1982.

———— 'Slaves or Serfs? A Comparitive Study of Slavery and Serfdom in Europe and Africa.' *The African Diaspora: African Origins and New World Identities*, edited by Isidore Okpewho, Carole Boyce Davies, and Ali Al'Amin Mazrui. United States, Indiana University Press, 2001.

Insoll, Timothy. 'Timbuktu the Less Mysterious?' *Researching Africa's Past: New contributions from British Archaeologists*, edited by P. J. Mitchell, *et al.* United Kingdom, Oxford University School of Archaeology, 2004.

Kemper, Steve. *A Labyrinth of Kingdoms: 10,000 Miles through Islamic Africa.* United States, W. W. Norton & Company, 2012.

Levtzion, Nehemia and J. F. P. Hopkins, editors. *Corpus of Early Arabic Sources for West African History.* United States, Markus Wiener Publishers, 2000.

——— 'A Seventeenth Century Chronicle by Ibn al-Mukhtar: A Critical Study of the Ta'rikh al-Fettash.' *Bulletin, School of Oriental and African Studies*, 34, 1971, pp. 571–593.

Lindqvist, Sven. *Exterminate All the Brutes.* United Kingdom, Granta Publications, 2021.

Magalhães, J. R. 'Africans, Indians, and Slavery in Portugal.' *Portuguese Studies*, 13, 1997, pp. 143–147.

Malio, Nouhou. *The Epic of Askia Mohammed.* Trans. Thomas A. Hale. United States, Indiana University Press, 1996.

M'bokolo, Elikia. 'The impact of the slave trade on Africa.' *Le Monde diplomatique*, 2 April 1998.

McKissack, Patricia and Fredrick McKissack. *The Royal Kingdoms of Ghana, Mali, and Songhay: Life in Medieval Africa.* Square Fish, 2016.

Miller, Joseph C. 'Mortality in the Atlantic Slave Trade: Statistical Evidence on Causality.' *The Journal of Interdisciplinary History*, vol. 11, no. 3, 1981, pp. 385–423.

Newitt, Malyn. *A History of Portuguese Overseas Expansion, 1400–1668.* United Kingdom, United States and Canada, Routledge, 2005.

——— editor. *The Portuguese in West Africa, 1415–1670: A Documentary History.* United States, Cambridge University Press, 2010.

Niane, Djibril Tamsir, editor. *General History of Africa, IV: Africa from the Twelfth to the Sixteenth Century.* UNESCO, 1984.

Ohaegbulam, Festus Ugboaja. *Towards an Understanding of the African Experience from Historical and Contemporary Perspectives.* University Press of America, 1990.

Phillips, William D. *Slavery from Roman Times to the Early Transatlantic Trade.* United Kingdom, Manchester University Press, 1985.

Prothero, R. Mansell. 'Heinrich Barth and the Western Sudan.' *The Geographical Journal*, vol. 124, no. 3, 1958, pp. 326–337.

Restall, Matthew. 'Black Conquistadors: Armed Africans in Early Spanish America.' *The Americas*, vol. 57, no. 2, 2000, pp. 171–205.

Rodney, Walter. *How Europe Underdeveloped Africa*. London, Bogle-L'Ouverture, 1972.

Sa'dī, 'Abd al-Rahmān ibn 'Abd Allāh. *Tarikh al-Sudan*. Trans. John Hunwick, in *Timbuktu and the Songhay Empire: Al-Sa'dī's Ta'rīkh al-sūdān down to 1613 and other contemporary documents*. Boston, Brill, 1999.

Saunders, A. *A Social History of Black Slaves and Freedmen in Portugal, 1441–1555*. United Kingdom, Cambridge University Press, 1982.

Scammell, Geoffrey Vaughn. *The First Imperial Age, European Overseas Expansion c.1400–1715*. Routledge, 1997.

Singleton, Brent. 'Rulers, Scholars, and Invaders: A Select Bibliography of the Songhay Empire.' *History in Africa*, vol. 31, 2004, pp. 357–368.

Spaulding, Jay and Nehemia Levtzion, editors. *Medieval West Africa: Views from Arab Scholars and Merchants*. United States, Markus Wiener Publishers, 2003.

Stoller, Paul. 'Social Interaction and the Management of Songhay Socio-Political Change.' *Africa: Journal of the International African Institute*, vol. 51, no. 3, 1981, pp. 765–780.

Thornton, John. *Africa and Africans in the Making of the Atlantic World, 1400–1800*. 2nd ed. United Kingdom, Cambridge University Press, 1998.

Timbuktī, Mahmūd Kutī ibn Mutawakkil Kutī. *Ta'rīkh al fattāsh: Timbuktu Chronicles 1493–1599*. Trans. Christopher Wise and Hala Abu Taleb. United Kingdom, Africa World Press, 2011.

Uzoigwe, G. N. 'The Slave Trade and African Societies.' *Transactions of the Historical Society of Ghana*, vol. 14, no. 2, 1973, pp. 187–212.

Vogt, John. 'Portuguese Gold Trade: An Account Ledger From Elmina, 1529–1531.' *Transactions of the Historical Society of Ghana*, vol. 14, no. 1, 1973, pp. 93–103.

Wright, John. *The Trans-Saharan Slave Trade*. United Kingdom, United States and Canada, Routledge, 2007.

12. The Aztecs

Andrews, James Richard. *Introduction to Classical Nahuatl*. United States, Norman: University of Oklahoma Press, 2003.

Arce, José Luis, *et al*. 'Geology and stratigraphy of the Mexico Basin.' *Journal of Maps*, vol. 15, no.2, 2019, pp. 320–332.

Barlow, Robert H. *Extent of the Empire of Culhua Mexica*. United States, University of California Press, 1949.

Berdan, Frances F. 'Mesoamerica: Mexica.' In: Michael S. Werner (ed.). *Encyclopedia of Mexico: History, Society & Culture*. Routledge, 1998.

Bernal Díaz del Castillo. *The True History of the Conquest of New Spain*. 1568. Trans. Alfred Percival Maudslay. 1908.

Boone, E. *The Aztec World*. Washington, DC, Smithsonian Books, 1994.

Calnek, Edward. 'Settlement Pattern and Chinampa Agriculture at Tenochtitlan.' *American Antiquity*, vol. 37, no. 1, 1973, pp. 190–95.

Carrasco, Davíd, editor. *The History of the Conquest of New Spain by Bernal Díaz del Castillo*. United States, University of New Mexico Press, 2008.

Carrasco, Pedro. *The Tenochca Empire of Ancient Mexico: The Triple Alliance of Tenochtitlan, Tetzcoco, and Tlacopan*. United States, University of Oklahoma Press, 1999.

Caso, Alfonso. *The Aztecs: People of the Sun*. Trans. Lowell Dunham. United States, University of Oklahoma Press, 1958.

Cervantes, Fernando. *Conquistadores*. United Kingdom, Penguin Books, 2020.

Chatters, James C., *et al*. 'Evaluating Claims of Early Human Occupation at Chiquihuite Cave, Mexico.' *PaleoAmerica*, vol. 8, no. 1, 2022, pp. 1–16.

Chimalpahin Quauhtlehuanitzin, Domingo Francisco De San Antón Muñón. *Codex Chimalpahin*. Ed. and trans. Arthur J. O. Anderson and Susan Schroeder, 2 vols. United States, Norman: University of Oklahoma Press, 1997.

Clendinnen, Inga. *Aztecs: An Interpretation*. United Kingdom, Cambridge University Press, 2014.

——————— '"Fierce and Unnatural Cruelty": Cortés and the Conquest of Mexico.' *Representations*, no. 33, 1991, pp. 65–100.

Cortés, Hernán. *Letters from Mexico*. Trans. Anthony Pagden. 1971. Revised Edition. United States, Yale University Press, 1986.

Cypess, Sandra Messinger. *La Malinche in Mexican Literature: From History to Myth*. Austin, TX, University of Texas Press, 1991.

Daniel, Douglas A. 'Tactical Factors in the Spanish Conquest of the Aztecs.' *Anthropological Quarterly*, vol. 65, no. 4, 1992, pp. 187–194.

Diamond, Jared. *Guns, Germs, and Steel: The Fates of Human Societies*. United Kingdom, W. W. Norton, 2017.

Durán, Diego. *The History of the Indies of New Spain*. 1964. New ed. United States, University of Oklahoma Press, 1994.

Duverger, Christian. *The Meaning of Sacrifice*. United States, University of Michigan: Zone, 1989.

Fehrenbach, T.R. *Fire & Blood: A History of Mexico*. United States, Open Road Media, 2014.

Frankopan, Peter. *The Silk Roads: A New History of the World*. London, Bloomsbury, 2015.

Hernández, Francisco. *Historia natural de nueva Espana*. 2 vols. Mexico, Universidad Nacional de Mexico, 1959.

Hirth, Kenneth, and Joanne Pillsbury, editors. *Merchants, Markets, and Exchange in the Pre-Columbian World*. United States, Dumbarton Oaks Research Library and Collection, 2013.

Ixtlilxóchitl, Fernando de Alva Cortés. *History of the Chichimeca Nation: Don Fernando de Alva Ixtlilxochitl's Seventeenth-Century Chronicle of Ancient Mexico*. Ed. and trans. Amber Brian, *et al*. United States, University of Oklahoma Press, 2019.

Karttunen, Frances. *Between Worlds: Interpreters, Guides, and Survivors*. New Brunswick, NJ, Rutgers University Press, 1994.

Lee, Jongsoo. *The Allure of Nessahualcoyotl: Pre-Hispanic History, Religion, and Nahua Poetics*. United States, UNM Press, 2008.

León-Portilla, Miguel. *The Broken Spears: The Aztec Account of the Conquest of Mexico*. 1962. Trans. Lysander Kemp. New ed. Boston, MA. Beacon Press, 1992.

———— *Aztec Thought and Culture: A Study of the Ancient Nahuatl mind*. Trans. Jack Emory Davis. United States, University of Oklahoma Press, 1963.

———— *La filosofía náhuatl estudiada en sus fuentes: con un nuevo apéndice*. Mexico, Universidad Nacional Autónoma de México, Instituto de Investigaciones Históricas, 1993.

Lockhart, James. *The Nahuas After the Conquest: A Social and Cultural History of the Indians of Central Mexico, Sixteenth Through Eighteenth Centuries*. Stanford, Stanford University Press, 1992.

———— *We People Here: Nahuatl Accounts of The Conquest of Mexico*. United States, University of California Press, 1993.

López de Gómara, Francisco. *Cortes: The Life of the Conqueror of Mexico by*

His Secratary. 1552. Trans. Lesley Byrd Simpson. United States, University of California Press, 1965.

Martin, Rodger. 'The Colonization of Paradise: Milton's Pandemonium and Montezuma's Tenochtitlan.' *Comparative Literature Studies*, vol. 35, no. 4, 1998, pp. 321–355.

Moctezuma, Eduardo Matos. 'Archaeology & Symbolism in Aztec Mexico: The Templo Mayor of Tenochtitlan.' *Journal of the American Academy of Religion*, vol. 53, no. 4, 1985, pp. 797–813.

Mundy, Barbara E. 'Mapping the Aztec Capital: The 1524 Nuremberg Map of Tenochtitlan, Its Sources and Meanings.' *Imago Mundi*, vol. 50, 1998, pp. 11–33.

———— *The Death of Aztec Tenochtitlan, the Life of México City*. United States, University of Texas Press, 2015.

Neale-Silva, Eduardo. 'An Incident in the Life of Cortés. Its Possible Source.' *Hispanic Review*, vol. 6, no. 1, 1938, pp. 69–74.

Nicholson, Henry B. 'Religion in Pre-Hispanic Central Mexico.' *Handbook of Middle American Indians, Volumes 10 and 11: Archaeology of Northern Mesoamerica*, edited by Robert Wauchope, *et al*. University of Texas Press, 1971, pp. 395–446.

Nicholson, Irene. *Firefly in the Night*. London, Faber and Faber, 1959.

———— *Mexican and Central American Mythology*. London, Hamlyn, 1967.

Parsons, Jeffrey R. 'The Aquatic Component of Aztec Subsistence: Hunters, Fishers, and Collectors in an Urbanized Society.' United States, University of Michigan Library, 2005.

———— *The Last Saltmakers of Nexquipayac, Mexico: An Archaeological Ethnography*. United States, University of Michigan Press, 2001.

Peterson, Jeanette Favrot and Kevin Terraciano, editors. *The Florentine Codex: An Encyclopedia of the Nahua World in Sixteenth-Century Mexico*. Spain, University of Texas Press, 2019.

Posth, Cosimo, *et al*. 'Pleistocene Mitochondrial Genomes Suggest a Single Major Dispersal of Non-Africans and a Late Glacial Population Turnover in Europe.' *Current Biology*, vol. 26, no. 6, March 2016, pp. 827–833.

Potter, Ben, *et al*. 'Current evidence allows multiple models for the peopling of the Americas.' *Science Advances*, vol. 4,8, 8 Aug. 2018. ncbi.nlm.nih.gov/pmc/articles/PMC6082647. Accessed 31 March 2021.

Raynal-Villasenor, Jose. 'The remarkable hydrological works of the Aztec civilization.' *Water for the Future: Hydrology in Perspective (Proceedings of the Rome Symposium, April 1987)*. IAHS Publ. no. 164, 1987.

Restall, Matthew. *Seven Myths of the Spanish Conquest*. United States, Oxford University Press, 2021.

————— *When Montezuma Met Cortes: The True Story of the Meeting that Changed History*. United States, Ecco, 2018.

Rinke, Stefan. *Conquistadors and Aztecs: A History of the Fall of Tenochtitlan*. United States, Oxford University Press, 2023.

Sagan, Eli. *Cannibalism: Human Aggression and Cultural Form*. New York, Harper Torchbooks, 1974.

Sahagún, Fray Bernardino de. *Florentine Codex: General History of the Things of New Spain*. Ed. and trans. Arthur J. O. Anderson and Charles E. Dibble. 13 vols. Santa Fe, NM, School of American Research; Salt Lake City, University of Utah Press, 1950–1982.

————— *General History of the Things of New Spain by Fray Bernardino de Sahagún: The Florentine Codex*. In Edward King, Viscount Kingsborough (ed.). *Antiquities of Mexico*, vol. 7. London, Havell, Colnaghi Son & Co., 1831.

Sanday, Peggy Reeves. *Divine Hunger: Cannibalism as a Cultural System*. United Kingdom, Cambridge University Press, 1986.

Schroeder, Susan. *Tlacaelel Remembered: Mastermind of the Aztec Empire*. United States, University of Oklahoma Press, 2016.

Schwaller, John F. 'Research Note: Broken Spears or Broken Bones: Evolution of the Most Famous Line in Nahuatl.' *The Americas*, vol. 66, no. 2, 2009, pp. 241–252.

Smith, Michael E. *The Aztecs*. Malden, MA, Blackwell Publishing, 1997.

Stokes, Gale. 'The Fates of Human Societies: A Review of Recent Macrohistories.' *The American Historical Review*, vol. 106, no. 2, 2001, pp. 508–525.

Thomas, Hugh. *Rivers of Gold: The Rise of the Spanish Empire*. United Kingdom, Penguin Books, 2013.

————— *The Conquest of Mexico*. 1993. New ed. United States, Simon & Schuster, 2014.

Todorov, Tzvetan. *The Conquest of America: The Question of the Other*. United States, University of Oklahoma Press, 1999.

Toribio de Benavente Motolinía. *Motolinia's History of the Indians of New*

Spain. 1950. Trans. Elizabeth Andros Foster. New ed. Westport, CT: Greenwood Press, 1973.

Townsend, Camilla. 'Burying the White Gods: New Perspectives on the Conquest of Mexico.' *The American Historical Review*, vol. 108, no. 3, 2003, pp. 659–687.

——— *Fifth Sun: A New History of the Aztecs*. United States, Oxford University Press, 2019.

——— *Malintzin's Choices: An Indian Woman in the Conquest of Mexico*. Albuquerque, NM, University of New Mexico Press, 2006.

Townsend, Richard F. *The Aztecs*. London, Thames & Hudson, 2009.

Van Tuerenhout, Dirk R. *The Aztecs: New Perspectives*. United Kingdom, Bloomsbury Publishing, 2005.

Willermet, Cathy, *et al*. 'Biodistances Among Mexica, Maya, Toltec, and Totonac Groups of Central and Coastal Mexico / Las Distancias Biológicas Entre Los Mexicas, Mayas, Toltecas, y Totonacas de México Central y Zona Costera.' *Chungara: Revista De Antropología Chilena* 45, no. 3, 2013.

13. The Inca

Andagoya, Pascual de. *Narrative of the Proceedings of Pedrarias Davila in the Provinces of Tierra Firme or Catilla Del Oro: And of the Discovery of the South Sea and the Coasts of Peru and Nicaragua*. Trans. Sir Clements Robert Markham. United Kingdom, Hakluyt Society, 1865.

Arredondo, Jaime Marroquín, *et al*., editors. *Translating Nature: Cross-Cultural Histories of Early Modern Science*. United States, University of Pennsylvania Press, Inc., 2019.

Bauer, Brian. *Ancient Cuzco: Heartland of the Inca*. United States, University of Texas Press, 2004.

——— and R. Alan Covey. 'Processes of State Formation in the Inca Heartland (Cuzco, Peru).' *American Anthropologist*, vol. 104, no. 3, 2002, pp. 846–864.

Bauer, Brian, *et al*. *Voices from Vilcabamba: Accounts Chronicling the Fall of the Inca Empire*. United States, University Press of Colorado, 2015.

Betanzos, Juan de. *Narrative of the Incas*. United States, University of Texas Press, 2010.

Bingham, Hiram. 'In the Wonderland of Peru: The Work Accomplished by the Peruvian Expedition of 1912, under the Auspices of Yale University and the National Geographic Society.' *National Geographic Magazine*, Apr. 1913.

———— *Lost City of the Incas*. 1948. Ed. Hugh Thomson. United Kingdom, Orion, 2010.

Brading, D. A. 'The Incas and the Renaissance: The Royal Commentaries of Inca Garcilaso de La Vega.' *Journal of Latin American Studies*, vol. 18, no. 1, 1986, pp. 1–23.

Burger, Richard, and Lucy C. Salazar, editors. *Machu Picchu: Unveiling the Mystery of the Incas*. United States, Yale University Press, 2004.

Castro-Klarén, Sara. '"May We Not Perish": The Incas and Spain.' *The Wilson Quarterly* (1976–), vol. 4, no. 3, 1980, pp. 166–175.

Cieza de León, Pedro de. *The Discovery and Conquest of Peru*. Trans. Alexandra Parma Cook and Noble David Cook. United States, Duke University Press, 1999.

———— *The Second Part of the Chronicle of Peru*. Trans. Sir Clements Robert Markham. United Kingdom, Hakluyt Society, 1883.

———— *The Travels of Pedro de Cieza de Leon, a.d. 1532–50, Contained in the First Part of His Chronicle of Peru*. Trans. Sir Clements Robert Markham. United Kingdom, Hakluyt Society, 1864.

Cornejo Polar, Antonio. *Writing in the Air: Heterogeneity and the Persistence of Oral Tradition in Andean Literatures*. United Kingdom, Duke University Press, 2013.

Covey, R. Alan. *Inca Apocalypse: The Spanish Conquest and the Transformation of the Andean World*. United Kingdom, Oxford University Press, 2020.

Crosby, Alfred W. 'Conquistador y Pestilencia: The First New World Pandemic and the Fall of the Great Indian Empires.' *The Hispanic American Historical Review*, vol. 47, no. 3, 1967, pp. 321–337.

Curl, John. 'Ancient American Poets.' *Bilingual Review / La Revista Bilingüe*, vol. 26, no. 2/3, 2001, pp. iii–163.

Gómara, Francisco López de. *Historia general de las Indias y vida de Hernán Cortés*. 1552. vol. 1. Trans. Lynda Jentsch. Caracas: Bibioteca Ayacucho, 1979.

Guamán Poma de Ayala, Felipe. *Letter to a King: A Peruvian chief's Account of Life Under the Incas and Under Spanish Rule*. 1613. Trans. Christopher Wentworth Dilke. New York, E. P. Dutton, 1978.

———— *The First New Chronicle and Good Government: On the History of the World and the Incas Up to 1615*. Trans. Roland Hamilton. United States, University of Texas Press, 2010.

Harris, Kevin R. 'Was the Inca Empire A Socialist State? A Historical Discussion.' *Historia*, vol. 16, 2007.

Hemming, John. *The Conquest of the Incas*. New York, Harcourt, Brace, Jovanovich, Inc., 1970.

Hopkins, Donald R. *The Greatest Killer: Smallpox in History*. United Kingdom, University of Chicago Press, 2002.

Julien, Catherine J. 'How Inca Decimal Administration Worked.' *Ethnohistory*, vol. 35, no. 3, 1988, pp. 257–279.

Karttunen, Frances E. *Between Worlds: Interpreters, Guides, and Survivors*. United States, Rutgers University Press, 1994.

Kieke, Gerrit. 'A Text Analysis of the Huarochirí Manuscript with Focus on Afterlife and Worship.' *Thesis*. University of Gothenburg, 2014.

Lee, Vincent R. *Forgotten Vilcabamba: Final Stronghold of the Incas*. United States, Sixpac Manco Publications, 2000.

MacCormack, Sabine. 'Atahualpa and the Book.' *Dispositio*, vol. 14, no. 36/38, 1989, pp. 141–168.

——————— 'Demons, Imagination, and the Incas.' *Representations*, no. 33, 1991, pp. 121–146.

——————— 'History, Historical Record, and Ceremonial Action: Incas and Spaniards in Cuzco.' *Comparative Studies in Society and History*, vol. 43, no. 2, 2001, pp. 329–63.

MacQuarrie, Kim. *The Last Days of the Incas*. United Kingdom, Little, Brown Book Group, 2007.

Malpass, Michael A. *Daily Life in the Inca Empire*. United States, Greenwood Press, 2009.

Mann, Charles C. *1491: New Revelations of the Americas Before Columbus*. United Kingdom, Knopf Doubleday Publishing Group, 2006.

Markham, Sir Clements Robert. *The Incas of Peru*. J. Murray, 1912.

Marsh, Erik. 'The Founding of Tiwanaku: Evidence from Kk'araña.' *Ñawpa Pacha*, vol. 32, 2012, pp. 169–188.

McEwan, Gordon F. *The Incas: New Perspectives*. Santa Barbara, CA: ABC-CLIO, 2006.

Menzel, Dorothy. 'The Inca Occupation of the South Coast of Peru.' *Southwestern Journal of Anthropology*, vol. 15, no. 2, 1959, pp. 125–142.

Moses, Bernard. *The Spanish Dependencies in South America.* 2 vols. New York, Harper and Brothers, 1914.

Nishi, Dennis. *The Inca Empire*. San Diego, Lucent, 2000.

Ocampo, Baltasar de, and Pedro Sarmiento De Gamboa. *History of the Incas by Pedro Sarmiento De Gamboa and the Execution of the Inca Tupac Amaru by Captain Baltasar De Ocampo.* Trans. Sir Clements Robert Markham. Cambridge, Hakluyt Society, 1897.

Petroski, Henry. 'Engineering: Machu Picchu.' *American Scientist*, vol. 97, no. 1, 2009, pp. 15–19.

Pizarro, Hernando. 'Letter from Hernando Pizarro to the Royal Audience of Santo Domingo.' 1533. *Works Issued by the Hakluyt Society.* United Kingdom, The Hakluyt Society, 1847.

Pizarro, Pedro. *Relation of the Discovery and Conquest of the Kingdoms of Peru.* 2 vols. Trans. Philip Ainsworth Means. United States, New York Cortes Society, 1921.

Polar, Antonio Cornejo. *Writing in the Air: Heterogeneity and the Persistence of Oral Tradition in Andean Literatures.* United States, Duke University Press, 2013.

Prescott, William H. *History of the Conquest of Peru, With a Preliminary View of the Civilisation of the Incas.* London, George Routledge and Sons, 1847.

Restall, Matthew. *Seven Myths of the Spanish Conquest.* United States, Oxford University Press, 2003.

Rostworowski de Diez Canseco, María. *History of the Inca Realm.* Trans. Harry B. Iceland. United Kingdom, Cambridge University Press, 1999.

Rowe, John Howland. *Inca Culture at the Time of the Spanish Conquest.* Washington, DC, U.S. G.P.O., 1946.

———— 'The Inca Civil War and the Establishment of Spanish Power in Peru.' *Ñawpa Pacha: Journal of Andean Archaeology*, no. 28, 2006, pp. 1–9.

Sarmiento de Gamboa, Pedro. *History of the Incas.* 1572. Trans. Clements Robert Markham. United Kingdom, Hakluyt Society, 1897.

Seed, Patricia. '"Failing to Marvel": Atahualpa's Encounter with the Word.' *Latin American Research Review*, vol. 26, no. 1, 1991, pp. 7–32.

Silverblatt, Irene. 'Andean Women in the Inca Empire.' *Feminist Studies*, vol. 4, no. 3, 1978, pp. 37–61.

———— *Moon, Sun, and Witches: Gender Ideologies and Class in Inca and Colonial Peru.* United States, Princeton University Press, 1987.

Stirling, Stuart. *Pizarro: Conqueror of the Inca*. United Kingdom, History Press, 2005.

———— *The Last Conquistador: Mansio Serra De Lequizamon and the Conquest of the Incas*. United Kingdom, History Press, 1999.

The Book of Chilam Balam of Chumayel. Trans. Ralph Roys. 1933. 2nd ed. United States, University of Oklahoma Press, 1967.

Titu Cusi Yupanqui, Don Diego de Castro. *An Inca Account of the Conquest of Peru*. Trans. Ralph Bauer. United States, University Press of Colorado, 2011.

Trujillo, Diego de, and Porras Barrenechea, Raúl. *Relación del descubrimiento del reyno del Perú*. Spain, Escuela de Estudios Hispano-Americanos, 1948.

Vega, Garcilaso de la. *The Incas: The Royal Commentaries of the Inca*. Trans. Alain Gheerbrant. United States, Avon, 1966.

Wood, Michael. *Conquistadors*. United Kingdom, Ebury Publishing, 2000.

Xerez, Francisco de. *Reports on the Discovery of Peru*. Trans. Sir Clements Robert Markham. United Kingdom, Hakluyt Society, 1872.

14. Easter Island

Bahn, Paul, and John Flenley. *Easter Island, Earth Island*. United Kingdom, Thames and Hudson, 1992.

Barthel, Thomas S. *The Eighth Land: The Polynesian Discovery and Settlement of Easter Island*. Trans. Anneliese Martin. Honolulu, University Press of Hawaii, 1978.

Behrens, Carl Friedrich. 'Another Narrative of Jacob Roggeveen's Visit.' In: *The Voyage of Captain Don Felipe Gonzalez*. Trans. Bolton Glanvill Corney. Cambridge, The Hakluyt Society, 1908, pp. 131–137.

Beighton, Peter. 'Easter Island People.' *The Geographical Journal*, vol. 132, no. 3, 1966, pp. 347–357.

Bendrups, Dan. *Singing and Survival: The Music of Easter Island*. United States, Oxford University Press, 2019.

Boersema, Jan J. *The Survival of Easter Island: Dwindling Resources and Cultural Resilience*. United Kingdom, Cambridge University Press, 2015.

Bullis, Douglas. 'Painting the Buddha's Eyes.' Bodhi Leaves 126. Kandy, Sri Lanka: Buddhist Publication Society, 1992.

Capek, Michael. *Easter Island*. United States, Twenty-First Century Books, 2008.

Corney, Bolton Glanvill, editor. *The Voyage of Captain Don Felipe Gonzalez*. Cambridge, The Hakluyt Society, 1908.

Cook, Captain James. *The Journals of Captain James Cook on His Voyages of Discovery: Volume II: The Voyage of the Resolution and Adventure 1772–1775*. Ed. J. C. Beaglehole. United Kingdom, Taylor & Francis, 2017.

Delsing, Riet. *Articulating Rapa Nui: Polynesian Cultural Politics in a Latin American Nation-State*. Germany, University of Hawaii Press, 2015.

Diamond, Jared. *Collapse: How Societies Choose to Fail or Survive*. United Kingdom, Penguin Books, 2013.

———— 'Easter Island's end.' *Discover Magazine*, vol. 16, no. 8, 1995, pp. 63–69.

Emory, Kenneth P. 'Easter Island's Position in the Prehistory of Polynesia.' *The Journal of the Polynesian Society*, vol. 81, no. 1, 1972, pp. 57–69.

Esen-Baur, Heide-Margaret. 'Towards an Understanding of "Rongorongo".' *Anthropos*, vol. 106, no. 2, 2011, pp. 439–461.

Finney, Ben. *Voyage of Rediscovery: A Cultural Odyssey Through Polynesia*. Germany, University of California Press, 2023.

Fischer, Steven Roger. *Island at the End of the World: The Turbulent History of Easter Island*. United Kingdom, Reaktion Books, 2006.

Gill, George W. and Vincent H. Stefan, editors. *Skeletal Biology of the Ancient Rapanui (Easter Islanders)*. United Kingdom, Cambridge University Press, 2016.

Haun, Beverley. *Inventing 'Easter Island'*. United Kingdom, University of Toronto Press, 2008.

Heyerdahl, Thor. *Easter Island: The Mystery Solved*. New York, Random House, 1989.

———— and Edwin N. Ferdon Jr, editors. *Reports of the Norwegian Archaeological Expedition to Easter Island and the East Pacific*. United States, Rand McNally & Company, 1961.

Hiatt, Alfred, *et al.*, editors. *European Perceptions of Terra Australis*. United Kingdom, Taylor & Francis, 2016.

Hunt, Terry and Carl Lipo. 'Late Colonization of Easter Island.' *Science*, vol. 311, 2006, pp. 1603–1606.

———— *The Statues that Walked: Unraveling the Mystery of Easter Island*. United Kingdom, Free Press, 2011.

———— 'Rethinking the Fall of Easter Island: New Evidence Points to an Alternative Explanation for a Civilization's Collapse.' *American Scientist*, vol. 94, no. 5, 2006, pp. 412–419.

Ioannidis, Alexander G., *et al.* 'Native American gene flow into Polynesia predating Easter Island settlement.' *Nature*, vol. 583, 2021, pp. 572–577.

Kalakaua, David. *The Legends and Myths of Hawaii: The Fables and Folk-lore of a Strange People*. United States, C. L. Webster, 1888.

Kjellgren, Eric, *et al. Splendid Isolation: Art of Easter Island*. United States, Metropolitan Museum of Art, 2001.

La Pérouse, Jean-François de Galaup. *A Voyage Round the World, Performed in the Years 1785, 1786, 1787, and 1788 by the* Boussole *and* Astrolabe. 2 vols. London, A. Hamilton, 1799.

Langdon, Robert, *et al.* 'The Settlement of Easter Island.' *The Journal of the Polynesian Society*, vol. 110, no. 3, 2001, pp. 329–333.

Lanyon-Orgill, P. A. 'The Easter Island Script.' *The Journal of the Polynesian Society*, vol. 51, no. 3, 1942, pp. 187–190.

Lipo, Carl and Terry Hunt. 'A.D. 1680 and Rapa Nui Prehistory.' *Asian Perspectives*, vol. 48, no. 2, 2009, pp. 309–317.

Lipo, Carl, Terry Hunt, Rene Horneman and Vincent Bonhomme. 'Weapons of war? Rapa Nui Mata'a Morphometric Analyses.' *Antiquity*, vol. 90, iss. 349, February 2016, pp. 172–187.

Lipo, Carl P., Terry L. Hunt and Sergio Rapu Haoa. 'The "walking" megalithic statues (moai) of Easter Island.' *Journal of Archaeological Science*, vol. 40, iss. 6, 2013, pp. 2859–2866.

Luke, Harry. 'Easter Island.' *The Geographical Journal*, vol. 120, no. 4, 1954, pp. 422–430.

Martinsson-Wallin, Helène and Susan J. Crockford. 'Early Settlement of Rapa Nui (Easter Island).' *Asian Perspectives*, vol. 40, no. 2, 2001, pp. 244–278.

Middleton, Guy D. *Understanding Collapse: Ancient History and Modern Myths*. United Kingdom, Cambridge University Press, 2017.

Mückler, Hermann and Ian Conrich, editors. *Rapa Nui-Easter Island: Cultural and Historical Perspectives*. Germany, Frank & Timme, Verlag für Wissenschaftliche Literatur, 2016.

Palmer, J. Linton. 'A Visit to Easter Island, or Rapa Nui, in 1868.' *The Journal of the Royal Geographical Society of London*, vol. 40, 1870, pp. 167–181.

Pavel, Pavel. 'Reconstruction of the Transport of the Moai statues and Pukao

Hats,' *Rapa Nui Journal: Journal of the Easter Island Foundation*, vol. 9, iss. 3, article 2, 1995.

Peiser, Benny. 'From Genocide to Ecocide: The Rape of "Rapa Nui".' *Energy & Environment*, vol. 16, no. 3/4, 2005, pp. 513–539.

Pinart, Alphonse. 'Voyage à l'Ile de Pâques (Océan Pacifique)'. *Le Tour du Monde: Nouveau Journal des Voyages*. 36: 225, 1877.

Quanchi, Max, and John Robson, editors. *Historical Dictionary of the Discovery and Exploration of the Pacific Islands*. Ukraine, Scarecrow Press, 2005.

Roggeveen, Jacob. 'Extract From the Official Log of Mr Jacob Roggeveen, Relating to His Discovery of Easter Island.' 1722. In: *The Voyage of Captain Don Felipe Gonzalez*. Trans. Bolton Glanville Corney. Cambridge, The Hakluyt Society, 1908, pp. 1–24.

Routledge, Katherine. *The Mystery of Easter Island*. United Kingdom, Hazell, Watson, and Viney Ltd, 1919.

——————— William Scoresby, *et al*. 'Easter Island: Discussion.' *The Geographical Journal*, vol. 49, no. 5, 1917, pp. 340–349.

——————— 'The Bird Cult of Easter Island.' *Folklore*, vol. 28, no. 4, 1917, pp. 337–355.

Ryan, Kay. 'Easter Island.' *The American Scholar*, vol. 77, no. 3, 2008, pp. 65–65.

Skinner, H. D. 'Easter Island Masonry.' *The Journal of the Polynesian Society*, vol. 64, no. 3, 1955, pp. 292–294.

——————— 'The Easter Island Figures.' *Folklore*, vol. 33, no. 3, 1922, pp. 296–299.

Stevenson, Christopher and Rull Valentí, editors. *The Prehistory of Rapa Nui (Easter Island): Towards an Integrative Interdisciplinary Framework*. Switzerland, Springer International Publishing, 2022.

——————— *et al*. 'Variation in Rapa Nui (Easter Island) land use indicates production and population peaks prior to European contact.' *Proceedings of the National Academy of Sciences*, 112 (4), 2015, pp. 1025-1030.

Stimson, John Francis. *Songs and Tales of the Sea Kings: Interpretations of the Oral Literature of Polynesia*. United States, Peabody Museum of Salem, 1957.

Tainter, Joseph A. 'Archaeology of Overshoot and Collapse.' *Annual Review of Anthropology*, vol. 35, 2006, pp. 59–74.

Thomson, William J. 'Te Pito te Henua, or Easter Island.' *Report of the US*

National Museum for the year ending June 30, 1889. US Government Printing Office, Washington DC, 1889, pp. 447–552.

Trachtman, Paul. 'The Secrets of Easter Island.' *Smithsonian*, 1 Mar. 2002. Online. www.smithsonianmag.com/history/the-secrets-of-easter-island-59989046. Accessed 7 November 2023.

Tregear, Edward. 'Easter Island.' *The Journal of the Polynesian Society*, vol. 1, no. 2, 1892, pp. 95–102.

Van Tilburg, Jo Anne and Ted Ralston. 'Engineers of Easter Island.' *Archaeology*, vol. 52, no. 6, 1999, pp. 40–45.

———— 'Moving the Moai.' *Archaeology*, vol. 48, no. 1, 1995, pp. 34–43.

———— 'Symbolic Archaeology on Easter Island.' *Archaeology*, vol. 40, no. 2, 1987, pp. 26–33.

Wilmshurst, Janet M., *et al.* 'High-Precision Radiocarbon Dating Shows Recent and Rapid Initial Human Colonization of East Polynesia.' *Proceedings of the National Academy of Sciences of the United States of America*, vol. 108, no. 5, 2011, pp. 1815–1820.

Epilogue

'A Proclamation', *Punch*, 48, 7 January 1865, p. 9.

Arrhenius, Svante. 'On the Influence of Carbonic Acid in the Air upon the Temperature of the Ground.' *Philosophical Magazine and Journal of Science*, ser. 5, vol. 41, April 1896, pp. 237–276.

———— *Worlds in the Making: The Evolution of the Universe*. United States, Harper & Brothers Publishers, 1908.

Bendell, Jem and Rupert Read, editors. *Deep Adaptation: Navigating the Realities of Climate Chaos*. United Kingdom, Polity Press, 2021.

Carrington, Damian. '"Insanity": Petrostates Planning Huge Expansion of Fossil Fuels, Says UN Report.' *Guardian*, 8 November 2023.

———— 'New Zealand Rated Best Place to Survive Global Societal Collapse.' *Guardian*, 28 July 2021.

Cernev, Tom. 'Global sustainability targets: Planetary boundary, global catastrophic risk, and disaster risk reduction considerations.' *Progress in Disaster Science*, vol. 16, 2022, 100264.

Dartnell, Lewis. 'Could We Reboot a Modern Civilisation without Fossil Fuels?: Aeon Essays.' Aeon, aeon.co/essays/could-we-reboot-a-modern-civilisation-without-fossil-fuels. Accessed 15 November 2023.

Fragile States Index Annual Report 2023. Ed. Ediye Bassey. United States, Fund For Peace, 2023.

Goldsmith, Steven. *Unbuilding Jerusalem: Apocalypse and Romantic Representation*. Ithaca, Cornell University Press, 1993.

Institute for Economics & Peace (IEP). 'Ecological Threat Register 2020: Understanding Ecological Threats, Resilience and Peace.' Sydney, September 2020, http://visionofhumanity.org/reports. Accessed 15 November 2023.

International Energy Agency (IEA). 'CO2 Emissions in 2022.' *IEA*, Paris, 2023. https://www.iea.org/reports/co2-emissions-in-2022. Accessed 14 November 2023.

Lenton, Timothy M., *et al*. 'Climate tipping points—too risky to bet against.' *Nature*, 575, 2019, pp. 592–595.

Lindqvist, Sven. *Exterminate All the Brutes*. United Kingdom, Granta Publications, 2021.

Lynch, Tommy. 'Why Hope Is Dangerous When It Comes to Climate Change.' *Slate*, 25 July 2017, slate.com/technology/2017/07/why-climate-change-discussions-need-apocalyptic-thinking.html. Accessed 14 November 2023.

Macaulay, Thomas Babington. 'Ranke's History of the Popes.' *Critical and Historical Essays Contributed to the Edinburgh Review by Thomas Babington Macaulay*, vol. 4, Germany, Bernhard Tauchnitz, 1850, pp. 97–143.

Macfarlane, Robert. 'Life in Ruins.' *Life*, edited by William Brown and Andrew Fabian, United Kingdom, Cambridge University Press, 2014, pp. 124–146.

Ripple, William J, *et al*. 'The 2023 state of the climate report: Entering uncharted territory.' *BioScience*, 2023, pp. 1–10.

———————— 'World Scientists' Warning of a Climate Emergency.' *BioScience*, vol. 70, iss. 1, January 2020, pp. 8–12.

Rosenberg, Scott. 'Virtual Reality Check Digital Daydreams, Cyberspace Nightmares.' *San Francisco Examiner*. p. C1., 19 April 1992.

Skilton, David. 'Contemplating the Ruins of London, Macaulay's New Zealander and Others.' *Literary London, Interdisciplinary Studies in the Representation of London*, vol. 2, no. 1, March 2004.

Steel, Daniel, *et al*. 'Climate change and the threat to civilization.' *PNAS*, vol. 119 no. 42, 2022.

Tainter, Joseph. *The Collapse of Complex Societies.* United Kingdom, Cambridge University Press, 1988.

Tirone, Jonathan. 'Global Warming Will Kill 83 Million People by 2100: New Study.' *Bloomberg*, 29 July 2021, www.bloomberg.com/news/articles/2021-07-29/warming-planet-means-83-million-face-death-from-heat-this-century. Accessed 14 November 2023.

United Nations Office for Disaster Risk Reduction. *Global Assessment Report on Disaster Risk Reduction 2022: Our World at Risk: Transforming Governance for a Resilient Future.* www.undrr.org/GAR2022. Geneva, 2022.

Vallet, Élisabeth. 'The World Is Witnessing a Rapid Proliferation of Border Walls.' *Migration Policy Institute*, 15 March 2022, www.migrationpolicy.org/article/rapid-proliferation-number-border-walls. Accessed 14 November 2023.

Victor, Daniel and Kenneth Chang. 'Starship Exploded, but SpaceX Had Reason to Pop Champagne Anyway.' *The New York Times*, 20 April 2023, www.nytimes.com/2023/04/20/science/rapid-unscheduled-disassembly-starship-rocket.html. Accessed 14 November 2023.

Wadhams, Peter. *A Farewell to Ice: A Report from the Arctic.* United Kingdom, Oxford University Press, 2017.

Weisman, Alan. *The World Without Us.* United Kingdom, Ebury Publishing, 2012.

Welzer, Harald. *Climate Wars: What People Will Be Killed For in the 21st Century.* Germany, Polity Press, 2015.

Yeon-Hee Kim, Seung-Ki Min, Nathan P. Gillett, *et al.* 'Observationally-constrained projections of an ice-free Arctic even under a low emission scenario.' *Nature Communications*, 14, 3139 (2023).

INDEX